一九七二年十一月八日
山田義行

MANUAL FOR READING
JAPANESE

PALI Language Texts: Japanese
(Pacific and Asian Linguistics Institute)

MANUAL FOR READING
JAPANESE

DALE P. CROWLEY
with the assistance of
YOSHIYUKI AND YOKO KAWATA

The University Press of Hawaii
Honolulu, 1972

Copyright © 1972 by The University Press of Hawaii
All rights reserved
Library of Congress Catalog Card Number 72-75796
ISBN 0-8248-0231-4
Manufactured in the United States of America

福音のため
日本語を学ぶのに
私が苦心したように
苦心している人々に献ぐ

CONTENTS

Foreword	ix
Appreciation	xi
Introduction	xiii
Characters 1-500	
Romanized Version of Phrases and Sentences	
Index	
Appendix: Officially Recommended Changes, 1971	

Foreword

It is with great pleasure that I take this opportunity to write the foreword to Dale P. Crowley's *Manual for Reading Japanese*. As a skillful and dedicated language teacher and administrator, Mr. Crowley is eminently suited to produce this text. Having lived and studied in Japan for many years and having benefited greatly from several years of graduate studies in Japanese language and linguistics at the Waseda University, he brings a wealth of experience and perception to his task. Further study at Georgetown University produced his exciting *Linguistics and Japanese Reading*. But he also brings a great deal of very practical experience to this text.

For some eight years he has served as both a linguist and language coordinator for the University of Hawaii's Peace Corps Training Center, devising texts and running training programs in such diverse languages as Indonesian, Thai, Hindustani, Samoan, Fijian, Tongan, and Gujarati. Mr. Crowley designed and directed a United States Office of Education Cooperative Research Project for the Hawaii State Department of Education to study the effects of modern aural-oral language pedagogy in standard English for boys and girls who come to school speaking only a nonstandard variety of English, namely, pidgin English. The results of this study have striking implications on a broad scale for all English-speaking nations.

In 1969 he was asked to serve as senior linguist for the Pilot Japanese Language Program for the Department of Education, State of Hawaii. The program for selected high school juniors necessitated a new approach to language learning. Mr. Crowley was asked to design and develop a course in Japanese reading to proceed concurrently with an intensive course in Japanese conversation. This work then brings together some twenty years of experience in Japanese and a practical proven method for learning what has too long been regarded as a most mystifying language.

John N. Stalker
Professor of History
University of Hawaii
Director
The Bridge

Appreciation

To all those, including my beloved parents, who sent us to Japan and helped us stay there eight wonderful years, where we learned, and learned to use, Japanese in the most important work in the world.

To my professors of the graduate schools of the University of Oklahoma (S.I.L.), Waseda University, and Georgetown University, who gave me the inspiration and tools needed to produce this manual.

To Hiroshi Kubo, who helped with the alphabetical listing of the morphographs.

To Kooichi Kitano, who helped organize the NLRI research for the task.

To Yoshiyuki and Yoko Kawata, who composed every phrase and sentence and wrote every character on the pages that follow.

To my colleagues of the University of Hawaii for their continual encouragement to finish the task.

To Jake Stalker, who, at the right time, got me started on the final manuscript.

To the Department of Education of the State of Hawaii, which helped support work on 100 of the pages that follow.

To the Center for Cross-Cultural Training and Research of the University of Hawaii at Hilo, whose office space, desks, chairs, and typewriters were so heavily used.

To my students at the Hilo College of the University of Hawaii, who used some of the pages that follow on a trial basis.

To my wife and children, whom I missed so many evenings, weekends, and holidays.

And finally, to Fud, who had to wait, and whom, because of this work, I may never meet.

INTRODUCTION

"One can't see the forest for the trees." To my mind, never is this saying more true than when a person sets out to learn to read Chinese and Japanese. Many a student, overwhelmed with the vastness and complexity of these two orthographies, has simply given up. Charged, in 1969, with the task of developing a "crash" course in reading Japanese for 100 high school juniors in the State of Hawaii, I decided that I would make an all-out effort to consolidate my experience and research of the foregoing ten years to help them see both the forest and the trees, through a program based on sound principles of linguistics and language education. That program turned out to be only a beginning toward such an ambitious goal, but it did prove to be the impetus needed for the completion of this manual, nearly three years later.

It was in 1958 that I decided a systematic and scientific presentation of the complex Japanese writing system was needed. But in order to produce it I had to wait twelve years, drawing upon work and study experiences at Waseda University, Georgetown University, the Peace Corps Training Center of the University of Hawaii at Hilo, the State of Hawaii Department of Education's high school pilot project, and, finally, my Japanese language course at the Hilo College (University of Hawaii at Hilo). At the critical time when authentic samples of the language needed to be supplied and the final manuscripts prepared, my long-time friends and colleagues, Mr. and Mrs. Yoshiyuki Kawata, were in Hawaii and offered to undertake the enormous task that lay ahead.

*Language research
and principles
of learning psychology*

Although various measures have been taken to simplify the task of reading Japanese (and, therefore, *learning* to read it), none to date has taken advantage of the most significant research in history on the frequency of occurrence of Chinese characters in Japanese orthography, as well as the frequency of occurrence of words that are formed by combinations of the characters. The studies to which I refer were published in Tokyo by the National Language Research Institute, an agency of the Japanese government: *Research on Vocabulary in Cultural Reviews,* Part 1, Vocabulary Tables, 1957; and *The Use of Written Forms in Japanese Cultural Reviews,* 1960. (Note: Instead of "Cultural Reviews" in the titles of these two reports, a more accurate translation is "General Magazines.") By combining the results of these two studies, it has been possible to identify a list of the most frequently occurring words that are formed by the most frequently occurring characters. (Obviously, we can expect a high correlation.) The next step to make this information useful to students of the language would be to present these characters and character compounds in a systematic, functional way.

*Function
as a factor
in efficient learning*

The discipline of educational psychology tells us that when the student knows *what* he is studying (the content of the course) and *why* (function, usefulness, etc.), he can enjoy a productive learning experience. Therefore, based on the NLRI investigation, the student of Japanese reading can be apprised of the relative importance of every character and word that he studies, and this, I insist, is important when one is confronted with such a vast system of written symbols as Japanese.

For example (and it should be of some consolation to the student of Japanese reading and writing), one-fourth of all the characters used in modern Japanese occur in three-fourths of all the most frequently occurring words. This means that by concentrating on learning approximately 500 select characters, the student is assured of being able to read 75 percent of all the high-frequency words he will encounter in modern literature. No one would argue, of course, that the 500 are sufficient; obviously, however, they constitute a good beachhead to establish.

*Aural-oral
base*

It is not that a list of words in the traditional orthography of a language is the language. Not at all. The author is deeply committed to the principles of modern aural-oral pedagogy. But he has discovered with many others that the secondary code system of a language--its orthography--is best learned through the medium of its primary code system, the sounds and patterns of speech.

*Purpose
of the manual*

The rationale underlying the development of this manual is very simple, but compelling--*that every student of Japanese should have at his fingertips immediate access to information about the relative importance of the characters and character compounds used to represent the language, as well as to all the most germane facts about each character.* This goal is achieved by featuring each character on a separate page, by ordering the pages according to the frequency rank order of characters as determined by the NLRI study, and by including on each page numerous facts about how the character occurs and is employed to represent spoken forms.

Therefore, through this manual, the serious student of Japanese can know immediately, with the turn of its pages, the relative importance and scope of use of a particular character, as well as other important characters that occur with it in compounds.

*Significance
of the NLRI study*

No one would insist that the National Language Research Institute's ranking of characters is sacred or inviolate, or unchangeable. Neither would anyone maintain that character 134 is really significantly more important than 144. Everyone would agree, however, that the characters in the second hundred (101 to 200) are certainly more important for the student to concentrate on in the beginning stages of language study than those in the fifth hundred (401 to 500) and that those are likewise more important than the characters in the twelfth hundred.

*The nature
of the present work*

My manual is not another book on Japanese writing, stroke counting, or stroke order. Neither does it present the traditional or a novel way to classify and locate characters. Such a shy and ill-equipped person as I would never have the temerity required to offer the public another book on these subjects when there are already so many good ones available. Neither is it a textbook, or series of lessons, as such. Lexicons and manuals usually do not have lessons appended.

Every author must decide what limitations and constraints he will work within. I decided that this work would be a reference manual, filled with thousands of bits of absolutely essential information about how Chinese characters and the words they represent occur in both spoken and written Japanese.

*Who should
use it?*

Since this manual is not a textbook, there is no clear guideline as to when the student of the language might begin using it most profitably. The only rule of thumb is, we might say, that when the student of Japanese is sufficiently advanced in beginning conversation and sufficiently curious and motivated to learn to read the language, he is then ready to take advantage of the features of the manual and use it efficiently and profitably. (Some have suggested that the greatest users of the manual will be the youngsters of Japan's elementary schools!)

FEATURES OF THE MANUAL

*Page numbers
correspond to
frequency of occurrence
ranking*

Characters are presented in the manual in the order of their frequency of occurrence in modern Japanese literature, as determined by the NLRI investigation. This system is considered by the author to have valid pedagogical implications. The relative position that a character occupies in the manual immediately suggests its comparative importance in the language and to the language learner.

The frequency rank order number is cited twice on each page--in an upper corner for quick location and in the data list for quick reference.

Occurrences per 1000 (in the NLRI research sample) are listed in the data list for those who are interested in these statistics.

Cross references

The page on which the character is treated in one of Japan's most popular compact lexicons, Sanseido's *Kanwa Jiten*, is cited in the data list, for quick reference.

The page on which the character is treated in a popular lexicon designed for foreign students of Japanese, Nelson's *The Modern Reader's Japanese-English Character Dictionary,* is cited in the data list. (Searching for characters is not particularly easy in this lexicon. It is a valuable work, however, and the citation will make quick reference possible.)

Related morphographs

Characters that exemplify certain identical orthographical elements and that are used to represent the same homophonous morpheme are listed at the top of each page, if there are such. If the character was assigned a frequency rank number in the NLRI investigation, that number is noted.

(Note: *Character* and *morphograph* are synonymous. In my thesis, done at the Georgetown University Graduate School, Institute of Languages and Linguistics, I suggested the word *morphograph* to best describe the function of Chinese characters in modern Japanese. Since the characters are not *logographs* or *ideographs* in the strict sense of these words, I had hoped that *morphograph* might catch on as a more scientific and convenient designation. If we are to be precise, we must say that the Chinese characters that occur in Japanese writing are used to represent approximately 3,000 *morphemes* of the language.)

Character categories

If the character presented on a particular page is among the 996 Educational Characters, the letter *A* appears in the lower left- or right-hand corner of the small character box. (*Educational Characters* are the KYOOIKU KANJI that the Japanese Ministry of Education has decided children must learn during their first six years of school.)

If the character is among the 1850 Current or General Use Characters, but not among the 996 Educational Characters, the letter *B* appears in the box. (*Current Use* or *General Use Characters* are the TOOYOO KANJI that the Japanese student must master during the remaining years of his compulsory education, especially if he wishes to progress to high school and college. Most publishers of books, magazines, newspapers, etc., restrict their use of characters to those in the TOOYOO KANJI list. *Important note:* The 996 Educational Characters are included among the 1850 General Use Characters.)

If the character is not among the 1850 the letter *x* appears in the box.

Under the small character box, the *KUN-yomi* (historical Japanese reading, or readings) and the *ON-yomi* (borrowed Chinese reading, or readings) are listed, and some, if not all, of the basic meanings of the character are cited.

*Compounds and
cross references*

Under "High Frequency Compounds" the words in which the character in question appears most frequently in modern Japanese literature are listed, with their English meanings.

(Note: Since it is probably impossible to render isolated Japanese words into English with the precise articles, determiners, or part of speech in every instance, the student is advised to view the definitions of single words and syllables as parts of an area of general meaning and to strive, as the years go by, to learn the whole range of meanings represented by a character in a variety of contexts. Whether the English translation should be a noun or verb, or a singular, plural, or mass noun is not always clear or important. The general concept of the wide range of meaning is.)

Under the same category and directly under the other character in each compound ("the other" meaning the character not under consideration on a particular page) is the frequency of occurrence rank number of that character. This gives another indication to the student of the relative importance of the compound and provides a valuable, quick cross-reference system for the study of compounds.

Under the list of compounds on many pages is another cross-reference, to additional compounds in which a character occurs, introduced by *See* or *Also*, or both. The number or numbers after *See* are the pages on which additional compounds that feature the character in question are found. The compounds after *Also* are compounds of relatively high frequency but not dealt with elsewhere in the manual.

Typical usage
in phrases and sentences

Under "Typical Phrases and Expanded Compounds," expressions that one might use or hear used in conversation are listed. (This is only a small sample of the possibilities, of course. Native speakers of Japanese can offer many others for reference and study.)

Under "Typical Conversational Usage," conversational sentences that demonstrate the use of the character or its compounds are listed. (This, likewise, is only a small sample of the possibilities.)

(Note: The thousands of examples of usage of Japanese lexical and orthographical items in this manual are fully authentic and rich in idiomatic and cultural content. Every typical phrase and sentence in the pages that follow were created by native speakers of Japanese who were instructed to put the compounds into the most commonly occurring and natural-sounding contexts imaginable. I myself am amazed as my mind flashes back to familiar scenes and cultural situations in Japan through the stimulation of these living examples of Japanese usage. Thus the student is well advised not to pass lightly over the typical phrases and conversational usage sections, but to store them away for certain future reference.)

The phrases and sentences in the first one hundred pages are slightly simpler than those in the following pages of the manual.

*Romanized version
of typical usage*

Following the basic section of the manual, which demonstrates the use of Japanese orthography, is a section that presents the Romanized version of all the phrases and sentences on the pages of the basic section. The Romanized versions are thus separated from the main body of the manual to minimize the "crutch effect" of Romanization. The student is advised to use these pages sparingly.

Romanization is useful, however, in making it possible for the student to consult a dictionary when information is needed on unfamiliar items that come up in the typical phrases and sentence sections. The tradition of representing *ON-yomi* with capital letters and *KUN-yomi* with lower-case letters is followed in this section.

*Translations
and lessons*

Translations of the "Typical Phrases and Expanded Compounds" and "Typical Conversational Usage" sections appear in a separate volume, together with situational lessons (dialogues and narratives) based on the sequential listing of the characters.

*The
Index*

One of the first needs that I recognized as a student of Japanese was for a comprehensive, alphabetical listing of all the words and syllables that were officially selected by the Ministry of Education to be represented by the 1850 General Use Characters.

Indeed, speakers of other languages often have clues to the identification of Chinese characters that amaze even native speakers of Japanese. One category of such clues is the recall of syllables by their sound and corresponding Romanized spelling. Access to an alphabetical listing of the syllables and words that are represented by Chinese characters would, then, save the student many hours of painful searching through other unfamiliar arrangements of the characters. Of course, if the student prefers or is forced to identify a character by its radical, number of strokes, etc., he can do so and then very quickly find its page in this manual through the use of the alphabetical index.

*Early preparation
for the Index*

In 1963, with the assistance of Mr. Hiroshi Kubo, I produced the first complete alphabetical listing of the morphemes represented by the 1850 General Use Characters. The purpose of that effort was twofold--to serve as a tool in the development of this *Manual for Reading Japanese* and as a feature to be included in it.

*Features
of the Index*

The following features of the Index of this manual should be noted:

1. It is an alphabetical listing of the morphemes (words and syllables) that are represented by the 1850 General Use Characters, to be used as a quick way to locate the page on which a character is treated. A Romanized morpheme is listed with each entry in order to provide an additional visual stimulus for learning.

2. Borrowed Chinese morphemes (*ON-yomi*) are spelled with capital letters. Historical Japanese morphemes (*KUN-yomi*) are spelled with lower-case letters.

3. When similarly spelled morphemes are represented by the same character, not every morpheme is listed, since the purpose of the Index is merely to locate the page on which complete listings can be found. Invariably, such similar spellings would be located in close proximity, such as *agaru* and *ageru*. Thus a character that is used to represent similarly spelled morphemes is immediately locatable.

4. The first number following the listing is the frequency rank order of the character, as determined by the NLRI study. For those characters from 1 to 500, the number in the first column is also the page in this manual on which the character, its usages, etc., are treated. Characters over 1417 are not assigned a number, since the NLRI study did not rank them.

5. The second number following the character listing is a cross-reference to Nelson's *Japanese-English Character Dictionary*, indicating the page on which the character is treated in that work. Since Nelson has now included a similar listing, this feature serves just a single purpose--the immediate identification of those characters that are among the 1850 General Use Characters. (Nelson's work lists 5000 characters.)

(Note: Long vowels are spelled with the double vowel but are listed immediately after the short-vowel syllables, despite the fact that other morphemes might occur in between in a strict alphabetical sequence. For example, DOO follows DO, then comes DOKU.)

*Additional comments
on the NLRI listing
of lexical items*

Since this work claims to be based on a scientifically determined selection of vocabulary, the following must be understood:

1. Although this manual presupposes conversational usage as the medium for learning reading, it must be remembered that the popularly read journals of the 1950s were the basis for the NLRI investigation, not conversational samples.

2. There are many orthographical items that represent everyday conversational usage but that do not appear early in the frequency of occurrence list--such as, *nomu, machi, o-matsuri,* and *kuwashii*. All such words are usually presented rather early in popular conversational courses, of course, and the student would do well to identify their corresponding Chinese character and make a list of such words. (Also in this category are compounds that appear frequently in signs but infrequently in the National Language Research Institute's sample, such as *kin'en* 禁煙 "No Smoking.")

3. A few characters and character compounds that came up in the NLRI research are not officially recognized by the Ministry of Education. Such characters are included in this work, nevertheless, identified by an *x* in the character box (e.g., No. 145). Most unrecognized "readings" of morphographs, such as *ikaga* are enclosed in parentheses.

4. In some cases, I selected words to demonstrate meaning and usage that do not appear in the NLRI research, simply because I knew intuitively that they were high in conversational occurrence. (See "For the Future," No. 4.)

5. Current preoccupations at the time of the research dictated the extreme use of certain characters and words. 戦前 SENZEN, 原子 GENSHI, and 共産 KYOOSAN are typical examples. But it should be remembered that these kinds of words are still used heavily and should be added early to the student's conversational and reading tools.

6. Frequent references to former Prime Minister Yoshida (吉田), and the then Prime Minister Ikeda (池田) resulted in a heavy use of certain otherwise less-used characters, such as 田 . There are similar examples throughout the manual. (See "For the Future.")

Pedagogical advice for teachers and students

Basic assumptions:

Speech is the fundamental form of language.

Japanese writing is a system for recording Japanese speech.

In learning to read, the voice and ear must guide the eye. (Teachers in Japan require children to read orally.)

Only through frequent, repeated attempts at reading the same material over and over again can a person acquire the skill of reading new materials.

Practice in reading can and must contribute to the strengthening of conversational skills.

Implications:

The student should have a native-speaker guide to read the "Typical Phrases and Expanded Compounds" and "Typical Conversational Usage" sections of each page, especially as a beginner in the language.

The student should read the phrases and sentences orally, character by character, repeating after the native-speaker guide and concentrating on the meaning.

The student's goal should be to read orally and fluently, and with full understanding, the phrases and sentences on each page that are commensurate with his own level of proficiency. More difficult items should be postponed until a later date.

As each page is studied, the teacher should create additional examples of how a character and the words in which it occurs can be used in speech and writing, by writing them on the chalkboard, by reading them aloud for the student to hear, and by having the student practice reading aloud.

Not too much time should be spent in class learning to write the characters. Students should be encouraged to buy any of the excellent books that have been written to guide the learner into the proper method of writing Japanese *kana* and Chinese characters.

As the examples on each page are mastered and as additional examples of usage are supplied the student, the student and the teacher should engage in free conversation in order to put acquired skills to use. Functional communication is the ultimate purpose of language study.

During periods of time when the student will be using this manual as a reference work for self-study, examples should be read aloud, the Romanized versions should be referred to when necessary, companion lexicons should be referred to frequently, and all cross-reference systems of the manual should be utilized.

Rapid silent reading with full understanding is the goal of readers of any language. But in order to reach that goal in Japanese, persistent, continual *oral reading* is unquestionably the most powerful and productive device at the student's disposal.

Conventions:
The system
of Romanized Transcription
employed

The guiding principle in this work is the convenience of the learner and the practical accuracy of the materials to be learned. Therefore, strict adherence to phonemic transcription, or an exclusive use of any one of the systems of Romanized transcription, was decided against. Note:

1. *sh* is used for the *s* in /si/, and in analogous syllables.

2. *ch* is used for the *t* in /ti/, and in analogous syllables.

3. *ts* is used for the *t* in /tu/, and in analogous syllables.

4. Nasal-final syllables are spelled with *M* or *N*, depending on the homorganic consonant that follows. *N* also occurs before consonants *K* and *G*, as in GENKI and BENGI.

5. /hu/ is used throughout simply because it reflects the articulatory realities more accurately than the more popular *fu*.

*The use
of the apostrophe
to separate morphemes*

The apostrophe to separate morphemes (often employed following nasal-final syllables) is used sparingly, and only when necessary to avoid ambiguity. Examples: *KEN'I* (though the knowledgeable student would never say *KE'NI*); *HAN'EI* (though *NEI* is a very uncommon morpheme in Japanese); and *KI'NEMBI* (though it is doubtful that a student would "naturally" say *KIN'EMBI* "smoking prohibition day," simply because of the articulatory difficulties inherent in such a variation). The use of the apostrophe after *all* nasal-final syllables, as in words like *KENRI*, is avoided.

As a matter of fact, the use of the apostrophe is, in most cases, unnecessary for one reason or another. The guidance of a native speaker, as suggested earlier, will help preclude mispronunciations.

*Variant
pronunciations*

Although the process becomes automatic in time, the beginning student is advised to consult the following chart when searching for syllables, the first consonant of which might have undergone a change because of its occurrence as the second or third syllable in a multisyllabic word.

日 , for example, is listed *hi* on page 3, but when it occurs in the days of the week it becomes *bi,* as in NICHIYOO*bi*. The spelling, or pronunciation, *bi* is not, however, listed in the Index. The following key should be kept in mind:

Syllables beginning with *b,* check under *h.* Ex.: 三本
SAMBON

" *p,* " *h.* Ex.: 発表
HAPPYOO

" *d,* " *t,* Ex.: 一粒種
hitotsubudane

" *j,* " *sh.* Ex.: 患者
KANJA

" *j,* " *ch.* Ex.: 一日中
ICHINICHIJUU

" *z,* " *s.* Ex.: 青空
aozora

" *z,* " *ts.* Ex.: 力強い
chikarazuyoi

" *g,* " *k.* Ex.: 手紙
tegami

It must be remembered that not all syllables that begin with the consonants in the left column above are variations of related sounds in the second column. As a matter of fact, most are not. Compare the listings under CHOO, CHOO, and JOO in the Index, for example. By and large, Japanese words and syllables maintain their dictionary forms regardless of the position of their occurrence in compounds. The most notable exceptions to this rule are among *KUN* readings and in proper names, as in 本田 *Honda*.

Appendix--
Changes made in 1971
by the Ministry of Education

After two decades of pressure and the evidence of irreversible reading and writing tradition, the Ministry of Education published a list of changes in the 1946 promulgation of accepted usage of Chinese characters.

For the most part, these changes fall into two categories: The reinstatement of certain readings, or pronunciations of characters (*ON-yomi* and *KUN-yomi*), and the reinstatement of words formed by compounds. All of the reinstated words in both categories were a part of accepted usage prior to 1946 and continued to be used by educated people even after the 1946 ruling.

The news of this change came too late to be incorporated into the main body of the *Manual for Reading Japanese,* but the Appendix features the complete list of changes.

xxxv

FOR THE FUTURE

I am not fully satisfied with this manual and propose the following.

*Research
and
curriculum development
proposals*

1. An updated investigation of the occurrence of characters and compounds in Japanese popular literature and a revision of this manual based on it.

2. Research based on the hypothesis that the governmental mandate embodied in the determination of the categories of General Use Characters and Educational Characters has continued to have a drastic and measurable effect on Japanese orthographical usage during the decade since the NLRI investigation.

3. A study of the frequency of occurrence of Japanese lexical items in speech and a study of the correlation of conversational and written usage.

4. A reading manual based on the frequency of occurrence of lexical items in conversation (not popular literature), since the effect of the multisensory stimuli of the same items in speech and reading would be even more powerful than the approach followed in this manual.

5. The completion of a page, or portion of a page, devoted to all the General Use Characters through 1850. As one approaches character 1850 there is usually *only one* important word for which the use of the Chinese character is retained! It would be valuable for the student of the language to have such information for all the characters at his fingertips.

                                Dale P. Crowley

Hilo, Hawaii
October, 1971

Graphically-Phonetically Related Morphographs:

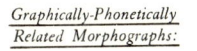

一
A

Occurrences/1000 15
Frequency Rank 1
Sanseido Page 1
Nelson Page 19

ON: ICHI, ITSU
kun: hito(tsu)

Basic Meaning(s): one, a unit, the same, just

High Frequency Compounds:

一部 ICHIBU -- a part, a copy (of a publication)
52

一般 IPPAN -- general, ordinary, liberal
460

一体 ITTAI -- one body, in fact, what on earth
96

一番 ICHIBAN -- number one, the first, most
519

統一 TOOITSU -- unity, uniformity, concentration
273

See 9, 25, 44, 208, 362, 417

Also 一時, 一致, 一同, 一家, 一瞬

Typical Phrases and Expanded Compounds:

一部分
一般的
一体全体
一番高い
統一をはかる
計画の一つ

Typical Conversational Usage:

ここは大学の一部です。
それは一般的な考えです。
一体全体どうしたのですか。
このビルは東京で一番高いビルです。
統一行動をとりましょう。
このすいかを一つください。

2 人

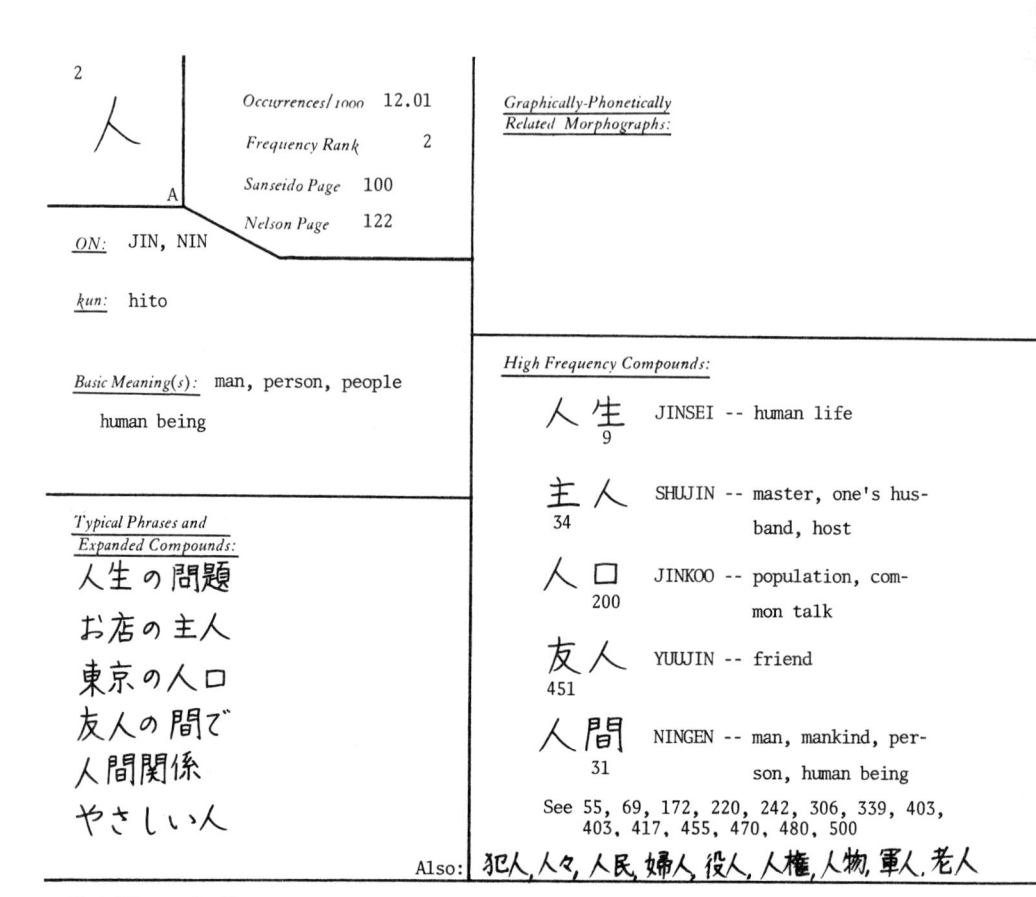

Occurrences/1000: 12.01
Frequency Rank: 2
Sanseido Page: 100
Nelson Page: 122

ON: JIN, NIN

kun: hito

Basic Meaning(s): man, person, people, human being

Graphically-Phonetically Related Morphographs:

High Frequency Compounds:

人生 (9) JINSEI -- human life
主人 (34) SHUJIN -- master, one's husband, host
人口 (200) JINKOO -- population, common talk
友人 (451) YUUJIN -- friend
人間 (31) NINGEN -- man, mankind, person, human being

See 55, 69, 172, 220, 242, 306, 339, 403, 403, 417, 455, 470, 480, 500

Also: 犯人, 人々, 人民, 婦人, 役人, 人権, 人物, 軍人, 老人

Typical Phrases and Expanded Compounds:

人生の問題
お店の主人
東京の人口
友人の間で
人間関係
やさしい人

Typical Conversational Usage:

人生にはいろいろな問題があります。
ご主人はおるすですか。
東京の人口は世界一です。
本田さんは私の友人です。
人間関係はむずかしいです。
あの人はとてもやさしい人です。

Graphically-Phonetically
Related Morphographs:

Occurrences/1000 10.6	3
Frequency Rank 3	日
Sanseido Page 481	
Nelson Page 473	A

<u>ON</u>: JITSU, NICHI

<u>kun</u>: hi, ka

High Frequency Compounds:

日本 NIHON, NIPPON -- Japan
6

今日 KONNICHI (KYOO) -- today, this day
50

毎日 MAINICHI -- everyday, daily
592

朝日 asahi -- morning sun, rising sun
217

昨日 SAKUJITSU (KINOO) -- yesterday
663

See 11, 21, 22, 39, 116, 147, 155, 190, 209

Also: 一日, 日々, 日曜日

Basic Meaning(s): day, sun, date, Sunday, Japanese

Typical Phrases and
Expanded Compounds:

日本人

今日の問題

毎日の仕事

朝日新聞

昨日の出来事

Typical Conversational Usage:

日本をいつたちますか。
今日の世界は大きな問題をかかえています。
毎日何をしていますか。
うちでは朝日新聞をとっています。
昨日上田さんにお会いしました。

4

国

Occurrences/1000 10.28
Frequency Rank 4
Sanseido Page 236
Nelson Page 261

A

ON: KOKU

kun: kuni

Basic Meaning(s): country, land, province, place, native land

Typical Phrases and Expanded Compounds:

米国市民
中国大陸
日本国民
外国製品
国際的
国をあげて

Graphically-Phonetically Related Morphographs:

High Frequency Compounds:

米国 155 — BEIKOKU -- U.S.A.

中国 12 — CHUUGOKU -- China, middle of a country, Hiroshima area

国民 30 — KOKUMIN -- the people, a national

外国 69 — GAIKOKU -- foreign country, foreign

国際 189 — KOKUSAI -- international (intercourse)

See 6, 16, 36, 46, 70, 77, 101, 211, 263, 265, 268, 272, 277, 326, 361, 379

Also: 帝国, 自国, 国務, 国立, 国々

Typical Conversational Usage:

米国へぜひ行ってみたいです。
中国は大きい国です。
それは国民にとって大きな問題です。
あの方は外国人ですか。
その方は国際的によく知られています。
お国はどちらですか。

Graphically-Phonetically Related Morphographs:

Occurrences/1000   9.52
Frequency Rank   5
Sanseido Page   257
Nelson Page   288

大 5
A

ON: DAI, TAI

kun: oo(kii), oo(i ni), oo(ki ni)

Basic Meaning(s): big, large, huge, very, severe

High Frequency Compounds:

大学   DAIGAKU -- college, university
15

大戦   TAISEN -- great war, world war
32

大変   TAIHEN -- serious, terrible, awful
254

大切   TAISETSU -- importance, value, important
208

大事   DAIJI -- great thing, serious affair, importance
10

See 99, 136, 232, 239, 299, 389, 390, 445, 447, 452

Also: 大体, 大会, 大臣, 拡大, 大抵, 大幅, 大分, 偉大

Typical Phrases and Expanded Compounds:

大学生
第二次世界大戦
大変な事件
大切な本
大事な物
大きい学校

Typical Conversational Usage:

東京大学はどこですか。
大戦前、私は中国にいました。
ピアノが大変じょうずになりました。
この本を大切にしてください。
大事な物をわすれてきました。
そんなに大きな木は見たことがありません。

6 本 A

ON: HON

kun:

Occurrences/1000 8.34
Frequency Rank 6
Sanseido Page 533
Nelson Page 64

Basic Meaning(s): book, the present, main, true, counter for long things

Graphically-Phonetically Related Morphographs:

High Frequency Compounds:

日本 — NIHON, NIPPON -- Japan
 3

資本 — SHIHON -- capital, fund
 141

本当 — HONTOO -- true, real, genuine
 68

根本 — KOMPON -- root, origin, basis, fundamental
 390

本国 — HONGOKU -- one's own country
 4

See 359

Also: 本年, 本部, 本物, 本気

Typical Phrases and Expanded Compounds:

日本政府
会社の資本
本当の話
根本的
本国へ帰る

Typical Conversational Usage:

日本には山がたくさんあります。
資本金はいくらですか。
東京は本当に人が多いです。
根本的にやりなおさなければなりません。
スミスさんは本国へ帰りました。
この本はだれの本ですか。

Graphically-Phonetically Related Morphographs:

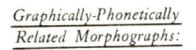

	7
Occurrences/1000 7.5	的
Frequency Rank 7	
Sanseido Page 583	
Nelson Page 637	A

ON: TEKI

kun: mato

Basic Meaning(s): noun-adjective ending, mark, target, object

High Frequency Compounds:

目的　　MOKUTEKI -- aim, purpose, intention
91

的中　　TEKICHUU -- hit the mark, come true
12

的確　　TEKIKAKU -- precision, accuracy,
343　　　　　　　　　　　infallibility

一般的　IPPANTEKI -- generally, commonly
1 460

Typical Phrases and Expanded Compounds:

人生の目的
予想が的中する
的確な回答
一般的な意見
的がはずれる

Typical Conversational Usage:

人生の目的は何ですか。
予想がみごとに的中しました。
的確な回答がほしいんです。
一般的にそういわれています。
あの人の考えは的がはずれています。

8

出

A

Occurrences/1000 7.00
Frequency Rank 8
Sanseido Page 310
Nelson Page 66

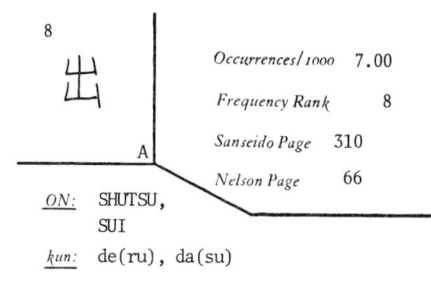

ON: SHUTSU, SUI
kun: de(ru), da(su)

Basic Meaning(s): come out, put out, born of, appearing from

Typical Phrases and Expanded Compounds:
出発点
輸出品
出身校
支出が多い
ふとした出来事
月が出る

Graphically-Phonetically Related Morphographs:

High Frequency Compounds:

出発 SHUPPATSU -- departure
102

輸出 YUSHUTSU -- export, exports, exportation
444

出身 SHUSSHIN -- hailing from, graduate from
174

支出 SHISHUTSU -- expenditure, disbursement
185

出来事 (dekigoto) -- incident, affair
27 10

See 185, 376, 472

Also: 出版, 出席, 出現, 出入, 出世

Typical Conversational Usage:

何時に出発しますか。
日本は輸出がさかんです。
私の出身地は岡山です。
今月の支出はとても多かったです。
きのうの出来事について話してください。
毎朝うちを七時に出ます。

生 {9}

Occurrences/1000 6.96
Frequency Rank 9
Sanseido Page 207
Nelson Page 616

ON: SEI, SHOO

kun: i(kiru), i(ki), i(kasu), u(mareru), u(mu), u(mi), ki, nama

Basic Meaning(s): life, live, birth, revive, pure, raw, simple

Graphically-Phonetically Related Morphographs:

牲 SEI
性 SEI, SHOO (119)
姓 SEI, SHOO (1385)
星 SEI, SHOO (1230)

High Frequency Compounds:

生産 (92) SEISAN -- production
学生 (15) GAKUSEI -- student
生活 (132) SEIKATSU -- life, livelihood
先生 (115) SENSEI -- teacher, master, doctor, professional person
一生 (1) ISSHOO -- a lifetime, one's (whole) life

See 2, 238, 249, 252, 287

Also: 生徒, 発生, 生涯, 誕生

Typical Phrases and Expanded Compounds:

自動車の生産
学生時代
東京の生活
きびしい先生
一生の問題
生き物

Typical Conversational Usage:

この工場では何を生産していますか。
学生の意見をまとめました。
東京で生活したことがありますか。
化学を山田先生にならっています。
しあわせな一生をおくりたいと思います。
その魚は生きていますか。

10 事

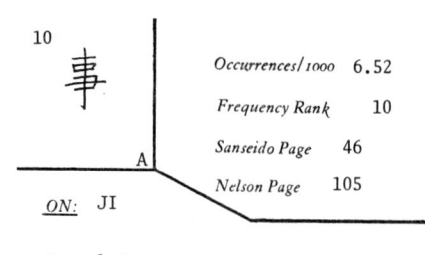

Occurrences/1000: 6.52
Frequency Rank: 10
Sanseido Page: 46
Nelson Page: 105

ON: JI
kun: koto

Basic Meaning(s): thing, matter, fact, business, experience

Graphically-Phonetically Related Morphographs:

High Frequency Compounds:

事実 JIJITSU -- fact, reality, as a matter of fact (37)

軍事 GUNJI -- naval and military affairs, military (36)

事業 JIGYOO -- enterprise, business, industry, activities (74)

事務 JIMU -- business, clerical work (244)

仕事 SHIgoto -- work, employment, occupation (271)

See 171, 173, 183, 187, 207, 209, 330, 477

Also: 理事, 事柄, 事変

Typical Phrases and Expanded Compounds:

事実がわかる
軍事的
事業の内容
事務所
大変な仕事

Typical Conversational Usage:

事実をうったえました。
アメリカは軍事的につよい国です。
父は事業に成功しました。
事務所で毎日働いています。
もう仕事がおわりましたか。

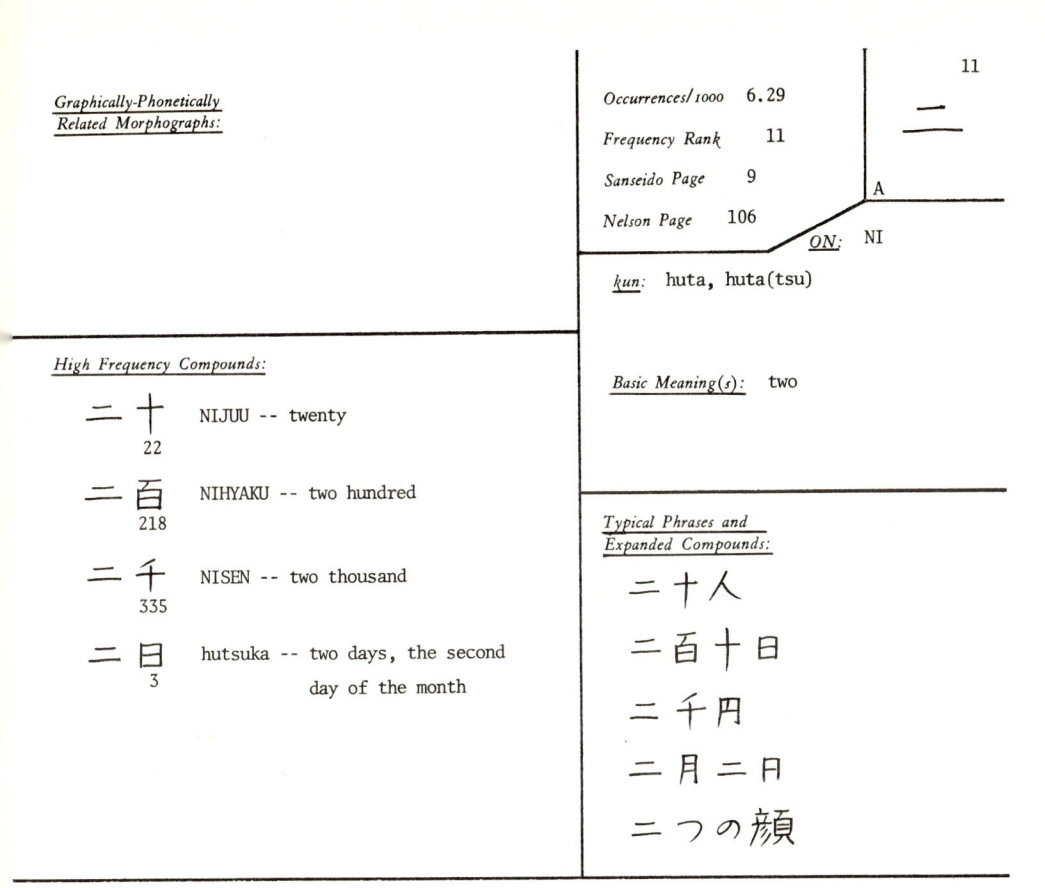

Graphically-Phonetically Related Morphographs:

Occurrences/1000 6.29
Frequency Rank 11
Sanseido Page 9
Nelson Page 106

二 11 A

ON: NI

kun: huta, huta(tsu)

High Frequency Compounds:

二十   NIJUU -- twenty
22

二百   NIHYAKU -- two hundred
218

二千   NISEN -- two thousand
335

二日   hutsuka -- two days, the second
3   day of the month

Basic Meaning(s): two

Typical Phrases and Expanded Compounds:

二十人

二百十日

二千円

二月二日

二つの顔

Typical Conversational Usage:

校庭にさくらの木を二十本うえました。
きのうの大会に二百人ぐらいあつまりました。
このシャツは二千円でかいました。
二日もすれば、よくなるでしょう。
りんごを二つたべました。

12

中

ON: CHUU

kun: naka

Occurrences/1000 6.00
Frequency Rank 12
Sanseido Page 228
Nelson Page 56

Basic Meaning(s): center, middle, mean, average, inside

Typical Phrases and Expanded Compounds:
中国地方
中心地
町の中央
中立国家
中学三年生
家の中

Graphically-Phonetically Related Morphographs:

忠 CHUU (1184)

虫 CHUU (1183)

仲 CHUU (951)

High Frequency Compounds:

中国 CHUUGOKU -- China, middle of a country, Hiroshima area
 4

中心 CHUUSHIN -- center, heart, emphasis
 64

中央 CHUUOO -- center, middle
 919

中立 CHUURITSU -- neutrality
 35

中学 CHUUGAKU -- middle school, junior high school
 15

See 101, 318, 478

Also: 中共, 女中, 途中, 背中

Typical Conversational Usage:

広島県は中国地方にあります。
このへんは町の中心にあたります。
町の中央に小学校があります。
スイスは中立国です。
一郎君は中学何年生ですか。
おもちゃはそのはこの中にあります。

Graphically-Phonetically Related Morphographs:

Occurrences/1000 5.90	年 13
Frequency Rank 13	
Sanseido Page 209	
Nelson Page 87	A
	ON: NEN
	kun: toshi

Basic Meaning(s): year, term of service, age, time of life

High Frequency Compounds:

毎年   MAINEN, MAItoshi -- every year, annually
592

青年   SEINEN -- youth, boy, young people
393

去年   KYONEN -- last year
496

年齢   NENREI -- age
1305

今年   KONNEN, KOtoshi -- this year
50

See 153

Also: 昨年, 本年

Typical Phrases and Expanded Compounds:

毎年の行事
青年会
去年の暮
年齢の差
今年の計画
年をとる

Typical Conversational Usage:

毎年あきに運動会をもようします。
この町の青年会は活発です。
去年の夏、北海道へ行ってきました。
あの方の年齢はよくわかりません。
今年はどこへも行きません。
お年はいくつですか。

14

自 A

Occurrences/1000 5.84
Frequency Rank 14
Sanseido Page 64
Nelson Page 755

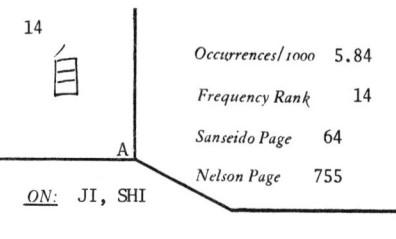

ON: JI, SHI

kun: mizuka(ra)

Basic Meaning(s): oneself, personally, naturally, of itself

Typical Phrases and Expanded Compounds:
自分自身
自由行動
自動車
不自然
自衛隊
自ら進んで

Graphically-Phonetically Related Morphographs:

High Frequency Compounds:

自分 28 JIBUN -- self, oneself

自由 134 JIYUU -- independence, freedom, liberty

自動 47 JIDOO -- automatic action

自然 144 SHIZEN -- nature

自衛 287 JIEI -- self defense, bodyguard

See 88, 174, 181, 242, 363, 380, 470

Also: 自己, 自国, 自体, 自覚, 自主

Typical Conversational Usage:

それは自分の問題です。
自由に質問してください。
このエレベーターは自動です。
けがが自然になおりました。
おとうとは自衛隊に入隊しました。
自らはんせいしてみてください。

Graphically-Phonetically Related Morphographs:

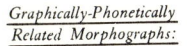

Occurrences/1000 5.67	学 15
Frequency Rank 15	
Sanseido Page 619	A
Nelson Page 309	
	ON: GAKU
	kun: mana(bu), mana(bi)

Basic Meaning(s): learning, learn

High Frequency Compounds:

大学   DAIGAKU -- college, university
 5

学生   GAKUSEI -- student
 9

学校   GAKKOO -- school
 233

科学   KAGAKU -- science
 369

学問   GAKUMON -- learning, study
 41

See 12, 19, 65, 89, 104, 126, 318, 345, 369, 387

Also: 哲学, 医学, 学部

Typical Phrases and Expanded Compounds:

大学四年
学生生活
学校の先生
科学者
学問の世界
英語を学ぶ

Typical Conversational Usage:

大学を出たら、先生になるつもりです。
学生生活は一番たのしいです。
あした学校へ行きますか。
小さい時から科学がすきでした。
大川さんはなかなか学問があります。
今英語とフランス語を学んでいます。

16

会

Occurrences/1000 5.55
Frequency Rank 16
Sanseido Page 104
Nelson Page 136

ON: KAI, E

kun: a(u), a(waseru), a(wasu)

Basic Meaning(s): meeting, meet, join

Graphically-Phonetically Related Morphographs:

絵 KAI (1100)

High Frequency Compounds:

会議 KAIGI -- meeting, council, conference
130

社会 SHAKAI -- society
82

会社 KAISHA -- company, firm
82

国会 KOKKAI -- national assembly, parliament, Diet
4

教会 KYOOKAI -- church
58

See 125, 127, 130, 158, 193, 224, 252, 394

Also: 会合, 大会, 会見, 会長, 都合, 会館

Typical Phrases and Expanded Compounds:

会議中
社会問題
会社の重役
国会議員
教会員
友だちに会う

Typical Conversational Usage:

あしたは大切な会議があります。
社会にはいろいろな問題があります。
となりの根本さんは会社の重役です。
中学生の時、国会を見学しました。
日曜日にはいつも教会へ行きます。
きのう東京駅で山本さんに会いました。

Graphically-Phonetically Related Morphographs:

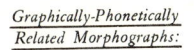

Occurrences/1000 5.28
Frequency Rank 17
Sanseido Page 600
Nelson Page 663

17

私

A

<u>ON</u>: SHI

<u>kun</u>: watakushi

Basic Meaning(s): I, myself, private affairs

High Frequency Compounds:

公私 KOOSHI -- government and people, public and personal affairs
212

私立 SHIRITSU -- private, nongovernment
 35

私書 SHISHO -- private document, private letter
121

Typical Phrases and Expanded Compounds:

公私混同

私立大学

私書箱

私の ~~母~~

Typical Conversational Usage:

公私混同してはいけません。

私の大学は私立です。

私書箱は何番ですか。

そこにある本は私のです。

18

行

A

Occurrences/1000 5.46
Frequency Rank 18
Sanseido Page 355
Nelson Page 801

<u>ON</u>: KOO, GYOO, AN

<u>kun</u>: i(ku), yu(ku), yu(ki), oko(nau), oko(nai)

Basic Meaning(s): go, leave, do, perform, performance, action

Typical Phrases and Expanded Compounds:
あやしい行動
日本銀行
実行力
流行のドレス
修学旅行
東京へ行く

Graphically-Phonetically Related Morphographs:

High Frequency Compounds:

行動　KOODOO -- action, conduct, behavior
47

銀行　GINKOO -- bank
574

実行　JIKKOO -- practice, deed, action
37

流行　RYUUKOO -- fashion, popularity
235

旅行　RYOKOO -- journey, trip
752

See 23, 156, 235, 446

Also: 飛行

Typical Conversational Usage:

あの人の行動は何となくあやしいです。
銀行でお金をおろしてきます。
何事も実行することが大切です。
これは流行のドレスです。
旅行はとてもたのしいです。
まだ九州へ行ったことがありません。

者 19

Graphically-Phonetically Related Morphographs:

煮 SHA

Occurrences/1000 5.31
Frequency Rank 19
Sanseido Page 561
Nelson Page 729

ON: SHA
kun: mono

Basic Meaning(s): person, somebody, agent, actor

High Frequency Compounds:

学者 GAKUSHA -- scholar, learned man, scribe
15

読者 DOKUSHA -- reader, subscriber
323

記者 KISHA -- journalist, reporter
209

患者 KANJA -- patient, victim of a disease
1016

医者 ISHA -- medical doctor
772

Also: 筆者, 作者, 業者, 役者

Typical Phrases and Expanded Compounds:

学者の意見
愛読者
記者会見
入院患者
若者

Typical Conversational Usage:

学会に学者が大ぜいあつまります。
私は毎日新聞の愛読者です。
山本さんは新聞記者です。
八号室の患者はきのう入院しました。
医者にみてもらいました。
私は山口という者です。

20 見

Occurrences/1000 5.29
Frequency Rank 20
Sanseido Page 587
Nelson Page 813

A

ON: KEN

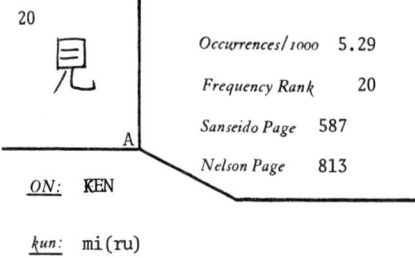

kun: mi(ru)

Basic Meaning(s): see, look at, hopes, chances

Graphically-Phonetically Related Morphographs:

Typical Phrases and Expanded Compounds:

意見をのべる
大発見
見解をことにする
見物人
見当違い
テレビを見る

High Frequency Compounds:

意見 IKEN -- opinion
86

発見 HAKKEN -- discovery
102

見解 KENKAI -- opinion, view
142

見物 KEMBUTSU -- sightseeing, sight, spectacle
95

見当 KENTOO -- aim, mark, estimate, guess
68

See 396

Typical Conversational Usage:

みんなの意見を聞いてみましょう。
コロンブスはアメリカを発見しました。
二人の見解がことなりました。
おじいちゃんは東京見物に行きました。
まったく見当がつきません。
きのう、おもしろい映画を見ました。

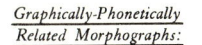

Graphically-Phonetically Related Morphographs:

参 SAN (350)

惨 SAN (1175)

Occurrences/1000 5.19
Frequency Rank 21
Sanseido Page 13
Nelson Page 28

21
三
A

ON: SAN

kun: mi(tsu), mi(ttsu)

Basic Meaning(s): three

High Frequency Compounds:

三十 (22) SANJUU -- thirty

三百 (218) SAMBYAKU -- three hundred, many

三日 (3) mikka -- three days, the third day (of the month)

Typical Phrases and Expanded Compounds:

三十代
三百円
三日ぼうず
三つの子

Typical Conversational Usage:

私はもう三十をすぎました。
手もとに三百円しかありません。
会議は三日間です。
この子はまだ三つです。

22

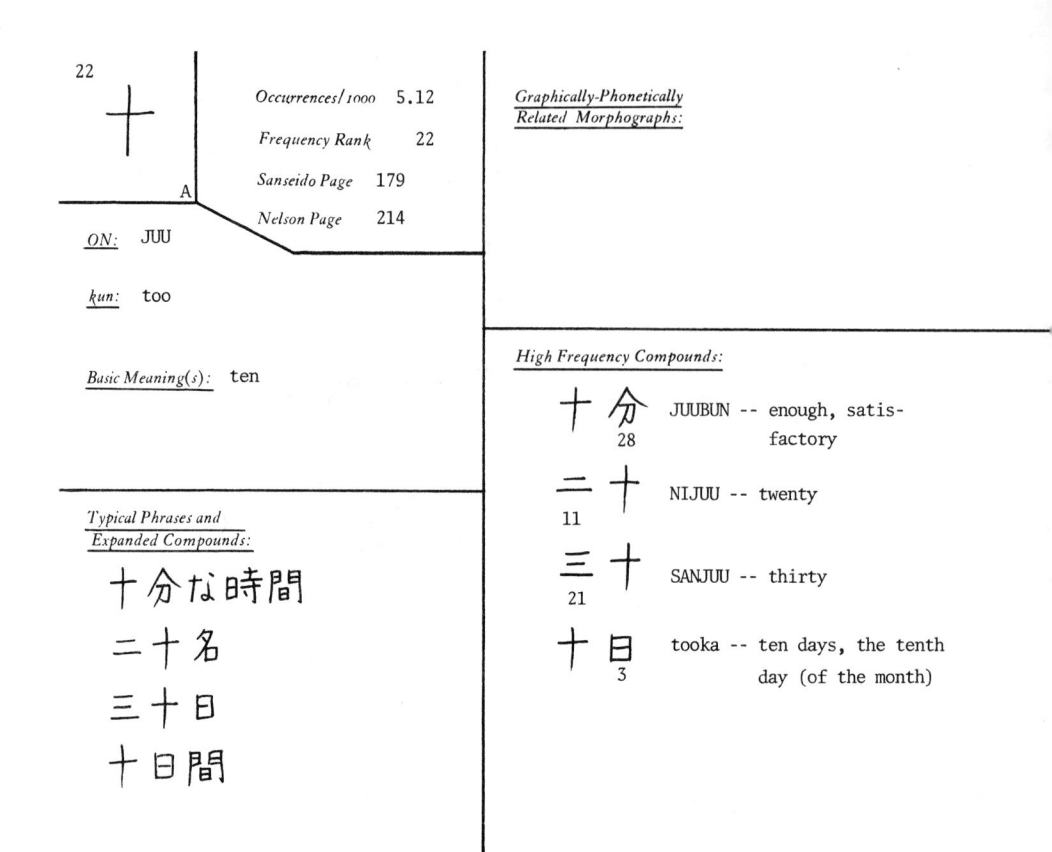

十 A

Occurrences/1000 5.12
Frequency Rank 22
Sanseido Page 179
Nelson Page 214

ON: JUU

kun: too

Basic Meaning(s): ten

Graphically-Phonetically Related Morphographs:

High Frequency Compounds:

十分 JUUBUN -- enough, satis-
 28   factory

二十 NIJUU -- twenty
 11

三十 SANJUU -- thirty
 21

十日 tooka -- ten days, the tenth
 3   day (of the month)

Typical Phrases and Expanded Compounds:

十分な時間
二十名
三十日
十日間

Typical Conversational Usage:

もう十分です。
その仕事は二十人ぐらいでできるでしょう。
私のたんじょう日は四月三十日です。
今月の十日に東京へ行きます。

		23
	Occurrences/1000 4.99	政
	Frequency Rank 23	
	Sanseido Page 471	A
	Nelson Page 456	

Graphically-Phonetically Related Morphographs:

正 SEI, SHOO (139)   証 SHOO (448)
征 SEI (1231)   症 SHOO
整 SEI (825)

ON: SEI, SHOO

kun: matsurigoto

Basic Meaning(s): government, rule

High Frequency Compounds:

政府 SEIHU -- the government, the administration
168

政治 SEIJI -- government, administration, politics
88

政策 SEISAKU -- policy, political measures
256

政党 SEITOO -- political party
76

政権 SEIKEN -- political powers, reins of government, administration
162

行政 GYOOSEI -- administration
18

Typical Phrases and Expanded Compounds:

政府の方針
政治問題
政府の政策
二大政党
政権をとる
地方行政

Typical Conversational Usage:

政府の方針が明らかにされました。
政治家にはなりたくありません。
政府の政策が変わりました。
アメリカの二大政党は何と何ですか。
今は自由民主党が政権をにぎっています。
行政がすこしみだれています。

24

時

Occurrences/1000 4.88
Frequency Rank 24
Sanseido Page 488
Nelson Page 481

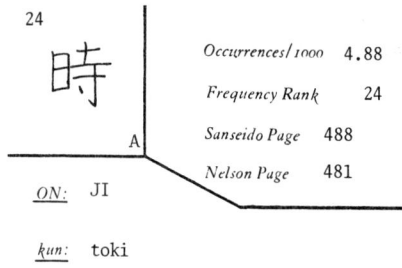

ON: JI
kun: toki

Basic Meaning(s): time, hour, o'clock, occasion, opportunity

Typical Phrases and Expanded Compounds:

明治時代
何時間
時間制
戦争当時
腕時計
その時

Graphically-Phonetically Related Morphographs:

寺 JI (763)
持 JI (94)
侍 JI

High Frequency Compounds:

時代 JIDAI -- period, age
 87
何時 nanJI -- what time
 43
時間 JIKAN -- an hour, time,
 31   period
当時 TOOJI -- at that time, in those
 68   days, in these days
時計 toKEI -- clock, watch
 210

See 54, 247

Also: 一時, 時刻

Typical Conversational Usage:

学生時代のことはわすれられません。
毎日、何時間ぐらいべんきょうしますか。
もう学校へ行く時間です。
戦争当時どこにいましたか。
この時計はスイス製です。
町へ行く時は、いっしょに行きましょう。

方 25

Graphically-Phonetically Related Morphographs:

放 HOO (325)　　訪 HOO (957)
芳 HOO
倣 HOO

Occurrences/1000	4.80
Frequency Rank	25
Sanseido Page	81
Nelson Page	470

ON: HOO
kun: kata

Basic Meaning(s): direction, way, person, settlement, manner

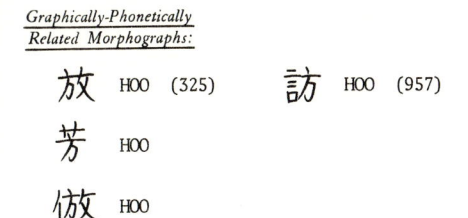

High Frequency Compounds:

地方 (45) CHIHOO -- locality, the country, vicinity
方法 (100) HOOHOO -- way, method, means
一方 (1) IPPOO -- one direction, (on) the other hand, a quarter
方面 (117) HOOMEN -- direction, side, district
両方 (288) RYOOHOO -- both

See 169, 172, 192, 256, 356

Also: 夕方, 方針, 双方

Typical Phrases and Expanded Compounds:

関東地方
やさしい方法
一方通行
東京方面
両方とも
その方

Typical Conversational Usage:

きのうこの地方に大雨がふりました。
その方法はむずかしいですか、やさしいですか。
ここは一方通行です。
このバスは上野方面へ行きますか。
東京大学と大阪大学は両方とも国立大学です。
その方をごぞんじですか。

26

思

Occurrences/1000 4.78
Frequency Rank 26
Sanseido Page 576
Nelson Page 622

A

ON: SHI

kun: omo(u), omo(i)

Basic Meaning(s): think, believe, consider, guess

Typical Phrases and Expanded Compounds:

中国の思想
思慮のある人
思うように

Graphically-Phonetically Related Morphographs:

志、SHI (681)

誌、SHI (737)

High Frequency Compounds:

思想 SHISOO -- thought, idea, ideas, conception
197

思慮 SHIRYO -- thought, consideration
831

Typical Conversational Usage:

中川さんの思想はゆたかです。
思慮のない事をしてはいけません。
なかなか思うようにいきません。

Graphically-Phonetically Related Morphographs:

Occurrences/1000 4.66	27
Frequency Rank 27	来
Sanseido Page 44	
Nelson Page 91	A

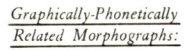

ON: RAI

kun: ku(ru)

High Frequency Compounds:

来年 RAINEN -- next year, the coming year
13

将来 SHOORAI -- future, one's future, prospects
447

以来 IRAI -- since
118

未来 MIRAI -- future, future life, future tense
624

Basic Meaning(s): coming, come, arrive, become, since

Typical Phrases and Expanded Compounds:

来年の今ごろ
近い将来
先月以来
未来のアメリカ
ご飯を食べて来る

Typical Conversational Usage:

来年アメリカに行くつもりです。
将来のことはまだはっきりわかりません。
大学を出て以来、中山さんに会っていません。
未来の世界はどうなりますか。
うちでご飯を食べて来ました。

28 分

A

Occurrences/1000 4.57
Frequency Rank 28
Sanseido Page 148
Nelson Page 171

ON: BUN, HUN, BU
kun: wa(keru), wa(kareru)

Basic Meaning(s): division, part, a minute of time, understand, separate

Typical Phrases and Expanded Compounds:
自分の問題
十分な答
部分的
気分が悪い
半分以上
多分の

See 170, 418

Graphically-Phonetically Related Morphographs:

粉 HUN
紛 HUN

High Frequency Compounds:

自分 JIBUN -- self, oneself
14

十分 JUUBUN -- enough, sufficient, satisfactory, perfect
22

部分 BUBUN -- part, portion, section
52

気分 KIBUN -- feeling, mood, spirit
55

半分 HAMBUN -- half
324

多分 TABUN -- perhaps, maybe, probably, a great deal
128

Also: 分裂,随分,大分,分子,分析

Typical Conversational Usage:

自分でやってみてください。
もう十分です。
それはほんの一部分です。
どうも気分がすぐれません。
半分でけっこうです。
多分あらしになるかもしれません。

Graphically-Phonetically Related Morphographs:

上 [29]

Occurrences/1000 4.56
Frequency Rank 29
Sanseido Page 191
Nelson Page 223

<u>ON</u>: JOO
<u>kun</u>: ue, kami, a(garu), a(geru), nobo(ru), nobo(ri), nobo(su)

Basic Meaning(s): up, top, best, surface, go up, give (to one's superiors)

High Frequency Compounds:

以上 [118] IJOO -- more than, beyond, the above-mentioned

向上 [192] KOOJOO -- advancement, progress, improvement

地上 [45] CHIJOO -- terrestrial, on the ground, on earth

See 300, 445

Typical Phrases and Expanded Compounds:

十人以上
教育の向上
地上十二階
たなの上

Typical Conversational Usage:

これ以上できません。
戦後、女性の地位が向上しました。
あのビルは地下二階、地上十階だてです。
テーブルの上にある本をとってください。

30 民

Occurrences/1000 4.43
Frequency Rank 30
Sanseido Page 219
Nelson Page 42

A

ON: MIN

kun: tami

Basic Meaning(s): people, subjects, nation

Graphically-Phonetically Related Morphographs:

眠 MIN (832)

High Frequency Compounds:

国民 (4) KOKUMIN -- the people, the citizens, the nationals

民主 (34) MINSHU -- democracy, the head of the nation

市民 (305) SHIMIN -- citizen, townspeople

民間 (31) MINKAN -- private, civil, unofficial

農民 (229) NOOMIN -- peasants, farmers

See 232, 301

Also: 人民, 植民

Typical Phrases and Expanded Compounds:

国民性
民主主義
市民権
民間放送
農民の生活

Typical Conversational Usage:

この本には、日本の国民性がよくあらわされています。
アメリカは民主主義の国です。
公害は市民にとって大きな問題です。
民間放送局は東京にいくつありますか。
農民の生活がよくなりました。

間 — 31

Graphically-Phonetically Related Morphographs:

閑 KAN (1201)

関 KAN (84)

簡 KAN (882)

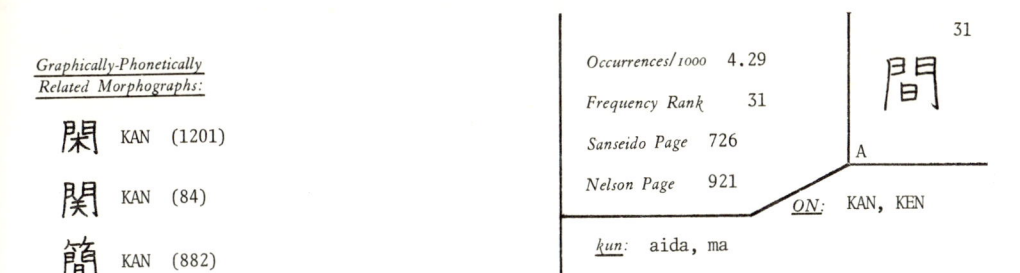

High Frequency Compounds:

人間 NINGEN -- man, person, human being
(2)

時間 JIKAN -- an hour, time, period
(24)

世間 SEKEN -- world, society, the public, rumor
(01)

期間 KIKAN -- term, period
(247)

週間 SHUUKAN -- week
(1141)

See 30, 274, 281, 399

Also: 仲間, 瞬間

Occurrences/1000 4.29
Frequency Rank 31
Sanseido Page 726
Nelson Page 921

ON: KAN, KEN

kun: aida, ma

Basic Meaning(s): interval, space, between, among, time

Typical Phrases and Expanded Compounds:

人間社会

長時間

世間話

売出し期間

一週間

三年の間

Typical Conversational Usage:

人間関係はなかなかむずかしいです。
時間的にみて、その仕事はちょっとむりです。
オリンピックは、今、世間の話題になっています。
テストの期間がながすぎます。
三週間あれば、国内をまわれるでしょう。
山田さんには、この間、会ったばかりです。

32

戦

A

Occurrences/1000 4.08
Frequency Rank 32
Sanseido Page 268
Nelson Page 413

ON: SEN

kun: tataka(u), tataka(i)

Basic Meaning(s): war, battle, game, fight, strife

Graphically-Phonetically Related Morphographs:

High Frequency Compounds:

戦争 SENSOO -- war, battle, campaign
107

戦前 SENZEN -- before the war, prewar days
53

戦後 SENGO -- after the war
48

大戦 TAISEN -- World War, great war
5

終戦 SHUUSEN -- end of the war
392

See 420, 478

Also: 休戦

Typical Phrases and Expanded Compounds:

ベトナム戦争
戦前の日本
戦後の経済
大戦前
終戦後

Typical Conversational Usage:

戦争が、はやくおわればいいと思います。
戦前、私は九州にいました。
戦後のふっこうぶりは大したものです。
大戦がおわるまで、北海道にいました。
終戦後、父は事業をはじめました。
その問題で戦っています。

Graphically-Phonetically Related Morphographs:

33

合

A

Occurrences/1000 4.03
Frequency Rank 33
Sanseido Page 105
Nelson Page 138

ON: GOO (GAS)

kun: a(u), a(wasu), a(waseru)

Basic Meaning(s): fit, agree with, join together, unite, one-tenth SHOO

High Frequency Compounds:

合衆国 GASSHUUKOKU -- United States of America, a federal state
232 4

場合 baai -- occasion, case, instance, situation, circumstances
49

合理 GOORI -- rationality
59

具合 GUai -- fitness, condition, state of health
534

連合 RENGOO -- union, federation, alliance
101

See: 73, 122, 210, 267, 307, 371

Also: 会合, 知合

Typical Phrases and Expanded Compounds:

アメリカ合衆国
その場合
合理的
車の具合
国際連合
似合う

Typical Conversational Usage:

ハワイは合衆国で五十番目の州です。
行く場合には、知らせてください。
それは合理的ではありません。
体の具合が思わしくありません。
国際連合の働きは大きいと思います。
このドレスはよく似合いますか。

34 主

Occurrences/1000 3.85
Frequency Rank 34
Sanseido Page 84
Nelson Page 110

A

<u>ON:</u> SHU, SU

<u>kun:</u> nushi

Basic Meaning(s): master, lord, husband, owner

Graphically-Phonetically Related Morphographs:

High Frequency Compounds:

主義 (62) SHUGI -- principle, policy, -ism

民主 (30) MINSHU -- democracy, the head of the nation

主人 (2) SHUJIN -- master, landlord, one's husband

主張 (553) SHUCHOO -- insistence, assertion, emphasis

主権 (162) SHUKEN -- sovereignty, dominion

See 78

Also: 主婦, 主食, 自主, 主催

Typical Phrases and Expanded Compounds:

共産主義
自由民主党
主人の出張
意見の主張
主権在民

Typical Conversational Usage:

あの方は平和主義者です。
ケネディは民主党でした。
主人は仕事で出張しました。
自分の意見ばかり主張してはいけません。
主権は国民にあります。

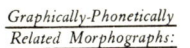

Graphically-Phonetically Related Morphographs:

	35
Occurrences/1000 3.75	立
Frequency Rank 35	
Sanseido Page 85	
Nelson Page 676	A

ON: RITSU

kun: ta(tsu), ta(teru)

Basic Meaning(s): standing, stand, be built, set up, depart

High Frequency Compounds:

独立   DOKURITSU -- independence, freedom,
205   self-reliance

立派   RIPPA -- fine, excellent, honorable
286

中立   CHUURITSU -- neutrality
13

立場   tachiba -- standpoint, position,
49   situation

対立   TAIRITSU -- opposition, antagonism
39

See 160, 343

Also: 国立, 自立

Typical Phrases and Expanded Compounds:

独立国家
立派な人
中立の立場
わるい立場
対立者
上に立つ人

Typical Conversational Usage:

イスラエルはいつ独立しましたか。
民子さんのおとうさんは立派な方です。
本田さんの立場はいつも中立です。
私の立場がありません。
アラブの国々はよくイスラエルと対立します。
あそこに立っている方はどなたですか。

36 軍

A

Occurrences/1000   3.71
Frequency Rank   36
Sanseido Page   154
Nelson Page   187

ON: GUN

kun:

Basic Meaning(s): army, troops

Graphically-Phonetically Related Morphographs:

High Frequency Compounds:

軍事   GUNJI -- naval and military
 10   affairs

軍隊   GUNTAI -- army, troops
 225

海軍   KAIGUN -- navy
 206

軍国   GUNKOKU -- nation at war,
  4   militant nation

軍備   GUMBI -- armament, military
 201   preparation

See 155, 304, 445, 477

Also: 軍人, 米軍, 軍部, 軍需, 軍閥

Typical Phrases and Expanded Compounds:

軍事教育
米国軍隊
海軍と陸軍
軍国主義
再軍備

Typical Conversational Usage:

戦前、兄は軍事教育をうけました。
軍隊に入って、間もなく戦地に行きました。
海軍と陸軍では、どちらの方がすきですか。
戦前の日本は軍国的でした。
あのデモは再軍備反対のデモです。

実 37

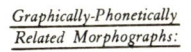

Occurrences/1000 3.71
Frequency Rank 37
Sanseido Page 283
Nelson Page 204

A

ON: JITSU

kun: mi, mino(ru)

Basic Meaning(s): truth, reality, sincerity, seed, ripen, bear fruit

Graphically-Phonetically Related Morphographs:

High Frequency Compounds:

現実 (67) GENJITSU -- actuality, reality
事実 (10) JIJITSU -- fact, reality, as a matter of fact
実行 (18) JIKKOO -- practice, performance, action
実現 (67) JITSUGEN -- realization, fruition, materialization
実際 (189) JISSAI -- truth, fact, actually

See 105, 195, 343, 385

Also: 実業, 実施, 実質, 実践

Typical Phrases and Expanded Compounds:

現実の問題
事実をうったえる
実行力
ゆめの実現
実際問題として
実りの秋

Typical Conversational Usage:

それは現実の問題として考えなければなりません。
事実、そんな事をしたことはありません。
思ったことを実行してみてください。
ゆめが実現して、とてもうれしいです。
それは実際に聞いた話です。
みかんがたくさん実りました。

38 力

Occurrences/1000 3.70
Frequency Rank 38
Sanseido Page 168
Nelson Page 204

A

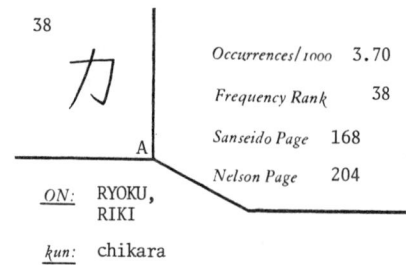

ON: RYOKU, RIKI
kun: chikara

Basic Meaning(s): strength, energy, power

Graphically-Phonetically Related Morphographs:

High Frequency Compounds:

努力 DORYOKU -- endeavor, effort, exertion
634

協力 KYOORYOKU -- cooperation
193

能力 NOORYOKU -- ability, capacity, faculty
285

暴力 BOORYOKU -- violence, force, terrorism
556

勢力 SEIRYOKU -- influence, power, might
293

See 133, 162, 243, 263, 332, 397

Also: 魅力, 全力

Typical Phrases and Expanded Compounds:
努力をおしまない
協力的な人
能力におうじて
暴力行為
勢力家
力持ち

Typical Conversational Usage:

できるだけ努力してみましょう。
みんなの協力がなければ、この仕事はできません。
子どもの能力をのばしてあげましょう。
暴力をふるってはいけません。
いつも勢力争いがたえません。
力のあるかぎり、がんばりましょう。

対 [39]

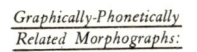

Graphically-Phonetically Related Morphographs:

Occurrences/1000 3.66
Frequency Rank 39
Sanseido Page 476
Nelson Page 464

A

ON: TAI, TSUI
kun:

Basic Meaning(s): the opposite, even, equal, pair

High Frequency Compounds:

反対 [146] — HANTAI -- opposition, resistance, contrast

絶対 [613] — ZETTAI -- absolute, positive, categorical

対立 [35] — TAIRITSU -- opposition, antagonism, co-ordination

対策 [256] — TAISAKU -- countermeasure

対日 [3] — TAINICHI -- toward Japan, with Japan

See 111, 279, 418

Also: 対外, 対照

Typical Phrases and Expanded Compounds:

反対側
絶対多数
意見の対立
対策をこうずる
対日感情
相手に対して

Typical Conversational Usage:

その意見には反対です。
その政策には絶対反対です。
二人の意見は対立しています。
水害地に対して対策をねっています。
アメリカの対日感情はとてもいいと思います。
この問題に対して、どう思いますか。

40 五 A

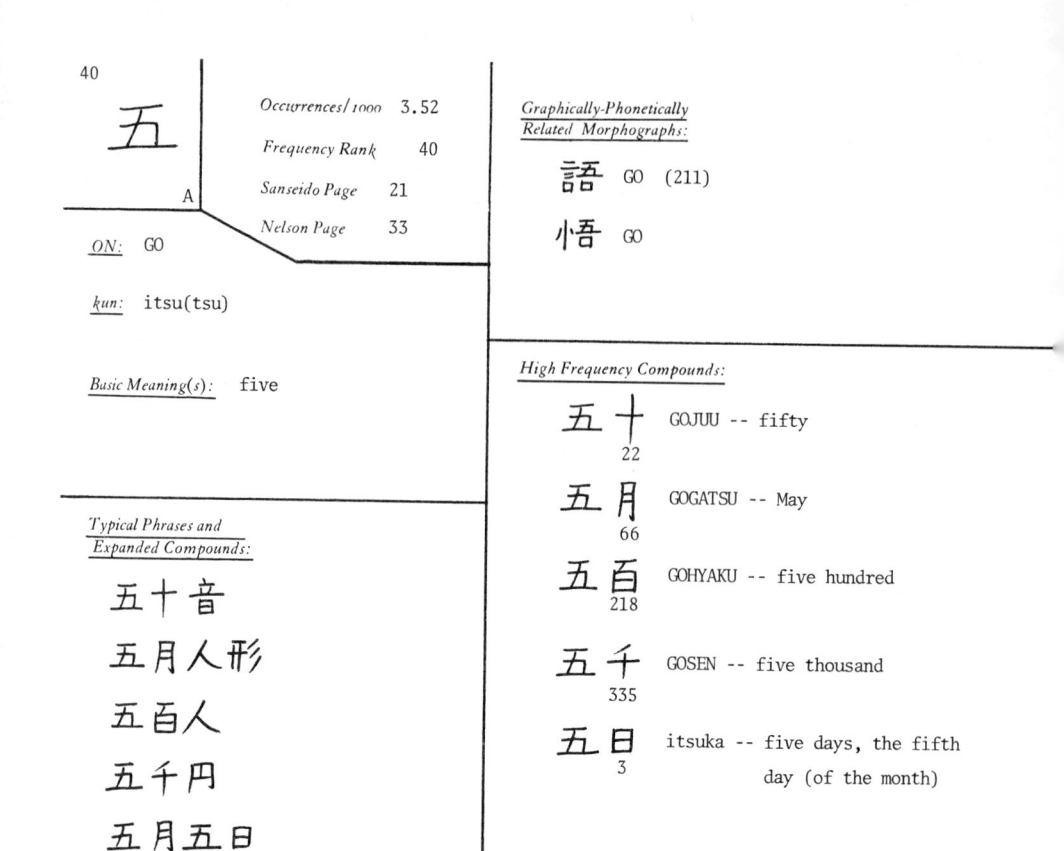

Occurrences/1000 3.52
Frequency Rank 40
Sanseido Page 21
Nelson Page 33

<u>ON</u>: GO

<u>kun</u>: itsu(tsu)

Basic Meaning(s): five

Graphically-Phonetically Related Morphographs:

語 GO (211)

悟 GO

Typical Phrases and Expanded Compounds:

五十音
五月人形
五百人
五千円
五月五日

High Frequency Compounds:

五十 GOJUU -- fifty
22

五月 GOGATSU -- May
66

五百 GOHYAKU -- five hundred
218

五千 GOSEN -- five thousand
335

五日 itsuka -- five days, the fifth
3   day (of the month)

Typical Conversational Usage:

父は満五十さいになりました。
五月五日は子どもの日です。
この中学校の一年生は、全部で五百人ぐらいです。
この五月人形は五千円でかいました。
五日で北海道をまわるつもりです。

Graphically-Phonetically Related Morphographs:

門　MON　(376)

Occurrences/1000　3.47
Frequency Rank　41
Sanseido Page　725
Nelson Page　920

問　41

A

ON:　MON

kun:　to(u), toi

Basic Meaning(s):　question, problem, subject

High Frequency Compounds:

問題　MONDAI -- problem, question, issue
　51

学問　GAKUMON -- learning, studies, scholarship
　15

質問　SHITSUMON -- question, interrogation
　359

疑問　GIMON -- doubt, question, problem
　488

問屋　tonya -- wholesaler, forwarding agent
　236

Typical Phrases and Expanded Compounds:

練習問題

学問的

むずかしい質問

疑問がはれる

くすり問屋

Typical Conversational Usage:

どのくらいできるかが問題です。

今、学問的な見地から、その問題をしらべています。

何か質問がありますか。

疑問の点は、どしどしたずねてください。

うちはくすり問屋をしています。

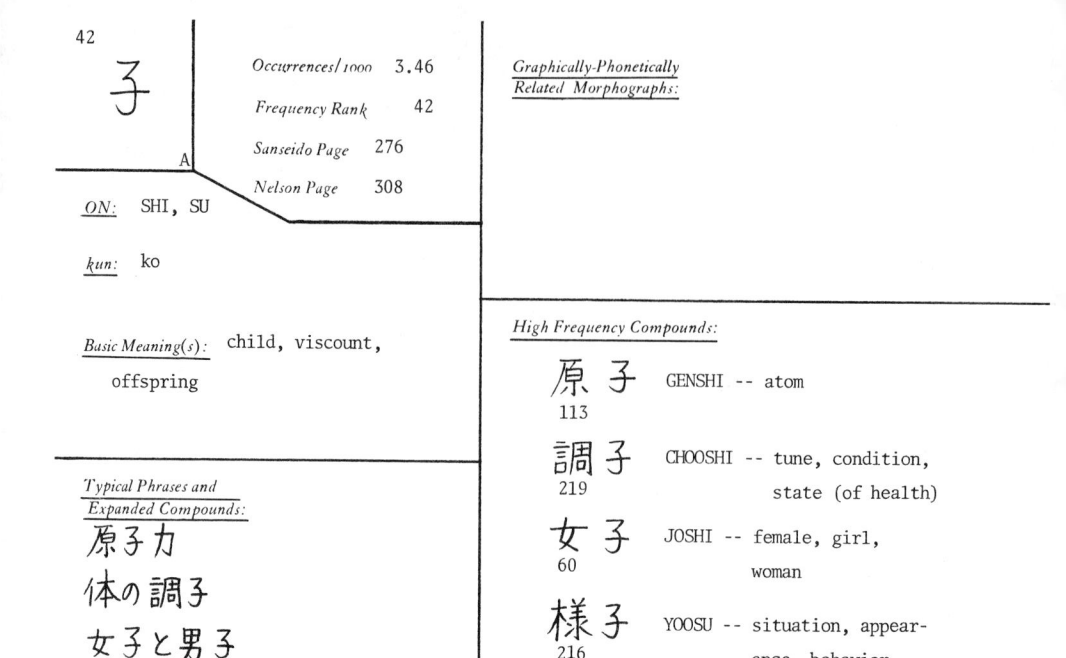

42

子

Occurrences/1000 3.46
Frequency Rank 42
Sanseido Page 276
Nelson Page 308

ON: SHI, SU

kun: ko

Basic Meaning(s): child, viscount, offspring

Typical Phrases and Expanded Compounds:
原子力
体の調子
女子と男子
おかしな様子
息子の会社
あの子

Graphically-Phonetically Related Morphographs:

High Frequency Compounds:

原子 GENSHI -- atom
113

調子 CHOOSHI -- tune, condition,
219   state (of health)

女子 JOSHI -- female, girl,
60   woman

様子 YOOSU -- situation, appear-
216   ance, behavior

息子 musuko -- son, boy, young
786   man

See 60, 315

Also: 男子

Typical Conversational Usage:

原子の力は大きいです。
何だか体の調子が思わしくありません。
そこには女子しかおりません。
ちょっと仕事の様子を見てきます。
息子は東京の大学に行っています。
あの子はよく働くいい子でした。

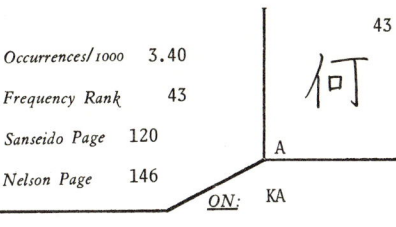

何

Occurrences/1000: 3.40
Frequency Rank: 43
Sanseido Page: 120
Nelson Page: 146

ON: KA
kun: nani, nan

Basic Meaning(s): what, why, anything, something

Graphically-Phonetically Related Morphographs:

荷 KA (1254)
可 KA (463)
河 KA (614)
歌 KA (486)

High Frequency Compounds:

何時 (24) nanJI -- what time, when
何故 (523) naze, naniyue -- why, how
如何 (337) ikaga, ika -- how (about it), how (are you)
何事 (10) nanigoto -- what, something, everything
何者 (19) nanimono -- who, what kind of person

Typical Phrases and Expanded Compounds:

何時ごろ
何故か
如何様師
何事でも
何者かにおそわれる

Typical Conversational Usage:

おじさんは何時ごろつきますか。
何故そんなことをしたのですか。
毎日如何おすごしですか。
何事でもまじめに仕事をすることが大切です。
何者かにさいふをぬすまれました。

44 言

Occurrences/1000 3.35
Frequency Rank 44
Sanseido Page 676
Nelson Page 821

A

ON: GEN, GON

kun: i(u), koto

Basic Meaning(s): word, phrase, speech, speak, say, tell

Graphically-Phonetically Related Morphographs:

Typical Phrases and Expanded Compounds:

言論界
発言が多い
証言をもとめる
予言者
一言二言
何を言っても

High Frequency Compounds:

言論 110 — GENRON — speech, discussion

発言 102 — HATSUGEN — speaking, speech, utterance

証言 448 — SHOOGEN — testimony, evidence

予言 283 — YOGEN — prediction, prophecy

一言 1 — hitokoto — a word, a single word

Also: 宣言

Typical Conversational Usage:

日本には言論の自由があります。
どしどし発言してください。
公判で証言をもとめられました。
来年の出来事について、予言した人がいます。
私にも一言いわせてください。
何も言うことがありません。

Graphically-Phonetically Related Morphographs:

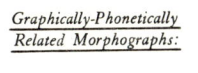

池 CHI (650)

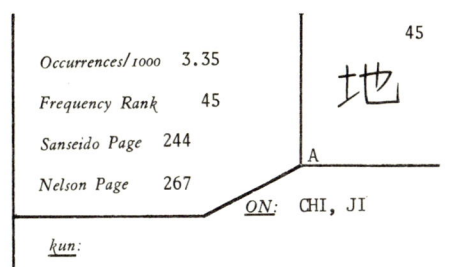

Occurrences/1000 3.35
Frequency Rank 45
Sanseido Page 244
Nelson Page 267

地 45

ON: CHI, JI

kun:

Basic Meaning(s): earth, land, ground

High Frequency Compounds:

地方 CHIHOO -- locality, region, area
25

土地 TOCHI -- land, estate, locality
360

地位 CHII -- position, status, office
319

基地 KICHI -- base
251

地震 JISHIN -- earthquake
908

See 229, 363

Also: 地域, 地球, 地区, 地理

Typical Phrases and Expanded Compounds:

地方選挙
わるい土地
高い地位
米軍基地
大地震

Typical Conversational Usage:

きのう、東京地方はあめでした。
いなかの方に土地をかいました。
おじさんは会社でも上の方の地位にいます。
川村さんは立川の米軍基地で働いていたそうです。
最近、各地で地震がよくおこっています。

46 家

Occurrences/1000 3.31
Frequency Rank 46
Sanseido Page 286
Nelson Page 321

ON: KA, KE

kun: ie, ya

Basic Meaning(s): house, home, family, profession, specialist

Graphically-Phonetically Related Morphographs:

嫁 KA (1309)

High Frequency Compounds:

国家 KOKKA -- nation, country
4

家庭 KATEI -- home
600

作家 SAKKA -- writer, novelist, artist
120

家族 KAZOKU -- family, household
301

画家 GAKA -- painter, artist
176

See 229, 236

Also: 一家

Typical Phrases and Expanded Compounds:

国家権力
家庭用品
現代作家
家族会議
天才画家
新しい家

Typical Conversational Usage:

国家の安全は大切です。
中山さんのご主人はとても家庭的です。
どんな作家がすきですか。
ご家族はみなさんお元気ですか。
ピカソはゆうめいな画家です。
あの新しい家は和子さんの家です。

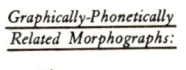

Graphically-Phonetically Related Morphographs:

働 DOO (137)

Occurrences/1000 3.30
Frequency Rank 47
Sanseido Page 73
Nelson Page 208

動   47
A

ON: DOO

kun: ugo(ku), ugo(ki), ugo(kasu)

Basic Meaning(s): motion, change, move, operate

High Frequency Compounds:

運動 UNDOO -- motion, movement, exercise (sports)
157

活動 KATSUDOO -- activity, action
132

自動 JIDOO -- automatic action
14

動物 DOOBUTSU -- animal
95

行動 KOODOO -- conduct, action, movements
18

See 146

Also: 感動, 暴動

Typical Phrases and Expanded Compounds:

学生運動
活動家
自動のカメラ
動物園
行動派
手を動かす

Typical Conversational Usage:

毎日、すこし運動することにしています。
山本さんは社会的によく活動しています。
このカメラは自動です。
子どもを連れて、動物園へ行きました。
変な行動をとってはいけません。
思うように体が動きません。

48

後

Occurrences/1000 3.18
Frequency Rank 48
Sanseido Page 357
Nelson Page 383

A

ON: KOO, GO

kun: nochi, ushiro

Basic Meaning(s): back, rear, behind, after

Typical Phrases and Expanded Compounds:
最後の手段
今後の成り行き
戦後の日本
以後の問題
午後三時
この後

Graphically-Phonetically Related Morphographs:

High Frequency Compounds:

最後 SAIGO -- the last, the end, final
99

今後 KONGO -- after this, hereafter
50

戦後 SENGO -- after the war
32

以後 IGO -- hereafter, thereafter
118

午後 GOGO -- afternoon, p.m.
1106

See 156

Also: 直後

Typical Conversational Usage:

きのうは学校の最後の日でした。
今後気をつけます。
おとうとは戦後生まれました。
それ以後、まだ何にもしていません。
田中さんと午後一時に会うつもりです。
その後、ずっと東京にいました。

Graphically-Phonetically Related Morphographs:

場 49

Occurrences/1000 3.17
Frequency Rank 49
Sanseido Page 247
Nelson Page 275

A

ON: JOO
kun: ba

Basic Meaning(s): place, ground, site, space, scene

High Frequency Compounds:

立場 35 — tachiba -- standpoint, position, situation

工場 173 — KOOJOO -- factory, workshop, mill (KOOba)

場所 129 — baSHO -- place, area, locality

場面 117 — baMEN -- place, scene, spectacle

現場 67 — GEMba -- the scene, the spot, the construction site

See 33, 253, 305

Also: 役場

Typical Phrases and Expanded Compounds:

人の立場
工場見学
会議の場所
映画の場面
工事の現場

Typical Conversational Usage:

人の立場をよく考えなければなりません。
ソニーの工場へ見学に行きました。
場所をまちがえました。
どの場面が一番よかったですか。
部長は現場にいます。

50

今

Occurrences/1000 3.15
Frequency Rank 50
Sanseido Page 103
Nelson Page 127

ON: KON, KIN

kun: ima

Basic Meaning(s): now, the present, this, the coming

Graphically-Phonetically Related Morphographs:

琴 KIN

Typical Phrases and Expanded Compounds:

今度の機会
今日の世界
今年の話題
今後の問題
今夜の月
今から

High Frequency Compounds:

今度 KONDO -- this time, now, next time
72

今日 KONNICHI (KYOO) -- today
3

今年 KONNEN (KOtoshi) -- this year
13

今後 KONGO -- after this, hereafter
48

今夜 KONYA -- this evening, tonight
318

Typical Conversational Usage:

今度は東京で会いましょう。
今日の天気はよくありません。
今年大学を出たばかりです。
今後そんなことはしないつもりです。
今夜の月はとてもきれいです。
今からどこへ行きますか。

Graphically-Phonetically Related Morphographs:

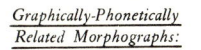

Occurrences/1000 3.06	51
Frequency Rank 51	題
Sanseido Page 743	
Nelson Page 488	A
	ON: DAI
	kun:

Basic Meaning(s): subject, topic, theme, title

High Frequency Compounds:

問題 MONDAI -- problem, question, issue
41

課題 KADAI -- lesson, section, department
755

主題 SHUDAI -- subject, theme, motif
34

Typical Phrases and Expanded Compounds:

問題が多い
研究課題
主題歌

Typical Conversational Usage:

問題が多くて、あたまがいたいです。
私の研究課題は「日本の文化」についてです。
論文の主題がもうきまりましたか。

52 部

Occurrences/1000 3.03
Frequency Rank 52
Sanseido Page 436
Nelson Page 897

A

ON: BU

kun:

Basic Meaning(s): part, section, department, set

Graphically-Phonetically Related Morphographs:

High Frequency Compounds:

内部 NAIBU -- interior, inside
77

一部 ICHIBU -- a part, a copy
1

全部 ZEMBU -- all, the whole, entirely
70

部分 BUBUN -- part, section, portion
28

部長 BUCHOO -- head of a division or department
90

See 185, 225, 236, 327

Also: 学部, 軍部, 本部

Typical Phrases and Expanded Compounds:
学校の内部
体の一部
全部の人
部分的
営業部長
夜間部

Typical Conversational Usage:

軍の内部のことはわかりません。
手は体の一部です。
これで全部です。
こわれた部分をなおしてください。
部長は今会議中です。
おとうとは夜間部の学生です。

Graphically-Phonetically Related Morphographs:

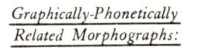

Occurrences/1000	2.97
Frequency Rank	53
Sanseido Page	364
Nelson Page	178

前 53

A

ON: ZEN

kun: mae

Basic Meaning(s): before, front, ago, ahead

High Frequency Compounds:

戦前 (32) SENZEN -- prewar days, before the war

以前 (118) IZEN -- ago, since, before

前進 (188) ZENSHIN -- advance, drive, progress

午前 (1106) GOZEN -- forenoon, a.m.

前途 (590) ZENTO -- one's future prospects, outlook, the journey ahead

名前 (140) namae -- name, given name

See 214, 278, 472   Also: 直前

Typical Phrases and Expanded Compounds:

戦前戦後を通じて
ルネサンス以前
一歩前進する
午前二時
前途有望
おもしろい名前

Typical Conversational Usage:

この本は戦前に出た本です。
以前はそんなことはありませんでした。
二、三歩前進してください。
この仕事は午前中におわるでしょう。
前田さんの前途は有望です。
このいぬの名前はポチといいます。

54

同

Occurrences/1000 2.96
Frequency Rank 54
Sanseido Page 159
Nelson Page 184

A

<u>ON</u>: DOO

<u>kun</u>: ona(ji), ona(jiku suru)

Basic Meaning(s): same, the same, identical, equal

Typical Phrases and Expanded Compounds:

同時に
アメリカと同様に
三国同盟
共同事業
同情をよぶ
同じ目的

Graphically-Phonetically Related Morphographs:

胴 DOO (745)
銅 DOO (715)

High Frequency Compounds:

同時 DOOJI -- the same time, simultaneous
24

同様 DOOYOO -- same, same kind, same way, like
216

同盟 DOOMEI -- alliance, league
603

共同 KYOODOO -- cooperation, collaboration, association
106

同情 DOOJOO -- sympathy
183

Also: 同意, 同一, 同志, 一同, 協同

Typical Conversational Usage:

二人は日本に同時につきました。
アメリカと同様に、日本では工業がさかんです。
ドイツとイタリアは、かつて軍事同盟をむすびました。
この水道は共同でつかっています。
そんなことに同情するわけにはいきません。
いもうとと同じドレスをかいました。

55 気

Graphically-Phonetically Related Morphographs:

汽 KI

Occurrences/1000	2.89
Frequency Rank	55
Sanseido Page	208
Nelson Page	529

ON: KI, KE

kun:

Basic Meaning(s): spirit, feeling, air

High Frequency Compounds:

気持 (94) KImochi -- feeling, mood

人気 (2) NINKI -- popularity, popular feeling, business conditions

空気 (384) KUUKI -- air, atmosphere

病気 (502) BYOOKI -- sickness, disease, ailment, fault

電気 (332) DENKI -- electricity, electric light

See 28, 98, 169, 361, 386, 408

Also: 雰囲気, 景気, 本気

Typical Phrases and Expanded Compounds:

気持が変わる
人気が上がる
新鮮な空気
わるい病気
電気会社

Typical Conversational Usage:

何だか気持がよくありません。
あけみちゃんは家の人気者です。
会議の空気はおもくるしかったです。
病気で学校をやすみました。
電気のはたすやくわりは大きいです。

56 彼

Occurrences/1000 2.88
Frequency Rank 56
Sanseido Page 357
Nelson Page 382

B

ON: HI

kun: kare, kano

Basic Meaning(s): he, that

Graphically-Phonetically Related Morphographs:

皮 HI (1242)
被 HI (555)
疲 HI

High Frequency Compounds:

彼女 (60) kanoJO -- she, girl friend
彼岸 (815) HIGAN -- the other side of the water, the equinoctial week, Buddhist services during that week

Typical Phrases and Expanded Compounds:

彼女の大学
彼岸の入り
彼の仕事

Typical Conversational Usage:

彼女にあした会うつもりです。
彼岸もすぎ、日が少しずつ長くなりました。
彼のお父さんは実業家です。

Graphically-Phonetically Related Morphographs:

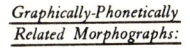

	57
Occurrences/1000　2.87	手
Frequency Rank　57	
Sanseido Page　59	A
Nelson Page　418	
	ON: SHU
kun:　te	

High Frequency Compounds:

手段　　SHUDAN -- resources, way, means
425

手紙　　tegami -- letter, note
456

相手　　aite -- companion, partner
111

勝手　　katte -- kitchen, condition, one's
419　　　　　　own convenience, wilful

両手　　RYOOte -- both hands
288

上手　　JOOZU -- skill, dexterity
29

　　See 341　　Also: 下手

Basic Meaning(s):　hand

Typical Phrases and Expanded Compounds:

手段をえらぶ
手紙を受け取る
相手の人
勝手気ままに
両手で持つ
口の上手な人

Typical Conversational Usage:

どんな手段をこうじますか。
九州にいるあねから手紙をもらいました。
もう相手の方がきまりましたか。
勝手なことをしてはいけません。
両手がしびれました。
大山さんはピアノがとても上手です。

58

教 A

Occurrences/1000 2.82
Frequency Rank 58
Sanseido Page 472
Nelson Page 457

ON: KYOO

kun: oshi(eru), oshi(e)

Basic Meaning(s): teaching, teach, faith

Typical Phrases and Expanded Compounds:
義務教育
英語教授法
宗教家
近くの教会
化学の教師
国語を教える

Graphically-Phonetically Related Morphographs:

High Frequency Compounds:

教育 259 — KYOOIKU -- education

教授 457 — KYOOJU -- professor, teaching

宗教 579 — SHUUKYOO -- religion, faith, a creed

教会 16 — KYOOKAI -- church, church building

教師 438 — KYOOSHI -- teacher, minister, rabbi

See 369

Also: 教員, 教室, 教養

Typical Conversational Usage:

アメリカの義務教育は何年ですか。
おじさんは大学の教授でした。
アジアの宗教について学んでいますか。
家の近くに教会があります。
父は高校の教師です。
兄は中学校で英語を教えています。

Graphically-Phonetically Related Morphographs:

里 RI (857)

Occurrences/1000 2.81
Frequency Rank 59
Sanseido Page 567
Nelson Page 610

理 59

A

ON: RI

kun:

Basic Meaning(s): reason, justice, principle

High Frequency Compounds:

理由 RIYUU -- cause, reason
134

理論 RIRON -- theory
110

心理 SHINRI -- mentality, psychology
64

理想 RISOO -- ideal
197

理解 RIKAI -- understanding, comprehension
142

See 33, 62, 179, 195, 307, 395

Also: 地理, 整理, 理事, 理屈, 管理

Typical Phrases and Expanded Compounds:

理由がたつ
理論的
心理学
理想的
理解にくるしむ

Typical Conversational Usage:

どんな理由がありますか。
その理論はむずかしいです。
大学で心理学を学んでいます。
小説家になるのが私の理想です。
大川さんのお父さんは、とても理解のある方です。

60 女

A

Occurrences/1000: 2.79
Frequency Rank: 60
Sanseido Page: 269
Nelson Page: 299

ON: JO, NYO

kun: onna

Basic Meaning(s): woman, girl, female

Typical Phrases and Expanded Compounds:
彼女の家
女性美
女子大生
かわいい少女
男女同権
女の人

Graphically-Phonetically Related Morphographs:

如 JO, NYO (337)

High Frequency Compounds:

彼女 (56) — kanoJO -- she, girl friend

女性 (119) — JOSEI -- female, woman

女子 (42) — JOSHI -- girl, female, woman

少女 (153) — SHOOJO -- daughter, young lady, virgin

男女 (203) — DANJO -- men and women, both sexes

Also: 女中

Typical Conversational Usage:

彼女は来年大学を出るそうです。
このクリームは女性用です。
東京に女子大がいくつありますか。
あの少女はかわいらしいです。
この学校は男女共学です。
あそこにいる女の方はどなたですか。

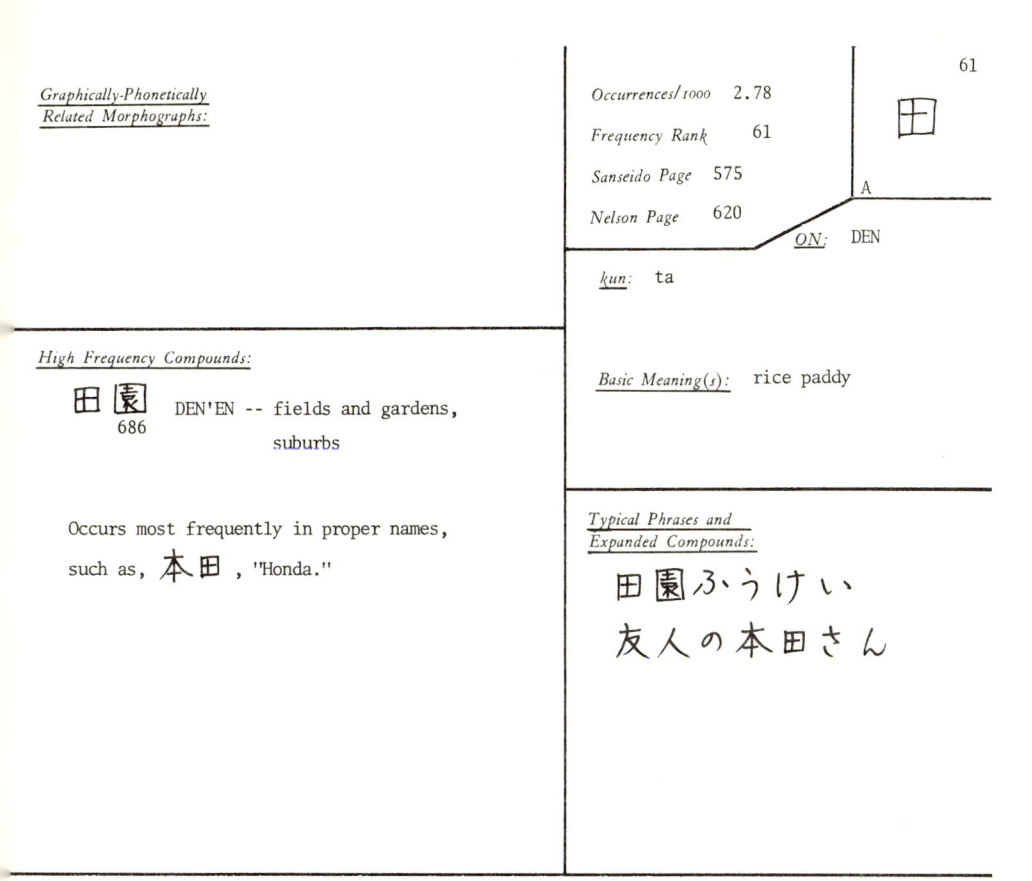

Graphically-Phonetically Related Morphographs:

	61
Occurrences/1000 2.78	田
Frequency Rank 61	
Sanseido Page 575	A
Nelson Page 620	
	ON: DEN
kun: ta	

High Frequency Compounds:

田園 DEN'EN -- fields and gardens, suburbs
686

Occurs most frequently in proper names, such as 本田, "Honda."

Basic Meaning(s): rice paddy

Typical Phrases and Expanded Compounds:

田園ふうけい
友人の本田さん

Typical Conversational Usage:

いなかの田園ふうけいが大すきです。
本田さんといっしょに、来月、四国へ行くつもりです。

62 義

Occurrences/1000 2.66
Frequency Rank 62
Sanseido Page 652
Nelson Page 724

A

ON: GI

kun:

Basic Meaning(s): justice, righteousness

*Graphically-Phonetic.
Related Morphographs:*

儀 GI (966)
犠 GI
議 GI (130)

High Frequency Compounds:

主義 SHUGI -- principle, policy, ideology, -ism
34

意義 IGI -- meaning, significance
86

講義 KOOGI -- lecture, exposition
469

義務 GIMU -- duty, obligation, responsibility
244

義理 GIRI -- sense of duty, sense of honor, obligation
59

*Typical Phrases and
Expanded Compounds:*

自由主義
意義がふかい
大学の講義
義務をはたす
義理がたい

Typical Conversational Usage:

どちらかと言えば、私は自由主義かも知れません。
意義のある人生をおくりたいと思います。
論理学の講義はおもしろいです。
自分の義務ははたすべきです。
本田さんはとても義理がたい人です。

考 (63)

Graphically-Phonetically Related Morphographs:

酵 KOO
孝 KOO

Occurrences/1000 2.65
Frequency Rank 63
Sanseido Page 559
Nelson Page 729

ON: KOO
kun: kanga(eru), kanga(e)

Basic Meaning(s): thought, think, consideration

High Frequency Compounds:

考慮 (800) KOORYO -- careful thought, consideration
参考 (350) SANKOO -- reference, consultation
考古 (320) KOOKO -- study of antiquities

Typical Phrases and Expanded Compounds:

考慮してから
参考人
考古学
考えがうかぶ

Typical Conversational Usage:

よく考慮してから、きめることにいたします。
これは英文法の参考書です。
考古学の研究のために、ヨーロッパへ行きました。
考えがなかなかまとまりません。

64

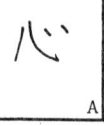

心 A

Occurrences/1000 2.63
Frequency Rank 64
Sanseido Page 457
Nelson Page 393

<u>ON</u>: SHIN

<u>kun</u>: kokoro

Basic Meaning(s): heart, mind, spirit

Typical Phrases and Expanded Compounds:
中心人物
心配事
心理状態
感心にも
決心がにぶる
心もとない

Graphically-Phonetically Related Morphographs:

High Frequency Compounds:

中心 CHUUSHIN -- center, heart,
 12   pivot

心配 SHIMPAI -- anxiety, worry,
 308   care

心理 SHINRI -- psychology, men-
 59   tality

感心 KANSHIN -- admiration, wonder
 105

決心 KESSHIN -- determination, reso-
 138   lution, decision

See 479

Also: 熱心, 用心

Typical Conversational Usage:

上田さんが中心になって、その仕事をしました。
何も心配はいりません。
その心理がわかりません。
あの子には感心させられます。
アメリカへ行く決心をしました。
一人で行くのは心もとないです。

65 入 A

Graphically-Phonetically Related Morphographs:

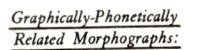

Occurrences/1000 2.63
Frequency Rank 65
Sanseido Page 102
Nelson Page 169

<u>ON</u>: NYUU
<u>kun</u>: i(reru), i(ru), i(ri)

<u>Basic Meaning(s)</u>: enter, go in, come in, contain

High Frequency Compounds:

入学 NYUUGAKU -- matriculation
15

輸入 YU'NYUU -- imports, importation
444

収入 SHUU'NYUU -- income, receipts, earnings, revenue
516

侵入 SHINNYUU -- invasion, raid, aggression
741

入口 iriguchi -- entrance
200

Typical Phrases and Expanded Compounds:

入学式
輸入品
収入源
侵入者
会場の入口
はこに入れる

Typical Conversational Usage:

あしたは小学校の入学式です。
日本ではあぶらを輸入しています。
今月から収入が少し多くなりました。
てきの侵入をふせがなければなりません。
会場の入口はどちらですか。
むすこを東京の大学に入れるつもりです。

66

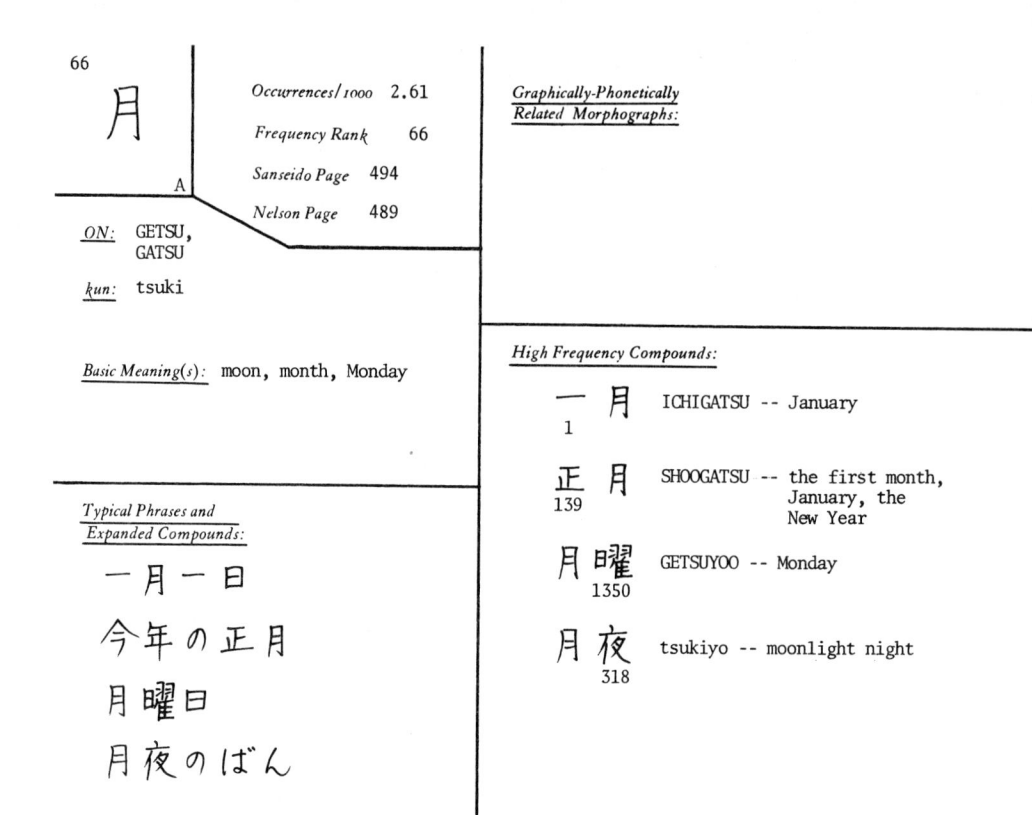

月 A

Occurrences/1000 2.61
Frequency Rank 66
Sanseido Page 494
Nelson Page 489

ON: GETSU, GATSU
kun: tsuki

Basic Meaning(s): moon, month, Monday

Graphically-Phonetically Related Morphographs:

Typical Phrases and Expanded Compounds:

一月一日
今年の正月
月曜日
月夜のばん

High Frequency Compounds:

一月 ICHIGATSU -- January
1

正月 SHOOGATSU -- the first month, January, the New Year
139

月曜 GETSUYOO -- Monday
1350

月夜 tsukiyo -- moonlight night
318

Typical Conversational Usage:

私は一月十五日に生まれました。
正月にかるたをしてあそびました。
月曜日にまた会いましょう。
内田さんにはじめて会ったのは、月夜のばんでした。

現 [67]

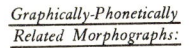

Occurrences/1000 2.61
Frequency Rank 67
Sanseido Page 567
Nelson Page 610

ON: GEN
kun: ara(wareru), ara(wasu)

Basic Meaning(s): present, existing, actual, appear, show

Graphically-Phonetically Related Morphographs:

High Frequency Compounds:

現在 [182] GENZAI -- the present time, now
現実 [37] GENJITSU -- actuality, reality
現代 [87] GENDAI -- present age, today, modern times
表現 [176] HYOOGEN -- expression, presentation
実現 [37] JITSUGEN -- realization, fruition, materialization

See 49, 430

Also: 現状, 現象

Typical Phrases and Expanded Compounds:

現在の立場
現実主義
現代式
ゆたかな表現
理想が実現する
うわさの人が現われる

Typical Conversational Usage:

社長は現在ニューヨークにいます。
理想と現実はちがいます。
現代作家の中で、だれが一番すきですか。
ことばの表現はなかなかむずかしいです。
東京オリンピックがとうとう実現しました。
うわさをしていたところへ、川上さんが現われました。

68 当

Occurrences/1000 2.61
Frequency Rank 68
Sanseido Page 266
Nelson Page 337

A

ON: TOO

kun: a(taru), a(teru)

Basic Meaning(s): hit, strike, right, appropriateness

Graphically-Phonetically Related Morphographs:

High Frequency Compounds:

本当 HONTOO -- true, real, actual
6

当時 TOOJI -- in these days, in those days, at that time
24

当然 TOOZEN -- justly, properly, necessarily
144

相当 SOOTOO -- suitable, proper, befit
111

当局 TOOKYOKU -- the authorities concerned, the powers that be
228

See 20, 139

Also: 担当, 弁当, 不当

Typical Phrases and Expanded Compounds:

本当の話
終戦当時
当然の事
相当の値段
当局者
くじが当たる

Typical Conversational Usage:

トルコに地震があったそうですが、本当ですか。
当時、よくハイキングに行きました。
それは当然の事です。
一ドルはいくらに相当しますか。
わからない時は、当局におたずねください。
くじが当たりました。

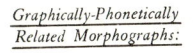

69

外

Occurrences/1000 2.60
Frequency Rank 69
Sanseido Page 253
Nelson Page 283

A

ON: GAI, GE

kun: soto, hoka

Basic Meaning(s): outside, without, beside

Graphically-Phonetically Related Morphographs:

High Frequency Compounds:

外国 — GAIKOKU -- foreign country, foreign
 4

以外 — IGAI -- with the exception of, excepting
 118

外交 — GAIKOO -- diplomacy, foreign relations
 269

外務 — GAIMU -- foreign affairs
 244

外人 — GAIJIN -- foreigner, alien
 2

See 77, 206

Also: 対外, 外相, 意外

Typical Phrases and Expanded Compounds:

外国人
男性以外
外交手段
外務省
外人墓地
家の外

Typical Conversational Usage:

まだ外国へ行ったことがありません。
英語以外の外国語はわかりません。
兄は保険会社の外交員です。
今の外務大臣はだれですか。
あの外人はアメリカ人ですか、フランス人ですか。
子どもは外であそんでいます。

70 全

Occurrences/1000: 2.60
Frequency Rank: 70
Sanseido Page: 106
Nelson Page: 139

ON: ZEN

kun: matta(ku), matta(ku suru)

Basic Meaning(s): completeness, totality, absolutely, wholly

Graphically-Phonetically Related Morphographs:

High Frequency Compounds:

完全 KANZEN -- perfection, completeness
559

安全 ANZEN -- safety, security
165

全部 ZEMBU -- all, the whole, entirely
52

全国 ZENKOKU -- the whole country, nationwide
4

全体 ZENTAI -- the whole, general
96

See 117, 144

Also: 健全, 全力

Typical Phrases and Expanded Compounds:

完全な状態
安全第一
全部をまとめる
全国大会
全体的に見て
全くのところ

Typical Conversational Usage:

人はだれでも完全ではありません。
工事現場では安全が第一です。
その本を全部よみました。
代理店は全国にあります。
全体の意見をまとめてください。
その話をきいて、全くおどろきました。

経 71

Occurrences/1000	2.59
Frequency Rank	71
Sanseido Page	637
Nelson Page	702

A

ON: KEI, KYOO

kun: he(ru)

Basic Meaning(s): pass, elapse, sutra, longitude

Graphically-Phonetically Related Morphographs:

径 KEI
茎 KEI
軽 KEI (814)

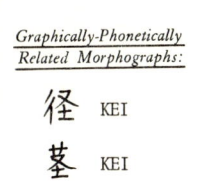

High Frequency Compounds:

経済 (131) KEIZAI -- economy, economics, finance
経験 (385) KEIKEN -- experience
経営 (388) KEIEI -- construction, management, operation
経過 (230) KEIKA -- progress, course, lapse
経歴 (389) KEIREKI -- personal history, career, pilgrimage

See 191

Typical Phrases and Expanded Compounds:

家庭の経済
経験を通して
経営こんなん
時間の経過
ふくざつな経歴
ホノルルを経る

Typical Conversational Usage:

国の経済が安定しています。
まだ経験があさいので、これからが大変です。
会社の経営がむずかしくなりました。
あの時から、どのくらい経過したかわかりません。
あの人の経歴はふくざつです。
サンフランシスコを経て、ニューヨークへむかいます。

72 度

Occurrences/1000: 2.59
Frequency Rank: 72
Sanseido Page: 319
Nelson Page: 364

A

ON: DO

kun:

Basic Meaning(s): degree, extent, time

Graphically-Phonetically Related Morphographs:

High Frequency Compounds:

今度 (50) KONDO -- this time, now, the next time

態度 (330) TAIDO -- attitude, posture, manner

制度 (161) SEIDO -- system, organization, institution

程度 (276) TEIDO -- degree, extent, limit

限度 (370) GENDO -- limit, limitation

Also: 温度

Typical Phrases and Expanded Compounds:

今度の授業
態度を決める
社会制度
ある程度
限度をこす

Typical Conversational Usage:

今度の正月をたのしくすごしましょう。
はやく態度を決めなければなりません。
中世ヨーロッパの社会制度について学びました。
どの程度の地震かまだわかりません。
体力には限度があります。

Graphically-Phonetically Related Morphographs:

痴 CHI

Occurrences/1000 2.59	73
Frequency Rank 73	知
Sanseido Page 591	
Nelson Page 646	A

<u>ON</u>: CHI

<u>kun</u>: shi(ru)

Basic Meaning(s): knowledge, understanding, understand, know

High Frequency Compounds:

知識 CHISHIKI -- knowledge, learning, information
611

承知 SHOOCHI -- consent, assent, acknowledgement
701

知恵 CHIE -- wisdom, sense, sagacity
1208

知事 CHIJI -- governor
10

Also 知合

Typical Phrases and Expanded Compounds:

ゆたかな知識
ご承知の通り
知恵熱
都知事
知らない人

Typical Conversational Usage:

本田さんは知識があります。
承知いたしました。
この子はなかなか知恵があります。
今の都知事はとても人気があります。
それは知りませんでした。

74 業

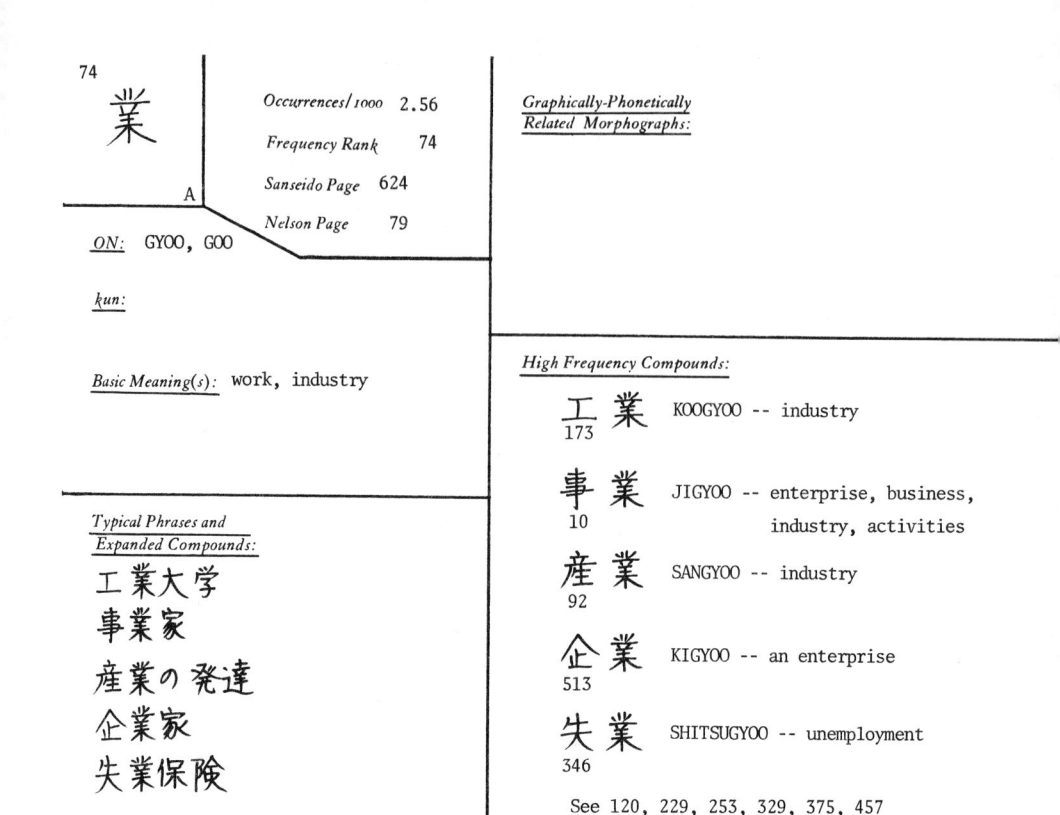

Occurrences/1000 2.56
Frequency Rank 74
Sanseido Page 624
Nelson Page 79

A

<u>ON</u>: GYOO, GOO

kun:

Basic Meaning(s): work, industry

Graphically-Phonetically Related Morphographs:

High Frequency Compounds:

工業 KOOGYOO -- industry
173

事業 JIGYOO -- enterprise, business,
10   industry, activities

産業 SANGYOO -- industry
92

企業 KIGYOO -- an enterprise
513

失業 SHITSUGYOO -- unemployment
346

See 120, 229, 253, 329, 375, 457

Also: 卒業, 業者, 実業

Typical Phrases and Expanded Compounds:

工業大学
事業家
産業の発達
企業家
失業保険

Typical Conversational Usage:

日本の工業は戦後さかんになりました。
おじさんは事業にしっぱいしました。
電気自動車は、今、産業界の話題です。
めずらしいものは、何でも企業化されています。
あの人は、今失業しているそうです。

Graphically-Phonetically Related Morphographs:

Occurrences/1000	2.55
Frequency Rank	75
Sanseido Page	10
Nelson Page	30

75

下

A

<u>ON</u>: KA, GE

<u>kun</u>: shita, shimo, moto, sa(geru), sa(garu), kuda(ru), kuda(ri), kuda(su)

Basic Meaning(s): below, down, under, low class, inferiority, come down, put down, descend

High Frequency Compounds:

以下 — IKA -- less than, under, below, the following
118

廊下 — ROOKA -- corridor, hall, lobby
1249

天下 — TENKA -- the whole country, the public, the world
277

地下 — CHIKA -- underground, basement, subterranean
45

See 376

Also: 下駄

Typical Phrases and Expanded Compounds:

以下同文
わたり廊下
天下一品
地下鉄
えんの下
手を下す

Typical Conversational Usage:

そのセーターは、千円以下ではかえないでしょう。
廊下をそうじしてください。
この品物は天下一品です。
地下鉄にのったことがありますか。
あの木の下のベンチにすわりましょう。
この時計はおばが下さったものです。

76 党

Occurrences/1000 2.55
Frequency Rank 76
Sanseido Page 620
Nelson Page 339

ON: TOO

kun:

Basic Meaning(s): party, faction, clique, companions

Typical Phrases and Expanded Compounds:

日本の政党
共産党員
与党側の意見
野党の反論

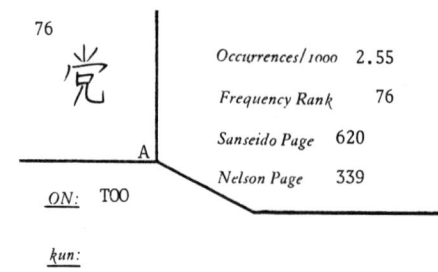

Graphically-Phonetically Related Morphographs:

High Frequency Compounds:

政党 (23)   SEITOO -- political party

党員 (127)   TOOIN -- party member, partisan

与党 (334)   YOTOO -- party in power

野党 (170)   YATOO -- opposition party

Typical Conversational Usage:

アメリカの二大政党は民主党と共和党です。
和田君は共産党員として知られています。
与党と野党ははげしく対立しました。
野党はその意見に反対です。

77

内

Graphically-Phonetically Related Morphographs:

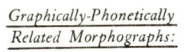

Occurrences/1000	2.51
Frequency Rank	77
Sanseido Page	156
Nelson Page	58

ON: NAI, DAI

kun: uchi

Basic Meaning(s): inside, interior, within

High Frequency Compounds:

内閣 504 — NAIKAKU -- Cabinet Ministry
内部 52 — NAIBU -- interior, inside
内容 402 — NAIYOO -- contents, detail, import
国内 4 — KOKUNAI -- domestic, the interior of a country
内外 69 — NAIGAI -- inside and outside

See 118, 369

Typical Phrases and Expanded Compounds:

内閣総理大臣
内部の事情
むずかしい内容
国内事情
国の内外
内側と外側

Typical Conversational Usage:

もう内閣が決まりましたか。
会社の内部がふくざつです。
その本の内容を知っていますか。
国内問題がたくさんあります。
内田さんは国の内外の事情に明るいです。
内かぎをかけて、外出しました。

78 要 A

Occurrences/1000 2.50
Frequency Rank 78
Sanseido Page 666
Nelson Page 811

<u>ON</u>: YOO

<u>kun</u>:

Basic Meaning(s): essence, main point, require, need

Typical Phrases and Expanded Compounds:
必要品
組合側の要求
重要な地位
重大な要素
主要都市
要するに

Graphically-Phonetically Related Morphographs:

腰 YOO (1041)

High Frequency Compounds:

必要 HITSUYOO -- need, necessity
188

要求 YOOKYUU -- requirement, demand, request
297

重要 JUUYOO -- important, momentous, essential
136

要素 YOOSO -- element, essential, requisite
500

主要 SHUYOO -- main, principal, chief
34

See 314

Also: 要請

Typical Conversational Usage:

どんな物が必要ですか。
組合側の要求が通りました。
もっと重要なことを考えなさい。
かけている要素をおぎなわなければなりません。
東京や大阪は日本の主要都市です。
車で行けば、二時間は要するでしょう。

Graphically-Phonetically Related Morphographs:

Occurrences/1000	2.49
Frequency Rank	79
Sanseido Page	712
Nelson Page	904

金 79

A

ON: KIN, KON

kun: kane

Basic Meaning(s): gold, money, metal, Friday

High Frequency Compounds:

資金 141 — SHIKIN -- fund, capital

金融 751 — KIN'YUU -- money market, credit situation, financial

税金 909 — ZEIKIN -- tax, duty

金額 659 — KINGAKU -- amount of money

Typical Phrases and Expanded Compounds:

会社の資金
金融機関
税金をおさめる
支払い金額
お金持

Typical Conversational Usage:

仕事をはじめるのに、資金が必要です。
兄は金融会社につとめています。
もう税金をおさめましたか。
支払った金額は全部でいくらですか。
お金が少したりません。

80 新

Occurrences/1000 2.40
Frequency Rank 80
Sanseido Page 611
Nelson Page 467

A

ON: SHIN

kun: atara(shii), ara(ta)

Basic Meaning(s): new, fresh, newness

Graphically-Phonetically Related Morphographs:

薪 SHIN

High Frequency Compounds:

新聞 SHIMBUN -- newspaper
184

革新 KAKUSHIN -- reform, innovation
487

新鮮 SHINSEN -- freshness
471

Typical Phrases and Expanded Compounds:

新聞記事
革新的
新鮮なくだもの
新しい家

Typical Conversational Usage:

まいあさ新聞をよむことにしています。
それはなかなか革新的な方法です。
このはなしはあまり新鮮ではありません。
内野さん家族は先月新しい家にひっこしました。

Graphically-Phonetically Related Morphographs:

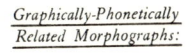

Occurrences/1000	2.40
Frequency Rank	81
Sanseido Page	32
Nelson Page	63

世 81

ON: SE, SEI
kun: yo

Basic Meaning(s): generation, world, age, society

High Frequency Compounds:

世界 (164) SEKAI -- the world, society, the universe
世間 (31) SEKEN -- world, society, life
世紀 (616) SEIKI -- century, era
世論 (110) SERON -- public opinion
世話 (125) SEWA -- help, aid, good offices

Also: 出世

Typical Phrases and Expanded Compounds:

世界中
世間のうわさ
二十世紀
世論調査
世話人
世の中

Typical Conversational Usage:

エベレスト山は世界で一番高い山です。
その事件は世間をおどろかせました。
東京オリンピックは、世紀のさいてんでした。
今、全国で世論調査が行われています。
中山さんはとても世話ずきな方です。
世の中にはいろいろな事があります。

82

社

Occurrences/1000 2.39
Frequency Rank 82
Sanseido Page 570
Nelson Page 655

A

ON: SHA

kun: yashiro

Basic Meaning(s): Shinto shrine, association, firm

Graphically-Phonetically Related Morphographs:

High Frequency Compounds:

社会   SHAKAI -- society, community,
 16   the world

会社   KAISHA -- company, corporation
 16

社長   SHACHOO -- firm president
 90

Typical Phrases and Expanded Compounds:

社会主義
会社員
社長室

Typical Conversational Usage:

社会全体のことを考えなければなりません。
もう十五年も今の会社につとめています。
社長はただ今会議中です。

83
第

Graphically-Phonetically Related Morphographs:

弟 DAI (548)

Occurrences/1000 2.39
Frequency Rank 83
Sanseido Page 625
Nelson Page 683

ON: DAI

kun:

Basic Meaning(s): No. (indicator of ordinal numbers), residence

High Frequency Compounds:

次第 SHIDAI -- order, precedence, circumstances
150

第一 DAIICHI -- No. 1, the first, the best
 1

See 327

Typical Phrases and Expanded Compounds:

次第に

第一人者

Typical Conversational Usage:

人口が次第に多くなっています。
安全に運転することが第一です。

84 関

Occurrences/1000 2.38
Frequency Rank 84
Sanseido Page 727
Nelson Page 924

A

ON: KAN
kun: seki

Basic Meaning(s): barriar, gate, related to, concern

Graphically-Phonetically Related Morphographs:

間 KAN (31)
閑 KAN (1201)
簡 KAN (882)

High Frequency Compounds:

関係 221 KANKEI -- relation, connection, concern
機関 158 KIKAN -- engine, machine, means
関連 101 KANREN -- connection, relation, association
関心 64 KANSHIN -- concern, interest, regard
関東 108 KANTOO -- the Kanto District

See 198

Typical Phrases and Expanded Compounds:

関係者
通信機関
関連のない話
関心事
関東地方

Typical Conversational Usage:

これは、その話と何も関係がありません。
これは、労働問題に関連した記事です。
今は通信機関がとてもよく発達しています。
あなたは政治に関心がありますか。
関東平野は日本で一番大きい平野です。
関口さんが来てから、いっしょに行きましょう。

Graphically-Phonetically Related Morphographs:

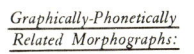

Occurrences/1000 2.37
Frequency Rank 85
Sanseido Page 602
Nelson Page 664

85

和

A

<u>ON</u>: WA
<u>kun</u>: yawa(ragu), yawa(rageru)

High Frequency Compounds:

平和 HEIWA -- peace, harmony
98

昭和 SHOOWA -- the name of the era
508   beginning in 1926

緩和 KANWA -- relief, mitigation,
                         alleviation

共和 KYOOWA -- republic
106

講和 KOOWA -- making peace with
469

Basic Meaning(s): peace, harmony, be reconciled

Typical Phrases and Expanded Compounds:

平和共存
昭和二十年
きんちょうの緩和
共和国
講和会議

Typical Conversational Usage:

あの人は平和な毎日をおくっています。
昭和二十年は終戦の年です。
問題が大分緩和されました。
ブラジルは大きな共和国です。
吉田茂は講和会議の全権大使でした。

86 意

A

Occurrences/1000 2.35
Frequency Rank   86
Sanseido Page   610
Nelson Page   955

ON: I

kun:

Basic Meaning(s): mind, heart, care, will

Typical Phrases and Expanded Compounds:

意味ありげに
全体の意見
注意ぶかい
決意を新たにする
意義のない事

Graphically-Phonetically Related Morphographs:

High Frequency Compounds:

意味 (169) IMI -- meaning, significance

意見 (20) IKEN -- opinion, idea

注意 (459) CHUUI -- attention, care, warning

決意 (138) KETSUI -- resolution, determination

意義 (62) IGI -- meaning, significance

See 177, 262

Also: 同意, 意外, 意志

Typical Conversational Usage:

彼女は意味ありげな事を言いました。
みんなの意見をきいてください。
あの子には注意をあたえた方がいいです。
決意を新たにして、その仕事をするつもりです。
人生の意義はふかいです。

Graphically-Phonetically Related Morphographs:

代   87

Occurrences/1000 2.33
Frequency Rank 87
Sanseido Page 115
Nelson Page 132

ON: DAI

kun: ka(waru), ka(wari), ka(eru), yo

Basic Meaning(s): period, age, generation, change, replace

High Frequency Compounds:

時代   JIDAI -- period, age, stage
24

代表   DAIHYOO -- representation, type, delegate
178

近代   KINDAI -- modern times
149

現代   GENDAI -- present age, today, modern times
67

代議   DAIGI -- representing others in a conforonco
130

See 320

Typical Phrases and Expanded Compounds:

時代おくれ
代表者
近代的
現代の人々
代議士
代わりに

Typical Conversational Usage:

そんな考えは時代おくれです。
「ハムレット」はシェークスピアの代表作です。
私たちの学校はとても近代的です。
現代のわかい人々は、何をもとめていますか。
この地区から代議士が三名出ています。
和子さんの代わりに、私が来ました。

88

治

Occurrences/1000　2.33
Frequency Rank　88
Sanseido Page　398
Nelson Page　540

ON: CHI, JI

kun: osa(meru), osa(maru)

Basic Meaning(s): peace, government, cure, heal, rule

Graphically-Phonetically Related Morphographs:

High Frequency Compounds:

政治　SEIJI -- government, administration, politics
23

明治　MEIJI -- Meiji
152

自治　JIJI -- self-government
14

治療　CHIRYOO -- medical treatment
1303

Typical Phrases and Expanded Compounds:

政治学
明治の人
自治会
治療法

Typical Conversational Usage:

中田さんは政治家になりたいそうです。
明治時代に、西洋の学問が、さかんにとりいれられました。
二時から学校の自治会があります。
手をけがして、毎日治療をうけています。

Graphically-Phonetically Related Morphographs:

	89
Occurrences/1000 2.33	文
Frequency Rank 89	
Sanseido Page 79	A
Nelson Page 462	
	ON: BUN, MON

kun:

Basic Meaning(s): literary text, sentence, civil affairs

High Frequency Compounds:

文化 — BUNKA -- culture, civilization
104

文学 — BUNGAKU -- literature
15

文章 — BUNSHOO -- sentence, article, composition
717

文句 — MONKU -- phrase, expression, complaint
860

文明 — BUMMEI -- civilization, culture
152

論文 — ROMBUN -- dissertation, thesis, essay
110

See 459   Also: 文字, 文芸, 文部省

Typical Phrases and Expanded Compounds:

文化人
日本文学
うつくしい文章
文句を言う
ヨーロッパ文明
卒業論文

Typical Conversational Usage:

中国の文化はふるいです。
どんな文学作品がすきですか。
文句ばかり言ってはいけません。
明治になって、日本の文明はひらけました。
もう卒業論文は書きおわりましたか。

90 長

Occurrences/1000 2.30
Frequency Rank 90
Sanseido Page 723
Nelson Page 918

A

ON: CHOO

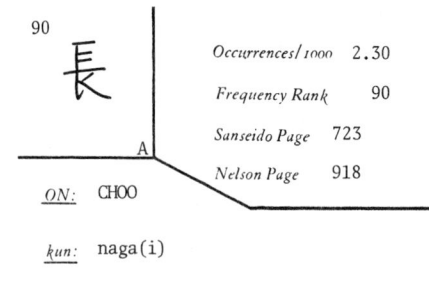

kun: naga(i)

Basic Meaning(s): long, length, head, chief, grow up, prolong

Typical Phrases and Expanded Compounds:
社長のいす
官房長官
経理部長
経済の高度成長
中学校長
長い話

Graphically-Phonetically Related Morphographs:

帳 CHOO
張 CHOO (553)
脹 CHOO

High Frequency Compounds:

社長 (82) SHACHOO -- firm president
長官 (202) CHOOKAN -- magistrate, chief, governor
部長 (52) BUCHOO -- head of a division, department, section
成長 (160) SEICHOO -- growth (usually of animals)
校長 (233) KOOCHOO -- principal, schoolmaster

See 241

Also: 会長, 議長

Typical Conversational Usage:

父は二年前に社長のいすにつきました。
アメリカの国務長官はだれですか。
部長は今やすんでおります。
関さんのむすこはりっぱに成長しました。
校長先生はみんなにすかれています。
このひもは長すぎますか。

Graphically-Phonetically Related Morphographs:

	91
Occurrences/1000 2.29	目
Frequency Rank 91	
Sanseido Page 586	A
Nelson Page 641	

ON: MOKU

kun: me

Basic Meaning(s): eye, look, notice, item, class

High Frequency Compounds:

目的 (7) MOKUTEKI -- aim, purpose, intention

目標 (706) MOKUHYOO -- sign, mark, target, objective

駄目 (1031) DAme -- bad, useless, impossible, ruined

注目 (459) CHUUMOKU -- attention, observation, notice

役目 (266) YAKUME -- duty, office, business

Typical Phrases and Expanded Compounds:

目的を達成する
目標を目ざす
駄目おし
注目をあびる
大切な役目
三番目

Typical Conversational Usage:

どうやら目的を達成しました。
目標まであとひといきです。
そんなことをしては駄目です。
キュリー夫人は、ラジウムの発見で、世界の注目をあびました。
とんだ役目をおおせつかりました。
前から四番目の子が私のむすこです。

92

産

A

Occurrences/1000 2.28
Frequency Rank 92
Sanseido Page 95
Nelson Page 679

ON: SAN

kun: u(mu)

Basic Meaning(s): produce, product
bear (a child), childbirth

Graphically-Phonetically Related Morphographs:

High Frequency Compounds:

共産 KYOOSAN -- common property,
106 commun(ism)

生産 SEISAN -- production
9

産業 SANGYOO -- industry
74

財産 ZAISAN -- property, estate,
491 fortune

Typical Phrases and Expanded Compounds:

共産軍
かんずめの生産
産業経済
財産家

Typical Conversational Usage:

ブルガリアは共産国ですか。
ハワイでは何を生産していますか。
デトロイトは自動車産業で有名です。
おじさんは、財産をたくさんのこして、なくなりました。

定

93

Occurrences/1000 2.28
Frequency Rank 93
Sanseido Page 284
Nelson Page 316

A

ON: TEI, JOO
kun: sada(meru), sada(me), sada(maru)

Basic Meaning(s): deciding, be decided, establish

Graphically-Phonetically Related Morphographs:

錠　JOO
提　TEI (472)
堤　TEI (1335)

High Frequency Compounds:

協定 193　KYOOTEI -- pact, agreement
規定 453　KITEI -- bylaws, provisions, regulations
決定 139　KETTEI -- decision, determination, conclusion
安定 165　ANTEI -- stability, equilibrium, composure
否定 549　HITEI -- denial

See 161, 186, 283

Typical Phrases and Expanded Compounds:

協定を結ぶ
きびしい規定
決定権
物価の安定
否定文
位置を定める

Typical Conversational Usage:

アメリカとどんな協定が結ばれていますか。
規定はまもらなければなりません。
社長のアメリカ行が決定しました。
国の経済が安定しています。
そのアイデアは、あたまから否定されてしまいました。
あの人は、何をやっても定まりがありません。

94

持

A

Occurrences/1000 2.27
Frequency Rank 94
Sanseido Page 383
Nelson Page 435

ON: JI

kun: mo(tsu)

Basic Meaning(s): hold, maintain, have, possess

Graphically-Phonetically Related Morphographs:

寺 JI (763)
侍 JI
時 JI (24)

High Frequency Compounds:

気持 KImochi -- feeling, mood
55

支持 SHIJI -- support, maintenance
185

Typical Phrases and Expanded Compounds:

気持がわるい
支持をうける
手で持つ

Typical Conversational Usage:

今日は、天気がよくて、気持がいいです。
山口さんは、みんなの支持をうけています。
そのはこは、あまり重いので、一人では持てません。

Graphically-Phonetically Related Morphographs:

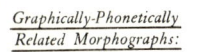

Occurrences/1000 2.24	95
Frequency Rank 95	物
Sanseido Page 547	
Nelson Page 597	A

ON: BUTSU, MOTSU

kun: mono

Basic Meaning(s): thing, object, matter, something

High Frequency Compounds:

動物 DOOBUTSU -- animal
47

物価 BUKKA -- prices
342

物資 BUSSHI -- commodities, resources
141

物質 BUSSHITSU -- matter, substance
359

着物 kimono -- clothes, kimono
410

See 20, 121, 207, 278, 312, 372

Also: 人物, 何物, 本物, 植物

Typical Phrases and Expanded Compounds:

動物園

物価が高い

物資の不足

物質的

きれいな着物

Typical Conversational Usage:

小さい時、よく動物園に連れて行ってもらいました。

最近、また物価が上がりました。

戦時中、物資が不足しました。

この国は物質的にめぐまれています。

定子さんは、着物の方がよくにあいます。

96 体

Occurrences/1000 2.22
Frequency Rank 96
Sanseido Page 122
Nelson Page 143

<u>ON</u>: TAI, TEI

<u>kun</u>: karada

Basic Meaning(s): body, substance, appearance

Graphically-Phonetically Related Morphographs:

Typical Phrases and Expanded Compounds:

体制がととのう
大きな団体
具体的
一体化する
全体主義
体がいたい

High Frequency Compounds:

体制 — TAISEI -- structure, system, set-up
161

団体 — DANTAI -- organization, body, corporation
336

具体 — GUTAI -- concreteness
534

一体 — ITTAI -- one body, one flesh, after all, what on earth
1

全体 — ZENTAI -- the whole, whatever
70

See 307, 385

Also: 肉体, 大体

Typical Conversational Usage:

これでどうにか体制がととのいました。
団体でりょこうすると、安くつきます。
具体的に説明してください。
一体何があったのですか。
全体の意見を聞いてみなければなりません。
体がいたくてたまりません。

通 97

Occurrences/1000 2.21
Frequency Rank 97
Sanseido Page 444
Nelson Page 882

<u>ON</u>: TSUU

<u>kun</u>: too(ru), too(ri), too(su), too(shi), kayo(u), kayo(i)

Basic Meaning(s): pass, pass through, expert, prevail, commute, attend

Graphically-Phonetically Related Morphographs:

痛 TSUU (768)

High Frequency Compounds:

普通 (894) HUTSUU -- ordinary, common, usual
共通 (106) KYOOTSUU -- common
通過 (230) TSUUKA -- passage, transit
通信 (181) TSUUSHIN -- correspondence, communication, intelligence
交通 (269) KOOTSUU -- traffic, communication, transport

Typical Phrases and Expanded Compounds:

普通の感覚
共通の立場
急行の通過
通信社
交通公社
バスが通る

Typical Conversational Usage:

あの方のあたまは普通ではありません。
二人は共通の意見を持っています。
今通過した急行は大阪行です。
本田君は通信員としてパリにいます。
このへんの交通はとてもはげしいです。
この通りはバスが通りますか。

98

平

Occurrences/1000: 2.21
Frequency Rank: 98
Sanseido Page: 34
Nelson Page: 43

ON: HEI, BYOO

kun: tai(ra), hira(tai), tai(rageru), tai(ragu)

Basic Meaning(s): level, peaceful

Graphically-Phonetically Related Morphographs:

Typical Phrases and Expanded Compounds:

平和主義者
平等の権利
平均時速
平凡な人
平気なかお
平らにする

High Frequency Compounds:

平和 HEIWA -- peace, harmony
85

平等 BYOODOO -- equality
151

平均 HEIKIN -- average, balance, equilibrium
1021

平凡 HEIBON -- common, ordinary, mediocre
1156

平気 HEIKI -- composure, unconcern
55

See 212

Typical Conversational Usage:

平君はいつも平和運動をしています。
戦後、男女平等になりました。
平均五十キロで行けば、二時間でつくでしょう。
このところ、一人で平凡な毎日をおくっています。
しかられても平気です。
ブルドーザーで土地を平らにならしています。

Graphically-Phonetically Related Morphographs:

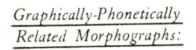

Occurrences/1000 2.19
Frequency Rank 99
Sanseido Page 490
Nelson Page 484

最 99

A

ON: SAI

kun: motto(mo)

Basic Meaning(s): most, greatest, the utmost, exceedingly

High Frequency Compounds:

最近 — SAIKIN -- recently, latest, newest
 149

最後 — SAIGO -- the last, the end, final
 48

最高 — SAIKOO -- maximum, supreme, highest
 135

最大 — SAIDAI -- maximum, greatest, largest
 5

最初 — SAISHO -- the first, the beginning
 279

Also: 最低

Typical Phrases and Expanded Compounds:

最近の出来事
最後の仕上げ
最高速度
世界最大
最初の一年
最も大きい

Typical Conversational Usage:

最近の大きな問題は何だと思いますか。
今は最後の学期なので、とてもいそがしいです。
このへんの最高速度は六十キロです。
太平洋は世界最大の海です。
社会に出てから、最初の一年はとてもつらかったです。
アメリカで、最も高い山は何という山ですか。

100

法

A

Occurrences/1000 2.81
Frequency Rank 100
Sanseido Page 399
Nelson Page 543

ON: HOO

kun:

Basic Meaning(s): law, rule, legislation, method

Typical Phrases and Expanded Compounds:

日本国憲法
正しい方法
法律事務所
新法案

Graphically-Phonetically Related Morphographs:

High Frequency Compounds:

憲法   KEMPOO -- constitution, con-
429   stitutional law

方法   HOOHOO -- way, method, means
25

法律   HOORITSU -- law
898

法案   HOOAN -- bill, measure
353

See 369

Typical Conversational Usage:

五月三日は憲法記念日です。
方法がわかりません。
どこの法律事務所につとめていますか。
新方案が国会を通過しました。

連

101

Graphically-Phonetically Related Morphographs:

Occurrences/1000 2.18
Frequency Rank 101
Sanseido Page 446
Nelson Page 881

ON: REN
kun: tsu(reru), tsura(naru), tsura(neru)

Basic Meaning(s): set, party, put in a row, take (someone) along

High Frequency Compounds:

関連 (84) KANREN -- connection, relation, association

国連 (4) KOKUREN -- United Nations

連中 (12) RENCHUU -- party, group, clique

連絡 RENRAKU -- connection, contact, communication

See 33

Also 連盟

Typical Phrases and Expanded Compounds:

関連のある
国連大使
あの連中
連絡事項
連れて行く

Typical Conversational Usage:

それはこの問題には全く関連していません。
国連には世界のいろいろな問題があります。
あの連中は何をしていますか。
何かあったら連絡してください。
きのう子どもを公園に連れて行きました。

102

発 A

Occurrences/1000 2.13
Frequency Rank 102
Sanseido Page 582
Nelson Page 633

ON: HATSU, HOTSU
kun:

Basic Meaning(s): start, departure, discharge, announce

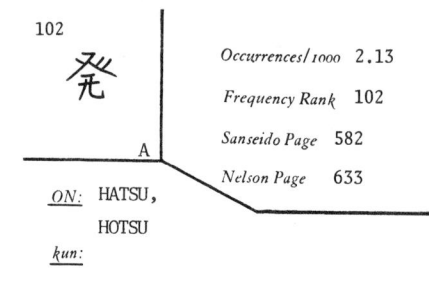

Graphically-Phonetically Related Morphographs:

High Frequency Compounds:

発表 HAPPYOO -- announcement, communique
178

発見 HAKKEN -- discovery, detection, revelation
20

発展 HATTEN -- expansion, extension, development
443

出発 SHUPPATSU -- departure
8

発達 HATTATSU -- growth, development, progress
154

発作 HOSSA -- fit, spasm, an attack
120

See 44, 290 Also 発生, 発音

Typical Phrases and Expanded Compounds:

研究発表
アメリカの発見
発展の途上にある
出発の時間
科学の発達
発作を起こす

Typical Conversational Usage:

論文を発表しました。
アメリカはいつ発見されましたか。
自動車産業は発展の途上にあります。
何時に出発しますか。
工業が発達しました。
おじいさんは時々心臓の発作を起こします。

Graphically-Phonetically Related Morphographs:

Occurrences/1000	2.12
Frequency Rank	103
Sanseido Page	25
Nelson Page	37

103

不

A

ON: HU

kun:

Basic Meaning(s): negation, bad

High Frequency Compounds:

不足 (338) — HUSOKU -- shortage, lack, deficiency

不満 (466) — HUMAN -- dissatisfaction, displeasure, discontent

不安 (165) — HUAN -- anxiety, uneasiness, insecurity

不幸 (423) — HUKOO -- unhappiness, sorrow, disaster

不思議 (26, 130) — HUSHIGI -- wonder, mystery, marvel

不正 (139) — HUSEI -- injustice, iniquity, irregularity
See 479

Typical Phrases and Expanded Compounds:

手不足
不平不満
不安がともなう
不幸な人
不思議な話
不正事件

Typical Conversational Usage:

何の不足もありません。
不満がばくはつしました。
一人で行くのは不安です。
山田家に不幸がありました。
不思議なこともあればあるものです。
不正を行なってはいけません。

104 化 A

Occurrences/1000 2.09
Frequency Rank 104
Sanseido Page 111
Nelson Page 126

<u>ON</u>: KA, KE

<u>kun</u>: ba(keru)

Basic Meaning(s): influence, bewitch, appear in disguise, change into

Typical Phrases and Expanded Compounds:

日本の文化
変化に富む
化学工場
消化がいい
お化け

Graphically-Phonetically Related Morphographs:

貨 KA (687)
花 KA (642)

High Frequency Compounds:

文化 BUNKA -- culture, civilization
89

変化 HENKA -- change, variation, transformation
254

化学 KAGAKU -- chemistry
15

消化 SHOOKA -- digestion, assimilation
458

See 133, 265, 295

Also 感化

Typical Conversational Usage:

中国の文化を研究しています。
この辺はあまり変化がありません。
高校の時、化学が大好きでした。
このくすりは消化を助けます。
化けのかわがはがれました。

Graphically-Phonetically Related Morphographs:

憾 KAN

Occurrences/1000	2.09
Frequency Rank	105
Sanseido Page	463
Nelson Page	406

感 105

A

<u>ON</u>: KAN

<u>kun</u>:

Basic Meaning(s): feeling, sense, emotion, impression

High Frequency Compounds:

感情 183   KANJOO -- feelings, emotion, sentiment

感謝 1026   KANSHA -- thanks, appreciation

感心 64   KANSHIN -- admiration, wonder

実感 37   JIKKAN -- actual sensation, realization, low passions

感想 197   KANSOO -- thoughts, impressions, sentiments

感激 733   KANGEKI -- deep emotion, inspiration, impression

See 235   Also 感覚, 感化, 感動

Typical Phrases and Expanded Compounds:

感情をおさえる
感謝の気持
感心な子ども
実感がわく
感想をのべる
感激する

Typical Conversational Usage:

感情的になってはいけません。
感謝の気持でいっぱいです。
あの子はいつも感心に家の手つだいをします。
試験に受かっても、まだ実感がわきません。
試合の感想をのべてください。
映画を見て感激しました。

共

Occurrences/1000 2.07
Frequency Rank 106
Sanseido Page 552
Nelson Page 175

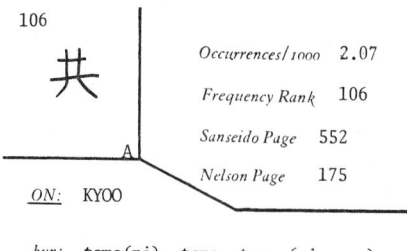

ON: KYOO

kun: tomo(ni), tomo, tomo (ni suru),

Basic Meaning(s): both, neither (with neg.), as well as, together with, share with

Graphically-Phonetically Related Morphographs:

供 KYOO (340)
恭

High Frequency Compounds:

共産 KYOOSAN -- communism, collectivism
 92

共同 KYOODOO -- cooperation, collaboration, association
 54

公共 KOOKYOO -- society, community, the public
 212

共通 KYOOTSUU -- common
 97

共和 KYOOWA -- republicanism, republic
 85

Also 中共, 反共

Typical Phrases and Expanded Compounds:

共産党
共同通信
公共団体
共通の問題
共和党
共に

Typical Conversational Usage:

ソ連は共産主義の国です。
私たちは共同でその仕事をしています。
公共のためにつくしたいと思います。
共通点が見出せません。
ニクソン氏は共和党です。
その問題は私共にはよくわかりません。

Graphically-Phonetically Related Morphographs:

Occurrences/1000 2.06	107 争
Frequency Rank 107	
Sanseido Page 214	A
Nelson Page 87	
	ON: SOO
	kun: araso(u), araso(i)

High Frequency Compounds:

戦争   SENSOO -- war, battle, game
32

競争   KYOOSOO -- rivalry, contest,
1019   competition

闘争   TOOSOO -- fight, combat, labor
367   strife

論争   RONSOO -- dispute, controversy,
110   argument

Basic Meaning(s): dispute, argue, compete, conflict

Typical Phrases and Expanded Compounds:

戦争と平和
競争相手
賃上げ闘争
論争をよぶ
人と争う

Typical Conversational Usage:

小さい時、よく戦争ごっこをしました。
競争がはげしくなりました。
春季闘争が近ずきました。
その問題は論争をよびそうです。
人と争わないように気をつけています。

108 東

Occurrences/1000	2.05
Frequency Rank	108
Sanseido Page	46
Nelson Page	93

A

ON: TOO

kun: higashi

Basic Meaning(s): east, Eastern Japan

Graphically-Phonetically Related Morphographs:

凍 TOO

High Frequency Compounds:

東京 303 TOOKYOO -- Tokyo

東西 198 TOOZAI -- east and west, Orient and Occident, "Your attention please"

東大 5 TOODAI -- Tokyo University

関東 84 KANTOO -- Kanto District

See 311

Also 東欧, 東独

Typical Phrases and Expanded Compounds:

東京駅
東西南北
東大生
関東平野
東ドイツ

Typical Conversational Usage:

きのう東京タワーにのぼりました。
この町は東西にひろがっています。
来年東大を受けるつもりです。
台風が関東地方をおそいました。
ドイツは東と西にわかれています。

Graphically-Phonetically Related Morphographs:

Occurrences/1000 2.04
Frequency Rank 109
Sanseido Page 640
Nelson Page 705

結 109
A

ON: KETSU
kun: musu(bu), yu(u), musu(bi)

Basic Meaning(s): tie, make, do up, knot, organize

High Frequency Compounds:

結果 KEKKA -- consequences, result, effect
250

結局 KEKKYOKU -- after all, in conclusion
228

結論 KETSURON -- conclusion
110

結婚 KEKKON -- marriage
693

See 336, 498

Also 結集

Typical Phrases and Expanded Compounds:

相談の結果
結局のところ
結論として
結婚の日取り
協定を結ぶ

Typical Conversational Usage:

テストの結果がまだわかりません。
結局何もやりませんでした。
結論がまだ出ません。
ご結婚おめでとうございます。
これをひもで結んでください。

110 論

Occurrences/1000: 2.04
Frequency Rank: 110
Sanseido Page: 686
Nelson Page: 835

ON: RON

kun:

Basic Meaning(s): argument, discourse, discuss, argue

Graphically-Phonetically Related Morphographs:

Typical Phrases and Expanded Compounds:

理論と実際
言論界
はげしい議論
卒業論文
論理的

High Frequency Compounds:

理論 (59) RIRON -- theory
言論 (44) GENRON -- speech, discussion
議論 (130) GIRON -- argument, controversy, discussion
論文 (89) ROMBUN -- dissertation, thesis, article
論理 (59) RONRI -- logic

See 81, 109, 179, 358

Also 討論

Typical Conversational Usage:

理論と実際はちがいます。
日本には言論の自由があります。
もう議論はやめましょう。
ようやく論文を書き上げました。
論理的に説明してください。

相　111

Occurrences/1000　2.03
Frequency Rank　111
Sanseido Page　521
Nelson Page　498

ON: SHOO, SOO
kun: ai

Basic Meaning(s): minister of state, aspect, together, each other, fellow

Graphically-Phonetically Related Morphographs:

想　SOO (197)
霜　SOO

High Frequency Compounds:

首相　SHUSHOO -- prime minister
525

相対　SOOTAI -- relativity, reciprocity
39

相談　SOODAN -- consultation, proposal, conference
394

相互　SOOGO -- mutual, reciprocal
524

相手　aite -- companion, partner, the other party
57

See 68, 274

Also: 外相, 相対

Typical Phrases and Expanded Compounds:

佐藤首相
相対的
相談役
相互関係
相手の人

Typical Conversational Usage:

イギリスの首相はだれですか。
アインシュタインの相対性理論は有名です。
先生によく相談するつもりです。
相互の理解が必要です。
相手の方はどんな方ですか。

112

九

Occurrences/1000 2.01
Frequency Rank 112
Sanseido Page 55
Nelson Page 80

A

<u>ON</u>: KYUU, KU

<u>kun</u>: kokono(tsu)

<u>Basic Meaning(s)</u>: nine

Graphically-Phonetically Related Morphographs:

究 KYUU (261)

High Frequency Compounds:

九百 KYUUHYAKU -- nine hundred
218

九州 KYUUSHUU -- Kyushu
865

九月 KUGATSU -- September
66

九日 kokonoka -- the ninth day
9   (of the month)

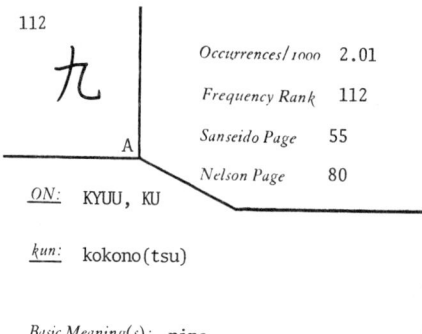

Typical Phrases and Expanded Compounds:

九百円
北九州市
九月十日
九日の日

Typical Conversational Usage:

このシャツは九百八十円でした。
まだ九州へ行ったことがありません。
アメリカでは九月に学校が始まります。
九日の日に会いましょう。

原 — 113

Graphically-Phonetically Related Morphographs:

源 GEN (626)

Occurrences/1000	1.99
Frequency Rank	113
Sanseido Page	198
Nelson Page	231

A

ON: GEN

kun: hara

Basic Meaning(s): original, primitive, field, plain

High Frequency Compounds:

原子 — GENSHI -- atom (42)

原爆 — GEMBAKU -- atom bomb (309)

原因 — GEN'IN -- root cause, factor, origin (485)

原則 — GENSOKU -- principle, general rule (746)

原料 — GENRYOO -- raw materials (395)

See 321

Typical Phrases and Expanded Compounds:

原子力
原爆記念日
原因不明
原則として
生地の原料
野原

Typical Conversational Usage:

原子力は平和に利用されています。
原爆には絶対反対です。
火事の原因がまだわかりません。
原則として、子どもは入場できません。
原料が不足しています。
うちのそばに野原があります。

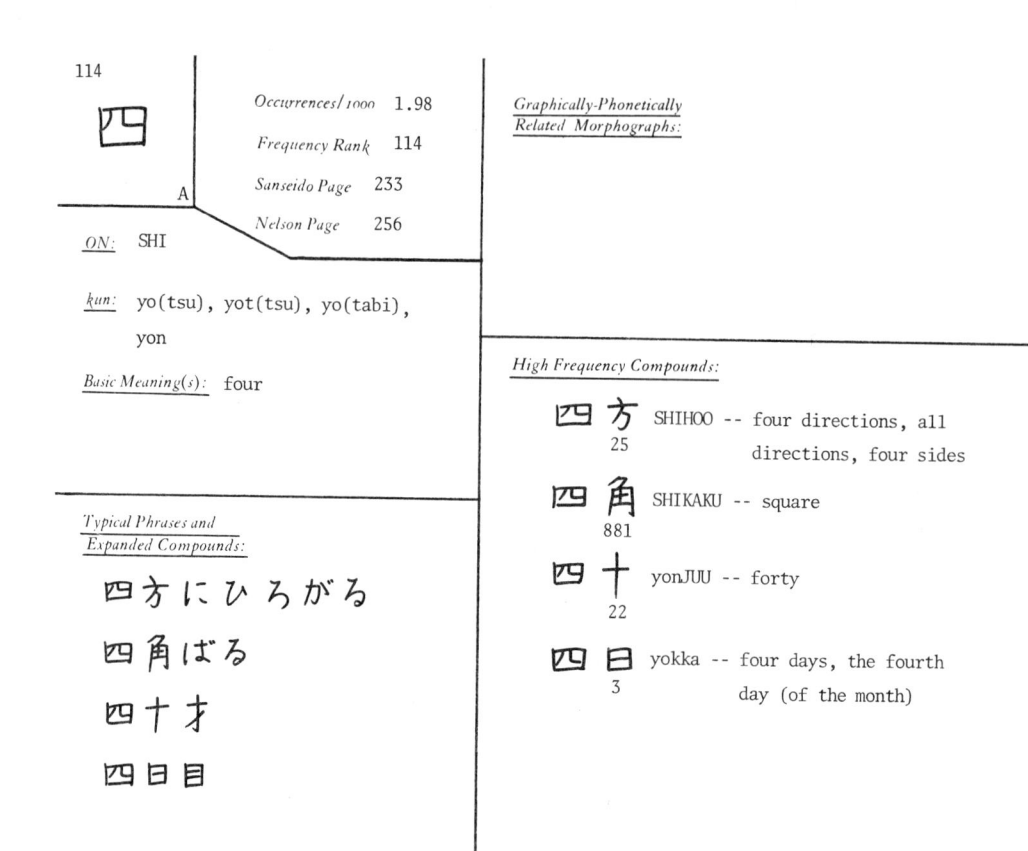

114

四

A

Occurrences/1000 1.98
Frequency Rank 114
Sanseido Page 233
Nelson Page 256

ON: SHI

kun: yo(tsu), yot(tsu), yo(tabi), yon

Basic Meaning(s): four

Graphically-Phonetically Related Morphographs:

High Frequency Compounds:

四方 SHIHOO -- four directions, all directions, four sides
25

四角 SHIKAKU -- square
881

四十 yonJUU -- forty
22

四日 yokka -- four days, the fourth day (of the month)
3

Typical Phrases and Expanded Compounds:

四方にひろがる
四角ばる
四十才
四日目

Typical Conversational Usage:

山火事が四方にひろがっています。
その四角なはこを取ってください。
工事は四十日で終わりました。
この仕事は四日あれば十分です。

Graphically-Phonetically Related Morphographs:

洗 SEN (1232)

銑 SEN

Occurrences/1000	1.96
Frequency Rank	115
Sanseido Page	549
Nelson Page	166

先 115

A

ON: SEN

kun: saki

Basic Meaning(s): precede, priority, the future point

High Frequency Compounds:

先生 SENSEI -- teacher, master, doctor, professional person
9

先日 SENJITSU -- the other day, a few days ago
3

先頭 SENTOO -- the head, the lead
234

先進 SENSHIN -- seniority, advance, leadership
156

Typical Phrases and Expanded Compounds:

山田先生
先日の件
先頭に立つ
先進的
先に行く

Typical Conversational Usage:

国語の先生はだれですか。
先日の件、どうなりましたか。
先頭に立っているのが弟です。
日本はアジアの先進国です。
お先に失礼します。

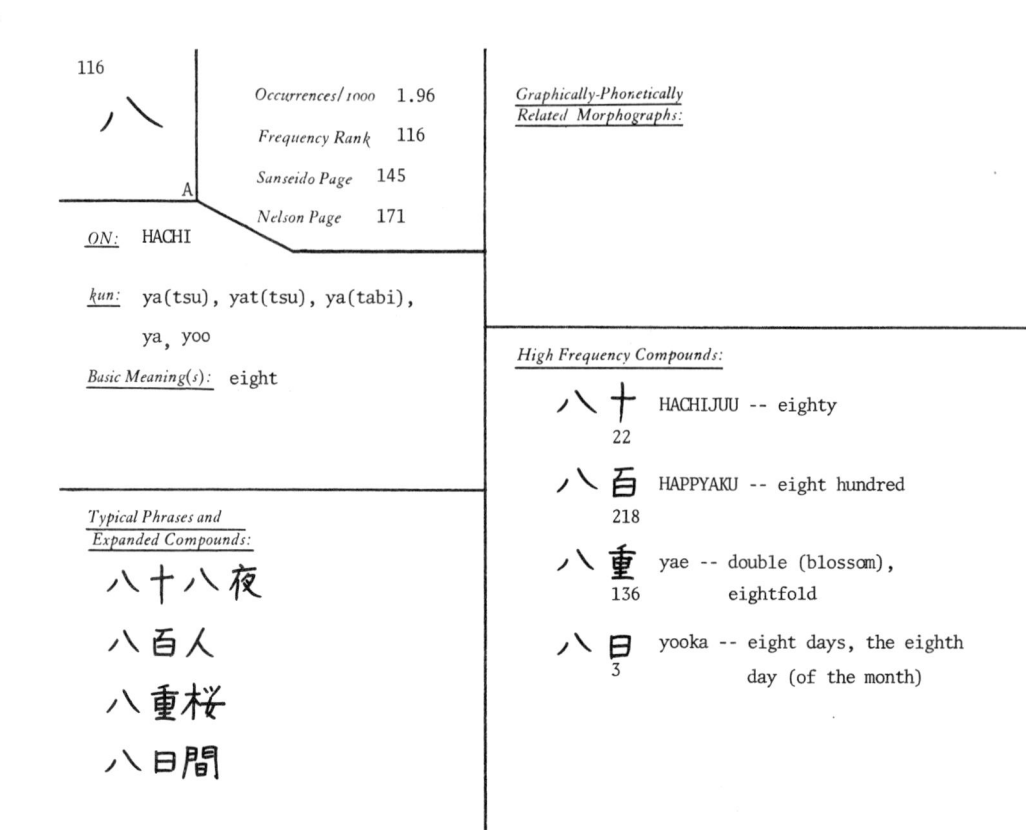

116

八

Occurrences/1000 1.96
Frequency Rank 116
Sanseido Page 145
Nelson Page 171

A

<u>ON</u>: HACHI

<u>kun</u>: ya(tsu), yat(tsu), ya(tabi), ya, yoo

Basic Meaning(s): eight

Graphically-Phonetically Related Morphographs:

High Frequency Compounds:

八十 HACHIJUU -- eighty
22

八百 HAPPYAKU -- eight hundred
218

八重 yae -- double (blossom), eightfold
136

八日 yooka -- eight days, the eighth day (of the month)
3

Typical Phrases and Expanded Compounds:

八十八夜
八百人
八重桜
八日間

Typical Conversational Usage:

おじいさんは今年八十才です。
生徒の数は八百人ぐらいです。
八重桜はとてもきれいです。
かぜで八日間、学校をやすみました。
ハワイには八つの島があります。

Graphically-Phonetically Related Morphographs:

Occurrences/1000 1.93
Frequency Rank 117
Sanseido Page 48
Nelson Page 951

面 117

ON: MEN
kun: omote, omo

Basic Meaning(s): face, mask, surface, side

High Frequency Compounds:

方面 HOOMEN -- direction, side, district
25

直面 CHOKUMEN -- face, confront
214

表面 HYOOMEN -- surface, outside, appearance
178

全面 ZEMMEN -- the whole surface, overall
70

See 49, 279, 399

Also: 正面

Typical Phrases and Expanded Compounds:

東京方面
問題に直面する
表面的
全面的
面長な顔

Typical Conversational Usage:

犯人は関西方面ににげました。
むずかしい問題に直面して、こまっています。
月の表面の写真を見ましたか。
その仕事には全面的に協力します。
あの方の顔は面長です。

118

以　A

Occurrences/1000 1.92
Frequency Rank 118
Sanseido Page 53
Nelson Page 126

ON: I

kun:

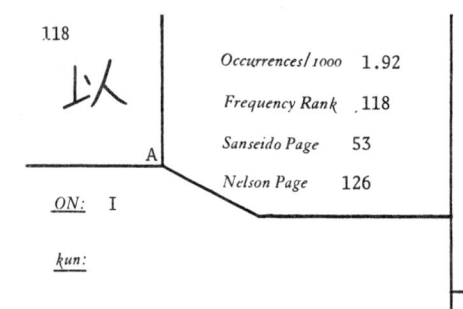

Basic Meaning(s): with, by means of, because

Typical Phrases and Expanded Compounds:

これ以上
日曜以外
先月以来
十日以後
以前のように
一週間以内

Graphically-Phonetically Related Morphographs:

High Frequency Compounds:

以上 29 — IJOO -- more than, above, beyond
以外 69 — IGAI -- with the exception of, excepting
以来 27 — IRAI -- since
以後 48 — IGO -- hereafter, thereafter
以前 53 — IZEN -- ago, since, before
以内 77 — INAI -- within, less than

See 75

Typical Conversational Usage:

これ以上がまんできません。
日曜以外はうちにいません。
その時以来お会いしていません。
以後気をつけます。
以前とあまり変わりありません。
レポートを三日以内に提出してください。

性 — 119

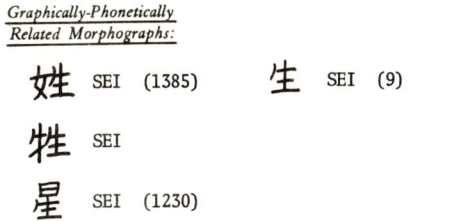

Occurrences/1000: 1.91
Frequency Rank: 119
Sanseido Page: 368
Nelson Page: 398

ON: SEI, SHOO
kun:

Basic Meaning(s): sex, nature, disposition, quality

Graphically-Phonetically Related Morphographs:

姓 SEI (1385) 　生 SEI (9)
牲 SEI
星 SEI (1230)

High Frequency Compounds:

性質 (359) SEISHITSU -- nature, disposition, qualities
性格 (403) SEIKAKU -- character, personality
性能 (285) SEINOO -- performance, efficiency
女性 (60) JOSEI -- woman, womanhood, feminine gender
本性 (6) HONSHOO -- original nature, real character, oneself

See 203, 295

Typical Phrases and Expanded Compounds:

おとなしい性質
強い性格
自動車の性能
女性的
本性を現わす

Typical Conversational Usage:

その問題の性質がちがいます。
あの二人は性格が合って、うらやましいです。
性能がよければ、買うことにします。
その本は女性の間で人気があります。
ついに本性を現わしました。

120 作

Occurrences/1000 1.90
Frequency Rank 120
Sanseido Page 121
Nelson Page 144

A

<u>ON</u>: SAKU, SA

<u>kun</u>: tsuku(ru)

Basic Meaning(s): work, a work, a production, make, create

Graphically-Phonetically Related Morphographs:

昨 SAKU (663)   詐 SAKU
酢 SAKU
搾 SAKU

High Frequency Compounds:

作家 SAKKA -- writer, novelist, artist
46

作品 SAKUHIN -- work, performance, production
372

作業 SAGYOO -- work, operations, manufacturing
74

作曲 SAKKYOKU -- musical composition
1020

Also: 作者

Typical Phrases and Expanded Compounds:

現代作家
ロダンの作品
作業時間
作曲家
たなを作る

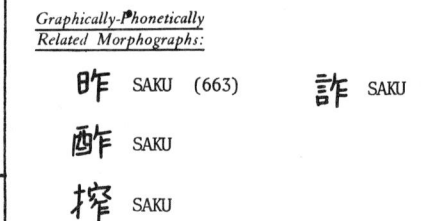

Typical Conversational Usage:

大きくなったら、作家になりたいと思います。
トルストイの作品を読んだことがありますか。
作業が終わりました。
このうたはだれの作曲かわかりません。
おいしいケーキを作りました。

Graphically-Phonetically Related Morphographs:

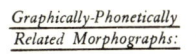

書   121

Occurrences/1000   1.89
Frequency Rank   121
Sanseido Page   352
Nelson Page   736

A

ON: SHO
kun: ka(ku)

Basic Meaning(s): handwriting, letter, book, write, compose

High Frequency Compounds:

書記 209   SHOKI -- clerk, secretary, scribe
書物 95   SHOMOTSU -- books
聖書 1030   SEISHO -- Bible, Scriptures
読書 323   DOKUSHO -- reading a book
図書 719   TOSHO -- books

See 323

Typical Phrases and Expanded Compounds:

書記長
おもしろい書物
聖書研究
読書にふける
図書館
手紙を書く

Typical Conversational Usage:

社会党の書記長はだれですか。
先生はよく書物を読んでいます。
聖書物語を読みました。
妹は読書が大好きです。
図書館で本を借りました。
ちょうど手紙を書いたところです。

122

組 A

Occurrences/1000 1.89
Frequency Rank 122
Sanseido Page 639
Nelson Page 699

ON: SO

kun: ku(mu), ku(mi), kumi

Basic Meaning(s): take part in, braid, contract, unite with

Typical Phrases and Expanded Compounds:

組織的
国鉄労組
組合活動
ラジオの番組
うでを組む

Graphically-Phonetically Related Morphographs:

阻 SO (1117)　　粗 SO
祖 SO (702)
租 SO

High Frequency Compounds:

組織　SOSHIKI -- organization,
416　　　　　　structure, system

労組　ROOSO -- labor union
145

組合　kumiai -- association, league
33　　　　　　union

番組　BANGUMI -- program
519

Typical Conversational Usage:

組織がまだできていません。
国鉄労組の力は強いです。
職場には組合がありますか。
テレビの人気番組は何ですか。
二人ずつ組んであそびましょう。

Graphically-Phonetically Related Morphographs:

導 DOO (501)

	123
Occurrences/1000 1.88	道
Frequency Rank 123	
Sanseido Page 449	A
Nelson Page 887	

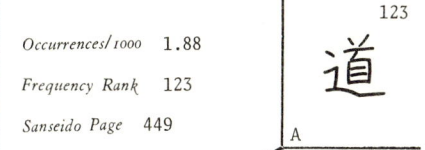

ON: DOO

kun: michi

Basic Meaning(s): road, district, morality, teachings

High Frequency Compounds:

鉄道 TETSUDOO -- railway, railroad
449

道徳 DOOTOKU -- morals, morality, virtue
635

報道 HOODOO -- news, report, information
310

道具 DOOGU -- tool, instrument, utensil
534

道路 DOORO -- road, way, street
835

See 267, 282

Typical Phrases and Expanded Compounds:

日本国有鉄道
道徳教育
報道機関
古道具
道路工事
悪い道

Typical Conversational Usage:

日本の鉄道は発達しています。
道徳をみだしてはいけません。
アポロ十一号の成功が全世界に報道されました。
高速道路を行けば、早くつきます。
道が悪かったので、時間がかかりました。

124

六

Occurrences/1000 1.88
Frequency Rank 124
Sanseido Page 82
Nelson Page 110

ON: ROKU

kun: mu(tsu), mut(tsu), mu, mu(tabi)

Basic Meaning(s): six

Graphically-Phonetically Related Morphographs:

High Frequency Compounds:

六月 ROKUGATSU -- June
66

六法 ROPPOO -- six law codes
100

六日 muika -- six days, the sixth day (of the month)
3

六感 ROKKAN -- the six senses
105

Typical Phrases and Expanded Compounds:

六月ごろ
六法全書
六日の旅
第六感
六つになる

Typical Conversational Usage:

六月にアメリカへ立つつもりです。
大学へ入って、すぐ六法全書を求めました。
あと六日程かかるでしょう。
第六感ですぐわかりました。
弟はようやく六つになりました。

Graphically-Phonetically Related Morphographs:

Occurrences/1000 1.88
Frequency Rank 125
Sanseido Page 682
Nelson Page 828

話

<u>ON</u>: WA

<u>kun</u>: hanashi
      hana(su)

Basic Meaning(s): talk, speak, tell, story, conversation

High Frequency Compounds:

話題 WADAI -- topic of conversation
 51

世話 SEWA -- help, service, care
 81

電話 DENWA -- telephone
332

会話 KAIWA -- conversation
 16

See 191

Typical Phrases and Expanded Compounds:

宇宙の話題
世話好きな人
電話番号
英会話
外人と話す

Typical Conversational Usage:

今は月の話題で持ち切りです。
弟がお世話になり、ありがとうございました。
お宅の電話番号は何番ですか。
大野さんは英会話を習っています。
もっと大きい声で話して下さい。

126

小 A

Occurrences/1000 1.87
Frequency Rank 126
Sanseido Page 264
Nelson Page 331

ON: SHOO

kun: chii(sai), o, ko

Basic Meaning(s): small, little, smallness, short, minor

Typical Phrases and Expanded Compounds:

恋愛小説
小学校
小児科
最小限
小さい国

Graphically-Phonetically Related Morphographs:

少 SHOO (153)   渉 SHOO (740
抄 SHOO
省 SHOO (546)

High Frequency Compounds:

小説 240   SHOOSETSU -- novel, romance, story

小学 15   SHOOGAKU -- elementary education

小児 597   SHOONI -- little child, infant

最小 99   SAISHOO -- the smallest, the minimum

Typical Conversational Usage:

「雪国」という小説を読みましたか。
あした小学校で父兄会があります。
小田先生は小児科専門です。
出費を最小限にとどめてください。
生れた時、私はとても小さかったそうです。

員   127

Occurrences/1000   1.85
Frequency Rank   127
Sanseido Page   232
Nelson Page   249

ON: IN
kun:

Basic Meaning(s):   member, number, the one in charge

Graphically-Phonetically Related Morphographs:

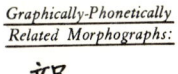

韻 IN

High Frequency Compounds:

委員 540 — IIN -- committeeman, committee, commission

議員 130 — GIIN -- member of an assembly

職員 253 — SHOKUIN -- employee, staff, personnel

会員 16 — KAIIN -- member, the membership

満員 466 — MAN'IN -- no vacancy, full house

See 76, 266, 329

Also: 教員

Typical Phrases and Expanded Compounds:

委員会
国会議員
教職員組会
会員制
超満員

Typical Conversational Usage:

あしたクラスの委員会があります。
小沢氏は県会議員に当選しました。
先生は今職員室にいます。
先月スキークラブの会員になりました。
その電車はいつも満員です。

128

多

A

Occurrences/1000 1.85
Frequency Rank 128
Sanseido Page 254
Nelson Page 285

ON: TA

kun: oo(i)

Basic Meaning(s): much, many, abundant, frequent

Graphically-Phonetically Related Morphographs:

Typical Phrases and Expanded Compounds:

多数の参加
ご多分にもれず
多少遅れる
多額納税者
人が多い

High Frequency Compounds:

多数 159 TASUU -- a large number, multitude, majority

多分 28 TABUN -- perhaps, maybe, probably, very likely

多少 153 TASHOO -- a little, somewhat, any

多額 659 TAGAKU -- large sum

Typical Conversational Usage:

多数の参加を希望しています。
多田さんは多分あした来ると思います。
事故のため、列車は多少遅れるかもしれません。
多額の寄附が集まりました。
この地方は雨が多いです。

所 129

Graphically-Phonetically Related Morphographs:

Occurrences/1000 1.82
Frequency Rank 129
Sanseido Page 469
Nelson Page 416

ON: SHO
kun: tokoro

Basic Meaning(s): place, locality, room, address

High Frequency Compounds:

住所 JUUSHO -- residence, address
377

場所 BASHO -- place, position, seat
49

近所 KINJO -- neighborhood, vicinity
149

所得 SHOTOKU -- income, earnings, possessions
167

See 245, 266, 436, 446

Also: 箇所

Typical Phrases and Expanded Compounds:

住所が変わる
場所が悪い
近所の家
年間所得
神田という所

Typical Conversational Usage:

多田さんの住所がわかりますか。
この場所がいいでしょう。
正男は近所の子供たちと遊んでいます。
所得税は何パーセントぐらいとられますか。
私は東京の中野という所に住んでいました。

130 議

Occurrences/1000: 1.81
Frequency Rank: 130
Sanseido Page: 690
Nelson Page: 841

A

ON: GI

kun:

Basic Meaning(s): consultation, deliberation, debate, consideration

Typical Phrases and Expanded Compounds:

会議室
議会の延期
都会議員
不思議な話
議論好きな人
協議の結果

See 87

Graphically-Phonetically Related Morphographs:

儀 GI (966)
犠 GI
義 GI (62)

High Frequency Compounds:

会議 KAIGI -- conference, assembly, council
16

議会 GIKAI -- deliberative assembly
16

議員 GIIN -- member of an assembly
127

不思議 HUSHIGI -- wonder, strange, mystery, curiosity
103 26

議論 GIRON -- argument, discussion, controversy
110

協議 KYOOGI -- conference, deliberation
193

Also: 審議, 抗議, 決議, 討議

Typical Conversational Usage:

あした、ここで会議が行われます。
議会は明後日に延期されました。
市会議員は全部で何人ですか。
それは全く不思議です。
議論の余地がありません。
協議会が終わりました。

131 済

Occurrences/1000: 1.81
Frequency Rank: 131
Sanseido Page: 406
Nelson Page: 555

ON: SAI
kun: su(mu)
　　　su(masu)

Basic Meaning(s): end, finish up, settle, do without

Graphically-Phonetically Related Morphographs:

High Frequency Compounds:

経済 (71) KEIZAI -- economy, economics, finance

返済 (477) HENSAI -- payment, refunding, redemption

救済 (804) KYUUSAI -- relief, salvation, rescue

Typical Phrases and Expanded Compounds:

経済学者
返済金
救済事業
仕事が済む

Typical Conversational Usage:

日本の経済はとてもよくなりました。
あの人は借金の返済になやんでいました。
水害地に救済の手を伸べましょう。
仕事はあと何分ぐらいで済みますか。

132

活

A

Occurrences/1000 1.80
Frequency Rank 132
Sanseido Page 401
Nelson Page 547

ON: KATSU

kun:

Basic Meaning(s): resuscitation, living, being helped, live, revive

Graphically-Phonetically Related Morphographs:

括 KATSU

Typical Phrases and Expanded Compounds:

楽な生活
活動範囲
大活躍
復活祭

High Frequency Compounds:

生活 SEIKATSU -- life, livelihood
9

活動 KATSUDOO -- activity, energy, service
47

活躍 KATSUYAKU -- be active in, jump into action
1039

復活 HUKKATSU -- revival, resuscitation, resurrection
537

Typical Conversational Usage:

都会の生活は活気があります。
小山さんはなかなかの活動家です。
国友先生の活躍ぶりは大したものです。
昔の歌が復活して、また歌われています。

Graphically-Phonetically Related Morphographs:

		133
Occurrences/1000	1.80	強
Frequency Rank	133	
Sanseido Page	303	
Nelson Page	376	A

ON: KYOO, GOO

kun: tsuyo(meru), tsuyo(mi), tsuyo(i)

Basic Meaning(s): strength, might, strong, strengthen, force

High Frequency Compounds:

勉強　BENKYOO -- study, diligence,
749　　　　　　　discount

強化　KYOOKA -- strengthening
104

強調　KYOOCHOO -- emphasis
219

強盗　GOOTOO -- burglary
953

See 161

Typical Phrases and Expanded Compounds:

英語の勉強

警備を強化する

強調が足りない

三人組の強盗

強い風

Typical Conversational Usage:

弟は一生懸命勉強しています。
町では美化運動を強化しています。
その点をもう少し強調して下さい。
ホテルに強盗が入りました。
きのうは強い北風が吹きました。

134

由 A

Occurrences/1000   1.80
Frequency Rank   134
Sanseido Page   482
Nelson Page   60

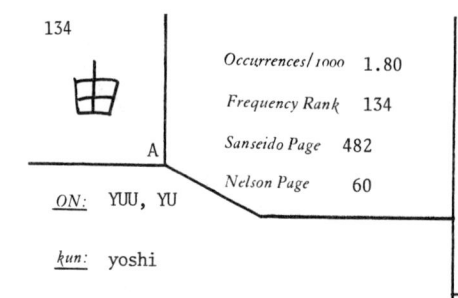

ON: YUU, YU

kun: yoshi

Basic Meaning(s): reason, means, effect, depend upon

Typical Phrases and Expanded Compounds:

自由な気持
欠席の理由
ホノルル経由

Graphically-Phonetically Related Morphographs:

油 YU (879)

High Frequency Compounds:

自由 14   JIYUU -- independence, freedom, liberty

理由 59   RIYUU -- reason, cause, pretext

経由 71   KEIYU -- via, go by way of

Typical Conversational Usage:

日本には宗教や言論の自由があります。
理由もなしに欠席してはいけません。
この列車は名古屋経由大阪行です。
先生があさって来られる由、うかがいました。

Graphically-Phonetically Related Morphographs:

稿 KOO

Occurrences/1000	1.79
Frequency Rank	135
Sanseido Page	91
Nelson Page	976

高 135

A

ON: KOO

kun: taka(i)

Basic Meaning(s): high, tall, eminent, noble

High Frequency Compounds:

最高 99 SAIKOO -- highest, maximum, supreme

高校 233 KOOKOO -- senior high school

高等 151 KOOTOO -- high class, high grade

高級 373 KOOKYUU -- high rank, high grade, seniority

See 347

Typical Phrases and Expanded Compounds:

最高裁判所
高校一年生
高等学校
高級ホテル
高い山

Typical Conversational Usage:

おとといの暑さは今年最高だそうです。
弟はまだ高校生です。
高橋さんは高等学校の先生です。
きのう、銀座でフランスの高級料理を食べました。
あまり高ければ、その品物は買いたくありません。

136

重

Occurrences/1000 1.79
Frequency Rank 136
Sanseido Page 69
Nelson Page 96

ON: JUU, CHOO

kun: omo(i), omo(ku suru), omo(sa), e, kasa(naru), kasa(neru), kasa(ne)

Basic Meaning(s): heavy, weight, fold, pile up, heap up, nest of boxes

Typical Phrases and Expanded Compounds:

重要書類
重大ニュース
意見を尊重する
貴重な時間
重い物
本を重ねる

Graphically-Phonetically Related Morphographs:

High Frequency Compounds:

重要 JUUYOO -- important, essential, principal
78

重大 JUUDAI -- important, serious
5

尊重 SONCHOO -- respect, esteem, regard
704

貴重 KICHOO -- precious
676

Typical Conversational Usage:

そんなに重要視する必要はありません。
きのう重大な事件が起こりました。
父はいつも人の意見を尊重します。
これは貴重品ですから、大事に使ってください。
その荷物は重そうです。
本を机の上に重ねておいてください。

137

働

Graphically-Phonetically Related Morphographs:

動 DOO (47)

Occurrences/1000　1.79
Frequency Rank　137
Sanseido Page　141
Nelson Page　162

ON: DOO
kun: hatara(ku), hatara(ki)

High Frequency Compounds:

労働 ROODOO -- labor, manual labor, work, toil
145

Basic Meaning(s): work, labor, movement, motion

Typical Phrases and Expanded Compounds:

労働組合
働きざかり

Typical Conversational Usage:

あなたの会社には労働組合がありますか。
小野田さんはよく働く方です。

138 決 A

Occurrences/1000 1.78
Frequency Rank 138
Sanseido Page 395
Nelson Page 538

ON: KETSU

kun: ki(meru), ki(maru), ki(me)

Basic Meaning(s): decision, vote, fix, be settled

Graphically-Phonetically Related Morphographs:

欠 KETSU (774)

穴 KETSU

Typical Phrases and Expanded Compounds:

解決策
決定権
判決を言い渡す
決意を新たにする
決心がつく
人数を決める

High Frequency Compounds:

解決 142 KAIKETSU -- solution, settlement

決定 93 KETTEI -- decision, determination, conclusion

判決 187 HANKETSU -- judgment, decision, sentence

決意 86 KETSUI -- resolution, determination

決心 64 KESSHIN -- determination, resolution, decision

Also: 決議

Typical Conversational Usage:

その問題はすでに解決しました。
就職先が決定しました。
裁判でどんな判決が下されましたか。
中川さんは何とかその仕事をやりとげる決意です。
まだそこへ行く決心をしていません。
どこの大学へ行くか、もう決めましたか。

正

139

Occurrences/1000 1.77
Frequency Rank 139
Sanseido Page 30
Nelson Page 44

A

ON: SEI, SHOO
kun: tada(shikusuru), tada(su), tada(shii)

Basic Meaning(s): right, just, honest, correct

Graphically-Phonetically Related Morphographs:

征 SEI (1231)
政 SEI, SHOO (23)
整 SEI (825)

High Frequency Compounds:

改正 (289) KAISEI -- revision, amendment, improvement

正常 (190) SEIJOO -- normalcy, normality, normal

正式 (356) SEISHIKI -- proper form, formality

正当 (68) SEITOO -- just, right, proper

正直 (214) SHOOJIKI -- honesty, integrity, frankness

See 66, 103

Also: 大正, 正面, 正義

Typical Phrases and Expanded Compounds:

法律の改正
正常に戻る
正式発表
正当防衛
正直な人
正しい答

Typical Conversational Usage:

その法律の一部が改正されました。
そんな考えは正常ではありません。
それがまだ正式に決まったわけではありません。
正当な手続きをふんでください。
正男君はとても正直です。
それは正しくありません。

140

名 A

Occurrences/1000 1.77
Frequency Rank 140
Sanseido Page 255
Nelson Page 286

ON: MEI, MYOO

kun: na

Basic Meaning(s): name, fame, distinguished, reputation

Graphically-Phonetically Related Morphographs:

銘 MEI

Typical Phrases and Expanded Compounds:

有名になる
名人芸
名誉教授
署名入りで
女優の本名
名前をつける

High Frequency Compounds:

有名 YUUMEI -- famous, notorious, proverbial
245

名人 MEIJIN -- master, expert
2

名誉 MEIYO -- honor, glory, dignity

署名 SHOMEI -- signature, autograph
1221

本名 HOMMYOO -- real name
6

名前 namae -- name, given name
53

See 299

Typical Conversational Usage:

本田さんは実業界で有名になりました。
大山さんは何の名人ですか。
それは名誉にかかわる問題です。
ここに署名してください。
美空ひばりの本名は何ですか。
その子の名前がわかりません。

141

資

Occurrences/1000   1.76
Frequency Rank   141
Sanseido Page   696
Nelson Page   850

A

ON: SHI
kun:

Graphically-Phonetically Related Morphographs:

次 JI (150)
諮 SHI
姿 SHI (560)

Basic Meaning(s): resources, capital, materials, quality

High Frequency Compounds:

資本 SHIHON -- capital, fund
  6

資金 SHIKIN -- fund, capital
  79

資格 SHIKAKU -- qualifications, requirements, capabilities
  403

資源 SHIGEN -- resources
  626

投資 TOOSHI -- investment
  510

See 95, 395

Typical Phrases and Expanded Compounds:

資本主義
資金不足
資格がある
資源に富む
多額の投資

Typical Conversational Usage:

その会社の資本金はいくらですか。
会社の運転資金は十分ですか。
去年中学校の教員の資格をもらいました。
日本は石油の資源が少ないです。
私は土地に投資することにしました。

142 解 A

Occurrences/1000: 1.75
Frequency Rank: 142
Sanseido Page: 675
Nelson Page: 820

ON: KAI, GE

kun: to(ku), to(keru)

Basic Meaning(s): explanation, understanding, untie, solve

Typical Phrases and Expanded Compounds:
問題の解決
理解を深める
見解の相違
英文解釈
国会の解散
なぞを解く

Graphically-Phonetically Related Morphographs:

High Frequency Compounds:

解決 138 — KAIKETSU -- solution, settlement

理解 59 — RIKAI -- understanding, appreciation, comprehension

見解 20 — KENKAI -- opinion, view

解釈 775 — KAISHAKU -- interpretation, explanation

解散 969 — KAISAN -- dispersion, disbanding, dissolution

Typical Conversational Usage:

その問題はまだ解決されていません。
山田さんのお父さんはとても理解があります。
二人の見解は大分違っています。
この文をどういうふうに解釈しますか。
衆議院はきのう解散しました。
その問題を解くのに二時間かかりました。

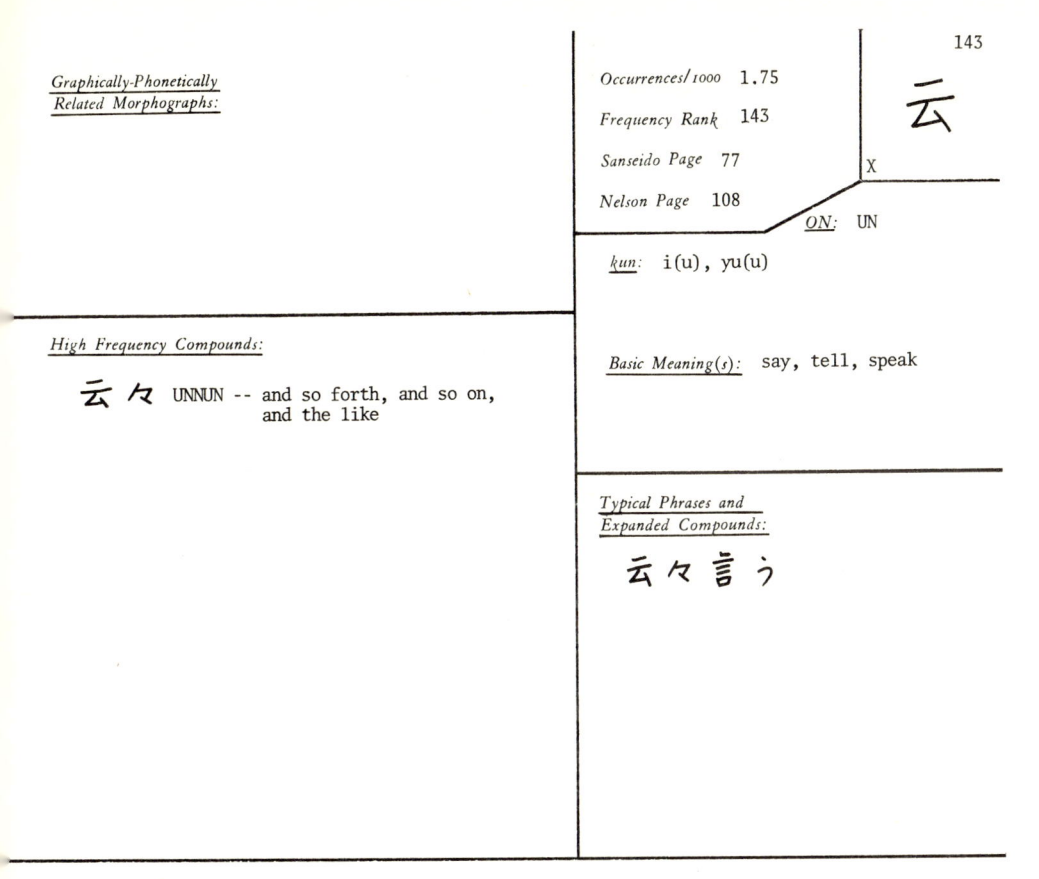

Graphically-Phonetically Related Morphographs:

Occurrences/1000 1.75
Frequency Rank 143
Sanseido Page 77
Nelson Page 108

云

X

ON: UN

kun: i(u), yu(u)

Basic Meaning(s): say, tell, speak

High Frequency Compounds:

云々 UNNUN -- and so forth, and so on, and the like

Typical Phrases and Expanded Compounds:

云々言う

Typical Conversational Usage:

云々言っても始まりません。

144

然
A

Occurrences/1000 1.75
Frequency Rank 144
Sanseido Page 562
Nelson Page 577

ON: ZEN, NEN

kun:

Basic Meaning(s): decree, but, proper, and

Typical Phrases and Expanded Compounds:

当然の結果
全然わからない
突然起こる
偶然に
天然資源
自然現象

Graphically-Phonetically Related Morphographs:

燃 NEN

High Frequency Compounds:

当然 TOOZEN -- justly, properly, naturally
68

全然 ZENZEN -- wholly, entirely, completely, not at all
70

突然 TOTSUZEN -- suddenly, unexpectedly
542

偶然 GUUZEN -- chance, accident
1267

天然 TENNEN -- nature, spontaneity
277

自然 SHIZEN -- nature
14

See 188

Typical Conversational Usage:

親が子供を愛するのは当然です。
フランス語は全然わかりません。
姉の留学が決まったのは突然です。
銀座で上田さんに偶然に会いました。
その映画は天然色ですか。
あの子は泳ぎを自然におぼえるでしょう。

145

労

ON: ROO

kun:

Occurrences/1000 1.72
Frequency Rank 145
Sanseido Page 619
Nelson Page 206

Basic Meaning(s): labor, toil, trouble

Graphically-Phonetically Related Morphographs:

High-Frequency Compounds:

労働 ROODOO -- manual labor, work, toil
137

苦労 KUROO -- hardships, difficulties, toil
344

勤労 KINROO -- labor, exertion
690

Typical Phrases and Expanded Compounds:

労働者
苦労のない人
勤労感謝の日

Typical Conversational Usage:

今の労働大臣はだれですか。
あの方は若い時大変苦労しました。
十一月二十三日は勤労感謝の日です。

146

反

A

Occurrences/1000 1.71
Frequency Rank 146
Sanseido Page 196
Nelson Page 229

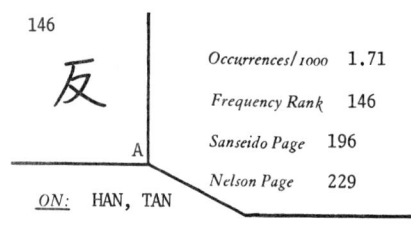

ON: HAN, TAN

kun:

Basic Meaning(s): antithesis, opposite, anti-, roll of cloth

Typical Phrases and Expanded Compounds:

反対側

反省を求める

反動的

違反者

Graphically-Phonetically Related Morphographs:

板 HAN (876)   版 HAN (892)
販 HAN (1121) 飯 HAN (932)
坂 HAN (1037)

High Frequency Compounds:

反対 HANTAI -- opposition, resistance, antagonism
39

反省 HANSEI -- reflection, reconsideration, meditation
546

反動 HANDOO -- reaction, recoil, kick
47

違反 IHAN -- violation, infringement, breach (of contract)
274

See 368

Also: 反米, 反共

Typical Conversational Usage:

この意見に賛成ですか、反対ですか。

その点をよく反省してください。

そのグループはすごく反動的です。

それは規則違反です。

七

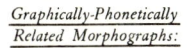

Occurrences/1000 1.70
Frequency Rank 147
Sanseido Page 7
Nelson Page 102

A

<u>ON</u>: SHICHI

<u>kun</u>: nana(tsu), nana, nanu, nana(tabi)

Basic Meaning(s): seven

Graphically-Phonetically Related Morphographs:

High Frequency Compounds:

七人₂　SHICHININ -- seven people

七日₃　nanuka, nanoka -- seven days, the seventh day of the month

Typical Phrases and Expanded Compounds:

七人集まる

七日間

世界の七不思議

Typical Conversational Usage:

全部で七人集まりました。
一週間は七日です。
きのうは世界の七不思議について勉強しました。

148

山 A

Occurrences/1000 1.69
Frequency Rank 148
Sanseido Page 304
Nelson Page 346

<u>ON</u>: SAN

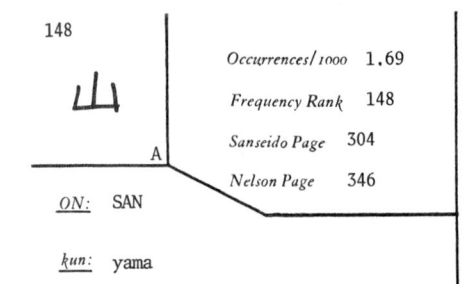

<u>kun</u>: yama

Basic Meaning(s): mountain, mount, hill, pile, climax

Typical Phrases and Expanded Compounds:

沢山の人々
火山帯
山頂をめざして
登山隊
山の多い

Graphically-Phonetically Related Morphographs:

High Frequency Compounds:

沢山 TAKUSAN -- a great man, a large
442   quantity, abundance

火山 KAZAN -- volcano
595

山頂 SANCHOO -- mountain top
1062

登山 TOZAN -- mountain climbing,
1151   mountain ascent

Occurs frequently in proper names, such as, 山田 , "Yamada."

Typical Conversational Usage:

きゅうりが沢山とれました。
日本には火山が多いです。
山頂は雪におおわれています。
兄と来年日本アルプスを登山するつもりです。
仕事が山ほどあります。

149 近

Graphically-Phonetically Related Morphographs:

斤 KIN

Occurrences/1000 1.68
Frequency Rank 149
Sanseido Page 439
Nelson Page 873

ON: KIN
kun: chika(i), chika(zuku)
       chika(shii), chika(zuku
       chika(goro)
Basic Meaning(s): near, early

High Frequency Compounds:

最近 SAIKIN -- recently, lately, latest
99

近代 KINDAI -- modern times
87

付近 HUKIN -- neighborhood, vicinity
792

近所 KINJO -- neighborhood, vicinity
129

Typical Phrases and Expanded Compounds:

最近の模様
近代的設備
付近一帯
近所の人々
近いうちに

Typical Conversational Usage:

私は最近九州から来たばかりです。
あのビルはとても近代的です。
この付近はまだ家が少ないです。
山本さんは近所に越してきました。
プリンスホテルは家の近くにあります。

150

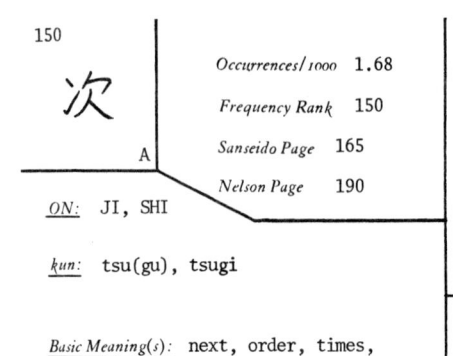

次　A

Occurrences/1000　1.68
Frequency Rank　150
Sanseido Page　165
Nelson Page　190

ON: JI, SHI

kun: tsu(gu), tsugi

Basic Meaning(s): next, order, times, then, rank next to, below

Typical Phrases and Expanded Compounds:

本の目次
事の次第
その次

Graphically-Phonetically Related Morphographs:

諮　SHI
姿　SHI (560)
資　SHI (141)

High Frequency Compounds:

目次　MOKUJI -- table of contents
91

次第　SHIDAI -- order, precedence, reason, as soon as
83

Typical Conversational Usage:

目次を見てください。
そこへ行くか、行かないかはお天気次第です。
次の人はどなたですか。

151 等

Occurrences/1000: 1.68
Frequency Rank: 151
Sanseido Page: 626
Nelson Page: 684

A

ON: TOO
kun: hito(shii)

Graphically-Phonetically Related Morphographs:

Basic Meaning(s): class, grade, and so forth, equal, and others

High Frequency Compounds:

高等₁₃₅ KOOTOO -- high class, high grade

等々 TOOTOO -- etc., and so forth

平等₉₈ BYOODOO -- equality, impartiality

何等₄₃ nanra -- what, whatever, any kind of

Typical Phrases and Expanded Compounds:

高等学校
ラジオやテレビ等々
平等にする
何等かの方法
数字が等しい

Typical Conversational Usage:

私は今高等動物について勉強しています。
物理や化学等々、いろいろな本を買いました。
人はみな平等です。
何等かの問題があるに違いありません。
そんな苦労は無に等しいです。

152 明

A

Occurrences/1000 1.68
Frequency Rank 152
Sanseido Page 485
Nelson Page 477

ON: MEI, MYOO

kun: aki(raka), aka(rui), a(keru), a(kasu), a(kari), a(ke), a(kashi), a(ki)

Basic Meaning(s): clearness, clear, light, discernment, open, reveal

Graphically-Phonetically Related Morphographs:

盟 MEI (603)

High Frequency Compounds:

明治 MEIJI -- Meiji
88

説明 SETSUMEI -- explanation, interpretation, description
240

声明 SEIMEI -- declaration, statement, proclamation
299

文明 BUMMEI -- civilization, culture
89

発明 HATSUMEI -- invention, contrivance, cleverness
102

See 448

Also: 明確, 表明

Typical Phrases and Expanded Compounds:

明治維新
説明を要する
声明を発表する
文明の発達
発明者
明るい部屋

Typical Conversational Usage:

明治時代に工業が発達しはじめました。
これを簡単に説明してください。
政府は重大な声明を発表しました。
日本はアジアの文明国です。
エジソンは何を発明しましたか。
吉田さんはとても明るい方です。

少

Graphically-Phonetically Related Morphographs:

小 SHOO (126)   渉 SHOO (740)

抄 SHOO

省 SHOO (546)

Occurrences/1000 1.64
Frequency Rank 153
Sanseido Page 265
Nelson Page 83

ON: SHOO
kun: suku(nai), suko(shi)

High Frequency Compounds:

少年 13	SHOONEN -- boy
少女 60	SHOOJO -- daughter, girl, young lady, virgin
少数 159	SHOOSUU -- few, minority
多少 128	TASHOO -- a little, somewhat, slightly

Basic Meaning(s): few, small, young, a small quantity, a little, few

Typical Phrases and Expanded Compounds:

少年野球
少女趣味
少数派
多少の違い
雨が少ない
ほんの少し

Typical Conversational Usage:

どこの国にも青少年の問題があります。
きのう妹に少女雑誌を買って来ました。
会議に少数の人しか集まりませんでした。
多少の違いはあるかも知れません。
先月は雨が少なかったです。
ほんの少しで結構です。

154

達

A

Occurrences/1000 1.64
Frequency Rank 154
Sanseido Page 449
Nelson Page 886

ON: TATSU

kun:

Basic Meaning(s): reach, become expert, accomplish, plural ending

Graphically-Phonetically Related Morphographs:

High Frequency Compounds:

達成 TASSEI -- achievement, accomplishment
160

到達 TOOTATSU -- arrival
777

発達 HATTATSU -- growth, development, progress
102

友達 tomoDACHI -- friend, companion
451

Typical Phrases and Expanded Compounds:

目的を達成する
目標に到達する
工業の発達
友達に会う

Typical Conversational Usage:

森さんは努力して、自分の目的を達成しました。
井上さんは、あきらめの境地に到達したそうです。
戦後、日本の科学は急速に発達しました。
きのう銀座で友達に会いました。

Graphically-Phonetically Related Morphographs:

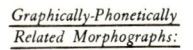

Occurrences/1000	1.64
Frequency Rank	155
Sanseido Page	631
Nelson Page	690

155

米

A

ON: BEI, MAI

kun: kome

Basic Meaning(s): rice, U.S.A.

High Frequency Compounds:

米国   BEIKOKU -- U.S.A.
 4

日米   NICHIBEI -- Japan and the U.S.A.
 3

欧米   OOBEI -- Europe and the U.S.A.
641

米軍   BEIGUN -- U. S. Armed Forces
 36

Also: 反米

Typical Phrases and Expanded Compounds:

米国政府

日米関係

欧米諸国

米軍基地

米の配給

Typical Conversational Usage:

あの方は米国人だそうです。
日米医学会議が来月東京で開かれます。
それは欧米諸国にとって大きな問題です。
原君は、立川の米軍基地でしばらく働いていました。
この地方は、お米がよくとれます。

156

進

Occurrences/1000 1.62
Frequency Rank 156
Sanseido Page 447
Nelson Page 885

ON: SHIN

kun: susu(mu), susu(meru), susu(mi)

Basic Meaning(s): advancing, proceed, progress, move forward

Typical Phrases and Expanded Compounds:

進行状態
大学へ進学する
後進国
産業を促進する
行進曲
どんどん進む

Graphically-Phonetically Related Morphographs:

High Frequency Compounds:

進行   SHINKOO -- go forward, advance
  18

進学   SHINGAKU -- entrance to a
  15   higher school

後進   KOOSHIN -- retreat, moving back-
  48   ward, former generation

促進   SOKUSHIN -- promote, encourage,
 1007   facilitate

行進   KOOSHIN -- advance, march,
  18   parade

See 53, 373, 443

Also: 改進, 推進

Typical Conversational Usage:

工事は、どのくらい進行していますか。
今、弟は進学をめざして勉強しています。
アジアには、まだ後進国がたくさんあります。
県では山林の開発を促進しています。
一体あれは何の行進ですか。
ピアノのレッスンは大分進みました。

Graphically-Phonetically Related Morphographs:

	157
Occurrences/1000 1.59	運
Frequency Rank 157	
Sanseido Page 448	A
Nelson Page 888	

<u>ON</u>: UN

<u>kun</u>: hako(bu), hako(bi)

High Frequency Compounds:

運動 UNDOO -- motion, exercise,
 47   campaign

運命 UMMEI -- destiny, fate
249

運転 UNTEN -- operation, motion,
554   driving a car

See 423

Basic Meaning(s): destiny, fortune, carry, progress, arrangements

Typical Phrases and Expanded Compounds:

運動会

運命に任せる

自動車の運転

荷物を運ぶ

Typical Conversational Usage:

毎朝少し運動することにしています。
友人の石田君は船と運命を共にしました。
西村さんはトラックの運転手をしています。
この机を向こうへ運んでください。

158 機

Occurrences/1000 1.58
Frequency Rank 158
Sanseido Page 531
Nelson Page 513

A

ON: KI

kun: hata

Basic Meaning(s): loom, machine, opportunity, occasion

Typical Phrases and Expanded Compounds:

機械工業
機会があれば
経済危機
動機をつかむ
交通機関

Graphically-Phonetically Related Morphographs:

幾 KI (464)

High Frequency Compounds:

機械 KIKAI -- machine, mechanism, gear
937

機会 KIKAI -- opportunity, chance
16

危機 KIKI -- crisis, emergency
495

動機 DOOKI -- motive, incentive
47

機関 KIKAN -- engine, machine, facilities, organ
84

See 285, 498

Typical Conversational Usage:

この機械の調子があまりよくありません。
本田さんに会う機会がありますか。
南ベトナムは危機にさらされました。
先生になった動機は何ですか。
日本の交通機関は発達しています。

数
159

Graphically-Phonetically Related Morphographs:

Occurrences/1000 1.57
Frequency Rank 159
Sanseido Page 474
Nelson Page 460

ON: SUU
kun: kazu, kazo(eru)

Basic Meaning(s): numbers, count, strength

High Frequency Compounds:

多数 TASUU -- a large number, majority
128

少数 SHOOSUU -- few, minority
153

数字 SUUJI -- figure, numeral, tabular matter
515

数学 SUUGAKU -- mathematics
15

偶数 GUUSUU -- even number
1267

Also: 無数

Typical Phrases and Expanded Compounds:

多数決
少数の人々
数字が合わない
数学の先生
偶数と奇数
人数を数える

Typical Conversational Usage:

それは多数決で決まりました。
そこに集まった人はごく小数でした。
私は数字に強くありません。
兄は数学が得意です。
二や四は偶数で、一や三は奇数です。
この部屋に何人いるか数えてください。

160 成

Occurrences/1000 1.56
Frequency Rank 160
Sanseido Page 615
Nelson Page 412

A

ON: SEI, JOO

kun: na(ru), na(su)

Basic Meaning(s): become, get or grow (old), mature, do, accomplish

Typical Phrases and Expanded Compounds:

大成功
法案の成立
賛成を求める
完成に近い
良い成績
成り上がる

See 154, 498

Graphically-Phonetically Related Morphographs:

誠 SEI (848)
盛 SEI (808)

High Frequency Compounds:

成功 SEIKOO -- success, achievement, prosperity
735

成立 SEIRITSU -- materialization, realization
35

賛成 SANSEI -- approval, agreement, support
1324

完成 KANSEI -- finish, be finished
559

成績 SEISEKI -- results, marks, score
1056

Also: 成立, 結成, 編成

Typical Conversational Usage:

その仕事は大変成功しました。
新しい法案が成立しました。
その意見に賛成です。
このビルはもう完成に近いです。
小田さんは二学期の成績が上がったそうです。
このチームは二十人から成っています。

161

制

Graphically-Phonetically Related Morphographs:

製 SEI (521)

Occurrences/1000 1.55
Frequency Rank 161
Sanseido Page 172
Nelson Page 200

<u>ON</u>: SEI
<u>kun</u>:

Basic Meaning(s): system, organization, laws, control, hold back

High Frequency Compounds:

制度 SEIDO -- system, organization
72

制限 SEIGEN -- limit, limitation, restriction
370

強制 KYOOSEI -- coercion, compulsion, enforcement
133

抑制 YOKUSEI -- control, restrain, suppress
798

See 96, 258, 273

Also: 専制

Typical Phrases and Expanded Compounds:

封建制度
制限速度
強制的
感情を抑制する

Typical Conversational Usage:

教育制度は戦後だいぶ変わりました。
時間に制限がありますか。
人を強制してはいけません。
感情を抑制するのはむずかしいです。

162 権

Occurrences/1000 1.54
Frequency Rank 162
Sanseido Page 529
Nelson Page 511

A

ON: KEN, GON

kun:

Basic Meaning(s): authority, power, rights, concession

Typical Phrases and Expanded Compounds:

政権を失う
権力争い
権利金
権威的
特権階級

Graphically-Phonetically Related Morphographs:

High Frequency Compounds:

政権 23 — SEIKEN -- political power, reins of government, administration

権力 38 — KENRYOKU -- power, authority, influence

権利 180 — KENRI -- rights, claim, powers

権威 728 — KEN'I -- authority, power, dignity

特権 186 — TOKKEN -- privilege, special rights, liberties (civil)

See 34

Also: 人権

Typical Conversational Usage:

イギリスでは何党が政権を担当していますか。
兄は家でいつも権力をふるっています。
小野さんにはそれだけの事をいう権利があります。
あの方はいつも権威的に物を言います。
そこへ行けるのは特権だと思います。

保

163

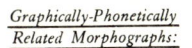

Occurrences/1000 1.52
Frequency Rank 163
Sanseido Page 131
Nelson Page 154

A

<u>ON</u>: HO
<u>kun</u>: tamo(tsu)

Graphically-Phonetically Related Morphographs:

Basic Meaning(s): keep, maintain, guarantee, support, last

High Frequency Compounds:

- 保安 (165) — HOAN -- peace preservation, security
- 保守 (364) — HOSHU -- conservatism
- 保証 (448) — HOSHOO -- guarantee, security
- 保護 (474) — HOGO -- care, protection, patronage
- 保存 (431) — HOZON -- preservation, conservation, storage

Also: 保障, 確保

Typical Phrases and Expanded Compounds:

海上保安官
保守的
保証人
保護者
保存がきく
地位を保つ

Typical Conversational Usage:

弟は海上保安官になりました。
保子さんの考えはとても保守的です。
その機械は何年ぐらい保証されていますか。
和子ちゃんは迷子になって、警察に保護されました。
これはあまり長く保存できません。
小野さんは重役の地位を保っています。

164 界 A

Occurrences/1000 1.50
Frequency Rank 164
Sanseido Page 576
Nelson Page 622

ON: KAI

kun:

Basic Meaning(s): circle, world, boundary, limits

Graphically-Phonetically Related Morphographs:

介 KAI (658)

High Frequency Compounds:

世界 81 — SEKAI -- the world, society, the universe

限界 370 — GENKAI -- boundary, limit, bounds

財界 491 — ZAIKAI -- financial world, money market

業界 74 — GYOOKAI -- business world, industry, trade

Typical Phrases and Expanded Compounds:

全世界
能力の限界
財界人
業界の話題

Typical Conversational Usage:

成田さんはスポーツの世界で活躍しています。
もう能力の限界に達しました。
野沢氏は財界きっての人物と言われています。
それは業界で今大きな問題となっています。

安

Occurrences/1000 1.49
Frequency Rank 165
Sanseido Page 278
Nelson Page 312

ON: AN

kun: yasu(i), yasu(raka), yasun(jiru), yasun(zuru)

Basic Meaning(s): peaceful, cheap, be contented, tranquil

Graphically-Phonetically Related Morphographs:

案 AN (353)

High Frequency Compounds:

安定 — ANTEI -- stability, equilibrium, stabilization
93

安全 — ANZEN -- safety, security
70

不安 — FUAN -- anxiety, uneasiness, insecurity
103

安心 — ANSHIN -- peace of mind, freedom of care, sense of relief, security
64

See 163

Typical Phrases and Expanded Compounds:

職業安定所
安全運転
不安がともなう
安心感
安っぽい品物

Typical Conversational Usage:

国の経済は今安定しています。
車を運転する時、安全が第一です。
全く不安がなくなりました。
試験が終わるまでは、まだ安心できません。
安物は買わないことにしています。

166

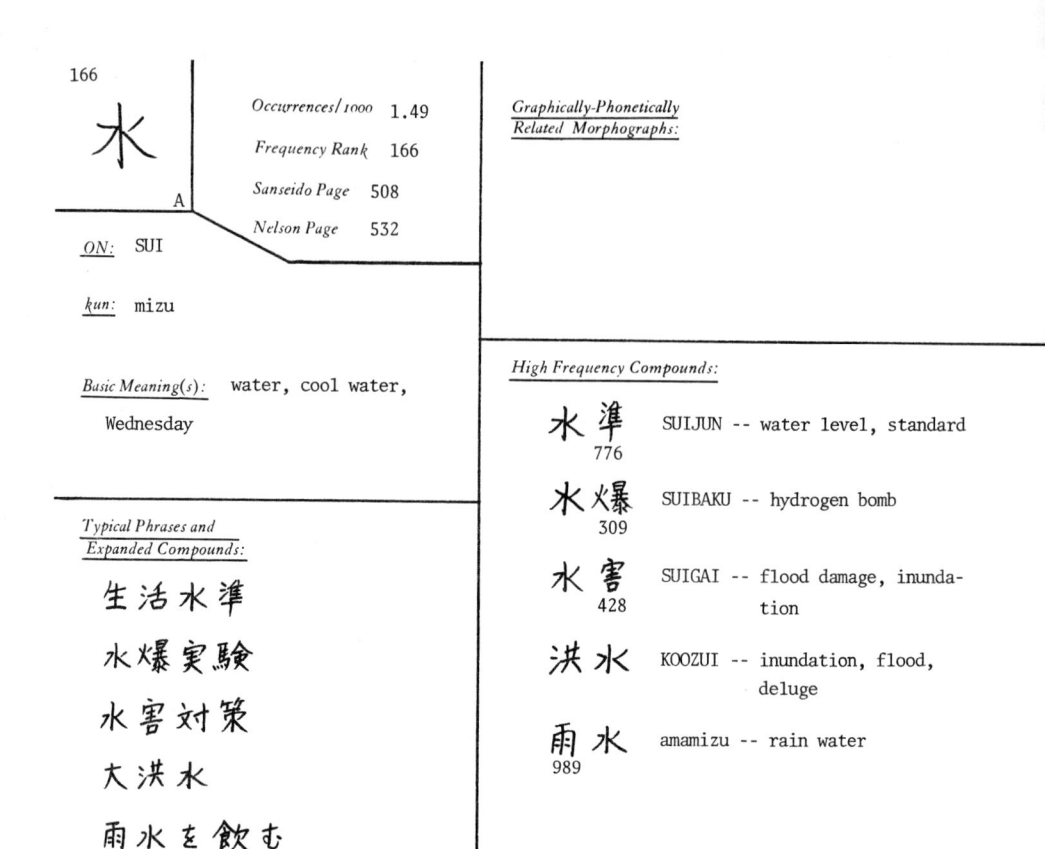

水　A

Occurrences/1000　1.49
Frequency Rank　166
Sanseido Page　508
Nelson Page　532

ON: SUI

kun: mizu

Basic Meaning(s):　water, cool water, Wednesday

Typical Phrases and Expanded Compounds:

生活水準
水爆実験
水害対策
大洪水
雨水を飲む

Graphically-Phonetically Related Morphographs:

High Frequency Compounds:

水準　SUIJUN -- water level, standard
776

水爆　SUIBAKU -- hydrogen bomb
309

水害　SUIGAI -- flood damage, inunda-
428　　　　tion

洪水　KOOZUI -- inundation, flood,
　　　　　　　deluge

雨水　amamizu -- rain water
989

Typical Conversational Usage:

日本の生活水準は高くなりました。
アメリカは水爆実験をどこでやりましたか。
首相は水害地を訪れました。
大雨でこの辺一帯は洪水になりました。
雨水を飲んだことがありますか。

167 得

Graphically-Phonetically Related Morphographs:

Occurrences/1000 1.48
Frequency Rank 167
Sanseido Page 360
Nelson Page 386

A

ON: TOKU

kun: e(ru)

Basic Meaning(s): profit, benefit, advantage, get, earn, gain

High Frequency Compounds:

獲得 1132 — KAKUTOKU -- acquisition, possession

納得 1337 — NATTOKU -- assent, understanding, agreement, consent

所得 129 — SHOTOKU -- income, earnings, possessions

損得 1058 — SONTOKU -- loss and gain, disadvantages and advantages

Typical Phrases and Expanded Compounds:

票を獲得する
納得済み
所得税
損得を考える
得がたい品物

Typical Conversational Usage:

票をどのくらい獲得すれば、当選できますか。
その話は納得できません。
少し所得がふえました。
損得を考えないで、その仕事をやりました。
それは得がたい品物です。

168

府

Occurrences/1000 1.48
Frequency Rank 168
Sanseido Page 319
Nelson Page 363

A

ON: HU

kun:

Basic Meaning(s): urban prefecture, government office, representative body, storehouse

Typical Phrases and Expanded Compounds:

日本政府
徳川幕府
大阪府

Graphically-Phonetically Related Morphographs:

付 HU (792)   腐 HU (1243)
符 HU
附 HU (778)

High Frequency Compounds:

政府 SEIHU -- the government, administration
23

幕府 BAKUHU -- shogunate
1036

Typical Conversational Usage:

政府でその問題を検討しています。
鎌倉幕府は何年つづいたか知っていますか。
京都府の人口はどのくらいですか。

味

Occurrences/1000 1.48
Frequency Rank 169
Sanseido Page 223
Nelson Page 247

A

ON: MI

kun: aji, aji(wau)
　　　aji(wai)

Basic Meaning(s): taste, flavor, experience, zest

Graphically-Phonetically Related Morphographs:

未 MI (624)

魅 MI

High Frequency Compounds:

意味　IMI -- meaning, significance
86

趣味　SHUMI -- taste, zest, interest, hobby
971

興味　KYOOMI -- interest, entertainment, pleasure
490

気味　KIMI -- feeling, touch, tendency
55

味方　MIkata -- friend, ally, supporter
25

Also: 味噌

Typical Phrases and Expanded Compounds:

意味が深い
趣味が違う
興味を持つ
かぜ気味
味方する
にがい経験を味わう

Typical Conversational Usage:

その言葉には深い意味があります。
弟は切手を集めるのが趣味です。
そんな事には全く興味がありません。
きのう気味の悪い話を聞きました。
どちらのチームを味方していますか。
今までどんな経験を味わいましたか。

170

野

Occurrences/1000 1.44
Frequency Rank 170
Sanseido Page 709
Nelson Page 903

A

ON: YA

kun: no

Basic Meaning(s): field, plain, rustic, the opposition

Typical Phrases and Expanded Compounds:

プロ野球
医学の分野
野党大会
美しい野原

Graphically-Phonetically Related Morphographs:

High Frequency Compounds:

野球 YAKYUU -- baseball
688

分野 BUN'YA -- field, sphere, division
28

野党 YATOO -- opposition party
76

野原 nohara -- plain, field, moor
113

Typical Conversational Usage:

東京六大学野球は有名です。
山野さんは科学の分野で活躍しています。
野党側はみなそれに反対しています。
小野さんと野原をさんぽしました。

171 件

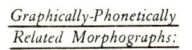

Occurrences/1000 1.42
Frequency Rank 171
Sanseido Page 118
Nelson Page 282

A

ON: KEN
kun:

Basic Meaning(s): matter, case, item

Graphically-Phonetically Related Morphographs:

High Frequency Compounds:

事件 JIKEN -- event, incident
10

条件 JOOKEN -- proviso, stipulation, condition
213

要件 YOOKEN -- requisite, important matter, essentials
78

Typical Phrases and Expanded Compounds:

殺人事件
条件を出す
要件を済ます

Typical Conversational Usage:

その事件はまだ解決されていません。
私は無条件にその会社を選びました。
もう要件は済みましたか。

172

他 A

Occurrences/1000   1.42
Frequency Rank   172
Sanseido Page   114
Nelson Page   129

ON: TA

kun: hoka

Basic Meaning(s):   the other, another, the rest

Graphically-Phonetically Related Morphographs:

High Frequency Compounds:

他人 TA'NIN -- another person, unrelated person, stranger
 2

他方 TAHOO -- another side, on the other hand, different direction
 25

自他 JITA -- oneself and others, transitive and intransitive
 14

排他 HAITA -- exclusion
1288

Typical Phrases and Expanded Compounds:

他人に干渉する
他方においては
自他共に
排他的
他の人

Typical Conversational Usage:

他人に迷惑をかけてはいけません。
その意見は他方では受け入れられていません。
原さんの声がきれいなのは、自他共に認めるところです。
あの人の考えはいつも排他的です。
誰か他の人にたのんでください。

173

工

Occurrences/1000 1.40
Frequency Rank 173
Sanseido Page 312
Nelson Page 352

ON: KOO, KU
kun:

Graphically-Phonetically Related Morphographs:

貢 KOO (1321)   項 KOO (1138)   江 KOO (761)
巧 KOO (1373)   功 KOO (735)   攻 KOO (588)
紅 KOO (1137)   控 KOO

Basic Meaning(s): artisan, mechanic, manufacture, work

High Frequency Compounds:

工場 KOOJOO -- factory, workshop, mill
  49
工業 KOOGYOO -- industry
  74
人工 JINKOO -- human work, human skill,
  2   artificial, man-made
工事 KOOJI -- construction
  10
大工 DAIKU -- carpenter, carpentry
  5

See 237

Also: 工作

Typical Phrases and Expanded Compounds:

工場見学
工業地帯
人工衛星
工事中
大工仕事

Typical Conversational Usage:

あそこに見えるのはソニーの工場です。
この辺は工業地帯で有名です。
弟は人工呼吸で助かりました。
その道は工事中で、今は通れません。
小川さんは大工さんです。

174 身

Occurrences/1000 1.40
Frequency Rank 174
Sanseido Page 67
Nelson Page 862

ON: SHIN

kun: mi

Basic Meaning(s): body, person, heart, flesh

Typical Phrases and Expanded Compounds:

自分自身の問題
出身校
身体検査
身長をはかる
身にあまる思い

Graphically-Phonetically Related Morphographs:

High Frequency Compounds:

自身 14 — JISHIN -- self, oneself, itself

出身 8 — SHUSSHIN -- graduate from, hailing from

身体 96 — SHINTAI -- the body

身長 90 — SHINCHOO -- height, stature

Typical Conversational Usage:

それは野口さん自身の問題でしょう。
私の出身校は九州大学です。
きのう身体検査を受けました。
身長はどのくらいありますか。
北海道の寒さは身にしみます。

175

点

Graphically-Phonetically Related Morphographs:

店 TEN (632)

Occurrences/1000 1.39
Frequency Rank 175
Sanseido Page 194
Nelson Page 227

ON: TEN

kun:

Basic Meaning(s): point, score, standpoint, vote

High Frequency Compounds:

焦点 SHOOTEN -- focus
1276

欠点 KETTEN -- faults, defect, weakness
774

要点 YOOTEN -- gist, essentials, substance
78

氷点 HYOOTEN -- freezing point

See 246, 351

Typical Phrases and Expanded Compounds:

焦点を合わす
欠点だらけ
要点をつかむ
氷点下
点がからい

Typical Conversational Usage:

よく焦点を合わせて、写真をとってください。
だれにも欠点があります。
要点だけをのべてください。
きのうは氷点下五度でした。
その点がよくわかりません。

176

画　A

Occurrences/1000　1.37
Frequency Rank　176
Sanseido Page　45
Nelson Page　50

ON: GA, KAKU

kun:

Basic Meaning(s): picture, drawing, painting, sketch, stroke (in a character)

Typical Phrases and Expanded Compounds:

映画の画面
フランスの画家
計画通り
企画部

Graphically-Phonetically Related Morphographs:

High Frequency Compounds:

映画　EIGA -- movie, cinema, film
368

画家　GAKA -- painter, artist
46

計画　KEIKAKU -- plan, scheme, project
210

企画　KIKAKU -- plan, planning
513

Typical Conversational Usage:

「風と共に去りぬ」という映画を見ましたか。
将来画家になるつもりです。
夏休みにどこへ行く計画を立てていますか。
今会社で何を企画していますか。

用 177

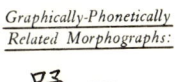

Occurrences/1000 1.36
Frequency Rank 177
Sanseido Page 158
Nelson Page 619

ON: YOO
kun: mochi(iru)

Graphically-Phonetically Related Morphographs:

踊 YOO

High Frequency Compounds:

利用 (180) RIYOO -- use, utilization, improvement (of opportunities)

使用 (239) SHIYOO -- employ, use, utilize

応用 (362) OOYOO -- practical application, adaptation, improvement

信用 (181) SHINYOO -- confidence, trust, reputation, credit

用意 (86) YOOI -- preparation, arrangement

See 263, 268

Also: 作用, 用心

Basic Meaning(s):

Typical Phrases and Expanded Compounds:

利用価値
使用中
応用問題
信用のある人
用意周到な人
重く用いる

Typical Conversational Usage:

これはまだ利用できます。
この部屋は当分使用できません。
彼はあまり応用がききません。
それは信用にかかわる問題です。
今すぐ出かける用意をしなければなりません。
この言葉は一般に用いられています。

178

表

Occurrences/1000 1.35
Frequency Rank 178
Sanseido Page 564
Nelson Page 71

ON: HYOO

kun: omote, ara(wasu), ara(wareru)

Basic Meaning(s): table, chart, schedule, surface, appear, reveal

Graphically-Phonetically Related Morphographs:

俵 HYOO

High Frequency Compounds:

代表 (87) DAIHYOO -- representation, representative, delegate, type

発表 (102) HAPPYOO -- announcement, communique

表現 (67) HYOOGEN -- expression, presentation

表面 (117) HYOOMEN -- surface, face, outside

Also: 表情, 表明

Typical Phrases and Expanded Compounds:

代表団
合格発表
愛情の表現
表面化する
表立って
言葉で表わす

Typical Conversational Usage:

日本美術の代表的なものは何ですか。
試験の結果がもう発表されましたか。
先生の文の表現はとてもきれいです。
その事件は表面に現われました。
地震で、あわてて表へ飛び出しました。
何と言ったらよいか、言葉で表わせません。

179 無

Occurrences/1000 1.35
Frequency Rank 179
Sanseido Page 210
Nelson Page 579

ON: MU, BU
kun: na(i)

Graphically-Phonetically Related Morphographs:

舞 BU (634)

Basic Meaning(s): nothing, nil, negation, none

High Frequency Compounds:

無理 (59) MURI -- unreasonable, unjustifiable, impossible

無限 (370) MUGEN -- infinite, endless, eternity

無視 (513) MUSHI -- disregard, ignore, defy

無論 (110) MURON -- of course, naturally

無事 (10) BUJI -- safety, peace, good health

Also: 無数, 無駄

Typical Phrases and Expanded Compounds:

無理な事
無限に広がる
信号無視
無論のこと
無事を祈る
無しで済ます

Typical Conversational Usage:

それは無理な注文です。
宇宙は無限ですか。
彼は信号無視でつかまったそうです。
兄は無論のこと、両親も賛成してくれました。
上原さんは、きのう無事に帰国しました。
そこには何も無さそうです。

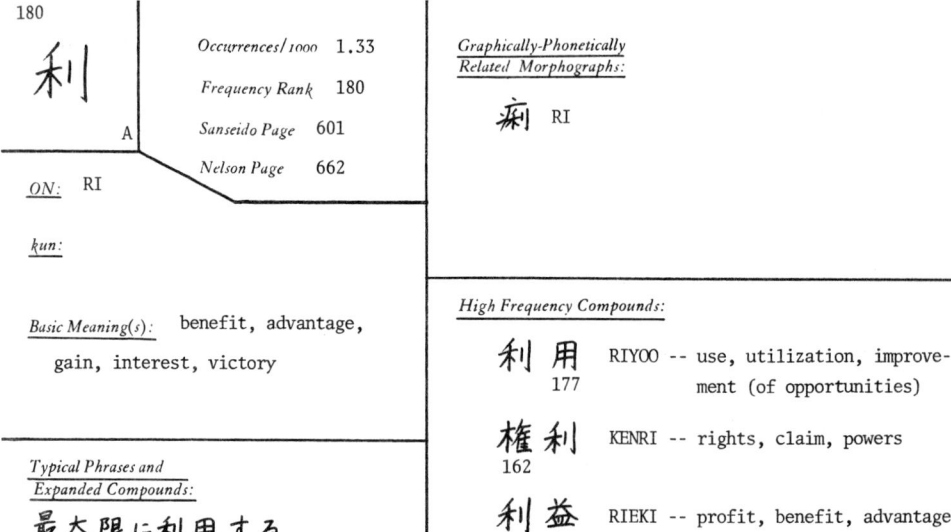

180

利

Occurrences/1000　1.33
Frequency Rank　180
Sanseido Page　601
Nelson Page　662

ON: RI

kun:

Basic Meaning(s): benefit, advantage, gain, interest, victory

Typical Phrases and Expanded Compounds:

最大限に利用する
権利を主張する
利益をあげる
有利な条件
勝利に導く
便利な機械

See 388

Graphically-Phonetically Related Morphographs:

痢　RI

High Frequency Compounds:

利用　RIYOO -- use, utilization, improvement (of opportunities)
177

権利　KENRI -- rights, claim, powers
162

利益　RIEKI -- profit, benefit, advantage
605

有利　YUURI -- advantageous, profitable, better
245

勝利　SHOORI -- victory
419

便利　BENRI -- convenient, handy, useful
769

Also: 利潤

Typical Conversational Usage:

これは何かに利用できるはずです。
あの人はいつも権利ばかり主張しています。
この仕事の利益はあまりよくありません。
この試合は相手の方がかなり有利です。
勝利投手は誰ですか。
学校は便利な所にあります。

信

181

Graphically-Phonetically Related Morphographs:

Occurrences/1000 1.32
Frequency Rank 181
Sanseido Page 129
Nelson Page 153

ON: SHIN
kun:

Basic Meaning(s): truth, faith, sincerity, trust, confidence

High Frequency Compounds:

信頼 (604) SHINRAI -- reliance, trust, confidence

信用 (177) SHINYOO -- confidence, trust, reputation, credit

通信 (97) TSUUSHIN -- correspondence, communication, information

信仰 (1363) SHINKOO -- belief, creed, religious faith

自信 (14) JISHIN -- self-confidence

信念 (333) SHINNEN -- belief, faith, conviction

See 343   Also: 信者

Typical Phrases and Expanded Compounds:

信頼できる人
信用取引
共同通信社
信仰の自由
自信がある
信念をもって

Typical Conversational Usage:

父は松下さんをいつも信頼しています。
その会社は大変信用があります。
兄は大学の通信教育を受けています。
日本には信仰の自由があります。
野村さんは自信満々です。
何事をするにも強い信念が必要です。

182

在

Occurrences/1000 1.31
Frequency Rank 182
Sanseido Page 184
Nelson Page 266

A

ON: ZAI

kun:

Basic Meaning(s): exist, be located, outskirts, suburbs, country

Graphically-Phonetically Related Morphographs:

High Frequency Compounds:

現在   GENZAI -- the present time, now,
67   present tense

存在   SONZAI -- existence, subsistence,
431   being

不在   HUZAI -- absence
103

健在   KENZAI -- good health
734

駐在   CHUUZAI -- residence, stay
888

Typical Phrases and Expanded Compounds:

過去と現在
存在価値
不在投票
健在である
駐在所

Typical Conversational Usage:

高木さんは現在大阪にいます。
人の存在を無視してはいけません。
父は京都へ行って不在です。
両親は健在です。
この辺に駐在所がありますか。

情

183

Occurrences/1000: 1.31
Frequency Rank: 183
Sanseido Page: 370
Nelson Page: 404

ON: JOO
kun: nasake

Basic Meaning(s): feeling, passion, affection, sympathy

Graphically-Phonetically Related Morphographs:

High Frequency Compounds:

事情 (10) — JIJOO -- circumstances, reasons

情勢 (293) — JOOSEI -- state of affairs, condition, indication

感情 (105) — KANJOO -- feelings, emotion, sentiment

愛情 (268) — AIJOO -- love, affection

同情 (54) — DOOJOO -- sympathy

Typical Phrases and Expanded Compounds:

国内事情
情勢を見ながら
感情のもつれ
愛情のある
同情をよせる
情無い

Typical Conversational Usage:

石井さんは海外の事情にくわしいです。
情勢をよく見てから、判断したいと思います。
彼女は感情的です。
これは親子の愛情の物語です。
あの子はみんなの同情を引きました。
それは情無い話です。

聞

184

A

Occurrences/1000 1.31
Frequency Rank 184
Sanseido Page 728
Nelson Page 924

ON: BUN

kun: ki(ku), ki(koeru), ki(koe), ki(kaseru)

Basic Meaning(s): hear, listen to, inquire, inform, be heard, sound

Graphically-Phonetically Related Morphographs:

High Frequency Compounds:

新聞 (80)　SHIMBUN -- newspaper

見聞 (20)　KEMBUN -- information, experience, observation

外聞 (69)　GAIBUN -- reputation, honor, respectability

Typical Phrases and Expanded Compounds:

新聞を読む
見聞を広める
外聞の悪い
音楽を聞く
音が聞こえる

Typical Conversational Usage:

何新聞をとっていますか。
海外へ行って見聞を広めたいと思います。
それは外聞がよくありません。
美しい音楽を聞きました。
水の音が聞こえます。

185 支

Occurrences/1000 1.28
Frequency Rank 185
Sanseido Page 181
Nelson Page 454

A

ON: SHI
kun:

Basic Meaning(s): branch, support, maintain, hold

Graphically-Phonetically Related Morphographs:

枝 SHI (1050)

High Frequency Compounds:

支配 308 SHIHAI -- management, control, rule

支持 94 SHIJI -- support, maintenance

支出 8 SHISHUTSU -- expenditure, disbursement

収支 516 SHUUSHI -- income and expenditure

支部 52 SHIBU -- branch, branch office

Typical Phrases and Expanded Compounds:

支配下にある
支持を受ける
支出が多い
収支決算する
名古屋支部

Typical Conversational Usage:

石田さんはホテルの支配人です。
池田さんはみんなの支持を受けています。
先月の支出は大分多かったようです。
去年の国際収支は黒字です。
その問題は、あしたの支部会で協議されます。

186

特

A

Occurrences/1000 1.28
Frequency Rank 186
Sanseido Page 548
Nelson Page 598

ON: TOKU

kun:

Basic Meaning(s): special, especially, particularly

Typical Phrases and Expanded Compounds:

特別国会
特殊技術
特権階級
特定財産
特に

Graphically-Phonetically Related Morphographs:

High Frequency Compounds:

特別 TOKUBETSU -- special, extraordinary
227

特殊 TOKUSHU -- special, unique, characteristic
1027

特権 TOKKEN -- privilege, special rights, liberties (civil)
162

特定 TOKUTEI -- specify
93

Typical Conversational Usage:

この洋服は特別にあつらえたものです。
これは特殊な機械です。
それは会員だけに与えられた特権です。
ここでは特定の品物だけ扱っています。
特に変わった事はありません。

判 — 187

Graphically-Phonetically Related Morphographs:

半 HAN (324)
伴 HAN (930)
畔 HAN

Occurrences/1000 1.28
Frequency Rank 187
Sanseido Page 170
Nelson Page 198

ON: HAN
kun:

Basic Meaning(s): stamp, seal, signature, understand

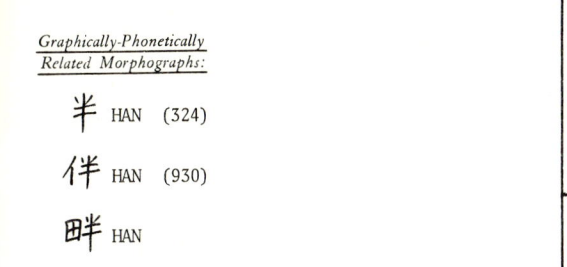

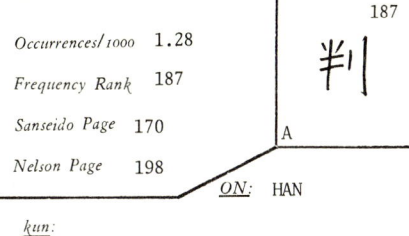

High Frequency Compounds:

批判 536	HIHAN --	criticism, comment
判決 138	HANKETSU --	judgment, decision, sentence
裁判 577	SAIBAN --	trial, adjudication
判断 426	HANDAN --	judgment, decision, conclusion
判事 10	HANJI --	judge
評判 358	HYOOBAN --	fame, reputation, rumor

Typical Phrases and Expanded Compounds:

批判を受ける
判決を言い渡す
裁判所
判断を誤る
判事席
評判が高い

Typical Conversational Usage:

その論文は強い批判を受けました。
被告は無罪の判決を受けました。
その事件の裁判は来月行われます。
なかなか判断がつきません。
叔父は先月判事になりました。
その品物の評判はとてもいいです。

188 必

Occurrences/1000	1.28
Frequency Rank	188
Sanseido Page	458
Nelson Page	74

ON: HITSU

kun: kanara(zu), kanara(zushimo)

Basic Meaning(s): certainly, positively, invariably, not always, not necessarily

Graphically-Phonetically Related Morphographs:

泌 HITSU

High Frequency Compounds:

必要 78 — HITSUYOO -- need, necessity

必然 144 — HITSUZEN -- necessity

必死 238 — HISSHI -- inevitable death, desperation, frantic

Typical Phrases and Expanded Compounds:

必要に迫られて
必然的に
必死になって
必ず

Typical Conversational Usage:

もっと本を読む必要があります。
それは必然的に起こりました。
弟は必死になって勉強しています。
あした必ずそこへ行きます。

際

189

Graphically-Phonetically Related Morphographs:

祭　SAI (1214)

Occurrences/1000	1.27
Frequency Rank	189
Sanseido Page	434
Nelson Page	934

A

ON: SAI

kun:

Basic Meaning(s): time, occasion, when, then

High Frequency Compounds:

国際　KOKUSAI -- international, international intercourse
4

実際　JISSAI -- truth, reality, fact, actuality
37

交際　KOOSAI -- association, intercourse, acquaintance
269

Typical Phrases and Expanded Compounds:

国際会議
実際の問題として
交際費

Typical Conversational Usage:

それは国際的な問題に発展しました。
実際むずかしい問題でした。
山田さんに交際を求められました。

190 常

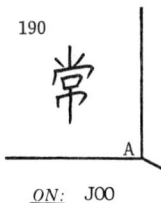

Occurrences/1000 1.26
Frequency Rank 190
Sanseido Page 620
Nelson Page 339

A

ON: JOO

kun: tsune

Basic Meaning(s): normal conditions, regular course of events, ordinary

Graphically-Phonetically Related Morphographs:

High Frequency Compounds:

非常 HIJOO -- emergency, unusual, exceedingly
222

正常 SEIJOO -- normalcy, normality, normal
139

日常 NICHIJOO -- everyday, ordinary, usually, always
3

常識 JOOSHIKI -- common sense
416

Typical Phrases and Expanded Compounds:

非常手段をとる
正常化する
日常生活
常識を欠く
常日頃

Typical Conversational Usage:

非常の際は、このベルを鳴らしてください。
列車のダイヤが正常に戻りました。
それは日常欠くことのできないものです。
非常識な事をしてはいけません。
夏休みに私はアルバイトをするのが常です。

神 191

Graphically-Phonetically Related Morphographs:

申 SHIN (509)
伸 SHIN (1330)
紳 SHIN

Occurrences/1000 1.26
Frequency Rank 191
Sanseido Page 571
Nelson Page 657

ON: SHIN, JIN
kun: kami

Basic Meaning(s): god, diety, mind, soul

High Frequency Compounds:

精神 (439) SEISHIN -- mind, spirit, intention
神経 (71) SHINKEI -- nerves
神社 (82) JINJA -- Shinto shrine
神話 (125) SHINWA -- myth, mythology

Typical Phrases and Expanded Compounds:

精神的
神経質
神社参拝
ギリシャ神話
神と人間

Typical Conversational Usage:

兄は精神的に大分つかれています。
母は神経痛でねています。
和田さんは神社へお参りに行きました。
学生時代に、よくギリシャ神話を読みました。
原さんと「神の存在」について論じました。

192 向

Occurrences/1000 1.25
Frequency Rank 192
Sanseido Page 64
Nelson Page 69

A

ON: KOO

kun: mu(kau), mu(ku), mu(kaseru), mu(ki), mu(kai), mu(koo)

Basic Meaning(s): opposite, the other side, face, turn, turn towards, look out on, aspect, direction

Typical Phrases and Expanded Compounds:

そんな傾向がある
方向を変える
生活の向上
向かって
向こう側
右を向く

Graphically-Phonetically Related Morphographs:

High Frequency Compounds:

傾向 KEIKOO -- tendency, trend, disposition
759

方向 HOOKOO -- direction, bearings, course
25

向上 KOOJOO -- advancement, progress, improvement
29

Typical Conversational Usage:

あの子は学校を休む傾向があります。
山で方向がわからなくなって困りました。
戦後日本の生活は向上しました。
向かって右側にあるのが私達の学校です。
向こうから男の人が来ました。
あなたは先生に向いていると思います。

協

193

Occurrences/1000: 1.24
Frequency Rank: 193
Sanseido Page: 186
Nelson Page: 217

A

ON: KYOO
kun:

Basic Meaning(s): cooperation

Graphically-Phonetically Related Morphographs:

脅 KYOO (1362)

High Frequency Compounds:

協定 (93) KYOOTEI -- pact, agreement
協力 (38) KYOORYOKU -- cooperation
妥協 (979) DAKYOO -- compromise, understanding, agreement
協議 (130) KYOOGI -- conference, deliberation
協会 (16) KYOOKAI -- association, society

Also: 協同

Typical Phrases and Expanded Compounds:

協定を結ぶ
みんなの協力
妥協点
協議会
作家協会

Typical Conversational Usage:

ソ連との航空協定が結ばれました。
この仕事にはみんなの協力が必要です。
妥協の余地が全くありません。
その事は協議の上、決めることにいたしましょう。
上田さんは、野球協会の役員になったそうです。

194

取 A

Occurrences/1000 1.24
Frequency Rank 194
Sanseido Page 654
Nelson Page 731

ON: SHU

kun: to(ru)

Basic Meaning(s): take, receive, pick, engage

Graphically-Phonetically Related Morphographs:

趣 SHU (971)

High Frequency Compounds:

取材 SHUZAI -- choice of subject
806

取引 torihiki -- transaction, deal, business
263

See 298

Typical Phrases and Expanded Compounds:

取材班
取引銀行
取るに足らない

Typical Conversational Usage:

今どんな記事を取材していますか。
ようやくその取引を成立させました。
そこにある新聞を取ってください。

真

195
A

Occurrences/1000 1.23
Frequency Rank 195
Sanseido Page 188
Nelson Page 220

ON: SHIN
kun: ma

Basic Meaning(s): truth, reality, genuineness, just, right

Graphically-Phonetically Related Morphographs:

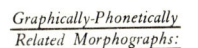

High Frequency Compounds:

真実 (37) SHINJITSU -- truth, reality, truly
写真 (696) SHASHIN -- photograph
真理 (59) SHINRI -- truth
真剣 (818) SHINKEN -- real sword, earnestness
真心 (64) magokoro -- sincerity, devotion

Typical Phrases and Expanded Compounds:

真実性
写真屋
真理の探究
真剣勝負
真心こめて

Typical Conversational Usage:

川上さんは真実性にあふれています。
これは学生時代の写真です。
真理とは何ですか。
もう少し真剣に勉強しなければいけません。
これは真心こめて作ったものです。

196

川

A

Occurrences/1000 1.23
Frequency Rank 196
Sanseido Page 312
Nelson Page 351

ON: SEN

kun: kawa

Basic Meaning(s): river, stream, brook

Graphically-Phonetically Related Morphographs:

High Frequency Compounds:

河川 KASEN -- rivers
614

川上 kawakami -- upper stream, upstream
29

Occurs most frequently in proper names, such as, 吉川, "Yoshikawa."

Typical Phrases and Expanded Compounds:

河川工事
川上の方

Typical Conversational Usage:

この会社は河川工事が得意です。
発電所は川上の方にあります。

想 197

Graphically-Phonetically Related Morphographs:

相 SOO (111)
霜 SOO

Occurrences/1000 1.22
Frequency Rank 197
Sanseido Page 464
Nelson Page 405

ON: SOO
kun:

Basic Meaning(s): idea, conception, thought

High Frequency Compounds:

理想 59 — RISOO -- ideal
想像 720 — SOOZOO -- imagination, supposition, conjecture
思想 26 — SHISOO -- thought, idea
感想 105 — KANSOO -- thoughts, impressions, sentiments
予想 283 — YOSOO -- anticipation, forecast, estimate

See 304

Typical Phrases and Expanded Compounds:

理想的
想像力
思想問題
感想をのべる
予想に反して

Typical Conversational Usage:

理想が実現したらと思っています。
そんなことはとても想像できません。
中国の思想について研究しています。
その感想はいかがですか。
成績が予想外によかったです。

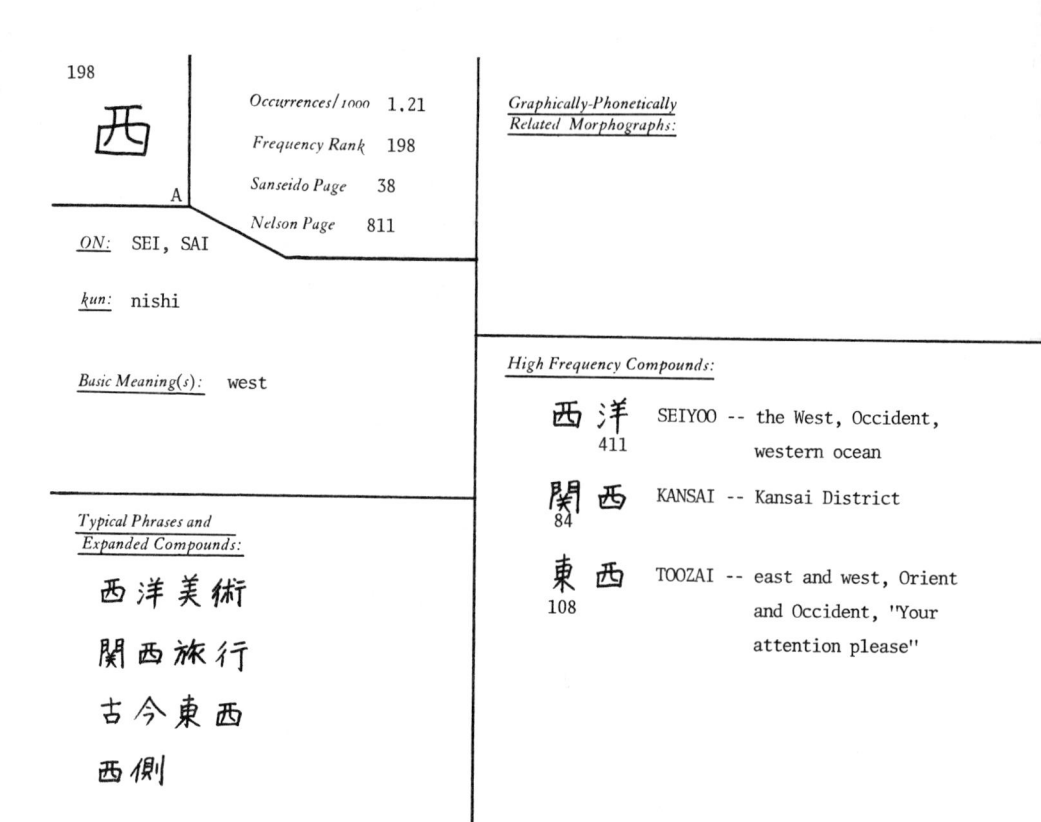

198

西 A

Occurrences/1000 1.21
Frequency Rank 198
Sanseido Page 38
Nelson Page 811

<u>ON</u>: SEI, SAI

<u>kun</u>: nishi

Basic Meaning(s): west

Graphically-Phonetically Related Morphographs:

High Frequency Compounds:

西洋 SEIYOO -- the West, Occident,
411　　　　　　western ocean

関西 KANSAI -- Kansai District
84

東西 TOOZAI -- east and west, Orient
108　　　　　　and Occident, "Your
　　　　　　　attention please"

Typical Phrases and Expanded Compounds:

西洋美術

関西旅行

古今東西

西側

Typical Conversational Usage:

大学で西洋史を勉強しました。
私は関西で育ちました。
洋の東西を問わず、人々は流行を追っています。
この窓は西向きです。

Graphically-Phonetically Related Morphographs:

Occurrences/1000 1.20	199
Frequency Rank 199	吉
Sanseido Page 240	
Nelson Page 265	A

ON: KICHI

kun:

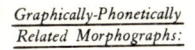

High Frequency Compounds:

吉報　KIPPOO -- good news
310

不吉　HUKITSU -- bad luck, ill omen,
103　　　　inauspicious

Occurs most frequently in proper names, such as, 吉田 , "Yoshida."

Basic Meaning(s): good luck, joy, congratulations

Typical Phrases and Expanded Compounds:

吉報を受け取る
不吉な予感
吉野の桜

Typical Conversational Usage:

西さんから吉報を受け取りました。
何だか不吉な予感がしました。
吉田さんときのう東京へ行って来ました。

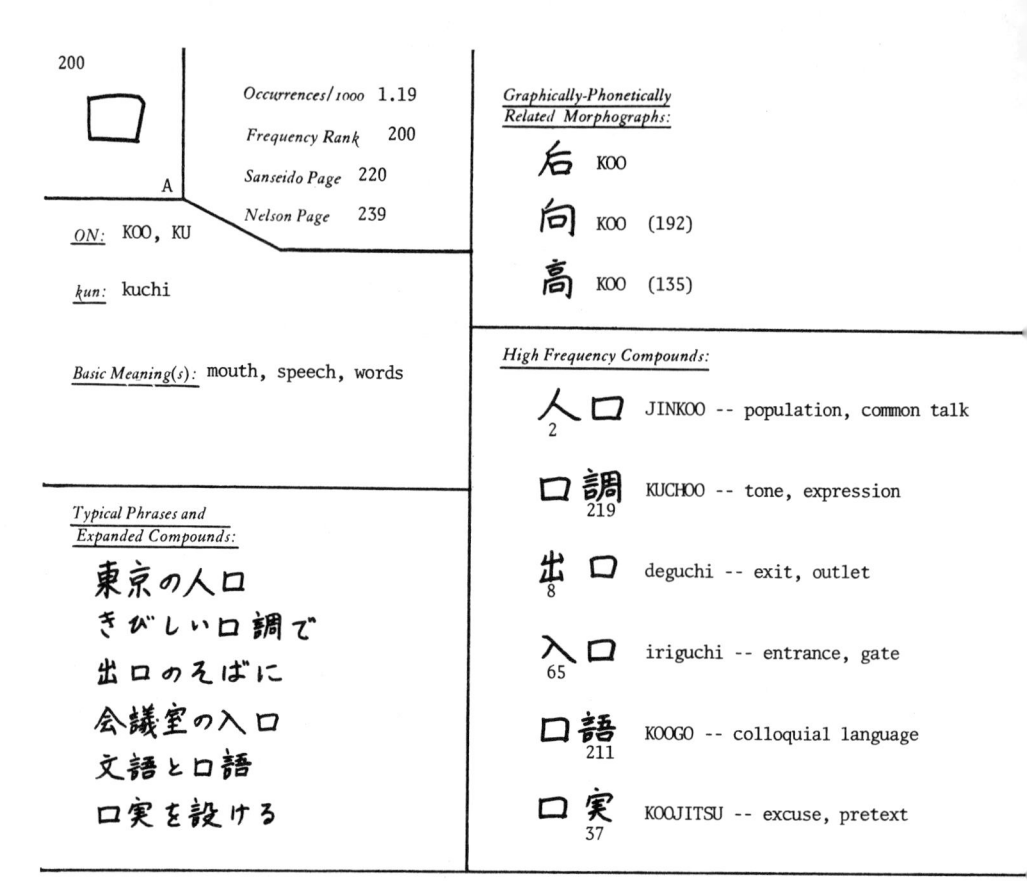

200

口

A

Occurrences/1000 1.19
Frequency Rank 200
Sanseido Page 220
Nelson Page 239

ON: KOO, KU

kun: kuchi

Basic Meaning(s): mouth, speech, words

Graphically-Phonetically Related Morphographs:

右 KOO

向 KOO (192)

高 KOO (135)

High Frequency Compounds:

人口 — JINKOO -- population, common talk
2

口調 — KUCHOO -- tone, expression
219

出口 — deguchi -- exit, outlet
8

入口 — iriguchi -- entrance, gate
65

口語 — KOOGO -- colloquial language
211

口実 — KOOJITSU -- excuse, pretext
37

Typical Phrases and Expanded Compounds:

東京の人口
きびしい口調で
出口のそばに
会議室の入口
文語と口語
口実を設ける

Typical Conversational Usage:

この町の人口はどのくらいですか。
先生にはげしい口調でしかられました。
出口はどこですか。
入口はあそこです。
この文体は口語体です。
そんなのは口実です。

Graphically-Phonetically Related Morphographs:

Occurrences/1000 1.19	備 201
Frequency Rank 201	
Sanseido Page 139	
Nelson Page 161	

<u>ON</u>: BI

<u>kun</u>: sona(e), sona(eru), sona(waru)

High Frequency Compounds:

設備 SETSUBI -- equipment, fixtures
270

準備 JUMBI -- preparation, provision
776

Basic Meaning(s): preparation, provision, furnish, provide, be furnished with

Typical Phrases and Expanded Compounds:

工場の設備
準備が整う
まさかの時に備えて

Typical Conversational Usage:

学校の設備がよくなりました。
今、旅行の準備をしています。
現在、大学の入試に備えて勉強しています。

202

官
A

Occurrences/1000 1.19
Frequency Rank 202
Sanseido Page 281
Nelson Page 315

ON: KAN

kun:

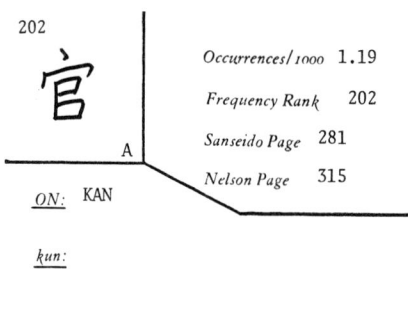

Basic Meaning(s): government, court, authorities

Typical Phrases and Expanded Compounds:

警官隊
官房長官
官僚あがり

Graphically-Phonetically Related Morphographs:

棺 KAN
管 KAN (996)
館 KAN (532)

High Frequency Compounds:

警官 KEIKAN -- police officer
454

長官 CHOOKAN -- magistrate, chief, governor
90

官僚 KANRYOO -- bureaucracy, officialdom
917

Typical Conversational Usage:

父はもと警官でした。
アメリカの国務長官は誰ですか。
彼は官僚あがりです。

男

Occurrences/1000 1.19
Frequency Rank 203
Sanseido Page 575
Nelson Page 621

ON: DAN, NAN

kun: otoko

Basic Meaning(s): man, male, baron, counter for sons

Graphically-Phonetically Related Morphographs:

High Frequency Compounds:

男女 (60) DANJO -- men and women, both sexes

男性 (119) DANSEI -- male, masculinity

長男 (90) CHOONAN -- eldest son

Typical Phrases and Expanded Compounds:

男女共学
男性用
長男の仕事
男の子

Typical Conversational Usage:

日本は今男女同権です。
ここは男性だけに限られています。
こちらは、うちの長男と次男です。
あの男の人はセールスマンです。

204 君 A

Occurrences/1000 1.16
Frequency Rank 204
Sanseido Page 351
Nelson Page 245

ON: KUN

kun: kimi

Basic Meaning(s): ruler, master, Mister, you

Graphically-Phonetically Related Morphographs:

High Frequency Compounds:

諸君 SHOKUN -- gentlemen, ladies and gentlemen, my friends, you
272

細君 SAIKUN -- wife, my wife
736

Typical Phrases and Expanded Compounds:

学生諸君
君の細君
君の家

Typical Conversational Usage:

これもみな学生諸君のおかげです。
細君と一緒に行くことにします。
日本の国歌は「君が代」です。

Graphically-Phonetically Related Morphographs:

Occurrences/1000	1.16
Frequency Rank	205
Sanseido Page	423
Nelson Page	602

独

ON: DOKU

kun:

Basic Meaning(s): alone, on one's one, spontaneously

High Frequency Compounds:

独立 (35) DOKURITSU -- independence, freedom, self-reliance

孤独 KODOKU -- solitude, isolation, lonliness

独自 (14) DOKUJI -- original, peculiar, characteristic

独身 (174) DOKUSHIN -- single life, celibacy

独占 (378) DOKUSEN -- exclusive possession, monopoly

Typical Phrases and Expanded Compounds:

独立記念日
孤独な人
独自の考え
独身のころ
独占事業
独り舞台

Typical Conversational Usage:

七月四日はアメリカの独立記念日です。
叔父はいなかで孤独な生活を送っています。
これは独自に考え出したものです。
私はまだ独身です。
これは独占事業じゃありません。
私は独り歩きをするのが好きです。

206 海

Occurrences/1000: 1.16
Frequency Rank: 206
Sanseido Page: 400
Nelson Page: 547

A

<u>ON</u>: KAI

<u>kun</u>: umi

Basic Meaning(s): sea, ocean

Graphically-Phonetically Related Morphographs:

High Frequency Compounds:

海軍 (36) KAIGUN -- navy

海外 (69) KAIGAI -- overseas, foreign, abroad

海岸 (815) KAIGAN -- seashore, coast, beach

北海道 (282) (123) HOKKAIDOO -- Hokkaido

Typical Phrases and Expanded Compounds:

米国海軍
海外事情
海岸を散歩する
北海道の出身
海があれる

Typical Conversational Usage:

昔、日本の海軍は強かったそうです。
上野さんは海外事情にくわしいです。
海岸へ行って船を見ましょう。
北海道の名産は何ですか。
今日は海があれています。

Graphically-Phonetically Related Morphographs:

	207
Occurrences/1000 1.15	食
Frequency Rank 207	
Sanseido Page 108	
Nelson Page 964	A

ON: SHOKU, JIKI

kun: ta(beru), ku(u)

Basic Meaning(s): food, meal, provisions, eat

High Frequency Compounds:

食糧 (935) SHOKURYOO -- food, provisions, rations

食事 (10) SHOKUJI -- meal, diet, board

食堂 (789) SHOKUDOO -- dining hall

食べ物 tabemono -- food

Also: 主食, 食物

Typical Phrases and Expanded Compounds:

食糧不足
おいしい食事
きれいな食堂
食べすぎる
食べ物がよい

Typical Conversational Usage:

食糧が少し足りません。
食事を終えてから、いつもテレビを見ます。
あそこの食堂に入りましょう。
何が食べたいですか。
どんな食べ物が好きですか。

208

切

Occurrences/1000 1.15
Frequency Rank 208
Sanseido Page 220
Nelson Page 195

<u>ON</u>: SETSU, SAI

<u>kun</u>: ki(ru), ki(reru), ki(ri), ki(re)

Basic Meaning(s): cut, chop, slice, sharp

Graphically-Phonetically Related Morphographs:

窃 SETSU

Typical Phrases and Expanded Compounds:

大切にする
親切な人
一切引き受ける
電話を切る
期限が切れる
踏切をわたる

High Frequency Compounds:

大切 TAISETSU -- important, significant
5

親切 SHINSETSU -- kindness
315

一切 ISSAI -- all, everything
1

踏切 fumikiri -- railway crossing
1033

Typical Conversational Usage:

今水が少ないので、大切に使ってください。
山野さんは、親切にも本をかしてくれました。
一切私にまかせてください。
電話をまだ切らないでください。
彼はなかなか頭が切れます。
早く踏切をわたりましょう。

記 — 209

Occurrences/1000: 1.14
Frequency Rank: 209
Sanseido Page: 676
Nelson Page: 824

ON: KI
kun:

Basic Meaning(s): account, history, remembering

Graphically-Phonetically Related Morphographs:

- 起 KI (246)
- 紀 KI (616)
- 忌 KI

High Frequency Compounds:

- 記事 KIJI -- description, news item
- 記念 KINEN -- remembrance, commemoration
- 記録 KIROKU -- record, document, archives
- 日記 NIKKI -- diary, journal
- 記者 KISHA -- journalist, reporter

See 121, 331

Also: 記憶

Typical Phrases and Expanded Compounds:

おもしろい記事
卒業記念
記録やぶり
日記をつける
新聞記者

Typical Conversational Usage:

最近、日本のおもしろい記事を読みました。
それは何の記念切手ですか。
このところ、記録やぶりの天気が続いています。
今年から日記をつけることにしました。
あの人は新聞記者です。

210 計

Occurrences/1000 1.14
Frequency Rank 210
Sanseido Page 676
Nelson Page 823

A

<u>ON</u>: KEI

<u>kun</u>: haka(ru)

Basic Meaning(s): measure, total, plan, scheme, devise

Graphically-Phonetically Related Morphographs:

High Frequency Compounds:

計画 KEIKAKU -- plan, scheme, project
176

計算 KEISAN -- computation, calculation
499

時計 TOKEI -- clock, watch
24

合計 GOOKEI -- total
33

See 270, 273

Typical Phrases and Expanded Compounds:

計画を立てる
めんどうな計算
時計屋
合計すれば
身長を計る

Typical Conversational Usage:

来年北海道へ行く計画を立てています。
計算はめんどうくさいので、好きじゃありません。
この腕時計はスイス製です。
出席者は合計三十六名でした。
身長がどの位か計ってみましょう。

語

211

Graphically-Phonetically Related Morphographs:

五 GO (40)
悟 GO
互 GO (524)

High Frequency Compounds:

英語 EIGO -- the English language
361

国語 KOKUGO -- national language, Japanese
4

語学 GOGAKU -- language study, linguistics
15

物語 monogatari -- story, legend
95

Occurrences/1000 1.14
Frequency Rank 211
Sanseido Page 682
Nelson Page 832

ON: GO

kun: kata(ru), kata(rau), kata(ri)

Basic Meaning(s): word, speech, language, talk, tell

Typical Phrases and Expanded Compounds:

英語の表現
国語の能力
語学の研究
イソップ物語
友人と語る

Typical Conversational Usage:

英語が話せますか。
学校の科目で、国語が一番好きです。
大学で語学の研究をしています。
日本の竹取物語は有名です。
ひさしぶりで、旧友と語り合いました。

212

公 A

Occurrences/1000 1.14
Frequency Rank 212
Sanseido Page 146
Nelson Page 173

ON: KOO

kun: ooyake

Basic Meaning(s): public, official

Graphically-Phonetically Related Morphographs:

High Frequency Compounds:

公園 KOOEN -- park
686

公共 KOOKYOO -- society, the community
106

公平 KOOHEI -- justice, fairness
98

See 239, 244, 290

Typical Phrases and Expanded Compounds:

国立公園
公共事業
公平に分ける
公にする

Typical Conversational Usage:

公園に美しい花がたくさんあります。
叔父は町の公共のためにつくしています。
彼はいつも公平で、みんなの信用があります。
その計画が公にされました。

Graphically-Phonetically Related Morphographs:

Occurrences/1000 1.14
Frequency Rank 213
Sanseido Page 257
Nelson Page 282

213

条

ON: JOO

kun:

Basic Meaning(s): article, clause, line, column

High Frequency Compounds:

条約   JOOYAKU -- treaty
258

条件   JOOKEN -- provision, condition
171

Typical Phrases and Expanded Compounds:

安全保障条約
条件つきで

Typical Conversational Usage:

日米間にどんな条約がありますか。
条件がよければ、入社したいと思います。

214 直

Occurrences/1000 1.14
Frequency Rank 214
Sanseido Page 186
Nelson Page 217

A

ON: CHOKU, JIKI

kun: tada(chi ni), nao(su), nao(ru), nao(shi)

Basic Meaning(s): right, frank, direct, personal, at once, immediately, be mended, mend, heal, repair

Typical Phrases and Expanded Compounds:

直接話す
問題に直面する
正直な人
直ちにうかがう
時計を直す

Graphically-Phonetically Related Morphographs:

High Frequency Compounds:

直接 CHOKUSETSU -- direct
399

直面 CHOKUMEN -- face, confront
117

正直 SHOOJIKI -- honesty
139

Also: 直後, 直前

Typical Conversational Usage:

直接本田さんから聞きました。
むずかしい問題に直面しました。
あの子は正直ないい子です。
それでは、直ちにうかがいます。
車を直してから行きます。

215

万

Graphically-Phonetically Related Morphographs:

Occurrences/1000 1.13
Frequency Rank 215
Sanseido Page 18
Nelson Page 27

ON: MAN, BAN

kun: (yorozu)

Basic Meaning(s): ten thousand, myriad, all, everything

High Frequency Compounds:

三万 SAMMAN -- thirty thousand
21

万一 MANICHI, MANgaICHI -- if by any chance
1

万国 BANKOKU -- all nations
4

万屋 yorozuya -- general merchant jack-of-all-trades
236

Typical Phrases and Expanded Compounds:

三万円
万一の場合
万国標準時
情報の万屋

Typical Conversational Usage:

この町の人口は三万人を越えました。
万一失敗したら、どうしますか。
今度の万国博覧会に行く予定です。
彼は万屋です。

216 様

Occurrences/1000: 1.13
Frequency Rank: 216
Sanseido Page: 529
Nelson Page: 509

A

ON: YOO

kun: sama

Basic Meaning(s): manner, way, Mr., Mrs., Miss, etc.

Graphically-Phonetically Related Morphographs:

羊 YOO

洋 YOO (411)

養 YOO (586)

High Frequency Compounds:

同様 DOOYOO -- same, identical (54)

様子 YOOSU -- situation, state of affairs (42)

模様 MOYOO -- pattern, appearance (797)

Typical Phrases and Expanded Compounds:

それと同様に
変な様子
きれいな模様
皆様

Typical Conversational Usage:

これは新品も同様です。
少し様子がおかしいです。
これは私の好きな模様です。
皆様いかがお過ごしですか。

217 朝

Graphically-Phonetically Related Morphographs:

潮　CHOO (1149)

Occurrences/1000	1.12
Frequency Rank	217
Sanseido Page	738
Nelson Page	749

ON: CHOO
kun: asa

Basic Meaning(s): morning, dynasty, epoch

High Frequency Compounds:

今朝　KONCHOO -- this morning
50

朝鮮　CHOOSEN -- Korea
471

朝食　CHOOSHOKU -- breakfast
207

朝日　asahi -- morning sun, rising sun
3

Typical Phrases and Expanded Compounds:

今朝の会議
北朝鮮
朝食をとる
朝日がのぼる

Typical Conversational Usage:

今朝八時に会議が始まります。
北朝鮮に帰国した人がたくさんいます。
朝食をとりましたか。
きのうの朝日新聞を読みましたか。

218

百
A

Occurrences/1000 1.12
Frequency Rank 218
Sanseido Page 39
Nelson Page 46

ON: HYAKU

kun: (momo)

Basic Meaning(s): hundred, a great number

Graphically-Phonetically Related Morphographs:

High Frequency Compounds:

百科 HYAKKA -- many subjects (for study)
369

四百 YONHYAKU -- four hundred
114

百点 HYAKUTEN -- hundred points, perfect
175

Also: 百姓

Typical Phrases and Expanded Compounds:

百科辞典

四百人

百点満点

Typical Conversational Usage:

百科辞典を調べて下さい。
この工場には四百人の人が働いています。
きのうの試験で百点をとりました。

調

219

A

Occurrences/1000 1.11
Frequency Rank 219
Sanseido Page 686
Nelson Page 835

ON: CHOO
kun: shira(beru), shira(be)

Basic Meaning(s): examine, test, tune, tone

Graphically-Phonetically Related Morphographs:

彫 CHOO

High Frequency Compounds:

調査 (576) CHOOSA -- investigation, examination
調子 (42) CHOOSHI -- tune, tone, rhythm, condition
強調 (133) KYOOCHOO -- emphasis
調和 (85) CHOOWA -- harmony, accord

See 262, 267

Also: 調印

Typical Phrases and Expanded Compounds:

調査の結果
調子が悪い
強調する
調和がとれる
人数を調べる

Typical Conversational Usage:

その事件の調査をしています。
この車の調子はあまりよくありません。
その重要性を強調しました。
この家は庭と調和がよくとれています。
何を調べていますか。

220 夫

Occurrences/1000: 1.11
Frequency Rank: 220
Sanseido Page: 29
Nelson Page: 82

A

ON: HU, (HUU)

kun: otto

Basic Meaning(s): husband, man, spouse

Graphically-Phonetically Related Morphographs:

扶 HU

High Frequency Compounds:

夫人 (2) HUJIN -- wife, Mrs.

夫妻 (629) HUSAI -- man and wife, Mr. and Mrs.

夫婦 (591) HUUHU -- husband and wife, couple

Also: 大丈夫

Typical Phrases and Expanded Compounds:

夫人同伴で
皇太子御夫妻
夫婦そろって
夫の会社

Typical Conversational Usage:

山村氏は夫人同伴で行きました。
きのう内原さん御夫妻に会いました。
本田さんはおしどり夫婦です。
夫はデパートに勤めています。

係 221

Graphically-Phonetically Related Morphographs:

系 KEI (884)

Occurrences/1000	1.1
Frequency Rank	221
Sanseido Page	128
Nelson Page	151

ON: KEI

kun: kaka(ru), kaka(ri)

High Frequency Compounds:

関係 (84) KANKEI -- relation, connection

係長 (90) kakariCHOO -- chief clerk

Basic Meaning(s): duty, person in charge, is the work of, concern oneself in

Typical Phrases and Expanded Compounds:

関係のない
係長の指示により
問題に係わる

Typical Conversational Usage:

その人に何か関係がありますか。
係長に相談してから、返事をします。
その問題に何も係わりたくありません。

222 非

Occurrences/1000: 1.10
Frequency Rank: 222
Sanseido Page: 736
Nelson Page: 949

ON: HI

kun:

Basic Meaning(s): mistake, misdeed, injustice, wrong

Typical Phrases and Expanded Compounds:

非常にむずかしい
ごうごうたる非難
非行少年
是非とも

Graphically-Phonetically Related Morphographs:

悲 HI (748)

High Frequency Compounds:

非常 HIJOO -- emergency, calamity
190

非難 HINAN -- criticism, denunciation
351

非行 HIKOO -- misdemeanor, evil deed, immoral act
18

是非 ZEHI -- by all means, right or wrong, pro and con
1229

Typical Conversational Usage:

あそこに非常口があります。
彼の意見はみんなに非難されました。
非行少年を補導しています。
今度の日曜日、是非遊びに来てください。

223 氏

Graphically-Phonetically Related Morphographs:

紙　SHI　(456)

High Frequency Compounds:

氏名　SHIMEI -- surname
140

Occurrences/1000　1.08
Frequency Rank　223
Sanseido Page　59
Nelson Page　529

ON: SHI

kun: uji

Basic Meaning(s): Mr., family clan surname

Typical Phrases and Expanded Compounds:

氏名がわからない
氏も素性もない人

Typical Conversational Usage:

ここに氏名をはっきり書いてください。
「氏より育ち」と、よく言われます。

224 集

Occurrences/1000   1.08
Frequency Rank   224
Sanseido Page   730
Nelson Page   937

ON: SHUU

kun: atsu(maru), atsu(meru), atsu(mari)

Basic Meaning(s): gathering, collection, meet, assemble, gather, collect, meeting

Graphically-Phonetically Related Morphographs:

Typical Phrases and Expanded Compounds:

集団となって
編集者
集中的に
集会を開く
ここに集まる

High Frequency Compounds:

集団 (336)   SHUUDAN -- group, body

編集 (877)   HENSHUU -- editing, compilation

集中 (12)   SHUUCHUU -- concentration, convergence, centralization

集会 (16)   SHUUKAI -- meeting

Also: 結集

Typical Conversational Usage:

それは集団心理だと思います。
どんな記事を編集していますか。
今、数学を集中的に勉強しています。
何時に集会が始まりますか。
あしたここに三時に集まってください。

Graphically-Phonetically Related Morphographs:

Occurrences/1000	1.07
Frequency Rank	225
Sanseido Page	432
Nelson Page	933

225

隊

ON: TAI

kun:

High Frequency Compounds:

軍隊 36 — GUNTAI -- army, troops

兵隊 243 — HEITAI -- soldier, sailor

入隊 65 — NYUUTAI -- enlistment

部隊 52 — BUTAI -- corps, unit, force

Basic Meaning(s): party, company, corps

Typical Phrases and Expanded Compounds:

軍隊の規則
兵隊にとられる
自衛隊に入隊する
歩兵部隊

Typical Conversational Usage:

軍隊の規則はきびしいです。
兄は兵隊にとられて、戦死しました。
山本君は自衛隊に入隊しました。
あの方は、私たちの部隊長です。

226 父

Occurrences/1000: 1.07
Frequency Rank: 226
Sanseido Page: 148
Nelson Page: 591

A

ON: HU

kun: chichi

Basic Meaning(s): father

Graphically-Phonetically Related Morphographs:

High Frequency Compounds:

父母 HUBO, chichi-haha -- father and mother
317

父兄 HUKEI -- parents and brothers, parents and children
575

叔父 oji -- uncle

Also: 伯父

Typical Phrases and Expanded Compounds:

父母のおもかげ
父兄会
叔父の会社
父の仕事

Typical Conversational Usage:

父母に相談してみます。
きのうの父兄会は大変重要でした。
叔父は現在北海道にいます。
父は学校の先生です。

Graphically-Phonetically Related Morphographs:

Occurrences/1000 1.07	227
Frequency Rank 227	別
Sanseido Page 170	
Nelson Page 198	A

<u>ON</u>: BETSU

<u>kun</u>: waka(reru), waka(re)

High Frequency Compounds:

特別 TOKUBETSU -- special, extraordinary
186

区別 KUBETSU -- distinction, difference
544

別居 BEKKYO -- separation, living apart
281

See 281

Basic Meaning(s): separate, branch off, farewell

Typical Phrases and Expanded Compounds:

特別扱いにする
老若男女の区別なく
別居生活
友人と別れる

Typical Conversational Usage:

彼は特別です。
いいのと悪いのと区別してください。
あの方は御主人と別居しています。
きのう山口さんと銀座で別れました。

228

局

Occurrences/1000 1.06
Frequency Rank 228
Sanseido Page 297
Nelson Page 342

ON: KYOKU

kun:

Basic Meaning(s): bureau, office, conclusion

Graphically-Phonetically Related Morphographs:

High Frequency Compounds:

結局 KEKKYOKU -- after all, in conclusion
109

当局 TOOKYOKU -- the authorities concerned, the powers-that-be
68

郵便局 YUUBINKYOKU -- post office
1348 769

Typical Phrases and Expanded Compounds:

結局のところ
当局にたずねる
郵便局長

Typical Conversational Usage:

結局、誰にも会えませんでした。
疑問の点は当局までおたずねください。
郵便局へ手紙を出しに行って来ます。

Graphically-Phonetically Related Morphographs:

濃　NOO　(1152)

Occurrences/1000	1.06
Frequency Rank	229
Sanseido Page	669
Nelson Page	870

農　229

ON:　NOO

kun:

Basic Meaning(s):　agriculture, farm

High Frequency Compounds:

農民　NOOMIN -- peasants, farmers
30

農村　NOOSON -- farm village, rural community
241

農業　NOOGYOO -- agriculture
74

農家　NOOKA -- farmers, farm house
46

農地　NOOCHI -- agricultural land
46

Typical Phrases and Expanded Compounds:

農民の支持
農村の人々
農業を営む
農家の出
農地解放

Typical Conversational Usage:

池田氏は農民の支持を受けています。
農村の生活は最近よくなりました。
この辺は農業がさかんです。
あそこの農家は大きいようです。
宅地がふえ、農地がだんだん少なくなってきました。

230

過

A

Occurrences/1000   1.05
Frequency Rank   230
Sanseido Page   448
Nelson Page   887

ON: KA

kun: su(giru), su(gosu), su(gi)

Basic Meaning(s):   pass, spend, past, error, fault

Graphically-Phonetically Related Morphographs:

禍   KA

High Frequency Compounds:

過去   KAKO -- the past, previous life, past tense
496

過程   KATEI -- process
276

経過   KEIKA -- progress, course, interim
71

Typical Phrases and Expanded Compounds:

過去の思い出

生産の過程

手術後の経過

時が過ぎるにつれ

いなかで過ごす

Typical Conversational Usage:

過去十年間には、いろいろな事が起こりました。

今、生産はどの辺の過程にありますか。

その後の経過はいかがですか。

春はもう過ぎました。

兄は冬休みをパリで過ごしました。

Graphically-Phonetically Related Morphographs:

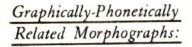

Occurrences/1000 1.05	車 231
Frequency Rank 231	
Sanseido Page 700	A
Nelson Page 864	
	ON: SHA
	kun: kuruma

Basic Meaning(s): wheel, wagon, automobile, vehicle

High Frequency Compounds:

電車 — DENSHA -- electric car, street car, electric train
332

汽車 — KISHA -- train (steam)

自動車 — JIDOOSHA -- automobile
14 47

列車 — RESSHA -- train (the line of connected cars)
656

Typical Phrases and Expanded Compounds:

電車で通う
汽車の切符
自動車事故
貨物列車
車の調子

Typical Conversational Usage:

東京駅まで電車賃はいくらですか。
汽車の旅行はとても楽しいです。
今、自動車学校で運転を習っています。
次の列車で行きましょうか。
この車は新車ですか。

232

衆

Occurrences/1000 1.05
Frequency Rank 232
Sanseido Page 666
Nelson Page 801

<u>ON</u>: SHUU, SHU

<u>kun</u>:

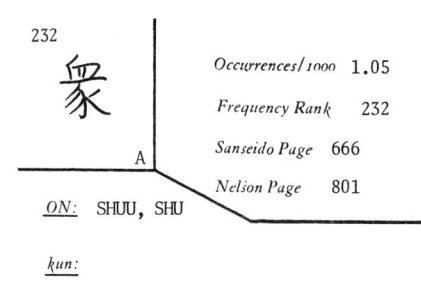

Basic Meaning(s): great numbers, multitude, populace

Typical Phrases and Expanded Compounds:

大衆向き
民衆心理
アメリカ合衆国

Graphically-Phonetically Related Morphographs:

High Frequency Compounds:

大衆 TAISHUU -- a crowd, the masses
民衆 MINSHUU -- people, populace
合衆国 GASSHUUKOKU -- United States (of America), a federal state

Typical Conversational Usage:

彼は大衆作家です。
駅に民衆がおしよせました。
月にアメリカ合衆国のはたが立てられました。

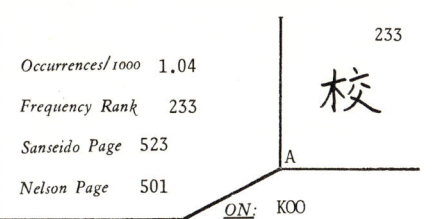

Graphically-Phonetically Related Morphographs:

交 KOO (269)   絞 KOO
効 KOO (714)
郊 KOO

High Frequency Compounds:

学校 15 GAKKOO -- school
高校 135 KOOKOO -- senior high school
校長 90 KOOCHOO -- principal
校正 139 KOOSEI -- proofreading

Occurrences/1000 1.04
Frequency Rank   233
Sanseido Page   523
Nelson Page   501

校 233
A

ON: KOO

kun:

Basic Meaning(s): school, correction, proof

Typical Phrases and Expanded Compounds:

学校の運動会
高校三年生
校長先生
印刷物の校正

Typical Conversational Usage:

きのうは三時きで学校にいました。
高校を出たら、会社に勤めるつもりです。
校長先生は、今日、東京へ出張しました。
今、印刷物の校正をしています。

234

頭

A

Occurrences/1000 1.04
Frequency Rank 234
Sanseido Page 692
Nelson Page 843

ON: TOO, ZU

kun: atama

Basic Meaning(s): head, intellect, counter for cattle

Graphically-Phonetically Related Morphographs:

闘 TOO (367)

豆 TOO

Typical Phrases and Expanded Compounds:

先頭に立つ
三井銀行の頭取
頭脳流出
頭痛の種
頭がいい

High Frequency Compounds:

先頭 SENTOO -- the head, the lead
115

頭取 TOOdori -- president (of private bank), manager
194

頭脳 ZUNOO -- head, brains
829

頭痛 ZUTSUU -- headache, worry
768

到頭 TOOTOO -- finally, at last
777

Typical Conversational Usage:

先頭に立っているのが私の兄です。
山本さんは、どこの銀行の頭取ですか。
彼はいつも頭脳的に物事を考えます。
きのうは頭痛がしたので、早く帰りました。
あの子は頭がいいです。

235

流

Graphically-Phonetically Related Morphographs:

硫 RYUU

Occurrences/1000 1.04
Frequency Rank 235
Sanseido Page 404
Nelson Page 553

A

ON: RYUU, RU

kun: naga(reru), naga(su), naga(re), naga(shi)

Basic Meaning(s): flow, stream, drain, shed, pour

High Frequency Compounds:

流行 RYUUKOO -- fashion, popularity
18

流感 RYUUKAN -- flu, influenza
105

Typical Phrases and Expanded Compounds:

流行歌
流感がはやる
川が流れる
水を流す

Typical Conversational Usage:

これは今流行のドレスです。
流感にかからないように、気をつけてください。
水がよく流れません。
洪水で橋が流されました。

236

屋

A

ON: OKU

kun: ya

Basic Meaning(s): roof, house, shop, seller

Occurrences/1000 1.03
Frequency Rank 236
Sanseido Page 298
Nelson Page 344

Graphically-Phonetically Related Morphographs:

High Frequency Compounds:

家屋　KAOKU -- house, building
46

屋敷　yashiki -- mansion, residence
955

部屋　heya -- room.
52

Typical Phrases and Expanded Compounds:

家屋が焼ける
広い屋敷
部屋を借りる

Typical Conversational Usage:

この間の火事で、家屋が全焼しました。
安井さんは立派な屋敷に住んでいます。
成田さんはとなりの部屋にいます。

加

237

Occurrences/1000 1.03
Frequency Rank 237
Sanseido Page 168
Nelson Page 204

A

ON: KA

kun: kuwa(eru), kuwa(waru)

Graphically-Phonetically Related Morphographs:

架 KA

Basic Meaning(s): addition, increase, join in

High Frequency Compounds:

増加 ZOOKA -- increase, add
365

参加 SANKA -- participation, joining
350

加工 KAKOO -- processing, manufacturing
173

Typical Phrases and Expanded Compounds:

人員の増加
オリンピックに参加する
加工品
圧力を加える
組識に加わる

Typical Conversational Usage:

人員の増加をはかりました。
今度の会議に参加してくださいませんか。
その工場ではどんな物を加工していますか。
もう少し力を加えてみてください。
今度その団体に加わりました。

238

死

A

Occurrences/1000   1.03
Frequency Rank   238
Sanseido Page   37
Nelson Page   521

ON: SHI

kun: shi(nu), shi

Basic Meaning(s): death, die

Graphically-Phonetically Related Morphographs:

High Frequency Compounds:

死亡   SHIBOO -- death
795

生死   SEISHI -- life or death, life
9   and death

必死   HISSHI -- inevitable, despera-
188   tion

Typical Phrases and Expanded Compounds:

死亡を確認する
生死の境をさまよう
必死の努力
ぽっくり死ぬ

Typical Conversational Usage:

きのう父の死亡届を出しました。
アルプスに登った友人の生死が不明です。
必死の努力で泳ぎました。
それは死ぬか生きるかの大問題です。

Graphically-Phonetically Related Morphographs:

	239
Occurrences/1000 1.03	使
Frequency Rank 239	
Sanseido Page 126	A
Nelson Page 150	

ON: SHI
kun: tsuka(u), tsuka(i)

High Frequency Compounds:

使用　SHIYOO -- utilize, employ
177

使命　SHIMEI -- mission, errand
249

大使　TAISHI -- ambassador
5

Basic Meaning(s): use, employ, spend, messenger

Typical Phrases and Expanded Compounds:

使用禁止
使命を全うする
米国大使
部屋を使う

Typical Conversational Usage:

今この部屋は使用中です。
平井さんは重大な使命をおびています。
新しい駐日米国大使が任命されました。
この鉛筆を使ってもよろしいですか。

240 説

Occurrences/1000 1.02
Frequency Rank 240
Sanseido Page 683
Nelson Page 832

ON: SETSU, ZEI

kun: to(ku)

Basic Meaning(s): comment, opinion, explain

Graphically-Phonetically Related Morphographs:

設 SETSU (270)
税 ZEI (909)

High Frequency Compounds:

演説 ENZETSU -- speech, lecture
413

小説 SHOOSETSU -- novel, fiction
126

説明 SETSUMEI -- explain
152

遊説 YUUZEI -- electioneering tour, campaign speech
585

Typical Phrases and Expanded Compounds:

へたな演説
小説家
じょうずに説明する
地方を遊説する
意味を説く

Typical Conversational Usage:

首相の演説をきのうラジオで聞きました。
誰の小説が好きですか。
それは説明の必要がないと思います。
上村氏は地方を遊説しています。
先生は、その意味をわかりやすく説いてくれました。

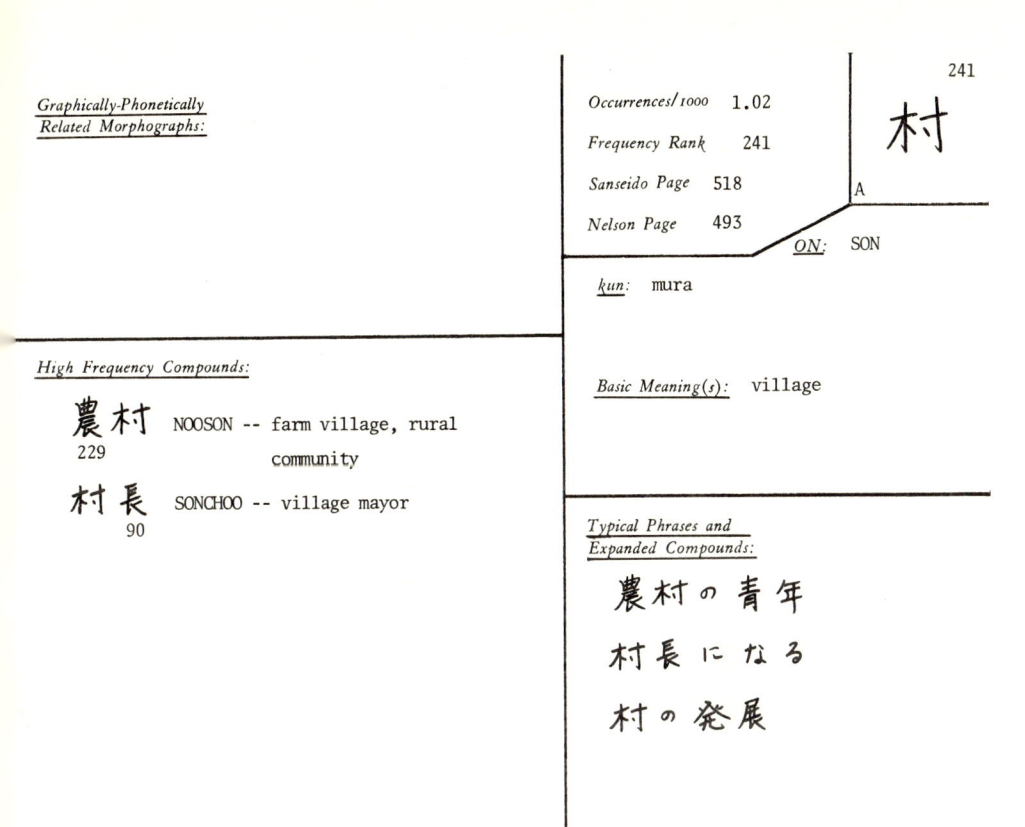

Graphically-Phonetically
Related Morphographs:

	241
Occurrences/1000 1.02	村
Frequency Rank 241	
Sanseido Page 518	A
Nelson Page 493	

ON: SON

kun: mura

Basic Meaning(s): village

High Frequency Compounds:

農村　　NOOSON -- farm village, rural
229　　　　　　community

村長　　SONCHOO -- village mayor
90

Typical Phrases and
Expanded Compounds:

農村の青年

村長になる

村の発展

Typical Conversational Usage:

その新しい機械は農村に受けがいいです。

村長は評判がいいです。

水野さんは、村の発展のためにつくしています。

242

白 A

Occurrences/1000 1.02
Frequency Rank 242
Sanseido Page 61
Nelson Page 635

ON: HAKU, BYAKU

kun: shiro(i), shiro

Basic Meaning(s): white

Graphically-Phonetically Related Morphographs:

伯 HAKU (891)   迫 HAKU (698)
拍 HAKU   舶 HAKU
泊 HAKU (1405)

High Frequency Compounds:

告白 KOKUHAKU -- confession
398

白人 HAKUJIN -- Caucasian, white man
2

真白 masshiro -- pure white
195

Typical Phrases and Expanded Compounds:

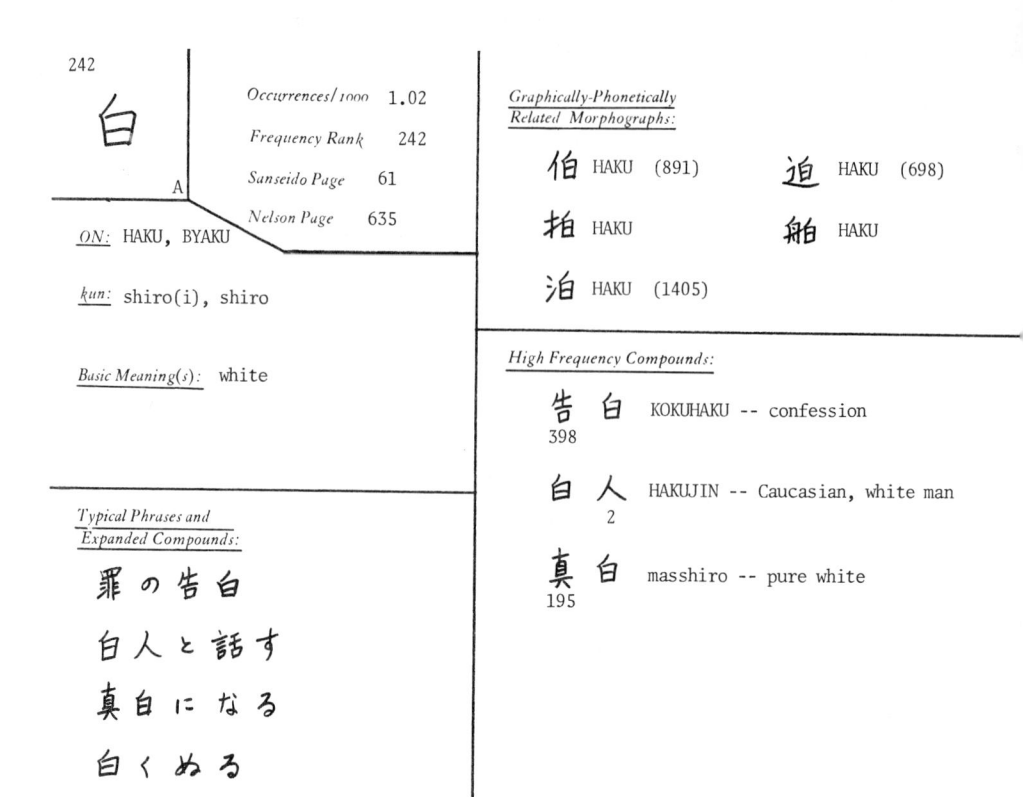

罪の告白
白人と話す
真白になる
白くぬる

Typical Conversational Usage:

彼は罪を告白しました。
あの白人は何という人ですか。
山が雪で真白になりました。
かべを白くぬりました。

Graphically-Phonetically Related Morphographs:

Occurrences/1000 1.02
Frequency Rank 243
Sanseido Page 67
Nelson Page 90

243
兵
A

ON: HEI

kun:

Basic Meaning(s): soldier, army

High Frequency Compounds:

兵器 HEIKI -- arms, ordnance
520

兵隊 HEITAI -- soldier, sailor
225

兵力 HEIRYOKU -- military force
38

Typical Phrases and Expanded Compounds:

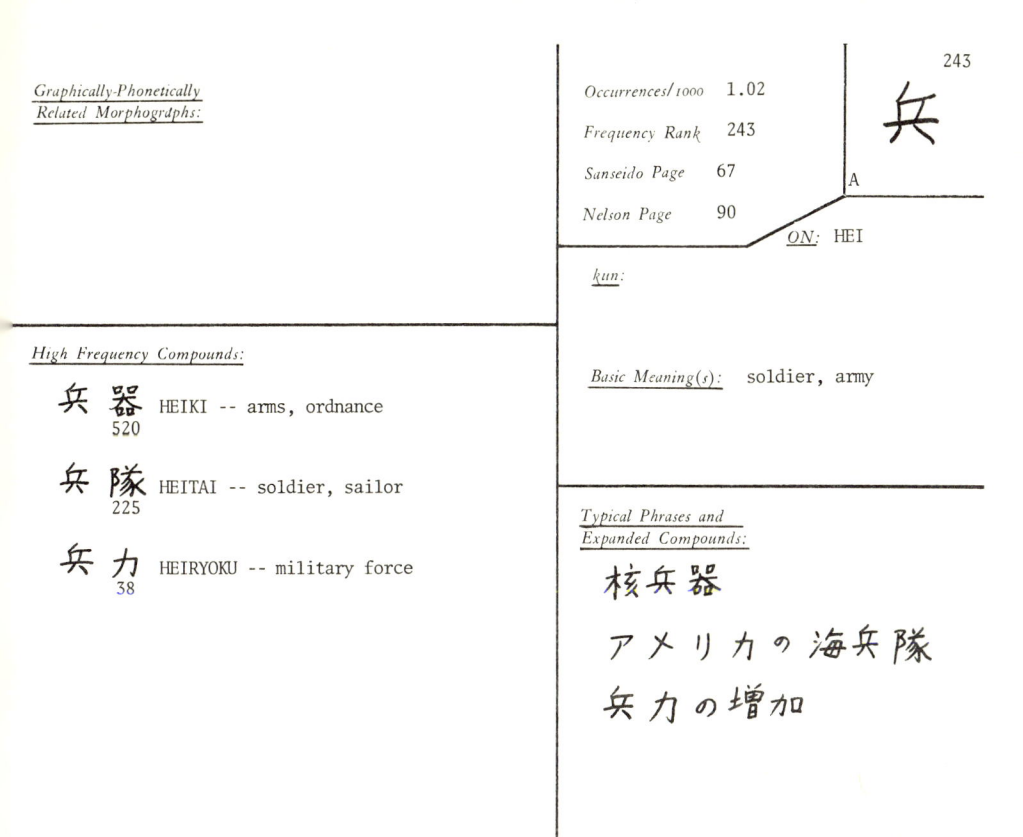

核兵器
アメリカの海兵隊
兵力の増加

Typical Conversational Usage:

あれは核兵器反対のデモです。
小さい時、よく兵隊ごっこをしました。
敵の兵力が弱まりました。

244

務

Occurrences/1000: 1.02
Frequency Rank: 244
Sanseido Page: 591
Nelson Page: 646

ON: MU

kun: tsuto(me)

Basic Meaning(s): duty, service, business

Graphically-Phonetically Related Morphographs:

予 MU (1246)
霧 MU

Typical Phrases and Expanded Compounds:

事務的に
外務大臣
義務を果す
勤務時間
公務執行妨害
務めを果す

High Frequency Compounds:

事務 JIMU -- business, clerical work
10

外務 GAIMU -- foreign affairs
69

義務 GIMU -- duty, obligation, responsibility
62

勤務 KIMMU -- service, duty, work
690

公務 KOOMU -- public service, official business
212

See 349

Typical Conversational Usage:

あそこが私の事務所です。
兄は東大を出て、外務省に入りました。
アメリカの義務教育は何年ですか。
御主人の勤務先はどちらですか。
父は公務員です。
務めをおこたってはいけません。

Graphically-Phonetically Related Morphographs:

右 YUU (384)

友 YUU (451)

High Frequency Compounds:

有名 YUUMEI -- famous
140

有効 YUUKOO -- effectiveness, validity
714

所有 SHOYUU -- possession, ownership
129

有利 YUURI -- advantageous, profitable
180

Occurrences/1000 1.02
Frequency Rank   245
Sanseido Page   185
Nelson Page   738

245

有

A

ON: YUU, U

kun: a(ru)

Basic Meaning(s): being, existence, possession, there is/are

Typical Phrases and Expanded Compounds:

有名な人

有効期間

所有地

有利な条件

Typical Conversational Usage:

ワイキキは有名な海岸です。
この定期はあしたまで有効です。
この土地は誰の所有地ですか。
この試合は相手の方が有利です。

246 起

Occurrences/1000 1.01
Frequency Rank 246
Sanseido Page 698
Nelson Page 855

ON: KI

kun: o(kiru), o(koru), o(kosu), o(kori)

Basic Meaning(s): get up, raise up, happen, originate

Graphically-Phonetically Related Morphographs:

危 KI (495)   忌 KI
紀 KI (616)
記 KI (209)

High Frequency Compounds:

起源 (626) KIGEN -- origin, beginning

再起 (252) SAIKI -- comeback, recovery, restoration

起点 (175) KITEN -- starting point, terminus, home port

Typical Phrases and Expanded Compounds:

中世に起源を発して
再起不能
ここを起点として
六時に起きる
事件が起こる

Typical Conversational Usage:

「種の起源」という本を読みましたか。
彼の再起が危ぶまれています。
ここを起点として、出発しましょう。
毎朝何時に起きますか。
重大な事件が起こりました。

247

期

Graphically-Phonetically Related Morphographs:

基 KI (251)
棋 KI (1315)
旗 KI (1316)

High Frequency Compounds:

期待 KITAI -- expectation, hope
366

時期 JIKI -- time, the times, season
24

期間 KIKAN -- term, period
31

初期 SHOKI -- early days, early years, beginning
279

Occurrences/1000 1.01
Frequency Rank 247
Sanseido Page 670
Nelson Page 748

ON: KI

kun:

Basic Meaning(s): time, period, expectation

Typical Phrases and Expanded Compounds:

期待がはずれる
時期が早い
期間が短い
明治の初期
最期をとげる

Typical Conversational Usage:

何とか皆さんの期待にこたえたいと思います。
どうも時期が悪かったようです。
試験の期間が長すぎました。
昭和の初期にはどんな作家がいましたか。
彼は立派な最期をとげました。

248 助 A

Occurrences/1000 1.01
Frequency Rank 248
Sanseido Page 587
Nelson Page 205

ON: JO

kun: tasu(keru), tasu(karu), tasu(ke), suke

Basic Meaning(s): help, rescue, save, be saved, assistance

Graphically-Phonetically Related Morphographs:

High Frequency Compounds:

援助 ENJO -- assistance, support, help
354

助言 JOGEN -- advice, suggestion
44

助長 JOCHOO -- promotion, fostering
90

Typical Phrases and Expanded Compounds:

援助をほどこす
助言を受ける
進歩を助長する
人を助ける
大いに助かる

Typical Conversational Usage:

被害地に援助の手をさしのべましょう。
先生の助言が必要です。
悪いことを助長してはいけません。
川でおぼれている子どもを助けました。
手伝っていただき、大いに助かりました。

命

249

Graphically-Phonetically Related Morphographs:

Occurrences/1000 1.01
Frequency Rank 249
Sanseido Page 108
Nelson Page 149

ON: MEI, MYOO

kun: inochi

Basic Meaning(s): life, destiny, command

High Frequency Compounds:

革命 KAKUMEI -- revolution
487

生命 SEIMEI -- life, soul
9

運命 UMMEI -- destiny, fate
157

命令 MEIREI -- command, decree
587

See 239

Also: 一生懸命

Typical Phrases and Expanded Compounds:

革命が起こる
生命保険
人の運命
命令にそむく
命があぶない

Typical Conversational Usage:

フランス革命はいつ起こりましたか。
いつ生命保険に入りましたか。
人の運命はわからないものです。
命令にそむいてはいけません。
かめの寿命は長いです。
命がちぢまるような思いをしました。

250

果

A

Occurrences/1000 1.00
Frequency Rank 250
Sanseido Page 484
Nelson Page 71

ON: KA

kun: ha(tasu), ha(teru)

Basic Meaning(s): fruit, reward, carry out, achieve, end

Graphically-Phonetically Related Morphographs:

菓 KA

課 KA (755)

High Frequency Compounds:

結果 (109) KEKKA -- consequences, result, effect

効果 (714) KOOKA -- efficacy, effect

果実 (37) KAJITSU -- fruit, nut, berry

Typical Phrases and Expanded Compounds:

その結果
効果があがる
果実の生産
責任を果す
疲れ果てる

Typical Conversational Usage:

調査の結果がまだわかりません。
大分勉強の効果があがりました。
この辺は果実の生産で有名です。
何事にも責任を果すことが大切です。
彼はもう疲れ果てたという感じです。

251

基

Graphically-Phonetically Related Morphographs:

期 KI (247)

棋 KI (1315)

旗 KI (1316)

Occurrences/1000 1.00
Frequency Rank 251
Sanseido Page 670
Nelson Page 274

ON: KI

kun: motoi, moto(zuku)

Basic Meaning(s): foundation, basis, be based on

High Frequency Compounds:

基地 KICHI -- base, military base
45

基礎 KISO -- foundation, base, basis
927

Also: 基盤

Typical Phrases and Expanded Compounds:

昭和基地
基礎工事
基がない
事実に基づいて

Typical Conversational Usage:

以前米軍基地で働いていました。
英語を勉強するのに基礎が大切です。
仕事の基を築きました。
何に基づいて、その研究をしましたか。

252

再 A

Occurrences/1000 1.00
Frequency Rank 252
Sanseido Page 36
Nelson Page 47

ON: SAI

kun: hutata(bi)

Basic Meaning(s): again, twice, second time

Graphically-Phonetically Related Morphographs:

High Frequency Compounds:

再会 SAIKAI -- another meeting, reunion
 16

再生 SAISEI -- return to life, regeneration
 9

再建 SAIKEN -- reconstruction, rebuilding
 278

See 246

Typical Phrases and Expanded Compounds:

再会を喜ぶ
テープの再生
会社の再建
二度と再び

Typical Conversational Usage:

五年前に別れた友と再会しました。
このテープを再生してください。
父は会社の再建にのり出しました。
村田氏は議長に再び選ばれました。

253

職

Graphically-Phonetically Related Morphographs:

織 SHOKU (611)

Occurrences/1000 1.00
Frequency Rank 253
Sanseido Page 657
Nelson Page 735

ON: SHOKU

kun:

Basic Meaning(s): employment, work, profession, office

High Frequency Compounds:

職場 (49) SHOKUBA -- place of work, workshop

職員 (127) SHOKUIN -- employee, staff, personnel

職業 (74) SHOKUGYOO -- occupation, business, *profession*

就職 (906) SHUUSHOKU -- finding employment

Typical Phrases and Expanded Compounds:

楽しい職場

教職員

職業安定所

就職先

Typical Conversational Usage:

職場がとても明るいです。
職員室はどこですか。
職業は何ですか。
ようやく就職が決まりました。

254 変

Occurrences/1000 1.00
Frequency Rank 254
Sanseido Page 90
Nelson Page 117

ON: HEN

kun: ka(waru), ka(eru), ka(wari)

Basic Meaning(s): change, vary, different, revise, alteration

Graphically-Phonetically Related Morphographs:

High Frequency Compounds:

大変 TAIHEN -- serious, terrible
5

変化 HENKA -- change, alteration
104

Also: 事変

Typical Phrases and Expanded Compounds:

大変な事になる
変化がない
色が変わる
予定を変える
変な人

Typical Conversational Usage:

きのうは大変あつかったです。
日本では四季の変化がはっきりしています。
何か変わった事がありますか。
この計画を変えるわけにはいきません。
その話はどうも変です。

Graphically-Phonetically Related Morphographs:

	255
Occurrences/1000 1.00	木
Frequency Rank 255	
Sanseido Page 511	
Nelson Page 490	
	ON: BOKU, MOKU
kun: ki	

Basic Meaning(s): tree, wood, timber, lumber

High Frequency Compounds:

大木 TAIBOKU -- large tree
5

木材 MOKUZAI -- lumber, wood
806

木曜日 MOKUYOOBI -- Thursday
1350 3

Occurs most frequently in proper names; such as, 木村 "Kimura."

Typical Phrases and Expanded Compounds:

大木を切りたおす
木材業を営む
先週の木曜日
木を植える

Typical Conversational Usage:

この辺には、みごとな大木がたくさんあります。
この家はどんな木材でできていますか。
来週の木曜日に、東京へ行くことにしました。
これは桜の木です。
木村さんは、とても親切ないい方です。

256

策

A

Occurrences/1000 .98
Frequency Rank 256
Sanseido Page 626
Nelson Page 683

ON: SAKU

kun:

Basic Meaning(s): plan, scheme, policy, measure

Typical Phrases and Expanded Compounds:

外交政策
失業対策
方策がつきる

Graphically-Phonetically Related Morphographs:

High Frequency Compounds:

政策 SEISAKU -- political measures, policy
  23
対策 TAISAKU -- countermeasure
  39
方策 HOOSAKU -- plan, policy, means, measure, strategy
  25

Typical Conversational Usage:

政府はどんな外交政策をうち出しましたか。
何かいい対策をねらなければなりません。
もう方策がつきて、どうしようもありません。

257

太

Occurrences/1000 .97
Frequency Rank 257
Sanseido Page 261
Nelson Page 296

ON: TAI, TA
kun: futo(i)

Basic Meaning(s): big, fat

Graphically-Phonetically Related Morphographs:

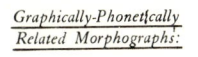

大 TAI (5)

High Frequency Compounds:

太陽 TAIYOO -- sun
856

太平洋 TAIHEIYOO -- Pacific Ocean
98 411

Typical Phrases and Expanded Compounds:

太陽が沈む
太平洋を航行中
太い木

Typical Conversational Usage:

ハワイは太陽の光線が強いです。
大西洋に比べて、太平洋はずっと大きいです。
その木はかなり太い木です。

258

約

Occurrences/1000 .97
Frequency Rank 258
Sanseido Page 635
Nelson Page 695

A

ON: YAKU

kun:

Basic Meaning(s): promise, approximately

Graphically-Phonetically Related Morphographs:

Typical Phrases and Expanded Compounds:

条約の締結
約束を守る
契約書
制約をうける

High Frequency Compounds:

条約 JOOYAKU -- treaty
213

約束 YAKUSOKU -- promise, appointment
911

契約 KEIYAKU -- contract, agreement
1209

制約 SEIYAKU -- condition, limitation, restriction
161

Typical Conversational Usage:

対日講和条約は何年に締結されましたか。
あした池田さんに会う約束をしました。
まだ取引の契約をしていません。
参加するのに、何か制約がありますか。

259

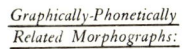

育

Occurrences/1000 .96
Frequency Rank 259
Sanseido Page 88
Nelson Page 114

A

ON: IKU
kun: soda(teru), soda(tsu)

Basic Meaning(s): be brought up, be raised, grow, raise

Graphically-Phonetically Related Morphographs:

High Frequency Compounds:

教育 KYOOIKU -- education
58

育成 IKUSEI -- rearing, training
160

育児 IKUJI -- care of children
597

Typical Phrases and Expanded Compounds:

道徳教育
幹部の育成
育児法

Typical Conversational Usage:

子供の教育はとても大切です。
今村先生は選手の育成に力を入れています。
彼女は育児に追われています。

260

円   A

Occurrences/1000 .96
Frequency Rank 260
Sanseido Page 156
Nelson Page 183

ON: EN

kun:

Basic Meaning(s): round, circle, Yen

Graphically-Phonetically Related Morphographs:

High Frequency Compounds:

円満 ENMAN -- perfection, peace, harmony
466

円熟 ENJUKU -- ripeness, maturity
1219

Typical Phrases and Expanded Compounds:

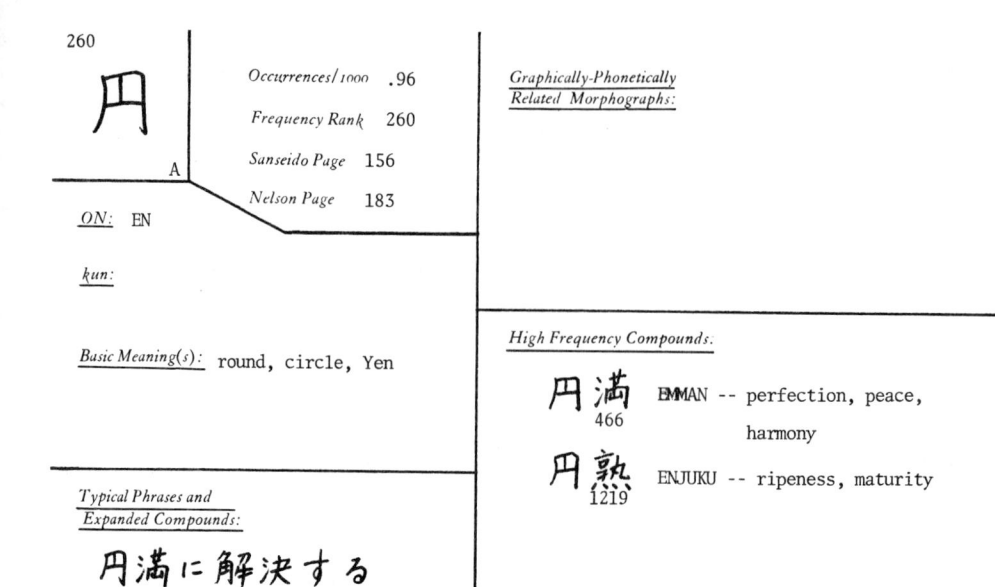

円満に解決する
円熟した選手
百五十円

Typical Conversational Usage:

竹田御夫妻はとても円満です。
あの選手は最近とみに円熟してきました。
全部で三百五十円になります。

Graphically-Phonetically Related Morphographs:

九 KYUU (112)

究 261

Occurrences/1000 .95
Frequency Rank 261
Sanseido Page 280
Nelson Page 671

ON: KYUU
kun:

Basic Meaning(s): investigate, carry to extremes, thorough

High Frequency Compounds:

研究 KENKYUU -- research, study
284

探究 TANKYUU -- search, research, inquiry
871

究明 KYUUMEI -- investigation, inquiry
152

Typical Phrases and Expanded Compounds:

研究室
探究心が強い
原因を究明する

Typical Conversational Usage:

先生は現在何を研究していますか。
あの子は探究心がとても強いです。
今その原因を究明しているところです。

262 好

Occurrences/1000 .95
Frequency Rank 262
Sanseido Page 270
Nelson Page 301

ON: KOO

kun: kono(mu), su(ku), kono(mi), su(ki), kono(mashii)

Basic Meaning(s): like, be fond of, taste, liking, desirable

Graphically-Phonetically Related Morphographs:

High Frequency Compounds:

好意 KOOI -- good will, friendliness, kindness
86

好物 KOOBUTSU -- something good, favorite dish
95

好評 KOOHYOO -- public favor, favorable criticism
358

好調 KOOCHOO -- favorable, promising, satisfactory
219

Typical Phrases and Expanded Compounds:

好意的に
大好物
好評を博する
万事好調

Typical Conversational Usage:

友人の好意を無にするわけにはいきません。
おすしは私の大好物です。
中村氏の演説は好評を博しました。
仕事は今好調です。

引

Occurrences/1000 .94
Frequency Rank 263
Sanseido Page 301
Nelson Page 372

ON: IN

kun: hi(ku), hi(ki)

Basic Meaning(s): pull, withdraw

Graphically-Phonetically Related Morphographs:

High Frequency Compounds:

引用 IN'YOO -- quotation, quote, citation
177

引退 INTAI -- retirement, drawback, retreat
666

引力 INRYOKU -- gravity, attraction
38

取引 torihiki -- transaction, business
194

Typical Phrases and Expanded Compounds:

本から引用する
引退生活
引力が強い
取引が成立する

Typical Conversational Usage:

これは何の本から引用したものですか。
葉山先生はいつ引退しましたか。
ニュートンの「万有引力の法則」を知っていますか。
外国と取引をしています。

264

郎

B

ON: ROO

kun:

Basic Meaning(s): man, husband

Occurrences/1000 .94
Frequency Rank 264
Sanseido Page 673
Nelson Page 896

Graphically-Phonetically Related Morphographs:

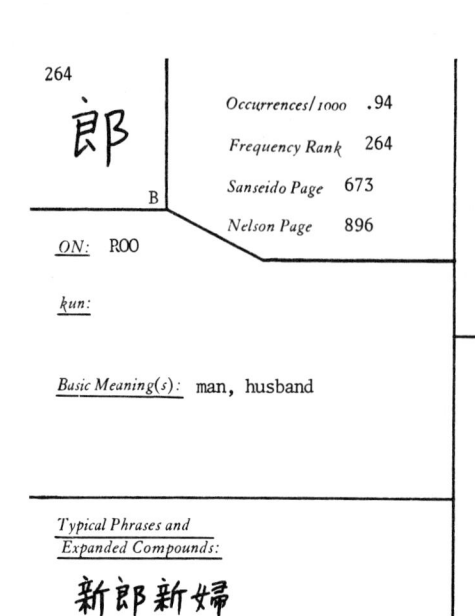

朗 ROO

廊 ROO (1249)

浪 ROO

High Frequency Compounds:

新郎 SHINROO --bridegroom
80

Occurs most frequently in proper names, such as 太郎, "Taroo."

Typical Phrases and Expanded Compounds:

新郎新婦
一郎

Typical Conversational Usage:

私は新郎の友人です。
一郎はうちの長男です。

帰

Graphically-Phonetically Related Morphographs:

Occurrences/1000 .93
Frequency Rank 265
Sanseido Page 151
Nelson Page 378

A

ON: KI

kun: kae(ru), kae(su), kae(ri)

Basic Meaning(s): return, send (someone) back

High Frequency Compounds:

帰国 KIKOKU -- returning to one's country
 4

帰省 KISEI -- homecoming
 546

復帰 HUKKI -- return, comeback, reinstatement
 537

帰化 KIKA -- naturalization
 104

Typical Phrases and Expanded Compounds:

帰国の途につく
帰省中に
日本に復帰する
日本に帰化する

Typical Conversational Usage:

ブラウンさんはもう帰国しました。
両親に相談するために、帰省する予定です。
小笠原諸島は日本に復帰しました。
あの方は最近日本に帰化したそうです。

266 役

Occurrences/1000: .93
Frequency Rank: 266
Sanseido Page: 356
Nelson Page: 381

A

ON: EKI, YAKU
kun:

Basic Meaning(s): war, office, duty, help

Typical Phrases and Expanded Compounds:

現役を退く
重要な役割を演ずる
役所の仕事
会社の役員
幹事の役をつとめる

Graphically-Phonetically Related Morphographs:

疫 EKI

High Frequency Compounds:

現役 (67) GEN'EKI -- active service, commissioned (battleship)

役割 (414) YAKUwari -- role, allotment of duties

役所 (129) YAKUSHO -- government office

役員 (127) YAKUIN -- officer, official, staff

See 91

Also: 役場, 役者, 役人, 役立つ

Typical Conversational Usage:

彼はまだ現役の選手です。
父はその仕事で重要な役割を演じました。
どこの役所に勤めていますか。
会社の役員に選ばれました。
これは何かの役にたちますか。

Graphically-Phonetically
Related Morphographs:

Occurrences/1000	.92
Frequency Rank	267
Sanseido Page	536
Nelson Page	519

267

歩

A

<u>ON</u>: HO, BU

<u>kun</u>: aru(ku), ayu(mu), aru(ki), ayu(mi)

Basic Meaning(s): walk, step, rate

High Frequency Compounds:

歩道 — HODOO -- path, footpath, sidewalk
123

歩調 — HOCHOO -- pace, step, cadence
219

散歩 — SAMPO -- stroll, walk
969

歩合 — BUAI -- rate, ratio, percentage
33

Typical Phrases and
Expanded Compounds:

歩道を歩く
歩調を合わせる
散歩に出かける
歩合がいい

Typical Conversational Usage:

いつも歩道を歩きましょう。
彼と歩調をそろえて下さい。
主人は散歩に出かけています。
この仕事は歩合がとてもいいです。

268

愛

Occurrences/1000 .91
Frequency Rank 268
Sanseido Page 544
Nelson Page 590

ON: AI

kun:

Basic Meaning(s): love, affection, favorite, beloved, dear

Typical Phrases and Expanded Compounds:

愛情が足りない
愛国心
恋愛小説
愛用車

Graphically-Phonetically Related Morphographs:

High Frequency Compounds:

愛情 AIJOO -- love, affection
183

愛国 AIKOKU -- patriotism
4

恋愛 REN'AI -- love, love-making, passion
899

愛用 AIYOO -- favorite, habitual use
177

Typical Conversational Usage:

あの子は愛情にうえかわいています。
彼は愛国心に燃えています。
彼女は今恋愛中です。
どんな車を愛用していますか。

交

Graphically-Phonetically Related Morphographs:

効 KOO (714)　　絞 KOO
郊 KOO
校 KOO (233)

Occurrences/1000　.91
Frequency Rank　269
Sanseido Page　86
Nelson Page　113

ON: KOO
kun: maji(waru), maji(eru), ma(zeru), ma(jiru), maji(wari), ma(jiri)
Basic Meaning(s): association, mix, mingle with, coming and going

High Frequency Compounds:

外交 GAIKOO -- foreign relations, diplomacy
　69
交渉 KOOSHOO -- negotiation, discussion, connection
　740
交換 KOOKAN -- exchange, reciprocity
　660
交通 KOOTSUU -- traffic, communication, transport
　97
交際 KOOSAI -- association, intercourse, acquaintance
　189

Typical Phrases and Expanded Compounds:

外交政策
値段の交渉
意見を交換する
交通整理
交際を広める
友人と交わる

Typical Conversational Usage:

山野さんは外交がじょうずです。
値段を交渉してみましょう。
電話交換手に聞いてください。
東京は交通が便利です。
彼女は交際が広いです。
悪い友とは交わらない方がいいです。

270 設

Occurrences/1000 .91
Frequency Rank 270
Sanseido Page 678
Nelson Page 825

A

ON: SETSU

kun: moo(keru), moo(ke)

Basic Meaning(s): provide, prepare, establish, found, get

Typical Phrases and Expanded Compounds:
近代設備
建設会社
設計図
会社の設立
娯楽施設
規則を設ける

Graphically-Phonetically Related Morphographs:

説 SETSU (240)

High Frequency Compounds:

設備 SETSUBI -- equipment, fixtures, facilities
201

建設 KENSETSU -- construction, building, establishment
278

設計 SEKKEI -- plan, design
210

設立 SETSURITSU -- establish, found, organize
35

施設 SHISETSU -- institution, establishment, equipment
783

Typical Conversational Usage:

工場の設備はとてもいいです。
その建設工事はいつ終わりますか。
大下さんは自分の設計で家を建てたそうです。
この大学は五十年前に設立されました。
この町の公共施設は毎年改善されています。
市では来年新しい公園を設ける計画です。

271

仕

Occurrences/1000 .90
Frequency Rank 271
Sanseido Page 113
Nelson Page 129

A

ON: SHI
kun: tsuka(eru)

Basic Meaning(s): serve, service, official

Graphically-Phonetically Related Morphographs:

士 SHI (386)
誌 SHI (737)

High Frequency Compounds:

仕事 (10) SHIgoto -- work, employment, occupation

奉仕 (1193) HOOSHI -- service, serving, ministering

給仕 (404) KYUUJI -- office boy or girl, waiter, waitress, table service

Typical Phrases and Expanded Compounds:

会社の仕事
奉仕品
学校の給仕
父母に仕える

Typical Conversational Usage:

何だか仕事が手につきません。
大沢さんはよく社会奉仕をする方です。
お給仕をしていただけませんか。
長年彼は川村さん宅に仕えています。

272

諸

Occurrences/1000 .90
Frequency Rank 272
Sanseido Page 684
Nelson Page 836

ON: SHO

kun:

Basic Meaning(s): many, several, various, every, together

Typical Phrases and Expanded Compounds:

ヨーロッパ諸国
学生諸君
ハワイ諸島

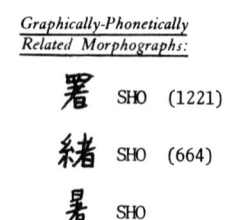

Graphically-Phonetically Related Morphographs:

署 SHO (1221)
緒 SHO (664)
暑 SHO

High Frequency Compounds:

諸国 (4) SHOKOKU -- all nations, various countries, all provinces
諸君 (204) SHOKUN -- gentlemen, ladies and gentlemen, my friends
諸島 (379) SHOTOO -- group of islands, archipelago

Typical Conversational Usage:

青野氏は東南アジア諸国をまわって来ました。
諸君に大いに期待をよせています。
東インド諸島ではどんな物がとれますか。

273 統

Occurrences/1000: .90
Frequency Rank: 273
Sanseido Page: 641
Nelson Page: 703

A

ON: TOO
kun: su(beru)

Basic Meaning(s): relationship, control, supervise

Graphically-Phonetically Related Morphographs:

High Frequency Compounds:

統一₁ TOOITSU -- unity, uniformity, rule

伝統₃₃₁ DENTOO -- tradition

統計₂₁₀ TOOKEI -- statistics

統制₁₆₁ TOOSEI -- control, regulation

Typical Phrases and Expanded Compounds:

統一行動
伝統を守る
統計をとる
統制がとれる
国を統べおさめる

Typical Conversational Usage:

皆さんの意見を統一してください。
この学校の伝統はとても古いです。
統計によれば、先月の生産は最高です。
少しも仕事の統制がとれません。
バビロニアは昔どんな国を統べおさめましたか。

274 違

Occurrences/1000: .90
Frequency Rank: 274
Sanseido Page: 451
Nelson Page: 886

B

ON: I

kun: chiga(u), chiga(eru), chiga(i)

Basic Meaning(s): differ, difference, disagree with, no, change, make a mistake

Graphically-Phonetically Related Morphographs:

偉 I (987)
緯 I

High Frequency Compounds:

違反 IHAN -- violation
146

相違 SOOI -- difference, disparity, gap
111

間違い machigai -- mistake
31

Typical Phrases and Expanded Compounds:

交通違反
見解の相違
間違った考え
違いない

Typical Conversational Usage:

交通違反をしてはいけません。
これは高橋さんの物に相違ありません。
どうも道を間違えたようです。
あれはホテルに違いありません。

275

葉

Occurrences/1000 .90
Frequency Rank 275
Sanseido Page 339
Nelson Page 782

ON: YOO

kun: ha

Basic Meaning(s): leaf, foliage, counter for flat things

Graphically-Phonetically Related Morphographs:

High Frequency Compounds:

紅葉 KOOYOO -- fall colors
1137

青葉 aoba -- foliage, green leaves
393

言葉 (kotoba) -- words, speech, language
44

Typical Phrases and Expanded Compounds:

美しい紅葉
青葉がかおる
お言葉に甘えて
木の葉

Typical Conversational Usage:

私は紅葉の秋が大好きです。
今は青葉がとてもきれいです。
返す言葉もありません。
そんな事は根も葉もない事です。

276 程

ON: TEI

kun:

Basic Meaning(s): degree, limits, distance, about

Occurrences/1000: .89
Frequency Rank: 276
Sanseido Page: 606
Nelson Page: 667

Graphically-Phonetically Related Morphographs:

呈 TEI

Typical Phrases and Expanded Compounds:

程度が高い
研究の過程
仕事の日程
余程注意しなければ

High Frequency Compounds:

程度 TEIDO -- degree, extent, standard
72

過程 KATEI -- process, course
230

日程 NITTEI -- day's schedule
3

余程 YOhodo -- very, greatly, much
468

Typical Conversational Usage:

その子の能力はどの程度かよくわかりません。
それは研究の過程にあります。
仕事の日程を組んでみました。
余程勉強しなければ、大学に入れません。

天

277

Graphically-Phonetically Related Morphographs:

Occurrences/1000 .89
Frequency Rank 277
Sanseido Page 23
Nelson Page 34

A

<u>ON</u>: TEN

<u>kun</u>: ame, (ama)

Basic Meaning(s): sky, heaven(s), celestial, God

High Frequency Compounds:

天皇 (535) — TENNOO -- Emperor of Japan

天気 (55) — TENKI -- weather, fine weather

天国 (4) — TENGOKU -- heaven, paradise, Kingdom of Heaven

天下 (75) — TENKA -- the world, the whole country, the public

Typical Phrases and Expanded Compounds:

天皇陛下
天気予報
天国と地獄
天下を取る
天の助け

Typical Conversational Usage:

歴代の天皇の名前が言えますか。
山の天気は変わりやすいです。
聖書には天国が記されています。
今は天下泰平です。
入試に受かって、天にも上るような心地でした。

278 建

Occurrences/1000: .88
Frequency Rank: 278
Sanseido Page: 326
Nelson Page: 370

A

ON: KEN

kun: ta(teru), ta(tsu)

Basic Meaning(s): build, erect, set up, be built, be established

Graphically-Phonetically Related Morphographs:

健 KEN (734)

Typical Phrases and Expanded Compounds:

建設的な意見
封建的
建築材料
家の建前
工場を建てる
ビルが建つ

High Frequency Compounds:

建設 270 KENSETSU -- building, construction, establishment
封建 724 HOOKEN -- feudalism
建築 872 KENCHIKU -- building, architecture
建前 53   tatemae -- framework, erection ceremony, framing a house, fundamental principles
建物 95   tatemono -- building

Typical Conversational Usage:

石川君は建設会社に入りました。
あの村は封建的です。
兄は今自分の家を建築中です。
そんな時、一般に挨拶するのが建前です。
来年、新しい事務所を建てる計画です。
あのビルは最近建ちました。

初

Graphically-Phonetically Related Morphographs:

Occurrences/1000 .88
Frequency Rank 279
Sanseido Page 596
Nelson Page 803

ON: SHO
kun: haji(me), haji(mete), hatsu

Basic Meaning(s): first, beginning, origin, new

High Frequency Compounds:

最初 SAISHO -- the first, the beginning
99

初期 SHOKI -- early days, early years, beginning
247

初対面 SHOTAIMEN -- first meeting, first interview
39 117

初耳 HATSUmimi -- something heard for the first time
923

Typical Phrases and Expanded Compounds:

最初の頃
ルネサンスの初期
初対面の人
全くの初耳
初めて習う

Typical Conversational Usage:

最初誰が誰だかわかりませんでした。
ルネサンスの初期と末期では大分違います。
内野さんとは初対面でした。
それは初耳です。
大学に行って、初めてフランス語を習いました。

280 側

Occurrences/1000 .88
Frequency Rank 280
Sanseido Page 137
Nelson Page 159

A

ON: SOKU

kun: kawa

Basic Meaning(s): a side, row, surroundings, vicinity

Typical Phrases and Expanded Compounds:

側面から

首相の側近筋

向って右側に

Graphically-Phonetically Related Morphographs:

則 SOKU (746)

測 SOKU

High Frequency Compounds:

側面 SOKUMEN -- side, flank
117

側近 SOKKIN -- close associate, braintruster
149

右側 migigawa -- right hand, right side
384

Typical Conversational Usage:

側面から援助したいと思います。

彼は首相の側近です。

アメリカでは車は道の右側を走ります。

281

居

Graphically-Phonetically Related Morphographs:

Occurrences/1000 .87
Frequency Rank 281
Sanseido Page 297
Nelson Page 343

ON: KYO

kun: i(ru)

Basic Meaning(s): be, stay, live, residence

High Frequency Compounds:

住居 JUUKYO -- dwelling, residence, address
377

別居 BEKKYO -- separation, limited divorce
227

居間 ima -- living room, private room
31

鳥居 torii -- Shinto gateway
852

Typical Phrases and Expanded Compounds:

住居が定まる
別居生活
広い居間
大きな鳥居
家に居る

Typical Conversational Usage:

彼の住居はまだ定まりません。
彼女は御主人と長い間別居しています。
居間が少し狭すぎます。
明治神宮の鳥居はとても大きいです。
一男君は家に居るかどうかわかりません。

282 北

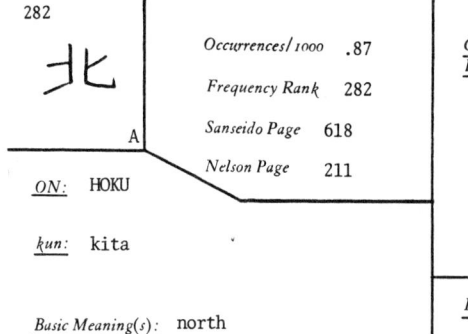

Occurrences/1000 .87
Frequency Rank 282
Sanseido Page 618
Nelson Page 211

A

ON: HOKU

kun: kita

Basic Meaning(s): north

Graphically-Phonetically Related Morphographs:

Typical Phrases and Expanded Compounds:

敗北の原因
北海道旅行
東北地方
東西南北
北極探検
北風

High Frequency Compounds:

敗北 HAIBOKU -- defeat, reversal, rout
420

北海道 HOKKAIDOO -- Hokkaido
206 123

東北 TOOHOKU -- the Northeast, northeast
108

南北 NAMBOKU -- north and south
401

北極 HOKKYOKU -- North Pole
311

Typical Conversational Usage:

今度の試合ではみごとに敗北しました。
夏休みには北海道を旅行する予定です。
松下さんは東北で育ったそうです。
アメリカの南北戦争は有名です。
北極を初めて探検した人は誰ですか。
きのうはつめたい北風が吹きました。

予

283

Occurrences/1000 .87
Frequency Rank 283
Sanseido Page 203
Nelson Page 104

ON: YO

kun:

Basic Meaning(s): beforehand, in advance, previous

Graphically-Phonetically Related Morphographs:

預 YO (1300)

High Frequency Compounds:

予算 (499) YOSAN -- estimate, appropriation, budget

予想 (197) YOSOO -- forcast, estimate, anticipation

予言 (44) YOGEN -- prediction, prophecy

予定 (93) YOTEI -- prearrangement, plan, expectation

予報 (310) YOHOO -- forecast, prediction, prior notification

Typical Phrases and Expanded Compounds:

国家予算
予想外に
予言者
予定通り
天気予報

Typical Conversational Usage:

今月はそれを買う予算がありません。
全然予想がつきません。
よく予言する人がいます。
飛行機は予定通り着きました。
あしたの天気予報を聞きましたか。

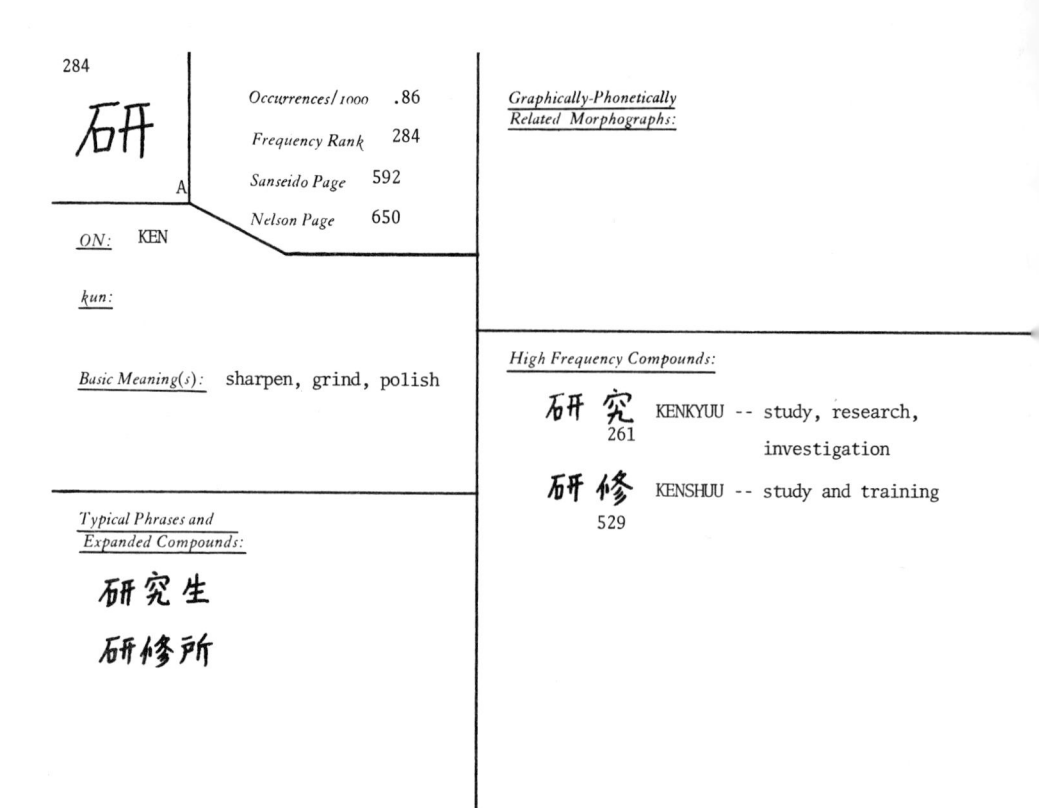

284

研 A

Occurrences/1000 .86
Frequency Rank 284
Sanseido Page 592
Nelson Page 650

ON: KEN

kun:

Basic Meaning(s): sharpen, grind, polish

Graphically-Phonetically Related Morphographs:

High Frequency Compounds:

研究　KENKYUU -- study, research, investigation
261

研修　KENSHUU -- study and training
529

Typical Phrases and Expanded Compounds:

研究生
研修所

Typical Conversational Usage:

研究がまだ足りません。
今外交官の研修を受けています。

能

285

Graphically-Phonetically Related Morphographs:

Occurrences/1000 .86
Frequency Rank 285
Sanseido Page 202
Nelson Page 236

ON: NOO

kun:

Basic Meaning(s): ability, talent, skill, Noh play

High Frequency Compounds:

可能 KANOO -- possibility
463

能力 NOORYOKU -- ability, faculty, capability
38

才能 SAINOO -- talent, ability
885

機能 KINOO -- faculty, function, process
158

Typical Phrases and Expanded Compounds:

可能性がある
学生の能力
語学の才能
機能障害

Typical Conversational Usage:

試合に勝つ可能性は十分にあります。
あの選手にはまだまだ伸びる能力があります。
あの子は生れつき音楽の才能があります。
心臓の機能が弱っています。

286 派

Occurrences/1000: .86
Frequency Rank: 286
Sanseido Page: 402
Nelson Page: 545

ON: HA

kun:

Basic Meaning(s): group, party, sect, school

Graphically-Phonetically Related Morphographs:

High Frequency Compounds:

立派 (35) RIPPA -- fine, excellent, honorable

左派 (374) SAHA -- left wing, left faction, leftist

右派 (384) UHA -- right wing, right faction, rightist

派遣 HAKEN -- send, dispatch

Typical Phrases and Expanded Compounds:

立派な青年
左派の動向
右派系
外国に派遣する

Typical Conversational Usage:

彼女は立派な演技を見せてくれました。
新聞で左派の動向がきびしく非難されました。
社会党の右派と左派が対立しました。
北野さんは会社から香港に派遣されました。

287 衛

Graphically-Phonetically Related Morphographs:

Occurrences/1000 .85
Frequency Rank 287
Sanseido Page 362
Nelson Page 392

ON: EI
kun:

Basic Meaning(s): protection

High Frequency Compounds:

防衛 (326) BOOEI -- defense, protection
自衛 (14) JIEI -- self defense, bodyguard
衛生 (0) EISEI -- health, hygiene, sanitation
守衛 (364) SHUEI -- a guard, watchman, doorkeeper

Typical Phrases and Expanded Compounds:

防衛庁
自衛官
公衆衛生
大学の守衛

Typical Conversational Usage:

あそこは防衛庁です。
今国では自衛官を募集しています。
その件については、衛生局に問い合わせてください。
橋本さんは大学の守衛です。

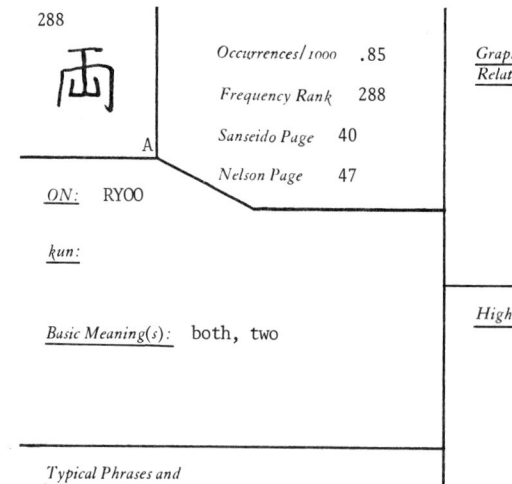

288

両

A

Occurrences/1000   .85
Frequency Rank   288
Sanseido Page   40
Nelson Page   47

ON: RYOO

kun:

Basic Meaning(s):   both, two

Graphically-Phonetically Related Morphographs:

High Frequency Compounds:

両親 RYOOSHIN -- parents, both parents
315

両者 RYOOSHA -- both persons, both things
19

両方 RYOOHOO -- both
25

両手 RYOOte -- both hands
57

Typical Phrases and Expanded Compounds:

両親を失う
両者の間で
両方とも
両手両足

Typical Conversational Usage:

中島君は小さい時、両親を失ったそうです。
両者の間で契約が成立しました。
両方とも悪かったと思います。
小山さんは両手両足をけがしました。

Graphically-Phonetically Related Morphographs:

289

改

Occurrences/1000 .84
Frequency Rank 289
Sanseido Page 301
Nelson Page 355

<u>ON</u>: KAI

<u>kun</u>: arata(meru), arata(maru), arata(me)

Basic Meaning(s): renew, be renewed, reform, mend, improve, change

High Frequency Compounds:

改正 KAISEI -- revision, improvement
139

改革 KAIKAKU -- reform, reformation
487

改良 KAIRYOO -- improvement, reform
479

改善 KAIZEN -- improvement, reform
665

Also: 改進

Typical Phrases and Expanded Compounds:

条約改正
宗教改革
品種の改良
生活改善
改まって
席を改めて

Typical Conversational Usage:

時刻表が改正されました。
きのう学校で宗教改革について学びました。
米の品質が改良されています。
現在の生活を改善しなければなりません。
そんなに改まる必要はありません。
改めて言うまでもありません。

290 開

Occurrences/1000	.84
Frequency Rank	290
Sanseido Page	725
Nelson Page	922

ON: KAI

kun: hira(ku), hira(keru), hira(ki)

Basic Meaning(s): open, opening, development

Typical Phrases and Expanded Compounds:

開始時間
未開発地域
局面の展開
開放的
公開討論会
会を開く

Graphically-Phonetically Related Morphographs:

High Frequency Compounds:

開始 (321) KAISHI -- commencement, inauguration

開発 (102) KAIHATSU -- development, enlightenment, colonization

展開 (443) TENKAI -- unfold, develop, evolve

開放 (325) KAIHOO -- open, throw open, leave open

公開 (212) KOOKAI -- open to the public

Typical Conversational Usage:

何時に授業が開始されますか。
この辺はまだよく開発されていません。
政局はどんな方向に展開していますか。
彼女は開放的です。
きのう国宝が公開されました。
今度はいつ会議を開きますか。

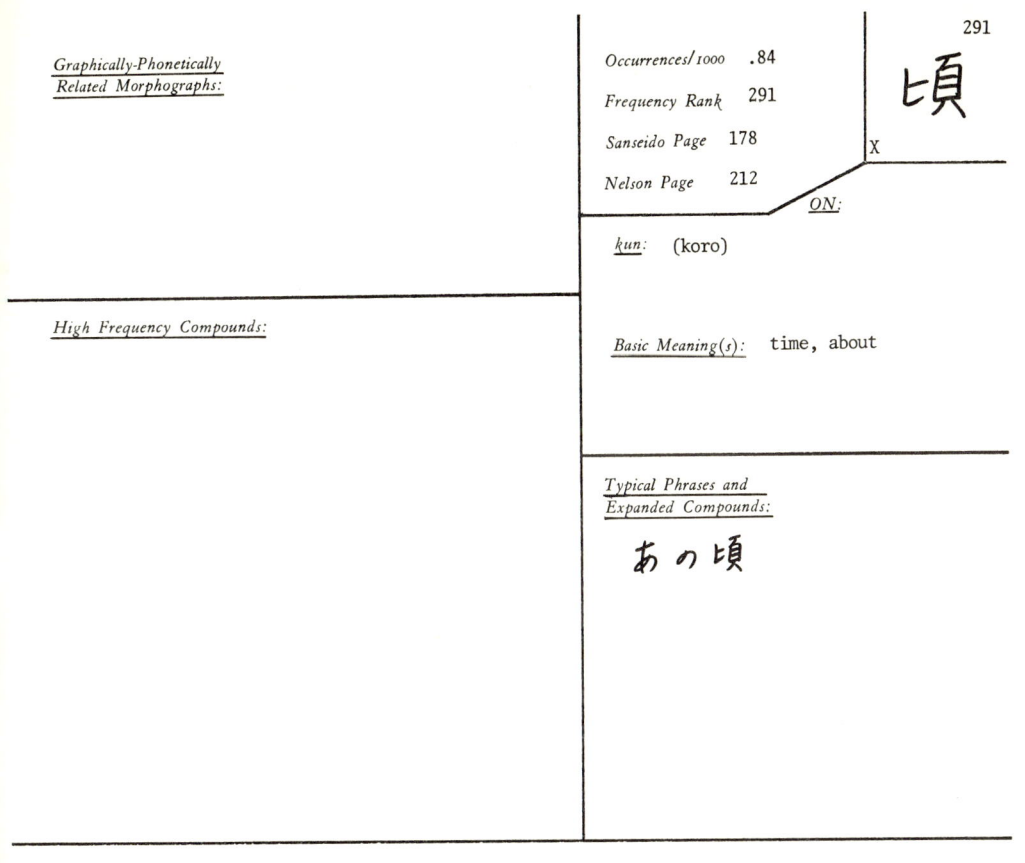

Graphically-Phonetically Related Morphographs:	*Occurrences/1000* .84 *Frequency Rank* 291 *Sanseido Page* 178 *Nelson Page* 212	291 頃 X
	ON:	
	kun: (koro)	
High Frequency Compounds:	*Basic Meaning(s):* time, about	
	Typical Phrases and Expanded Compounds: あの頃	

Typical Conversational Usage:

学生の頃、よく旅行しました。

292

指
A

Occurrences/1000   .84
Frequency Rank   292
Sanseido Page   383
Nelson Page   436

<u>ON</u>:   SHI

<u>kun</u>:   yubi

Basic Meaning(s):   finger

Graphically-Phonetically Related Morphographs:

High Frequency Compounds:

指導   SHIDOO -- guidance, leadership
501

指摘   SHITEKI -- pointing out, indication
874

指揮   SHIKI -- command, supervision, instructions

指示   SHIJI -- indication, instructions, directions
465

Typical Phrases and Expanded Compounds:

指導者
間違いを指摘する
楽団の指揮
先生の指示に従って
指をけがする

Typical Conversational Usage:

ピアノを母に指導してもらっています。
間違いがあったら、指摘してください。
みんなの指揮をとってください。
よく先生の指示に従わなければいけません。
指先がいたみます。

293

勢

Occurrences/1000 .84
Frequency Rank 293
Sanseido Page 251
Nelson Page 209

A

ON: SEI

kun: ikio(i)

Basic Meaning(s): energy, strength, force, power, military strength, tendency

Graphically-Phonetically Related Morphographs:

High Frequency Compounds:

勢力 SEIRYOKU -- influence, power, force
38

情勢 JOOSEI -- state of affairs, condition,
183   indication

攻勢 KOOSEI -- offensive, aggression
588

大勢 ooZEI -- crowd, multitude
5

Typical Phrases and Expanded Compounds:

勢力争い
社会情勢
労働攻勢
大勢の人々
勢いが強い

Typical Conversational Usage:

台風の勢力がおとろえました。
情勢が悪化しました。
今度の試合で、相手はかなり攻勢に出ました。
彼女の家族は大勢です。
彼はお酒の勢いであんな事をしたようです。

294

例

Occurrences/1000 .84
Frequency Rank 294
Sanseido Page 127
Nelson Page 149

ON: REI

kun:

Basic Meaning(s): custom, usage, example, illustration

Graphically-Phonetically Related Morphographs:

High Frequency Compounds:

例外 REIGAI -- exception
69

例文 REIBUN -- model sentence
89

例題 REIDAI -- example, exercises (in
51　　　　　　a textbook)

前例 ZENREI -- precedent
53

Typical Phrases and Expanded Compounds:

例外なく
例文に従って
例題にある通り
前例のない
例をあげる

Typical Conversational Usage:

これは例外です。
例文に従って、文を作ってください。
例題をこなすと、よく覚えられます。
それは前例のない事です。
一つ例をあげて下さい。

295

悪

Occurrences/1000 .84
Frequency Rank 295
Sanseido Page 461
Nelson Page 53

ON: AKU
kun: waru(i)

Basic Meaning(s): evil, wrong, vice, wickedness, bad

Graphically-Phonetically Related Morphographs:

High Frequency Compounds:

悪化 AKKA -- worsening, deterioration, aggravation
104

罪悪 ZAIAKU -- crime, sin, vice
645

悪性 AKUSEI -- virulence, vicious, malignancy, pernicious
119

凶悪 KYOOAKU -- atrocious, brutal, fiendish

Typical Phrases and Expanded Compounds:

病状が悪化する
罪悪感
悪性のかぜ
凶悪犯罪
気持が悪い

Typical Conversational Usage:

事態が悪化しました。
彼等には罪悪感が全くないようです。
今悪性のかぜがはやっています。
殺人は凶悪犯罪です。
悪い遊びをしてはいけません。

296 僕

Occurrences/1000: .84
Frequency Rank: 296
Sanseido Page: 142
Nelson Page: 164

ON: BOKU

kun:

Basic Meaning(s): first person personal pronoun for men and boys "I", manservant, servant (of God)

Graphically-Phonetically Related Morphographs:

撲 BOKU

High Frequency Compounds:

僕達 BOKUtachi -- we (males)
154

Typical Phrases and Expanded Compounds:

僕達の学校
僕の兄

Typical Conversational Usage:

僕達は去年九州を旅行しました。
それは僕の本です。

求

Occurrences/1000 .83
Frequency Rank 297
Sanseido Page 42
Nelson Page 77

ON: KYUU
kun: moto(meru), moto(me)

Graphically-Phonetically Related Morphographs:

High Frequency Compounds:

探求 (871) TANKYUU -- quest, pursuit, research

求人 (2) KYUUJIN -- help wanted

要求 (78) YOOKYUU -- request, demand, requirement

追求 (547) TSUIKYUU -- pursue, follow up, seek for

Basic Meaning(s):

Typical Phrases and Expanded Compounds:

物事を探求する
求人広告
要求に応じて
原因を追求する
本を求める

Typical Conversational Usage:

その原理を探求しなければなりません。
会社で求人の広告を出しました。
組合側の要求が通りました。
事故の原因を追求しています。
今度の会議の出席を求められました。

298 受

Occurrences/1000: .83
Frequency Rank: 298
Sanseido Page: 543
Nelson Page: 589

ON: JU

kun: u(keru), u(karu), u(ke)

Basic Meaning(s): receive, accept, take, answer, undergo, pass

Graphically-Phonetically Related Morphographs:

High Frequency Compounds:

受験 385 — JUKEN -- take an examination

受諾 — JUDAKU -- acceptance

受付 792 — uketsuke -- receptionist, information, receipt

受取 194 — uketori -- receipt, acknowledgment

Typical Phrases and Expanded Compounds:

受験勉強
申し出を受諾する
受付係
受取証
試験を受ける
試験に受かる

Typical Conversational Usage:

兄は夜遅くまで受験勉強をしています。
山村氏はその申し出を受諾しました。
受付でおたずね下さい。
これは、昨日買った品物の受取書です。
彼女は大学まで教育を受けました。
入社試験に受かりました。

Graphically-Phonetically Related Morphographs:

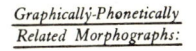

Occurrences/1000	.83
Frequency Rank	299
Sanseido Page	241
Nelson Page	270

声 299

A

<u>ON</u>: SEI

<u>kun</u>: koe

High Frequency Compounds:

声明 (152) SEIMEI -- declaration, statement, proclamation

名声 (140) MEISEI -- fame, reputation

声楽 (481) SEIGAKU -- vocal music

歌声 (486) utagoe -- singing, singing voice

大声 (5) oogoe -- loud voice

Basic Meaning(s): voice, tone, cry, song (birds)

Typical Phrases and Expanded Compounds:

共同声明
名声を博する
声楽家
歌声が聞こえる
大声でさけぶ

Typical Conversational Usage:

両国代表は共同声明を発表しました。
音楽家として、彼は世界的名声を博しています。
今彼女は声楽を勉強しています。
となりの部屋から美しい歌声が聞こえました。
大声で話してはいけません。

300

史

A

Occurrences/1000 .82
Frequency Rank 300
Sanseido Page 230
Nelson Page 60

ON: SHI

kun:

Basic Meaning(s): history, chronicles, historian, book

Typical Phrases and Expanded Compounds:

歴史上

沢村女史

史上まれな

史料に基づいて

史跡に富んでいる

Graphically-Phonetically Related Morphographs:

High Frequency Compounds:

歴史 387   REKISHI -- history

女史 60   JOSHI -- Mrs., Miss, Madame

史上 29   SHIJOO -- historical, in history

史料 395   SHIRYOO -- historical records

史跡 1145   SHISEKI -- historical landmark

Typical Conversational Usage:

この大学は歴史がまだ浅いです。

あの方は沢村女史です。

それは史上まれな出来事です。

江戸時代の史料に基づいて、論文を書きました。

私は史跡を訪れるのが大好きです。

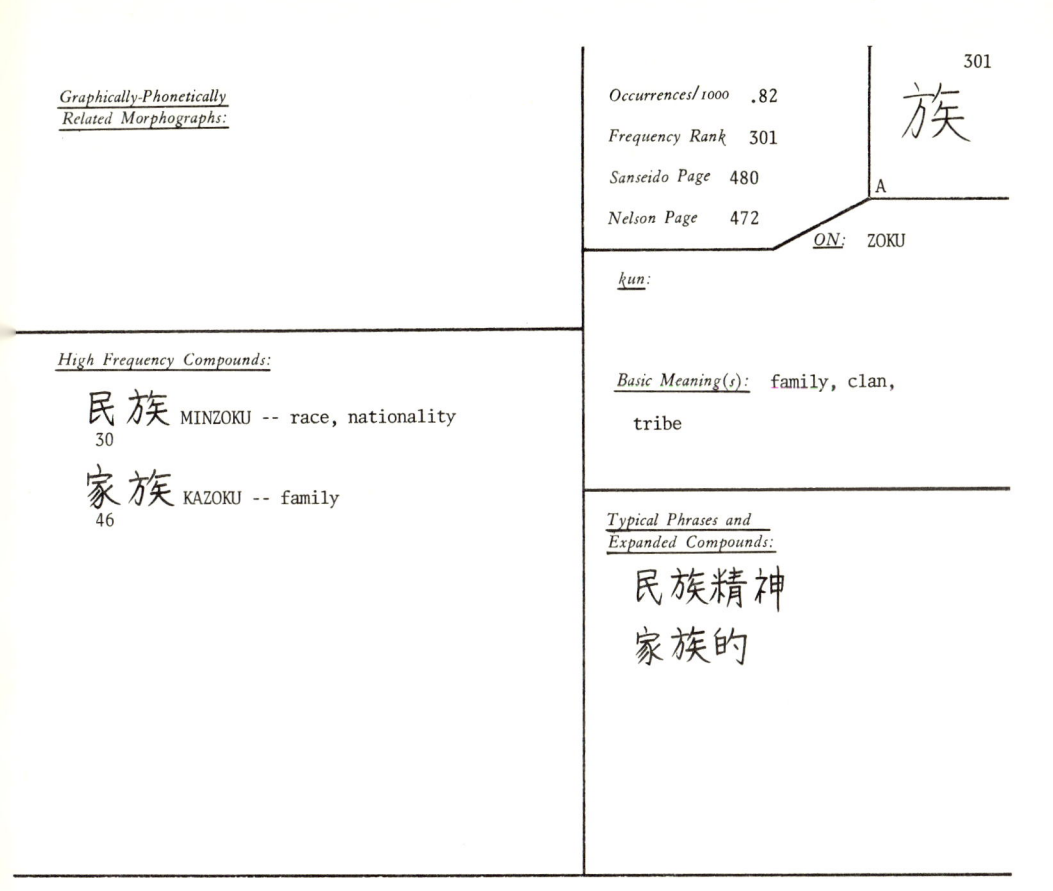

Graphically-Phonetically Related Morphographs:

High Frequency Compounds:

民族 MINZOKU -- race, nationality
30
家族 KAZOKU -- family
46

	301
Occurrences/1000 .82	族
Frequency Rank 301	
Sanseido Page 480	A
Nelson Page 472	
	ON: ZOKU
kun:	

Basic Meaning(s): family, clan, tribe

Typical Phrases and Expanded Compounds:

民族精神
家族的

Typical Conversational Usage:

アイヌ民族の大部分は北海道に住んでいます。
家族は全部で八人です。

302

観

A

Occurrences/1000 .81
Frequency Rank 302
Sanseido Page 762
Nelson Page 818

ON: KAN

kun:

Basic Meaning(s): look, appearance, view, outlook

Typical Phrases and Expanded Compounds:

経済観念
動物の観察
観光旅行
客観的な見方

Graphically-Phonetically Related Morphographs:

勧 KAN (1076)
歓 KAN (1259)

High Frequency Compounds:

観念 KANNEN -- idea, meditation, conviction
333

観察 KANSATSU -- observation, survey
492

観光 KANKOO -- sightseeing
345

客観 KYAKKAN -- the object
606

Typical Conversational Usage:

あの人には、経済観念が少しもありません。
何を観察していますか。
父は日光へ観光旅行に出かけました。
客観的に物事を考えてみてください。

京 303

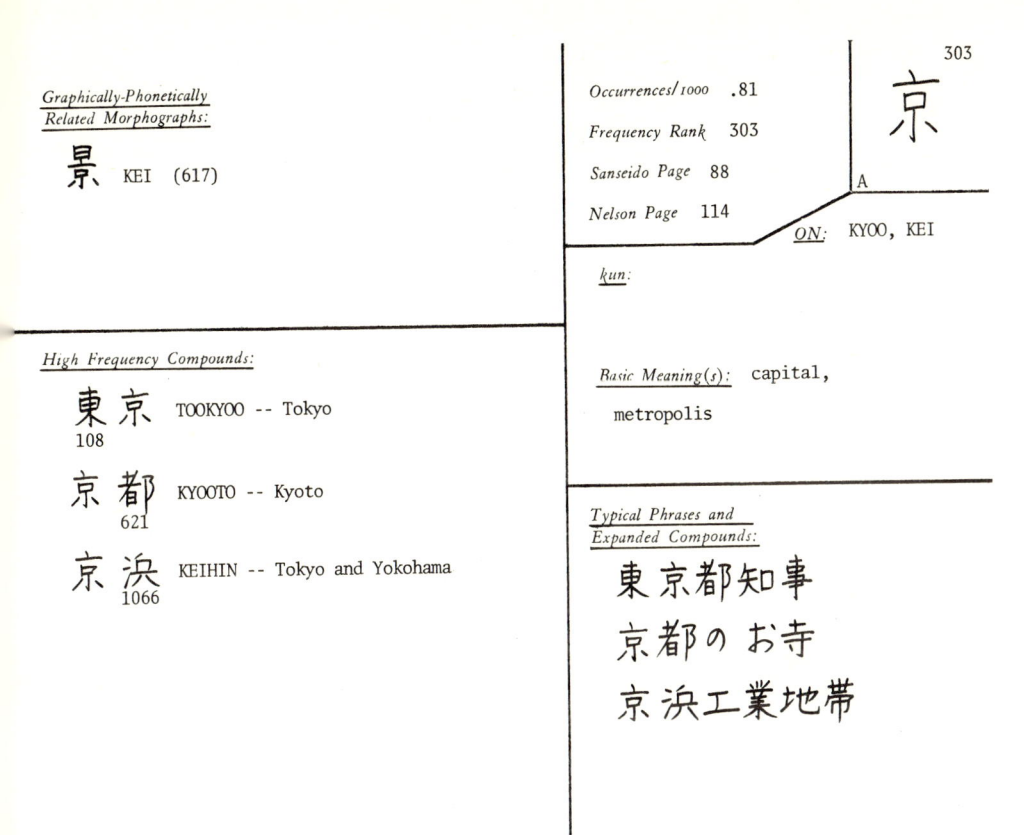

Occurrences/1000 .81
Frequency Rank 303
Sanseido Page 88
Nelson Page 114

ON: KYOO, KEI
kun:

Basic Meaning(s): capital, metropolis

Graphically-Phonetically Related Morphographs:

景 KEI (617)

High Frequency Compounds:

東京 TOOKYOO -- Tokyo
108

京都 KYOOTO -- Kyoto
621

京浜 KEIHIN -- Tokyo and Yokohama
1066

Typical Phrases and Expanded Compounds:

東京都知事
京都のお寺
京浜工業地帯

Typical Conversational Usage:

東京に行って、友人に会いました。
京都は日本の代表的な観光都市です。
京浜工業地帯には、工場がたくさんあります。

304

空

Occurrences/1000: .81
Frequency Rank: 304
Sanseido Page: 282
Nelson Page: 672

ON: KUU

kun: sora

Basic Meaning(s): sky, air, emptiness

Typical Phrases and Expanded Compounds:

米国空軍
空気の圧力
空想家
すみきった青空

Graphically-Phonetically Related Morphographs:

High Frequency Compounds:

空軍 KUUGUN -- air force
36

空気 KUUKI -- air, atmosphere
55

空想 KUUSOO -- daydream, imagination
197

青空 aozora -- blue sky
393

Typical Conversational Usage:

きのう米国空軍のパレードを見ました。
少しタイヤの空気が足りないようです。
弟はとてつもない空想家です。
ハワイの青空はとてもきれいです。

Graphically-Phonetically Related Morphographs:

Occurrences/1000 .81	305
Frequency Rank 305	市
Sanseido Page 83	
Nelson Page 110	A

ON: SHI
kun: ichi

High Frequency Compounds:

市場 ichiba, SHIJOO -- market
49

都市 TOSHI -- cities, towns and cities
621

市民 SHIMIN -- citizens, townspeople
30

Basic Meaning(s): city, town
market

Typical Phrases and Expanded Compounds:

市の衛生局
青果市場
都市計画
善良な市民

Typical Conversational Usage:

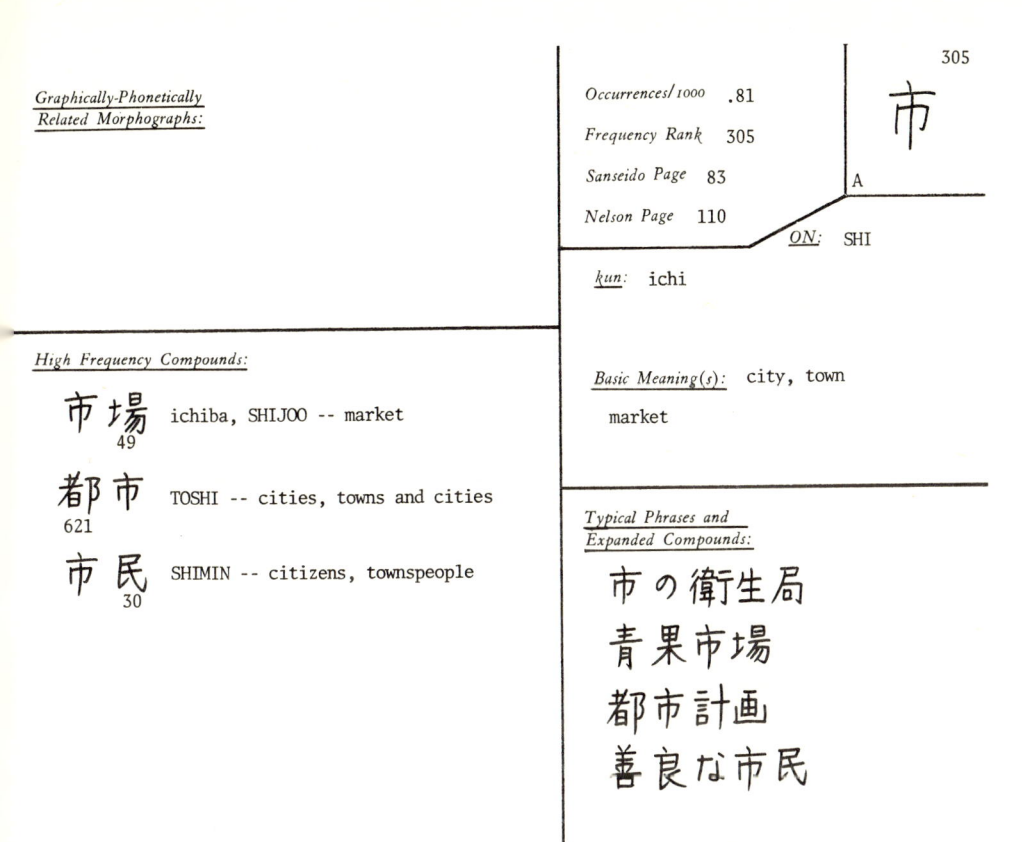

四日市はいつ市になりましたか。
東京の青果市場を見学しました。
大都市では商工業がさかんです。
三年たったら、アメリカの市民権を取るつもりです。

306

形　A

Occurrences/1000　.81
Frequency Rank　306
Sanseido Page　555
Nelson Page　380

ON: KEI, GYOO

kun: katachi, kata

Basic Meaning(s): shape, form, pattern

Typical Phrases and Expanded Compounds:

形式的なもの
京人形
人間形成
いい形

Graphically-Phonetically Related Morphographs:

High Frequency Compounds:

形式　KEISHIKI -- form, formality
356

人形　NINGYOO -- doll, puppet
 2

形成　KEISEI -- formation
160

Typical Conversational Usage:

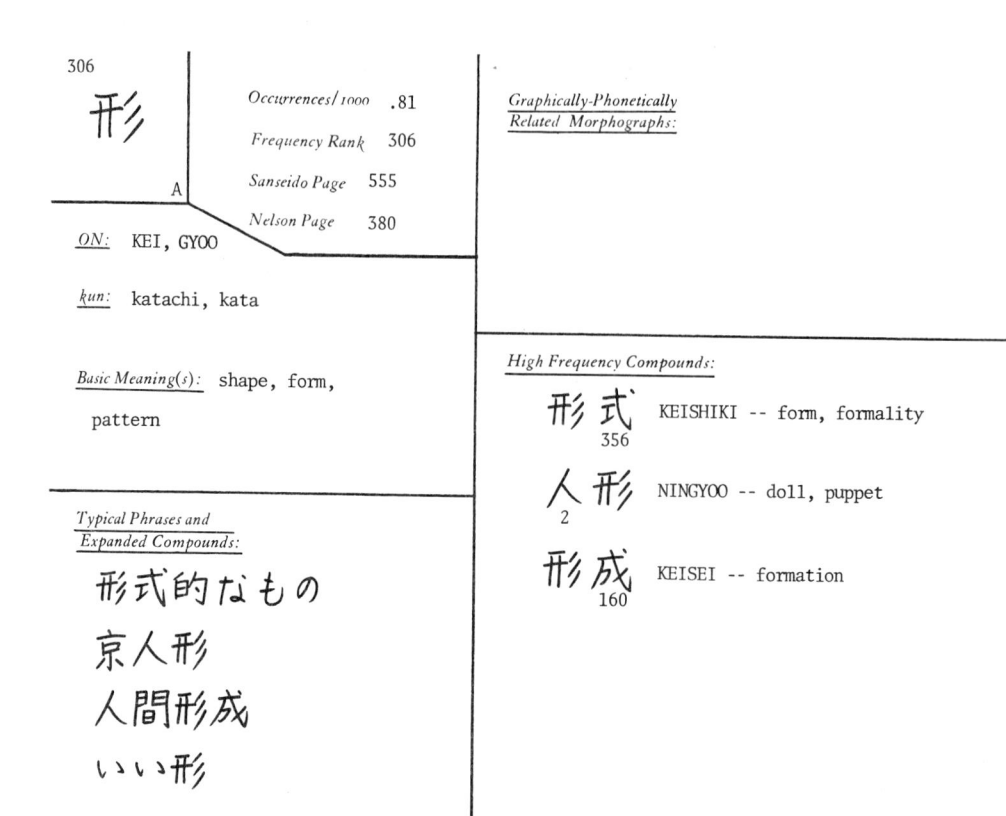

あまり形式にとらわれない方がいいと思います。
今度京都へ行った時、京人形を求めるつもりです。
このチームは二十八人で形成されています。
これは形のいい石です。

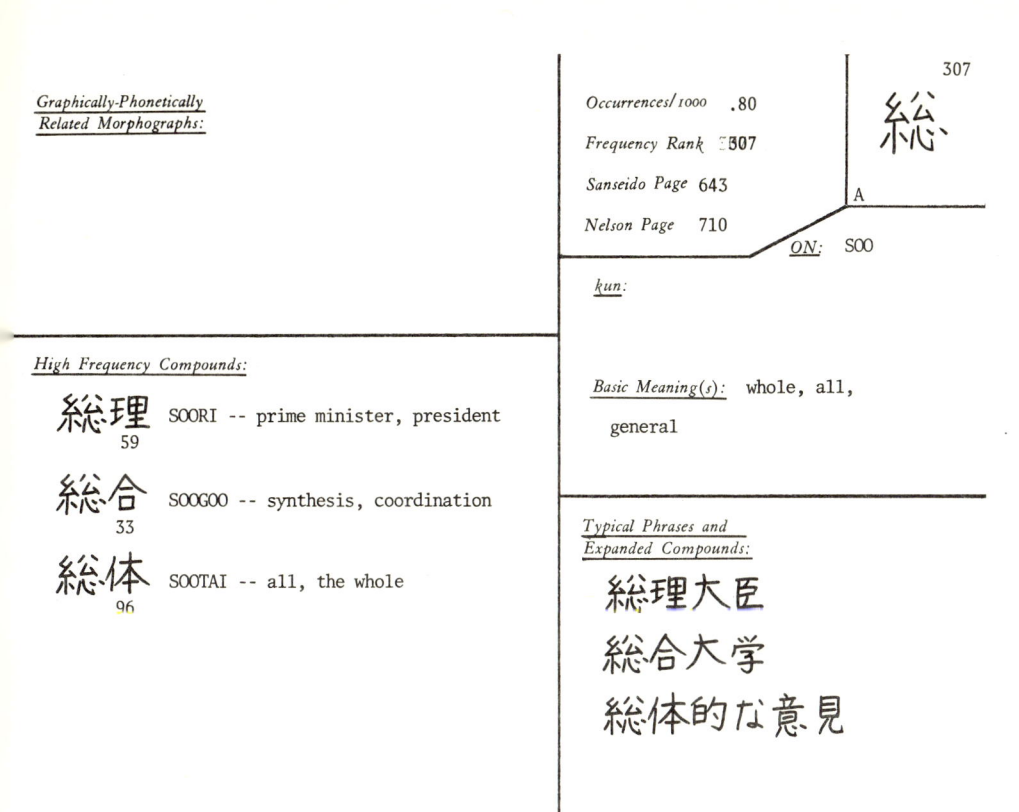

Graphically-Phonetically Related Morphographs:

Occurrences/1000 .80	307
Frequency Rank 307	総
Sanseido Page 643	
Nelson Page 710	A
	ON: SOO
	kun:

Basic Meaning(s): whole, all, general

High Frequency Compounds:

総理 SOORI -- prime minister, president
59

総合 SOOGOO -- synthesis, coordination
33

総体 SOOTAI -- all, the whole
96

Typical Phrases and Expanded Compounds:

総理大臣
総合大学
総体的な意見

Typical Conversational Usage:

吉田茂は立派な総理大臣だったと思います。
東京大学は総合大学です。
総体的な意見をまとめてください。

308 配

Occurrences/1000 .80
Frequency Rank 308
Sanseido Page 705
Nelson Page 899

A

_ON_: HAI

kun: kuba(ru)

Basic Meaning(s): distribute, allot, spouse

Graphically-Phonetically Related Morphographs:

High Frequency Compounds:

支配   SHIHAI -- management, control
185

心配   SHIMPAI -- anxiety, worry, care
64

配給   HAIKYUU -- distribution, rationing
404

Typical Phrases and Expanded Compounds:

支配力
心配事
お米の配給
新聞を配る

Typical Conversational Usage:

昔、ローマはいろいろな国を支配していました。
何も心配はいりません。
日本ではお米の配給があります。
そんなに気を配らなくても結構です。

Graphically-Phonetically Related Morphographs:

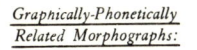

Occurrences/1000	.80
Frequency Rank	309
Sanseido Page	508
Nelson Page	588

爆 309

B

ON: BAKU

kun:

Basic Meaning(s): burst open, pop, split

High Frequency Compounds:

原爆 113 — GEMBAKU -- atom bomb
爆撃 407 — BAKUGEKI -- bombing
爆発 102 — BAKUHATSU -- explosion, blasting
爆弾 705 — BAKUDAN -- bomb

See 166

Typical Phrases and Expanded Compounds:

原爆の実験
爆撃機
火山の爆発
爆弾を落とす

Typical Conversational Usage:

この前、原爆の実験が中国で行われたようです。
この町は戦争中、爆撃を受けたことがありますか。
三原山がまた爆発しました。
戦争中、この辺に爆弾が落ちたそうです。

310 報

Occurrences/1000 .80
Frequency Rank 310
Sanseido Page 251
Nelson Page 276

A

ON: HOO

kun: muku(iru), muku(i)

Basic Meaning(s): news, report, reward

Graphically-Phonetically Related Morphographs:

High Frequency Compounds:

報告 HOOKOKU -- report, information
398

報道 HOODOO -- news, report
123

電報 DEMPOO -- telegram
332

See 283

Typical Phrases and Expanded Compounds:

近況報告
報道機関
至急電報
恩に報いる

Typical Conversational Usage:

研究の結果を報告しました。
重大ニュースが報道されました。
この電報を打ってください。
親の恩に報いたいと思います。

Graphically-Phonetically Related Morphographs:

Occurrences/1000 .80
Frequency Rank 311
Sanseido Page 525
Nelson Page 506

極 311

A

ON: KYOKU, GOKU

kun:

Basic Meaning(s): end, the poles, highest rank, extremely

High Frequency Compounds:

積極 SEKKYOKU -- the positive
1056

極東 KYOKUTOO -- the Far East
108

極限 KYOKUGEN -- limit, extremity
370

See 282

Typical Phrases and Expanded Compounds:

積極的な態度
極東問題
極限に達する
極わずか

Typical Conversational Usage:

前田さんは大変積極的な方です。
日本は極東で重要な役割を果しています。
もう極限に達しました。
極わずかで結構です。

312 置

A

Occurrences/1000: .80
Frequency Rank: 312
Sanseido Page: 585
Nelson Page: 719

ON: CHI

kun: o(ku)

Basic Meaning(s): place, put, set

Graphically-Phonetically Related Morphographs:

值 CHI (828)

High Frequency Compounds:

措置 SOCHI -- measure, action
975

位置 ICHI -- situation, position, location
319

置物 okimono -- ornament for display
95

Typical Phrases and Expanded Compounds:

寛大な措置
適当な位置
きれいな置物
本を置いた所

Typical Conversational Usage:

どんな措置をとったらよろしいでしょうか。
学校の位置は町の南の方です。
この置物は石でできています。
ペンは本を置いた所にあります。

売 313

Graphically-Phonetically Related Morphographs:

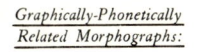

Occurrences/1000	.79
Frequency Rank	313
Sanseido Page	242
Nelson Page	270

ON: BAI

kun: u(ru), u(reru), u(ri)

Basic Meaning(s): sell, selling, betray

High Frequency Compounds:

商売 SHOOBAI -- trade, business
375

販売 HAMBAI -- sale, selling
1121

読売 yomiuri -- Yomiuri Newspaper
323

Typical Phrases and Expanded Compounds:

商売道具
教科書の販売
読売新聞
千円で売る
品物の売れ行き

Typical Conversational Usage:

商売があまり思わしくありません。
あそこで今教科書の販売をしています。
家では朝日新聞と読売新聞をとっています。
あの車を二十万円で売りました。
友人の佐々木さんは名前がよく売れています。

314

望

A

ON: BOO, MOO

kun: nozo(mu), nozo(mi), nozo(mashii)

Basic Meaning(s): hope, desire, aspire to, desirable

Occurrences/1000 .79
Frequency Rank 314
Sanseido Page 242
Nelson Page 609

Graphically-Phonetically Related Morphographs:

亡 BOO (795)   盲 MOO (1347)
忙 BOO (1411)   網 MOO (1091)
忘 BOO (726)

High Frequency Compounds:

希望 KIBOO -- hope
816

失望 SHITSUBOO -- disappointment,
346   despair

要望 YOOBOO -- demand, longing for
78

欲望 YOKUBOO -- desire, ambition
1043

See 366

Typical Phrases and Expanded Compounds:

希望通り
失望せずに
要望に応えて
欲望を満たす
望んでいる所

Typical Conversational Usage:

何とか御希望にそいたいと思います。
妹は大学の入試に落ちて失望しています。
先方からどんな要望がありましたか。
人間の欲望には限りがありません。
将来、医者になることを望んでいます。

親 315

Occurrences/1000 .78
Frequency Rank 315
Sanseido Page 612
Nelson Page 816

A

ON: SHIN

kun: oya, shita(shimu), shita(shimi), shita(shii)

Basic Meaning(s): intimacy, familiar, friendly, parent

Graphically-Phonetically Related Morphographs:

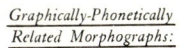

新 SHIN (80)
薪 SHIN

High Frequency Compounds:

親切 SHINSETSU -- kindness
 208

両親 RYOOSHIN -- parents
 288

親子 oyako -- parent(s) and child,
 42   chicken and eggs (over rice)

Typical Phrases and Expanded Compounds:

親切な人
両親のおかげ
親子の関係
親しい間柄

Typical Conversational Usage:

見知らぬ人に、親切に道を教えていただきました。
両親は今ヨーロッパを旅行しています。
お昼に親子丼を食べました。
大山さんは私の親しい友人です。

316 風

Occurrences/1000 .78
Frequency Rank 316
Sanseido Page 162
Nelson Page 960

A

ON: HUU

kun: kaze

Basic Meaning(s): wind, air

Graphically-Phonetically Related Morphographs:

High Frequency Compounds:

風景 HUUKEI -- landscape, scenery
617

台風 TAIHUU -- typhoon
436

風呂 HURO -- bath, bathtub

Typical Phrases and Expanded Compounds:

美しい風景
台風の影響
ぬるい風呂
からっ風

Typical Conversational Usage:

私は風景画が好きなので、よく外で写生します。
今度の台風は大分大きいようです。
お風呂は熱いのよりぬるい方が好きです。
きのうは風が強かったので、畑が荒されました。

Graphically-Phonetically Related Morphographs:

Occurrences/1000 .78	317
Frequency Rank 317	母
Sanseido Page 622	
Nelson Page 525	A
	ON: BO
	kun: haha

Basic Meaning(s): mother

High Frequency Compounds:

母体 BOTAI -- mother's body, parent organization
96

母国語 BOKOKUGO -- mother tongue
4 211

叔母 oba -- aunt

母親 hahaoya -- mother
315

Typical Phrases and Expanded Compounds:

健全な母体
母国語で話す
叔母さんの家
母親の責任

Typical Conversational Usage:

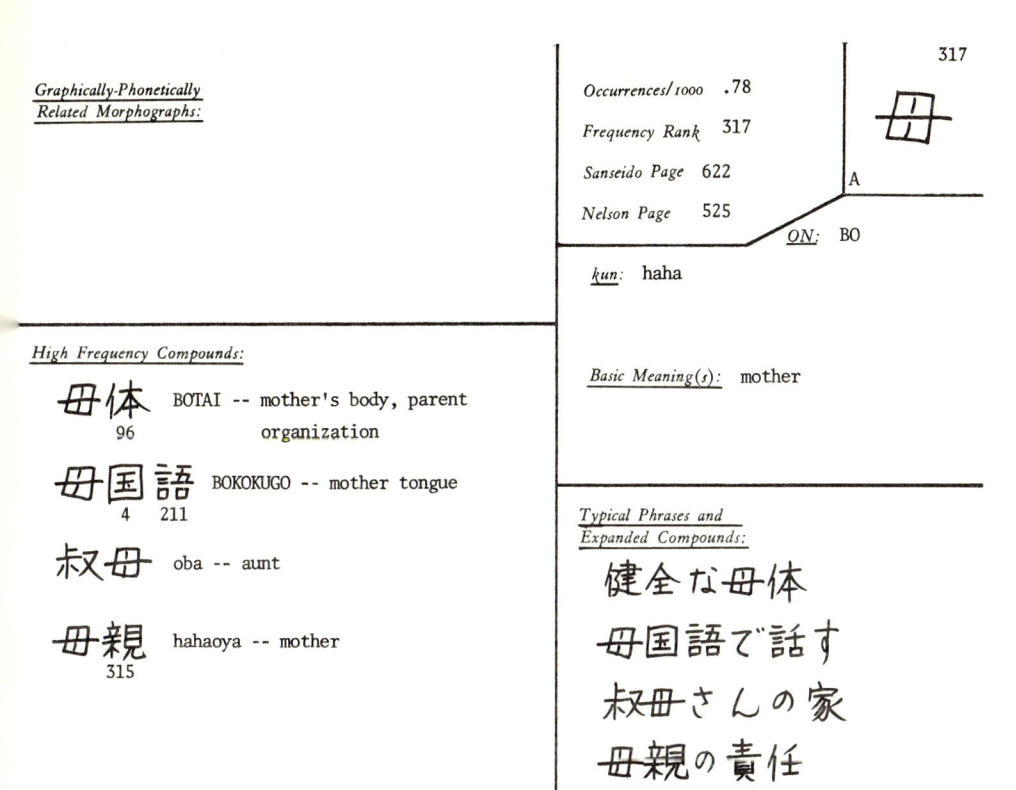

団体の母体がしっかりしていれば大丈夫です。
私の母国語は日本語です。
叔母さんの家はそんなに遠くありません。
私は二十二才の時、母親になりました。

318 夜

Occurrences/1000: .78
Frequency Rank: 318
Sanseido Page: 89
Nelson Page: 115

A

<u>ON</u>: YA

<u>kun</u>: yo, yoru

Basic Meaning(s): night, evening, night time

Graphically-Phonetically Related Morphographs:

High Frequency Compounds:

今夜 (50) KON'YA -- tonight

夜学 (15) YAGAKU -- night school, night classes

夜中 (12) yonaka -- midnight

Typical Phrases and Expanded Compounds:

今夜のテレビ番組
夜学の勉強
夜中の二時頃
夜遅くまで

Typical Conversational Usage:

叔父は今夜の飛行機で帰って来ます。
山田さんは夜学に通っています。
きのうは夜中まで仕事をしました。
いつも夜何時頃まで起きていますか。

位 319

Graphically-Phonetically Related Morphographs:

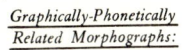

Occurrences/1000 .77
Frequency Rank 319
Sanseido Page 120
Nelson Page 142

ON: I

kun: kurai

Basic Meaning(s): rank, place, grade, dignity

High Frequency Compounds:

地位 CHII -- position, status, post
45

位置 ICHI -- situation, position
312

単位 TAN'I -- unit, credit (in school)
348

Typical Phrases and Expanded Compounds:

いい地位
位置を変える
科目の単位
位のある人

Typical Conversational Usage:

彼はかなりいい地位にいます。
机の位置が悪いので、なおしましょう。
化学は何単位ですか。
防衛庁で、山本氏は位が大分上の方です。

320

古

A

Occurrences/1000 .77
Frequency Rank 320
Sanseido Page 182
Nelson Page 215

ON: KO

kun: huru(i)

Basic Meaning(s): old, aged, ancient

Graphically-Phonetically Related Morphographs:

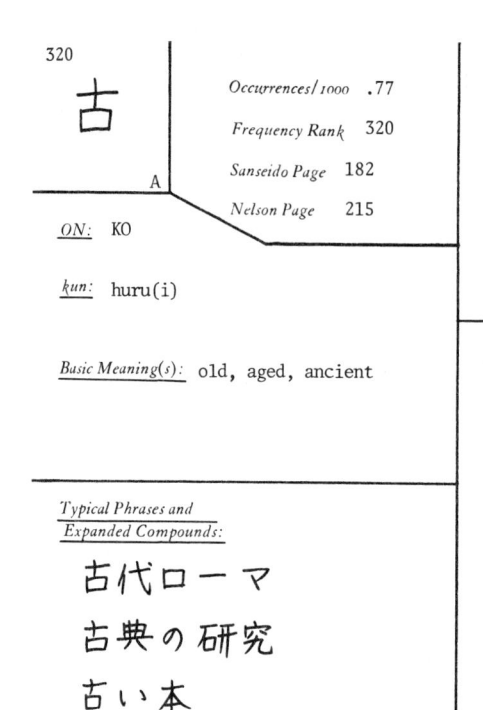

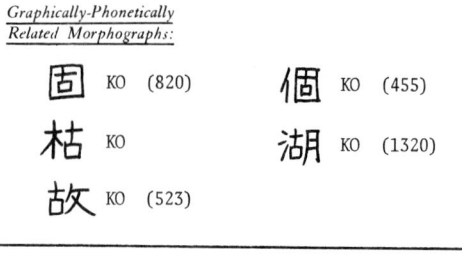

固 KO (820)   個 KO (455)
枯 KO   湖 KO (1320)
故 KO (523)

High Frequency Compounds:

古代 KODAI -- ancient times
87
古典 KOTEN -- old book, classics
1011

Typical Phrases and Expanded Compounds:

古代ローマ
古典の研究
古い本
古びた建物

Typical Conversational Usage:

古代ギリシャについて、研究しています。
古典を読むのが好きです。
その考えはもう古いです。
あの建物は古びています。

321

始

Occurrences/1000 .77
Frequency Rank 321
Sanseido Page 272
Nelson Page 304

A

ON: SHI

kun: haji(meru), haji(maru)

Graphically-Phonetically Related Morphographs:

High Frequency Compounds:

始末 SHIMATSU -- circumstances, management
531

原始 GENSHI -- origin, primitive
113

開始 KAISHI -- commencement, inauguration
290

See 392

Basic Meaning(s): beginning, begin, start, for the first time

Typical Phrases and Expanded Compounds:

あと始末
原始時代
授業の開始
学校が始まる
会議を始める

Typical Conversational Usage:

始末が悪くて手がつけられません。
原始時代の人間は、どんなものを食べましたか。
授業の開始は毎朝八時です。
いつ学校が始まりますか。
そろそろ会議が始まる時間です。

322

術

A

Occurrences/1000 .77
Frequency Rank 322
Sanseido Page 360
Nelson Page 386

ON: JUTSU

kun:

Basic Meaning(s): art, technique, skill, trick, magic

Typical Phrases and Expanded Compounds:

すぐれた技術
芸術家
学術会議
美術展覧会

Graphically-Phonetically Related Morphographs:

述 JUTSU (631)

High Frequency Compounds:

技術 GIJUTSU -- art, technique, skill
528

芸術 GEIJUTSU -- art, the arts
551

学術 GAKUJUTSU -- science, learning, scholarship
15

美術 BIJUTSU -- art, the fine arts
339

Typical Conversational Usage:

日本の建築の技術はすぐれています。
あしたから大学の芸術祭が始まります。
それは学術的な問題です。
今、東洋の美術を学んでいます。

Graphically-Phonetically Related Morphographs:

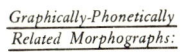

Occurrences/1000 .77	323
Frequency Rank 323	読
Sanseido Page 683	
Nelson Page 833	A

ON: TOKU, DOKU

kun: yo(mu), yo(mi)

Basic Meaning(s): reading, read, understand

High Frequency Compounds:

読本 TOKUHON -- reader, reading book
6

読者 DOKUSHA -- reader, subscriber
19

読書 DOKUSHO -- reading a book
121

Scc 313

Typical Phrases and Expanded Compounds:

英語の読本
愛読者
読書の秋
読みやすい本

Typical Conversational Usage:

本屋で英語の読本を買いました。
私はその本の愛読者です。
今は読書の秋です。
新聞を毎日読みます。

324

半　A

Occurrences/1000　.77
Frequency Rank　324
Sanseido Page　150
Nelson Page　75

ON: HAN

kun: naka(ba)

Basic Meaning(s): half, odd number, semi-, middle, partly

Graphically-Phonetically Related Morphographs:

伴　HAN (930)
判　HAN (187)
畔　HAN

High Frequency Compounds:

半分　HAMBUN -- half
　28

半信半疑　HANSHIN-HANGI --
181　488　dubious, incredulous

Typical Phrases and Expanded Compounds:

半分ずつ
半信半疑で
人生の半ば

Typical Conversational Usage:

仕事は半分できています。
その話を半信半疑で聞きました。
半ばあきらめています。

325 放

Graphically-Phonetically Related Morphographs:

方 HOO (25)　　芳 HOO

傲 HOO

訪 HOO (957)

Occurrences/1000　.77
Frequency Rank　325
Sanseido Page　478
Nelson Page　470

ON: HOO

kun: hana(su), hana(tsu)

High Frequency Compounds:

放棄 1045　HOOKI -- abandonment, resignation

放送 440　HOOSOO -- broadcasting

放射 823　HOOSHA -- emancipation, radiation, discharge

釈放 775　SHAKUHOO -- release, liberation, acquittal

See 290

Basic Meaning(s): set free, release, let go, free oneself from, give up

Typical Phrases and Expanded Compounds:

戦争放棄

野球放送

放射線

手を放す

かおりを放つ

Typical Conversational Usage:

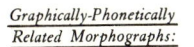

権利を放棄してはいけません。
野球放送は何時から始まりますか。
山田さんは今、放射線治療を受けています。
川上さんはいつ釈放されましたか。
手を放してください。
池にこいを放ちました。

326

防

A

Occurrences/1000 .77
Frequency Rank 326
Sanseido Page 426
Nelson Page 927

ON: BOO

kun: huse(gu), huse(gi)

Basic Meaning(s): defend, protect, resist, keep away

Typical Phrases and Expanded Compounds:

タイトルの防衛
国防長官
盗難の防止
火災を防ぐ

Graphically-Phonetically Related Morphographs:

妨 BOO (1410)
紡 BOO
肪 BOO
坊 BOO (1124)

High Frequency Compounds:

防衛 BOOEI -- defense, protection
287

国防 KOKUBOO -- national defense
4

防止 BOOSHI -- prevention
415

Typical Conversational Usage:

今年兄は防衛大学校に入学しました。
アメリカの国防長官はだれですか。
盗難防止に協力してください。
火災を防がなければなりません。

落

327

Graphically-Phonetically Related Morphographs:

酪 RAKU

絡 RAKU

Occurrences/1000 .77
Frequency Rank 327
Sanseido Page 339
Nelson Page 783

ON: RAKU

kun: o(chiru), o(tosu), o(chi), o(toshi)

Basic Meaning(s): fall, drop, come down, fail, lose

High Frequency Compounds:

部落 (52) BURAKU -- community, settlement, village

落第 (83) RAKUDAI -- failure (in an examination)

落選 (311) RAKUSEN -- election defeat, rejection

Typical Phrases and Expanded Compounds:

部落の行事
落第生
選挙で落選する
木から落ちる
信用を落とす

Typical Conversational Usage:

これは部落の行事です。
落第点をとってはいけません。
上田氏はおしくも今度の選挙で落選しました。
屋根から落ちて、けがをしました。
気を落とさないで、がんばってください。

328 階 A

Occurrences/1000 .76
Frequency Rank 328
Sanseido Page 432
Nelson Page 933

ON: KAI

kun:

Basic Meaning(s): stair, step, story, counter for stories (of a building)

Graphically-Phonetically Related Morphographs:

皆 KAI (780)

High Frequency Compounds:

階級 KAIKYUU -- class, estate, rank
373

段階 DANKAI -- grade, rank, step
425

階段 KAIDAN -- steps, stairway
425

Typical Phrases and Expanded Compounds:

上流階級
現段階において
階段の下

Typical Conversational Usage:

どの社会にも階級闘争があります。
現段階においては、何とも言えません。
出口は階段の右側にあります。

329

従

Graphically-Phonetically Related Morphographs:

縦 JUU (1273)

Occurrences/1000 .76
Frequency Rank 329
Sanseido Page 359
Nelson Page 385

ON: JUU
kun: shitaga(u), shitaga(eru)

High Frequency Compounds:

従来 JUURAI -- heretofore, existing
27

従順 JUUJUN -- submissive, obedient
1028

従業員 JUUGYOOIN -- employee, working force
74 127

従事 JUUJI -- engage in, carry on, practice medicine
10

Basic Meaning(s):

Typical Phrases and Expanded Compounds:

従来の問題
従順な子
従業員組合
仕事に従事する
先生の意見に従って
子どもを従える

Typical Conversational Usage:

私は従来、本を読むことが好きです。
あの子はとても従順な子です。
私はデパートの従業員です。
今、どんな仕事に従事していますか。
親の意見に従って、大学を選びました。
子どもを従えて、学校へ行きました。

330

態

A

Occurrences/1000 .76
Frequency Rank 330
Sanseido Page 465
Nelson Page 407

ON: TAI

kun:

Basic Meaning(s): condition, figure, appearance, voice (of verbs)

Typical Phrases and Expanded Compounds:

立派な態度
今の状態
緊急事態

Graphically-Phonetically Related Morphographs:

High Frequency Compounds:

態度 TAIDO -- attitude, posture, manner
72

状態 JOOTAI -- state of affairs, situation
430

事態 JITAI -- situation, state of affairs
10

Typical Conversational Usage:

あの方の態度はいつも立派です。
今の状態では、そちらへ行くことができません。
緊急事態が発生しました。

331 伝

Graphically-Phonetically Related Morphographs:

Occurrences/1000 .76
Frequency Rank 331
Sanseido Page 118
Nelson Page 135

A

ON: DEN
kun: tsuta(eru), tsuta(waru), tsuta(e)

Basic Meaning(s): legend, tradition, biography, go along, report, be transmitted

High Frequency Compounds:

伝統 (273) DENTOO -- tradition, convention
宣伝 (849) SENDEN -- publicity, propaganda
伝記 (209) DENKI -- biography

Typical Phrases and Expanded Compounds:

学校の伝統
商品の宣伝
伝記物語
話を伝える
うわさが伝わる

Typical Conversational Usage:

この学校には長い伝統があります。
まんまとその宣伝にのってしまいました。
私は伝記物語を読むのが大好きです。
この話を先方に伝えてください。
変なうわさが伝わりました。

332

電
A

Occurrences/1000   .76
Frequency Rank   332
Sanseido Page   732
Nelson Page   943

ON: DEN

kun:

Basic Meaning(s): electricity

Graphically-Phonetically Related Morphographs:

High Frequency Compounds:

電車   DENSHA -- electric car (train)
231   street car

電気   DENKI -- electricity, electric
55   light

電話   DENWA -- telephone
125

電力   DENRYOKU -- electric power,
                electricity

See 310

Typical Phrases and Expanded Compounds:

電車の便
電気料金
電話番号
電力資源

Typical Conversational Usage:

私の家は電車の便がいいです。
電気を消してください。
きのう島田さんと電話で話しました。
日本は電力資源にめぐまれています。

Graphically-Phonetically Related Morphographs:

Occurrences/1000 .76
Frequency Rank 333
Sanseido Page 459
Nelson Page 148

念 333

ON: NEN

kun:

Basic Meaning(s): sense, idea, feeling, desire, concern

High Frequency Compounds:

観念 302 — KANNEN -- meditation, idea, intention

残念 382 — ZANNEN -- regret, disappointment

記念 209 — KI'NEN -- remembrance, commemoration

信念 181 — SHINNEN -- belief, faith, conviction

概念 1258 — GAINEN -- general idea, notion, concept

Typical Phrases and Expanded Compounds:

時間の観念
残念ながら
記念品
固い信念
哲学の概念

Typical Conversational Usage:

彼には時間の観念がありません。
残念ながら、東京へ行くことができません。
これは卒業の記念写真です。
彼は自分の仕事に強い信念を持っています。
「しぶい」という概念について考えてみましょう。

334 与

B

Occurrences/1000: .76
Frequency Rank: 334
Sanseido Page: 19
Nelson Page: 26

<u>ON</u>: YO

<u>kun</u>: ata(eru)

Basic Meaning(s): give, award, provide, allot, cause

Graphically-Phonetically Related Morphographs:

High Frequency Compounds:

給与 KYUUYO -- grant, ration, compensation
404

与党 YOTOO -- party in power
76

Typical Phrases and Expanded Compounds:

給与体系
与党議員
機会を与える

Typical Conversational Usage:

教員の給与水準はどのくらいですか。
与党の間で意見の調整が行われています。
山田さんに会う機会が与えられました。

Graphically-Phonetically Related Morphographs:

Occurrences/1000 .75	335
Frequency Rank 335	千
Sanseido Page 58	
Nelson Page 81	A

ON: SEN

kun: chi

Basic Meaning(s): thousand, many

High Frequency Compounds:

二千 NISEN -- two thousand
11

千差万別 SENSABAMBETSU -- infinite
694 215 227　　　　　　variety

Typical Phrases and Expanded Compounds:

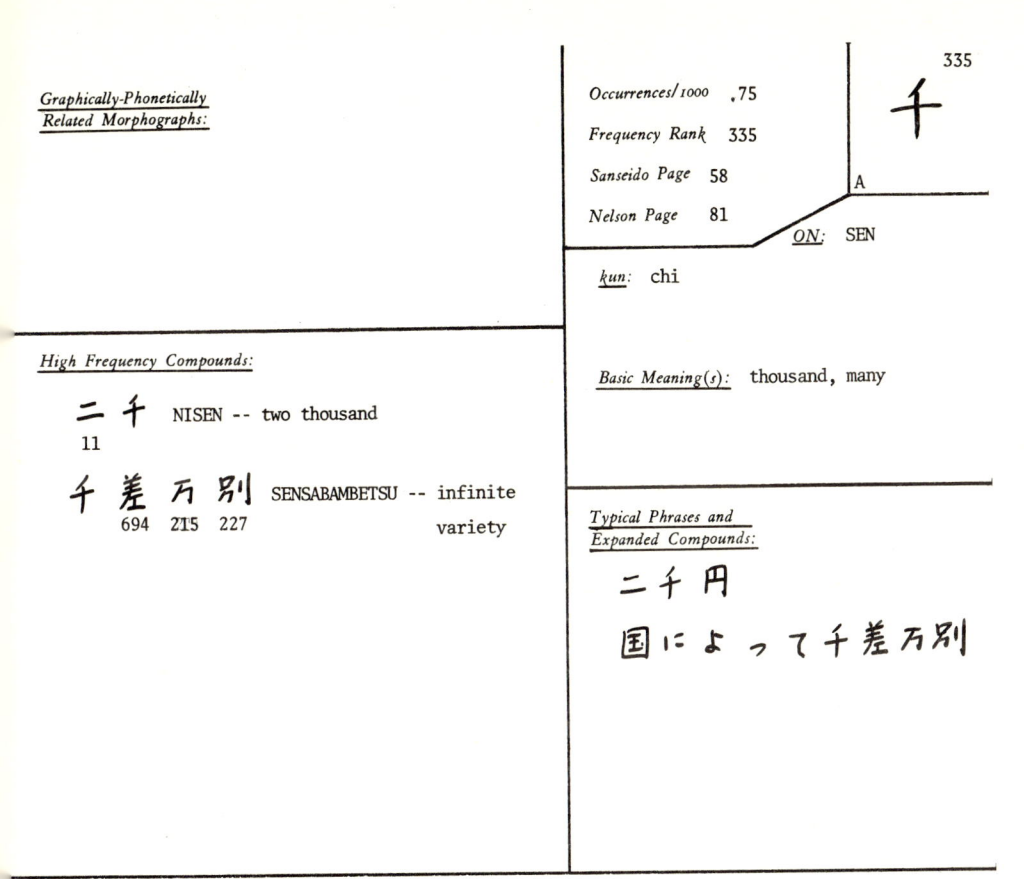

二千円

国によって千差万別

Typical Conversational Usage:

この辞書は二千円で買いました。
生徒は学校によって千差万別です。

336

団 A

Occurrences/1000   .76
Frequency Rank   336
Sanseido Page   235
Nelson Page   258

ON: DAN

kun:

Basic Meaning(s): body, group, corps, gang, party

Graphically-Phonetically Related Morphographs:

High Frequency Compounds:

団体 DANTAI -- corporation, party, organization
96

集団 SHUUDAN -- group, body, mass
224

団結 DANKETSU -- unity, union, combination
109

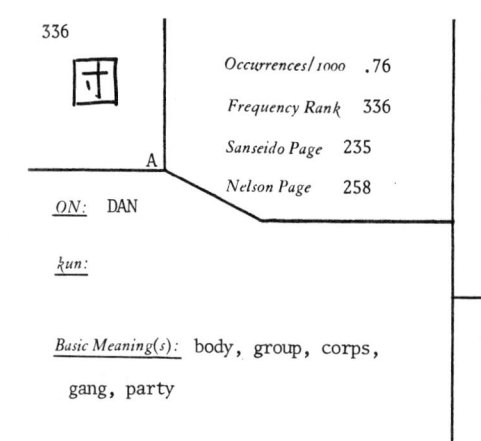

Typical Phrases and Expanded Compounds:

団体競技
集団農場
一致団結する

Typical Conversational Usage:

団体行動をとってください。
ソ連の集団農場は有名です。
一致団結してがんばりましょう。

Graphically-Phonetically Related Morphographs:

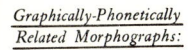

Occurrences/1000 .75	337
Frequency Rank 337	如
Sanseido Page 271	
Nelson Page 301	

ON: JO, NYO

kun: (gotoshi)

High Frequency Compounds:

如実 NYOJITSU -- truly, realistically
 37

如才無い JOSAInai -- clever, smart
885 179

如何程 (ikahodo) -- how much, how many,
 43 276   no matter how much

Basic Meaning(s):

Typical Phrases and Expanded Compounds:

如実に語る
如才無い人
如何程のもの
アメリカ人の如く

Typical Conversational Usage:

その小説に作者の生活が如実に描かれています。
山下さんは如才無い人です。
如何程さし上げましょうか。
大阪は東京の如く、人が多いです。

338

足　A

Occurrences/1000 .74
Frequency Rank 338
Sanseido Page 231
Nelson Page 857

ON: SOKU

kun: ashi, ta(su), ta(riru)

Basic Meaning(s): foot, leg, counter for pairs of footwear, add to, be sufficient

Typical Phrases and Expanded Compounds:

人手不足
満足感
早足で
物足りない

Graphically-Phonetically Related Morphographs:

促　SOKU (1007)

High Frequency Compounds:

不足　HUSOKU -- shortage, lack, deficiency
103

満足　MANZOKU -- satisfaction, contentment
466

Typical Conversational Usage:

今人手不足でよわっています。
今の仕事に満足しています。
早足で行けば、十分で着くでしょう。
何だか物足りないような気がします。

Graphically-Phonetically Related Morphographs:

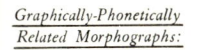

Occurrences/1000 .74
Frequency Rank 339
Sanseido Page 650
Nelson Page 721

339
美
A

ON: BI

kun: utsukushi(i)

Basic Meaning(s): beauty, grace, charm, beautiful, lovely

High Frequency Compounds:

美術 BIJUTSU -- art, fine arts
322

美人 BIJIN -- a beautiful woman
2

美容院 BIYOOIN -- beauty parlor
402 412

Typical Phrases and Expanded Compounds:

美術工芸品
美人コンテスト
行きつけの美容院

Typical Conversational Usage:

今、大学で日本の美術史を学んでいます。
大野さんはなかなかの美人です。
あそこの美容院でかみをセットしました。

340 供

Occurrences/1000 .73
Frequency Rank 340
Sanseido Page 125
Nelson Page 149

A

<u>ON</u>: KYOO, KU

<u>kun</u>: sona(eru), sona(waru)
tomo

Basic Meaning(s): offer, present, sacrifice, accompany

Graphically-Phonetically Related Morphographs:

High Frequency Compounds:

供給 KYOOKYUU -- supply
404

提供 TEIKYOO -- offer, tender
472

Typical Phrases and Expanded Compounds:

需要と供給
話題を提供する
おもちを供える
お供して

Typical Conversational Usage:

需要と供給のつり合いがとれません。
この番組は日立の提供です。
この花は何に供えるのですか。
ぜひお供させていただきます。

選 — 341

Graphically-Phonetically Related Morphographs:

Occurrences/1000: .73
Frequency Rank: 341
Sanseido Page: 454
Nelson Page: 893

ON: SEN
kun: era(bu)

Basic Meaning(s): selection, choice, choose, select, elect, prefer

High Frequency Compounds:

選挙 (434) — SENKYO -- election
選手 (57) — SENSHU -- athlete, player
選択 (1283) — SENTAKU -- selection, choice, option

See 327

Typical Phrases and Expanded Compounds:

総選挙
優秀な選手
学校の選択
道を選ぶ

Typical Conversational Usage:

来月、衆議員の総選挙があります。
兄はテニスの選手です。
今大学の選択にまよっています。
スピーチコンテストで、学校の代表に選ばれました。

342

価

A

_ON_: KA

kun:

Basic Meaning(s): price, cost, value, worth

Occurrences/1000 .72
Frequency Rank 342
Sanseido Page 125
Nelson Page 148

Graphically-Phonetically Related Morphographs:

Typical Phrases and Expanded Compounds:

物価の値上り
石油の価格
物の価値
高く評価する

High Frequency Compounds:

物価   BUKKA -- prices
95

価格   KAKAKU -- price, cost, value
403

価値   KACHI -- value, merit
828

評価   HYOOKA -- appraisal, valuation assessment
358

Typical Conversational Usage:

毎年物価が値上りしています。
その材料の価格はどの位ですか。
この品物はとても価値があります。
父の研究は高く評価されました。

343

確

Graphically-Phonetically Related Morphographs:

Occurrences/1000 .72
Frequency Rank 343
Sanseido Page 594
Nelson Page 654

ON: KAKU
kun: tashi(ka), tashi(kani), tashi(kameru)

Basic Meaning(s): firm, tight, hard, certainly, doubtless

High Frequency Compounds:

確実 (37) KAKUJITSU -- certainty, authenticity, reliability

確信 (181) KAKUSHIN -- conviction, confidence, assurance

確認 (357) KAKUNIN -- verify, certify, confirm

確立 (35) KAKURITSU -- settlement, establishment

Typical Phrases and Expanded Compounds:

確実性がある
確信して
再確認する
方針を確立する
確かな返事

Typical Conversational Usage:

高野さんがアメリカへ行くのは確実なのですか。
その試合には必ず勝つ確信があります。
明日西田さんが来られるかどうか、確認してください。
今年度の方針が確立したら、すぐお知らせします。
米国へ行くのが確かに決まったわけではありません。

344

苦

Occurrences/1000 .72
Frequency Rank 344
Sanseido Page 330
Nelson Page 774

ON: KU

kun: kuru(shii), kuru(shimu), kuru-(shimi), niga(i), niga(mi), niga(ru)

Basic Meaning(s): suffering, worry, hardship, painful, suffer, bitter, bitterness

Graphically-Phonetically Related Morphographs:

High Frequency Compounds:

苦労 KUROO -- hardships, difficulties, trials
145

苦心 KUSHIN -- pains, trouble, anxiety
64

苦痛 KUTSUU -- pain, agony, suffering
768

See 367

Typical Phrases and Expanded Compounds:

苦労のかいがあって
苦心して
苦痛を訴える
苦しい思い
返答に苦しむ
苦い経験

Typical Conversational Usage:

子どもを育てるのに大変苦労しました。
山本さんは苦心してこの家を建てたそうです。
そこへ行くのが何となく苦痛でたまりません。
試験に失敗して、苦しい思いをしたことがあります。
何といったらいいか、返答に苦しみました。
これはとても苦いくすりです。

345 光

Graphically-Phonetically Related Morphographs:

Occurrences/1000 .72
Frequency Rank 345
Sanseido Page 266
Nelson Page 336

ON: KOO
kun: hika(ru), hikari

Basic Meaning(s): light, shine, glitter, twinkle

High Frequency Compounds:

光景 KOOKEI -- scene, spectacle, aspect
617

光沢 KOOTAKU -- brilliance, polish, luster
442

光学 KOOGAKU -- optics
15

Typical Phrases and Expanded Compounds:

美しい光景
光沢のある
光学器械
ぴかぴか光る

Typical Conversational Usage:

テレビで月の光景を見ることができました。
この置物はずいぶん光沢がありますね。
父は光学関係の仕事をしています。
ゆかがぴかぴか光っています。

346

失

A

Occurrences/1000 .72
Frequency Rank 346
Sanseido Page 206
Nelson Page 85

<u>ON</u>: SHITSU

<u>kun</u>: ushina(u)

Basic Meaning(s): error, fault, disadvantage, lose, miss

Graphically-Phonetically Related Morphographs:

High Frequency Compounds:

失業 SHITSUGYOO -- unemployment
74

失敗 SHIPPAI -- failure, mistake, blunder
420

失望 SHITSUBOO -- disappointment, dispair
314

失礼 SHITSUREI -- impoliteness, rudeness, discourtesy
959

Typical Phrases and Expanded Compounds:

失業対策
大失敗
失望のあまり
失礼な事
自信を失う

Typical Conversational Usage:

あの人は今失業しています。
「失敗は成功のもと」とよく言われます。
そんなことに失望してはいけません。
きのうはどうも失礼しました。
すっかり自信を失ってしまいました。

Graphically-Phonetically Related Morphographs:

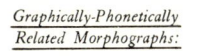

Occurrences/1000 .72
Frequency Rank 347
Sanseido Page 32
Nelson Page 648

347
石
A

ON: SEKI, SHAKU, KOKU
kun: ishi

Basic Meaning(s): stone, pebble, rock, jewel, 10 cubic feet

High Frequency Compounds:

石油 SEKIYU -- kerosene, petroleum
879

石炭 SEKITAN -- coal
1061

石高 KOKUdaka -- crop, yield, salary,
135　　　　　　　amount of rice

石屋 ishiya -- stone merchant, stone
236　　　　　　　mason

Typical Phrases and Expanded Compounds:

石油化学
石炭産業
米の石高
村の石屋

Typical Conversational Usage:

石油ストーブは一般の家庭でよく使われています。
石炭はどこで一番多くとれますか。
今年の米の石高を調べています。
この近所に石屋がありますか。

348

単

Occurrences/1000 .72
Frequency Rank 348
Sanseido Page 267
Nelson Page 78

ON: TAN

kun:

Basic Meaning(s): one, single, simple, singular, individual

Graphically-Phonetically Related Morphographs:

High Frequency Compounds:

簡単 KANTAN -- simplicity, brevity
882

単位 TAN'I -- unit, denomination, credit
319

単純 TANJUN -- simplicity
925

Typical Phrases and Expanded Compounds:

簡単な挨拶
計りの単位
単純な性格

Typical Conversational Usage:

その問題を簡単に説明してください。
この科目をとれば、全部で十六単位になります。
仕事がかなり単純化されてきました。

349

任

Graphically-Phonetically Related Morphographs:

妊 NIN

Occurrences/1000 .72
Frequency Rank 349
Sanseido Page 119
Nelson Page 133

ON: NIN
kun: maka(seru)

Basic Meaning(s): duty, responsibility, office, mission, entrust to, leave to

High Frequency Compounds:

責任 SEKININ -- responsibility, liability
599

任務 NIMMU -- duty, function, office, mission
244

任命 NIMMEI -- appointment, nomination, ordination
249

Typical Phrases and Expanded Compounds:

連帯責任
首相の任務
任命式
仕事を任せる

Typical Conversational Usage:

責任を果してください。
吉川さんは与えられた任務を全うしました。
山本さんはきのう部長に任命されました。
その仕事を全部任せられています。

350

参

Occurrences/1000 .71
Frequency Rank   350
Sanseido Page   201
Nelson Page   235

A

ON: SAN

kun: mai(ru)

Basic Meaning(s): three, going, coming, visiting

Typical Phrases and Expanded Compounds:

参加国
参考書
授業参観

Graphically-Phonetically Related Morphographs:

High Frequency Compounds:

参加 SANKA -- participation, joining,
237

参考 SANKOO -- reference, consultation
63

参観 SANKAN -- visit, inspection
302

Typical Conversational Usage:

日本はオリンピックにいつも参加しています。
この本を参考にして、レポートを書いてください。
宮城はいつ参観できますか。

351

難

Occurrences/1000 .71
Frequency Rank 351
Sanseido Page 348
Nelson Page 939

A

ON: NAN

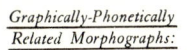

kun: kata(i)

Graphically-Phonetically Related Morphographs:

Basic Meaning(s): trouble, difficulty, accident, defect, criticism, difficult, impossible

High Frequency Compounds:

非難 HI'NAN -- criticism, denunciation
222

困難 KONNAN -- trouble, distress, perplexity
437

難点 NANTEN -- difficult point
175

Typical Phrases and Expanded Compounds:

はげしい非難
困難にぶつかる
難点がある
し難い

Typical Conversational Usage:

演説の後、山本氏ははげしい非難をあびました。
そこへ行くのは大分困難だったようです。
まだまだ難点があります。
これはなかなか解き難い問題です。

352 費

Occurrences/1000 .71
Frequency Rank 352
Sanseido Page 403
Nelson Page 847

ON: HI

kun: tsuiya(su)

Basic Meaning(s): expenses, cost, spend, consume, waste

Graphically-Phonetically Related Morphographs:

High Frequency Compounds:

費用 (177) HIYOO -- expense, cost

消費 (458) SHOOHI -- consumption, expenditure

Typical Phrases and Expanded Compounds:

旅行の費用
消費者
時間を費す

Typical Conversational Usage:

その旅行の費用はどの位かかりますか。
日常生活でいろいろな物を消費しています。
お金をむだに費してはいけません。

案 353

Graphically-Phonetically Related Morphographs:

安 AN (165)

Occurrences/1000 .71
Frequency Rank 353
Sanseido Page 286
Nelson Page 320

ON: AN

kun:

Basic Meaning(s): proposition, suggestion, plan, idea

High Frequency Compounds:

提案 TEIAN -- suggestion, proposition
472

案外 ANGAI -- surprisingly, disappointingly, unexpectedly
69

案内 ANNAI -- guidance, guide, announcement, invitation
77

See 100

Typical Phrases and Expanded Compounds:

考えを提案する
案外上手に
観光案内

Typical Conversational Usage:

何かよい考えがありましたら、提案してください。
今度の試験は案外やさしかったようです。
下山さんは観光案内の仕事をしています。

354

援

Occurrences/1000	.71
Frequency Rank	354
Sanseido Page	388
Nelson Page	446

B

ON: EN

kun:

Basic Meaning(s): help, save

Typical Phrases and Expanded Compounds:

援助額
応援団
後援会

Graphically-Phonetically Related Morphographs:

High Frequency Compounds:

援助 247 — ENJO -- assistance, help, support

応援 362 — OOEN -- aid, reinforcement, cheering

後援 48 — KOOEN -- assistance, support, backing

Typical Conversational Usage:

水害地から援助を求めて来ました。
テニスの試合の応援に行きませんか。
私は佐藤氏の後援会に入っています。

Graphically-Phonetically Related Morphographs:

願 GAN (711)

Occurrences/1000 .71	顔 355
Frequency Rank 355	
Sanseido Page 743	A
Nelson Page 959	
	ON: GAN
	kun: kao

Basic Meaning(s): face, countenance, expression

High Frequency Compounds:

洗顔 SENGAN -- washing the face
1232

顔色 kaoiro -- expression, counte-
405　　　　　　nance, complexion

Typical Phrases and Expanded Compounds:

洗顔用の石けん
顔色をうかがう
立派な顔触れ

Typical Conversational Usage:

この石けんは洗顔用です。
何だか顔色がよくありません。
選手の顔触れがそろいました。

356

式

A

Occurrences/1000 .71
Frequency Rank 356
Sanseido Page 351
Nelson Page 371

ON: SHIKI

kun:

Basic Meaning(s): ceremony, function, method, style, form, rite

Typical Phrases and Expanded Compounds:

形式ばらずに
正式な手続きをとる
公式発表
儀式ばる
古い方式

Graphically-Phonetically Related Morphographs:

High Frequency Compounds:

形式 KEISHIKI -- form, formality
306

正式 SEISHIKI -- proper form, formality
139

公式 KOOSHIKI -- formula, formality
212

儀式 GISHIKI -- ceremony, rite, ritual, service
966

方式 HOOSHIKI -- form, formula, method, process
25

Typical Conversational Usage:

論文の形式で書いてみてください。
結婚式の日取りが正式に決まりました。
いよいよ明日からプロ野球の公式戦が始まります。
何も儀式ばる必要はありません。
新しい方式で試みてみましょう。

*Graphically-Phonetically
Related Morphographs:*

Occurrences/1000 .71

Frequency Rank 357

Sanseido Page 684

Nelson Page 831

認

357

A

<u>ON</u>: NIN

<u>kun</u>: mito(meru), mito(me)

Basic Meaning(s): witness, sight, discern, recognize, believe

High Frequency Compounds:

認識   NINSHIKI -- recognition, under-
416   standing, knowledge

確認   KAKUNIN -- verify, certify, confirm
343

承認   SHOONIN -- approval, consent,
701   recognition

*Typical Phrases and
Expanded Compounds:*

認識不足
確認する
承認状
世に認められる

Typical Conversational Usage:

まだその仕事に対する認識が足りません。
その情報を確認しました。
国連で中共は承認されましたか。
あの方は作曲家として認められています。

358 評

A

Occurrences/1000 .71
Frequency Rank 358
Sanseido Page 679
Nelson Page 826

ON: HYOO

kun:

Basic Meaning(s): criticism, comment

Typical Phrases and
Expanded Compounds:

映画の批評
文芸評論
近所の評判

Graphically-Phonetically
Related Morphographs:

High Frequency Compounds:

批評 HIHYOO -- criticism, comment
536

評論 HYOORON -- criticism, review,
110   comment, editorial

評判 HYOOBAN -- fame, reputation,
187   sensation

See 262, 342

Typical Conversational Usage:

新聞でその映画の批評を読みました。
中西氏は文芸評論家です。
一郎君は近所の評判もよく、クラスの人気者です。

質

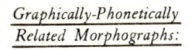

359

Occurrences/1000 .71
Frequency Rank 359
Sanseido Page 368
Nelson Page 851

<u>ON</u>: SHITSU, SHICHI
<u>kun</u>:

Basic Meaning(s): hostage, pawn, substance, matter, quality

Graphically-Phonetically Related Morphographs:

High Frequency Compounds:

質問 — SHITSUMON -- question
41

性質 — SEISHITSU -- nature, disposition, temperament
119

実質 — JISSHITSU -- substance, essence, material
37

物質 — BUSSHITSU -- matter, material, substance
95

Typical Phrases and Expanded Compounds:

むずかしい質問
仕事の性質
実質的に
物質的に
質に入れる

Typical Conversational Usage:

質問してもよろしいですか。
この子はまじめでおとなしい性質です。
その学校は実質的によくなったと思います。
アメリカの国は物質的にめぐまれています。
この前の質を流されました。

360

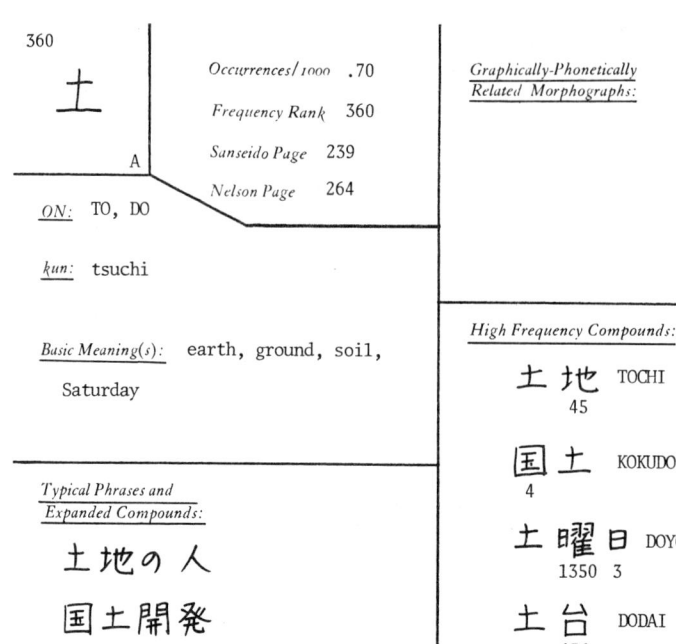

土

Occurrences/1000 .70
Frequency Rank 360
Sanseido Page 239
Nelson Page 264

A

ON: TO, DO

kun: tsuchi

Basic Meaning(s): earth, ground, soil, Saturday

Typical Phrases and Expanded Compounds:

土地の人
国土開発
先週の土曜日
家の土台
土をふむ

Graphically-Phonetically Related Morphographs:

High Frequency Compounds:

土地 TOCHI -- land, lot, soil, estate
45

国土 KOKUDO -- country, territory, domain
4

土曜日 DOYOOBI -- Saturday
1350 3

土台 DODAI -- foundation, groundwork
436

Typical Conversational Usage:

この辺の土地にはあまりくわしくありません。
国土発展のために努力するつもりです。
今度の土曜日に大沢さんに会う予定です。
この家は土台がしっかりしています。
まだカナダの土をふんだことがありません。

Graphically-Phonetically Related Morphographs:

映 EI (368)

Occurrences/1000 .69
Frequency Rank 361
Sanseido Page 329
Nelson Page 773

361
英
A

ON: EI

kun:

Basic Meaning(s): England, Britain, gifted person, English

High Frequency Compounds:

英語 EIGO -- the English language
211

英国 EIKOKU -- England, Great Britain, United Kingdom
4

英雄 EIYUU -- hero
538

英気 EIKI -- excellent talent
55

Typical Phrases and Expanded Compounds:

英語の勉強
英国の女王
世界の英雄
英気をやしなう

Typical Conversational Usage:

上原さんは英語の勉強に余念がありません。
ロンドンは英国の首都です。
かつてナポレオンはフランスの英雄でした。
大いに英気をやしなってください。

362

応

A

Occurrences/1000 .69
Frequency Rank 362
Sanseido Page 318
Nelson Page 363

ON: OO

kun:

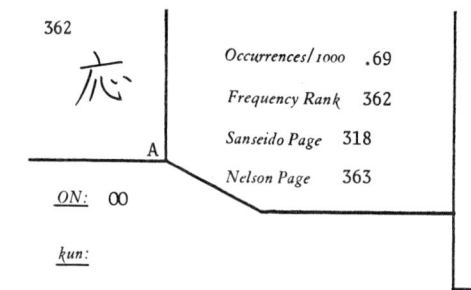

Basic Meaning(s): yes, all right, answer, reply to

Graphically-Phonetically Related Morphographs:

High Frequency Compounds:

一応   ICHIOO -- once, tentatively,
 1   in outline

応用   OOYOO -- practical application,
 177   adaptation, practice

応急   OOKYUU -- temporary, emergency
 533

応募   OOBO -- subscription, applica-
                  tion, enlistment

Typical Phrases and Expanded Compounds:

一応の手続き
応用問題
応急手当
応募規定

Typical Conversational Usage:

一応先生に聞いてみた方がよろしいでしょう。
先生の言われたことを応用してみました。
小山さんは病院で応急手当を受けました。
歌のコンクールに応募したことがありますか。

363 各

Graphically-Phonetically Related Morphographs:

客 KAKU (606)
格 KAKU (403)
閣 KAKU (504)

Occurrences/1000 .69
Frequency Rank 363
Sanseido Page 257
Nelson Page 282

ON: KAKU
kun: onoono

Basic Meaning(s): each, every, either, respectively

High Frequency Compounds:

各国 KAKKOKU -- all countries, various nations, each nation
4

各地 KAKUCHI -- each place, various areas
45

各種 KAKUSHU -- each kind, all kinds
417

各自 KAKUJI -- each one, every individual
14

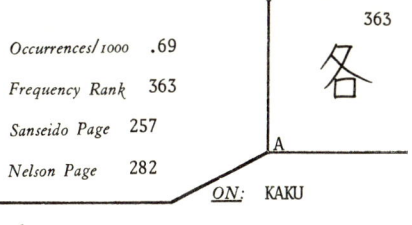

Typical Phrases and Expanded Compounds:

各国代表
各地をまわる
各種とりそろえて
各自の問題
各々の

Typical Conversational Usage:

もう各国代表がそろいましたか。
選挙運動が各地で行われています。
最近日本では各種の国際会議が行われています。
各自で考えたうえで、発表してください。
各々の意見をまとめてください。

364

守 A

Occurrences/1000 .69
Frequency Rank 364
Sanseido Page 279
Nelson Page 311

ON: SHU, SU

kun: mamo(ru), mamo(ri)

Basic Meaning(s): defend, protect, keep, observe, obey

Typical Phrases and Expanded Compounds:

保守的
留守中
意見を固守する
法律を守る

Graphically-Phonetically Related Morphographs:

狩 SHU

High Frequency Compounds:

保守 HOSHU -- conservatism
163

留守 RUSU -- absence, being away,
670   from home, neglecting

固守 KOSHU -- persistense, tena-
820   city, adhering

See 287

Typical Conversational Usage:

叔父の考えは非常に保守的です。
昨日、田中さんの家に行きましたが、留守でした。
上田さんはいつも自分の意見を固守します。
交通規則を守ることは大切です。

365 増

Occurrences/1000	.69
Frequency Rank	365
Sanseido Page	248
Nelson Page	279

A

ON: ZOO

kun: ma(su)

Basic Meaning(s): increase, add to, augment, gain, promote

Graphically-Phonetically Related Morphographs:

憎 ZOO

贈 ZOO

High Frequency Compounds:

増加 ZOOKA -- increase, multiply
237

増大 ZOODAI -- increase, enlarge, enhance
5

急増 KYUUZOO -- surge, sudden increase
533

Typical Phrases and Expanded Compounds:

人口増加

増大の一途をたどる

水が急増する

人数が増す

Typical Conversational Usage:

東京の人口は毎年増加しています。

電話の申し込みが増大しています。

この地方の住宅は急増し始めました。

今度の大雨で川の水が増しました。

366

待

A

Occurrences/1000 .69
Frequency Rank 366
Sanseido Page 359
Nelson Page 383

ON: TAI

kun: ma(tsu)

Basic Meaning(s): wait, waiting, expect, depend on

Graphically-Phonetically Related Morphographs:

High Frequency Compounds:

期待 KITAI -- expectation, hope,
247   anticipation

待望 TAIBOO -- expectant waiting
314

待遇 TAIGUU -- treatment, recep-
1206   tion, entertainment

Typical Phrases and Expanded Compounds:

期待はずれ
待望の夏休み
いい待遇
待ち遠しい

Typical Conversational Usage:

あまりあの人には期待をかけない方がいいです。
それは待望の映画です。
その会社の待遇はとてもいいと思います。
あと十五分ぐらい待ってみましょう。

Graphically-Phonetically Related Morphographs:

豆 TOO   頭 TOO (234)

登 TOO (1151)

痘 TOO

High Frequency Compounds:

闘争 TOOSOO -- fight, combat, conflict, labor strife
107

苦闘 KUTOO -- fight hard, struggle
344

Occurrences/1000 .69
Frequency Rank 367
Sanseido Page   729
Nelson Page   927

闘 367

B

<u>ON</u>: TOO

kun:

Basic Meaning(s): fighting, fight, struggle against

Typical Phrases and Expanded Compounds:

はげしい闘争
悪戦苦闘

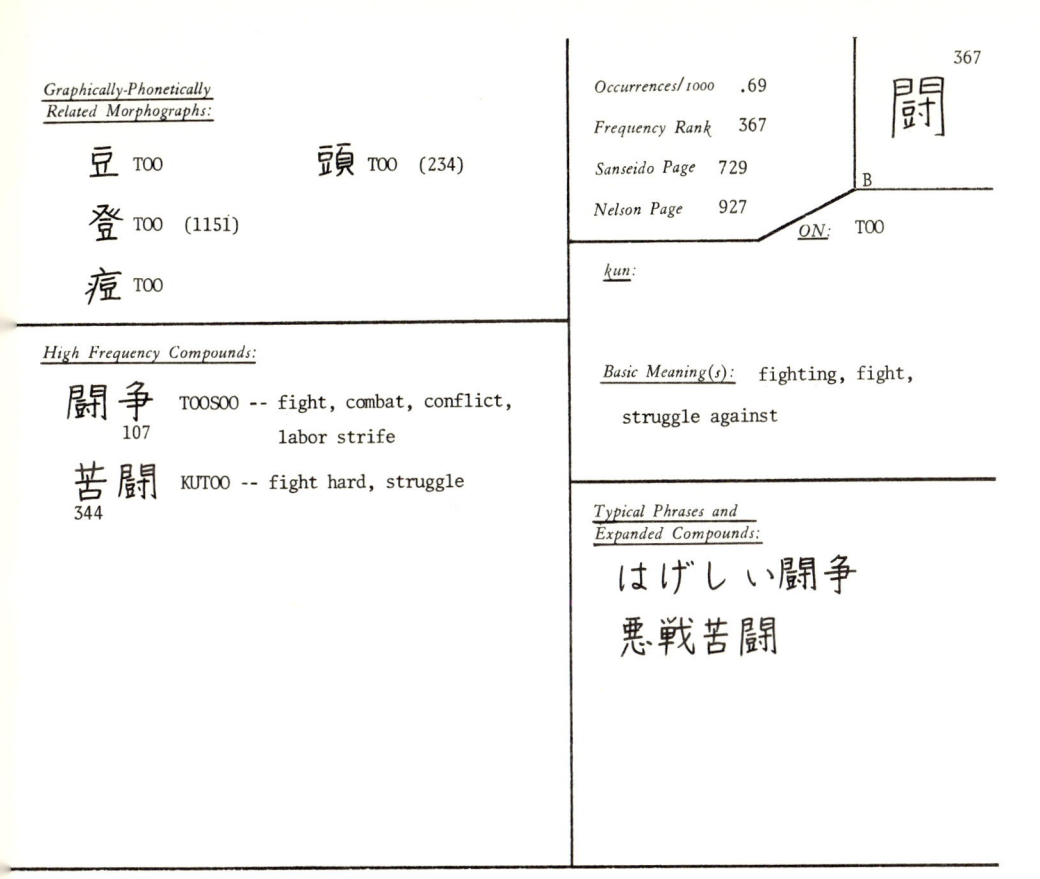

Typical Conversational Usage:

はげしい闘争の結果、組合側が勝ちました。
選挙運動で、原氏は悪戦苦闘しています。

368

映

A

Occurrences/1000 .68
Frequency Rank 368
Sanseido Page 486
Nelson Page 479

ON: EI

kun: utsu(ru)

Basic Meaning(s): reflecting, projection, be reflected, match

Graphically-Phonetically Related Morphographs:

英 EI (361)

High Frequency Compounds:

映画 EIGA -- movie, film
176

映写 EISHA -- projection
696

反映 HAN'EI -- reflection, influence
146

Typical Phrases and Expanded Compounds:

映画化する
映写機
世論の反映
目に映る

Typical Conversational Usage:

映画を見に行きましょう。
映写時間は一時間ぐらいでしょう。
その新聞は世論をよく反映しています。
山が水に映ってとても美しいです。

Graphically-Phonetically Related Morphographs:

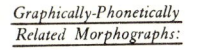

	369
Occurrences/1000 .68	科
Frequency Rank 369	
Sanseido Page 603	A
Nelson Page 665	
	ON: KA

kun:

Basic Meaning(s): course, branch, department, faculty

High Frequency Compounds:

教科 KYOOKA -- lesson, course, curriculum
  58

科学 KAGAKU -- science
  15

法科 HOOKA -- law course, law department
  100

内科 NAIKA -- internal medicine
  77

Typical Phrases and Expanded Compounds:

教科書
科学的に
法科の学生
内科にかかる

Typical Conversational Usage:

これは化学の教科書です。
二十世紀になって、科学が急速に発達しました。
兄は法科の学生で、将来弁護士になるそうです。
西山先生は内科ですか、外科ですか。

370

限 A

Occurrences/1000 .68
Frequency Rank 370
Sanseido Page 427
Nelson Page 929

ON: GEN

kun: kagi(ru), kagi(ri)

Basic Meaning(s): limit, restrict, confine, as far as possible

Typical Phrases and Expanded Compounds:

制限速度
限度がある
限界に来る
忙しい時に限って

Graphically-Phonetically Related Morphographs:

High Frequency Compounds:

制限 SEIGEN -- limit, limitation, restriction
161

限度 GENDO -- limit, limits, limitation
70

限界 GENKAI -- boundary, limit, limits, bounds
164

See 311, 376

Typical Conversational Usage:

このバスには人数の制限があって、五十人しか乗れません。
どんな仕事にも限度があります。
仕事でつかれて、もう限界に来ています。
この子に限って、そんなことはありません。

Graphically-Phonetically Related Morphographs:

	371
Occurrences/1000 .68	御
Frequency Rank 371	
Sanseido Page 360	B
Nelson Page 360	

ON: GYO, GO,
kun: ON

High Frequency Compounds:

御苑 GYOEN -- Imperial Garden

御法度 GOHATTO -- law, ordinance,
100 72   prohibition

御都合 GOTSUGOO -- your convenience
621 33

御曹子 ONZOOSHI -- son of a noble
    42

御陰 o-kage -- indebtedness, favor,
988   help, good offices

Basic Meaning(s): honorific prefix, imperial honorary prefix

Typical Phrases and Expanded Compounds:

新宿御苑
御法度である
御都合が悪ければ
小山家の御曹子
御陰様で

Typical Conversational Usage:

きのう民子さんと新宿御苑に行って来ました。
そんなことは御法度です。
今日御都合が悪ければ、明日でも結構です。
あの方は山田家の御曹子です。
長男が東京の会社に入れたのは吉田さんの御陰です。

372

品

Occurrences/1000 .68
Frequency Rank 372
Sanseido Page 232
Nelson Page 249

A

ON: HIN

kun: shina

Basic Meaning(s): refinement, dignity, article, goods, thing

Graphically-Phonetically Related Morphographs:

High Frequency Compounds:

作品 SAKUHIN -- work, performance, production
120

商品 SHOOHIN -- goods, stock, merchandise
375

製品 SEIHIN -- manufactured goods
521

品物 shinamono -- goods, stock, articles
95

Typical Phrases and Expanded Compounds:

すぐれた作品
商品価値
会社の製品
品物がきれる
品がある

Typical Conversational Usage:

シェイクスピアの作品の中で、どれが一番好きですか。
会社でどんな商品をあつかっていますか。
新しい製品をどんどん作るように心がけています。
この品物はなかなか手に入りません。
あの方はとても品があります。

Graphically-Phonetically Related Morphographs:

及 KYUU (422)

吸 KYUU (1168)

High Frequency Compounds:

階級 328 — KAIKYUU -- class, estate, caste, rank

高級 135 — KOOKYUU -- high rank, seniority, high grade

級友 451 — KYUUYUU -- classmate

進級 156 — SHINKYUU -- school promotion

Occurrences/1000 .67
Frequency Rank 373
Sanseido Page 636
Nelson Page 695

級 373

ON: KYUU

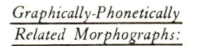

kun:

Basic Meaning(s): grade, class, rank, decapitated head

Typical Phrases and Expanded Compounds:

階級をつける
高級ホテル
親しい級友
進級する

Typical Conversational Usage:

父は軍隊で階級が上の方でした。
きのう銀座でイタリアの高級料理を食べました。
おととい、町でばったり昔の級友に会いました。
兄は大学の四年に進級しました。

374 左

Occurrences/1000	.67
Frequency Rank	374
Sanseido Page	183
Nelson Page	353

ON: SA

kun: hidari

Basic Meaning(s): left, the following, the left, leftist

Graphically-Phonetically Related Morphographs:

佐 SA (381)

High Frequency Compounds:

左派 286 SAHA -- leftwing, left faction, leftist

左右 384 SAYUU -- left and right, one's side, one's attendants

左翼 985 SAYOKU -- left flank, left wing, leftist

Typical Phrases and Expanded Compounds:

左派と右派
左右に気をつける
左翼がかる
左側に

Typical Conversational Usage:

その人は左派ですか。右派ですか。
左右に気をつけて、道を渡ってください。
あの学生は左翼がかっています。
あそこを左に曲れば、右側に学校があります。

Graphically-Phonetically Related Morphographs:

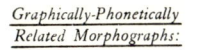

Occurrences/1000 .67	375
Frequency Rank 375	商
Sanseido Page 95	
Nelson Page 119	A

<u>ON</u>: SHOO

<u>kun</u>: akina(u)

High Frequency Compounds:

商業 (74) SHOOGYOO -- commerce, trade, business

商売 (313) SHOOBAI -- trade, business, occupation

商品 (372) SHOOHIN -- goods, merchandise

商店 (632) SHOOTEN -- shop, store

Basic Meaning(s): trade, merchant, sell, handle, trade in

Typical Phrases and Expanded Compounds:

商業化する
商売がら
商品の売れ行き
商店街
商って歩く

Typical Conversational Usage:

原君は商業高校を出てから、貿易会社に入りました。
最近北川さんは商売を変えたそうです。
会社の宣伝がよいせいか、商品の売行きが上々です。
この辺の商店は夜九時にしまります。
あの人は何を商って歩いていますか。

376

門

Occurrences/1000 .67
Frequency Rank 376
Sanseido Page 724
Nelson Page 920

A

ON: MON

kun: kado

Basic Meaning(s): gate, gateway, private school, door, class

Graphically-Phonetically Related Morphographs:

問 MON (41)

High Frequency Compounds:

門限 MONGEN -- closing time
370

部門 BUMON -- class, group, depart-
52   ment, category

門下 MONKA -- vicinity of the gate,
75   disciple, pupil

門出 kadode -- departure
8

専門 SEMMON -- specialty, special
589   subject of study

Typical Phrases and Expanded Compounds:

寮の門限
部門に分ける
門下生
門出を祝う
専門科目

Typical Conversational Usage:

寮の門限は十時なので、もう帰らなければなりません。
父は設計の部門で働いています。
私は平田先生の門下生です。
アメリカの大学に入った長男の門出を祝いました。
大学で、今、専門科目を勉強しています。

Graphically-Phonetically Related Morphographs:

	377
Occurrences/1000 .66	住
Frequency Rank 377	
Sanseido Page 122	
Nelson Page 142	

<u>ON</u>: JUU

<u>kun</u>: su(mu), su(mau), su(mai)

Basic Meaning(s): dwelling, living, live, reside, inhabit

High Frequency Compounds:

住宅 JUUTAKU -- residence, house
522

住所 JUUSHO -- address, residence
129

移住 IJUU -- migration, emigration,
625   immigration, moving

See 281

Typical Phrases and Expanded Compounds:

静かな住宅地
現住所
ハワイへ移住する
住めば都

Typical Conversational Usage:

この辺は最近住宅がふえてきました。
住所が変わったら、お知らせください。
叔母がハワイへ移住してから、もう四十年になります。
私達は今東京に住んでいます。

378

占

Occurrences/1000 .66
Frequency Rank 378
Sanseido Page 194
Nelson Page 226

ON: SEN

kun: urana(u), urana(i)

Basic Meaning(s): occupy, hold, have, divine, forecast

Graphically-Phonetically Related Morphographs:

High Frequency Compounds:

占領 452 — SENRYOO -- capture, possession, occupation

独占 205 — DOKUSEN -- exclusive possession, monopoly

Typical Phrases and Expanded Compounds:

占領軍
独占禁止法
星を占う
地位を占める

Typical Conversational Usage:

ここはかつて日本軍が占領した所です。
そんなに広い所を独占してはいけません。
あの人はよく星を占います
去年、日本の造船は世界で第一位を占めました。

Graphically-Phonetically Related Morphographs:

島 379

Occurrences/1000 .66
Frequency Rank 379
Sanseido Page 712
Nelson Page 97

A

ON: TOO

kun: shima

Basic Meaning(s): island

High Frequency Compounds:

島民 TOOMIN -- islanders
30

諸島 SHOTOO -- archipelago, group of
272 islands

島国 shimaguni -- island country
4

Typical Phrases and Expanded Compounds:

島民の歓迎
小笠原諸島
島国根性
小さい島

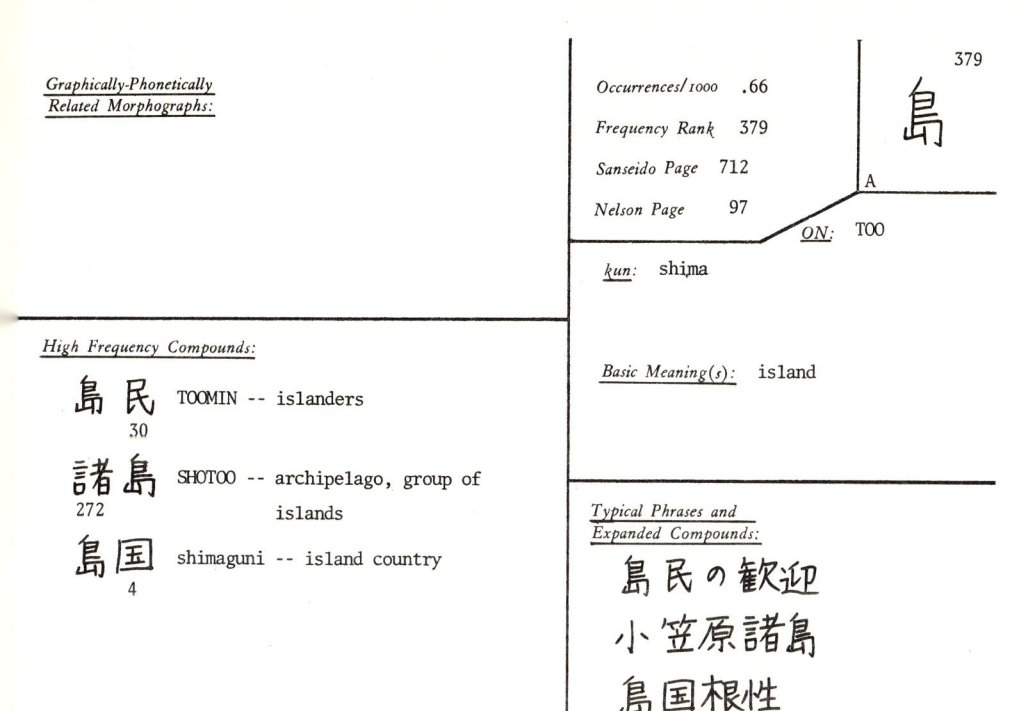

Typical Conversational Usage:

島民の盛大な歓迎を受けました。
小笠原諸島はいつ日本に復帰しましたか。
日本は南北に広がる細長い島国です。
向うの方に、かすかに見える島が大島です。

380

我

Occurrences/1000 .65
Frequency Rank 380
Sanseido Page 66
Nelson Page 90

ON: GA

kun: ware

Basic Meaning(s): I, self, ego, egotism, selfishness

Graphically-Phonetically Related Morphographs:

餓 GA

High Frequency Compounds:

我慢 1245 GAMAN -- patience, perseverance, endurance

自我 14 JIGA -- self, the ego

我流 235 GARYUU -- self-taught, one's own way

我々 wareware -- we

Typical Phrases and Expanded Compounds:

我慢強い
自我意識
我流の絵
我々の世代

Typical Conversational Usage:

もうすぐ終わりますから、我慢してください。
あの子は自我の強い子です。
この絵は我流でかいたものです。
それは他でもない我々の問題です。

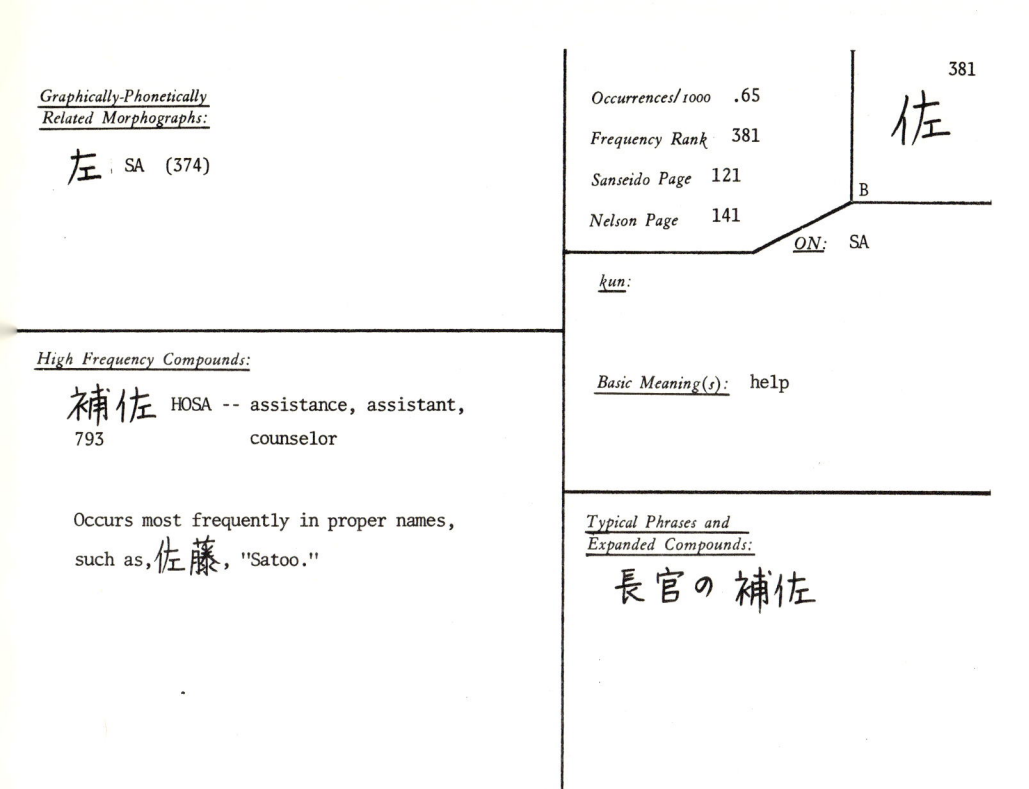

381

佐

Graphically-Phonetically Related Morphographs:

左 SA (374)

Occurrences/1000 .65
Frequency Rank 381
Sanseido Page 121
Nelson Page 141

B

ON: SA

kun:

Basic Meaning(s): help

High Frequency Compounds:

補佐 HOSA -- assistance, assistant, counselor
793

Occurs most frequently in proper names, such as, 佐藤, "Satoo."

Typical Phrases and Expanded Compounds:

長官の補佐

Typical Conversational Usage:

佐々木さんは佐藤氏の補佐です。

382 残

Occurrences/1000: .65
Frequency Rank: 382
Sanseido Page: 538
Nelson Page: 522

A

ON: ZAN

kun: noko(su), noko(ru)

Basic Meaning(s): remainder, balance, leave behind, keep back, remain, be left over, stay

Graphically-Phonetically Related Morphographs:

High Frequency Compounds:

残念 ZANNEN -- regret, disappointment
333

残暑 ZANSHO -- lingering summer heat

残酷 ZANKOKU -- cruelty, atrocity, brutality
1376

Typical Phrases and Expanded Compounds:

残念そうに
残暑がきびしい
残酷物語
仕事を残す
家に残る

Typical Conversational Usage:

残念ながら、まだ日光へ行ったことがありません。
今年の残暑はなかなかきびしいです。
彼等は残酷に扱われたそうです。
家に子どもを残して来ました。
これはきのうの残り物です。

Graphically-Phonetically Related Morphographs:

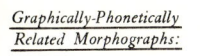

Occurrences/1000 .65
Frequency Rank 383
Sanseido Page 484
Nelson Page 477

383

易

A

ON: I, EKI

kun:

Basic Meaning(s): divination, fortune-telling, easiness

High Frequency Compounds:

容易 YOOI -- easy, simple
402

貿易 BOOEKI -- trade, commerce
550

易者 EKISHA -- fortuneteller
19

Typical Phrases and Expanded Compounds:

容易な事
対米貿易
易者にみてもらう

Typical Conversational Usage:

容易な事じゃありません。
日本の貿易はぐんぐんのびています。
大木さんは将来の運勢を易者にみてもらったそうです。

384

右 A

ON: U, YUU

kun: migi

Occurrences/1000 .65
Frequency Rank 384
Sanseido Page 184
Nelson Page 242

Basic Meaning(s): right, the right, right hand

Typical Phrases and Expanded Compounds:

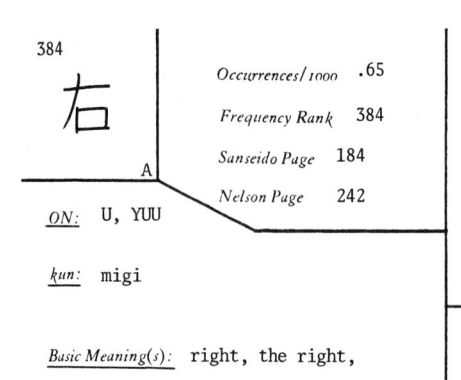

社会党右派
左右を見て
右翼団体
右手の方に

Graphically-Phonetically Related Morphographs:

有 YUU (245)
友 YUU (541)

High Frequency Compounds:

右派 286 — UHA -- rightists, the Right

左右 374 — SAYUU -- left and right, one's side, one's attendants

右翼 985 — UYOKU -- right wing, rightists, right field

右手 57 — migite -- right hand, right handed

Typical Conversational Usage:

どちらかと言えば、山田君は右派だと思います。
私は流行にあまり左右されません。
島原さんは右翼団体には属していません。
右手をあげてください。

385

験

Graphically-Phonetically Related Morphographs:

剣 KEN (818)　　検 KEN (473)
倹 KEN
険 KEN (662)

Occurrences/1000　.65
Frequency Rank　385
Sanseido Page　750
Nelson Page　974

ON: KEN
kun:

Basic Meaning(s): effect, testing

High Frequency Compounds:

実験 (37)　JIKKEN -- experimentation, experience
経験 (71)　KEIKEN -- experience
試験 (318)　SHIKEN -- examination, experiment, test
受験 (298)　JUKEN -- taking an examination
体験 (96)　TAIKEN -- experience

Typical Phrases and Expanded Compounds:

化学の実験
経験をつむ
試験に受かる
大学を受験する
体験談

Typical Conversational Usage:

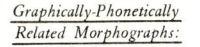

あそこに実験室があります。
経験がまだ浅いです。
試験に落ちて、残念です。
どこの大学を受験するつもりですか。
きのうおもしろいことを体験しました。

386

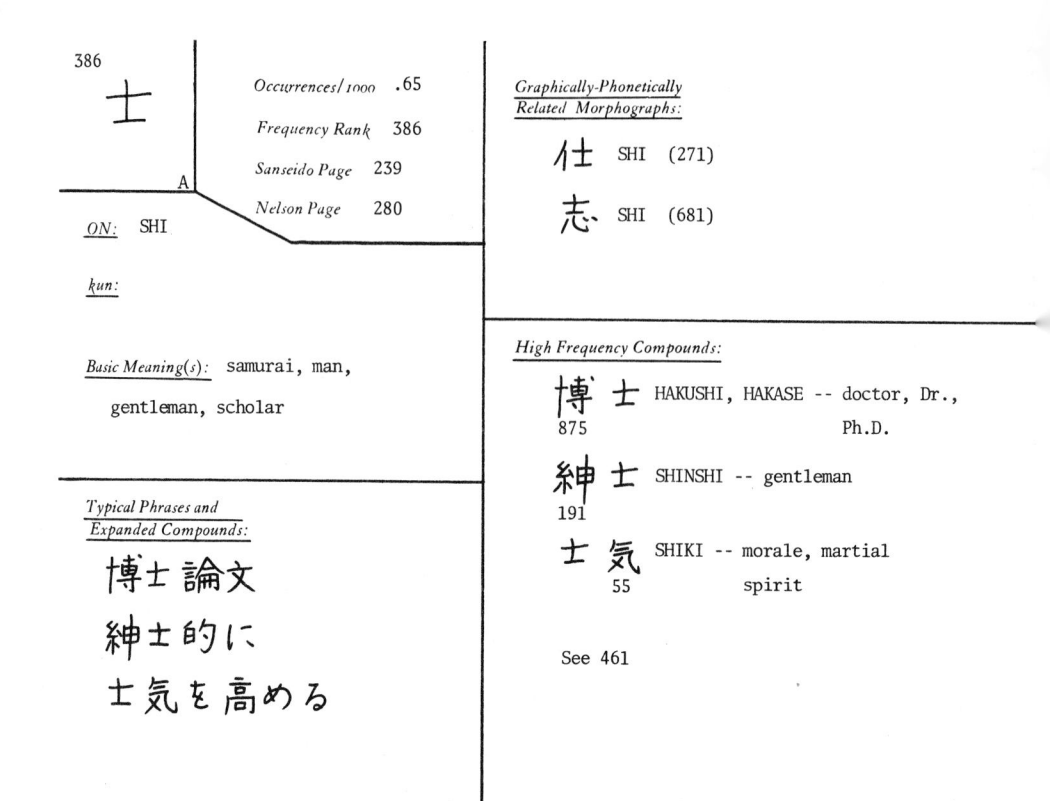

士

Occurrences/1000   .65
Frequency Rank   386
Sanseido Page   239
Nelson Page   280

A

ON: SHI

kun:

Basic Meaning(s): samurai, man, gentleman, scholar

Graphically-Phonetically Related Morphographs:

仕   SHI   (271)

志   SHI   (681)

High Frequency Compounds:

博士   HAKUSHI, HAKASE -- doctor, Dr., Ph.D.
875

紳士   SHINSHI -- gentleman
191

士気   SHIKI -- morale, martial spirit
55

See 461

Typical Phrases and Expanded Compounds:

博士論文
紳士的に
士気を高める

Typical Conversational Usage:

弟は博士号をとるために、一生懸命勉強しています。
あの方は紳士的で、とても感じがいい方です。
士気を失わないで、がんばってください。

Graphically-Phonetically Related Morphographs:

暦 REKI

High Frequency Compounds:

歴史 REKISHI -- history
300

経歴 KEIREKI -- personal history,
71   career, pilgrimage

履歴 RIREKI -- personal career history

学歴 GAKUREKI -- school career, academic
15   record

387

歴

Occurrences/1000 .65
Frequency Rank 387
Sanseido Page 200
Nelson Page 233

A

<u>ON</u>: REKI

<u>kun</u>:

Basic Meaning(s): continuation, passing of time

Typical Phrases and Expanded Compounds:

歴史の流れ
選手になった経歴
履歴書
学歴がある

Typical Conversational Usage:

本山さんは歴史家です。
原田さんは先生をした経歴があります。
明日履歴書を持って来てください。
大下さんは学歴があって、大変立派な人です。

388

営

Occurrences/1000 .64
Frequency Rank 388
Sanseido Page 621
Nelson Page 252

ON: EI

kun: itona(mu), itona(mi)

Basic Meaning(s): camp, performing, perform, build, conduct, follow

Typical Phrases and Expanded Compounds:

個人経営
営利事業
県営住宅
店を営む

Graphically-Phonetically Related Morphographs:

High Frequency Compounds:

経営 KEIEI -- construction, management, operation
71

営利 EIRI -- gain, money-making
180

県営 KEN'EI -- prefectural operation
842

Typical Conversational Usage:

この会社は誰が経営していますか。
これは営利事業じゃありません。
県営住宅が当たりました。
父は小さな店を営んでいます。

389 広

Occurrences/1000 .64
Frequency Rank 389
Sanseido Page 317
Nelson Page 362

A

<u>ON</u>: KOO

<u>kun</u>: hiro(i), hiro(geru), hiro(garu), hiro(maru), hiro(meru), hiro(me)

Basic Meaning(s): wide, broad, spread out, extend, expand, enlarge

Graphically-Phonetically Related Morphographs:

鉱 KOO

High Frequency Compounds:

広告 (398) KOOKOKU -- advertisement, public notice, poster

広大 (5) KOODAI -- vast, extensive, magnificent

Typical Phrases and Expanded Compounds:

新聞広告
広大な敷地
広い庭
うわさが広がる
道を広げる

Typical Conversational Usage:

きのうの新聞広告を見ましたか。
広大な土地に住宅が建てられています。
あの方は交際がとても広いです。
鈴木さんは変なうわさをたてられ、困っています。
今、道を広げているところです。

390

根

Occurrences/1000: .64
Frequency Rank: 390
Sanseido Page: 524
Nelson Page: 502

A

ON: KON

kun: ne

Basic Meaning(s): root, base, head

Graphically-Phonetically Related Morphographs:

恨 KON
墾 KON
懇 KON

High Frequency Compounds:

根本 KOMPON -- root, origin, cause
 6

根拠 KONKYO -- basis, foundation, authority
 756

大根 DAIKON -- daikon, the huge white radish
 5

Typical Phrases and Expanded Compounds:

根本的な問題
根拠のない話
大根役者
根に持つ

Typical Conversational Usage:

根本的にやり直さなければなりません。
その話に何か根拠がありますか。
その太い大根はいくらですか。
吉田さんは根が正直な人です。

391

若

Occurrences/1000 .64
Frequency Rank 391
Sanseido Page 331
Nelson Page 773

ON: JAKU
kun: waka(i)

Graphically-Phonetically Related Morphographs:

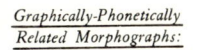

High Frequency Compounds:

若干 JAKKAN -- some, a number of
939

若年 JAKUNEN -- youth
13

老若 ROONYAKU -- young and old
640

Basic Meaning(s): young, immature, if, perhaps, or, otherwise

Typical Phrases and Expanded Compounds:

若干の原料
若年ながら
老若男女
若い人

Typical Conversational Usage:

まだ原料が若干残っています。
根本さんのいとこは若年で病死しました。
老若男女の別なく、誰でもその会に出席できます。
若いからといって、体を無理してはいけません。

392

終

Occurrences/1000 .64
Frequency Rank 392
Sanseido Page 638
Nelson Page 700

A

ON: SHUU

kun: o(waru), o(wari), o(eru)

Basic Meaning(s): end, finish, complete, be over

Graphically-Phonetically Related Morphographs:

High Frequency Compounds:

終戦   SHUUSEN -- end of the war
 32

終始   SHUUSHI -- beginning and end,
321   from first to last,
                always

Typical Phrases and Expanded Compounds:

終戦後
終始一貫
仕事を終える
映画が終わる

Typical Conversational Usage:

終戦当時、父は外地にいました。
その話を終始緊張して聞きました。
丁度食事を終えたところです。
もう授業が終わりました。

青 393

Graphically-Phonetically Related Morphographs:

清 SEI (569)　　静 SEI (744)
晴 SEI (949)　　請 SEI (743)
精 SEI (439)
　　SHOO

Occurrences/1000 .64
Frequency Rank 393
Sanseido Page 562
Nelson Page 947

ON: SEI, SHOO
kun: ao, ao(i)

Basic Meaning(s): blue, green, unripe, new, immature, pale

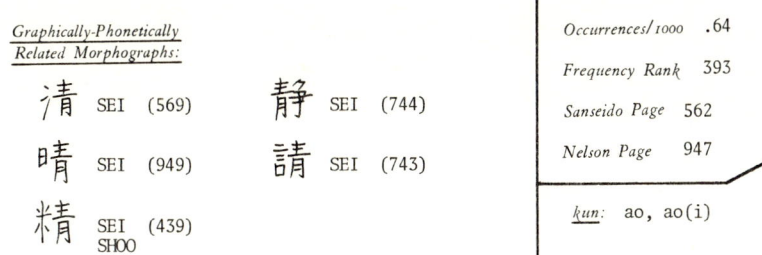

High Frequency Compounds:

青年 SEINEN -- youth, young people, boy
 13
青春 SEISHUN -- springtime of life, youth
609
青葉 aoba -- foliage, greenery, green leaves
275

See 304

Typical Phrases and Expanded Compounds:

青年会
青春を楽しむ
青葉のかおる夏
青い空

Typical Conversational Usage:

この町の青年会は活発です。
青春時代は本当に楽しいものです。
青葉の季節が大好きです。
このバナナはまだ青いです。

394

談

ON: DAN

kun:

Occurrences/1000 .64
Frequency Rank 394
Sanseido Page 685
Nelson Page 834

Basic Meaning(s): conversation, talk

Graphically-Phonetically Related Morphographs:

High Frequency Compounds:

会談 KAIDAN -- conversation, discussion, interview
16

相談 SOODAN -- consultation, conversation, talk
111

冗談 JOODAN -- joke

Typical Phrases and Expanded Compounds:

日米会談
相談がまとまる
冗談ばかり

Typical Conversational Usage:

今度の日米会談はいつですか。
先生に相談してください。
あの人は冗談ばかり言っています。

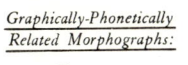

395

料

Occurrences/1000 .64
Frequency Rank 395
Sanseido Page 632
Nelson Page 690

ON: RYOO

kun:

Basic Meaning(s): charge, allowance, materials

Graphically-Phonetically Related Morphographs:

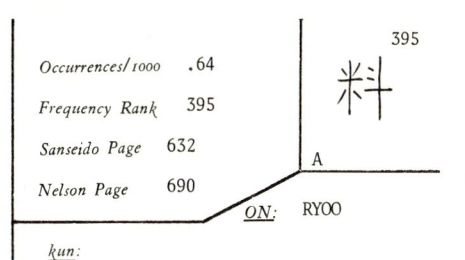

糧 RYOO (935)

High Frequency Compounds:

料理 RYOORI -- cooking, cuisine, food
59

材料 ZAIRYOO -- materials, factor,
806   data, ingredients

原料 GENRYOO -- raw materials
113

資料 SHIRYOO -- materials, data
141

See 300

Typical Phrases and Expanded Compounds:

日本料理
材料を買う
原料が入る
研究の資料

Typical Conversational Usage:

日本料理を食べたり、西洋料理を食べたりします。
手芸の材料を買って来ました。
原料が少し足りないので、すぐ仕入れなければなりません。
今、人類学の研究の資料を集めているところです。

396 込

Occurrences/1000 .64
Frequency Rank 396
Sanseido Page 438
Nelson Page 871

B

ON:

kun: ko(meru), ko(me), ko(mu), ko(mi)

Basic Meaning(s): be crowded, include, requiring, load

Graphically-Phonetically Related Morphographs:

High Frequency Compounds:

煮込み nikomi -- boiling

見込み mikomi -- hope, chance, estimate, judgment

Typical Phrases and Expanded Compounds:

煮込みおでん
完成の見込み
見込まれる

Typical Conversational Usage:

私は煮込みうどんが大好きです。
この建物は、来年の五月までに完成する見込みです。
広田部長は社長に見込まれています。
とんでもない事をして、姉にやり込められました。

Graphically-Phonetically Related Morphographs:

Occurrences/1000   .63
Frequency Rank   397
Sanseido Page   197
Nelson Page   230

397

圧

A

ON: ATSU

kun:

Basic Meaning(s): press, suppress, pressure, squeezing

High Frequency Compounds:

圧倒 667 ATTOO -- overwhelm, overpower, crush

圧力 38 ATSURYOKU -- pressure, stress

弾圧 705 DAN'ATSU -- pressure, oppression, suppression

圧迫 698 APPAKU -- pressure, oppression, tyranny

Typical Phrases and Expanded Compounds:

圧倒的に

団体の圧力

弾圧を受ける

Typical Conversational Usage:

相手が強いので、終始圧倒された試合になりました。
上より圧力がかかりました。
戦時中、キリスト教は政府の弾圧を受けました。
南さんは、仕事に圧迫を感じて、ノイローゼ気味です。

398

告

Occurrences/1000 .63
Frequency Rank 398
Sanseido Page 550
Nelson Page 245

ON: KOKU

kun: tsu(geru), tsu(ge)

Basic Meaning(s): tell, inform, announce, proclaim

Graphically-Phonetically Related Morphographs:

酷 KOKU (1376)

High Frequency Compounds:

報告 HOOKOKU -- report, information, returns
310

告白 KOKUHAKU -- confession, acknowledgment
242

忠告 CHUUKOKU -- advice, warning
1184

See 389

Typical Phrases and Expanded Compounds:

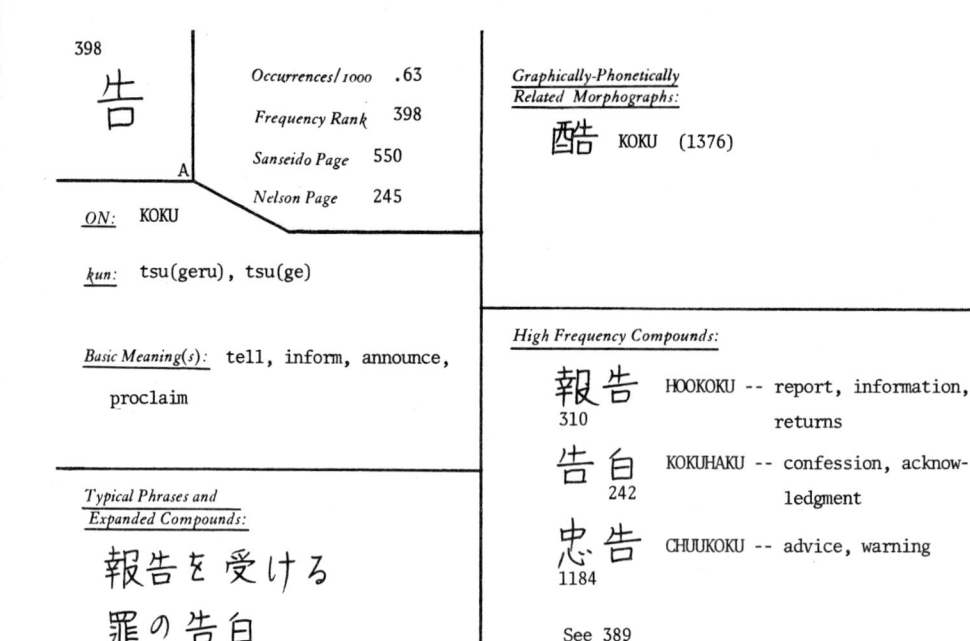

報告を受ける
罪の告白
忠告を受ける
別れを告げる

Typical Conversational Usage:

出張した小松部長から、きのう報告がありました。
犯人の告白によれば、その事件は真夜中に起こったものです。
うちの子は先生に忠告されてから、素直になりました。
告げ口をしてはいけません。

接 — 399

Graphically-Phonetically Related Morphographs:

折 SETSU (910)
拙 SETSU
摂 SETSU

Occurrences/1000: .63
Frequency Rank: 399
Sanseido Page: 387
Nelson Page: 444

ON: SETSU
kun:

Basic Meaning(s): touch, contact, adjoin, receive, encounter

High Frequency Compounds:

直接 CHOKUSETSU -- direct, immediate, personal
214

間接 KANSETSU -- indirect
31

面接 MENSETSU -- interview
117

Typical Phrases and Expanded Compounds:

直接話す
間接的に
面接試験

Typical Conversational Usage:

きのう直接先生に会って話しました。
間接的にその話を聞きました。
あした会社の面接試験があります。

400 続

Occurrences/1000 .63
Frequency Rank 400
Sanseido Page 642
Nelson Page 707

A

ON: ZOKU

kun: tsuzu(ku), tsuzu(keru), tsuzu(ki

Basic Meaning(s): continue, continuation

Graphically-Phonetically Related Morphographs:

High Frequency Compounds:

連続 101 RENZOKU -- continuity, continuation, series

相続 111 SOOZOKU -- continuation, inheritance

継続 1170 KEIZOKU -- continuation, continuance

Typical Phrases and Expanded Compounds:

不連続線
相続権
継続的な仕事
降り続く
研究を続ける

Typical Conversational Usage:

私は毎日テレビで連続家庭ドラマを見ています。
叔父は相続人として、たくさん財産をもらいました。
何とかこの仕事を継続させたいと思います。
もう雨が三日も続いて降っています。
この研究をあと二年も続けたら、アメリカへ渡るつもりです。

Graphically-Phonetically Related Morphographs:

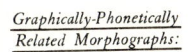

Occurrences/1000 .63
Frequency Rank 401
Sanseido Page 187
Nelson Page 219

南 401

ON: NAN

kun: minami

Basic Meaning(s): south

High Frequency Compounds:

南北 282 — NAMBOKU -- north and south

南極 311 — NANKYOKU -- South Pole

南洋 411 — NANYOO -- South Seas

Typical Phrases and Expanded Compounds:

南北に広がる
南極観測隊
南洋の島々
南アメリカ

Typical Conversational Usage:

アメリカの南北戦争は、奴隷解放の戦争として有名です。
鈴木さんは、観測隊員として、南極に越冬しています。
やしの木は、南洋の代表的な木だと思います。
ブラジルは、南アメリカで、一番大きい国です。

402

容

A

Occurrences/1000 .63
Frequency Rank 402
Sanseido Page 288
Nelson Page 320

ON: YOO

kun:

Basic Meaning(s): form, looks

Graphically-Phonetically Related Morphographs:

溶 YOO

High Frequency Compounds:

内容 NAIYOO -- contents, detail, import
77

容易 YOOI -- easy, simple
383

美容 BIYOO -- beautiful face
339

理容 RIYOO -- tonsorial art
59

See 339

Typical Phrases and Expanded Compounds:

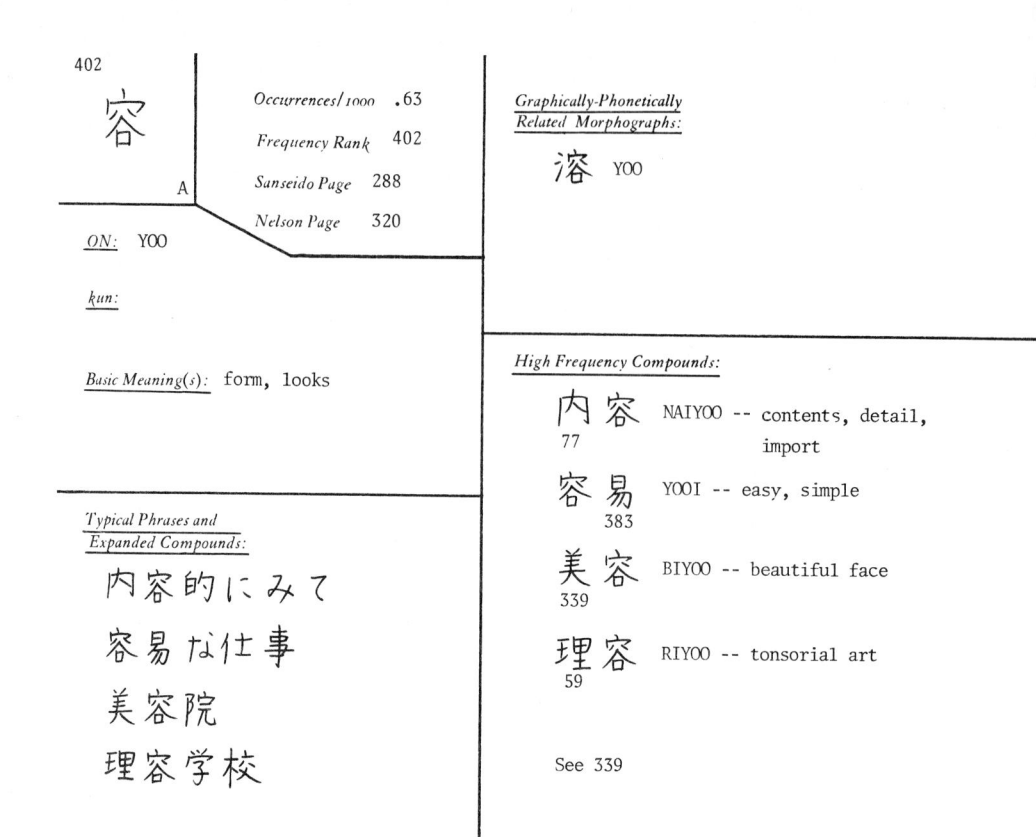

内容的にみて
容易な仕事
美容院
理容学校

Typical Conversational Usage:

仕事の内容はあまりおもしろくありません。
実際にやるのは容易ではありません。
母は、毎日、家で美容体操をしています。
理容師になるのはむずかしいですか。

格 403

Graphically-Phonetically Related Morphographs:

各 KAKU (363)
閣 KAKU (504)
客 KAKU (606)

Occurrences/1000 .62
Frequency Rank 403
Sanseido Page 523
Nelson Page 501

ON: KAKU

kun:

Basic Meaning(s): status, rank, capacity, character, standard

High Frequency Compounds:

性格 SEIKAKU -- character, personality
119

価格 KAKAKU -- price, cost, value
342

資格 SHIKAKU -- qualifications, requirements, capabilities
141

人格 JINKAKU -- character, personality, individuality
2

Typical Phrases and Expanded Compounds:

やさしい性格
価格の決定
理容師の資格
人格を重んずる

Typical Conversational Usage:

子どもは、やる事なす事に、素直に性格を表わします。
最近、大衆車の価格が少し安くなりました。
はやく看護婦の資格がとれればいいと思っています。
福沢先生の人格に心をひかれました。

404

給　A

Occurrences/1000　.62
Frequency Rank　404
Sanseido Page　639
Nelson Page　704

ON: KYUU

kun:

Basic Meaning(s): wage, gift, wage grade

*Graphically-Phonetic
Related Morphographs:*

High Frequency Compounds:

給与　KYUUYO -- grant, ration,
334　　　　　　compensation

供給　KYOOKYUU -- supply
340

給料　KYUURYOO -- wages, salary,
395　　　　　　payroll

Typical Phrases and Expanded Compounds:

公務員の給与
供給の不足
給料日

Typical Conversational Usage:

年々、公務員の給与はよくなっています。
ひでりが続いて、水の供給に困っています。
会社の給料日は毎月二十五日です。

Graphically-Phonetically Related Morphographs:

Occurrences/1000   .62
Frequency Rank   405
Sanseido Page   213
Nelson Page   768

色 405
A

ON: SHIKI, SHOKU

kun: iro

Basic Meaning(s): color, tint, complexion, look, charms

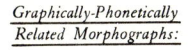

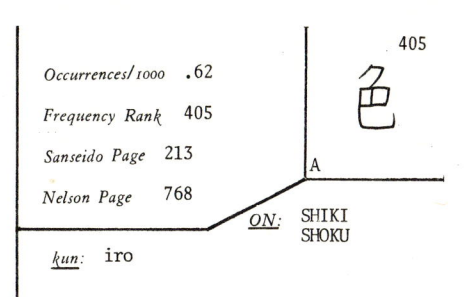

High Frequency Compounds:

景色 617 — KESHIKI -- scenery, landscape
血色 489 — KESSHOKU -- complexion
特色 186 — TOKUSHOKU -- characteristic, peculiarity
顔色 355 — kaoiro — complexion, countenance, expression

Typical Phrases and Expanded Compounds:

美しい景色
血色がいい
特色のある学校
顔色をうかがう

Typical Conversational Usage:

この絵を見ると、いなかを思い出します。
南さんは、食事がすすんで、血色もよくなってきたそうです。
この学校は、女生徒が多いのが特色です。
葉子さんは具合が悪く、顔色もよくありません。

406 赤

Occurrences/1000 .62
Frequency Rank 406
Sanseido Page 241
Nelson Page 853

ON: SEKI, SHAKU

kun: aka, aka(i)

Basic Meaning(s): red, crimson, scarlet

Graphically-Phonetically Related Morphographs:

跡 SEKI (1145)

High Frequency Compounds:

赤十字 SEKIJUUJI -- Red Cross
22 515

赤道 SEKIDOO -- equator
123

赤面 SEKIMEN -- a blush, shamefacedness
117

赤字 akaJI -- red figures, deficit
515

Typical Phrases and Expanded Compounds:

日本赤十字社
赤道直下
赤面のいたり
赤字財政

Typical Conversational Usage:

国際赤十字はとてもよい組織です。
船で赤道を通った時、赤道祭をしました。
人を赤面させるようなことを言ってはいけません。
運営が困難なので、赤字になってしまいました。
赤い花がきれいに咲いています。

Graphically-Phonetically Related Morphographs:

	407
Occurrences/1000 .61	撃
Frequency Rank 407	
Sanseido Page 471	B
Nelson Page 450	

<u>ON</u>: GEKI

<u>kun</u>:

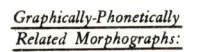

High Frequency Compounds:

攻撃 — KOOGEKI -- attack, assault, criticism
588

爆撃 — BAKUGEKI -- bombing
309

打撃 — DAGEKI -- blow, hit, shock
435

Basic Meaning(s): attack, defeat, destroy, conquer

Typical Phrases and Expanded Compounds:

攻撃を開始する
爆撃音
打撃をうける

Typical Conversational Usage:

共産側の攻撃がはげしくなったようです。
あの車の音は、まるで爆撃音です。
山口さんに会社をやめられて、仕事に大きな打撃をうけました。

408

元 A

ON: GAN, GEN
kun: moto

Occurrences/1000 .61
Frequency Rank 408
Sanseido Page 77
Nelson Page 108

Basic Meaning(s): beginning, origin, foundation, New Years Day, first year of an era

Graphically-Phonetically Related Morphographs:

High Frequency Compounds:

元気 GENKI -- vigor, energy, vitality
55

元日 GANJITSU -- New Years Day
3

紀元 GANJITSU -- era, epoch, A.D.
616

Typical Phrases and Expanded Compounds:

元気な子
元日早々
紀元前

Typical Conversational Usage:

いなかのおじいさんは元気にくらしています。
元日に、子どもたちはお年玉をもらいました。
バビロン帝国は、紀元前の何世紀頃でしたか。

Graphically-Phonetically Related Morphographs:

草 SOO (649)

High Frequency Compounds:

早速 SASSOKU -- at once, immediately, quick
766

早熟 SOOJUKU -- early maturity, premature growth
1219

早合点 hayaGATTEN -- hasty conclusion
33 175

Occurrences/1000   .61
Frequency Rank   409
Sanseido Page   483
Nelson Page   476

早 409
A

ON: SOO
kun: haya(i)

Basic Meaning(s): fast, quick, early

Typical Phrases and Expanded Compounds:

早速ですが
早熟な子
早合点する

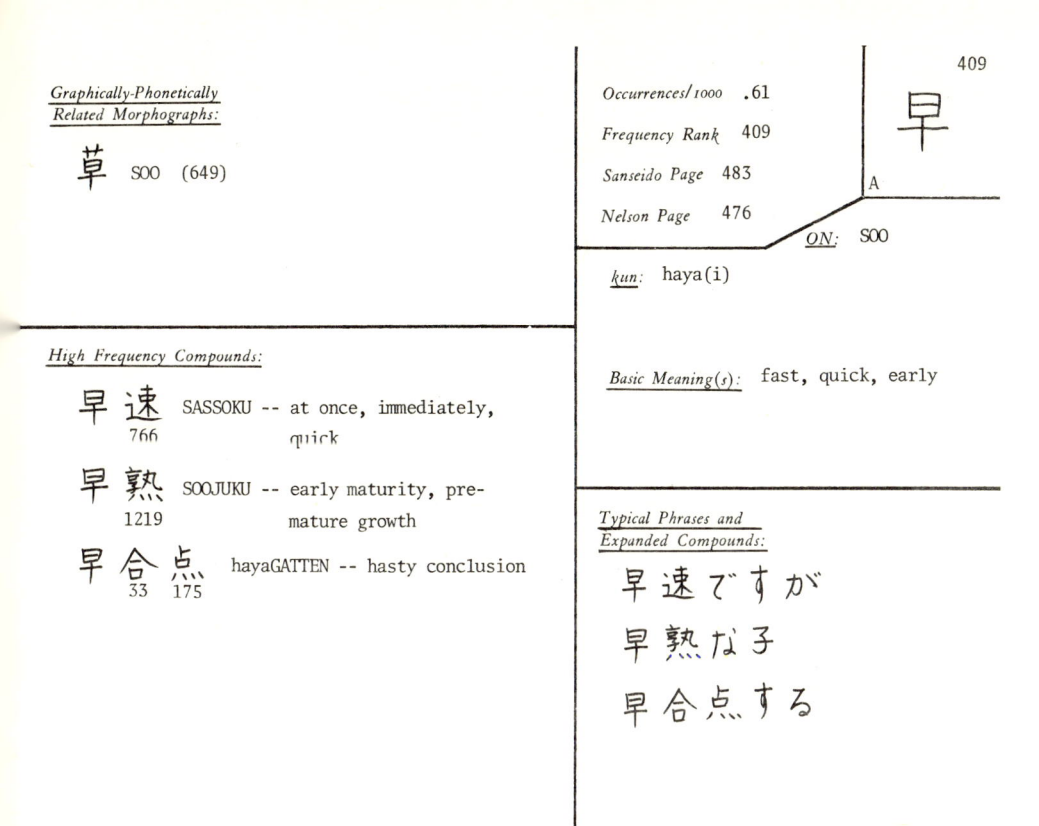

Typical Conversational Usage:

今日着いた小荷物、早速取りにうかがいます。
あの子は早熟で、あまり言うことが感心しません。
早合点して、とんでもない失敗をしてしまいました。

410

着

A

Occurrences/1000 .61
Frequency Rank 410
Sanseido Page 651
Nelson Page 723

ON: CHAKU

kun: ki(ru), ki(seru), tsu(ku)

Basic Meaning(s): wear, clothe, put on, arrive, arrive at

Graphically-Phonetically Related Morphographs:

High Frequency Compounds:

着物 kimono -- kimono, clothes, dress
95

着実 CHAKUJITSU -- sincerity, steadiness
37

先着 SENCHAKU -- early arrival, first arrival
115

Typical Phrases and Expanded Compounds:

着物の裏表
着実性をもって
先着順

Typical Conversational Usage:

私はドレスより着物の方が日本的で、とても好きです。
地下鉄の工事は着実に進行しています。
指定席がないので、先着順によい席が取れるそうです。

411

洋

Graphically-Phonetically Related Morphographs:

様　YOO　(216)
養　YOO　(586)
羊　YOO

Occurrences/1000　.60
Frequency Rank　411
Sanseido Page　402
Nelson Page　546

ON: YOO

kun:

Basic Meaning(s):　ocean, Western, foreign

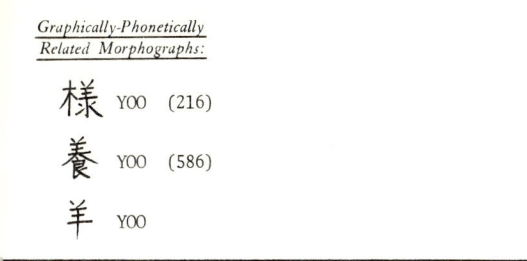

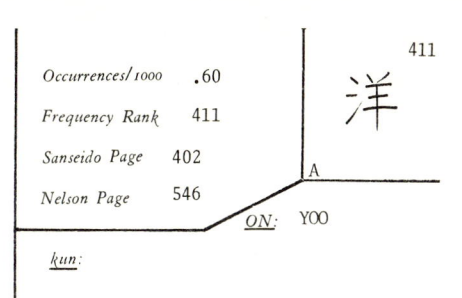

High Frequency Compounds:

西洋　SEIYOO -- Western countries,
198　　　　the West
東洋　TOOYOO -- Eastern countries, the
108　　　　East, the Orient
洋服　YOOHUKU -- European-style clothes,
176　　　　Western dress

Typical Phrases and Expanded Compounds:

西洋式
東洋風
こんの洋服

Typical Conversational Usage:

来年は、ぜひ西洋諸国を旅行してみたいと思います。
日本画は、東洋美術の中でも代表的なものです。
こんの洋服が似合うので、先日銀座の店であつらえました。

412 院

Occurrences/1000 .59
Frequency Rank 412
Sanseido Page 427
Nelson Page 929

ON: IN

kun:

Basic Meaning(s): institution, school, hospital, congress

Graphically-Phonetically Related Morphographs:

High Frequency Compounds:

上院 JOOIN -- Upper House, House of
29   Lords, Senate

病院 BYOOIN -- hospital
502

入院 NYUUIN -- admission to a hospi-
65   tal

大学院 DAIGAKUIN -- graduate
5 15   school

See 339

Typical Phrases and Expanded Compounds:

上院議員
病院の設備
入院患者
大学院生

Typical Conversational Usage:

アメリカの議会制度は、上院と下院に分れています。
弟は、現在、東大病院に入院しています。
早川さんが入院してから、もうまる一月になります。
大学院で、今、昭和文学の研究に取り組んでいます。

Graphically-Phonetically Related Morphographs:

Occurrences/1000 .59	演 413
Frequency Rank 413	
Sanseido Page 415	
Nelson Page 569	

ON: EN

kun:

Basic Meaning(s): act, perform

High Frequency Compounds:

演説 ENZETSU -- speech, lecture, address
240

講演 KOOEN -- lecture, address
469

演奏 ENSOO -- musical performance, recital

Typical Phrases and Expanded Compounds:

名演説
講演会
名演奏家

Typical Conversational Usage:

長い演説はもうこりごりです。
山下先生の講演は、日比谷公会堂で行われます。
今晩ピアノの演奏会がありますので、いっしょに行きませんか。

414 割

Occurrences/1000	.59
Frequency Rank	414
Sanseido Page	174
Nelson Page	202

A

ON: KATSU

kun: wa(ru), wari, wa(reru)

Basic Meaning(s): split, divide, cut, break, proportion, rate, ratio, 10%

Graphically-Phonetically Related Morphographs:

轄 KATSU

High Frequency Compounds:

役割 (266) YAKUwari -- role, part, allotment of duties

割合 (33) wariai -- rate, ratio, comparatively

分割 (89) BUNKATSU -- partition, division, dismemberment

割引 (263) waribiki -- discount, reduction

Typical Phrases and Expanded Compounds:

自分の役割
割合じょうずに
土地の分割
割引券
物事を割り切る

Typical Conversational Usage:

自分の役割を果たして、ほっとしました。
今度の選挙では、割合楽に勝つことができました。
テレビと冷蔵庫を分割払いで買いました。
いつも物事は、割り切って考えることにしています。

止　415

Graphically-Phonetically Related Morphographs:

歯　SHI　(1083)

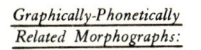

祉　SHI

紫　SHI

Occurrences/1000 .59
Frequency Rank 415
Sanseido Page 194
Nelson Page 518

ON: SHI
kun: to(meru), toma(ru)

Basic Meaning(s): stop, end, interrupt, cease

High Frequency Compounds:

禁止 KINSHI -- prohibition, ban, taboo
732

防止 BOOSHI -- prevention
326

中止 CHUUSHI -- suspension, stoppage, interruption
12

廃止 HAISHI -- abolition, discontinuance, abrogation
1120

Typical Phrases and Expanded Compounds:

立入禁止
水害防止対策
試合中止
制度の廃止

Typical Conversational Usage:

この土地は、測量のため立入禁止になっています。
水害防止対策がもうけられました。
雨のため、試合が中止になりました。
悪い制度は廃止しなければなりません。
車を止めて、少し休んでから行きましょう。

416 識

Occurrences/1000: .59
Frequency Rank: 416
Sanseido Page: 690
Nelson Page: 840

A

ON: SHIKI

kun:

Basic Meaning(s): know, knowledge, understanding

Typical Phrases and Expanded Compounds:

知識階級
認識不足
常識を欠く

Graphically-Phonetically Related Morphographs:

織 SHIKI (611)

High Frequency Compounds:

知識 CHISHIKI -- knowledge, information, learning
73

認識 NINSHIKI -- recognition, understanding, knowledge
357

常識 JOOSHIKI -- common sense
190

Typical Conversational Usage:

私は、いろいろな知識を身につけたいです。
もう少し認識があれば、よかったと思います。
あの方の行動は常識を欠いています。

Graphically-Phonetically Related Morphographs:

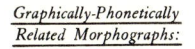

Occurrences/1000 .59	417
Frequency Rank 417	種
Sanseido Page 606	A
Nelson Page 668	

ON: SHU

kun: tane

Basic Meaning(s): seed, kind, class, species, variety

High Frequency Compounds:

一種 ISSHU -- a kind, a species
1

種々 SHUJU -- variety

種類 SHURUI -- kind, variety, class
480

人種 JINSHU -- race of people
2

Typical Phrases and Expanded Compounds:

一種の偏見

種々の問題

各種類

人種差別

一粒種

Typical Conversational Usage:

アベベ選挙の走り方は、一種独特でした。
種々の高山植物を集めて研究しています。
桜の花は全部で何種類ありますか。
人種問題はアメリカにとって、大きな問題と言えるでしょう。
和ちゃんは、一粒種でみんなにかわいがられています。

418

処

A

Occurrences/1000: .59
Frequency Rank: 418
Sanseido Page: 256
Nelson Page: 281

ON: SHO

kun:

Basic Meaning(s): deal with, manage, behave

Typical Phrases and Expanded Compounds:

退学処分
汚水の処理
問題に対処する

Graphically-Phonetically Related Morphographs:

High Frequency Compounds:

処分 ₂₈ SHOBUN -- disposition of, management

処理 ₅₉ SHORI -- procedure, management, treatment

対処 ₃₉ TAISHO -- dealing with, coping with

Typical Conversational Usage:

彼は過激な学生だったので、退学処分になりました。
その問題はもう処理してしまいました。
どのように対処したらよいか、わかりません。

Graphically-Phonetically Related Morphographs:

Occurrences/1000 .59	勝
Frequency Rank 419	
Sanseido Page 499	
Nelson Page 748	A

<u>ON</u>: SHOO

<u>kun</u>: ka(tsu)

Basic Meaning(s): victory, win, excel, surpass

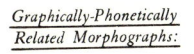

High Frequency Compounds:

勝利 SHOORI -- victory
180

勝敗 SHOOHAI -- victory or defeat,
420   the issue (of a battle)

勝手 katte -- kitchen, condition,
57   one's own convenience

Typical Phrases and Expanded Compounds:

勝利投手
勝敗を決める
勝手気まま

Typical Conversational Usage:

みんなの団結が勝利をもたらしたのです。
勝敗が決まらないまま、引き分けになりました。
自分勝手な事ばかりしてはいけません。
勝っても、敗けても、最後までがんばらなければ
なりません。

420

敗 A

Occurrences/1000 .59
Frequency Rank 420
Sanseido Page 693
Nelson Page 847

ON: HAI

kun: yabu(reru), yabu(ru)

Basic Meaning(s): defeat, be defeated

Graphically-Phonetically Related Morphographs:

High Frequency Compounds:

敗北 282 — HAIBOKU -- defeat, reversal, rout

敗戦 32 — HAISEN -- defeat, a lost battle

腐敗 1243 — HUHAI -- decay, decomposition, rottenness

失敗 346 — SHIPPAI -- failure, mistake, blunder

Typical Phrases and Expanded Compounds:

敗北の結果
敗戦後
腐敗した政治
大失敗

Typical Conversational Usage:

敗北の原因は練習不足だったからです。
軍事的に強かっただけに、敗戦の痛手は大きかったです。
誰でも失敗はするものです。
ほんのわずかの差で、試合に敗れました。

Graphically-Phonetically Related Morphographs:

Occurrences/1000 .58	421
Frequency Rank 421	回
Sanseido Page 235	A
Nelson Page 258	

ON: KAI, E

kun: mawa(su), mawa(ru)

High Frequency Compounds:

回復 KAIHUKU -- recovery, restoration, rehabilitation
537

回答 KAITOO -- reply
565

今回 KONKAI -- this time, lately
50

Basic Meaning(s): time, round, turn, spin, go around

Typical Phrases and Expanded Compounds:

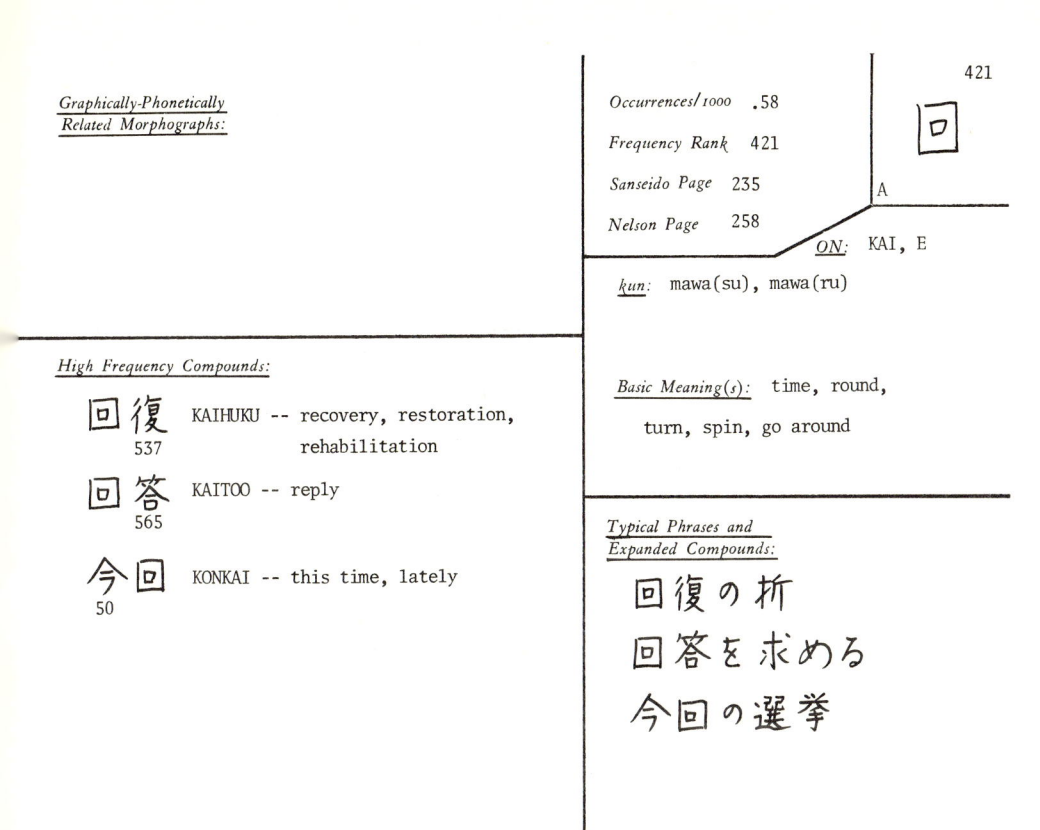

回復の折
回答を求める
今回の選挙

Typical Conversational Usage:

手術後の回復を待って、社長に話すつもりです。
会社側にいくら求めても、回答が得られませんでした。
今回のキャンプはとても楽しかったので、また来年行くつもりです。
小さい時、よくこまを回して遊びました。

422 及

Occurrences/1000 .58
Frequency Rank 422
Sanseido Page 59
Nelson Page 80

B

ON: KYUU

kun: oyo(bu), oyo(bi)

Basic Meaning(s): reach, cause, happen to, and

Typical Phrases and Expanded Compounds:

及第点
普及率
及びもつかない

Graphically-Phonetically Related Morphographs:

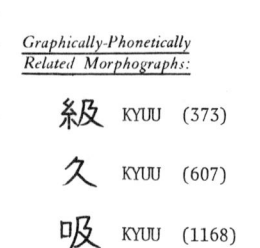

級 KYUU (373)
久 KYUU (607)
吸 KYUU (1168)

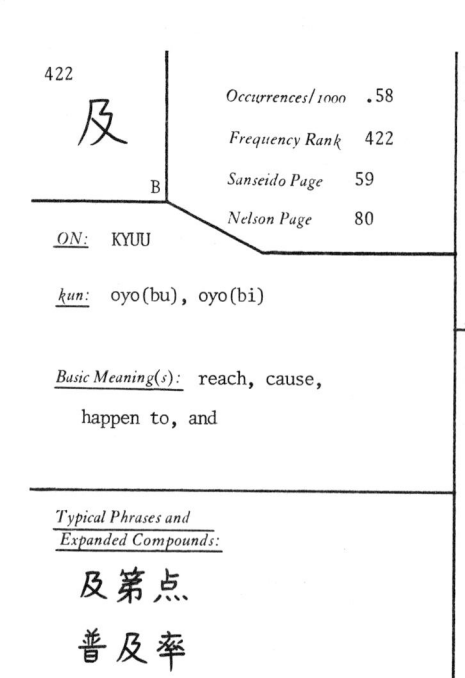

High Frequency Compounds:

及第 KYUUDAI -- passing an examination
83

普及 HUKYUU -- diffusion, dissemination
894

Typical Conversational Usage:

何とか及第点は、取らなければなりません。
日本のテレビの普及率は、大変高くなりました。
及ばずながら、何とかやってみましょう。

Graphically-Phonetically
Related Morphographs:

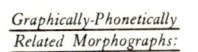

Occurrences/1000 .58	423
Frequency Rank 423	幸
Sanseido Page 242	
Nelson Page 272	A

<u>ON</u>: KOO

<u>kun</u>: saiwa(i)

High Frequency Compounds:

幸福　KOOHUKU -- happiness, welfare
583

不幸　HUKOO -- unhappiness, sorrow,
103　　　　　　　death

幸運　KOOUN -- good fortune, luck
157

Basic Meaning(s): happiness, fortune, blessing

Typical Phrases and
Expanded Compounds:

幸福な家庭
不幸な子ども
幸運な人
幸いにも

Typical Conversational Usage:

幸子さんが幸福であったとは、いちがいには言えません。
その子は、事故で両親をなくした不幸な子どもなんです。
幸運にも、今度ヨーロッパへ旅行することになりました。
ロンドンで、大山さんに会えて幸いでした。

424

深

Occurrences/1000 .58
Frequency Rank 424
Sanseido Page 407
Nelson Page 558

A

ON: SHIN

kun: huka(i), huka(meru), huka(maru)

Basic Meaning(s): deep, deepen, intensify

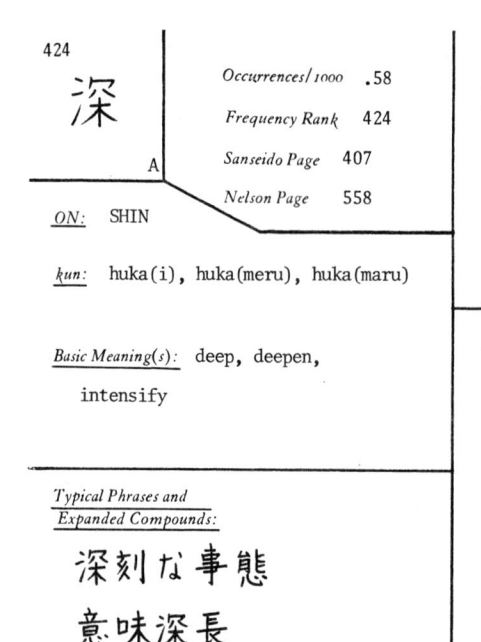

Graphically-Phonetically Related Morphographs:

High Frequency Compounds:

深刻　SHINKOKU -- deep, profound, serious, severe
844

深長　SHINCHOO -- deep, profound
90

Typical Phrases and Expanded Compounds:

深刻な事態
意味深長
深い海

Typical Conversational Usage:

公害は深刻な問題になっています。
あの方の言ったことばは、なかなか意味深長です。
田沢湖は、日本で一番深い湖です。

Graphically-Phonetically Related Morphographs:

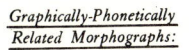

Occurrences/1000 .58	425
Frequency Rank 425	段
Sanseido Page 540	
Nelson Page 524	A

ON: DAN

kun:

Basic Meaning(s): steps, stair, column, paragraph, grade

High Frequency Compounds:

手段 SHUDAN -- resources, way, means
57

段階 DANKAI -- grade, rank, step
   328

段々 DANDAN -- gradually, steps, staircase

階段 KAIDAN -- steps, stairway
328

Typical Phrases and Expanded Compounds:

最後の手段
今の段階では
段々ばたけ
階段をのぼる

Typical Conversational Usage:

どうしようもないので、最後の手段をとることにしました。
今の段階では、まだ発表できません。
ドイツ語が段々話せるようになり、とてもおもしろいです。
階段からすべり落ちて、大けがをしました。

426 断

Occurrences/1000: .58
Frequency Rank: 426
Sanseido Page: 632
Nelson Page: 466

A

ON: DAN

kun: ta(tsu), kotowa(ru), kotowa(ri)

Basic Meaning(s): decision, judgment, decline, refuse, cut off

Typical Phrases and Expanded Compounds:

判断を誤る
断定を下す
横断歩道
断わりなく

Graphically-Phonetically Related Morphographs:

High Frequency Compounds:

判断 (187) HANDAN -- judgment, decision, adjudication
断定 (93) DANTEI -- decision, conclusion
横断 (511) OODAN -- crossing, intersection

Typical Conversational Usage:

判断を誤って、とんでもない失敗をしてしまいました。
すぐに断定を下すわけにはいきません。
道を横断する時は、気をつけなければなりません。
そんなことは、お断わりします。

破
427

Occurrences/1000 .58
Frequency Rank 427
Sanseido Page 592
Nelson Page 651

A

<u>ON</u>: HA

<u>kun</u>: yabu(ru), yabu(reru), yabu(re)

Basic Meaning(s): tear, rip, rend, crush, destroy

Graphically-Phonetically Related Morphographs:

波 HA (790)

High Frequency Compounds:

破壊 802 HAKAI -- destruction, demolition, collapse

打破 435 DAHA -- breaking, destruction, defeat

Typical Phrases and Expanded Compounds:

破壊的行為
因習の打破
約束を破る

Typical Conversational Usage:

この町は、戦争で見る影もなく破壊されました。
悪い習慣は、打破していかなければなりません。
約束は、いつも破らないようにしています。

428

害

A

Occurrences/1000 .58
Frequency Rank 428
Sanseido Page 287
Nelson Page 320

ON: GAI

kun:

Basic Meaning(s): harm, injury, damage, mischief

Typical Phrases and Expanded Compounds:

災害を防ぐ
身体障害者
水害対策
大被害

Graphically-Phonetically Related Morphographs:

High Frequency Compounds:

災害 863 — SAIGAI -- disaster, calamity, accident

障害 530 — SHOOGAI -- obstacle, hindrance, difficulty

水害 166 — SUIGAI -- flood damage, inundation

被害 555 — HIGAI -- damage, harm, casualties

Typical Conversational Usage:

事前に、災害を防ぐように気をつけましょう。
あの方は言語障害のため、小さい時から、大変苦労されているそうです。
この辺は、去年の台風で水害をうけました。
きのうの火災で、会社は大きな被害をこうむりました。

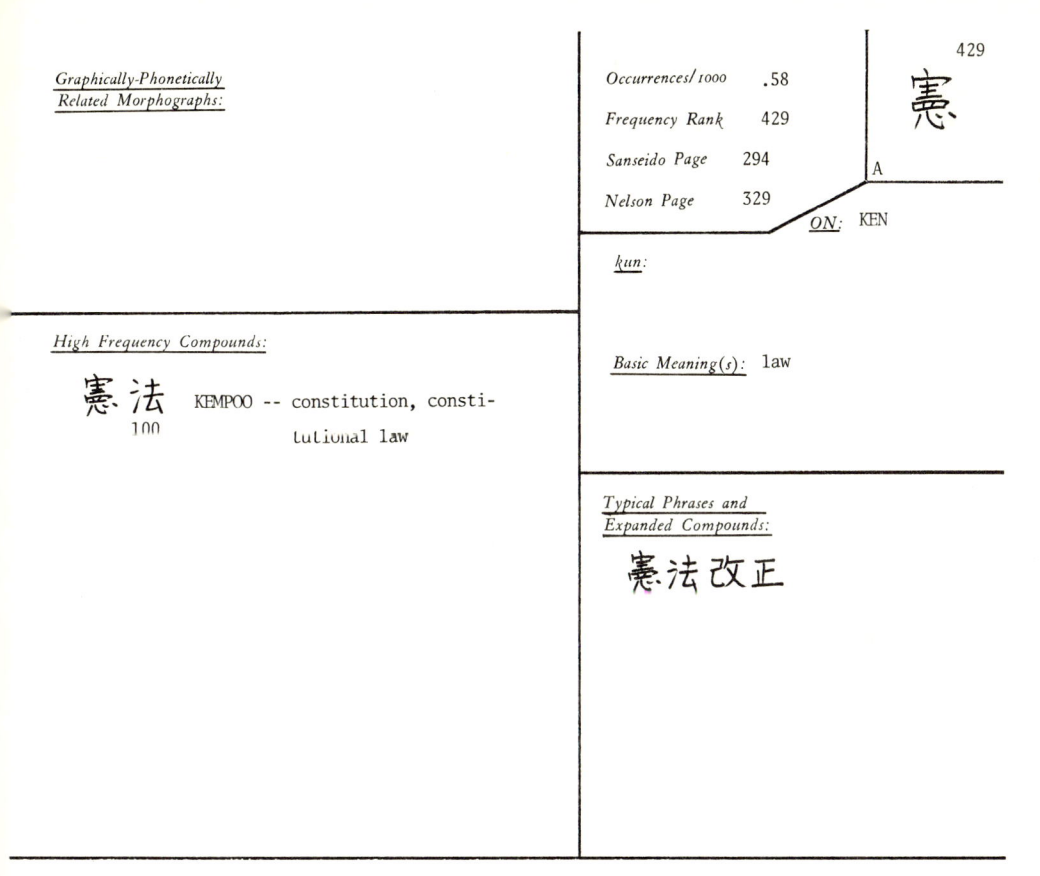

Graphically-Phonetically Related Morphographs:

Occurrences/1000	.58
Frequency Rank	429
Sanseido Page	294
Nelson Page	329

憲 429

A

ON: KEN

kun:

Basic Meaning(s): law

High Frequency Compounds:

憲法　KEMPOO -- constitution, consti-
100　　　　tutional law

Typical Phrases and Expanded Compounds:

憲法改正

Typical Conversational Usage:

五月三日は、憲法記念日で、祭日になっています。

430 状

A

Occurrences/1000: .58
Frequency Rank: 430
Sanseido Page: 456
Nelson Page: 592

ON: JOO

kun:

Basic Meaning(s): condition, circumstance, form

Typical Phrases and Expanded Compounds:

良い状態
現状維持
状況判断

Graphically-Phonetically Related Morphographs:

High Frequency Compounds:

状態 JOOTAI -- state of affairs, situation
330

現状 GENJOO -- existing state of affairs, status quo
67

状況 JOOKYOO -- circumstances
883

Typical Conversational Usage:

今の状態では、来年渡米できるかどうかわかりません。
調査団が現状を調べに来ました。
現在の状況では無理もありません。

Graphically-Phonetically Related Morphographs:

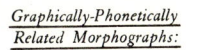

Occurrences/1000 .58	431
Frequency Rank 431	存
Sanseido Page 185	
Nelson Page 309	A

ON: SON, ZON

kun:

High Frequency Compounds:

存在　SONZAI -- existence, being, subsistence
182

依存　IZON -- dependence, reliance
961

保存　HOZON -- preservation, storage, conservation
163

Basic Meaning(s): know, be aware, exist, remain

Typical Phrases and Expanded Compounds:

大きな存在
依存性が強い
保存物

Typical Conversational Usage:

内原さんは、営業部で貴重な存在です。
もう一人前なので、親に依存しない生活をしています。
あまり長く保存しないで、めしあがった方がよろしいです。

432

藤

X

Occurrences/1000 .58
Frequency Rank 432
Sanseido Page 348
Nelson Page 792

ON: (TOO)

kun: (huji)

Basic Meaning(s): wisteria

Graphically-Phonetically Related Morphographs:

High Frequency Compounds:

藤色 hujiiro -- light purple, lavender
405

Occurs most frequently in proper names, such as, 佐藤, "Satoo," 加藤, "Katoo," and 藤本, "Fujimoto."

Typical Phrases and Expanded Compounds:

藤色の洋服
藤の花

Typical Conversational Usage:

加藤さんは、洋服屋に行って、藤色のワンピースを買いました。

Graphically-Phonetically Related Morphographs:

	433 買
Occurrences/1000 .58	
Frequency Rank 433	
Sanseido Page 585	A
Nelson Page 718	
	ON: BAI
	kun: ka(u)

High Frequency Compounds:

売買 BAIBAI -- trading, buying and
313　　　　　　selling, sale

買収 BAISHUU -- buying up, purchasing
516

買物 kaimono -- purchase, shopping,
95　　　　　　 bargain

Basic Meaning(s): buying, buy

Typical Phrases and Expanded Compounds:

土地の売買
家屋の買収
買物のメモ
本を買う

Typical Conversational Usage:

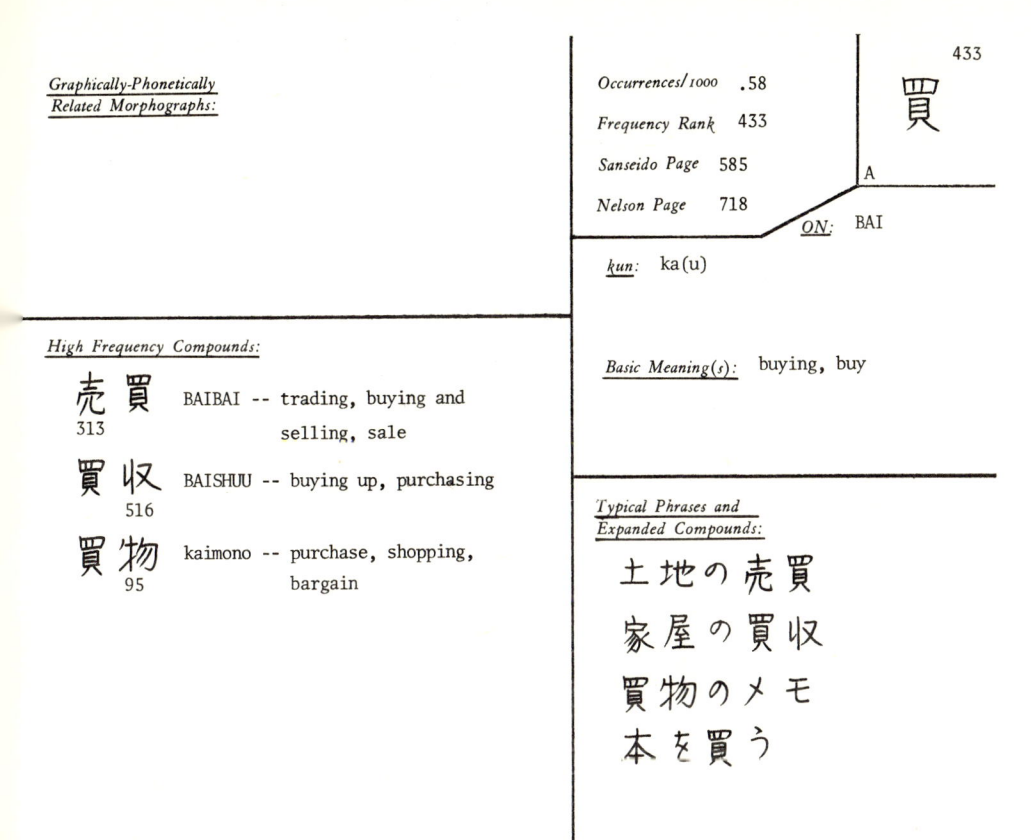

市場では、朝早くから、野菜の売買が行われます。
この土地は買収されることになりました。
買物をする時、メモを持っていると便利です。
おみやげに何を買ったらよいか、まだ決めていません。

434

挙

Occurrences/1000 .57
Frequency Rank 434
Sanseido Page 674
Nelson Page 435

ON: KYO

kun:

Basic Meaning(s): plan, project, celebrate, ceremony

Graphically-Phonetically Related Morphographs:

High Frequency Compounds:

選挙 SENKYO -- election
341

検挙 KENKYO -- arrest, roundup
473

挙式 KYOSHIKI -- holding a ceremony
356

Typical Phrases and Expanded Compounds:

選挙権
再検挙
挙式をあげる

Typical Conversational Usage:

今回の選挙は、まれにみる激戦でした。
検挙された者の中には、名の知られた人もいました。
来年の五月に、春子さんたちは、挙式をあげることに決まったそうです。

Graphically-Phonetically Related Morphographs:

Occurrences/1000 .57	435
Frequency Rank 435	打
Sanseido Page 375	
Nelson Page 423	A
	ON: DA
kun: u(tsu)	

Basic Meaning(s): hitting, striking, hit, strike, beat

High Frequency Compounds:

打撃 DAGEKI -- blow, hit, shock
407

打倒 DATOO -- overthrow, strike down
667

打算 DASAN -- calculation, self-
499　　　　 interest, selfishness

Typical Phrases and Expanded Compounds:

決定的な打撃
内閣の打倒
打算的

Typical Conversational Usage:

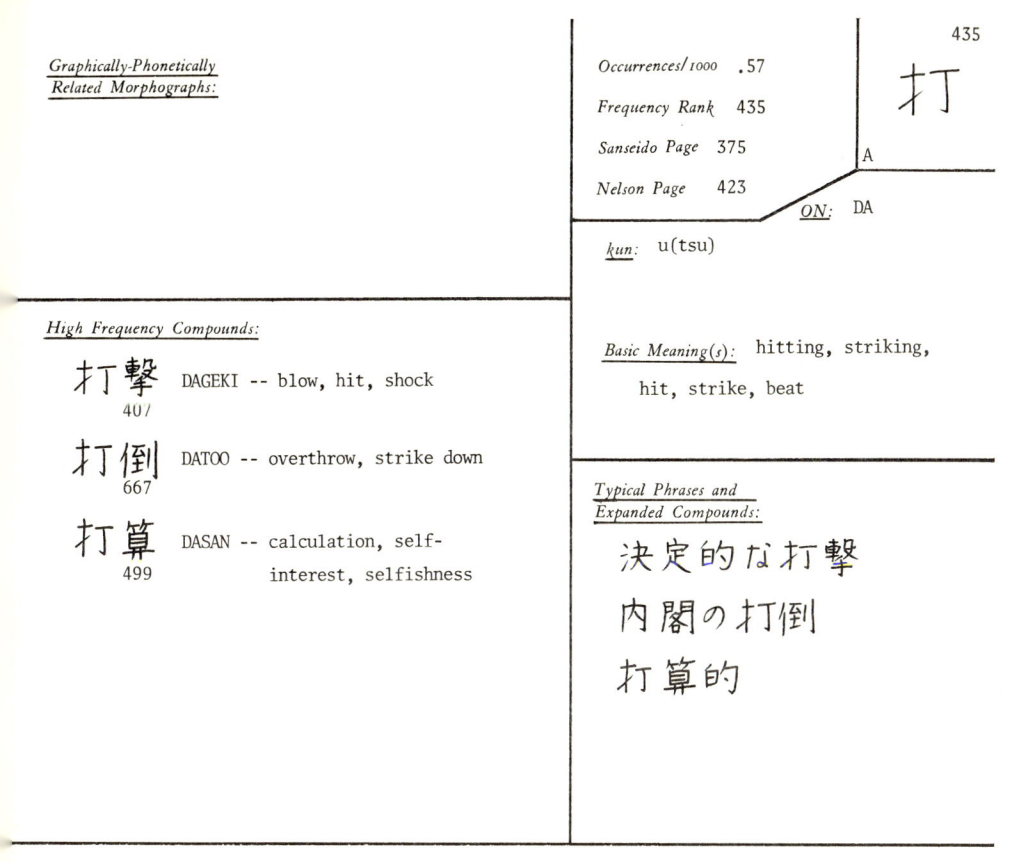

ストライキが長びけば、会社側にとって大きな打撃です。
野党は、内閣の打倒をめざして必死です。
あまり打算的なので、彼女はみんなからいやがられています。

436

台

A

Occurrences/1000   .57
Frequency Rank   436
Sanseido Page   200
Nelson Page   235

ON: DAI, TAI

kun:

Basic Meaning(s): pedestal, table, stand, bench

Graphically-Phonetically Related Morphographs:

High Frequency Compounds:

舞台   BUTAI -- stage
638

台所   DAIdokoro -- kitchen
129

土台   DODAI -- foundation, base, groundwork
360

台風   TAIHUU -- typhoon
316

Typical Phrases and Expanded Compounds:

舞台装置

台所の改造

土台の修理

台風の目

Typical Conversational Usage:

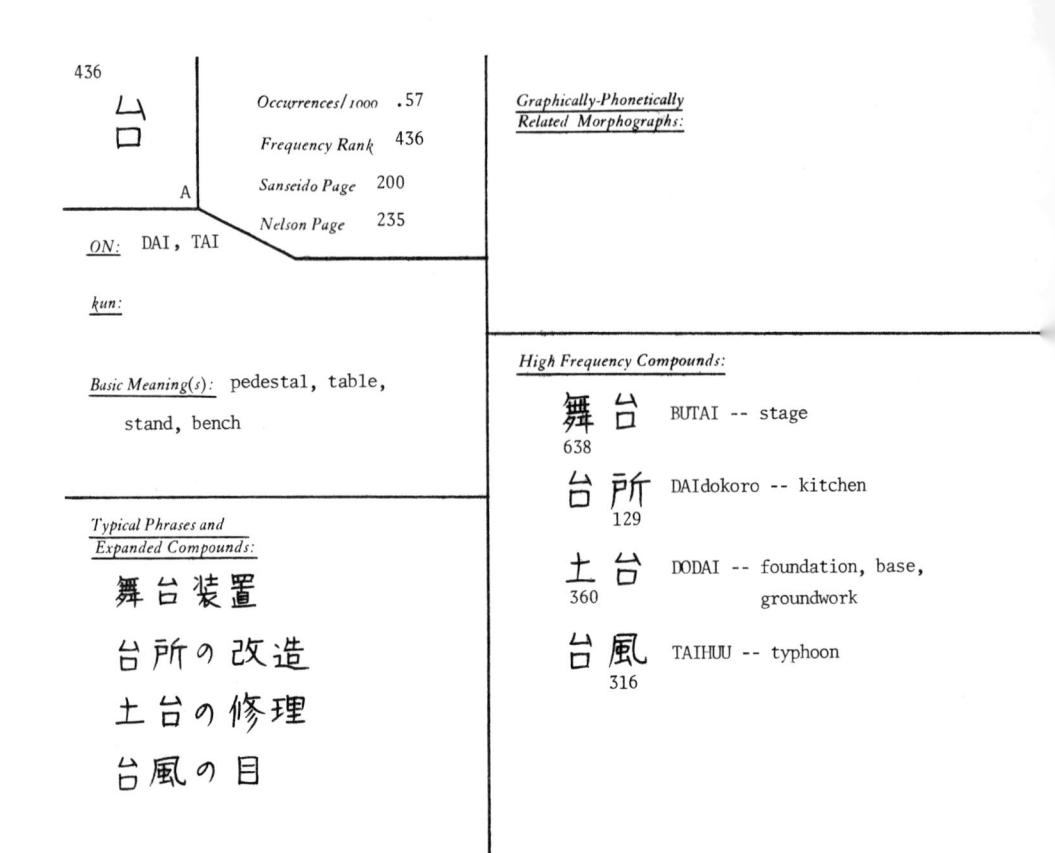

初舞台をいつふみましたか。
最近の家は、台所がモダンになりました。
あまり家が古いので、土台からしっかり直さなければなりません。
夏の終わりには、必ずと言っていい程、日本は台風におそわれます。

Graphically-Phonetically Related Morphographs:

	437
Occurrences/1000 .56	困
Frequency Rank 437	
Sanseido Page 236	
Nelson Page 259	A
	ON: KON
	kun: koma(ru)

High Frequency Compounds:

困難 KONNAN -- trouble, distress, perplexity
351

貧困 HINKON -- poverty, lack
507

Basic Meaning(s): be distressed, be in trouble, be destitute, embarrased

Typical Phrases and Expanded Compounds:

困難な作業
貧困対策
返事に困る

Typical Conversational Usage:

仕事には困難がつきものです。
政府は貧困対策に乗り出しました。
お金がなくて困りました。

438

師

Occurrences/1000: .57
Frequency Rank: 438
Sanseido Page: 72
Nelson Page: 73

A

ON: SHI

kun:

Basic Meaning(s): teacher, master, army, expedition

Graphically-Phonetically Related Morphographs:

市 SHI (305)
姉 SHI (1217)

High Frequency Compounds:

教師 KYOOSHI -- teacher, minister, rabbi
58

医師 ISHI -- doctor
772

Typical Phrases and Expanded Compounds:

家庭教師
医師の診断
山本師

Typical Conversational Usage:

あの方は、もう三十年も教師をしています。
入社するために、医師の診断書が必要です。
講師に吉田師を招いています。

精 439

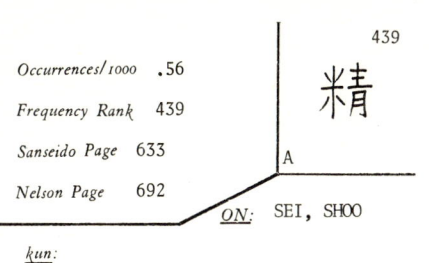

Graphically-Phonetically Related Morphographs:

青 SEI (393)   静 SEI (744)
清 SEI (596)   晴 SEI (949)
請 SEI (743)

High Frequency Compounds:

精神 191 — SEISHIN -- mind, spirit, soul, heart

精算 499 — SEISAN -- exact calculation, accurate account

Occurrences/1000 .56
Frequency Rank 439
Sanseido Page 633
Nelson Page 692

A

ON: SEI, SHOO

kun:

Basic Meaning(s): spirit, ghost, fairy, energy, details

Typical Phrases and Expanded Compounds:

精神薄弱
運賃の精算

Typical Conversational Usage:

あまり仕事が多いので、父は精神的に疲れています。
乗り越しの運賃をどこで精算したらよろしいですか。

440

送

A

Occurrences/1000   .56
Frequency Rank   440
Sanseido Page   441
Nelson Page   875

ON: SOO

kun: oku(ru)

Basic Meaning(s): send, sending

Graphically-Phonetically Related Morphographs:

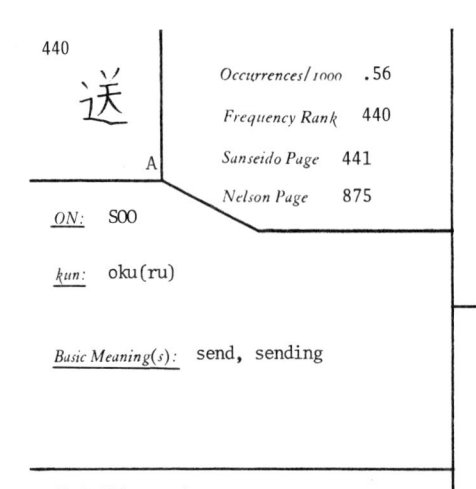

Typical Phrases and Expanded Compounds:

放送局
運送店
送迎会
プレゼントを送る

High Frequency Compounds:

放送   HOOSOO -- broadcasting
325

運送   UNSOO -- shipping, transpor-
157   tation, forwarding

送迎   SOOGEI -- seeing (someone)
805   off, and meeting
                       upon return

Typical Conversational Usage:

夕べの放送で、その事件を知りました。
車で運送した場合、何日くらいかかりますか。
きのう、古い先生と新しい先生の送迎会がありました。
東京にいる弟に、お金を送りました。

Graphically-Phonetically Related Morphographs:

441

造

Occurrences/*1000* .56
Frequency Rank 441
Sanseido Page 443
Nelson Page 880

A

ON: ZOO
kun: tsuku(ru), tsuku(ri)

Basic Meaning(s): build, make, workmanship

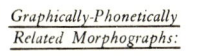

High Frequency Compounds:

造船 ZOOSEN -- shipbuilding
518

構造 KOOZOO -- construction, frame-
498   work, structure

製造 SEIZOO -- manufacture, produc-
521   tion, making

改造 KAIZOO -- remodeling, reconstruc-
289   tion

創造 SOOZOO -- creation
976

Typical Phrases and Expanded Compounds:

造船会社
人体の構造
製造元
建物の改造
創造力
家を造る

Typical Conversational Usage:

日本の造船は世界的に有名です。
きのう買った本は、自動車の構造についての本です。
私の会社では、おもちゃの製造をしています。
部屋を改造しましたので、いつか見に来てください。
聖書には、天地の創造が記されています。
山本さんの造った家は、なかなかモダンです。

442

沢

B

Occurrences/1000   .56
Frequency Rank   442
Sanseido Page   396
Nelson Page   537

ON: TAKU

kun: sawa

Basic Meaning(s): swamp, valley, marsh

Graphically-Phonetically Related Morphographs:

High Frequency Compounds:

沢山
148
TAKUSAN -- a large quantity, a great many, plenty, much

光沢
345
KOOTAKU -- brilliance, polish

Occurs frequently in proper names, such as 沢村, "Sawamura," and 大沢, "Oosawa."

Typical Phrases and Expanded Compounds:

盛り沢山

光沢のある石

Typical Conversational Usage:

招待されたところ、盛り沢山のごちそうが用意されてありました。

この品物は、金メッキして光沢を出した物です。

Graphically-Phonetically Related Morphographs:

	443
Occurrences/1000 .56	展
Frequency Rank 443	
Sanseido Page 299	A
Nelson Page 344	
	ON: TEN
kun:	

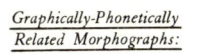

Basic Meaning(s): expand

High Frequency Compounds:

発展 HATTEN -- expansion, extension,
102   development, growth

展開 TENKAI -- unfold, develop,
290   evolve

進展 SHINTEN -- development, progress
156

Typical Phrases and Expanded Compounds:

都市の発展
展開する景色
交渉が進展する

Typical Conversational Usage:

この町は、ここ二、三年で著しく発展しました。
眼下に展開する景色は、実にすばらしかったです。
公害は、大きな社会問題に進展しました。

444

輸

Occurrences/1000 .56
Frequency Rank 444
Sanseido Page 703
Nelson Page 868

A

ON: YU

kun:

Basic Meaning(s): send, transport, be inferior to

Typical Phrases and Expanded Compounds:

輸出品
輸入税
多量の輸血

Graphically-Phonetically Related Morphographs:

愉 YU
諭 YU

High Frequency Compounds:

輸出 YUSHUTSU -- exports, exportation
 8

輸入 YU'NYUU -- imports, importation
 65

輸血 YUKETSU -- blood transfusion
 489

Typical Conversational Usage:

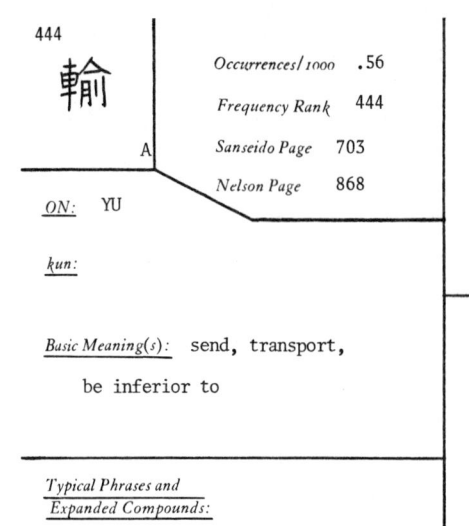

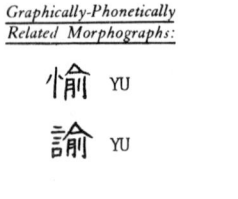

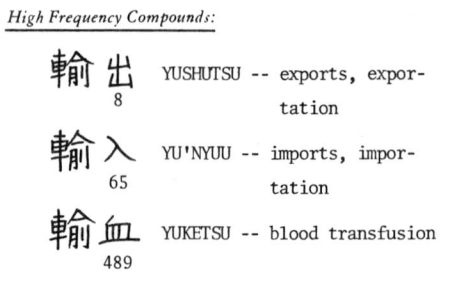

絹の輸出は、このところ毎年減少しつつあります。
輸入超過をめぐって、政府は臨時会議を開きました。
手術が大きかったので、あの方は多量の輸血をしたそうです。

Graphically-Phonetically Related Morphographs:

Occurrences/1000 .55	445
Frequency Rank 445	陸
Sanseido Page 431	
Nelson Page 932	A

ON: RIKU

kun:

Basic Meaning(s): land

High Frequency Compounds:

陸軍 36 — RIKUGUN -- army

大陸 5 — TAIRIKU -- continent, mainland, the Continent of Asia

上陸 29 — JOORIKU -- landing, disembarkation

Typical Phrases and Expanded Compounds:

陸軍司令官
大陸性気候
上陸の準備

Typical Conversational Usage:

父はもと陸軍少佐でしたが、今は大学教授です。
大沢さんは、長い間中国にいたせいか、大陸的な感じのする人です。
上陸を目前にひかえ、台風にみまわれ、船は危うく沈みそうになりました。

446

為

Occurrences/1000 .55
Frequency Rank 446
Sanseido Page 151
Nelson Page 77

B

ON: I

kun: (tame)

Basic Meaning(s): be of use, do, purpose, advantage

Graphically-Phonetically Related Morphographs:

High Frequency Compounds:

行為 KOOI -- deed, conduct, trans-
 18   action, practices

Typical Phrases and Expanded Compounds:

変な行為
人の為を思って

Typical Conversational Usage:

あなたの行為は、よい結果を生みました。
みんなの為になるような仕事をしたいと思っています。

447

将

Occurrences/1000 .55
Frequency Rank 447
Sanseido Page 456
Nelson Page 592

A

ON: SHOO

kun:

Graphically-Phonetically Related Morphographs:

奨 SHOO

Basic Meaning(s): commander, general, soon

High Frequency Compounds:

将来 SHOORAI -- future, prospects
27

将軍 SHOOGUN -- general, commander, shogun
36

将棋 SHOOGI -- chess
1315

大将 TAISHOO -- general, admiral, head leader
5

Typical Phrases and Expanded Compounds:

将来有望
大将軍
将棋倒し
陸軍大将

Typical Conversational Usage:

将来性のある仕事を、これからは、身につけた方がいいです。
徳川家康は、関ヶ原の戦いの後、征夷大将軍となって、政権をにぎりました。
電車が急に止まったので、みんなは将棋倒しになりました。
あの子は近所のがき大将です。

448

証 A

Occurrences/1000 .55
Frequency Rank 448
Sanseido Page 679
Nelson Page 827

ON: SHOO

kun:

Basic Meaning(s): proof, evidence, certificate, guarantee

Graphically-Phonetically Related Morphographs:

政 SEI, SHOO (23)
正 SEI, SHOO (139)
症 SHOO

High Frequency Compounds:

証拠 756 SHOOKO -- proof, evidence, testimony
保証 163 HOSHOO -- guarantee, security, pledge
証言 44   SHOOGEN -- testimony, evidence
証明 152 SHOOMEI -- proof, evidence, testimony, witness

Typical Phrases and Expanded Compounds:

証拠品
保証付き
被告の証言
成績証明書

Typical Conversational Usage:

裁判の時、検察側は被告の証拠品を並べました。
この品物は保証付きですから、安心して使うことができます。
裁判長が被告の証言を求めました。
大学へ進学するためには、高校の成績証明書が必要です。

Graphically-Phonetically Related Morphographs:

迭 TETSU

Occurrences/1000	.55
Frequency Rank	449
Sanseido Page	715
Nelson Page	910

449

鉄

A

ON: TETSU

kun:

Basic Meaning(s): iron, steel, reddish black, steel blue

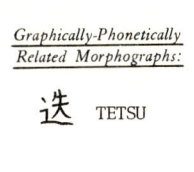

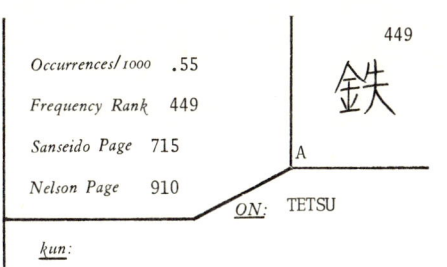

High Frequency Compounds:

鉄道 TETSUDOO -- railway, railroad
123

鉄鋼 TEKKOO -- iron and steel
1108

Typical Phrases and Expanded Compounds:

日本国有鉄道

鉄鋼業

Typical Conversational Usage:

日本国有鉄道を略して、国鉄と呼んでいます。
父は会社の鉄鋼第一課で働いています。

450
比
A

Occurrences/1000 .55
Frequency Rank 450
Sanseido Page 177
Nelson Page 527

ON: HI

kun: kura(beru)

Basic Meaning(s): ratio, comparison, compare, balance, contrast

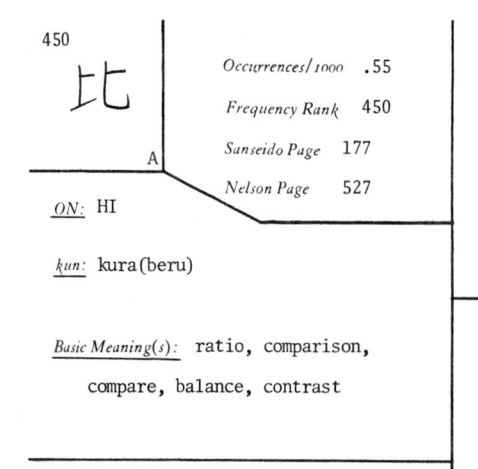

Graphically-Phonetically Related Morphographs:

批 HI (536)

High Frequency Compounds:

比較 HIKAKU -- comparison, comparative
858

比例 HIREI -- proportion, ration
294

Typical Phrases and Expanded Compounds:

比較にならぬ程
反比例

Typical Conversational Usage:

アメリカと比較して、日本の人口密度はものすごく高いです。
弟は、今、学校で比例と反比例の方式を勉強しています。
今度できたビルは、今までのに比べものになりません。

Graphically-Phonetically Related Morphographs:

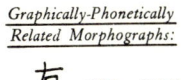

有 YUU (245)

右 YUU (384)

High Frequency Compounds:

友人 YUUJIN -- friend
2

友達 tomodachi -- friend, companion
154

友好 YUUKOO -- friendship, amity, companionship
262

友情 YUUJOO -- friendship, fellowship
183

451

友

A

Occurrences/1000 .55
Frequency Rank 451
Sanseido Page 181
Nelson Page 237

ON: YUU

kun: tomo

Basic Meaning(s): friend, companion, pal

Typical Phrases and Expanded Compounds:

思いがけない友人
学校の友達
友好関係
美しい友情

Typical Conversational Usage:

昨日電車の中で、思いがけない友人に出会いました。
野球の試合を、友達といっしょに見に行きました。
日本と中国の友好関係が、よくなって来ました。
あの二人は、美しい友情で結ばれています。

452 領

Occurrences/1000: .55
Frequency Rank: 452
Sanseido Page: 742
Nelson Page: 957

A

ON: RYOO

kun:

Basic Meaning(s): dominion, territory, possession, fief

Typical Phrases and Expanded Compounds:

占領した土地
大統領選挙
党の綱領

Graphically-Phonetically Related Morphographs:

High Frequency Compounds:

占領 SENRYOO -- capture, possession, occupation
378

大統領 DAITOORYOO -- president
5 273

綱領 KOORYOO -- general plan, main points, summary
1374

Typical Conversational Usage:

長い間占領されていた土地が、返還されました。
アメリカの大統領選挙は、四年に一度行われます。
党の綱領をまとめ上げるのに、一週間かかりました。

Graphically-Phonetically Related Morphographs:

Occurrences/1000	.54
Frequency Rank	453
Sanseido Page	556
Nelson Page	816

453

規

A

ON: KI

kun:

Basic Meaning(s): standard, measure

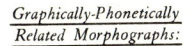

High Frequency Compounds:

規定   KITEI -- bylaws, provisions,
93   regulations

規模   KIBO -- scale, scope, plan
797

規則   KISOKU -- regulation, rule
746

Typical Phrases and Expanded Compounds:

郵便物の規定
大規模な捜査
規則正しい

Typical Conversational Usage:

給料は、会社の規定に従って支払われます。
まだこの仕事の規模は小さいですが、これから
だんだん大きくなるでしょう。
規則正しい生活をしていれば、体をこわさなくて
すむでしょう。

454 警

A

Occurrences/1000 .54
Frequency Rank 454
Sanseido Page 349
Nelson Page 840

ON: KEI

kun:

Basic Meaning(s): admonish, warn, prohibit, precept

Typical Phrases and Expanded Compounds:

警察所長
婦人警官
警戒体制

Graphically-Phonetically Related Morphographs:

敬 KEI (1079)

High Frequency Compounds:

警察 (492) KEISATSU -- police (force), police station
警官 (202) KEIKAN -- police officer, policeman
警戒 (1162) KEIKAI -- warning, admonition, vigilance

Typical Conversational Usage:

今度、警察の所長が代わりました。
この前のデモでは、警官隊側にも、かなり負傷者が出たそうです。
極悪犯人の捜査には、警戒が特に必要です。

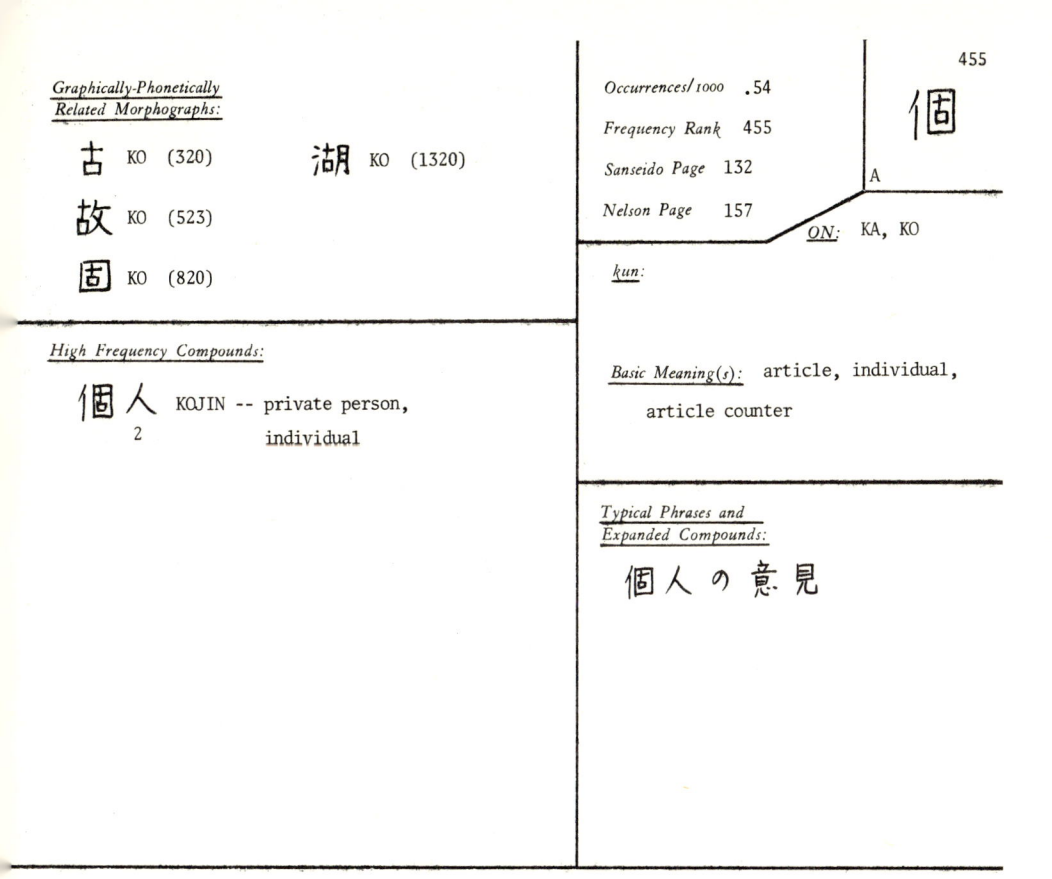

455

個

Graphically-Phonetically Related Morphographs:

古 KO (320)   湖 KO (1320)

故 KO (523)

固 KO (820)

Occurrences/1000 .54
Frequency Rank 455
Sanseido Page 132
Nelson Page 157

ON: KA, KO

kun:

High Frequency Compounds:

個人 KOJIN -- private person,
 2   individual

Basic Meaning(s): article, individual, article counter

Typical Phrases and Expanded Compounds:

個人の意見

Typical Conversational Usage:

民主主義の社会では、個人の意見が尊重されます。

456

紙

A

Occurrences/1000 .54
Frequency Rank 456
Sanseido Page 636
Nelson Page 698

<u>ON</u>: SHI

<u>kun</u>: kami

Basic Meaning(s): paper, newspaper

Typical Phrases and Expanded Compounds:

なつかしい手紙

新聞紙上

Graphically-Phonetically Related Morphographs:

氏 SHI (223)

High Frequency Compounds:

手紙 tegami -- letter, note
57

紙上 SHIJOO -- on paper, by letter,
29   in the newspaper or
                magazine

Typical Conversational Usage:

いなかの母から、なつかしい手紙を受け取りました。
その問題は、紙上でかなりはげしくたたかれていました。
買物に行ったついでに、質のいい紙を五、六枚買って
来てください。

Graphically-Phonetically Related Morphographs:

受 JU (298)

High Frequency Compounds:

教授 KYOOJU -- professor, teaching
133

授業 JUGYOO -- teaching, instruction, classwork
74

Occurrences/1000 .54
Frequency Rank 457
Sanseido Page 386
Nelson Page 443

授 457

A

ON: JU
kun: sazu(keru), sazu(karu)

Basic Meaning(s): give, grant, confer, bestow, award, be gifted with

Typical Phrases and Expanded Compounds:

大学の教授
授業の内容
博士号を授かる
手芸を授ける

Typical Conversational Usage:

藤本さんは、ダンス教習所で、今、タップダンスの教授を受けているそうです。
日野先生の授業の内容は、とても高度です。
あの美しい声は、天から授かったものでしょう。
うちの子は足が不自由なので、手芸を授けてもらっています。

458

消 A

Occurrences/1000   .54
Frequency Rank   458
Sanseido Page   403
Nelson Page   551

ON: SHOO

kun: kie(ru), ke(su)

Basic Meaning(s): extinguish, blow out, turn off, melt away, disappear

Typical Phrases and Expanded Compounds:

消費地
消化不良
火が消える
電気を消す

Graphically-Phonetically Related Morphographs:

硝   SHOO
肖   SHOO

High Frequency Compounds:

消費   SHOOHI -- consumption, expenditure
352

消化   SHOOKA -- digestion, assimilation
104

Typical Conversational Usage:

消費者の意見を参考にした新製品が、売り出されました。
とかく体力が弱っている時に、消化不良が起こりやすいです。
電気が消えたり、ついたりしています。
よく火を消してから、休んでください。

459

注

Graphically-Phonetically Related Morphographs:

駐 CHUU (888)
柱 CHUU (1032)

Occurrences/1000 .54
Frequency Rank 459
Sanseido Page 398
Nelson Page 541

ON: CHUU
kun: soso(gu)

Basic Meaning(s): pour into, pour on, sprinkle, flow into, notes, comment

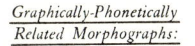

High Frequency Compounds:

注意 CHUUI -- attention, care, heed, warning
86

注目 CHUUMOKU -- attention, observation, notice
91

注文 CHUUMON -- order (for merchandise, etc.)
89

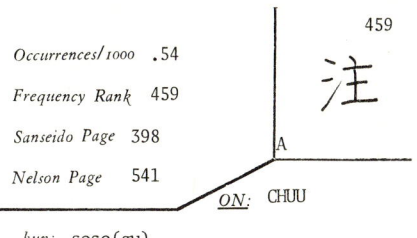

Typical Phrases and Expanded Compounds:

最大の注意
注目の的
注文の品物
水を注ぐ

Typical Conversational Usage:

雨の日の運転には、最大の注意が必要です。
アポロ11号は、世界の人々の注目の的になりました。
注文の品物を、お届けに参りました。
毎朝六時に起きて、花に水を注いでいます。

460

般

A

Occurrences/1000 .54
Frequency Rank 460
Sanseido Page 660
Nelson Page 763

ON: HAN

kun:

Basic Meaning(s): carry, all

Typical Phrases and Expanded Compounds:

一般の人々

全般的に

Graphically-Phonetically Related Morphographs:

搬 HAN

High Frequency Compounds:

一般 IPPAN -- general, liberal,
 1   universal, ordinary

全般 ZEMPAN -- the whole
 70

Typical Conversational Usage:

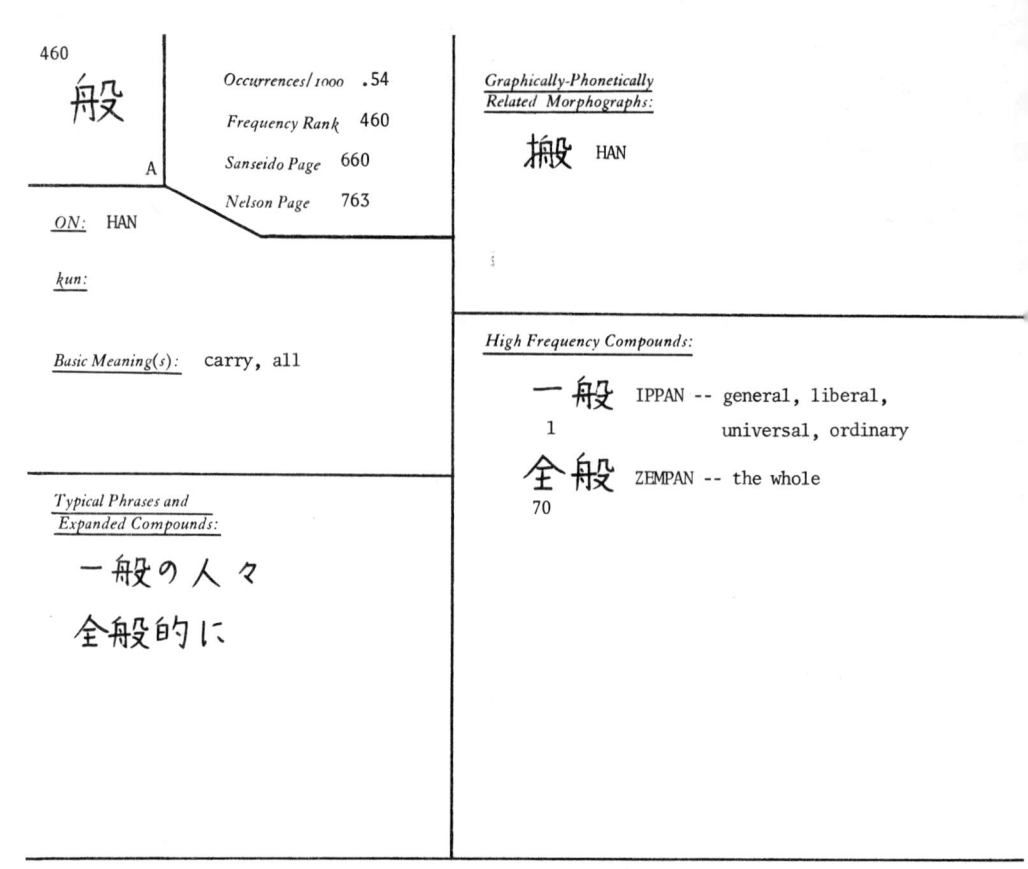

一般の人々は、場内に入ることができません。
全般的に見て、まだまだ改善されなければなりません。

Graphically-Phonetically Related Morphographs:

461

武

Occurrences/1000 .54
Frequency Rank 461
Sanseido Page 78
Nelson Page 51

A

<u>ON</u>: BU, MU

<u>kun</u>:

High Frequency Compounds:

武器   BUKI -- weapon, arms, ordnance
520

武装   BUSOO -- arms, armament, armed
648

武士   BUSHI -- samurai, warrior
386

Basic Meaning(s): military affairs, chivalry, military power, brave

Typical Phrases and Expanded Compounds:

武器とする
武装警官
武士道

Typical Conversational Usage:

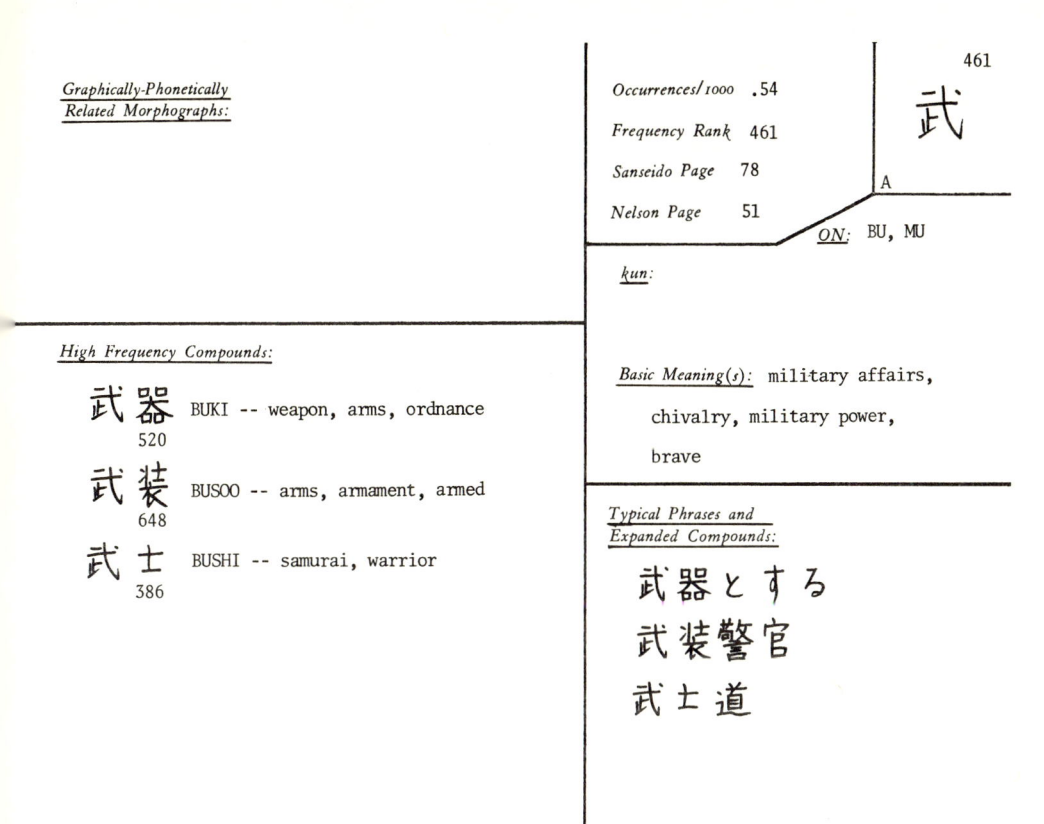

みんな手に手に武器を持って戦いました。
警官の武装が物々しいので、何事が起こったのかと思いました。
「武士に二言なし」と言われています。

462

億

A

Occurrences/1000 .53
Frequency Rank 462
Sanseido Page 142
Nelson Page 164

ON: OKU

kun:

Basic Meaning(s): 100,000,000

Graphically-Phonetically Related Morphographs:

憶 OKU (992)

High Frequency Compounds:

一億 ICHIOKU -- 100,000,000
 1

Typical Phrases and Expanded Compounds:

一億人

Typical Conversational Usage:

日本の人口は一億人を越えました。

Graphically-Phonetically Related Morphographs:

何 KA (43)　　荷 KA (1254)
歌 KA (486)
河 KA (614)

High Frequency Compounds:

可能 KANOO -- possibility
285

許可 KYOKA -- permission, approval,
689　　　　　　license, authorization

Occurrences/1000　.53
Frequency Rank　463
Sanseido Page　29
Nelson Page　42

463
可
A

ON: KA

kun:

Basic Meaning(s): good, passable, approval, shall, should, must

Typical Phrases and Expanded Compounds:

実現の可能性
許可の申請

Typical Conversational Usage:

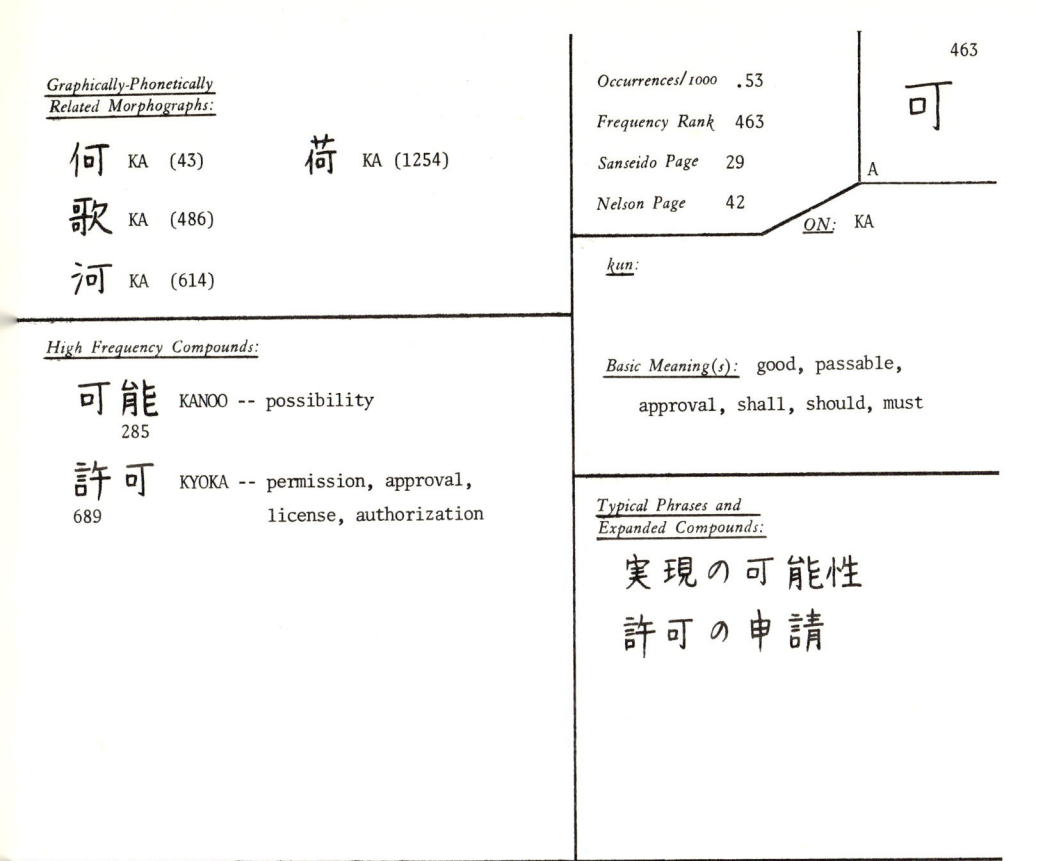

よい案ですが、可能性がうすいです。
申請して許可をもらわなければ、その会館は使用できません。

464

幾

B

Occurrences/1000 .53

Frequency Rank 464

Sanseido Page 317

Nelson Page 361

ON: KI

kun: iku, iku(ra)

Basic Meaning(s): how much, how many

Graphically-Phonetically Related Morphographs:

機 KI (158)

High Frequency Compounds:

幾人 ikuNIN -- how many people
2

Typical Phrases and Expanded Compounds:

幾人かの人々

Typical Conversational Usage:

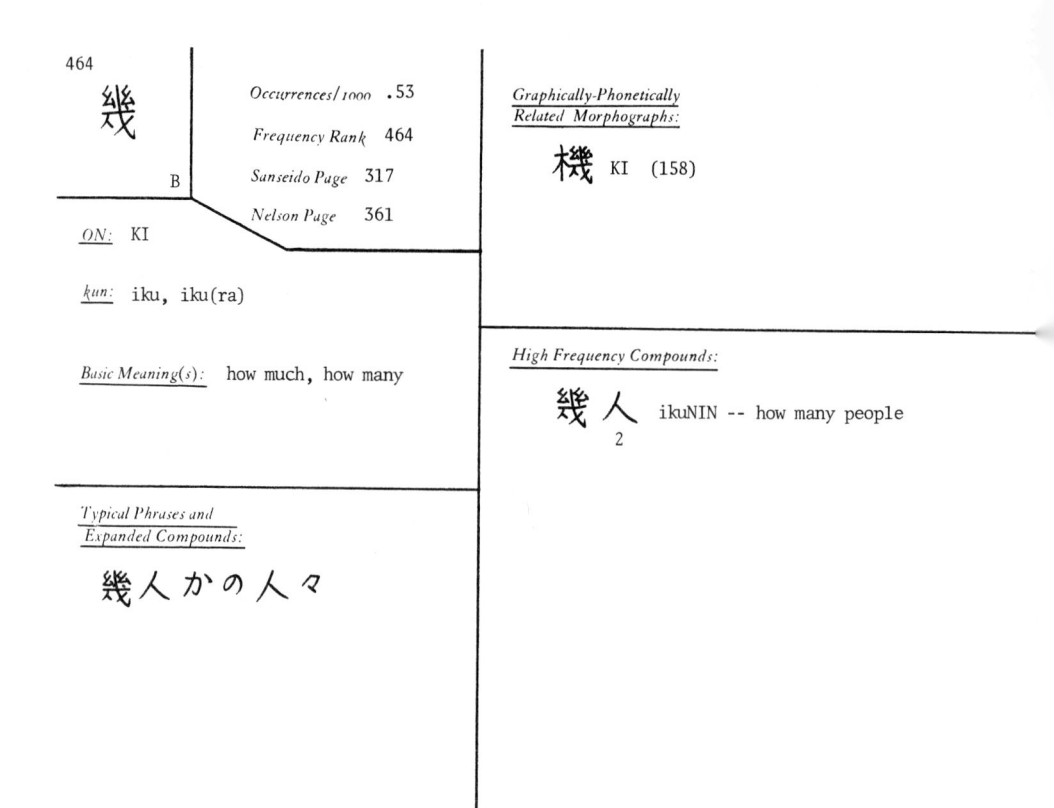

幾人かの人々は、最後まで自分の意見を主張しました。

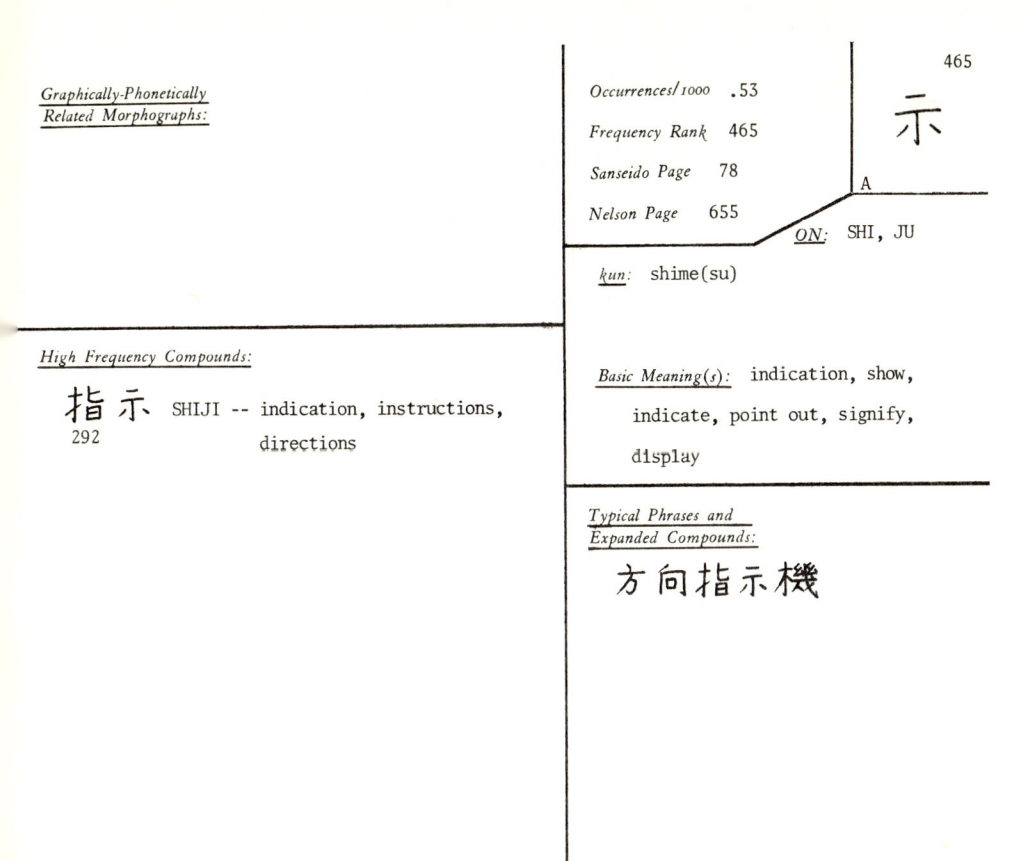

Graphically-Phonetically Related Morphographs:

465

示

Occurrences/1000 .53
Frequency Rank 465
Sanseido Page 78
Nelson Page 655

A

<u>ON</u>: SHI, JU

<u>kun</u>: shime(su)

High Frequency Compounds:

指示　SHIJI -- indication, instructions, directions
292

Basic Meaning(s): indication, show, indicate, point out, signify, display

Typical Phrases and Expanded Compounds:

方向指示機

Typical Conversational Usage:

先生の指示をあおいだうえで、決心するつもりです。
部長とよく示し合わせてから、商談に応ずることにします。

466

満

A

Occurrences/1000 .53
Frequency Rank 466
Sanseido Page 411
Nelson Page 562

ON: MAN

kun: mi(chiru), mi(tasu)

Basic Meaning(s): fullness, enough, pride, be full, fill

Typical Phrases and
Expanded Compounds:

満足感
満州鉄道
不平不満
潮が満ちる

Graphically-Phonetically
Related Morphographs:

High Frequency Compounds:

満足 MANZOKU -- satisfaction,
338   contentment

満州 MANSHUU -- Manchuria
865

不満 HUMAN -- dissatisfaction, dis-
103   pleasure, discontent

満員 MAN'IN -- no vacancy, full
127   house

Typical Conversational Usage:

満足に仕事もできないで、どうするのですか。
父は、戦前、満州で事業をしていました。
あの子はいつも不平ばかり言っていますが、何か
不満なのかしら。
満員電車をいつもさけて、乗るようにしています。
潮が満ちるのを見たことがありますか。

Graphically-Phonetically Related Morphographs:

Occurrences/1000 .53
Frequency Rank 467
Sanseido Page 203
Nelson Page 236

又

467

X

ON:

kun: mata

Basic Meaning(s): again, and, furthermore, on the other hand

High Frequency Compounds:

又聞き matagiki -- hearsay
184

Typical Phrases and Expanded Compounds:

又とない機会

Typical Conversational Usage:

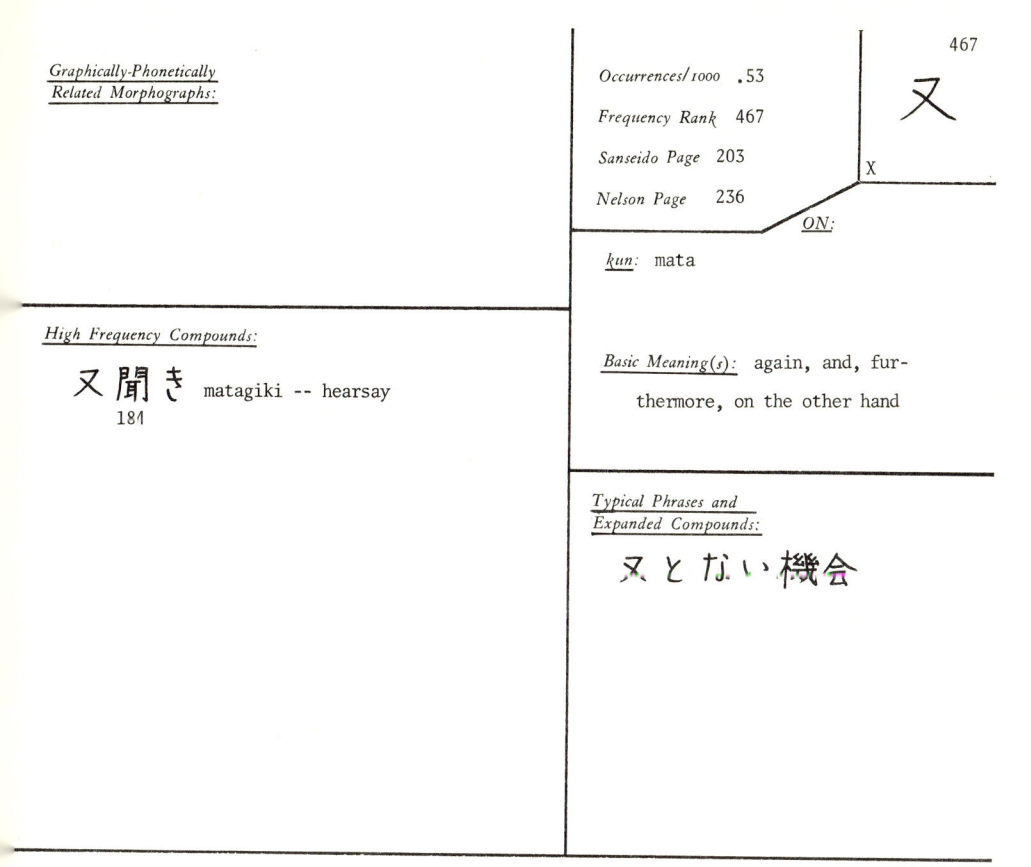

この話は又の機会にいたしましょう。

468

余

A

Occurrences/1000 .52
Frequency Rank 468
Sanseido Page 107
Nelson Page 145

ON: YO

kun: ama(ru), ama(ri), ama(su)

Basic Meaning(s): surplus, other, remainder

Typical Phrases and Expanded Compounds:

余程の注意
余裕たっぷり
話し合いの余地
余計なお世話
余り物

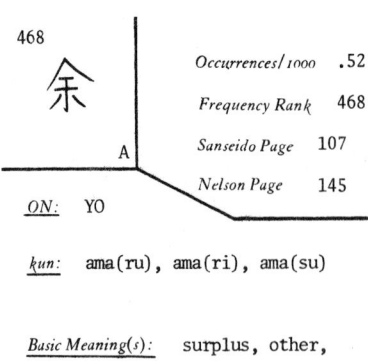

Graphically-Phonetically Related Morphographs:

High Frequency Compounds:

余程 (276) YOHODO -- very, greatly, much, to a large extent

余裕 YOYUU -- surplus, margin, room, time, allowance

余地 (45) YOCHI -- room, margin, scope

余計 (210) YOKEI -- excess, surplus, abundance

Typical Conversational Usage:

この辺は危いですから、余程の注意が必要です。
もうすぐ試合というのに、余裕満々です。
まだまだ話し合いの余地があると思います。
まちがって、少し余計に払ってしまいました。
時間が少し余ったので、あしたの予習をしました。

Graphically-Phonetically Related Morphographs:

構 KOO (498)

購 KOO (1213)

Occurrences/1000 .52
Frequency Rank 469
Sanseido Page 688
Nelson Page 839

469

講

A

ON: KOO

kun:

Basic Meaning(s): club, association, lecture, read aloud, lecture on

High Frequency Compounds:

講義 KOOGI -- lecture, exposition
62

講演 KOOEN -- lecture, address
413

講和 KOOWA -- make peace with
85

Typical Phrases and Expanded Compounds:

講義内容

講演会

講和条約

Typical Conversational Usage:

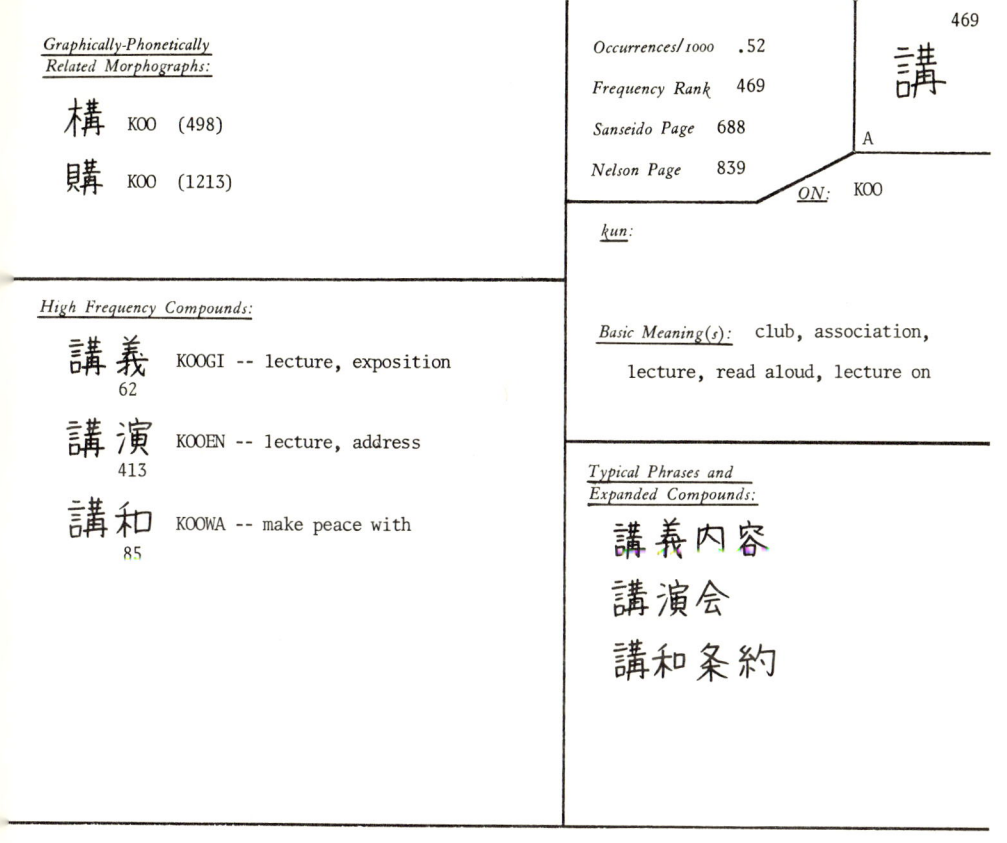

講義内容がとてもむずかしいので、よく聞かなければわかりません。

先生の講演会が、あした神田の共立講堂であるそうです。

いつ講和条約が結ばれたか、おぼえていますか。

470

殺

A

Occurrences/1000 .52
Frequency Rank 470
Sanseido Page 540
Nelson Page 524

ON: SATSU, SAI

kun: koro(su), koro(shi)

Basic Meaning(s): kill, murder, butcher, waste (money), suppress (anger)

Graphically-Phonetically Related Morphographs:

High Frequency Compounds:

殺人 SATSUJIN -- murder, homicide, manslaughter
 2
自殺 JISATSU -- suicide
 14

Typical Phrases and Expanded Compounds:

殺人犯

自殺未遂

息を殺す

Typical Conversational Usage:

警察では、先月起こった殺人事件を調査しています。
あの方の御主人は、病気に悩んで、鉄道自殺をしたそうです。
じっと息を殺して、その場を見まもりました。

Graphically-Phonetically
Related Morphographs:

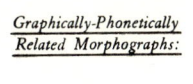

Occurrences/1000 .52	471
Frequency Rank 471	鮮
Sanseido Page 750	
Nelson Page 983	B

<u>ON</u>: SEN

<u>kun</u>:

High Frequency Compounds:

朝鮮 CHOOSEN -- Korea
217

新鮮 SHINSEN -- freshness
80

Basic Meaning(s): Korea, vivid, clear, brilliant

Typical Phrases and
Expanded Compounds:

北朝鮮の人々
新鮮な野菜

Typical Conversational Usage:

日赤を通じて、北朝鮮へ帰った人がたくさんいます。
新鮮な野菜を、できるだけ多く食べた方がよろしいです。

472

提

A

Occurrences/1000 .52
Frequency Rank 472
Sanseido Page 389
Nelson Page 447

ON: TEI

kun:

Basic Meaning(s): take along, carry in the hand

Typical Phrases and Expanded Compounds:

提案が通る
労力を提供する
提出期限
前提とする

Graphically-Phonetically Related Morphographs:

堤　TEI　(1335)

High Frequency Compounds:

提案 353 — TEIAN -- suggestion, proposition, overture

提供 340 — TEIKYOO -- offer, tender

提出 8 — TEISHUTSU -- present, introduce, tender

前提 53 — ZENTEI -- preamble, premise, reason, prerequisite

Typical Conversational Usage:

提案が通って、いよいよ実行されることになりました。
労力を提供してもらったので、この仕事は割合早く終わりました。
レポートの提出期限が迫っています。
米価審議会は、生産者と消費者の意見を前提として審議しました。

473 検

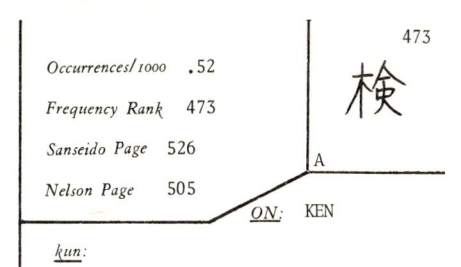

Graphically-Phonetically Related Morphographs:

験 KEN (385)
険 KEN (662)
剣 KEN (818)
倹 KEN

Occurrences/1000 .52
Frequency Rank 473
Sanseido Page 526
Nelson Page 505

ON: KEN
kun:

Basic Meaning(s): investigation, investigate

High Frequency Compounds:

検討 582 KENTOO -- investigation, examination, study
検挙 434 KENKYO -- arrest, roundup
検察 492 KENSATSU -- investigation and prosecution
探検 871 TANKEN -- exploration, expedition

Typical Phrases and Expanded Compounds:

原案の検討
直ちに検挙する
検察官
探検家

Typical Conversational Usage:

その件については、よく検討する必要があります。
あの人は盗みの現行犯で、直ちに検挙されました。
検察側は、証拠物件についてするどく追及しました。
ロジャーさんは、十年前、アフリカ探検隊に加わって行ったそうです。

474

護

A

Occurrences/1000 .52
Frequency Rank 474
Sanseido Page 690
Nelson Page 841

ON: GO

kun:

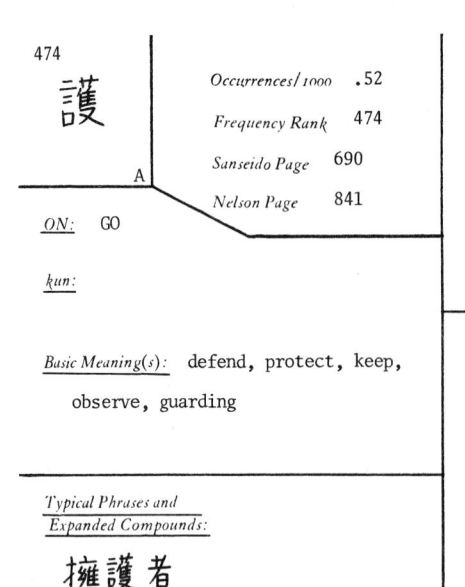

Basic Meaning(s): defend, protect, keep, observe, guarding

Graphically-Phonetically Related Morphographs:

High Frequency Compounds:

擁護   YOOGO -- protection, defense
984   assistance

保護   HOGO -- care, shelter, pro-
163   tection, favor

弁護   BENGO -- defense, vindication,
543   explanation, pleading

Typical Phrases and Expanded Compounds:

擁護者
保護者
弁護士

Typical Conversational Usage:

友人の立場を擁護してあげました。
いなかから出て来た14才の女の子は、警察に保護されました。
何と言ったらよいか、弁護に苦しみました。

Graphically-Phonetically Related Morphographs:

Occurrences/1000 .52	475
Frequency Rank 475	至
Sanseido Page 37	
Nelson Page 759	A

<u>ON</u>: SHI

<u>kun</u>: ita(ru), ita(ri)

High Frequency Compounds:

至急 SHIKYUU -- urgent
533

乃至 (NAISHI) -- from ... to; or
1060

Basic Meaning(s): go, proceed, come, reach, attain, the utmost, climax, to, until, imperfect

Typical Phrases and Expanded Compounds:

至急電報
一名乃至二名
今日に至る

Typical Conversational Usage:

きのう母から電報があり、至急帰らなければなりません。
一名乃至二名の求人広告がありました。
きのうに至って、その真相がはっきりしました。

476 服

Occurrences/1000	.52
Frequency Rank	476
Sanseido Page	496
Nelson Page	742

A

ON: HUKU

kun:

Basic Meaning(s): dress, costume, clothes, garment, uniform, yield to, obey

Graphically-Phonetically Related Morphographs:

High Frequency Compounds:

洋服 (411) YOOHUKU -- Western clothes

制服 (161) SEIHUKU -- uniform, regulation dress

服従 (329) HUKUJUU -- obedience, submission, subjection

Typical Phrases and Expanded Compounds:

新しい洋服
学校の制服
親に服従する

Typical Conversational Usage:

一昨日、デパートで新しい洋服を買いました。
高校の入学試験に受かったら、すぐ制服を買うつもりです。
その場合、親の意見に服従すべきだと思います。

Graphically-Phonetically Related Morphographs:

| | 477 |

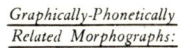

返

Occurrences/1000 .52
Frequency Rank 477
Sanseido Page 440
Nelson Page 872

A

<u>ON</u>: HEN

<u>kun</u>: kae(su), kae(shi), kae(ru), kae(ri)

Basic Meaning(s): answer, go back, return, repay

High Frequency Compounds:

返事 HENJI -- reply
10

Typical Phrases and Expanded Compounds:

手紙の返事
借金を返す
もとの職業に返る

Typical Conversational Usage:

あしたまでに、はっきりした返事がいただきたいんです。
あの人から、まだ、お金を返してもらっていません。
新井さんは、前の仕事に返ったそうです。

478

略

A

ON: RYAKU

kun:

Basic Meaning(s): abbreviation, abridgment, omit, shorten

Occurrences/1000	.52
Frequency Rank	478
Sanseido Page	577
Nelson Page	625

Graphically-Phonetically Related Morphographs:

High Frequency Compounds:

侵略 SHINRYAKU -- aggression, invasion, raid
741

戦略 SENRYAKU -- strategy, tactics
32

中略 CHUURYAKU -- omission of a part
12

Typical Phrases and Expanded Compounds:

侵略された領土
日本の戦略
文章の中略
略して書く

Typical Conversational Usage:

共産国からの侵略者と勇敢に戦いました。
戦略は勝敗の大きなポイントです。
この文を中略して書いてもいいですか。
あの人の字は余り略しているので、とても読みにくいです。

Graphically-Phonetically Related Morphographs:

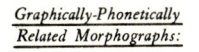

Occurrences/1000	.52
Frequency Rank	479
Sanseido Page	54
Nelson Page	766

479

良

A

<u>ON</u>: RYOO

<u>kun</u>: yo(i)

Basic Meaning(s): good, fine, good-natured, pleasing, noble, lovely, beautiful, lucky

High Frequency Compounds:

良心 — RYOOSHIN -- conscience
64

改良 — KAIRYOO -- improvement, reform
289

不良 — HURYOO -- bad, poor, inferior, wicked, delinquent
103

Typical Phrases and Expanded Compounds:

良心的
土地の改良
不良品

Typical Conversational Usage:

この品物は良心的にできています。
まだまだ改良の余地があります。
不良品は除いてください。

480

類

A

Occurrences/1000
Frequency Rank
Sanseido Page
Nelson Page

ON: RUI

kun:

Basic Meaning(s): kind, variety, class, genus, description, parallel case

Typical Phrases and Expanded Compounds:

人類学
花の種類

Graphically-Phonetically Related Morphographs:

High Frequency Compounds:

人類　JINRUI -- mankind, man,
 2　　　　　　humanity

種類　SHURUI -- kind, variety,
417　　　　　　class, species

Typical Conversational Usage:

原水爆は人類を破滅に導く危険があります。
あの人は花の種類をたくさん知っています。

Graphically-Phonetically Related Morphographs:

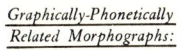

	481
Occurrences/1000 .51	楽
Frequency Rank 481	
Sanseido Page 516	A
Nelson Page 508	

ON: GAKU, RAKU

kun: tano(shii), tano(shimu), tano(shimi)

High Frequency Compounds:

音楽　ONGAKU -- music
558

楽器　GAKKI -- musical instrument
520

Basic Meaning(s): comfort, ease, relief, music, enjoy, amuse oneself, anticipate

Typical Phrases and Expanded Compounds:

宗教音楽
楽器を使う
楽しいひととき
休暇を楽しむ

Typical Conversational Usage:

あしたの音楽会に、いっしょに連れて行っていただけませんか。
楽器屋で、弟はギターを買って来ました。
一年中で夏は、私にとって一番楽しい季節です。
どのようにしたら、休暇を楽しみながら、有意義に
過ごせるかと考えています。

482

笑

A

Occurrences/1000   .51
Frequency Rank   482
Sanseido Page   625
Nelson Page   682

ON: SHOO

kun: wara(u)

Basic Meaning(s): laughter, laugh, smile, ridicule

Graphically-Phonetically Related Morphographs:

High Frequency Compounds:

微笑   BISHOO -- smile
1190

Typical Phrases and Expanded Compounds:

微笑を浮かべる
大きな笑い声
人に笑われる

Typical Conversational Usage:

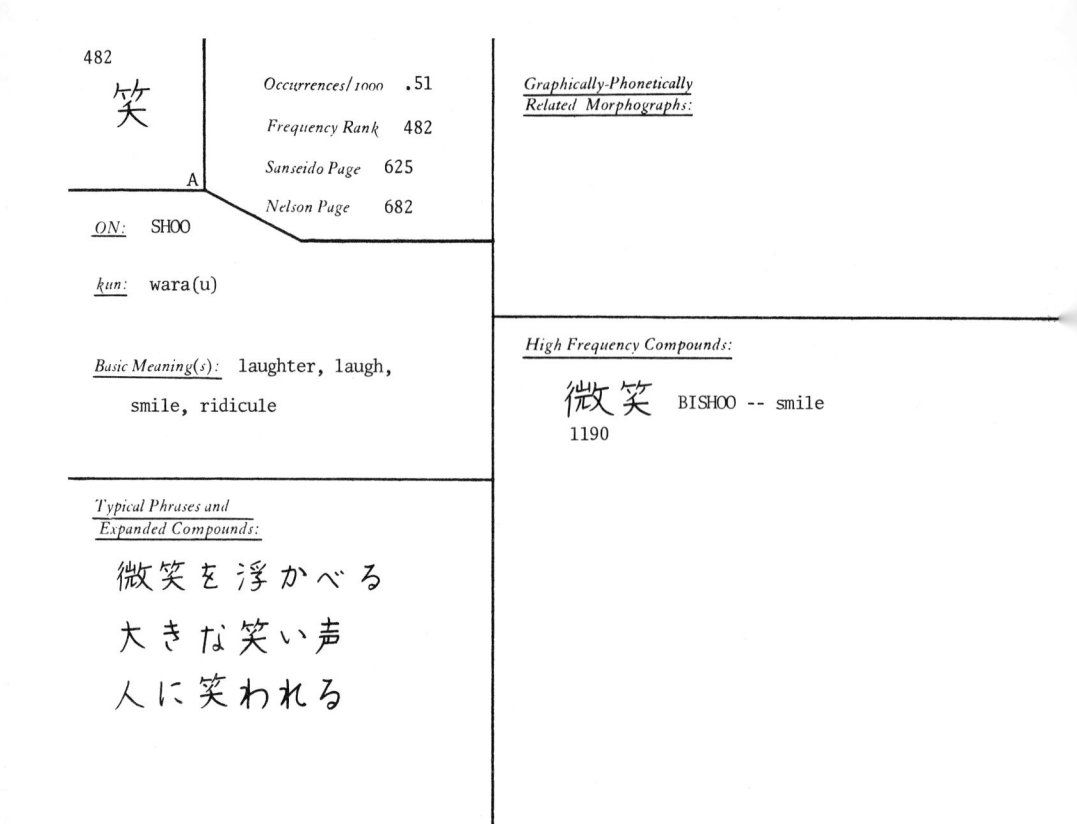

友人の松田さんは、いつも微笑を浮かべています。
あそこで大きな笑い声で話している方は、どなたですか。
そんなことをすると、人に笑われます。

Graphically-Phonetically
Related Morphographs:

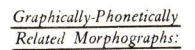

Occurrences/1000 .51
Frequency Rank 483
Sanseido Page 519
Nelson Page 494

483

松

B

ON: SHOO

kun: matsu

Basic Meaning(s): pine, pine tree

High Frequency Compounds:

松竹梅   SHOOCHIKUBAI -- pine-bamboo-plum
1009 1403   congratulatory
                       tree decoration

松林   matsubayashi -- pine forest
655

Occurs most frequently in proper names;
such as, 松村 "Matsumura."

Typical Phrases and
Expanded Compounds:

松竹梅の模様
海辺の松林

Typical Conversational Usage:

お正月に松竹梅の生け花をかざります。
私の家の近くに大きな松林があります。

484

誰

X

Occurrences/1000 .51
Frequency Rank 484
Sanseido Page 685
Nelson Page 834

ON:

kun: (dare)

Basic Meaning(s): who, someone, somebody

Graphically-Phonetically Related Morphographs:

High Frequency Compounds:

誰 一 人   dare hitori (mo) --
 1   2   no one

Typical Phrases and Expanded Compounds:

誰一人として
誰か

Typical Conversational Usage:

誰一人としてそこへ行きたがりません。
誰かおいでになりましたか。

Graphically-Phonetically Related Morphographs:

Occurrences/1000 .50
Frequency Rank 485
Sanseido Page 235
Nelson Page 258

485

因

A

ON: IN

kun: yo(ru)

High Frequency Compounds:

原因   GEN'IN -- root cause, factor, occasion, origin, reason, source
113

Basic Meaning(s): cause, factor, be associated with, depend on

Typical Phrases and Expanded Compounds:

原因結果

Typical Conversational Usage:

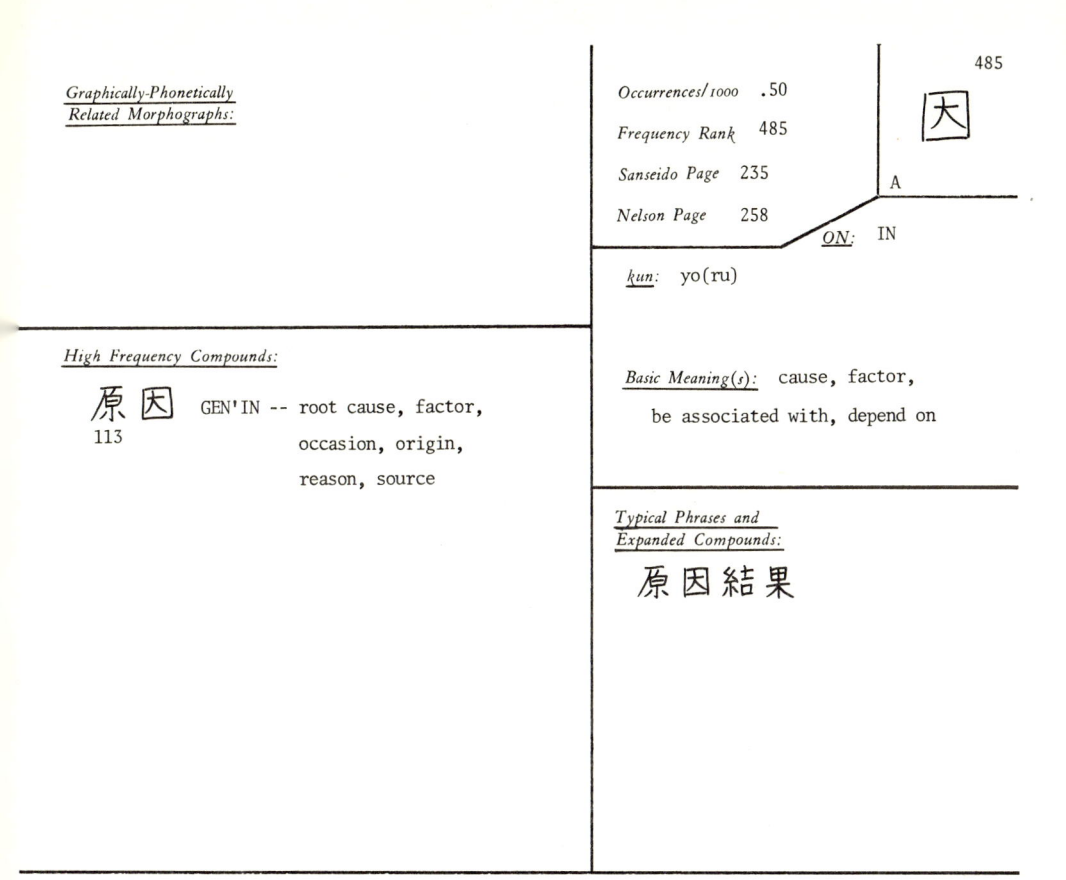

何か原因がなければ、そんなことは起こるはずがありません。

486

歌　A

Occurrences/1000　.50
Frequency Rank　486
Sanseido Page　535
Nelson Page　517

ON: KA

kun: uta, uta(u), uta(i)

Basic Meaning(s): sing, recite, chant, song, poem, singing

Graphically-Phonetically Related Morphographs:

何 KA (43)　荷 KA (1254)
可 KA (463)
河 KA (614)

High Frequency Compounds:

歌人 KAJIN -- poet
　2
歌舞伎 KABUKI -- kabuki, popu-
　638　　　　　　lar drama

Typical Phrases and Expanded Compounds:

有名な歌人
歌舞伎を見る
好きな歌
流行歌を歌う

Typical Conversational Usage:

与謝野晶子は私の好きな歌人です。
歌舞伎は古くからある日本の芸術です。
好きな歌から何曲か選んでひいてください。
歌を歌うのはどうも苦手です。

Graphically-Phonetically Related Morphographs:

Occurrences/1000 .50	487
Frequency Rank 487	革
Sanseido Page 553	A
Nelson Page 952	

<u>ON</u>: KAKU

<u>kun</u>:

Basic Meaning(s): tanned leather, become serious, renewal

High Frequency Compounds:

革命 KAKUMEI -- revolution
249

改革 KAIKAKU -- reform, reformation
289

革新 KAKUSHIN -- reform, innovation
80

Typical Phrases and Expanded Compounds:

暴力による革命
教育の改革
革新派の人々

Typical Conversational Usage:

暴力による革命をクーデターと言います。
２１世紀における教育の改革が叫ばれています。
学生には革新派が多いです。

488

疑

A

Occurrences/1000 .50
Frequency Rank 488
Sanseido Page 178
Nelson Page 212

ON: GI

kun: utaga(u), utaga(i), utaga(washii)

Basic Meaning(s): doubt, distrust, be suspicious of, question

Graphically-Phonetically Related Morphographs:

High Frequency Compounds:

疑問   GIMON -- question, problem,
41   doubt

疑獄   GIGOKU -- scandal, graft
1081

Typical Phrases and Expanded Compounds:

疑問文
疑獄事件
疑う余地がない
疑わしい足どり

Typical Conversational Usage:

疑問な点がありましたら、どんどん質問してください。
造船疑獄事件は世間を驚かせました。
もし疑ったら、きりがありません。
それは疑わしい事件として、まだ尾を引いています。

Graphically-Phonetically Related Morphographs:

Occurrences/1000 .50	489
Frequency Rank 489	血
Sanseido Page 63	A
Nelson Page 800	

ON: KETSU

kun: chi

Basic Meaning(s): blood

High Frequency Compounds:

血液   KETSUEKI -- blood

輸血   YUKETSU -- blood transfer
444

Typical Phrases and Expanded Compounds:

血液の検査

多量の輸血

血のにじむような努力

Typical Conversational Usage:

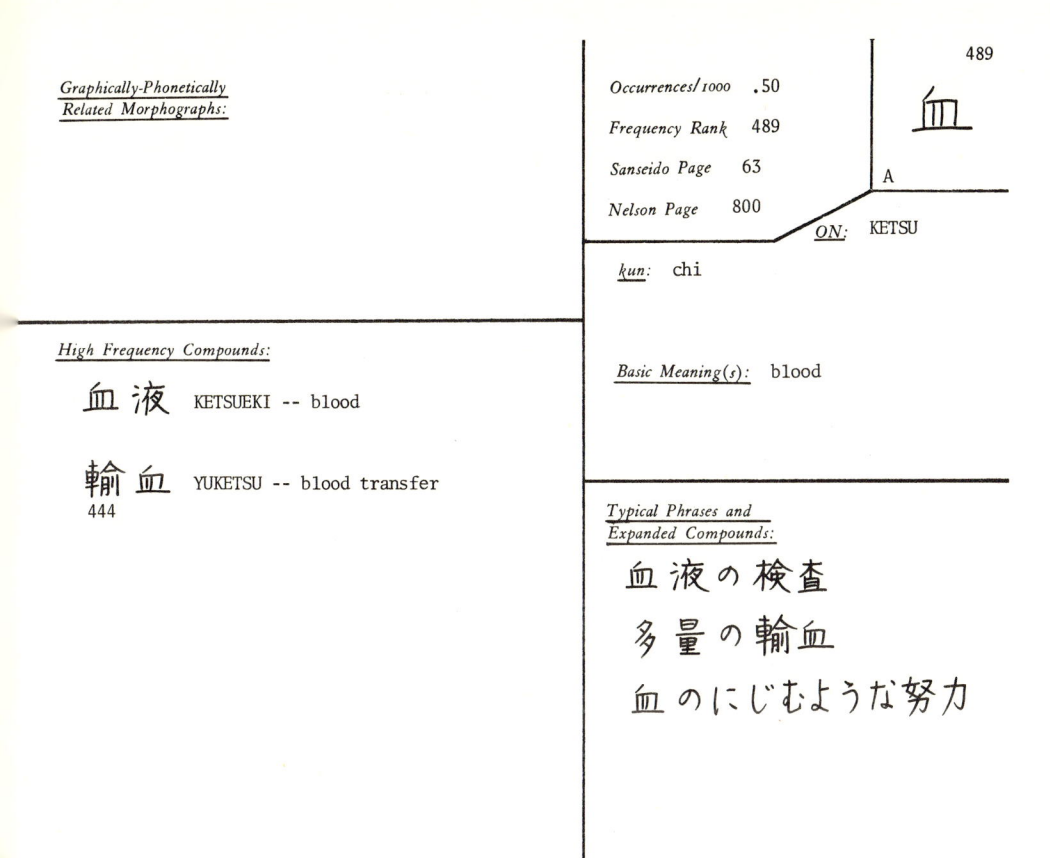

献血のため血液の検査を受けました。
おじは手術後、多量の輸血をしました。
妹は血を見ると、気が遠くなります。

490

興

A

Occurrences/1000 .50
Frequency Rank 490
Sanseido Page 551
Nelson Page 183

ON: KYOO, KOO

kun: oko(ru)

Basic Meaning(s): interest, entertainment, pleasure, be amused

Typical Phrases and Expanded Compounds:

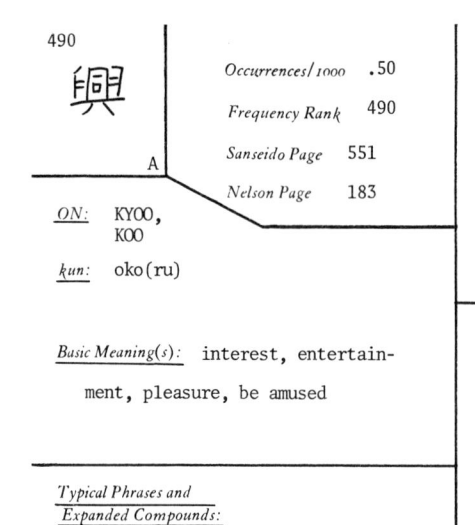

戦後の復興
興奮剤
興味を失う

Graphically-Phonetically Related Morphographs:

High Frequency Compounds:

復興 HUKKOO -- revival, resurgence, restoration
536

興奮 KOOHUN -- excitement, stimulation
1342

興味 KYOOMI -- interest
169

Typical Conversational Usage:

日本の産業は、戦後、めざましい復興ぶりを見せました。
コーヒーを飲み過ぎ、興奮して眠れなかったんです。
日本の歴史のことなら、興味があります。

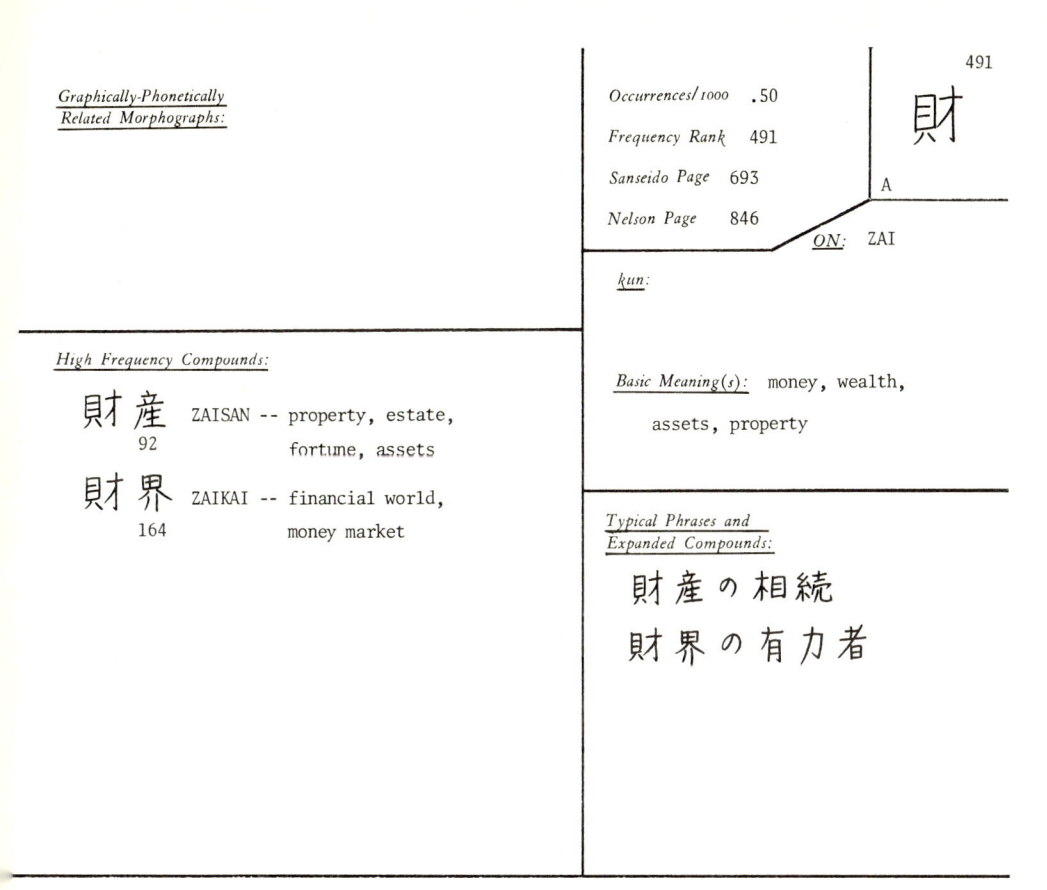

Graphically-Phonetically Related Morphographs:

Occurrences/1000 .50	491
Frequency Rank 491	財
Sanseido Page 693	
Nelson Page 846	A

ON: ZAI

kun:

High Frequency Compounds:

財産 ZAISAN -- property, estate,
 92   fortune, assets

財界 ZAIKAI -- financial world,
164   money market

Basic Meaning(s): money, wealth, assets, property

Typical Phrases and Expanded Compounds:

財産の相続
財界の有力者

Typical Conversational Usage:

おじは一生かかって、あれだけの財産を築き上げました。
政治家には財界の有力者が多いです。

492 察 A

Occurrences/1000	.50
Frequency Rank	492
Sanseido Page	293
Nelson Page	328

ON: SATSU

kun:

Basic Meaning(s): judge, presume, surmise, understand, realize

Graphically-Phonetically Related Morphographs:

擦 SATSU

High Frequency Compounds:

警察 454 KEISATSU -- police (force), police station

検察 473 KENSATSU -- investigation and prosecution

観察 302 KANSATSU -- observation, survey, investigation, supervision

Typical Phrases and Expanded Compounds:

警察官

検察側の立場

するどい観察力

Typical Conversational Usage:

警察の仕事は責任が重いので大変です。
今度の裁判で、検察側の主張が通りました。
自分で観察したことがらを、ありのままに記してごらんなさい。

Graphically-Phonetically Related Morphographs:

Occurrences/1000 .50	或
Frequency Rank 493	
Sanseido Page 468	X
Nelson Page 413	

ON:

kun: (a(ru)), (a(ruiwa))

High Frequency Compounds:

Basic Meaning(s): some, one, a certain, or, possibly

Typical Phrases and Expanded Compounds:

或る日

或るいは

Typical Conversational Usage:

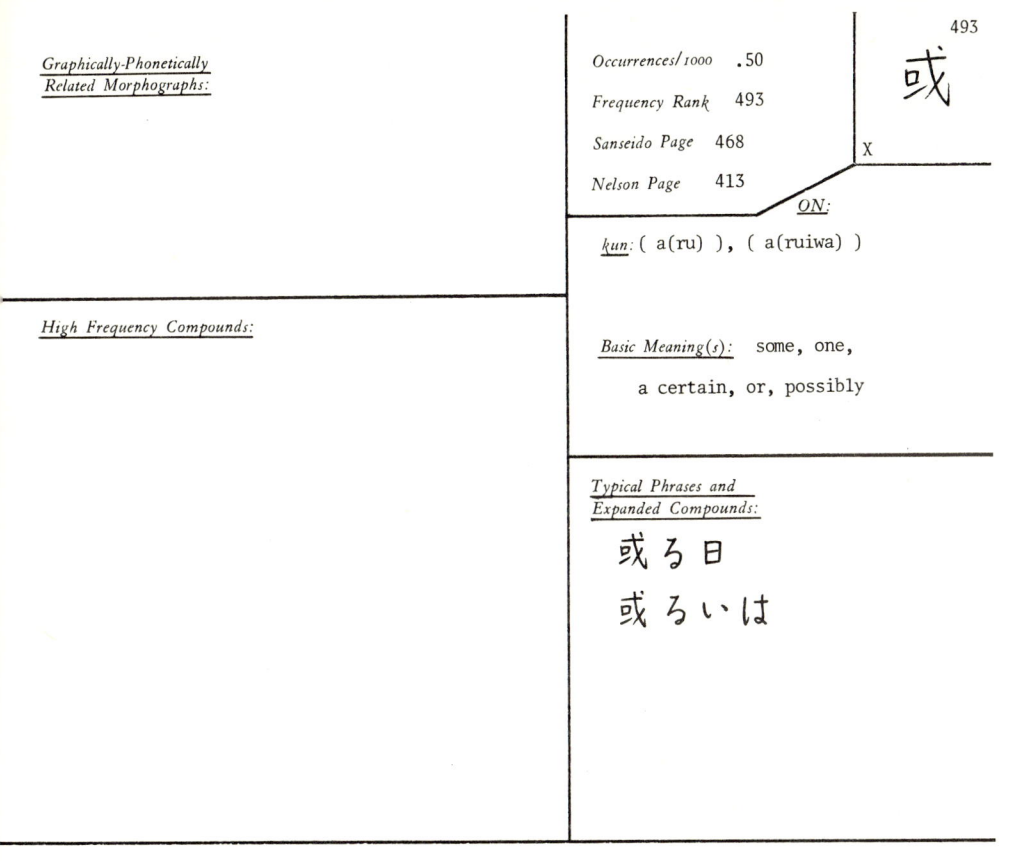

或る日、銀座で藤田さんに会ったことがあります。
まだはっきりしていませんが、或るいは山へ行くかも
知れません。

494

影 B

Occurrences/1000   .49
Frequency Rank   494
Sanseido Page   493
Nelson Page   380

ON: EI

kun: kage

Basic Meaning(s): shadow, light, silhouette

Typical Phrases and Expanded Compounds:

影響が大きい
まばらな人影
影も形もない

Graphically-Phonetically Related Morphographs:

High Frequency Compounds:

影響   EIKYOO -- influence, effect, consequences
757

人影   hitokage -- a person's shadow, a form
2

Typical Conversational Usage:

子どもにとって、テレビの影響力はとても大きいです。
夕方になったら、人影がまばらになりました。
あの方は、何となく影の薄い方です。

495

危 A

Graphically-Phonetically Related Morphographs:

Occurrences/1000	.49
Frequency Rank	495
Sanseido Page	213
Nelson Page	87

ON: KI

kun: ayau(i)

High Frequency Compounds:

危険 KIKEN -- danger, risk
662

危機 KIKI -- crisis, emergency
158

Basic Meaning(s): be afraid of, feel uneasy about, dangerous, uncertain

Typical Phrases and Expanded Compounds:

危険区域
危機が迫る
危いところ

Typical Conversational Usage:

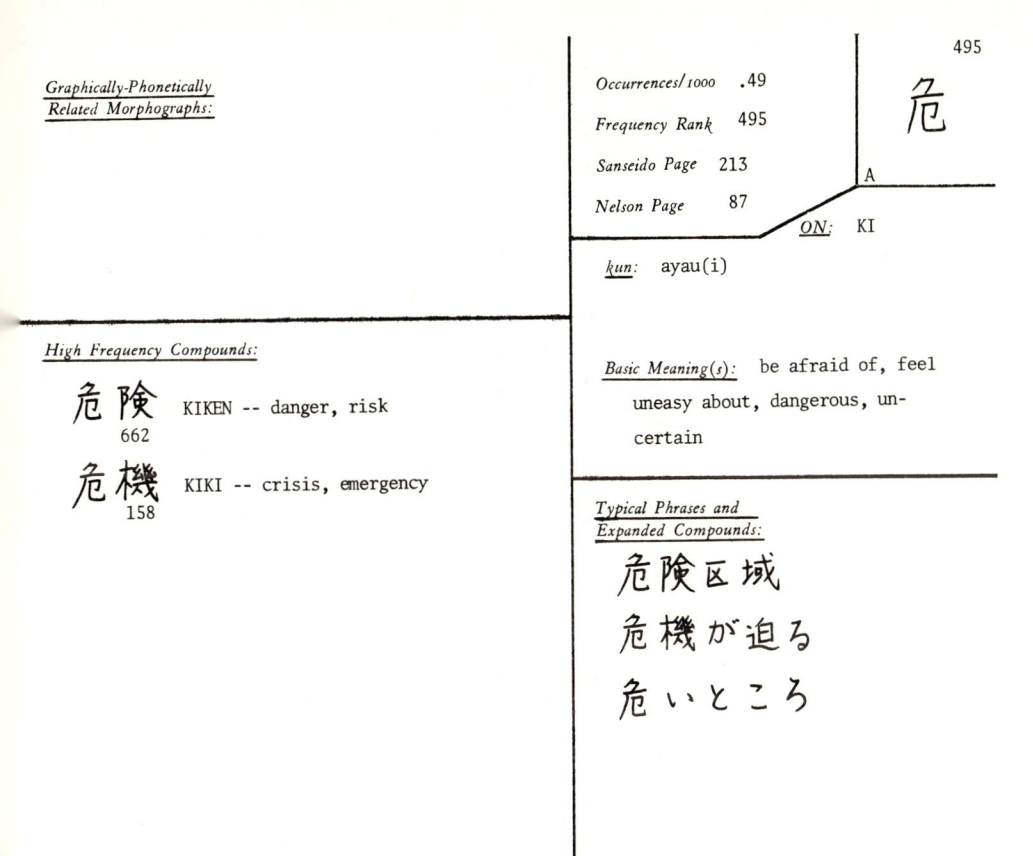

この辺は危険区域ですから、およぐことができません。
もう少し遅かったら、危機をのがれられなかったでしょう。
危ういところを助けていただき、ありがとうございました。

496

去

A

Occurrences/1000   .49
Frequency Rank   496
Sanseido Page   240
Nelson Page   265

ON: KYO, KO

kun: sa(ru)

Basic Meaning(s): leave, move away, quit, pass, elapse, be gone

Graphically-Phonetically Related Morphographs:

High Frequency Compounds:

過去 KAKO -- the past; previous life, past tense
230

去年 KYONEN -- last year
13

Typical Phrases and Expanded Compounds:

過去の思い出
去年の出来事
去る三月

Typical Conversational Usage:

過去のことにこだわっても、しかたがありません。
妹は、去年、バイオリンを習い始めたばかりです。
あつい夏が去り、いよいよ読書のシーズンになりました。

Graphically-Phonetically Related Morphographs:

High Frequency Compounds:

恐怖 KYOOHU -- fear, terror, panic
723

Occurrences/1000 .49
Frequency Rank 497
Sanseido Page 460
Nelson Page 401

恐   497

B

<u>ON</u>: KYOO

<u>kun</u>: oso(reru), oso(re)

Basic Meaning(s): fear, dread, be afraid, perhaps, possibly

Typical Phrases and Expanded Compounds:

恐怖心
恐らく
人を恐れる
恐ろしい夢

Typical Conversational Usage:

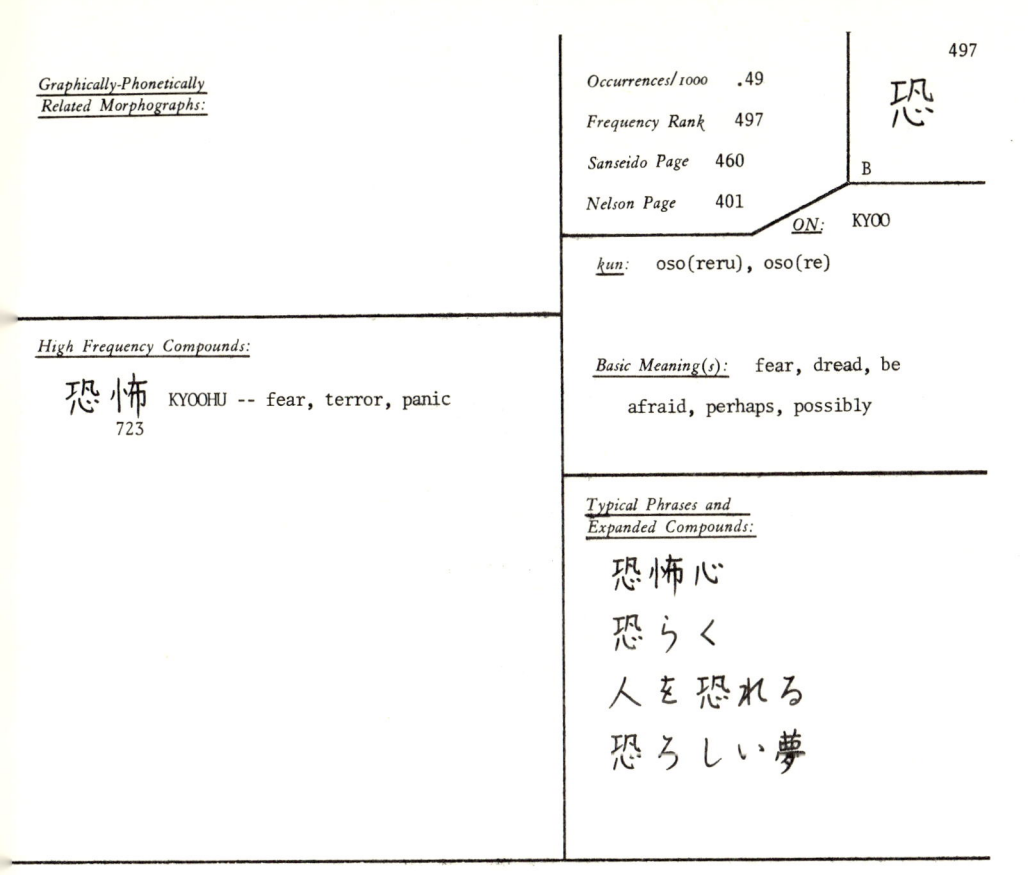

あの子は恐怖心が強くて、いつも何かにおびえています。
恐らくそれは問題になるでしょう。
死ぬわけでもあるまいし、何も恐れる必要はありません。
ゆうべ恐ろしい夢を見ました。

498 構

Occurrences/1000: .49
Frequency Rank: 498
Sanseido Page: 528
Nelson Page: 509

A

<u>ON</u>: KOO

<u>kun</u>: kama(eru), kama(e)

Basic Meaning(s): build, keep house, pose, assume an attitude, take a posture, be ready for

Typical Phrases and Expanded Compounds:

組合の機構
文章の構成
頭の構造
結構な話

Graphically-Phonetically Related Morphographs:

講 KOO (469)
購 KOO (1213)

High Frequency Compounds:

機構 158   KIKOO -- mechanism, structure, organization
構成 160   KOOSEI -- composition, organization, line-up
構造 441   KOOZOO -- construction, framework, set-up
結構 109   KEKKOO -- very well, set-up

Typical Conversational Usage:

組合の機構が変わり、規約の一部が改正されました。
沢村さんは、テレビ番組の構成を担当しています。
エンジンがどういう構造になっているのか、さっぱりわかりません。
それは大変結構な話だと思います。

Graphically-Phonetically Related Morphographs:

	499
Occurrences/1000 .49	算
Frequency Rank 499	
Sanseido Page 628	A
Nelson Page 686	

<u>ON</u>: SAN

<u>kun</u>:

High Frequency Compounds:

予算　YOSAN -- estimate, budget,
283　　　　　appropriation

計算　KEISAN -- computation, cal-
210　　　　　culation

Basic Meaning(s): calculation, numbers, divining block, count, plan

Typical Phrases and Expanded Compounds:

予算額
電子計算機

Typical Conversational Usage:

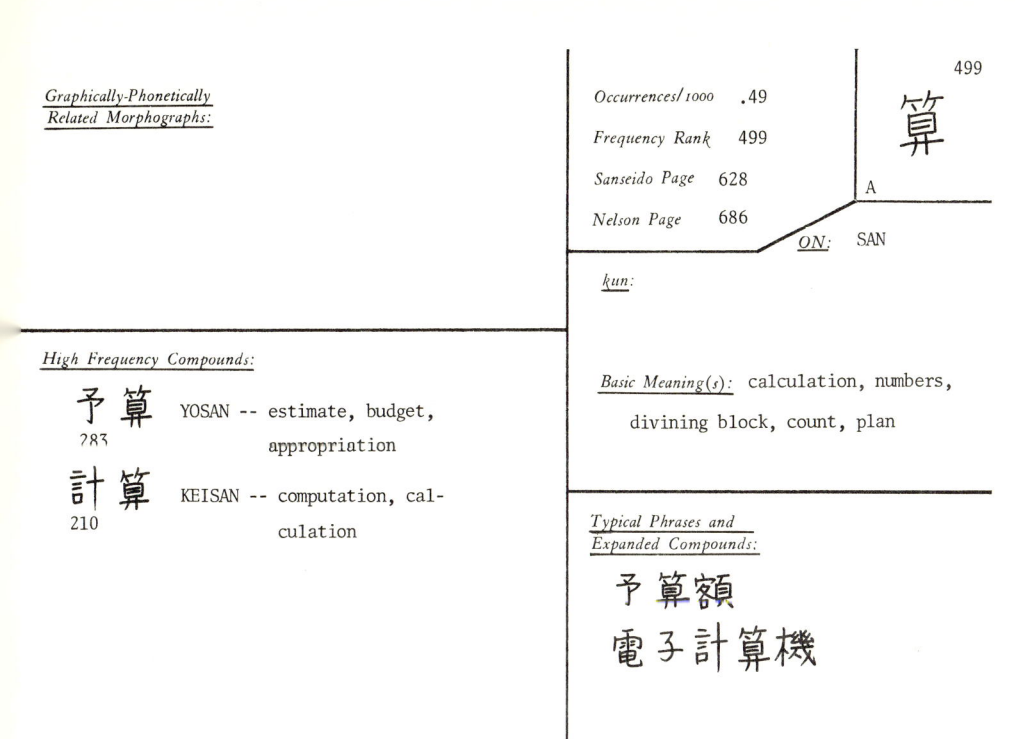

今度の総会で本年度の予算が決定します。
総額がいくらになるか、計算してみてください。

500 素 A

Occurrences/1000: .49
Frequency Rank: 500
Sanseido Page: 565
Nelson Page: 698

ON: SU, SO

kun:

Basic Meaning(s): principle, element, naked, uncovered, simple

Graphically-Phonetically Related Morphographs:

High Frequency Compounds:

要素 78 — YOOSO -- element, essential, constituent, requisite

素材 806 — SOZAI -- raw materials, matter, material, subject matter

素朴 1345 — SOBOKU -- simplicity, artlessness

素直 214 — SUnao -- gentle, meek, tame, obedient, honest, frank

素人 2 — shirooto -- amateur, novice, layman

Typical Phrases and Expanded Compounds:

大切な要素
彫刻の素材
素朴な住民
素直な子ども
ずぶの素人

Typical Conversational Usage:

成功の大切な要素は努力することです。
あの番組は、たくましい漁民の生活を素材にしたルポです。
この村の人々はみんな素朴な住民です。
子どもを素直に育てたいと願っています。
私の町で素人のど自慢大会が行われました。

ICHIBUBUN 1
IPPAN-TEKI   一
ITTAI ZENTAI
ICHIBAN takai
TOOITSU o hakaru
KEIKAKU no hitotsu

Koko wa DAIGAKU no ICHIBU desu.
Sore wa IPPAN-TEKI na kangae desu.
ITTAI ZENTAI doo shita no desu ka.
Kono biru wa TOOKYOO de ICHIBAN takai biru desu.
TOOITSU KOODOO o torimashoo
Kono SUIKA o hitotsu kudasai.

JINSEI no MONDAI 2
o-mise no SHUJIN   人
TOOKYOO no JINKOO
YUUJIN no aida de
NINGEN KANKEI
yasashii hito

JINSEI ni wa iroiro na MONDAI ga arimasu.
Go-SHUJIN wa o-RUSU desu ka.
TOOKYOO no JINKOO wa SEKAI-ICHI desu.
Honda-san wa watakushi no YUUJIN desu.
NINGEN KANKEI wa muzukashii desu.
Ano hito wa totemo yasashii hito desu.

NIHONJIN 3
KONNICHI no MONDAI   日
MAINICHI no SHIgoto
Asahi SHIMBUN
SAKUJITSU no dekigoto

NIHON o itsu tachimasu ka.
KONNICHI no SEKAI wa ookina MONDAI o kakaete imasu.
MAINICHI nani o shite imasu ka.
Uchi de wa Asahi SHIMBUN o totte imasu.
SAKUJITSU Ueda-san ni o-ai shimashita.

BEIKOKU SHIMIN 4
CHUUGOKU TAIRIKU
NIHON KOKUMIN   国
GAIKOKU SEIHIN
KOKUSAI-TEKI
kuni o agete

BEIKOKU e ZEHI itte mitai desu.
CHUUGOKU wa ookii kuni desu.
Sore wa KOKUMIN ni totte ookina MONDAI desu.
Ano kata wa GAIKOKUJIN desu ka.
Sono kata wa KOKUSAI-TEKI ni yoku shirarete imasu.
O-kuni wa dochira desu ka.

5 大

DAIGAKUSEI
DAI-NIJI SEKAI TAISEN
TAIHEN na JIKEN
TAISETSU na HON
DAIJI na mono
ookii GAKKOO

TOOKYOO DAIGAKU wa doko desu ka.
TAISEN-mae watakushi wa CHUUGOKU ni imashita.
Piano ga TAIHEN JOOZU ni narimashita.
Kono HON o TAISETSU ni shite kudasai.
DAIJI na mono o wasurete kimashita.

6 本

NIHON SEIHU
KAISHA no SHIHON
HONTOO no hanashi
KOMPON-TEKI
HONGOKU e kaeru

NIHON ni wa yama ga TAKUSAN arimasu.
SHIHONKIN wa ikura desu ka.
TOOKYOO wa HONTOO ni hito ga ooi desu.
KOMPON-TEKI ni yarinaosanakereba narimasen.
Sumisu-san wa HONGOKU e kaerimashita.
Kono HON wa dare no HON desu ka.

7 的

JINSEI no MOKUTEKI
YOSOO ga TEKICHUU suru
TEKIKAKU na KAITOO
IPPAN-TEKI na IKEN
mato ga hazureru

JINSEI no MOKUTEKI wa nan desu ka.
YOSOO ga mi goto ni TEKICHUU shimashita.
TEKIKAKU na KAITOO ga hoshii n' desu.
IPPAN-TEKI ni soo iwarete imasu.
Ano hito no kangae wa mato ga hazurete imasu.

8 出

SHUPPATSU TEN
YUSHUTSU HIN
SHUSSHIN KOO
SHISHUTSU ga ooi
hutoshita dekigoto
tsuki ga deru

NanJI ni SHUPPATSU shimasu ka.
NIHON wa YUSHUTSU ga sakan desu.
Watakushi no SHUSSHINCHI wa Okayama desu.
KONGETSU no SHISHUTSU wa totemo ookatta desu.
Kinoo no dekigoto ni tsuite hanashite kudasai.
MAIasa uchi o SHICHI-JI ni demasu.

JIDOOSHA no SEISAN						9
GAKUSEI JIDAI						生
TOOKYOO no SEIKATSU
kibishii SENSEI
ISSHOO no MONDAI
ikimono

Kono KOOJOO de wa nani o SEISAN shite imasu ka.
GAKUSEI no IKEN o matomemashita.
TOOKYOO de SEIKATSU shita koto ga arimasu ka.
KAGAKU o Yamada SENSEI ni naratte imasu.
Shiawase na ISSHOO o okuritai to omoimasu.
Sono sakana wa ikite imasu ka.

JIJITSU ga wakaru						10
GUNJI-TEKI						事
JIGYOO no NAIYOO
JIMUSHO
TAIHEN na SHIgoto

JIJITSU o uttaemashita.
Amerika wa GUNJI-TEKI ni tsuyoi kuni desu.
Chichi wa JIGYOO ni SEIKOO shimashita.
JIMUSHO de MAINICHI hataraite imasu.
Moo SHIgoto ga owarimashita.

NIJUU-NIN						11
NIHYAKU tooka						二
NISEN-EN
NIGATSU hutsuka
hutatsu no kao

KOOTEI ni sakura no ki o NIJUP-PON uemashita.
Kinoo no TAIKAI ni NIHYAKU-NIN gurai atsumarimashita.
Kono shatsu wa NISEN-EN de kaimashita.
Hutsuka mo sureba, yoku naru deshoo.
RINGO o hutatsu tabemashita.

CHUUGOKU CHIHOO						12
CHUUSHIN-CHI						中
machi no CHUUOO
CHUURITSU KOKKA
CHUUGAKU SANNENSEI
ie no naka

Hiroshima KEN wa CHUUGOKU CHIHOO ni arimasu.
Kono HEN wa machi no CHUUSHIN ni atarimasu.
Machi no CHUUOO ni SHOOGAKKOO ga arimasu.
Suisu wa CHUURITSU-KOKU desu.
ICHIROO-KUN wa CHUUGAKU nanNEN-SEI desu ka.
O-mocha wa sono hako no naka ni arimasu.

13 年
MAItoshi no GYOOJI
SEINEN-KAI
KYONEN no kure
NENREI no SA
KOtoshi no KEIKAKU
toshi o toru

MAItoshi aki ni UNDOOKAI o MOYOO shimasu.
Kono machi no SEINENKAI wa KAPPATSU desu.
KYONEN no natsu, HOKKAIDOO e itte kimashita.
Ano kata no NENREI wa yoku wakarimasen.
KOtoshi wa doko e mo ikimasen.
O-toshi wa ikutsu desu ka.

14 自
JIBUN JISHIN
JIYUU KOODOO
JIDOOSHA
HUSHIZEN
JIEITAI
mizukara susunde

Sore wa JIBUN no MONDAI desu.
JIYUU ni SHITSUMON shite kudasai.
Kono erebeetaa wa JIDOO desu.
Kega ga SHIZEN ni naorimashita.
O-tooto wa JIEITAI ni NYUUTAI shimashita.
Mizukara HANSEI shite mite kudasai.

15 学
DAIGAKU yoNEN
GAKUSEI SEIKATSU
GAKKOO no SENSEI
KAGAKU-SHA
GAKUMON no SEKAI
EIGO o manabu

DAIGAKU o detara, SENSEI ni naru tsumori desu.
GAKUSEI SEIKATSU wa ICHIBAN tanoshii desu.
Ashita GAKKOO e ikimasu ka.
Chiisai toki kara KAGAKU ga suki deshita.
Ookawa-san wa nakanaka GAKUMON ga arimasu.
Ima EIGO to HuransuGO o manande imasu.

16 会
KAIGI-CHUU
SHAKAI MONDAI
KAISHA no JUUYAKU
KOKKAI GIIN
KYOOKAI-IN
tomodachi ni au

Ashita wa TAISETSU na KAIGI ga arimasu.
SHAKAI ni wa iroiro na MONDAI ga arimasu.
Tonari no Nemoto-san wa KAISHA no JUUYAKU desu.
CHUUGAKU-SEI no toki, KOKKAI o KENGAKU shimashita.
NICHIYOObi ni wa itsumo KYOOKAI e ikimasu.
Kinoo TOOKYOO EKI de Yamamoto-san ni aimashita.

KOOSHI KONDOO SHIRITSU DAIGAKU SHISHO-bako watakushi no haha	17 私

KOOSHI KONDO shite wa ikemasen.
Watakushi no DAIGAKU wa SHIRITSU desu.
SHISHO-bako wa namBAN desu ka.
Soko ni aru HON wa watakushi no desu.

ayashii KOODOO NIHON GINKOO JIKKOORYOKU RYUUKOO no doresu SHUUGAKU RYOKOO TOOKYOO e iku	18 行

Ano hito no KOODOO wa nan to naku ayashii desu.
GINKOO de o-kane o oroshite kimasu.
Nanigoto mo JIKKOO suru koto ga TAISETSU desu.
Kore wa RYUUKOO no doresu desu.
RYOKOO wa totemo tanoshii desu.
Mada KYUUSHUU e itta koto ga arimasen.

GAKUSHA no IKEN AIDOKU-SHA KISHA KAIKEN NYUUIN KANJA wakamono	19 者

GAKKAI ni GAKUSHA ga ooZEI atsumarimasu.
Watakushi wa MAINICHI SHIMBUN no AIDOKU-SHA desu.
Yamamoto-san wa SHIMBUN KISHA desu.
HACHIGO-SHITSU no KANJA wa kinoo NYUUIN shimashita.
ISHA ni mite moraimashita.
Watakushi wa Yamaguchi to iu mono desu.

IKEN o noberu DAI-HAKKEN KENKAI o koto ni suru KEMBUTSUNIN KENTOO-chigai terebi o miru	20 見

Minna no IKEN o kiite mimashoo.
Korombusu wa Amerika o HAKKEN shimashita.
Hutari no KENKAI ga kotonarimashita.
O-jii-chan wa TOOKYOO KEMBUTSU ni ikimashita.
Mattaku KENTOO ga tsukimasen.
Kinoo, omoshiroi EIGA o mimashita.

SANJUU-DAI SAMBYAKU-EN mikka BOOZU mittsu no ko	21 三

con'd

21 con'd
三

Watakushi wa moo SANJUU o sugimashita.
Temoto ni SAMBYAKU-EN shika arimasen.
KAIGI wa mikka-KAN desu.
Kono ko wa mada mittsu desu.

22
十

JUUBUN na JIKAN
NIJUU-MEI
SANJUU NICHI
tooka-KAN

Moo JUUBUN desu.
Sono SHIgoto wa NIJUU-NIN gurai de dekiru deshoo.
Watakushi no TANJOObi wa SHIGATSU SANJUU-NICHI desu.
KONGETSU no tooka ni TOOKYOO e ikimasu.

23
政

SEIHU no HOOSHIN
SEIJI MONDAI
SEIHU no SEISAKU
NI-DAISEITOO
SEIKEN o toru
CHIHOO GYOOSEI

SEIHU no HOOSHIN ga akiraka ni saremashita.
SEIJI-KA ni wa naritaku arimasen.
SEIHU no SEISAKU ga kawarimashita.
Amerika no NI-DAISEITOO wa nani to nani desu ka.
Ima wa JIYUU-MINSHU-TOO ga SEIKEN o nigitte imasu.
GYOOSEI ga sukoshi midarete imasu.

24
時

MEIJI JIDAI
NAN-JIKAN
JIKANSEI
SENSOO TOOJI
udeDOKEI
sono toki

GAKUSEI JIDAI no koto wa wasureraremasen.
MAINICHI, NAN-JIKAN gurai BENKYOO shimasu ka.
Moo GAKKOO e iku JIKAN DESU.
SENSOO TOOJI doko ni imashita ka.
Kono TOKEI wa Suisu-SEI desu.
Machi e iku toki wa, ISSHOO ni ikimashoo.

25
方

KANTOO CHIHOO
yasashii HOOHOO
IPPOO TSUUKOO
TOOKYOO HOOMEN
RYOOHOO tomo
sono kata

Kinoo kono CHIHOO ni ooame ga hurimashita.
Sono HOOHOO wa muzukashii desu ka, yasashii desu ka.
Koko wa IPPOO TSUUKOO desu.
Kono basu wa Ueno HOOMEN e ikimasu ka.
TOOKYOO DAIGAKU to Oosaka DAIGAKU wa RYOOHOO tomo KOKURITSU DAIGAKU desu.
Sono kata o go-ZONji desu ka.

```
                CHUUGOKU no SHISOO                              26
                SHIRYO no aru hito
                omou yoo ni                                     思

                Nakagawa-san no SHISOO wa yutaka desu.
                SHIRYO no nai koto o shite wa ikemasen.
                Nakanaka omou yoo ni ikimasen.
```

```
                RAINEN no ima goro                              27
                chikai SHOORAI
                SENGETSU IRAI                                   来
                MIRAI no Amerika
                go-HAN o tabete kuru

                RAINEN Amerika ni iku tsumori desu.
                SHOORAI no koto wa mada hakkiri wakarimasen.
                DAIGAKU o dete IRAI, Nakayama-san ni atte imasen.
                MIRAI no SEKAI wa doo narimasu ka.
                Uchi de go-HAN o tabete kimashita.
```

```
                JIBUN no MONDAI                                 28
                JUUBUN na kotae
                BUBUN-TEKI                                      分
                KIBUN ga warui
                HAMBUN IJOO
                TABUN no

                JIBUN de yatte mite kudasai.
                Moo JUUBUN desu.
                Sore wa honno ICHIBUBUN desu.
                Doo mo KIBUN ga suguremasen.
                HAMBUN de KEKKOO desu.
                TABUN arashi ni naru kamo shiremasen.
```

```
                JUUNIN IJOO                                     29
                KYOOIKU no KOOJOO
                CHIJOO JUUNI-KAI                                上
                tana no ue

                Kore IJOO dekimasen.
                SENGO, JOSEI no CHII ga KOOJOO shimashita.
                Ano biru wa CHIKA NIKAI, CHIJOO JUKKAI-date desu.
                Teeburu no ue ni aru HON o totte kudasai.
```

```
                KOKUMIN-SEI                                     30
                MINSHU SHUGI
                SHIMINKEN                                       民
                MINKAN HOOSOO
                NOOMIN no SEIKATSU

                Kono HON ni wa NIHON no KOKUMINSEI ga yoku arawasarete imasu.
                Amerika wa MINSHU SHUGI no kuni desu.
                KOOGAI wa SHIMIN ni totte ookina MONDAI desu.
                MINKAN HOOSOOKYOKU wa TOOKYOO ni ikutsu arimasu ka.
                NOOMIN no SEIKATSU ga yoku narimashita.
```

31 間 NINGEN SHAKAI
CHOO-JIKAN
SEKEN-banashi
uridashi KIKAN
ISSHUU-KAN
SANNEN no aida

NINGEN KANKEI wa nakanaka muzukashii desu.
JIKAN-TEKI ni mite, sono SHIgoto wa chotto muri desu.
Orimpikku wa, ima, SEKEN no WADAI ni natte imasu.
Tesuto no KIKAN ga naga-sugimasu.
SANSHUU-KAN areba, KOKUNAI o mawareru deshoo.

32 戦 Betonamu SENSOO
SENZEN no NIHON
SENGO no KEIZAI
TAISENmae
SHUUSENGO

SENSOO ga hayaku owareba ii to omoimasu.
SENZEN, watakushi wa KYUUSHUU ni imashita.
SENGO no HUKKOO buri wa TAI-shita mono desu.
TAISEN ga owaru made, HOKKAIDOO ni imashita.
SHUUSENGO, chichi wa JIGYOO o hajimemashita.
Sono MONDAI de tatakatte imasu.

33 合 Amerika GASSHUUKOKU
sono baai
GOORI-TEKI
kuruma no GUai
KOKUSAI RENGOO
niau

Hawai wa GASSHUUKOKU de GOJUU BAMme no SHUU desu.
Iku baai ni wa, shirasete kudasai.
Sore wa GOORI-TEKI de wa arimasen.
Karada no GUai ga omowashiku arimasen.
KOKUSAI RENGOO no hataraki wa ookii to omoimasu.
Kono doresu wa yoku niaimasu ka.

34 主 KYOOSAN SHUGI
JIYUU MINSHU-TOO
SHUJIN no SHUTCHOO
IKEN no SHUCHOO
SHUKEN-ZAIMIN

Ano kata wa HEIWA SHUGI-SHA desu.
Kenedei wa MINSHU-TOO deshita.
SHUJIN wa SHIgoto de SHUTCHOO shimashita.
JIBUN no IKEN bakari SHUCHOO shite wa ikemasen.
SHUKEN wa KOKUMIN ni arimasu.

```
                DOKURITSU KOKKA                                    35
                RIPPA na hito
                CHUURITSU no tachiba                               立
                warui tachiba
                TAIRITSU-SHA
                ue ni tatsu hito

                Isuraeru wa itsu DOKURITSU shimashita ka.
                Tamiko-san no o-too-san wa RIPPA na kata desu.
                Honda-san no tachiba wa itsumo CHUURITSU desu.
                Watakushi no tachiba ga arimasen.
                Arabu no kuniguni wa yoku Isuraeru to TAIRITSU shimasu.
                Asoko ni tatte iru kata wa donata desu ka.
```
```
                GUNJI KYOOIKU                                      36
                BEIKOKU GUNTAI
                KAIGUN to RIKUGUN                                  軍
                GUNKOKU SHUGI
                SAIGUMBI

                SENZEN, ani wa GUNJI KYOOIKU o ukemashita.
                GUNTAI ni haitte, mamonaku SENCHI ni ikimashita.
                KAIGUN to RIKUGUN de wa, dochira no HOO ga suki desu ka.
                SENZEN no NIHON wa GUNKOKU-TEKI deshita.
                Ano demo wa SAIGUMBI HANTAI no demo desu.
```
```
                GENJITSU no MONDAI                                 37
                JIJITSU o uttaeru
                JIKKOORYOKU                                        実
                yume no JITSUGEN
                JISSAI MONDAI to shite
                minori no aki

                Sore wa GENJITSU no MONDAI to shite kangaenakereba narimasen.
                JIJITSU, sonna koto o shita koto wa arimasen.
                Omotta koto o JIKKOO shite mite kudasai.
                Yume ga JITSUGEN shite, totemo ureshii desu.
                Sore wa JISSAI ni kiita hanashi desu.
                MIKAN ga TAKUSAN minorimashita.
```
```
                DORYOKU o oshimanai                                38
                KYOORYOKU-TEKI na hito
                NOORYOKU ni oojite                                 力
                BOORYOKU KOOI
                SEIRYOKU KA
                chikara-mochi

                Dekiru dake DORYOKU shite mimashoo.
                Minna no KYOORYOKU ga nakereba, kono SHIgoto wa dekimasen.
                Kodomo no NOORYOKU o nobashite agemashoo.
                BOORYOKU o hurutte wa ikemasen.
                Itsumo SEIRYOKU arasoi ga taemasen.
                Chikara no aru kagiri, gambarimashoo.
```

39 対
HANTAI gawa
ZETTAI TASUU
IKEN no TAIRITSU
TAISAKU o KOOzuru
TAINICHI KANJOO
aite ni TAIshite

Sono IKEN ni wa HANTAI desu.
Sono SEISAKU ni wa ZETTAI HANTAI desu.
Hutari no IKEN wa TAIRITSU shite imasu.
SUIGAICHI ni TAIshite TAISAKU o nette imasu.
Amerika no TAINICHI KANJOO wa totemo ii to omoimasu.
Kono MONDAI ni TAIshite, doo omoimasu ka.

40 五
GOJUU ON
GOGATSU NINGYOO
GOHYAKU-NIN
GOSEN-EN
GOGATSU itsuka

Chichi wa MAN GOJUSSAI ni narimashita.
GOGATSU itsuka wa kodomo no hi desu.
Kono CHUUGAKKOO no ICHINEN-SEI wa, ZEMBU de GOHYAKU-NIN gurai desu.
Kono GOGATSU NINGYOO wa GOSEN-EN de kaimashita.
Itsuka de HOKKAIDOO o mawaru tsumori desu.

41 問
RENSHUU MONDAI
GAKUMON-TEKI
muzukashii SHITSUMON
GIMON ga hareru
kusuri tonya

Dono kurai dekiru ka ga MONDAI desu.
Ima, GAKUMON-TEKI na KENCHI kara, sono MONDAI o shirabete imasu.
Nani ka SHITSUMON ga arimasu ka.
GIMON no TEN wa, doshidoshi tazunete kudasai.
Uchi wa kusuri tonya o shite imasu.

42 子
GENSHI-RYOKU
karada no CHOOSHI
JOSHI to DANSHI
okashi na YOOSU
musuko no KAISHA
ano ko

GENSHI no chikara wa ookii desu.
Nan da ka karada no CHOOSHI ga omowashiku arimasen.
Soko ni wa JOSHI shika orimasen.
Chotto SHIgoto no YOOSU o mite kimasu.
Musuko wa TOOKYOO no DAIGAKU ni itte imasu.
Ano ko wa yoku hataraku ii ko deshita.

```
nanJI goro                                                    43
naze ka
ika-sama-SHI                                                  何
nanigoto de mo
nanimono ka ni osowareru

Oji-san wa nanJI goro tsukimasu ka.
Naze sonna koto o shita no desu ka.
MAINICHI ikaga o-sugoshi desu ka.
Nanigoto de mo MAJIME ni SHIgoto o suru koto ga TAISETSU desu.
Nanimono ka ni SAIHU o nusumaremashita.
```

```
GENRONKAI                                                     44
HATSUGEN ga ooi
SHOOGEN o motomeru                                            言
YOGEN-SHA
hitokoto hutakoto
nani o itte mo

NIHON ni wa GENRON no JIYUU ga arimasu.
Doshidoshi HATSUGEN shite kudasai.
KOOHAN de SHOOGEN o motomeraremashita.
RAINEN no dekigoto ni tsuite, YOGEN shita hito ga imasu.
Watakushi ni mo hitokoto iwasete kudasai.
Nani mo iu koto ga arimasen.
```

```
CHIHOO SENKYO                                                 45
warui TOCHI
takai CHII                                                    地
BEIGUN KICHI
DAIJISHIN

Kinoo, TOOKYOO CHIHOO wa ame deshita.
Inaka no hoo ni TOCHI o kaimashita.
Oji-san wa KAISHA de mo ue no hoo no CHII ni imasu.
Kawamura-san wa Tachikawa no BEIGUN KICHI de hataraite ita
SAIKIN, KAKUCHI de JISHIN ga yoku okotte imasu.    (soo desu.
```

```
KOKKA KENRYOKU                                                46
KATEI YOOHIN
GENDAI SAKKA                                                  家
KAZOKU KAIGI
TENSAI GAKA
atarashii ie

KOKKA no ANZEN wa TAISETSU desu.
Nakayama-san no go-SHUJIN wa totemo KATEI-TEKI desu.
Donna SAKKA ga suki desu ka.
Go-KAZOKU wa minasan o-GENKI desu ka.
Pikaso wa YUUMEI na GAKA desu.
Ano atarashii ie wa Kazuko-san no ie desu.
```

47 GAKUSEI UNDOO
動 KATSUDOO-KA
    JIDOO no kamera
    DOOBUTSUEN
    KOODOO-HA
    te o ugokasu

    MAINICHI, sukoshi UNDOO suru koto ni shite imasu.
    Yamamoto-san wa SHAKAI-TEKI ni yoku KATSUDOO shite imasu.
    Kono kamera wa JIDOO desu.
    Kodomo o tsurete, DOOBUTSUEN e ikimashita.
    HEN na KOODOO o totte wa ikemasen.
    Omou YOO ni karada ga ugokimasen.

48 SAIGO no SHUDAN
後 KONGO no nariyuki
    SENGO no NIHON
    IGO no MONDAI
    GOGO SANJI
    kono nochi

    Kinoo wa GAKKOO no SAIGO no hi deshita.
    KONGO KI o tsukemasu.
    Otooto wa SENGO umaremashita.
    Sore IGO, mada nan ni mo shite imasen.
    Tanaka-san to GOGO ICHIJI ni au tsumori desu.
    Sono GO, zutto TOOKYOO ni imashita.

49 hito no tachiba
場 KOOJOO KENGAKU
    KAIGI no baSHO
    EIGA no baMEN
    KOOJI no GEMba

    Hito no tachiba o yoku kangaenakereba narimasen.
    Sonii no KOOJOO e KENGAKU ni ikimashita.
    BaSHO o machigaemashita.
    Dono baMEN ga ICHIBAN yokatta desu ka.
    BUCHO wa GEMba ni imasu.

50 KONDO no KIKAI
今 KONNICHI no SEKAI
    KOtoshi no WADAI
    KONGO no MONDAI
    KON'YA no tsuki
    ima kara

    KONDO wa TOOKYOO de aimashoo.
    KYOO no TENKI wa yoku arimasen.
    KOtoshi DAIGAKU o deta bakari desu.
    KONGO sonna koto wa shinai tsumori desu.
    KON'YA no tsuki wa totemo kirei desu
    Ima kara doko e ikimasu ka.

MONDAI ga ooi 51
KENKYUU KADAI
SHUDAI-KA
題

MONDAI ga ookute, atama ga itai desu.
Watakushi no KENKYUU KADAI wa "NIHON no BUNKA" ni tsuite desu.
ROMBUN no SHUDAI ga moo kimarimashita ka.

GAKKOO no NAIBU 52
karada no ICHIBU
ZEMBU no hito
BUBUN-TEKI
EIGYOO BUCHOO
YAKAM-BU
部

GUN no NAIBU no koto wa wakarimasen.
Te wa karada no ICHIBU desu.
Kore de ZEMBU desu.
Kowareta BUBUN o naoshite kudasai.
BUCHOO wa ima KAIGI-CHUU desu.
Otooto wa YAKAM-BU no GAKUSEI desu.

SENZEN SENGO o TSUUjite 53
Runesansu IZEN
IPPO-ZENSHIN suru
GOZEN NIJI
ZENTO YUUBOO
omoshiroi namae
前

Kono HON wa SENZEN ni deta HON desu.
IZEN wa sonna koto wa arimasen deshita.
NISAM-PO ZENSHIN SHITE kudasai.
Kono SHIgoto wa GOZEN-CHUU ni owaru deshoo.
Maeda-san no ZENTO wa YUUDOO desu.
Kono inu no namae wa "Pochi" to iimasu.

DOOJI ni 54
Amerika to DOOYOO ni
SANGOKU DOOMEI
KYOODOO JIGYOO
DOOJOO o yobu
onaji MOKUTEKI
同

Hutari wa NIHON ni DOOJI ni tsukimashita.
Amerika to DOOYOO ni, NIHON de wa KOOGYOO ga SAKAN desu.
Doitsu to Itaria wa katsute GUNJI DOOMEI o musubimashita.
Kono SUIDOO wa KYOODOO de tsukatte imasu.
Sonna koto ni DOOJOO suru wake ni wa ikimasen.
Imooto to onaji doresu o kaimashita.

KImochi ga kawaru 55
NINKI ga agaru
SHINSEN na KUUKI
warui DYOOKI
DENKI-GAISHA
気
con'd

55
con'd
気

Nan da ka KImochi ga yoku arimasen.
Akemi-chan wa uchi no NINKImono desu.
KAIGI no KUUKI wa omokurushikatta desu.
BYOOKI de GAKKOO o yasumimashita.
DENKI no HATASU YAKUwari wa ookii desu.

56
彼

kanoJO no DAIGAKU
HIGAN no iri
kare no SHIgoto

KanoJO wa ashita au tsumori desu.
HIGAN mo sugi, hi ga sukoshi zutsu nagaku narimashita.
Kare no o-too-san wa JITSUGYOO-KA desu.

57
手

SHUDAN o erabu
tegami o uketoru
aite no hito
katte KImama ni
RYOOte de motsu
kuchi no JOOZU na hito

Donna SHUDAN o KOOjimasu ka.
KYUUSHUU ni iru ane kara tegami o moraimashita.
Moo aite no kata ga kimarimashita ka.
Katte na koto o shite wa ikemasen.
RYOOte ga shibiremashita.
Ooyama-san wa piano ga totemo JOOZU desu.

58
教

GIMU KYOOIKU
EIGO KYOOJU HOO
SHUUKYOO-KA
chikaku no KYOOKAI
KAGAKU no KYOOSHI
KOKUGO o oshieru

Amerika no GIMU KYOOIKU wa NANNEN desu ka.
Oji-san wa DAIGAKU no KYOOJU deshita.
Ajia no SHUUKYOO ni tsuite manande imasu ka.
Uchi no chikaku ni KYOOKAI ga arimasu.
Chichi wa KOOKOO no KYOOSHI desu.
Ani wa CHUUGAKKOO de EIGO o oshiete imasu.

59
理

RIYUU ga tatsu
RIRON-TEKI
SHINRIGAKU
RISOO-TEKI
RIKAI ni kurushimu

Donna RIYUU ga arimasu ka.
Sono RIRON wa muzukashii desu.
DAIGAKU de SHINRIGAKU o manande imasu.
SHOSETSU-KA ni naru no ga watakushi no RISOO desu.
Ookawa-san no o-too-san wa totemo RIKAI no aru kata desu.

```
                kanoJO no ie                                    60
                JOSEIBI
                JOSHIDAI-SEI                                    女
                kawaii SHOOJO
                DANJO DOOKEN
                onna no hito

                KanoJO wa RAINEN DAIGAKU o deru soo desu.
                Kono kuriimu wa JOSEI-YOO desu.
                TOOKYOO ni JOSHIDAI ga ikutsu arimasu ka.
                Ano SHOOJO wa kawairashii desu.
                Kono GAKKOO wa DANJO KYOOGAKU desu.
                Asoko ni iru onna no kata wa donata desu ka.
```

```
                DEN'EN HUUKEI                                   61
                YUUJIN no Honda-san                             田

                Inaka no DEN'EN HUUKEI ga DAIsuki desu.
                Honda-san to ISSHO ni, RAIGETSU, SHIKOKU e iku tsumori desu.
```

```
                JIYUU SHUGI                                     62
                IGI ga hukai
                DAIGAKU no KOOGI                                義
                GIMU o hatasu
                GIRI-gatai

                Dochira ka to ieba watakushi wa JIYUU SHUGI ka mo
                IGI no aru JINSEI o okuritai to omoimasu.    (shiremasen.
                RONRIGAKU no KOOGI wa omoshiroi desu.
                JIBUN no GIMU wa hatasu beki desu.
                Honda-san wa totemo GIRI-gatai hito desu.
```

```
                KOORYO shite kara                               63
                SANKOONIN
                KOOKOGAKU                                       考
                kangae ga ukabu

                Yoku KOORYO shite kara, kimeru koto ni itashimasu.
                Kore wa EIBUMPOO no SANKOOSHO desu.
                KOOKOGAKU no KENKYUU no tame ni Yooroppa e ikimashita.
                Kangae ga nakanaka matomarimasen.
```

```
                CHUUSHIN JIMBUTSU                               64
                SHIMPAI-goto
                SHINRI JOOTAI                                   心
                KANSHIN ni mo
                KESSHIN ga niburu
                kokoro moto nai

                Ueda-san ga CHUUSHIN ni natte, sono SHIgoto o shimashita.
                Nani mo SHIMPAI wa irimasen.
                Sono SHINRI ga wakarimasen.
                Ano ko ni wa KANSHIN saseraremasu.
                Amerika e iku KESSHIN o shimashita.
                Hitori de iku no wa kokoro moto nai desu.
```

65　NYUUGAKU-SHIKI
入　YU'NYUUHIN
　　SHUU'NYUU GEN
　　SHINNYUU-SHA
　　KAIJOO no iriguchi
　　hako ni ireru

　　Ashita wa SHOOGAKKOO no NYUUGAKU-SHIKI desu.
　　NIHON de wa abura o YU'NYUU shite imasu.
　　KONGETSU kara SHUU'NYUU ga sukoshi ooku narimashita.
　　Teki no SHINNYUU o huseganakereba narimasen.
　　KAIJOO no iriguchi wa dochira desu ka.
　　Musuko o TOOKYOO no DAIGAKU ni ireru tsumori desu.

66　ICHIGATSU tsuitachi
月　KOtoshi no SHOOGATSU
　　GETSUYOO-bi
　　tsukiyo no BAN

　　Watakushi wa ICHIGATSU JUUGONICHI ni umaremashita.
　　SHOOGATSU ni karuta o shite asobimashita.
　　GETSUYOO-bi ni mata aimashoo.
　　Uchida-san ni hajimete atta no wa, tsukiyo no BAN deshita.

67　GENZAI no tachiba
現　GENJITSU SHUGI
　　GENDAI-SHIKI
　　yutaka na HYOOGEN
　　RISOO ga JITSUGEN suru
　　uwasa no hito ga arawareru

　　SHACHOO wa GENZAI Nyuu Yooku ni imasu.
　　RISOO to GENJITSU wa chigaimasu.
　　GENDAI SAKKA no naka de, dare ga ICHIBAN suki desu ka.
　　Kotoba no HYOOGEN wa nakanaka muzukashii desu.
　　TOOKYOO Orimpikku ga tootoo JITSUGEN shimashita.
　　Uwasa o shite ita tokoro e, Kawakami-san ga arawaremashita.

68　HONTOO no hanashi
当　SENSOO TOOJI
　　TOOZEN no koto
　　SOOTOO no neDAN
　　TOOKYOKU-SHA
　　kuji ga ataru

　　Toruko ni JISHIN ga atta soo desu ga, HONTOO desu ka.
　　TOOJI, yoku haikingu ni ikimashita.
　　Sore wa TOOZEN no koto desu.
　　ICHI-doru wa ikura ni SOOTOO shimasu ka.
　　Wakaranai toki wa TOOKYOKU ni o-tazune kudasai.
　　Kuji ga atarimashita.

GAIKOKUJIN   69
DANSEI IGAI
GAIKOO SHUDAN   外
GAIMUSHO
GAIJIN BOCHI
ie no soto

Mada GAIKOKU e itta koto ga arimasen.
EIGO IGAI no GAIKOKUGO wa wakarimasen.
Ani wa HOKEN-GAISHA no GAIKOO-IN DESU.
Ima no GAIMU-DAIJIN wa dare desu ka.
Ano GAIJIN wa Amerika-JIN desu ka, Huransu-JIN desu ka.
Kodomo wa soto de asonde imasu.

KANZEN na JOOTAI   70
ANZEN DAIICHI
ZEMBU o matomeru   全
ZENKOKU TAIKAI
ZENTAI-TEKI ni mite
mattaku no tokoro

Hito wa dare de mo KANZEN de wa arimasen.
KOOJI GEMba de wa ANZEN ga DAIICHI desu.
Sono HON o ZEMBU yomimashita.
DAIRI-TEN wa ZENKOKU ni arimasu.
ZENTAI no IKEN o matomete kudasai.
Sono hanashi o kiite, mattaku odorokimashita.

KATEI no KEIZAI   71
KEIKEN o tooshite
KEIEI KONNAN   経
JIKAN no KEIKA
HUKUZATSU na KEIREKI
Honoruru o heru

Kuni no KEIZAI ga ANTEI shite imasu.
Mada KEIKEN ga asai no de, kore kara ga TAIHEN desu.
KAISHA no KEIEI ga muzukashiku narimashita.
Ano toki kara, dono kurai KEIKA shita ka wakarimasen.
Ano hito no KEIREKI wa HUKUZATSU desu.
San Huranshisuko o hete, Nyuu Yooku e mukaimasu.

KONDO no JUGYOO   72
TAIDO o kimeru
SHAKAI SEIDO   度
aru TEIDO
GENDO o kosu

KONDO no SHOOGATSU o tanoshiku sugoshimashoo.
Hayaku TAIDO o kimenakereba narimasen.
CHUUSE Yooroppa no SHAKAI SEIDO ni tsuite manabimashita.
Dono TEIDO no JISHIN ka mada wakarimasen.
TAIRYOKU ni wa GENDO ga arimasu.

73   yutaka na CHISHIKI
知   go-SHOOCHI no toori
       CHIE'NETSU
       TOCHIJI
       shiranai hito

       Honda-san wa CHISHIKI ga arimasu.
       SHOOCHI itashimashita.
       Kono ko wa nakanaka CHIE ga arimasu.
       Ima no TOCHIJI wa totemo NINKI ga arimasu.
       Sore wa shirimasen deshita.

74   KOOKYOO DAIGAKU
業   JIGYOO-KA
       SANGYOO no HATTATSU
       KIGYOO-KA
       SHITSUGYOO HOKEN

       NIHON no KOOGYOO wa SENGO SAKAN ni narimashita.
       Oji-san wa JIGYOO ni SHIPPAI shimashita.
       DENKI JIDOOSHA wa ima, SANGYOOKAI no WADAI desu.
       Mezurashii mono wa nan de mo KIGYOOKA sarete imasu.
       Ano hito wa ima SHITSUGYOO shite iru soo desu.

75   IKA DOOBUN
下   watari ROOKA
       TENKA IPPIN
       CHIKATETSU
       EN no shita
       itte kudasaru

       Sono seetaa wa, SEN'EN de wa kaenai deshoo.
       ROOKA o SOOJI shite kudasai.
       Kono shinamono wa TENKA IPPIN desu.
       CHIKATETSU ni notta koto ga arimasu ka.
       Ano ki no shita no benchi ni suwarimashoo.
       Kono TOKEI wa oba ga kudasatta mono desu.

76   NIHON no SEITOO
党   KYOOSANTOO-IN
       YOTOO-gawa no IKEN
       YATOO no HANRON

       Amerika no NI-DAI-SEITOO wa MINSHUTOO to KYOOWATOO desu.
       Wada-kun wa KYOOSANTOO-IN to shite shirarete imasu.
       YOTOO to YATOO wa hageshiku TAIRITSU shimashita.
       YATOO wa sono IKEN ni HANTAI desu.

77   NAIKAKU SOORI DAIJIN
内   NAIBU no JIJOO
       muzukashii NAIYOO
       KOKUNAI JIJOO
       kuni no NAIGAI
       uchigawa to sotogawa

con'd

	Moo NAIKAKU ga kimarimashita ka. KAISHA no NAIBU ga HUKUZATSU desu. Sono HON no NAIYOO o shitte imasu ka. KOKUNAI MONDAI ga TAKUSAN arimasu. Uchida-san wa kuni no NAIGAI no JIJOO ni akarui desu. Uchi kagi o kakete, GAISHUTSU shimashita.	77 con'd 内
	HITSUYOOHIN kumiai-gawa no YOOKYUU JUUYOO na CHII JUDAI na YOOSO SHUYOO TOSHI YOOsuru ni Donna mono ga HITSUYOO desu ka. Kumiai-gawa no YOOKYUU ga toorimashita. Motto JUUYOO na koto o kangaenasai. Kakete iru YOOSU o oginawanakereba narimasen. TOOKYOO ya Oosaka wa NIHON no SHUYOO TOSHI desu. Kuruma de ikeba, NIJI-KAN wa YOOsuru deshoo.	78 要
	KAISHA no SHIKIN KIN'YUU KIKAN ZEIKIN o osameru shiharai KINGAKU o-kanemochi SHIgoto o hajimeru no ni, SHIKIN ga HITSUYOO desu. Ani wa KIN'YUU-GAISHA ni tsutomete imasu. Moo ZEIKIN o osamemashita ka. Shiharatta KINGAKU wa ZEMBU de ikura desu ka. O-kane ga sukoshi tarimasen.	79 金
	SHIMBUN KISHA KAKUSHIN-TEKI SHINSEN na kudamono atarashii ie MAIasa SHIMBUN o yomu koto ni shite imasu. Sore wa nakanaka KAKUSHIN-TEKI na HOOHOO desu. Kono nashi wa amari SHINSEN de wa arimasen. Uchino-san KAZOKU wa SENGETSU atarashii ie ni hikkoshimashita.	80 新
	SEKAI-JUU SEKEN no uwasa NIJUSSEIKI SERON CHOOSA SEWA-NIN yo no naka Eberesuto-san wa SEKAI de ICHIBAN takai yama desu. Sono JIKEN wa SEKEN o odorokasemashita. TOOKYOO Orimpikku wa, SEIKI no SAITEN deshita. Ima, ZENKOKU de SERON CHOOSA ga okonawarete imasu. Nakayama-san wa totemo SEWA-zuki na kata desu. Yo no naka ni wa iroiro na koto ga arimasu.	81 世

82 社
SHAKAI SHUGI
KAISHA-IN
SHACHOO-SHITSU

SHAKAI ZENTAI no koto o kangaenakereba narimasen.
Moo JUUGONEN mo ima no KAISHA ni tsutomete imasu.
SHACHOO wa tadaima KAIGI-CHUU desu.

83 第
SHIDAI ni
DAIICHININ-SHA

JINKOO ga SHIDAI ni ooku natte imasu.
ANZEN ni UNTEN suru koto ga DAIICHI desu.

84 関
KANKEI-SHA
TSUUSHIN KIKAN
KANREN no nai hanashi
KANSHIN-goto
KANTOO CHIHOO

Kore wa sono hanashi to nani mo KANKEI ga arimasen.
Kore wa ROODOO MONDAI ni KANREN shita KIJI desu.
Ima wa TSUUSHIN KIKAN ga totemo yoku HATTATSU shite imasu.
Anata wa SEIJI ni KANSHIN ga arimasu ka.
KANTOO HEIYA wa NIHON de ICHIBAN ookii HEIYA desu.
Sekiguchi-san ga kite kara, issho ni ikimashoo.

85 和
HEIWA KYOOZON
SHOOWA NIJUUNEN
KINCHOO no KANWA
KYOOWA-KOKU
KOOWA KAIGI

Ano hito wa HEIWA na MAINICHI o okutte imasu.
SHOOWA NIJUU-NEN wa SHUUSEN no toshi desu.
MONDAI ga DAIBU KANWA saremashita.
Burajiru wa ooki na KYOOWA-KOKU desu.
Yoshida Shigeru wa KOOWA KAIGI no ZENKEN TAISHI deshita.

86 意
IMI ari ge ni
ZENTAI no IKEN
CHUUI-bukai
KETSUI o arata ni suru
IGI no nai koto

KanoJO wa IMI arige na koto o iimashita.
Minna no IKEN o kiite kudasai.
Ano ko ni wa CHUUI o ataeta ga ii desu.
KETSUI o arata ni shite, sono SHIGOTO o suru tsumori desu.
JINSEI no IGI wa hukai desu.

JIDAI okure
DAIHYOO-SHA
KINDAI-TEKI
GENDAI no hitobito
DAIGISHI
kawari ni

87 代

Sonna kangae wa JIDAI okure desu.
"Hamuretto" wa Sheekusupia no DAIHYOOSAKU desu.
Watakushi-tachi no GAKKOO wa totemo KINDAI-TEKI desu.
GENDAI no wakai hitobito wa, nani o motomete imasu ka.
Kono CHIKU kara DAIGISHI ga SAMMEI dete imasu.
Kazuko-san no kawari ni, watakushi ga kimashita.

SEIJIGAKU
MEIJI no hito
JIJIKAI
CHIRYOOHOO

88 治

Nakata-san wa SEIJI-KA ni naritai soo desu.
MEIJI JIDAI ni SEIYOO no GAKUMON ga sakan ni toriirerare-
NIJI kara GAKKOO no JIJIKAI ga arimasu.   (mashita.
Te o kega shite, MAINICHI CHIRYOO o ukete imasu.

BUNKAJIN
NIHON BUNGAKU
utsukushii BUNSHOO
MONKU o iu
Yooroppa BUMMEI
SOTSUGYOO ROMBUN

89 文

CHUUGOKU no BUNKA wa hurui desu.
Donna BUNGAKU SAKUHIN ga suki desu ka.
MONKU bakari itte wa ikemasen.
MEIJI ni natte, NIHON no BUMMEI wa hirakemashita.
Moo SOTSUGYOO ROMBUN wa kakiowarimashita ka.

SHACHOO no isu
KAMBOO CHOOKAN
KEIRI BUCHOO
KEIZAI no KOODO SEICHOO
CHUUGAKU KOOCHOO
nagai hanashi

90 長

Chichi wa NI'NEN mae ni SHACHOO no isu ni tsukimashita.
Amerika no KOKUMU CHOOKAN wa dare desu ka.
BUCHOO wa ima yasunde orimasu.
Seki-san no musuko wa rippa ni SEICHOO shimashita.
KOOCHOO SENSEI wa minna ni sukarete imasu.
Kono himo wa nagasugimasu ka.

91 目
MOKUTEKI o TASSEI suru
MOKUHYOO o mezasu
DAme oshi
CHUUMOKU o abiru
TAISETSU na YAKUME
SAMBAMME

Dooyara MOKUTEKI o TASSEI shimashita.
MOKUHYOO made ato hitoiki desu.
Sonna koto o shite wa DAme desu.
Kyuurii HUJIN wa Rajiumu no HAKKEN de SEKAI no CHUUMOKU o abimashita.
Tonda YAKUME o oose tsukarimashita.
Mae kara YOMBAMME no ko ga watakushi no musuko desu.

---

92 産
KYOOSANGUN
kanzume no SEISAN
SANGYOO KEIZAI
ZAISAN-KA

Burugaria wa KYOOSANKOKU desu ka.
Hawai de wa nani o SEISAN shite imasu ka.
Detoroito wa JIDOOSHA SANGYOO de YUUMEI desu.
Oji-san wa ZAISAN o TAKUSAN nokoshite, nakunarimashita.

---

93 定
KYOOTEI o musubu
kibishii KITEI
KETTEIKEN
BUKKA no ANTEI
HITEIBUN
ICHI o sadameru

Amerika to donna KYOOTEI ga musubarete imasu ka.
KITEI wa mamoranakereba narimasen.
SHACHOO no Amerika yuki ga KETTEI shimashita.
Kuni no KEIZAI ga ANTEI shite imasu.
Sono aidea wa, atama kara HITEI sarete shimaimashita.
Ano hito wa, nani o yatte mo sadamari ga arimasen.

---

94 持
KImochi ga warui
SHIJI o ukeru
te de motsu

Kyoo wa, TENKI ga yokute, KImochi ga ii desu.
Yamaguchi-san wa, minna no SHIJI o ukete imasu.
Sono hako wa amari omoi no de, hitori de wa motemasen.

---

95 物
con'd
DOOBUTSUEN
BUKKA ga takai
BUSSHI no HUSOKU
BUSSHITSU-TEKI
kirei na kimono

Chiisai toki, yoku DOOBUTSUEN ni tsurete itte moraimashita. 95
SAIKIN, mata BUKKA ga agarimashita.   con'd
SENJICHUU, BUSSHI ga HUSOKU shimashita.   物
Kono kuni wa BUSSHITSU-TEKI ni megumarete imasu.
Sadako-san wa kimono no HOO ga yoku niaimasu.

TAISEI ga totonou   96
ooki na DANTAI
GUTAI-TEKI   体
ITTAIKA suru
ZENTAI-SHUGI
karada ga itai

Kore de doo ni ka TAISEI ga totonoimashita.
DANTAI de RYOKOO suru to yasuku tsukimasu.
GUTAI-TEKI ni SETSUMEI shite kudasai.
ITTAI nani ga atta no desu ka.
ZENTAI no IKEN o kiite minakereba narimasen.
Karada ga itakute tamarimasen.

HUTSUU no KANKAKU   97
KYOOTSUU no tachiBA
KYUUKOO no TSUUKA   通
TSUUSHIN-SHA
KOOTSUU KOOSHA
basu ga tooru

Ano kata no atama wa HUTSUU de wa arimasen.
Hutari wa KYOOTSUU no IKEN o motte imasu.
Ima TSUUKA shita KYUUKOO wa Oosaka yuki desu.
Honda-kun wa TSUUSHIN-IN to shite Pari ni imasu.
Kono HEN no KOOTSUU wa totemo hageshii desu.
Kono toori wa basu ga toorimasu ka.

HEIWA-SHUGI-SHA   98
BYOODOO no KENRI
HEIKIN JISOKU   平
HEIBON na hito
HEIKI na kao
taira ni suru

Taira-kun wa itsumo HEIWA UNDOO o shite imasu.
SENGO, DANJO BYOODOO ni narimashita.
HEIKIN GOJUK-kiro de ikeba, NIJIKAN de tsuku deshoo.
Kono tokoro, hitori de HEIBON na MAINICHI o okutte imasu.
Shikararete mo HEIKI desu.
Burudoozaa de TOCHI o taira ni narashite imasu.

SAIKIN no dekigoto   99
SAIGO no SHIage
SAIKOO SOKUDO   最
SEKAI SAIDAI
SAISHO no ICHINEN
mottomo ookii
                                                             con'd

99 con'd SAIKIN no ooki na MONDAI wa nan da to omoimasu ka.
最 Ima wa SAIGO no GAKKI na no de, totemo isogashii desu.
Kono HEN no SAIKOO SOKUDO wa ROKUJUK-kiro desu.
TAIHEIYOO wa SEKAI SAIDAI no umi desu.
SHAKAI ni dete kara, SAISHO no ICHINEN wa totemo tsurakatta desu.
Amerika de, mottomo takai yama wa nan to iu yama desu ka.

---

100 NIPPONKOKU-KEMPOO
法 tadashii HOOHOO
HOORITSU JIMUSHO
SHIN-HOOAN

GOGATSU mikka wa KEMPOO KI'NEMBI desu.
HOOHOO ga wakarimasen.
Doko no HOORITSU JIMUSHO ni tsutomete imasu ka.
SHIN-HOOAN ga KOKKAI o TSUUKA shimashita.

101 連

KANREN no aru
KOKUREN TAISHI
ano RENCHUU
RENRAKU JIKOO
tsurete yuku

Sore wa kono MONDAI ni wa mattaku KANREN shite imasen.
KOKUREN ni wa SEKAI no iroiro na MONDAI ga arimasu.
Ano RENCHUU wa nani o shite imasu ka.
Nani ka attara RENRAKU shite kudasai.
Kinoo kodomo o KOOEN ni tsurete ikimashita.

102 発

KENKYUU HAPPYOO
Amerika no HAKKEN
HAKKEN no TOJOO ni aru
SHUPPATSU no JIKAN
KAGAKU no HATTATSU
HOSSA o okosu

ROMBUN o HAPPYOO shimashita.
Amerika wa itsu HAKKEN saremashita ka.
JIDOOSHA SANGYOO wa HATTEN no TOJOO ni arimasu.
NanJI ni SHUPPATSU shimasu ka.
KOOGYOO ga HATTATSU shimashita.
O-jii-san wa tokidoki SHINZOO no HOSSA o okoshimasu.

103 不

TE-BUSOKU
HUHEI-HUMAN
HUAN ga tomonau
HUKOO na hito
HUSHIGI na hanashi
HUSEI JIKEN

Nan no HUSOKU mo arimasen.
HUMAN ga BAKUHATSU shimashita.
Hitori de yuku no wa HUMAN desu.
Yamada-KE ni HUKOO ga arimashita.
HUSHIGI na koto mo areba aru mono desu.
HUSEI o okonatte wa ikemasen.

104 化

NIHON no BUNKA
HENKA ni tomu
KAGAKU KOOJOO
SHOOKA ga ii
o-bake

CHUUGOKU no BUNKA o KENKYUU shite imasu.
Kono HEN wa amari HENKA ga arimasen.
KOOKOO no toki, KAGAKU ga DAISUKI deshita.
Kono kusuri wa SHOOKA o tasukemasu.
Bake no kawa ga hagaremashita.

105　KANJOO o osaeru
感　KANSHA no KImochi
　　KANSHIN na kodomo
　　JIKKAN ga waku
　　KANSOO o noberu
　　KANGEKI suru

　　KANJOO-TEKI ni natte wa ikemasen.
　　KANSHA no KImochi de IPPAI desu.
　　Ano ko wa itsu mo KANSHIN ni ie no tetsudai o shimasu.
　　SHIKEN ni ukatte mo, mada JIKKAN ga wakimasen.
　　SHIai no KANSOO o nobete kudasai.
　　EIGA o mite KANGEKI shimashita.

106　KYOOSAN-TOO
共　KYOODOO-TSUUSHIN
　　KOOKYOO DANTAI
　　KYOOTSUU no MONDAI
　　KYOOWA-TOO
　　tomo ni

　　SoREN wa KYOOSAN-SHUGI no kuni desu.
　　Watakushi-tachi wa KYOODOO de sono SHIgoto o shite imasu.
　　KOOKYOO no tame ni tsukushi-tai to omoimasu.
　　KYOOTSUU-TEN ga mi-dasemasen.
　　Nikuson-SHI wa KYOOWA-TOO desu.
　　Sono MONDAI wa watakushi-domo ni wa yoku wakarimasen.

107　SENSOO to HEIWA
争　KYOOSOO-aite
　　CHINage-TOOSOO
　　RONSOO o yobu
　　hito to arasou

　　Chiisai toki, yoku SENSOO-gokko o shimashita.
　　KYOOSOO ga hageshiku narimashita.
　　SHUNKI TOOSOO ga chikazukimashita.
　　Sono MONDAI wa RONSOO o yobi-soo desu.
　　Hito to arasowanai yoo ni KI o tsukete imasu.

108　TOOKYOO-eki
東　TOOZAI-NAMBOKU
　　TOODAI-SEI
　　KANTOO HEIYA
　　Higashi Doitsu

　　Kinoo TOOKYOO Tawaa ni noborimashita.
　　Kono machi wa TOOZAI ni hirogatte imasu.
　　RAINEN TOODAI o ukeru tsumori desu.
　　TAIHUU ga KANTOO CHIHOO o osoimashita.
　　Doitsu wa Higashi to Nishi ni wakarete imasu.

```
                SOODAN no KEKKA                                    109
                KEKKYOKU no tokoro
                KETSURON to shite                                   結
                KEKKON no hidori
                KYOOTEI o musubu

                Tesuto no KEKKA ga mada wakarimasen.
                KEKKYOKU nani mo yarimasen deshita.
                KETSURON ga mada demasen.
                Go-KEKKON o-medetoo gozaimasen.
                Kore o himo de musunde kudasai.
```

```
                RIRON to JISSAI                                    110
                GENRON-KAI
                hageshii GIRON                                      論
                SOTSUGYOO-ROMBUN
                RONRI-TEKI

                RIRON to JISSAI wa chigaimasu.
                NIHON ni wa GENRON no JIYUU ga arimasu.
                Moo GIRON wa yamemashoo.
                YOOYAKU ROMBUN o kakiagemashita.
                RONRI-TEKI ni SETSUMEI shite kudasai.
```

```
                Satoo SHUSHOO                                      111
                SOOTAI-TEKI
                SOODAN-YAKU                                         相
                SOOGO KANKEI
                aite no hito

                Igirisu no SHUSHOO wa dare desu ka.
                Ainshutain no SOOTAISEI RIRON wa YUUMEI desu.
                SENSEI ni yoku SOODAN suru tsumori desu.
                SOOGO no RIKAI ga HITSUYOO desu.
                Aite no kata wa donna kata desu ka.
```

```
                KYUUHYAKU-EN                                       112
                KITAKYUUSHUU SHI
                KUGATSU tooka                                       九
                kokonoka no hi

                Kono shatsu wa KYUUHYAKU HACHIJUU-EN deshita.
                Mada KYUUSHUU e itta koto ga arimasen.
                Amerika de wa KUGATSU ni GAKKOO ga hajimarimasu.
                Kokonoka ni hi ni aimashoo.
```

```
                GENSHI-RYOKU                                       113
                GEMBAKU KI'NENBI
                GEN'IN-HUMEI                                        原
                GENSOKU to shite
                KIJI no GENRYOO
                nohara                                            con'd
```

| 113 con'd | GENSHI-RYOKU wa HEIWA ni RIYOO sarete imasu. |
| 原 | GEMBAKU ni wa ZETTAI HANTAI desu. |

113 con'd
原

GENSHI-RYOKU wa HEIWA ni RIYOO sarete imasu.
GEMBAKU ni wa ZETTAI HANTAI desu.
KAJI no GEN'IN ga mada wakarimasen.
GENSOKU to shite, kodomo wa NYUUJOO dekimasen.
GENRYOO ga HUSOKU shite imasu.
Uchi no soba ni nohara ga arimasu.

114
四

SHIHOO ni hirogaru
SHIKAKU-baru
YONJUS-SAI
yokka-me

Yama-KAJI ga SHIHOO ni hirogatte imasu.
Sono SHIKAKU na hako o totte kudasai.
KOOJI wa yonJUU-NICHI de owarimashita.
Kono SHIgoto wa yokka areba JUUBUN desu.

115
先

Yamada SENSEI
SENJITSU no KEN
SENTOO ni tatsu
SENSHIN-TEKI
saki ni iku

KOKUGO no SENSEI wa dare desu ka.
SENJITSU no KEN, doo narimashita ka.
SENTOO ni tatte iru no ga otootoo desu.
NIHON wa Ajia no SENSHIN-KOKU desu.
O-saki ni SHITSUREI shimasu.

116
八

HACHIJUU HACHI-YA
HYAPPAKU-NIN
yae-zakura
yooka-KAN

O-jii-san wa kotoshi HACHIJUS-SAI desu.
SEITO no kazu wa HAPPYAKU-NIN gurai desu.
Yae-zakura wa totemo KIREI desu.
Kaze de yooka-KAN, GAKKOO o yasumimashita.
Hawai ni wa yattsu no shima ga arimasu.

117
面

TOOKYOO HOOMEN
MONDAI ni CHOKUMEN suru
HYOOMEN-TEKI
ZEMMEN-TEKI
omonaga na kao

HANNIN wa KANSAI HOOMEN ni nigemashita.
Muzukashii MONDAI ni CHOKUMEN shite, komatte imasu.
Tsuki no HYOOMEN no SHASHIN o mimashita ka.
Sono SHIgoto ni wa ZEMMEN-TEKI ni KYOORYOKU shimasu.
Ano kata no kao wa omonaga desu.

kore IJOO   118
NICHIYOO IGAI
SENGETSU IRAI   以
tooka IGO
IZEN no YOO ni
ISSHUU-KAN INAI

Kore IJOO GAMAN dekimasen.
NICHIYOO IGAI wa uchi ni imasen.
Sono toki IRAI o-ai shite imasu.
IGO KI o tsukemasu.
IZEN to amari kawari arimasen.
Repooto o mikka INAI ni TEISHUTSU shite kudasai.

---

otonashii SEISHITSU   119
tsuyoi SEIKAKU
JIDOOSHA no SEINOO   性
JOSEI-TEKI
HONSHOO o arawasu

Sono MONDAI no SEISHITSU ga chigaimasu.
Ano hutari wa SEIKAKU ga atte, urayamashii desu.
SEINOO ga yokereba, kau koto ni shimasu.
Sono HON wa JOSEI no aida de NINKI ga arimasu.
TSUI ni HONSHOO o arawashimashita.

GENDAI SAKKA   120
Rodan no SAKUHIN
SAGYOO JIKAN   作
SAKKYOKU-KA
tana o tsukuru

Ookiku nattara SAKKA ni naritai to omoimasu.
Torusutoi no SAKUHIN o yonda koto ga arimasu ka.
SAGYOO ga owarimashita.
Kono uta wa dare no SAKKYOKU ka wakarimasen.
Oishii keeki o tsukurimashita.

SHOKI-CHOO   121
omoshiroi SHOMOTSU
SEISHO KENKYUU   書
DOKUSHO ni hukeru
TOSHOKAN
tegami o kaku

SHAKAI-TOO no SHOKI-CHOO wa dare desu ka.
SENSEI wa yoku SHOMOTSU o yonde imasu.
SEISHO monogatari o yomimashita.
Imooto wa DOKUSHO ga DAISUKI desu.
TOSHOKAN de HON o karimashita.
CHOODO tegami o kaita tokoro desu.

122 SOSHIKI-TEKI
     KOKUTETSU ROOSO
組   kumiai KATSUDOO
     rajio no BANgumi
     ude o kumu

     SOSHIKI ga mada dekite imasen.
     KOKUTETSU ROOSO no chikara wa tsuyoi desu.
     SHOKUba ni wa kumiai ga arimasu ka.
     Terebi no NINKI BANgumi wa nan desu ka.
     Hutari zutsu kunde asobimashoo.

123 NIHON KOKUYUU TETSUDOO
     DOOTOKU KYOOIKU
道   HOODOO KIKAN
     huru-DOOGU
     DOORO KOOJI
     warui michi

     NIHON no TETSUDOO wa HATTATSU shite imasu.
     DOOTOKU o midashite wa ikemasen.
     Aporo JUUICHI-GOO no SEIKOO ga ZEN-SEKAI ni HOODOO saremashita.
     KOOSOKU-DOORO o ikeba, hayaku tsukimasu.
     Michi ga warukatta no de, JIKAN ga kakarimashita.

124 ROKUGATSU goro
     ROPPOO-ZENSHO
六   muika no tabi
     DAI-ROKKAN
     muttsu ni naru

     ROKUGATSU ni Amerika e tatsu tsumori desu.
     DAIGAKU e haitte, sugu ROPPOO-ZENSHO o motomemashita.
     Ato muika hodo kakaru deshoo.
     DAI-ROKKAN de sugu wakarimashita.
     Otooto wa YOOYAKU muttsu ni narimashita.

125 UCHUU no WADAI
     SEWA-zuki na hito
話   DENWA BANGOO
     EI-KAIWA
     GAIJIN to hanasu

     Ima wa tsuki no WADAI de mochikiri desu.
     Otooto ga o-SEWA ni nari, arigatoo gozaimashita.
     O-taku no DENWA BANGOO wa namBAN desu ka.
     Oono-san wa EI-KAWAI o naratte imasu.
     Motto ookii koe de hanashite kudasai.

126 REN'AI SHOOSETSU
     SHOO-GAKKOO
小   SHOONI-KA
     SAISHOOGEN
     chiisai kuni   con'd

"Yukiguni" to iu SHOOSETSU o yomimashita ka.　　　126
Ashita SHOO-GAKKOO de HUKEI-KAI ga arimasu.　　　con'd
Oda SENSEI wa SHOONI-KA SEMMON desu.
SHUPPI o SAISHOOGEN ni todomete kudasai.　　　小
Umareta toki, watakushi wa totemo chiisakatta soo desu.

IIN-KAI　　　127
KOKKAI GIIN
KYOOSHOKUIN kumiai　　　員
KAIINSEI
CHOOMAN'IN

Ashita kurasu no IIN-KAI ga arimasu.
Ozawa-SHI wa KENKAI-GIIN ni TOOSEN shimashita.
SENSEI wa ima SHOKUIN-SHITSU ni imasu.
SENGETSU, sukii kurabu no KAIIN ni narimashita.
Sono DENSHA wa itsumo MAN'IN desu.

TASUU no SANKA　　　128
go-TABUN ni morezu
TASHOO okureru　　　多
TAGAKU NOOZEI-SHA
hito ga ooi

TASUU no SANKA o KIBOO shite imasu.
Tada-san wa TABUN ashita kuru to omoimasu.
JIKO no tame, RESSHA wa TASHOO okureru kamo shiremasen.
TAGAKU no KIHU ga atsumarimashita.
Kono CHIHOO wa ame ga ooi desu.

JUUSHO ga kawaru　　　129
baSHO ga warui
KINJO no ie　　　所
NENKAN-SHOTOKU
Kanda to iu tokoro

Tada-san no JUUSHO ga wakarimasu ka.
Kono baSHO ga ii deshoo.
Masao wa KINJO no kodomo-tachi to asonde imasu.
SHOTOKU-ZEI wa nan paasento gurai toraremasu ka.
Watakushi wa TOOKYOO no Nakano to iu tokoro ni sunde imashita.

KAIGI-SHITSU　　　130
GIKAI no ENKI
TOKAI GIIN　　　議
HUSHIGI na hanashi
GIRON-zuki na hito
KYOOGI no KEKKA

Ashita, koko de KAIGI ga okonawaremasu.
GIKAI wa MYOOGONICHI ni ENKI saremashita.
SHIKAI GIIN wa ZEMBU de nanNIN desu ka.
Sore wa mattaku HUSHIGI desu.
GIRON no YOCHI ga arimasen.
KYOOGI-KAI ga owarimashita.

131 KEIZAI GAKUSHA
済   HENSAI-KIN
     KYUUSAI JIGYOO
     SHIgoto ga susumu

     NIHON no KEIZAI wa totemo yoku narimashita.
     Ano hito wa SHAKKIN no HENZAI ni nayande imasu.
     SUIGAI-CHI ni KYUUSAI no te o nobemashoo.
     SHIgoto wa ato namPUN gurai de sumimasu ka.

132 RAKU na SEIKATSU
活   KATSUDOO HAN'I
     DAI-KATSUYAKU
     HUKKATSU-SAI

     TOKAI no SEIKATSU wa KAKKI ga arimasu.
     Koyama-san wa nakanaka no KATSUDOO-KA desu.
     Kunitomo SENSEI no KATSUYAKU-buri wa TAIshita mono desu.
     Mukashi no uta ga HUKKATSU shite, mata utawarete imasu.

133 EIGO no BENKYOO
強   KEIBI o KYOOKA suru
     KYOOCHOO ga tarinai
     SANNIN-gumi no GOOTOO
     tsuyoi kaze

     Otooto wa ISSHOOKEMMEI BENKYOO shite imasu.
     Machi de wa BIKA UNDOO o KYOOKA shite imasu.
     Sono TEN o moo sukoshi KYOOCHOO shite kudasai.
     Hoteru ni GOOTOO ga hairimashita.
     Kinoo wa tsuyoi kitakaze ga hukimashita.

134 JIYUU na KImochi
由   KESSEKI no RIYUU
     Honoruru KEIYU

     NIHON ni wa SHUUKYOO ya GENRON no JIYUU ga arimasu.
     RIYUU mo nashi ni KESSEKI shite wa ikemasen.
     Kono RESSHA wa Nagoya KEIYU Oosaka yuki desu.
     SENSEI ga asatte korareru yoshi, ukagaimashita.

135 SAIKOO SAIBANSHO
高   KOOKOO ICHINEN-SEI
     KOOTOO GAKKOO
     KOOKYUU hoteru
     takai yama

     Ototoi no atsusa wa kotoshi SAIKOO da soo desu.
     Otooto wa mada KOOKOO-SEI desu.
     Takahashi-san wa KOOTOO GAKKOO no SENSEI desu.
     Kinoo, GINZA de Huransu no KOOKYUU RYOORI o tabemashita.
     Amari takakereba, sono shinamono wa kai-taku arimasen.

JUUYOO SHORUI   136
JUUDAI nyuusu
IKEN o SONCHOO suru   重
KICHOO na JIKAN
omoi mono
HON o kasaneru

Sonna ni JUUYOOSHI suru HITSUYOO arimasen.
Kinoo JUUDAI na JIKEN ga okorimashita.
Chichi wa itsumo hito no IKEN o SONCHOO shimasu.
Kore wa KICHOOHIN desu kara, DAIJI ni tsukatte kudasai.
Sono NIMOTSU wa omo-soo desu.
HON o tsukue no ue ni kasanete oite kudasai.

ROODOO kumiai   137
hataraki-zakari
                                                                            働
Anata no KAISHA ni wa ROODOO kumiai ga arimasu ka.
Onoda-san wa yoku hataraki kata desu.

KAIKETSU-SAKU   138
KETTEI-KEN
HANDAN o ii-watasu   決
KETSUI o arata ni suru
KESSHIN ga tsuku
NINZU o kimeru

Sono MONDAI wa sude ni KAIKETSU shimashita.
SHUUSHOKU-saki ga KETTEI shimashita.
SAIBAN de donna HANKETSU ga kudasaremashita ka.
Nakagawa-san wa nan toka sono SHIgoto o yari-togeru KETSUI desu.
Mada soko e iku KESSHIN o shite imasen.
Doko no DAIGAKU e iku ka, moo kimemashita ka.

HOORITSU no KAISEI   139
SEIJOO ni modoru
SEISHIKI HAPPYOO   正
SEITOO BOOEI
SHOOJIKI na hito
tadashii kotae

Sono HOORITSU no ICHIBU ga KAISEI saremashita.
Sonna kangae wa SEIJOO de wa arimasen.
Sore ga mada SEISHIKI ni kimatta wake de wa arimasen.
SEITOO na tetsuzuki o hunde kudasai.
Masao-kun wa totemo SHOOJIKI desu.
Sore wa tadashiku arimasen.

YUUMEI ni naru   140
MEIJIN-GEI
MEIYOO KYOOJI
SHOMEI iri de
JOYUU no HOMMYOO
namae o tsukeru

                                                                       con'd

140 Honda-san wa JITSUGYOOKAI de YUUMEI ni narimashita.
con'd Ooyama-san wa nan no MEIJIN desu ka.
       Sore wa MEIYO ni kakawaru MONDAI desu.
名   Koko ni SHOMEI shite kudasai.
       Misora Hibari no HOMMYOO wa nan desu ka.
       Sono ko no namae ga wakarimasen.

---

141 SHIHON SHUGI
     SHIKEN-BUSOKU
資   SHIKAKU ga aru
     SHIGEN ni tomu
     TAGAKU no TOOSHI

     Sono KAISHA no SHIHON-KIN wa ikura desu ka.
     KAISHA no UNTEN SHIKIN wa JUUBUN desu ka.
     KYONEN CHUUGAKKOO no KYOOIN no SHIKAKU o moraimashita.
     NIHON wa SEKIYU no SHIGEN ga sukunai desu.
     Watakushi wa TOCHI ni TOOSHI suru koto ni shimashita.

---

142 MONDAI no KAIKETSU
     RIKAI o hukameru
解   KENKAI no SOOI
     EIBUN KAISHAKU
     KOKKAI no KAISAN
     nazo o toku

     Sono MONDAI wa mada KAIKETSU sarete imasen.
     Yamada-san no o-too-san wa totemo RIKAI ga arimasu.
     Hutari no KENKAI wa DAIBU chigatte imasu.
     Kono BUN o doo iu huu ni KAISHAKU shimasu ka.
     SHUUGIIN wa kinoo KAISAN shimashita.
     Sono MONDAI o toku no ni NIJI-KAN kakarimashita.

---

143 UNNUN iu
云   UNNUN itte mo hajimarimasen.

---

144 TOOZEN no KEKKA
     ZENZEN wakaranai
然   TOTSUZEN okoru
     GUUZEN ni
     TENNEN SHIGEN
     SHIZEN GENSHOO

     Oya ga kodomo o AIsuru no wa TOOZEN desu.
     Huransu-GO wa ZENZEN wakarimasen.
     Ane no RYUUGAKU ga kimatta no wa TOTSUZEN desu.
     GINZA de Ueda-san ni GUUZEN ni aimashita.
     Sono EIGA wa TENNENSHOKU desu ka.
     Ano ko wa oyogi o SHIZEN ni oboeru deshoo.

ROODOO-SHA
KUROO no nai hito
KINROO KANSHA no hi

Ima no ROODOO DAIJIN wa dare desu ka.
Ano kata wa wakai toki TAIHEN KUROO shimashita.
JUUICHI-GATSU NIJUU-SAN-NICHI wa KINROO KANSHA no hi desu.

145
労

HANTAI-gawa
HANSEI o motomeru
HANDOO-TEKI
IHAN-SHA

Kono IKEN ni SANSEI desu ka, HANTAI desu ka.
Sono TEN o yoku HANSEI shite kudasai.
Sono guruupu wa sugoku HANDOO-TEKI desu.
Sore wa KISOKU IHAN desu.

146
反

SHICHININ atsumaru
nanoka-KAN
SEKAI no nana-HUSHIGI

ZEMBU de SHICHININ atsumarimashita.
ISSHUU-KAN wa nanoka desu
Kinoo wa SEKAI no nana-HUSHIGI ni tsuite BENKYOO shimashita.

147
七

TAKUSAN no hitobito
KAZANTAI
SANCHOO o mezashite
TOZANTAI
yama no ooi

Kyuuri ga TAKUSAN toremashita.
NIHON ni wa KAZAN ga ooi desu.
SANCHOO wa yuki ni oowarete imasu.
Ani to RAINEN NIHON Arupusu o TOZAN suru tsumori desu.
SHIgoto ga yama hodo arimasu.

148
山

SAIKIN no MOYOO
KINDAI-TEKI SETSUBI
HUKIN ITTAI
KINJO no hitobito
chikai uchi ni

Watakushi wa SAIKIN KYUUSHUU kara kita bakari desu.
Ano biru wa totemo KINDAI-TEKI desu.
Kono HUKIN wa mada ie ga sukunai desu.
Yamamoto-san wa KINJO ni koshite kimashita.
Purinsu Hoteru wa ie no chikaku ni arimasu.

149
近

HON no MOKUJI
koto ni SHIDAI
sono tsugi

150
次
con'd

150 MOKUJI o mite kudasai.
con'd Soko e iku ka ikanai ka wa o-TENKI SHIDAI desu.
次 Tsugi no hito wa donata desu ka.

---

151 KOOTOO GAKKOO
等 rajio ya terebi TOOTOO
BYOODOO ni suru
nanraka no HOOHOO
SUUJI ga hitoshii

Watakushi wa ima KOOTOO DOOBUTSU ni tsuite BENKYOO shite imasu.
BUTSURI ya KAGAKU TOOTOO, iroiro na HON o kaimashita.
Hito wa mina BYOODOO desu.
Nanraka no MONDAI ga aru ni chigai arimasen.
Sonna KUROO wa MU ni hitoshii desu.

---

152 MEIJI ISHIN
明 SETSUMEI o YOOsuru
SEIMEI o HAPPYOO suru
BUMMEI no HATTATSU
HATSUMEI-SHA
akarui HEYA

Meiji JIDAI ni KOOGYOO ga HATTATSU shi-hajimemashita.
Kore o KANTAN ni SETSUMEI shite kudasai.
SEIHU wa JUUDAI na SEIMEI o HAPPYOO shimashita.
NIHON wa Ajia no BUMMEI-KOKU desu.
Ejison wa nani o HATSUMEI shimashita ka.
Yoshida-san wa totemo akarui kata desu.

---

153 SHOONEN YAKYUU
少 SHOOJO SHUMI
SHOOSUUHA
TASHOO no chigai
ame ga sukunai
honno sukoshi

Doko no kuni ni mo SEISHOONEN no MONDAI ga arimasu.
Kinoo imooto ni SHOOJO ZASSHI o katte kimashita.
KAIGI ni SHOOSUU no hito shika atsumarimasen deshita.
TASHOO no chigai wa aru kamo shiremasen.
SENGETSU wa ame ga sukunakatta desu.
Honno sukoshi de KEKKOO desu.

---

154 MOKUTEKI o TASSEI suru
達 MOKUHYOO ni TOOTATSU suru
KOOGYOO no HATTATSU
tomodachi ni au

Mori-san wa DORYOKU shite, JIBUN no MOKUTEKI o TASSEI shimashita.
Inoue-san wa, akirame no KYOOCHI ni TOOTATSU shita soo desu.
SENGO, NIHON no KAGAKU wa KYUUSOKU ni HATTATSU shimashita.
Kinoo GINZA de tomodachi ni aimashita.

BEIKOKU SEIHU 155
NICHIBEI KANKEI
OOBEI SHOKOKU   米
BEIGUN KICHI
kome no HAIKYUU

Ano kata wa BEIKOKU-JIN da soo desu.
NICHIBEI IGAKU KAIGI ga RAIGETSU TOOKYOO de hirakaremasu.
Sore wa OOBEI SHOKOKU ni totte ooki na MONDAI desu.
Hara-kun wa Tachikawa no BEIGUN KICHI de shibaraku hataraite
Kono CHIHOO wa o-kome ga yoku toremasu.   (imashita.

SHINKOO JOOTAI 156
DAIGAKU e SHINGAKU suru
KOOSHIN-KOKU   進
SANGYOO o SOKUSHIN suru
KOOSHINKYOKU
dondon susumu

KOOJI wa dono kurai SHINKOO shite imasu ka.
Ima, otooto wa SHINGAKU o mezashite BENKYOO shite imasu.
Ajia ni wa, mada KOOSHIN-KOKU ga TAKUSAN arimasu.
KEN de wa SANRIN no KAIHATSU o SOKUSHIN shite imasu.
ITTAI, are wa nan no KOOSHIN desu ka.

UNDOO-KAI 157
UMMEI ni makaseru
JIDOOSHA no UNTEN   運
NIMOTSU o hakobu

MAIasa sukoshi UNDOO suru koto ni shite imasu.
Tomodachi no Ishida-kun wa hune to UMMEI o tomo ni shimashita.
Nishimura-san wa torakku no UNTEN-SHU o shite imasu.
Kono tsukue o mukoo e hakonde kudasai.

KIKAI KOOGYOO 158
KIKAI ga areba
KEIZAI KIKI   機
DOOKI o tsukamu
KOOTSUU KIKAN

Kono KIKAI no CHOOSHI ga amari yoku arimasen.
Honda-san ni au KIKAI ga arimasu ka.
Minami Betonamu wa KIKI ni sarasaramashita.
SENSEI ni natta DOOKI wa nan desu ka.
NIHON no KOOTSUU KIKAN wa HATTATSU shite imasu.

TASUU-KETSU 159
SHOOSUU no hitobito
SUUJI ga awanai   数
SUUGAKU no SENSEI
GUUSUU to KISUU
NINZUU o kazoeru

                                    con'd

159 con'd 数

Sore wa TASUU-KETSU de kimarimashita.
Soko ni atsumatta hito wa goku SHOOSUU deshita.
Watakushi wa SUUJI ni tsuyoku arimasen.
Ani wa SUUGAKU ga TOKUI desu.
NI ya yon wa GUUSUU de, ICHI ya SAN wa KISUU desu.
Kono HEYA ni nanNIN iru ka kazoete kudasai.

160 成

DAI-SEIKOO
HOOAN no SEIRITSU
SANSEI o motomeru
KANSEI ni chikai
yoi SEISEKI
nari-agaru

Sono SHIgoto wa TAIHEN SEIKOO shimashita.
Atarashii HOOAN ga SEIRITSU shimashita.
Sono IKEN ni SANSEI desu.
Kono biru wa moo KANSEI ni chikai desu.
Oda-san wa NI-GAKKI no SEISEKI ga agatta soo desu.
Kono chiimu wa NIJUU-NIN kara natte imasu.

161 制

HOOKEN SEIDO
SEIGEN SOKUDO
KYOOSEI-TEKI
KANJOO o YOKUSEI suru

KYOOIKU SEIDO wa SENGO DAIBU kawarimashita.
JIKAN ni SEIGEN ga arimasu ka.
Hito o KYOOSEI shite wa ikemasen.
KANJOO o YOKUSEI suru no wa muzukashii desu.

162 権

SEIKEN o ushinau
KENRYOKU arasoi
KENRI-KIN
KEN'I-TEKI
TOKKEN KAIKYUU

Igirisu de wa nani-TOO ga SEIKEN o TANTOO shite imasu ka.
Ani wa uchi de wa itsumo KENRYOKU o hurutte imasu.
Ono-san ni wa sore dake no koto o iu KENRI ga arimasu.
Ano kata wa itsumo KEN'I-TEKI ni mono o iimasu.
Soko e ikeru no wa TOKKEN da to omoimasu.

163 保

KAIJOO HOAN-KAN
HOSHU-TEKI
HOSHOO-NIN
HOGO-SHA
HOZON ga kiku
CHII o tamotsu

Otooto wa KAIJOO HOAN-KAN ni narimashita.
Yasuko-san no kangae wa totemo HOSHU-TEKI desu.
Sono KIKAI wa nanNEN gurai HOSHOO sarete imasu ka.
Kazuko-chan wa MAIgo ni natte, KEISATSU ni HOGO saremashita.
Ono-san wa JUUYAKU no CHII o tamotte imasu.

```
ZEN-SEKAI                                                    164
NOORYOKU no GENKAI
ZAIKAI-JIN                                                    界
GYOOKAI no WADAI

Narita-san wa supootsu no SEKAI de KATSUYAKU shite imasu.
Moo NOORYOKU no GENKAI ni TASshimashita.
Nozawa-shi wa ZAIKAI kitte no JIMBUTSU to iwarete imasu.
Sore wa GYOOKAI de ima ookina MONDAI to natte imasu.
```

```
SHOKUGYOO ANTEIJO                                             165
ANZEN UNTEN
HUAN ga tomonau                                               安
ANSHIN-KAN
yasuppoi shinamono

Kuni no KEIZAI wa ima ANTEI shite imasu.
Kuruma o UNTEN suru toki, ANZEN ga DAIICHI desu.
Mattaku HUAN ga nakunarimashita.
SHIKEN ga owaru made wa, mada ANSHIN dekimasen.
Yasumono wa kawanai koto ni shite imasu.
```

```
SEIKATSU SUIJUN                                               166
SUIBAKU JIKKEN
SUIGAI TAISAKU                                                水
DAI-KOOZUI
amamizu o nomu

NIHON no SEIKATSU SUIJUN wa takaku narimashita.
Amerika wa SUIBAKU JIKKEN o doko de yarimashita ka.
SHUSHOO wa SUIGAICHI o otozuremashita.
Ooame de kono HEN ITTAI wa KOOZUI ni narimashita.
Amamizu o nonda koto ga arimasu ka.
```

```
HYOO o KAKUTOKU suru                                          167
NATTOKU-zumi
SHOTOKU-ZEI                                                   得
SONTOKU o kangaeru
e-gatai shinamono

HYOO o dono kurai KAKUTOKU sureba, TOOSEN dekimasu ka.
Sono hanashi wa NATTOKU dekimasen.
Sukoshi SHOTOKU ga huemashita.
SONTOKU o kangaenaide, sono SHIgoto o yarimashita.
Sore wa e-gatai shinamono desu.
```

```
NIHON SEIHU                                                   168
TOKUGAWA BAKUHU
Oosaka-HU                                                     府

SEIHU de sono MONDAI o KENTOO shite imasu.
Kamakura BAKUHU wa nanNEN tsuzuita ka shitte imasu ka.
KYOOTO-HU no JINKOO wa dono kurai desu ka.
```

169　　IMI ga hukai
　　　 SHUMI ga chigau
味　　 KYOOMI o motsu
　　　 kaze-GIMI
　　　 MIkata suru
　　　 nigai KEIKEN o ajiwau

　　　 Sono kotoba ni wa hukai IMI ga arimasu.
　　　 Otooto wa kitte o atsumeru no ga SHUMI desu.
　　　 Sonna koto ni wa mattaku KYOOMI ga arimasen.
　　　 Kinoo KIMI no warui hanashi o kikimashita.
　　　 Dochira no chiimu o MIkata shite imasu ka.
　　　 Ima made donna KEIKEN o ajiwaimashita ka.

170　　puro YAKYUU
　　　 IGAKU no BUNYA
野　　 YATOO TAIKAI
　　　 utsukushii nohara

　　　 TOOKYOO ROKU-DAIGAKU YAKYUU wa YUUMEI desu.
　　　 Yamano-san wa KAGAKU no BUNYA de KATSUYAKU shite imasu.
　　　 YATOO-gawa wa mina sore ni HANTAI shite imasu.
　　　 Ono-san to nohara o SAMPO shimashita.

171　　SATSUJIN JIKEN
　　　 JOOKEN o dasu
件　　 YOOKEN o sumasu

　　　 Sono JIKEN wa mada KAIKETSU sarete imasen.
　　　 Watakushi wa MUJOOKEN ni sono KAISHA o erabimashita.
　　　 Moo YOOKEN wa sumimashita.

172　　TANIN ni KANSHOO suru
　　　 TAHOO ni oite wa
他　　 JITA tomo ni
　　　 HAITA-TEKI
　　　 hoka no hito

　　　 TANIN ni MEIWAKU o kakete wa ikemasen.
　　　 Sono IKEN wa TAHOO de wa uke-irerarete imasen.
　　　 Hara-san no koe ga KIREI na no wa, JITA tomo ni mitomeru tokoro desu.
　　　 Ano hito no kangae wa itsu mo HAITA-TEKI desu.
　　　 Dare ka hoka no hito ni tanonde kudasai.

173　　KOOJOO KENGAKU
　　　 KOOGYOO CHITAI
工　　 JINKOO EISEI
　　　 KOOJI-CHUU
　　　 DAIKU SHIgoto

　　　 Asoko ni mieru no wa Sonii no KOOJOO desu.
　　　 Kono HEN wa KOOGYOO CHITAI de YUUMEI desu.
　　　 Otooto wa JINKOO KOKYUU de tasukarimashita.
　　　 Sono michi wa KOOJI-CHUU de, ima wa tooremasen.
　　　 Ogawa-san wa DAIKU-san desu.

JIBUN JISHIN no MONDAI SHUSSHIN-KOO SHINTAI KENSA SHINCHOO o hakaru mi ni amaru omou	174	身

Sore wa Noguchi-san JISHIN no MONDAI deshoo.
Watakushi no SHUSSHIN-KOO WA KYUUSHUU DAIGAKU desu.
Kinoo SHINTAI KENSA o ukemashita.
SHINCHOO wa dono kurai arimasu ka.
HOKKAIDOO no samusa wa mi ni shimimasu.

SHOOTEN o awasu KETTEN-darake YOOTEN o tsukamu HYOOTEN-KA TEN ga karai	175	点

Yoku SHOOTEN o awasete, SHASHIN o totte kudasai.
Dare ni mo KETTEN ga arimasu.
YOOTEN dake o nobete kudasai.
Kinoo wa HYOOTEN-KA GODO deshita.
Sono TEN ga yoku wakarimasen.

EIGA no GAMEN Furansu no GAKA KEIKAKU-doori KIKAKU-BU	176	画

"Kaze to tomo ni sarinu" to iu EIGA o mimashita ka.
SHOORAI GAKA ni naru tsumori desu.
Natsu yasumi ni doko e yuku KEIKAKU o tatete imasu ka.
Ima KAISHA de nani o KIKAKU shite imasu ka.

RIYOO KACHI SHIYOO-CHUU OOYOO MONDAI SHINYOO no aru hito YOOI SHUUTOO na hito omoku mochiiru	177	用

Kore wa mada RIYOO dekimasu.
Kono HEYA wa TOOBUN SHIYOO dekimasen.
Kare wa amari OOYOO ga kikimasen.
Sore wa SHINYOO ni kakawaru MONDAI desu.
Ima sugu dekakeru YOOI o shinakereba narimasen.
Kono kotoba wa IPPAN ni mochiirarete imasu.

DAIHYOO-DAN GOOKAKU HAPPYOO AIJOO no HYOOGEN HYOOMEN-KAsuru omote datto kotoba de arawasu	178	表 con'd

178 NIHON BIJUTSU no DAIHYOO-TEKI na mono wa nan desu ka.
con'd SHIKEN no KEKKA ga moo HAPPYOO saremashita ka.
  SENSEI no BUN no HYOOGEN wa totemo KIREI desu.
表 Sono JIKEN wa HYOOMEN ni arawaremashita.
  JISHIN de, awatete omote e tobi-dashimashita.

---

179 MURI na koto
  MUGEN ni hirogaru
無 SHINGOO MUSHI
  MURON no koto
  BUJI o inoru
  nashi de sumasu

  Sore wa MURI na CHUUMON desu.
  UCHUU wa MUGEN desu ka.
  Kare wa SHINGOO MUSHI de tsukamatta soo desu.
  Ani wa MURON no koto, RYOOSHIN mo SANSEI shite kuremashita.
  Uehara-san wa, kinoo BUJI ni KIKOKU shimashita.
  Soko ni nani mo nasa-soo desu.

---

180 SAIDAIGEN ni RIYOO suru
  KENRI o SHUCHOO suru
利 RIEKI o ageru
  YUURI na JOOKEN
  SHOORI ni michibiku
  BENRI na KIKAI

  Kore wa nani ka ni RIYOO dekiru hazu desu.
  Ano hito wa itsumo KENRI bakari SHUCHOO shite imasu.
  Kono SHIgoto no RIEKI wa amari yoku arimasen.
  Kono SHIai wa aite no HOO ga kanari YUURI desu.
  SHOORI TOOSHU wa dare desu ka.
  GAKKOO wa BENRI na tokoro ni arimasu.

---

181 SHINRAI dekiru hito
  SHINYOO torihiki
信 KYOODOO TSUUSHIN-SHA
  SHINKOO no JIYUU
  JISHIN ga aru
  SHINNEN o motte

  Chichi wa Matsushita-san o itsumo SHINRAI shite imasu.
  Sono KAISHA wa TAIHEN SHINYOO ga arimasu.
  Ani wa DAIGAKU no TSUUSHIN KYOOIKU o ukete imasu.
  NIHON ni wa SHINKOO no JIYUU ga arimasu.
  Nomura-san wa JISHIN-MAMMAN desu.
  Nanigoto o suru ni mo tsuyoi SHINNEN ga HITSUYOO desu.

---

182 KAKO to GENZAI
  SONZAI KACHI
在 HUZAI TOOHYOO
  KENZAI de aru
  CHUUZAISHO

                    con'd

Takagi-san wa GENZAI Oosaka ni imasu. 182
Hito no SONZAI o MUSHI shite wa ikemasen. con'd
Chichi wa KYOOTO e itte HUZAI desu. 在
RYOOSHIN wa KENZAI desu.
Kono HEN ni CHUUZAISHO ga arimasu ka.

KOKUNAI JIJOO 183
JOOSEI o minagara
KANJOO no motsure 情
AIJOO no aru
DOOJOO o yoseru
nasake nai

Ishii-san wa KAIGAI no JIJOO ni kuwashii desu.
JOOSEI o yoku mite kara, HANDAN shi-tai to omoimasu.
KanoJO wa KANJOO-TEKI desu.
Kore wa oyako no AIJOO no monogatari desu.
Ano ko wa minna no DOOJOO o hikimashita.
Sore wa nasake nai hanashi desu.

SHIMBUN o yomu 184
KEMBUN o hiromeru
GAIBUN no warui 聞
ONGAKU o kiku
oto ga kikoeru

Nani SHIMBUN o totte imasu ka.
KAIGAI e itte KEMBUN o hirome-tai to omoimasu.
Sore wa GAIBUN ga yoku arimasen.
Utsukushii ONGAKU o kikimashita.
Mizu no oto ga kikoemashita.

SHIHAIKA ni aru 185
SHIJI o ukeru
SHISHUTSU ga ooi 支
SHUUSHI KESSAN suru
Nagoya SHIBU

Ishida-san wa hoteru no SHIHAI-NIN desu.
Ikeda-san wa minna no SHIJI o ukete imasu.
SENGETSU no SHISHUTSU wa DAIBU ookatta yoo desu.
KYONEN no KOKUSAI SHUUSHI wa kuroJI desu.
Sono MONDAI wa ashita no SHIBUKAI de KYOOGI saremasu.

TOKUBETSU KOKKAI 186
TOKUSHU GIJUTSU
TOKKEN KAIKYUU 特
TOKUTEI ZAISAN
TOKU ni

Kono YOOFUKU wa TOKUBETSU ni atsuraeta mono desu.
Kore wa TOKUSHU na KIKAI desu.
Sore wa KAIIN dake ni ataerareta TOKKEN desu.
Koko de wa TOKUTEI no shinamono dake atsukatte imasu.
Toku ni kawatta koto wa arimasen.

187 HIHAN o ukeru
判 HANKETSU o ii-watasu
    SAIBANSHO
    HANDAN o ayamaru
    HANJISEKI
    HYOOBAN ga takai

    Sono ROMBUN wa tsuyoi HIHAN o ukemashita.
    HIKOKU wa MUZAI no HANKETSU o ukemashita.
    Sono JIKEN no SAIBAN wa RAIGETSU okonawaremasu.
    Nakanaka HANDAN ga tsukimasen.
    Oji wa SENGETSU HANJI ni narimashita.
    Sono shinamono no HYOOBAN wa totemo ii desu.

188 HITSUYOO ni semerarete
必   HITSUZEN-TEKI ni
    HISSHI ni natte
    kanarazu

    Motto HON o yomu HITSUYOO ga arimasu.
    Sore wa HITSUZEN-TEKI ni okorimashita.
    Otooto wa HISSHI ni natte BENKYOO shite imasu.
    Ashita kanarazu soko e ikimasu.

189 KOKUSAI KAIGI
際   JISSAI no MONDAI to shite
    KOOSAIHI

    Sore wa KOKUSAI-TEKI na MONDAI ni HATTEN shimashita.
    JISSAI muzukashii MONDAI deshita.
    Yamada-san ni KOOSAI o motomeraremashita.

190 HIJOO SHUDAN o toru
常   SEIJOO-KAsuru
    NICHIJOO SEIKATSU
    JOOSHIKI o kaku
    tsune higoro

    HIJOO no SAI wa, kono beru o narashite kudasai.
    RESSHA no daiya ga SEIJOO ni modorimashita.
    Sore wa NICHIJOO kaku koto no dekinai mono desu.
    HIJOOSHIKI na koto o shite wa ikemasen.
    Natsu yasumi ni watakushi wa arubaito o suru no ga tsune desu.

191 SEISHIN-TEKI
神   SHINKEI-SHITSU
    JINJA SAMPAI
    Girisha SHINWA
    Kami to NINGEN
con'd

191 con'd 神

Ani wa SEISHIN-TEKI ni DAIBU tsukarete imasu.
Haha wa SHINKEI-TSUU de nete imasu.
Wada-san wa JINJA e o-mairi ni ikimashita.
GAKUSEI JIDAI yoku Girisha SHINWA o yomimashita.
Hara-san to "kami no SONZAI" ni tsuite RONjimashita.

---

192 向

sonna KEIKOO ga aru
HOOKOO o kaeru
SEIKATSU no KOOJOO
mukatte
mukoo-gawa
migi o muku

Ano ko wa GAKKOO o yasumu KEIKOO ga arimasu.
Yama de HOOKOO ga wakaranaku natte komarimashita.
SENGO NIHON no SEIKATSU wa KOOJOO shimashita.
Mukatte migi-gawa ni aru no ga watakushitachi no GAKKOO desu.
Anata wa SENSEI ni muite iru to omoimasu.

---

193 協

KYOOTEI o musubu
minna no KYOORYOKU
DAKYOO-TEN
KYOOGIKAI
SAKKA KYOOKAI

SoREN to no KOOKUU KYOOTEI ga musubaremashita.
Kono SHIgoto ni wa minna no KYOORYOKU ga HITSUYOO desu.
DAKYOO no YOCHI ga mattaku arimasen.
Sono koto wa KYOOGI no ue, kimeru koto ni itashimashoo.
Ueda-san wa YAKYUU KYOOKAI no YAKUIN ni natta soo desu.

---

194 取

SHUZAIHAN
torihiki GINKOO
toru ni taranai

Ima donna KIJI o SHUZAI shite imasu ka.
YOOYAKU sono torihiki o SEIRITSU sasemashita.
Soko ni aru SHIMBUN o totte kudasai.

---

195 真

SHINJITSU-SEI
SHASHIN-YA
SHINRI no TANKYUU
SHINKEN SHOOBU
magokoro komete

Kawakami-san wa SHINJITSU-SEI ni ahurete imasu.
Kore wa GAKUSEI JIDAI no SHASHIN desu.
SHINRI to wa nan desu ka.
Moo sukoshi SHINKEN ni BENKYOO shinakereba ikemasen.
Kore wa magokoro komete tsukutta mono desu.

196　KASEN KOOJI
　　　kawakami no HOO

川

　　　Kono KAISHA wa KASEN KOOJI ga TOKUI desu.
　　　HATSUDEN-SHO wa kawakami no HOO ni arimasu.

197　RISOO-TEKI
　　　SOOZOORYOKU
　　　SHISOO MONDAI
想　　KANSOO o noberu
　　　YOSOO ni HANshite

　　　RISOO ga JITSUGEN shitara to omotte imasu.
　　　Sonna koto wa totemo SOOZOO dekimasen.
　　　CHUUGOKU no SHISOO ni tsuite KENKYUU shite imasu.
　　　Sono KANSOO wa ikaga desu ka.
　　　SEISEKI ga YOSOOGAI ni yokatta desu.

198　SEIYOO BIJUTSU
　　　KANSAI RYOKOO
西　　KOKON TOOZAI
　　　nishi-gawa

　　　DAIGAKU de SEIYOO-SHI o BENKYOO shimashita.
　　　Watakushi wa KANSAI de sodachimashita.
　　　YOO no TOOZAI o towazu, hitobito wa RYUUKOO o otte imasu.
　　　Kono mado wa nishi muki desu.

199　KIPPOO o uketoru
　　　HUKITSU na YOKAN
吉　　Yoshino no sakura

　　　Nishi-san kara KIPPOO o uketorimashita.
　　　Nandaka HUKITSU na YOKAN ga shimashita.
　　　Yoshida-san to kinoo TOOKYOO e itte kimashita.

200　TOOKYOO no JINKOO
　　　sabishii KUCHOO de
口　　deguchi no soba ni
　　　KAIGI SHITSU no iriguchi
　　　BUNGO to KOOGO
　　　KOOJITSU o mookeru

　　　Kono machi no JINKOO wa dono kurai desu ka.
　　　SENSEI ni hageshii KUCHOO de shikararemashita.
　　　Deguchi wa doko desu ka.
　　　Iriguchi wa asoko desu.
　　　Kono BUNTAI wa KOOGO-TAI desu.
　　　Sonna no wa KOOJITSU desu.

KOOJOO no SETSUBI   201
JUMBI ga totonou
masaka no toki ni sonaete   備

GAKKOO no SETSUBI ga yoku narimashita.
Ima RYOKOO no JUMBI o shite imasu.
GENZAI DAIGAKU no NYUUSHI ni sonaete BENKYOO shite imasu.

KEIKANTAI   202
KAMBOO-CHOOKAN
KANRYOO-agari   官

Chichi wa moto KEIKAN deshita.
Amerika no KOKUMU-CHOOKAN wa dare desu ka.
Kare wa KANRYOO-agari desu.

DANJO-KYOOGAKU   203
DANSEIYOO
CHOONAN no SHIgoto   男

NIHON wa ima DANJO-DOOKEN desu.
Koko wa DANSEI daki ni kagirarete imasu.
Kochira wa uchi no CHOONAN to JINAN desu.
Ano otoko no hito wa seirusuman desu.

GAKUSEI-SHOKUN   204
kimi no SAIKUN
kimi no ie   君

Kore mo mina GAKUSEI-SHOKUN no o-kage desu.
SAIKUN to issho ni iku koto ni shimasu.
NIHON no KOKKA wa "Kimi-ga-yo" desu.

DOKURITSU-KINEMBI   205
KODOKU na hito
DOKUJI no kangae
DOKUSHIN no koro   独
DOKUSEN-JIGYOO
hitori-BUTAI

SHICHIGATSU YOKKA wa Amerika no DOKURITSU-KINEMBI desu.
Oji wa inaka de KODOKU na SEIKATSU o okutte imasu.
Kore wa DOKUJI ni kangae-dashita mono desu.
Watakushi wa mada DOKUSHIN desu.
Watakushi wa hitori-aruki o suru no ga suki desu.

BEIKOKU KAIGUN   206
KAIGAI JIJOO
KAIGAN o SAMPO suru   海
HOKKAIDOO no SHUSSHIN
umi ga areru   con'd

206 con'd 海

Mukashi NIHON no KAIGUN wa tsuyokatta soo desu.
Ueno-san wa KAIGAI-JIJOO ni kuwashii desu.
KAIGAN e itte, hune o mimashoo.
HOKKAIDOO no MEISAN wa nan desu ka.
KYOO wa umi ga arete imasu.

207 食

SHOKURYOO-BUSOKU
oishii SHOKUJI
kirei na SHOKUDOO
tabe-sugiru
tabemono ga yoi

SHOKURYOO ga sukoshi tarimasen.
SHOKUJI o oete kara, itsumo terebi o mimasu.
Asoko no SHOKUDOO ni hairimashoo.
Nani ga tabetai desu ka.
Donna tabemono ga suki desu ka.

208 切

TAISETSU ni suru
SHINSETSU na hito
ISSAI hikiukeru
DENWA o kiru
KIGEN ga kireru
humikiri o wataru

Ima mizu ga sukunai node TAISETSU ni tsukatte imasu.
Yamano-san wa SHINSETSU nimo HON o kashite kuremashita.
ISSAI watashi ni makasete kudasai.
DENWA o mada kiranaide kudasai.
Kare wa nakanaka atama ga kiremasu.
Hayaku humikiri o watarimashoo.

209 記

omoshiroi KIJI
SOTSUGYOO-KI'NEN
KIROKU-yaburi
NIKKI o tsukeru
SHIMBUN-KISHA

SAIKIN, NIHON no omoshiroi KIJI o yomimashita.
Sore wa nan no KI'NEN-kitte desu ka.
Kono tokoro, KIROKU-yaburi TENKI ga tsuzuite imasu.
Kotoshi kara NIKKI o tsukeru koto ni shimashita.
Ano hito wa SHIMBUN-KISHA desu.

210 計

KEIKAKU o tateru
MENDOO na KEISAN
TOKEIya
GOOKEI sureba
SHINCHOO o hakaru

RAINEN HOKKAIDOO e iku KEIKAKU o tatete imasu.
KEISAN wa MENDOO-kusai node, suki ja arimasen.
Kono udeDOKEI wa Suisu-SEI desu.
SHUSSEKISHA wa GOOKEI SANJUUROKU-MEI deshita.
SHINCHOO ga dono kurai ka hakatte mimashoo.

		211
	EIGO no HYOOGEN KOKUGO no NOORYOKU GOGAKU no KENKYUU Isoppu Monogatari YUUJIN to kataru	語
	EIGO ga hanasemasu ka. GAKKOO no KAMOKU de, KOKUGO ga ICHIBAN suki desu. DAIGAKU de GOGAKU no KENKYUU o shite imasu. NIHON no Taketori Monogatari wa YUUMEI desu. Hisashiburi de, KYUUYUU to katariaimashita.	

		212
	KOKURITSU KOOEN KOOKYOO JIGYOO KOOHEI ni wakeru ooyake ni suru	公
	KOOEN ni utsukushii hana ga TAKUSAN arimasu. Oji wa machi no KOOKYOO no tame ni tsukushite imasu. Kare wa itsumo KOOHEI de, minna no SHINYOO ga arimasu. Sono KEIKAKU ga ooyake ni saremashita.	

		213
	ANZEN-HOSHOO-JOOYAKU JOOKEN-zuki de NICHIBEIKAN ni donna JOOYAKU ga arimasu ka. JOOKEN ga yokereba, NYUUSHA shitai to omoimasu.	条

		214
	CHOKUSETSU hanasu MONDAI ni CHOKUMEN suru SHOOJIKI na hito tadachi ni ukagau TOKEI o naosu	直
	CHOKUSETSU Honda-san kara kikimashita. Muzukashii MONDAI ni CHOKUMEN shimashita. Ano ko wa SHOOJIKI na ii ko desu. Sore de wa, tadachi ni ukagaimasu. Kuruma o naoshite kara ikimasu.	

		215
	SAMMAN-EN MAN'ICHI no BAAI BANKOKU-HYOOJUNJI JOOHOO no yorozuya	万
	Kono machi no JINKOO wa SAMMAN-NIN o koemashita. MAN'ICHI SHIPPAI shitara, doo shimasu ka. KONDO no BANKOKU-HAKURANKAI ni iku YOTEI desu. Kare wa yorozuya desu.	

216 様
sore to DOOYOO ni
HEN na YOOSU
kirei na MOYOO
minasama

Kore wa SHIMPIN mo DOOYOO desu.
Sukoshi YOOSU ga okashii desu.
Kore wa watashi no suki na MOYOO desu.
Minasama ikaga o-sugoshi desu ka.

217 朝
KONCHOO no KAIGI
KitaCHOOSEN
CHOOSHOKU o toru
asahi ga noboru

KONCHOO HACHIJI ni KAIGI ga hajimarimasu.
KitaCHOOSEN ni KIKOKU shita hito ga takusan imasu.
CHOOSHOKU o torimashita ka.
Kinoo no Asahi SHIMBUN o yomimashita ka.

218 百
HYAKKA-JITEN
YONHYAKU-NIN
HYAKUTEN-MANTEN

HYAKKA-JITEN o shirabete kudasai.
Kono KOOJOO ni wa YONHYAKU-NIN no hito ga hataraite imasu.
Kinoo no SHIKEN de HYAKUTEN o torimashita.

219 調
CHOOSA no KEKKA
CHOOSHI ga warui
KYOOCHOO suru
CHOOWA ga toreru
NINZU o shiraberu

Sono JIKEN no CHOOSA o shite imasu.
Kono kuruma no CHOOSHI wa amari yoku arimasen.
Sono JUUYOOSEI o KYOOCHOO shimashita.
Kono ie wa niwa to CHOOWA ga yoku torete imasu.
Nani o shirabete imasu ka.

220 夫
HUJIN-DOOHAN de
KOOTAISHI go-HUSAI
HUUHU sorotte
otto no KAISHA

Yamamura-shi wa HUJIN-DOOHAN de ikimashita.
Kinoo Uchihara-san go-HUSAI ni aimashita.
Honda-san wa oshidori HUUHU desu.
Otto wa depaato ni tsutomete imasu.

221 係 con'd
KANKEI no nai
kakariCHOO no SHIJI ni yori
MONDAI ni kakawaru

Sono hito ni nani ka KANKEI ga arimasu ka. KakariCHOO ni SOODAN shite kara HENJI o shimasu. Sono MONDAI ni nani mo kakawari-taku arimasen.	221 con'd 係
HIJOO ni muzukashii GOOGOO taru HINAN HIKOO-SHOONEN ZEHI tomo Asoko ni HIJOOguchi ga arimasu. Kare no IKEN wa minna ni HI'NAN saremashita. HIKOO-SHOONEN o HODOO shite imasu. KONDO no NICHIYOOBI ZEHI asobi ni kite kudasai.	222 非
SHIMEI ga wakaranai uji mo SUJOO mo nai hito Koko ni SHIMEI o hakkiri o kaite kudasai. "Uji yori sodachi" to yoku iwaremasu.	223 氏
SHUUDAN to natte HENSHUUSHA SHUUCHUU-TEKI ni SHUUKAI o hiraku koko ni atsumaru Sore wa SHUUDAN-SHINRI da to omoimasu. Donna KIJI o HENSHUU shite imasu ka. Ima, SUUGAKU o SHUUCHUU-TEKI ni BENKYOO shite imasu. NanJI ni SHUUKAI ga hajimarimasu ka. Ashita koko ni SANJI ni atsumatte kudasai.	224 集
GUNTAI no KISOKU HEITAI ni torareru JIEITAI ni NYUUTAI suru HOHEI BUTAI GUNTAI no KISOKU wa kibishii desu. Ani wa HEITAI ni torarete, SENSHI shimashita. Yamamoto-kun wa JIEITAI ni NYUUTAI shimashita. Ano kata wa watashitachi no BUTAICHOO desu.	225 隊
HUBO no omokage HUKEIKAI oji no KAISHA chichi no SHIgoto HUBO ni SOODAN shite mimasu. Kinoo no HUKEIKAI wa TAIHEN JUUYOO deshita. Oji wa GENZAI HOKKAIDOO ni imasu. Chichi wa GAKKOO no SENSEI desu.	226 父

227 別

TOKUBETSU atsukai ni suru
ROONYAKU-DANJO no KUBETSU naku
BEKKYO-SEIKATSU
YUUJIN to wakareru

Kare wa TOKUBETSU desu.
Ii no to warui no to KUBETSU shite kudasai.
Ano kata wa go-SHUJIN to BEKKYO shite imasu.
Kinoo Yamaguchi-san to GINZA de wakaremashita.

---

228 局

KEKKYOKU no tokoro
TOOKYOKU ni tazuneru
YUUBIN-KYOKUCHOO

KEKKYOKU dare ni mo aemasen'deshita.
GIMON no TEN wa TOOKYOKU made o-tazune kudasai.
YUUBINKYOKU e tegami o dashi ni itte kimasu.

---

229 農

NOOMIN no SHIJI
NOOSON no hitobito
NOOGYOO o itonamu
NOOKA no de
NOOCHI KAIHOO

Ikeda-shi wa NOOMIN no SHIJI o ukete imasu.
NOOSON no SEIKATSU wa SAIKIN yoku narimashita.
Kono HEN wa NOOGYOO ga sakan desu.
Asoko no NOOKA wa ookii yoo desu.
TAKUCHI ga hue, NOOCHI ga DANDAN sukunaku natte kimashita.

---

230 過

KAKO no omoide
SEISAN no KATEI
SHUJU-TSUGO no KEIKA
toki ga sugiru ni tsure
inaka de sugosu

KAKO JUUNENKAN ni wa iroiro na koto ga okorimashita.
Ima SEISAN wa dono HEN no KATEI ni arimasu ka.
Sono GO no KEIKA wa ikaga desu ka.
Haru wa moo sugimashita.
Ani wa huyu-yasumi o Pari de sugoshimashita.

---

231 車

DENSHA de kayou
KISHA no KIPPU
JIDOOSHA JIKO
KAMOTSU RESSHA
kuruma no CHOOSHI

TOOKYOO EKI made DENSHA-CHIN wa ikura desu ka.
KISHA no RYOKOO wa totemo tanoshii desu.
Ima, JIDOOSHA GAKKOO de UNTEN o naratte imasu.
Tsugi no RESSHA de ikimashoo ka.
Kono kuruma wa SHINSHA desu ka.

TAISHUU-muki MINSHUU-SHINRI Amerika GASSHUUKOKU Kare wa TAISHUU-SAKKA desu. Eki ni MINSHUU ga oshiyosemashita. Tsuki ni Amerika GASSHUUKOKU no hata ga tateraremashita.	232	衆
GAKKOO no UNDOOKAI KOOKOO SANNENSEI KOOCHOO SENSEI INSATSUBUTSU no KOOSEI Kinoo wa SANJI made GAKKOO ni imashita. KOOKOO o detara, KAISHA ni tsutomeru tsumori desu. KOOCHOO SENSEI wa kyoo TOOKYOO e SHUTCHOO shimashita. Ima INSATSUBUTSU no KOOSEI o shite imasu.	233	校
SENTOO ni tatsu Mitsui GINKOO no TOOdori ZUNOO-RYUUSHUTSU ZUTSUU no tane atama ga ii SENTOO ni tatte iru no ga watashi no ani desu. Yamamoto-san wa doko no GINKOO no TOOdori desu ka. Kare wa itsumo ZUNOOTEKI ni monogoto o kangaemasu. Kinoo wa ZUTSUU ga shita no de, hayaku kaerimashita. Ano ko wa atama ga ii desu.	234	頭
RYUUKOOKA RYUUKAN ga hayaru kawa ga nagareru mizu o nagasu Kore wa ima, RYUUKOO no doresu desu. RYUUKAN ni kakaranai yoo ni ki o tsukete kudasai. Mizu ga yoku nagaremasen. KOOZUI de hashi ga nagasaremashita.	235	流
KAOKU ga yakeru hiroi yashiki heya o kariru Konoaida no KAJI de, KAOKU ga ZENSHOO shimashita. Yasui-san wa RIPPA na YASHIKI ni sunde imasu. Narita-san wa tonari no heya ni imasu.	236	屋
JIN'IN no ZOOKA orimpikku ni SANKA suru KAKOOHIN ATSURYOKU o kuwaeru SOSHIKI ni kuwawaru	237 con'd	加

237 con'd 加	JIN'IN no ZOOKA o hakarimashita. KONDO no KAIGI ni SANKA shite kudasaimasen ka. Sono KOOJOO de wa donna mono o KAKOO shite imasu ka. Moo sukoshi chikara o kuwaete mite kudasai. KONDO sono DANTAI ni kuwawarimashita.	

238 死	SHIBOO o KAKUNIN suru SEISHI no sakai o samayou HISSHI no DORYOKU pokkuri shinu	

Kinoo chichi no SHIBOO-todoke o dashimashita.
Arupusu ni nobotta YUUJIN no SEISHI ga HUMEI desu.
HISSHI no DORYOKU de oyogimashita.
Sore wa shinu ka ikiru ka no DAIMONDAI desu.

239 使	SHIYOO KINSHI SHIMEI o mattoo suru BEIKOKU TAISHI heya o tsukau	

Ima kono heya wa SHIYOOCHUU desu.
Hirai-san wa JUUDAI na SHIMEI o obite imasu.
Atarashii CHUUNICHI BEIKOKU TAISHI ga NIMMEI saremashita.

240 説	heta na ENZETSU SHOOSETSUKA JOOZU ni SETSUMEI suru CHIHOO o YUUZEI suru IMI o toku	

SHUSHOO no ENZETSU o kinoo rajio de kikimashita.
Dare no SHOOSETSU ga suki desu ka.
Sore wa SETSUMEI no HITSUYOO ga nai to omoimasu.
Uemura-shi wa CHIHOO o YUUZEI shite imasu.
SENSEI wa sono IMI o wakari-yasuku toite kuremashita.

241 村	NOOSON no SEINEN SONCHOO ni naru mura no HATTEN	

Sono atarashii KIKAI wa NOOSON ni uke ga ii desu.
SONCHOO wa HYOOBAN ga ii desu.
Mizuno-san wa mura no HATTEN no tame ni tsukushite imasu.

242 白	tsumi no KOKUHAKU HAKUJIN to hanasu masshiro ni naru shiroku nuru	

Kare wa tsumi o KOKUHAKU shimashita.
Ano HAKUJIN wa nan to iu hito desu ka.
Yama ga yuki de masshiro ni narimashita.
Kabe o shiroku nurimashita.

243 兵

KAKUHEIKI
Amerika no KAIHEITAI
HEIRYOKU no ZOOKA

Are wa KAKUHEIKI-HANTAI no demo desu.
Chiisai toki, yoku HEITAI-gokko o shimashita.
TEKI no HEIRYOKU ga yowamarimashita.

244 務

JIMUTEKI ni
GAIMU-DAIJIN
GIMU o hatasu
KIMMU-JIKAN
KOOMU-SHIKKOO-BOOGAI
tsutome o hatasu

Asoko ga watashi no JIMUSHO desu.
Ani wa TOODAI o dete, GAIMUSHOO ni hairimashita.
Amerika no GIMU-KYOOIKU wa nanNEN desu ka.
Go-SHUJIN no KIMMUsaki wa dochira desu ka.
Chichi wa KOOMUIN desu.
Tsutome o okotatte wa ikemasen.

245 有

YUUMEI na hito
YUUKOO-KIKAN
SHOYUUCHI
YUURI na JOOKEN

Waikiki wa YUUMEI na KAIGAN desu.
Kono TEIKI wa ashita made YUUKOO desu.
Kono TOCHI wa dare no SHOYUUCHI desu ka.
Kono SHIAI wa AITE no HOO ga YUURI desu.

246 起

CHUUSEI ni KIGEN o hasshite
SAIKI-HUNOO
koko o KITEN to shite
ROKUJI ni okiru
JIKEN ga okoru

"SHU no KIGEN" to iu HON o yomimashita ka.
Kare no SAIKI ga ayabumarete imasu.
Koko o KITEN to shite, SHUPPATSU shimashoo.
MAIasa nanJI ni okimasu ka.
JUUDAI na JIKEN ga okorimashita

247 期

KITAI ga hazureru
JIKI ga hayai
KIKAN ga mijikai
MEIJI no SHOKI
SAIGO o togeru

Nan toka minasan no KITAI ni kotaetai to omoimasu.
Doomo JIKI ga warukatta YOO desu.
SHIKEN no KIKAN ga naga-sugimashita
SHOOWA no SHOKI ni wa donna SAKKA ga imashita ka.
Kare wa RIPPA na SAIGO o togemashita.

248 助

ENJO o hodokosu
JOGEN o ukeru
SHIMPO o JOCHOO suru
hito o tasukeru
ooi ni tasukaru

HIGAICHI ni ENJO no te o sashi-nobemashoo.
SENSEI no JOGEN ga HITSUYOO desu.
Warui koto o JOCHOO shite wa ikemasen.
Kawa de oborete iru kodomo o tasukemashita.
Tetsudatte itadaki, ooi ni tasukarimashita.

249 命

KAKUMEI ga okoru
SETSUMEI-HOKEN
hito no UMMEI
MEIREI ni somuku
inochi ga abunai

Huransu-KAKUMEI wa itsu okorimashita ka.
Itsu SEIMEI-HOKEN ni hairimashita ka.
Hito no UMMEI wa wakaranai mono desu.
MEIREI ni somuite wa ikemasen.
Kame no JU'MYOO wa nagai desu.
Inochi ga chijimaru YOO na omoi o shimashita.

250 果

sono KEKKA
KOOKA ga agaru
KAJITSU no SEISAN
SEKININ o hatasu
tsukare-hateru

CHOOSA no KEKKA ga mada wakarimasen.
DAIBU BENKYOO no KOOKA ga agarimashita.
Kono HEN wa KAJITSU no SEISAN de YUUMEI desu.
Nanigoto ni mo SEKININ o hatasu koto ga TAISETSU desu.
Kare wa moo tsukare-hateta to iu KANji desu.

251 基

SHOOWA KICHI
KISO KOOJI
motoi ga nai
JIJITSU ni motozuite

IZEN BEIGUN-KICHI de hataraite imashita.
EIGO o BENKYOO suru no ni KISO ga TAISETSU desu.
SHIgoto no motoi o kizukimashita.
Nani ni motozuite, sono KENKYUU o shimashita ka.

252 再 con'd

SAIKAI o yorokobu
teepu no SAISEI
KAISHA no SAIKEN
NIDO to hutatabi

GONEN mae ni wakareta tomo to SAIKAI shimashita. 252
Kono teepu o SAISEI shite kudasai. con'd
Chichi wa KAISHA no SAIKEN ni nori-dashimashita.
Murata-shi wa GICHOO ni hutatabi erabaremashita. 再

---

tanoshii SHOKUBA 253
KYOOSHOKUIN
SHOKUGYOO-ANTEI-SHO 職
SHUUSHOKU-saki

SHOKUba ga totemo akarui desu.
SHOKUINSHITSU wa doko desu ka.
SHOKUGYOO wa nan desu ka.
Yooyaku SHOKUGYOO ga kimarimashita.

TAIHEN na koto ni naru 254
HENKA ga nai
iro ga kawaru 変
YOTEI o kaeru
HEN na hito

Kinoo TAIHEN atsukatta desu.
NIHON de wa SHIKI no HENKA ga hakkiri shite imasu.
Nani ka kawatta koto ga arimasu ka.
Kono KEIKAKU o kaeru wake ni wa ikimasen.
Sono hanashi wa doomo HEN desu.

TAIBOKU o kiri-taosu 255
MOKUZAIGYOO o itonamu
SENSHUU no MOKUYOOBI 木
ki o ueru

Kono HEN ni wa, migoto na TAIBOKU ga TAKUSAN arimasu.
Kono ie wa donna MOKUSAI de dekite imasu ka.
RAISHUU no MOKUYOOBI ni TOOKYOO e iku koto ni shimashita.
Kore wa sakura no ki desu.
Kimura-san wa, totemo SHINSETSU na ii kata desu.

GAIKOO SEISAKU 256
SHITSUGYOO TAISAKU
HOOSAKU ga tsukiru 策

SEIHU wa donna GAIKOO SEISAKU o uchi-dashimashita ka.
Nani ka ii TAISAKU o neranakereba narimasen.
Moo HOOSAKU ga tsukite, doo shiyoo mo arimasen.

TAIYOO ga shizumu 257
TAIHEIYOO o KOOKOOCHUU
hutoi ki 太

Hawaii wa TAIYOO no KOOSEN ga tsuyoi desu.
TAISEIYOO ni kurabete, TAIHEIYOO wa zutto ookii desu.
Sono ki wa kanari hutoi ki desu.

258　　JOOYAKU no TEIKETSU
約　　YAKUSOKU o mamoru
　　　KEIYAKUSHO
　　　SEIYAKU o ukeru

TAINICHI-KOOWA-JOOYAKU wa nanNEN ni TEIKETSU saremashita ka.
Ashita Ikeda-san ni au YAKUSOKU o shimashita.
Mada torihiki no KEIYAKU o shite imasen.
SANKA suru no ni, nani ka SEIYAKU ga arimasu ka.

259　　DOOTOKU KYOOIKU
育　　KAMBU no IKUSEI
　　　IKUJIHOO

Kodomo no KYOOIKU wa totemo TAISETSU desu.
Imamura SENSEI wa SENSHU no IKUSEI ni chikara o irete imasu.
Kanojo wa IKUJI ni owarete imasu.

260　　EMMAN ni KAIKETSU suru
円　　ENJUKU shita SENSHU
　　　HYAKU-GOJUU EN

Takeda go-husai wa totemo EMMAN desu.
Ano SENSHU wa SAIKIN tomi ni ENJUKU shite kimashita.
ZEMBU de SAMBYAKU-GOJUU EN ni narimasu.

261　　KENKYUUSHITSU
究　　TANKYUUSHIN ga tsuyoi
　　　GEN'IN o KYUUMEI suru

SENSEI wa GENZAI nani o KENKYUU shite imasu ka.
Ano ko wa TANKYUUSHIN ga totemo tsuyoi desu.
Ima sono GEN'IN o KYUUMEI shite iru tokoro desu.

262　　KOOITEKI ni
好　　DAIKOOBUTSU
　　　KOOHYOO o HAKUsuru
　　　BANJI-KOOCHOO

YUUJIN no KOOI o MU ni suru wake ni wa ikimasen.
O-sushi wa watashi no DAIKOOBUTSU desu.
Nakamura-shi no ENZETSU wa KOOHYOO o HAKUshimashita.
SHIgoto wa ima KOOCHOO desu.

263　　HON kara IN'YOO suru
引　　INTAI-SEIKATSU
　　　INRYOKU ga tsuyoi
　　　torihiki ga SEIRITSU suru

Kore wa nan no HON kara IN'YOO shita mono desu ka.
Hayama SENSEI wa itsu INTAI shimashita ka.
Nyuuton no "BAN'YUU-INRYOKU no HOOSOKU" o shitte imasu ka.
GAIKOKU no torihiki o shite imasu.

```
SHINROO-SHIMPU                                              264
ICHIROO
                                                            郎
Watakushi wa SHINROO no YUUJIN desu.
ICHIROO wa uchi no CHOONAN desu.
```

```
KIKOKU no TO ni tsuku                                       265
KISEICHUU ni
NIHON ni HUKKI suru                                         帰
NIHON ni KIKA suru

Buraun-san wa moo KIKOKU shimashita.
RYOOSHIN ni SOODAN suru tame ni KISEI suru YOTEI desu.
Ogasawara SHOTOO wa NIHON ni HUKKI shimashita.
Ano kata wa SAIKIN NIHON ni KIKA shita soo desu.
```

```
GEN'EKI o shirizoku                                         266
JUUYOO na YAKUwari o ENsuru
YAKUSHO no SHIgoto                                          役
KAISHA no YAKUIN
KANJI no YAKU o tsutomeru

Kare wa mada GEN'EKI no SENSHU desu.
Chichi wa sono SHIgoto de JUUYOO na YAKUwari o ENjimashita.
Doko no YAKUSHO ni tsutomete imasu ka.
KAISHA no YAKUIN ni erabaremashita.
Kore wa nani ka no YAKU ni tachimasu ka.
```

```
HODOO o aruku                                               267
HOCHOO o awaseru
SAMPO ni dekakeru                                           歩
BUai ga ii

Itsumo HODOO o arukimashoo.
Kare to HOCHOO o soroete kudasai.
SHUJIN wa SAMPO ni dekakete imasu.
Kono SHIgoto wa BUai ga totemo ii desu.
```

```
AIJOO ga tarinai                                            268
AIKOKUSHIN
REN'AI-SHOSETSU                                             愛
AIYOOSHA

Ano ko wa AIJOO ni ue-kawaite imasu.
Kare wa AIKOKUSHIN ni moete imasu.
Kanojo wa ima REN'AI-CHUU desu.
Donna kuruma o AIYOO shite imasu ka.
```

```
GAIKOO-SEISAKU                                              269
NEDAN no KOOSHOO
IKEN o KOOKAN suru                                          交
KOOTSUU-SEIRI
KOOSAI o hiromeru
YUUJIN to majiwaru                                          con'd
```

269 Yamano-san wa GAIKOO ga JOOZU desu.
con'd NEDAN o KOOSHOO shite mimashoo.
      DENWA KOOKANSHU ni kiite kudasai.
交   TOOKYOO wa KOOTSUU ga BENRI desu.
      Kanojo wa KOOSAI ga hiroi desu.
      Warui tomo to wa majiwaranai HOO ga ii desu.

270   KINDAI SETSUBI
      KENSETSU-GAISHA
設   SEKKEIZU
      KAISHA no SETSURITSU
      GORAKU-SHISETSU
      KISOKU o mookeru

      KOOJOO no SETSUBI wa totemo ii desu.
      Sono KENSETSU-KOOJI wa itsu owarimasu ka.
      Ooshita-san wa JIBUN no SEKKEI de ie o tateta soo desu.
      Kono DAIGAKU wa GOJUU-NEN mae ni SETSURITSU saremashita.
      Kono machi no KOOKYOO-SHISETSU wa MAINEN KAIZEN sarete imasu.
      SHI wa RAINEN atarashii KOOEN o mookeru KEIKAKU desu.

271   KAISHA no SHIgoto
      HOOSHIHIN
仕   GAKKOO no KYUUJI
      HUBO ni tsukaeru

      Nan da ka SHIgoto ga te ni tsukimasen.
      Oosawa-san wa yoku SHAKAI-HOOSHI o suru kata desu.
      O-KYUUJI o shite itadakemasen ka.
      NagaNEN kare wa Kawamura-san TAKU ni tsukaete imasu.

272   Yooroppa SHOKOKU
      GAKUSEI SHOKUN
諸   Hawaii SHOTOO

      Aono-shi wa TOONAN-Ajia SHOKOKU o mawatte kimashita.
      SHOKUN ni ooi ni KITAI o yosete imasu.
      Higashi Indo SHOTOO de wa donna mono ga toremasu ka.

273   TOOITSU-KOODOO
      DENTOO o mamoru
統   TOOKEI o toru
      TOOSEI ga toreru
      kuni o sube-osameru

      Minasan no IKEN o TOOITSU shite kudasai.
      Kono GAKKOO no DENTOO wa totemo hurui desu.
      TOOKEI ni yoreba, SENGETSU no SEISAN wa SAIKOO desu.
      Sukoshi mo SHIgoto no TOOSEI ga toremasen.
      Babironiya wa mukashi donna kuni o sube-osamemashita ka.

KOOTSUU IHAN   274
KENKAI no SOOI
machigatta kangae   違
chigai nai

KOOTSUU IHAN o shite wa ikemasen.
Kore wa Takahashi-san no mono ni SOOI arimasen.
Doo mo michi o machigaeta YOO desu.
Are wa hoteru ni chigai arimasen.

---

utsukushii KOOYOO   275
aoba ga kaoru
o-kotoba ni amaete   葉
ki no ha

Watashi wa KOOYOO no aki ga DAIsuki desu.
Ima wa aoba ga totemo KIREI desu.
Kaesu kotoba mo arimasen.
Sonna koto wa ne mo ha mo nai koto desu.

TEIDO ga takai   276
KENKYUU no KATEI
SHIgoto no NITTEI   程
YOhodo CHUUI shinakereba

Sono ko no NOORYOKU wa dono TEIDO ka yoku wakarimasen.
Sore wa KENKYUU no KATEI ni arimasu.
SHIgoto no NITTEI o kunde mimashita.
YOhodo BENKYOO shinakereba, DAIGAKU ni hairemasen.

TENNOO-HEIKA   277
TENKI YOHOO
TENGOKU to JIGOKU   天
TENKA o toru
TEN no tasuke

REKIDAI no TENNOO no namae ga iemasu ka.
Tama no TENKI wa kawari-yasui desu.
SEISHO ni wa TENGOKU ga KIsarete imasu.
Ima wa TENKA-TAIHEI desu.
NYUUSHI ni ukatte, TEN ni mo noboru YOO na kokochi deshita.

KENSETSU-TEKI na IKEN   278
HOOKEN-TEKI
KENCHIKU-ZAIRYOO   建
ie no tatemae
KOOJOO o tateru
biru ga tatsu

Ishikawa-kun wa KENSETSU-GAISHA ni hairimashita.
Ano mura wa HOOKEN-TEKI desu.
Ani wa ima JIBUN no ie o KENCHIKUCHUU desu.
Sonna toki, IPPAN ni AISATSU suru no ga tatemae desu.
RAINEN, atarashii JIMUSHO o tateru KEIKAKU desu.
Ano biru wa SAIKIN tachimashita.

279 　SAISHO no koro
初　Runesansu no SHOKI
　　SHOTAIMEN no hito
　　mattaku no hatsumimi
　　hajimete narau

　　SAISHO dare ga dare da ka wakarimasen deshita.
　　Runesansu no SHOKI to MAKKI de wa DAIBU chigaimasu.
　　Uchino-san to SHOTAIMEN deshita.
　　Sore wa hatsumimi desu.
　　DAIGAKU ni itte, hajimete HuransuGO o naraimashita.

280　SOKUMEN kara
側　 SHUSHOO no SOKKIN-suji
　　 mukatte migigawa ni

　　 SOKUMEN kara ENJO shitai to omoimasu.
　　 Kare wa SHUSHOO no SOKKIN desu.
　　 Amerika de wa kuruma wa michi no migigawa o hashirimasu.

281　JUUKYO ga sadamaru
居　 BEKKYO-SEIKATSU
　　 hiroi ima
　　 ooki na torii
　　 ie ni iru

　　 Kare no JUUKYO wa mada sadamarimasen.
　　 Kanojo wa GO-SHUJIN to nagai aida BEKKYO shite imasu.
　　 Ima ga sukoshi sema-sugimasu.
　　 MEIJI-JINGUU no torii wa totemo ookii desu.
　　 Kazuo-kun wa ie ni iru ka doo ka wakarimasen.

282　HAIBOKU no GEN'IN
北　 HOKKAIDOO-RYOKOO
　　 TOOHOKU-CHIHOO
　　 TOOZAI-NAMBOKU
　　 HOKKYOKU-TANKEN
　　 kitakaze

　　 KONDO no SHIai de wa migoto ni HAIBOKU shimashita.
　　 Natsuyasumi ni wa HOKKAIDOO o RYOKOO suru YOTEI desu.
　　 Matsushita-san wa TOOHOKU de sodatta soo desu.
　　 Amerika no NAMBOKU-SENSOO wa YUUMEI desu.
　　 HOKKYOKU o hajimete TANKEN shita hito wa dare desu ka.
　　 Kinoo wa tsumetai kitakaze ga hukimashita.

283　KOKKA YOSAN
予　 YOSOOGAI ni
　　 YOGENSHA
　　 YOTEI-doori
　　 TENKI YOHOO
　con'd

KONGETSU wa sore o kau YOSAN ga arimasen.　　　　　283
ZENZEN YOSOO ga tsukimasen.　　　　　　　　　　　　con'd
Yoku YOGEN suru hito ga imasu.
HIKOOKI wa YOTEI-doori tsukimashita.　　　　　　　　予
Ashita no TENKI YOHOO o kikimashita ka.

KENKYUUSEI　　　　　　　　　　　　　　　　　　　　284
KENKYUUJO
　　　　　　　　　　　　　　　　　　　　　　　　　研
KENKYUU ga mada tarimasen.
Ima GAIKOOKAN no KENSHUU o ukete imasu.

KANOOSEI ga aru　　　　　　　　　　　　　　　　　285
GAKUSEI no NOORYOKU
GOGAKU no SAINOO　　　　　　　　　　　　　　　　能
KINOO-SHOOGAI

SHIai ni katsu KANOOSEI wa JUUBUN ni arimasu.
Ano SENSHU ni wa madamada nobiru NOORYOKU ga arimasu.
Ano ko wa umaretsuki ONGAKU no SAINOO ga arimasu.
SHINZOO no KINOO ga yowatte imasu.

RIPPA na SEINEN　　　　　　　　　　　　　　　　　286
SAHA no DOOKOO
UHAKEI　　　　　　　　　　　　　　　　　　　　　派
GAIKOKU ni HAKEN suru

Kanojo wa RIPPA na ENGI o misete kuremashita.
SHIMBUN de SAHA no DOOKOO ga kibishiku HINAN saremashita.
SHAKAITOO no UHA to SAHA ga TAIRITSU shimashita.
Kitano-san wa KAISHA kara HONKON ni HAKEN saremashita.

BOOEICHOO　　　　　　　　　　　　　　　　　　　　287
JIEIKAN
KOOSHUU-EISEI　　　　　　　　　　　　　　　　　　衛
DAIGAKU no SHUEI

Asoko wa BOOEICHOO desu.
Ima kuni de wa JIEIKAN o BOSHUU shite imasu.
Sono KEN ni tsuite wa, EISEIKYOKU ni toi-awasete kudasai.
Hashimoto-san wa DAIGAKU no SHUEI desu.

RYOOSHIN o ushinau　　　　　　　　　　　　　　　288
RYOOSHA no aida de
RYOOHOO to mo　　　　　　　　　　　　　　　　　両
RYOOte-RYOOashi

Nakajima-kun wa chiisai toki, RYOOSHIN o ushinatta soo desu.
RYOOSHA no aida de KEIYAKU ga SEIRITSU shimashita.
RYOOHOO to mo warukatta to omoimasu.
Koyama-san wa RYOOte-RYOOashi o kegashimashita.

289   JOOYAKU KAISEI
改   SHUUKYOO-KAIKAKU
    HINSHU no KAIRYOO
    SEIKATSU-KAIZEN
    aratamatte
    seki o aratamete

    JIKOKUHYOO ga KAISEI saremashita.
    Kinoo GAKKOO de SHUUKYOO-KAIKAKU ni tsuite manabimashita.
    Kome no HINSHITSU ga KAIRYOO sarete imasu.
    GENZAI no SEIKATSU o KAIZEN shinakereba narimasen.
    Sonna ni aratamaru HITSUYOO wa arimasen.
    Aratamete iu made mo arimasen.

290   KAISHI JIKAN
開   MIKAIHATSU-CHIIKI
    KYOKUMEN no TENKAI
    KAIHOOTEKI
    KOOKAI-TOORONKAI
    KAI o hiraku

    NanJI ni JUGYOO ga KAISHI saremasu ka.
    Kono HEN wa mada yoku KAIHATSU sarete imasen.
    SEIKYOKU wa donna HOOKOO ni TENKAI shite imasu ka.
    Kanojo wa KAIHOOTEKI desu.
    Kinoo KOKUHOO ga KOOKAI saremashita.
    KONDO wa itsu KAIGI o hirakimasu ka.

291   ano goro
頃

    GAKUSEI no koro, yoku RYOKOO shimashita.

292   SHIDOOSHA
指   machigai o SHITEKI suru
    GAKUDAN no SHIKI
    SENSEI no SHIJI ni shitagatte

    Piano o haha ni SHIDOO shite moratte imasu.
    Machigai ga attara, SHITEKI shite kudasai.
    Minna no SHIKI o **totte** kudasai.
    Yoku SENSEI no SHIJI ni shitagawanakereba ikemasen.

293   SEIRYOKU arasoi
勢   SHAKAI JOOSEI
    ROODOO KOOSEI
    ooZEI no hitobito
    ikiyoi ga tsuyoi

    TAIHUU no SEIRYOKU ga otoroemashita.
    JOOSEI ga AKKA shimashita.
    KONDO no SHIai de, aite wa kanari KOOSEI ni demashita.
    Kanojo no KAZOKU wa ooZEI desu.
    Kare wa o-sake no ikioi de anna koto o shita YOO desu.

REIGAI naku
REIBUN ni shitagatte
REIDAI ni aru toori
ZENREI no nai
REI o ageru

294 例

Kore wa REIGAI desu.
REIBUN ni shitagatte, BUN o tsukutte kudasai.
REIDAI o konasu to, yoku oboeraremasu.
Sore wa ZENREI no nai koto desu.
Hitotsu REI o agete kudasai.

BYOOJOO ga AKKA suru
ZAIAKU-KAN
AKUSEI no kaze
KYOOAKU-HANZAI
KImochi ga warui

295 悪

JITAI ga AKKA shimashita.
Karera ni wa ZAIAKU-KAN ga mattaku nai YOO desu.
Ima AKUSEI no kaze ga hayatte imasu.
SATSUJIN wa KYOOAKU-HANZAI desu.
Warui asobi o shite wa ikemasen.

BOKUtachi no GAKKOO
BOKU no ani

296 僕

BOKUtachi wa KYONEN KYUUSHUU o RYOKOO shimashita.
Sore wa BOKU no HON desu.

---

monogoto o TANKYUU suru
KYUUJIN-KOOKOKU
YOOKYUU ni ojite
GEN'IN o TSUIKYUU suru
HON o motomeru

297 求

Sono GENRI o TANKYUU shinakereba narimasen.
KAISHA de KYUUJIN no KOOKOKU o dashimashita.
Kumiai-gawa no YOOKYUU ga toorimashita.
JIKO no GEN'IN o TSUIKYUU shite imasu.
KONDO no KAIGI no SHUSSEKI o motomeraremashita.

JUKEN-BENKYOO
mooshide o JUDAKU suru
uketsuke-gakari
uketoriSHOO
SHIKEN o ukeru
SHIKEN ni ukaru

298 受

Ani wa yoru osoku made JUKEN BENKYOO o shite imasu.
Yamamura-shi wa sono mooshide o JUDAKU shimashita.
Uketsuke de o-tazune kudasai.
Kore wa, kinoo katta shinamono no uketoriSHO desu.
Kanojo wa DAIGAKU made KYOOIKU o ukemashita.
NYUUSHA SHIKEN ni ukarimashita.

299　KYOODOO-SEIMEI
声　MEISEI o HAKUsuru
　　SEIGAKUKA
　　utagoe ga kikoeru
　　oogoe de sakebu

RYOOGOKU DAIHYOO wa KYOODOO-SEIMEI o HAPPYOO shimashita.
ONGAKUKA to shite, kare wa SEKAI-TEKI MEISEI o HAKUshite imasu.
Ima kanojo wa SEIGAKU o BENKYOO shite imasu.
Tonari no heya kara utsukushii utagoe o kikoemashita.
Oogoe de hanashite wa ikemasen.

300　REKISHIJOO
史　Sawamura-JOSHI
　　SHIJOO mare na
　　SHIRYOO ni motozuite
　　SHISEKI ni tonde iru

Kono DAIGAKU wa REKISHI ga mada asai desu.
Ano kata wa Sawamura-JOSHI desu.
Sore wa SHIJOO mare na dekigoto desu.
Edo JIDAI no SHIRYOO ni motozuite ROMBUN o kakimashita.
Watakushi wa SHISEKI o otozureru no ga DAIsuki desu.

MINZOKU-SEISHIN 301
KAZOKU-TEKI

Ainu MINZOKU no DAIBUBUN wa HOKKAIDOO ni sunde imasu.
KAZOKU wa ZEMBU de HACHININ desu.

族

KEIZAI-KANNEN 302
DOOBUTSU no KANSATSU
KANKOO-RYOKOO
KYAKKAN-TEKI na mikata

Ano hito ni wa, KEIZAI-KANNEN ga sukoshi mo arimasen.
Nani o KANSATSU shite imasu ka.
Chichi wa NIKKOO e KANKOO-RYOKOO ni dekakemashita.
KYAKKAN-TEKI ni monogoto o kangaete mite kudasai.

観

TOOKYOO TOCHIJI 303
KYOOTO no o-tera
KEIHIN KOOGYOO-CHITAI

TOOKYOO ni itte YUUJIN ni aimashita.
KYOOTO wa NIHON no DAIHYOO-TEKI na KANKOO-TOCHI desu.
KEIHIN KOOGYOO-CHITAI ni wa, KOOJOO ga TAKUSAN arimasu.

京

BEIKOKU KUUGUN 304
KUUKI no ATSURYOKU
KUUSOOKA
sumikitta oozora

Kinoo BEIKOKU KUUGUN no pareedo o mimashita.
Sukoshi taiya no KUUKI ga tarinai yoo desu.
Otootoo wa TOTETSU mo nai KUUSOOKA desu.
Hawai no aozora wa totemo kirei desu.

空

SHI no EISEIKYOKU 305
SEIKA SHIJOO
TOSHI KEIKAKU
ZENRYOO na SHIMIN

Yokkaichi wa itsu SHI ni narimashita ka.
TOOKYOO no SEIKA SHIJOO o KENGAKU shimashita.
DAITOSHI de wa SHOOKOOGYOO ga sakan desu.
SANNEN tattara, Amerika no SHIMENKEN o toru tsumori desu.

市

KEISHIKI-TEKI na mono 306
KYOO'NINGYOO
NINGEN-KEISEI
ii katachi

Amari KEISHIKI ni torawarenai HOO ga ii to omoimasu.
KONDO KYOOTO e itta toki, KYOO'NINGYOO o motomeru tsumori desu.
Kono chiimu wa NIJUUHACHI-NIN de KEISEI sarete imasu.
Kore wa katachi no ii ishi desu.

形

307 SOORI DAIJIN
　　 SOOGOO DAIGAKU
総 SOOTAI-TEKI na IKEN

Yoshida Shigeru wa RIPPA na SOORI DAIJIN datta to omoimasu.
TOOKYOO DAIGAKU wa SOOGOO DAIGAKU desu.
SOOTAI-TEKI na IKEN o matomete kudasai.

---

308 SHIHAIRYOKU
　　 SHIMPAI-goto
配 o-kome no HAIKYUU
　　 SHIMBUN o kubaru

Mukashi, Rooma wa iroiro na kuni o SHIHAI shite imashita.
Nani mo SHIMPAI wa irimasen.
NIHON de wa o-kome no HAIKYUU ga arimasu.
Sonna ni KI o kubaranakute mo KEKKOO desu.

---

309 GEMBAKU no JIKKEN
　　 BAKUGEKI-KI
爆 KAZAN no BAKUHATSU
　　 BAKUDAN o otosu

Konomae, GEMBAKU no JIKKEN ga CHUUGOKU de okonawareta yoo desu.
Kono machi wa SENSOOCHUU, BAKUGEKI o uketa koto ga arimasu.
Miharayama ga mata BAKUHATSU shimashita.
SENSOOCHUU, kono HEN ni BAKUDAN ga ochita soo desu.

---

310 KINKYOO-HOOKOKU
　　 HOODOO KIKAN
報 SHIKYUU DEMPOO
　　 ON ni mukuiru

KENKYUU no KEKKA o HOOKOKU shimashita.
JUUDAI nyuusu ga HOODOO saremashita.
Kono DEMPOO o utte kudasai.
Oya no ON ni mukuitai to omoimasu.

---

311 SEKKYOKU-TEKI na TAIDO
　　 KYOKUTOO MONDAI
極 KYOKUGEN ni tassuru
　　 goku wazuka

Maeda-san wa TAIHEN SEKKYOKU-TEKI na hito desu.
NIHON wa KYOKUTOO de JUUYOO na YAKUwari o hatashite imasu.
Moo KYOKUGEN ni tasshimashita.
Goku wazuka de KEKKOO desu.

---

312 KANDAI na SOCHI
　　 TEKITOO na ICHI
置 kirei na okimono
　　 HON o oita tokoro

con'd

```
            Donna SOCHI o tottara yoroshii deshoo ka.              312
            GAKKOO no ICHI wa machi no minami no HOO desu.         con'd
            Kono okimono wa ishi de dekite imasu.
            Pen wa HON o oita tokoro ni arimasu.                   置
```

```
            SHOOBAI DOOGU                                          313
            KYOOKASHO no HAMBAI
            Yomiuri SHIMBUN
            SEN'EN de uru                                          売
            shinamono no ureyuki

            SHOOBAI ga amari omowashiku arimasen.
            Asoko de ima KYOOKASHO no HAMBAI o shite imasu.
            Ie de wa Asahi SHIMBUN to Yomiuri SHIMBUN o totte imasu.
            Ano kuruma o NIJUU-MAN'EN de urimashita.
```

```
            KIBOO-doori                                            314
            SHITSUBOO sezu ni
            YOOBOO ni kotaete
            YOKUBOO o mitasu                                       望
            nozonde iru tokoro

            Nan to ka go-KIBOO ni soitai to omoimasu.
            Imooto wa DAIGAKU no NYUUSHI ni ochite SHITSUBOO shite
            SEMPOO kara donna YOOBOO ga arimasu ka.      (imasu.
            NINGEN no YOKUBOO ni wa kagiri ga arimasen.
            SHOORAI, ISHA ni naru koto o nozonde imasu.
```

```
            SHINSETSU na hito                                      315
            RYOOSHIN no o-kage
            oyako no KANKEI
            shitashii aidagara                                     親

            Mishiranu hito ni, SHINSETSU ni michi o oshiete itadakimashita.
            RYOOSHIN wa ima Yooroppa o RYOKOO shite imasu.
            O-hiru ni oyako-domburi o tabemashita.
            Ooyama-san wa watakushi no shitashii YUUJIN desu.
```

```
            utsukushii HUUKEI                                      316
            TAIHUU no EIKYOO
            nurui HUURO
            karakkaze                                              風

            Watakushi wa HUUKEIGA ga suki na no de, yoku soto de SHASEI
            KONDO no TAIHUU wa DAIBU ookii yoo desu.     (shimasu.
            O-HUURO wa atsui no yori nurui HOO ga suki desu.
            Kinoo wa kaze ga tsuyokatta no de, hatake ga arasaremashita.
```

```
            KENZEN na BOTAI                                        317
            BOKOKUGO de hanasu
            obasan no ie
            hahaoya no SEKININ                                     母

                                                                   con'd
```

317 con'd	DANTAI no BOTAI ga shikkari shite ireba DAIJOOBU desu.
母	Watakushi no BO-KOKUGO wa NIHONGO desu.
	Obasan no ie wa sonna ni tooku arimasen.
	Watakushi wa NIJUUNI-SAI no toki, hahaoya ni narimashita.

318	KON'YA no terebi BANGUMI
夜	YAGAKU no BENKYOO
	yonaka no NEJI goro
	yoru osoku made
	Oji wa KON'YA no HIKOOKI de kaette kimasu.
	Yamada-san wa YAGAKU ni kayotte imasu.
	Kinoo wa yonaka made SHIgoto o shimashita.
	Itsumo yoru nanJI goro made okite imasu ka.

319	ii CHII
位	ICHI o kaeru
	KAMOKU no TAN'I
	kurai no aru hito
	Kare wa kanari ii CHII ni imasu.
	Tsukue no ICHI wa warui no de, naoshimashoo.
	KAGAKU wa nan-TAN'I desu ka.
	BOOEICHOO de Yamamoto-shi wa DAIBU ue no HOO desu.

320	KODAI Rooma
古	KOTEN no KENKYUU
	hurui HON
	hurubita tatemono
	KODAI Girisha ni tsuite, KENKYUU shite imasu.
	KOTEN o yomu no ga suki desu.
	Sono kangae wa moo hurui desu.
	Ano tatemono wa hurubite imasu.

321	Ato SHIMATSU
始	GENSHI-JIDAI
	JUGYOO no KAISHI
	GAKKOO ga hajimaru
	KAIGI o hajimeru
	SHIMATSU ga warukute te ga tsukeraremasen.
	GENSHI-JIDAI no NINGEN wa, donna mono o tabemashita ka.
	JUGYOO no KAISHI wa MAIasa HACHI-JI desu.
	Itsu GAKKOO ga hajimarimasu ka.
	Sorosoro KAIGI ga hajimaru JIKAN desu.

322	sugureta GIJUTSU
術	GEIJUTSUKA
	GAKUJUTSU-KAIGI
	BIJUTSU TENRANKAI
	NIHON no KENCHIKU no GIJUTSU wa sugurete imasu.
	Ashita kara DAIGAKU no GEIJUTSU-SAI ga hajimarimasu.
	Sore wa GAKUJUTSU-TEKI na MONDAI desu.
	Ima, TOOYOO no BIJUTSU o manande imasu.

EIGO no TOKUHON
AIDOKUSHA
DOKUSHO no aki
yomi-yasui HON

323 読

HON'YA de EIGO no TOKUHON o kaimashita.
Watakushi wa sono HON no AIDOKUSHA desu.
Ima wa DOKUSHO no aki desu.
SHIMBUN o MAINICHI yomimasu.

HAMBUN-zutsu
HANSHIN-HANGI de
JINSEI no nakaba

324 半

SHIgoto wa HAMBUN dekite imasu.
Sono hanashi o HANSHIN-HANGI de kikimashita.
Nakaba akiramete imasu.

SENSOO HOOKI
YAKYUU HOOSOO
HOOSHASEN
te o hanasu
kaori o hanatsu

325 放

KENRI o HOOKI shite wa ikemasen.
YAKYUU HOOSOO wa nanJI kara hajimarimasu ka.
Yamada-san wa ima, HOOSHASEN-CHIRYOO o ukete imasu.
Kawakami-san wa itsu SHAKUHOO saremashita ka.
Te o hanashite kudasai.
Ike ni koi o hanachimashita.

---

taitoru no BOOEI
KOKUBOO-CHOOKAN
TOONAN no BOOSHI
KASAI o husegu

326 防

Kotoshi ani wa BOOEI DAIGAKKOO ni NYUUGAKU shimashita.
Amerika no KOKUBOO-CHOOKAN wa dare desu ka.
TOONAN BOOSHI ni KYOORYOKU shite kudasai.
KASAI o huseganakereba narimasen.

BURAKU no GYOOJI
RAKUDAISEI
SENKYO de RAKUSEN suru
ki kara ochiru
SHIN'YOO o otosu

327 落

Kore wa BURAKU no GYOOJI desu.
RAKUDAI-TEN o totte wa ikemasen.
Ueda-shi wa oshiku mo KONDO no SENKYO de RAKUSEN shimashita.
Yane kara ochite, KEGA o shimashita.
KI o otosanaide, gambatte kudasai.

328 階 JOORYUU KAIKYUU
GEN-DANKAI ni oite
KAIDAN no shita

Dono SHAKAI ni mo KAIKYUU TOOSOO ga arimasu.
GEN-DANKAI ni oite wa, nan to mo iemasen.
Deguchi wa KAIDAN no migigawa ni arimasu.

---

329 従 JUURAI no MONDAI
JUUJUN na ko
JUUGYOOIN kumiai
SHIgoto ni JUUJI suru
SENSEI no IKEN ni shitagatte
kodomo o shitagaeru

Watakushi wa JUURAI, HON o yomu koto ga suki desu.
Ano ko wa totemo JUUJUN na ko desu.
Watakushi wa depaato no JUUGYOOIN desu.
Ima, donna SHIgoto ni JUUJI shite imasu ka.
Oya no IKEN ni shitagatte, DAIGAKU o erabimashita.
Kodomo o shitagaete, GAKKOO e ikimashita.

---

330 態 RIPPA na TAIDO
ima no JOOTAI
KINKYUU JITAI

Ano kata no TAIDO wa itsu mo RIPPA desu.
Ima no JOOTAI de wa, sochira e iku koto ga dekimasen.
KINKYUU JITAI ga HASSEI shimashita.

---

331 伝 GAKKOO no DENTOO
SHOOHIN no SENDEN
DENKI monogatari
hanashi o tsutaeru
uwasa ga tsutawaru

Kono GAKKOO ni wa nagai DENTOO ga arimasu.
Mamma to sono SENDEN ni notte shimaimashita.
Watakushi wa DENKI monogatari o yomu no ga suki desu.
Kono hanashi o SEMPOO ni tsutaete kudasai.
HEN na uwasa ga tsutawarimashita.

---

332 電 DENSHA no BEN
DENKI RYOOKIN
DENWA BANGOO
DENRYOKU SHIGEN

Watakushi no ie wa DENSHA no BEN ga ii desu.
DENKI o kesshite kudasai.
Kinoo Shimada-san to DENWA de hanashimashita.
NIHON wa DENRYOKU SHIGEN ni megumarete imasu.

JIKAN no KANNEN 333
ZANNEN nagara
KI'NEN HIN
katai SHINNEN
TETSUGAKU no GAINEN

Kare ni wa JIKAN no KANNEN ga arimasen.
ZANNEN nagara, TOOKYOO e iku koto ga dekimasen.
Kore wa SOTSUGYOO no KI'NEN SHASHIN desu.
Kare wa JIBUN no SHIgoto ni tsuyoi SHINNEN o motte imasu.
"Shibui" to iu GAINEN ni tsuite kangaete mimashoo.

KYUUYOO TAIKEI 334
YOTOO GIIN
KIKAI o ataeru

KYOOIN no KYUUYOO SUIJUN wa dono kurai desu ka.
YOTOO no aida de IKEN no CHOOSEI ga okonawarete imasu.
Yamada-san ni au KIKAI ga ataeraremashita.

NISEN-EN 335
kuni ni yotte SENSABAMBETSU

Kono JISHO wa NISEN-EN de kaimashita.
SEITO wa GAKKOO ni yotte SENSABAMBETSU desu.

DANTAI KYOOGI 336
SHUUDAN-NOOJOO
ITCHI-DANKETSU suru

DANTAI-KOODOO o totte kudasai.
SoREN no SHUUDAN-NOOJOO wa YUUMEI desu.
ITCHI-DANKETSU shite gambarimashoo.

NYOJITSU ni kataru 337
JOSAInai hito
ikahodo no mono
AmerikaJIN no gotoku

Sono SHOOSETSU ni SAKUSHA no SEIKATSU ga NYOJITSU ni egakarete
Yamashita-san wa JOSAInai hito desu.   (imasu.
Ikahodo sashiagemashoo ka.
Oosaka wa TOOKYOO no gotoku, hito ga ooi desu.

---

hitode-busoku 338
MANZOKU-KAN
hayaashi de
monotarinai

Ima hitode-busoku de yowatte imasu.
Ima no SHIgoto ni MANZOKU shite imasu.
Hayaashi de ikeba, JIPPUN de tsuku deshoo.
Nandaka monotarinai yoo na KI ga shimasu.

339 美
BIJUTSU KOOGEIHIN
BIJIN kontesuto
ikitsuke no BIYOOIN

Ima, DAIGAKU de NIHON no BIJUTSU-SHI o manande imasu.
Oono-san wa nakanaka no BIJIN desu.
Asoko no BIYOOIN de kami o setto shimashita.

---

340 供
JUYOO to KYOOKYUU
WADAI o TEIKYOO suru
o-mochi o sonaeru
o-tomo shite

JUYOO to KYOOKYUU no tsuriai ga torimasen.
Kono BANGUMI wa Hitachi no TEIKYOO desu.
Kono hana wa nani ni sonaeru no desu ka.
ZEHI o-tomo sasete itadakimasu.

---

341 選
SOOSENKYO
YUUSHUU na SENSHU
GAKKOO no SENTAKU
michi o erabu

RAIGETSU, SHUUGIIN no SOOSENKYO ga arimasu.
Ani wa tenisu no SENSHU desu.
Ima DAIGAKU no SENTAKU ni mayotte imasu.
Supiichi kontesuto de, GAKKOO no DAIHYOO ni erabarete imasu.

---

342 価
BUKKA no neagari
SEKIYU no KAKAKU
mono no KACHI
takaku HYOOKA suru

MAItoshi BUKKA ga neagari shite imasu.
Sono ZAIRYOO no KAKAKU wa dono kurai desu ka.
Kono shinamono wa totemo KACHI ga arimasu.
Chichi no KENKYUU wa takaku HYOOKA saremashita.

---

343 確
KAKUJITSU-SEI ga aru
KAKUSHIN shite
SAIKAKUNIN suru
HOOSHIN o KAKURITSU suru
tashika na HENJI

Takano-san ga Amerika e iku no wa KAKUJITSU na no desu.
Sono SHIai ni wa kanarazu katsu KAKUSHIN ga arimasu.
MYOONICHI Nishida-san ga korareru ka doo ka KAKUNIN shite kudasai.
KONNENDO no HOOSHIN ga KAKURITSU shitara, sugu o-shirase kudasai.
BEIKOKU e iku no ga tashika ni kimatta wake de wa arimasen.

KUROO no kai ga atte 344
KUSHIN shite
KUTSUU o uttaeru   苦
kurushii omoi
HENTOO ni kurushimu
nigai KEIKEN

Kodomo o sodateru no ni TAIHEN KUROO shimashita.
Yamamoto-san wa KUSHIN shite kono ie o tateta soo desu.
Soko e iku no ga nan to naku KUTSUU de tamarimasen.
SHIKEN ni SHIPPAI shite, kurushii omoi o shita koto ga ari-
Nan to ittara ii ka, HENTOO ni kurushimimashita.   (masu.
Kore wa totemo nigai kusuri desu.

---

utsukushii KOOKEI   345
KOOTAKU no aru
KOOGAKU KIKAI   光
pikapika hikaru

Terebi de tsuki no KOOKEI o miru koto ga dekimashita.
Kono okimono wa ZUIBUN KOOTAKU ga arimasu ne.
Chichi wa KOOGAKU KANKEI no SHIgoto o shite imasu.
Yuka ga pikapika hikatte imasu.

SHITSUGYOO TAISAKU   346
DAI-SHIPPAI
SHITSUBOO no amari   失
SHITSUREI na koto
JISHIN o ushinau

Ano hito wa ima SHITSUGYOO shite imasu.
SHIPPAI wa SEIKOO no moto to yoku iwaremasu.
Sonna koto ni SHITSUBOO shite wa ikemasen.
Kinoo wa doo mo SHITSUREI shimashita.

SEKIYU KAGAKU   347
SEKITAN SANGYOO
kome no KOKUdaka   石
mura no ishiya

SEKIYU sutoobu wa IPPAN no KATEI de yoku tsukawarete imasu.
SEKITAN wa doko de ICHIBAN ooku toremasu ka.
Kotoshi no kome no KOKUdaka o shirabete imasu.
Kono KINJO ni ishiya ga arimasu ka.

KANTAN na AISATSU   348
hakari no TAN'I
TANJUN na SEIKAKU   単

Sono MONDAI o KANTAN ni SETSUMEI shite kudasai.
Kono KAMOKU o toreba, ZEMBU de JUUROKU TAN'I ni narimasu.
SHIgoto ga kanari TANJUNKA sarete kimashita.

349 任
RENTAI SEKININ
SHUSHOO no NIMMU
NIMMEI-SHIKI
SHIgoto o makaseru

SEKININ o hatashite kudasai.
Yoshikawa-san wa ataerareta SEKININ o mattoo shimashita.
Yamamoto-san wa kinoo BUCHOO ni NIMMEI saremashita.
Sono SHIgoto o ZEMBU makaserarete imasu.

---

350 参
SANKA-KOKU
SANKOO-SHOO
JUGYOO SANKAN

NIHON wa Orimpikku ni itsumo SANKA shite imasu.
Kono HON o SANKOO ni shite, repooto o kaite kudasai.
KYUUJOO wa itsu SANKAN dekimasu ka.

---

351 難
hageshii HI'NAN
KONNAN ni butsukaru
NANTEN ga aru
shigatai

ENZETSU no nochi, Yamamoto-san wa hageshii HI'NAN o abimashita.
Soko e iku no wa DAIBU KONNAN datta YOO desu.
Madamada NANTEN ga arimasu.
Kore wa nakanaka toki-gatai MONDAI desu.

---

352 費
RYOKOO no HIYOO
SHOOHI-SHA
JIKAN o tsuiyasu

Sono RYOKOO no HIYOO wa dono kurai kakarimasu ka.
NICHIJOO SEIKATSU de iroiro na mono o SHOOHI shite imasu.
O-kane o MUDA ni tuiyashite wa ikemasen.

---

353 案
kangae o TEIAN suru
ANGAI JOOZU ni
KANKOO ANNAI

Nani ka yoi kangae ga arimashitara, TEIAN shite kudasai.
KONDO no SHIKEN wa ANGAI yasashikatta YOO desu.
Shimoyama-san wa KANKOO ANNAI no SHIgoto o shite imasu.

---

354 援
ENJO-GAKU
OOEN-DAN
KOOEN-KAI

SUIGAI-CHI kara ENJO o motomete kimashita.
Tenisu no SHIAI no OOEN ni ikimasen ka.
Watakushi wa Satoo-shi no KOOEN-KAI ni haitte imasu.

355 顔

SENGAN-YOO no SEKKEN
kaoiro o ukagau
RIPPA na kaobure

Kono SEKKEN wa SENGAN-YOO desu.
Nandaka kaoiro wa yoku arimasen.
SENSHU no kaobure ga soroimashita.

---

356 式

KEISHIKI-barazu ni
SEISHIKI na tetsuzuki o toru
KOOSHIKI HAPPYOO
GISHIKI-baru
hurui HOOSHIKI

ROMBUN no KEISHIKI de kaite mite kudasai.
KEKKON-SHIKI no hidori ga SEISHIKI ni kimarimashita.
Iyoiyo MYOONICHI kara puro YAKYUU no KOOSHIKISEN ga haji-
Nani mo GISHIKI-baru HITSUYOO wa arimasen.   (marimasu.
Atarashii HOOSHIKI de kokoromite mimashoo.

---

357 認

NINSHIKI-BUSOKU
KAKUNIN suru
SHOONINJOO
yo ni mitomerareru

Mada sono SHIgoto ni TAIsuru NINSHIKI ga tarimasen.
Sono JOOHOO o KAKUNIN shimashita.
KOKUREN de CHUUKYOO wa SHOONIN saremashita ka.
Ano kata wa SAKKYOKU-KA to shite mitomerarete imasu.

---

358 評

EIGA no HIHYOO
BUNGEI HYOORON
KINJO no HYOOBAN

SHIMBUN de sono EIGA no HIHYOO o yomimashita.
Nakanishi-shi wa BUNGEI HYOORON-KA desu.
Ichiroo-kun wa KINJO no HYOOBAN mo yoku, kurasu no NINKI
                                               (mono desu.

---

359 質

muzukashii SHITSUMON
SHIgoto no SEISHITSU
JISSHITSU-TEKI ni
BUSSHITSU-TEKI ni
SHITSU ni ireru

SHITSUMON shite mo yoroshii desu ka.
Kono ko wa majime de otonashii SEISHITSU desu.
Sono GAKKOO wa JISSHITSU-TEKI ni yoku natta to omoimasu.
Amerika no kuni wa BUSSHITSU-TEKI ni megumarete imasu.
Kono mao no SHICHI o nagasaremashita.

360   TOCHI no hito
          KOKUDO KAIHATSU
土   SENSHUU no DOYOOBI
          uchi no DODAI
          tsuchi o humu

          Kono HEN no TOCHI ni wa amari kuwashiku arimasen.
          KOKUDO HATTEN no tame ni DORYOKU suru tsumori desu.
          KONDO no DOYOOBI ni Oosawa-san ni au YOTEI desu.
          Kono ie wa DODAI ga shikkari shite imasu.
          Mada Kanada no tsuchi o hunda koto ga arimasen.

361   EIGO no BENKYOO
          EIKOKU no JOOO
英   SEKAI no EIYUU
          EIKI o yashinau

          Uehara-san wa EIGO no BENKYOO ni YONEN ga arimasen.
          Rondon wa EIKOKU no SHUTO desu.
          Katsute Napoleon wa Huransu no EIYUU deshita.
          Ooi ni EIKI o yashinatte kudasai.

362   ICHIOO no tetsuzuki
          OOYOO MONDAI
応   OOKYUU teate
          OOBO KITEI

          ICHIOO SENSEI ni kiite mita HOO ga yoroshii deshoo.
          SENSEI no iwareta koto o OOYOO shite mimashita.
          Koyama-san wa BYOOKI de OOKYUU teate o ukemashita.
          Uta no konkuuru ni OOBO shita koto ga arimasu ka.

363   KAKKOKU DAIHYOO
          KAKUCHI o mawaru
各   KAKUSHU torisoroete
          KAKUJI no MONDAI
          onoono no

          Moo KAKKOKU DAIHYOO ga soroimashita.
          SENKYO UNDOO ga KAKUCHI de okonawarete imasu.
          SAIKIN NIHON de wa KAKUSHU no KOKUSAI KAIGI ga okonawarete imasu.
          KAKUJI de kangaeta ue de, HAPPYOO shite kudasai.
          Onoono no IKEN o matomete kudasai.

364   HOSHU-TEKI
          RUSU-CHUU
守   IKEN o KOSHU suru
          HOORITSU o mamoru

          Oji no kangae wa HIJOO ni HOSHU-TEKI desu.
          Kinoo Tanaka-san no ie ni ikimashita ga, RUSU deshita.
          Ueda-san wa itsumo JIBUN no IKEN o KOSHU shimasu.
          KOOTSUU KISOKU o mamoru koto wa TAISETSU desu.

365 増

JINKOO ZOOKA
ZOODAI no ITTO o tadoru
mizu ga KYUUZOO suru
NINZUU ga masu

TOOKYOO no JINKOO wa MAINEN ZOOKA shite imasu.
DENWA no mooshikomi ga ZOODAI shite imasu.
Kono CHIHOO no JUUTAKU wa KYUUZOO shihajimemashita.
KONDO no ooame de kawa no mizu ga mashimashita.

366 待

KITAI hazure
TAIBOO no natsu yasumi
ii TAIGUU
machidooshi

Amari ano hito ni wa KITAI o kakenai HOO ga ii desu.
Sore wa TAIBOO no EIGA desu.
Sono KAISHA no TAIGUU wa totemo ii to omoimasu.
Ato JUUGO-HUN gurai matte mimashoo

367 闘

hageshii TOOSOO
AKUSEN KUTOO

Hageshii TOOSOO no KEKKA, kumiai-gawa ga kachimashita.
SENKYO UNDOO de Hara-shi wa AKUSEN KUTOO shite imasu.

368 映

EIGA-KA suru
EISHAKI
SERON no HAN'EI
me ni utsuru

EIGA o mi ni ikimashoo.
EISHA JIKAN wa ICHI-JIKAN gurai deshoo.
Sono SHIMBUN wa SERON o yoku HAN'EI shite imasu.
Yama ga mizu ni utsutte totemo utsukushii desu.

369 科

KYOOKASHO
KAGAKU-TEKI ni
HOOKA no GAKUSEI
NAIKA ni kakaru

Kore wa KAGAKU no KYOOKASHO desu.
NIJUSSEIKI ni natte KAGAKU ga KYUUSOKU ni HATTATSU shimashita.
Ani wa HOOKA no GAKUSEI de, SHOORAI BENGOSHI ni naru soo desu.
Nishiyama SENSEI wa NAIKA desu ka, GEKA desu ka.

370 限

SEIGEN SOKUDO
GENDO ga aru
GENKAI ni kuru
isogashii toki ni kagitte

Kono basu ni wa NINZUU no SEIGEN ga atte, GOJUU-NIN shika
Donna SHIgoto ni mo GENDO ga arimasu.   (noremasen.
SHIgoto de tsukarete, moo GENKAI ni kite imasu.
Kono ko ni kagitte, sonna koto wa arimasen.

371 SHINJUKU GYOEN
御 GOHATTO de aru
    GO-TSUGOO ga warukereba
    Koyama-KE no ONZOOSHI
    o-kage-sama de

Kinoo Tamiko-san to SHINJUKU GYOEN ni itte kimashita.
Sonna koto wa GOHATTO desu.
Kyoo GO-TSUGOO ga warukereba, MYOONICHI de mo KEKKOO desu.
Ano kata wa Yamada-KE no ONZOOSHI desu.
CHOONAN ga TOOKYOO no KAISHA ni haireta no wa Yoshida-san no o-kage
                                                              (desu.

372 sugureta SAKUHIN
品   SHOOHIN KACHI
    KAISHA no SEIHIN
    shinamono ga kireru
    HIN ga aru

Sheikusupia no SAKUHIN no naka de, dore ga ICHIBAN suki desu ka.
KAISHA de donna SHOOHIN o atsukatte imasu ka.
Atarashii SEIHIN o dondon tsukuru yoo ni kokoro-gakete imasu.
Kono shinamono wa nakanaka te ni hairimasen.
Ano kata wa totemo HIN ga arimasu.

373 KAIKYUU o tsukeru
級   KOOKYUU hoteru
    shitashii KYUUYUU
    SHINKYUU suru

Chichi wa GUNTAI de KAIKYUU ga ue no HOO deshita.
Kinoo GINZA de Itaria no KOOKYUU RYOORI o tabemashita.
Ototoi, machi de battari mukashi no KYUUYUU ni aimashita.
Ani wa DAIGAKU no YONEN ni SHINKYUU shimashita.

374 SAHA to UHA
左   SAYUU ni KI o tsukeru
    SAYOKU-gakaru
    hidari-gawa ni

Sono hito wa SAHA desu ka, UHA desu ka.
SAYUU ni KI o tsukete, michi o watatte kudasai.
Ano GAKUSEI wa SAYOKU-gakatte imasu.
Asoko o hidari ni magareba, migi gawa ni GAKKOO ga arimasu.

375 SHOOGYOO-KA suru
商   SHOOBAI-gara
    SHOOHIN no ureyuki
    SHOOTENGAI
    akinatte aruku

Hara-kun wa SHOOGYOO KOOKOO o dete kara, BOOEKI-GAISHA ni hairimashita.
SAIKIN Kitagawa-san wa SHOOBAI o kaeta soo desu.
KAISHA no SENDEN ga yoi seika, SHOOHIN no ureyuki ga JOOJOO desu.
Kono HEN no SHOOTEN wa yoru KUJI ni shimarimasu.
Ano hito wa nani o akinatte aruite imasu ka.

RYOO no MONGEN 376
BUMON ni wakeru
MONKA-SEI 門
kadode o iwau
SEMMON KAMOKU

RYOO no MONGEN wa JUUJI na no de, moo kaeranakereba narimasen.
Chichi wa SEKKEI no BUMON de hataraite imasu.
Watakushi wa Hirata SENSEI no MONKASEI desu.
Amerika no DAIGAKU ni haitta CHOONAN no kadode o iwaimashita.
DAIGAKU de, ima, SEMMON KAMOKU o BENKYOO shite imasu.

---

shizuka na JUUTAKUCHI 377
GENJUUSHO
Hawai e IJUU suru 住
sumeba miyako

Kono HEN wa SAIKIN JUUTAKU ga huete kimashita.
JUUSHO ga kawattara, o-shirase kudasai.
Oba ga Hawai e IJUU shite kara, moo YONJUUNEN ni narimasu.
Watakushi-tachi wa ima TOOKYOO ni sunde imasu.

SENRYOOGUN 378
DOKUSEN KINSHI HOO
hoshi o uranau 占
CHII o shimeru

Koko wa katsute NIHONGUN ga SENRYOO shita tokoro desu.
Sonna ni hiroi tokoro o DOKUSEN shite wa ikemasen.
Ano hito wa yoku hoshi o uranaimasu.
KYONEN, NIHON no ZOOSEN wa SEKAI de DAIICHII o shimemashita.

TOOMIN no KANGEI 379
Ogasawara SHOTOO
shimaguni KONJOO 島
chiisai shima

TOOMIN no SEIDAI na KANGEI o ukemashita.
Ogasawara SHOTOO wa itsu NIHON ni HUKKI shimashita ka.
NIHON wa NAMPOKU ni hirogaru hosonagai shimaguni desu.
Mukoo no HOO ni kasuka ni mieru shima ga Ooshima desu.

GAMAN-zuyoi 380
JIGA ISHIKI
GARYUU no e 我
wareware no SEDAI

Moo sugu owarimasu kara, GAMAN shite kudasai.
Ano ko wa JIGA no tsuyoi ko desu.
Kono e wa GARYUU de kaita mono desu.
Sore wa hoka de mo nai wareware no MONDAI desu.

381 CHOOKAN no HOSA
佐
Sasaki-san wa Satoo-shi no HOSA desu.

---

382 ZANNEN soo ni
残 ZANSHO ga kibishii
ZANKOKU monogatari
SHIgoto o nokosu
ie ni nokoru

ZANNEN nagara, mada NIKKOO e itta koto ga arimasen.
KOtoshi no ZANSHO wa nakanaka kibishii desu.
Karera wa ZANKOKU ni atsukawareta soo desu.
Ie ni kodomo o nokoshite kimashita.
Kore wa kinoo no nokorimono desu.

---

383 YOOI na koto
易 TAIBEI BOOEKI
EKISHA ni mite morau

YOOI na koto ja arimasen.
NIHON no BOOEKI wa gungun nobite imasu.
Ooki-san wa SHOORAI no UNSEI o EKISHA ni mite moratta soo desu.

---

384 SHAKAITOO UHA
右 SAYUU o mite
UYOKU DANTAI
migite no HOO ni

Dochira ka to ieba, Yamada-kun wa UHA da to omoimasu.
Watakushi wa RYUUKOO ni amari SAYUU saremasen.
Shimabara-san wa UYOKU DANTAI ni wa ZOKUshite imasen.
Migite o agete kudasai.

---

385 KAGAKU no JIKKEN
験 KEIKEN o tsumu
SHIKEN ni ukaru
DAIGAKU o JUKEN suru
TAIKENDAN

Asoko ni JIKKENSHITSU ga arimasu.
KEIKEN ga mada asai desu.
SHIKEN ni ochite, ZANNEN desu.
Doko no DAIGAKU o JUKEN suru tsumori desu ka.
Kinoo omoshiroi koto o taiken shimashita.

---

386 HAKUSHI ROMBUN
士 SHINSHI-TEKI ni
SHIKI o takameru

Otooto wa HAKUSHIGOO o toru tame ni, ISSHOOKEMMEI BENKYOO shite imasu.
Ano kata wa SHINSHI-TEKI de, totemo KANji ga ii kata desu.
SHIKI o ushinawanaide, GAMbatte kudasai.

REKISHI no nagare 387
SENSHU ni natta KEIREKI
RIREKISHO   歴
GAKUREKI ga aru

Motoyama-san wa REKISHI-KA desu.
Harada-san wa SENSEI o shita KEIREKI ga arimasu.
MYOONICHI RIREKISHO o motte kite kudasai.
Ooshita-san wa GAKUREKI ga atte, TAIHEN RIPPA na hito desu.

KOJIN KEIEI 388
EIRI JIGYOO
KEN'EI JUUTAKU   営
mise o itonamu

Kono KAISHA wa dare ga KEIEI shite imasu ka.
Kore wa EIRI JIGYOO ja arimasen.
KEN'EI JUUTAKU ga atarimashita.
Chichi wa chiisana mise o itonande imasu.

SHIMBUN KOOKOKU 389
KOODAI na SHIKICHI
hiroi niwa   広
uwasa ga hirogaru
michi o hirogeru

Kinoo no SHIMBUN KOOKOKU o mimashita ka.
KOODAI na TOCHI ni JUUTAKU ga taterarete imasu.
Ano kata wa KOOSAI ga totemo hiroi desu.
Suzuki-san wa HEN na uwasa o taterare, komatte imasu.
Ima, michi o hirogete iru tokoro desu.

KOMPON-TEKI na MONDAI 390
KONKYO no nai hanashi
DAIKON YAKUSHA   根
ne ni motsu

KOMPON-TEKI ni yarinaosanakereba narimasen.
Sono hanashi ni nani ka KONKYO ga arimasen ka.
Sono hutoi DAIKON wa ikura desu ka.
Yoshida-san wa ne ga SHOOJIKI na hito desu.

JAKKAN no GENRYOO 391
JAKUNEN nagara
ROONYAKU DANJO   若
wakai hito

Mada GENRYOO ga JAKKAN nokotte imasu.
Nemoto-san no itoko wa JAKUNEN de BYOOSHI shimashita.
ROONYAKU DANJO no BETSU naku, dare de mo sono kai ni SHUSSEKI
Wakai kara to itte, karada o MURI shite wa ikemasen.(dekimasu.

392 終 SHUUSENGO
SHUUSHI IKKAN
SHIgoto o oeru
EIGA ga owaru

SHUUSEN TOOJI, chichi wa GAICHI ni imashita.
Sono hanashi o SHUUSHI KINCHOO shite kikimashita.
CHOODO SHOKUJI o oeta tokoro desu.
Moo JUGYOO ga owarimashita.

---

393 青 SEINENKAI
SEISHUN o tanoshimu
aoba no kaoru natsu
aoi sora

Kono machi no SEINENKAI wa KAPPATSU desu.
SEISHUN JIDAI wa HONTOO ni tanoshii mono desu.
Aoba no KISETSU ga DAISUKI desu.
Kono banana wa mada aoi desu.

---

394 談 NICHIBEI KAIDAN
SOODAN ga matomaru
JOODAN bakari

KONDO no NICHIBEI KAIDAN wa itsu desu ka.
SENSEI ni SOODAN shite kudasai.
Ano hito wa JOODAN bakari itte imasu.

---

395 料 NIHON RYOORI
ZAIRYOO o kau
GENRYOO ga hairu
KENKYUU no SHIRYOO

NIHON RYOORI o tabetari, SEIYOO RYOORI o tabetari shimasu.
SHUGEI no ZAIRYOO o katte kimashita.
GENRYOO ga sukoshi tarinai no de, sugu SHIirenakereba narimasen.
Ima, JINRUIGAKU no KENKYUU no SHIRYOO o atsumete iru tokoro desu.

---

396 込 nikomi o-den
KANSEI no mikomi
mikomareru

Watakushi wa nikomi udon ga DAISUKI desu.
Kono tatemono wa RAINEN no GOGATSU made ni KANSEI suru mikomi desu.
Hirota-BUCHOO wa SHACHOO ni mikomarete imasu.
Tonde mo nai koto o shite, ane ni yarikomeraremashita.

---

397 圧 ATTOO-TEKI ni
DANTAI no ATSURYOKU
DAN'ATSU o ukeru

Aite ga tsuyoi no de, SHUUSHI ATTOO sareta SHIAI ni narimashita.
Ue yori ATSURYOKU ga kakarimashita.
SENJICHUU, Kirisuto-KYOO wa SEIHU no DAN'ATSU o ukemashita.
Minami-san wa SHIgoto ni APPAKU o KANjite, noirooze-GIMI desu.

---

398 告 HOOKOKU o ukeru
tsumi no KOKUHAKU
CHUUKOKU o ukeru
wakare o tsugeru

SHUTCHOO shita Komatsu-BUCHOO kara, kinoo HOOKOKU ga arimashita.
HANNIN no KOKUHAKU ni yoreba, sono JIKEN wa mayonaka ni
        okotta mono desu.
Uchi no ko wa SENSEI ni CHUUKOKU sarete kara, SUnao ni
        narimashita.
Tsugeguchi o shite wa ikemasen.

```
                CHOKUSETSU hanasu                                          399
                KANSETSU-TEKI ni
                MENSETSU SHIKEN                                            接

                Kinoo CHOKUSETSU SENSEI ni atte hanashimashita.
                KANSETSU-TEKI ni sono hanashi o kikimashita.
                Ashita KAISHA no MENSETSU SHIKEN ga arimasu.
```

```
                HU-RENZOKUSEN                                              400
                SOOZOKUKEN
                KEIZOKU-TEKI na SHIgoto                                    続
                huritsuzuku
                KENKYUU o tsuzukeru

                Watakushi wa MAINICHI terebi de RENZOKU KATEI dorama o
                        mite imasu.
                Oji wa SOOZOKUNIN to shite, TAKUSAN ZAISAN o moraimashita.
                Nan to ka kono SHIgoto o KEIZOKU sasetai to omoimasu.
                Moo ame ga mikka mo tsuzuite hutte imasu.
                Kono KENKYUU o ato NINEN mo tsuzuketara, Amerika e wataru
                        tsumori desu.
```

```
                NAMBOKU ni hirogaru                                        401
                NANKYOKU KANSOKUTAI
                NANYOO no shimajima                                        南
                Minami Amerika

                Amerika no NAMBOKU SENSOO wa, DOREI KAIHOO no SENSOO to shite
                        YUUMEI desu.
                Suzuki-san wa, KANSOKU TAIIN to shite, NANKYOKU ni ETTOO
                        shite imasu.
                Yashi no ki wa, NAN'YOO no DAIHYOO-TEKI no ki da to omoimasu.
                Burajiru wa, Minami Amerika de, ICHIBAN ookii kuni desu.
```

```
                NAIYOO-TEKI ni mite                                        402
                YOOI na SHIgoto
                BIYOOIN                                                    容
                RIYOO GAKKOO

                SHIgoto no NAIYOO wa amari omoshiroku arimasen.
                JISSAI ni yaru no wa YOOI de wa arimasen.
                Haha wa, MAINICHI, ie de BIYOO TAISOO o shite imasu.
                RIYOOSHI ni naru no wa muzukashii desu ka.
```

```
                yasashii SEIKAKU                                           403
                KAKAKU no KETTEI
                RIYOOSHI no SHIKAKU                                        格
                JINKAKU o omonzuru

                Kodomo wa, yaru koto nasu koto ni, sunao ni SEIKAKU o
                        arawashimasu.
                SAIKIN, TAISHUUSHA no KAKAKU ga sukoshi yasuku narimashita.
                Hayaku KANGOHU no SHIKAKU ga torereba ii to omotte imasu.
                Hukuzawa SENSEI no JINKAKU ni kokoro o hikaremashita
```

```
                KOOMUIN no KYUUYO                                          404
                KYOOKYUU no HUSOKU
                KYUURYOOBI                                                 給

                NENNEN, KOOMUIN no KYUUYO wa yoku natte imasu.
                Hideri ga tsuzuite, mizu no KYOOKYUU ni komatte imasu.
                KAISHA no KYUURYOOBI wa MAItsuki NIJUU-GO NICHI desu.
```

405 色

utsukushii KESHIKI
KESSHOKU ga ii
TOKUSHOKU no aru GAKKOO
kaoiro o ukagau

Kono e o miru to, inaka o omoidashimasu.
Minami-san wa, SHOKUJI ga susunde, KESSHOKU mo yoku natte
　　　　kita soo desu.
Kono GAKKOO wa JOSEITO ga ooi no ga TOKUSHOKU desu.
Yooko-san wa GUai ga waruku, kaoiro mo yoku arimasen.

406 赤

NIHON SEKIJUUJI-SHA
SEKIDOO CHOKKA
SEKIMEN no itari
akaJI ZAISEI

KOKUSAI SEKIJUUJI wa totemo yoi SOSHIKI desu.
Hune de SEKIDOO o tootta toki, SEKIDOO matsuri o shimashita.
Hito o SEKIMEN saseru yoo na koto o itte wa ikemasen.
UN'EI ga KONNAN na no de, akaJI ni natte shimaimashita.
Akai hana ga KIREI ni saite imasu.

407 撃

KOOGEKI o KAISHI suru
BAKUGEKI-ON
DAGEKI o ukeru

KYOOSANgawa no KOOGEKI ga hageshiku natta yoo desu.
Ano kuruma no ato wa, marude BAKUGEKI-ON desu.
Yamaguchi-san ni KAISHA o yamerarete, SHIgoto ni ooki na DAGEKI o
　　　　ukemashita.

408 元

GENKI na ko
GANJITSU SOOSOO
KIGENZEN

Inaka no o-jii-san wa GENKI ni kurashite imasu.
GANJITSU ni, kodomo-tachi wa, o-toshidama o moraimashita.
Babiron TEIKOKU wa, KIGENZEN no NANSEIKI goro deshita ka.

409 早

SASSOKU desu ga
SOOJUKU na ko
hayaGATEN suru

Kyoo tsuita koniMOTSU, SASSOKU tori ni ukagaimasu.
Ano ko wa SOOJUKU de, amari iu koto ga KANSHIN shimasen.
HayaGATEN shite, tonde mo nai SHIPPAI o shite shimaimashita.

410 着

kimono no uraomote
CHAKUJITSUSEI o motte
SENCHAKUJUN

Watakushi wa doresu yori kimono no HOO ga Nihon-TEKI de, totemo
　　　　suki desu.
CHIKATETSU no KOOJI wa CHAKUJITSU ni SHINKOO shite imasu.
SHITEIseki ga nai no de, SENCHAKUJUN ni yoi seki ga toreru soo desu.

411 洋

SEIYOOSHIKI
TOOYOOHUU
kon no YOOHUKU

RAINEN wa ZEHI SEIYOO-SHOKOKU o RYOKOO shite mitai to omoimasu.
NihonGA wa, TOOYOO BIJUTSU no naka de mo DAIHYOO-TEKI na mono desu.
Kon no YOOHUKU ga niau no de, SENJITSU GINZA no mise de
　　　　atsuraemashita.

```
                    JOOIN GIIN                                          412
                    BYOOIN no SETSUBI
                    NYUUIN KANJA                                         院
                    DAIGAKUIN-SEI

         Amerika no GIKAI SEIDO wa JOOIN to KAIN ni wakarete imasu.
         Otooto wa, GENZAI, TOODAI BYOOIN ni NYUUIN shite imasu.
         Hayakawa-san ga NYUUIN shite kara, moo maru hitotsuki
              ni narimasu.
         DAIGAKUIN de, ima, SHOOWA BUNGAKU no KENKYUU ni torikunde
              imasu.
```

```
                    MEIENZETSU                                          413
                    KOOENKAI
                    MEIENSOOKA                                           演

         Nagai ENZETSU wa moo korigori desu.              (masu.
         Yamashita SENSEI no KOOEN wa, Hibiya KOOKAIDOO de okonaware-
         KOMBAN piano no ENSOOKAI ga arimasu no de, issho ni
              ikimasen ka.
```

```
                    JIBUN no YAKUwari                                   414
                    wariai JOOZU ni
                    TOchi no BUNKATSU                                    割
                    waribikiKEN
                    monogoto o warikiru

         JIBUN no YAKUwari o hatashite, hotto shimashita.  (mashita.
         KONDO no SENKYO de wa, wariai RAKU ni katsu koto ga deki-
         Terebi to REIZOOKO o BUNKATSU-barai de kaimashita.
         Itsumo monogoto wa, warikitte kangaeru koto ni shite imasu.
```

```
                    tachiiri KINSHI                                     415
                    SUIGAIBOOSHI TAISAKU
                    SHIaiCHUUSHI                                         止
                    SEIDO no HAISHI

         Kono TOchi wa, SOKURYOO no tame tachiiri KINSHI ni natte
         SUIGAIBOOSHI TAISAKU ga mookeraremashita.        (imasu.
         Ame no tame, SHIai ga CHUUSHI ni narimashita.
         Warui SEIDO wa HAISHI shinakereba narimasen.
         Kuruma o tomete, sukoshi yasunde kara ikimashoo.
```

```
                    CHISHIKI KAIKYUU                                    416
                    NINSHIKI-BUSOKU
                    JOOSHIKI o kaku                                      識

         Watakushi wa, iroiro na CHISHIKI o mi ni tsuketai desu.
         Moo sukoshi NINSHIKI ga areba, yokatta to omoimasu.
         Ano kata no KOODOO wa JOOSHIKI o kaite imasu.
```

417 種
ISSHU no HENKEN
SHUJU no MONDAI
KAKUSHURUI
JINSHU-SABETSU
hitotsubu-dane

Abebe SENSHU no hashirikata wa, ISSHU DOKUTOKU desu.
SHUJU no KOOZAN SHOKUBUTSU o atsumete KENKYUU shite imasu.
Sakura no hana wa ZEMBU de nan SHURUI arimasu ka.
JINSHU MONDAI wa Amerika ni totte, ooki na MONDAI to ieru deshoo.
Kazu-chan wa, hitotsubu-dane de minna ni kawaigararete imasu.

418 処
TAIGAKU SHOBUN
OSUI no SHORI
MONDAI ni TAISHO suru

Kare wa KAGEKI na GAKUSEI datta no de, TAIGAKU SHOBUN ni narimashita.
Sono MONDAI wa moo SHORI shite shimaimashita.
Dono yoo ni TAISHO shitara yoi ka, wakarimasen.

419 勝
SHOORI TOOSHU
SHOOHAI o kimeru
katte kimama

Minna no DANKETSU ga SHOORI o motarashita no desu.
SHOOHAI ga kimaranai mama, hikiwake ni narimashita.
JIBUN katte na koto bakari shite wa ikemasen.
Katte mo, makete mo, SAIGO made gambaranakereba narimasen.

420 敗
HAIBOKU no KEKKA
HAISENGO
HUHAI shita SEIJI
DAISHIPPAI

HAIBOKU no GEN'IN wa RENSHUU-BUSOKU datta kara desu.
GUNJI-TEKI ni tsuyokatta dake ni, HAISEN no itade wa ookikatta desu.
Dare demo SHIPPAI wa suru mono desu.
Honno wazuka no SA de, SHIai ni yaburemashita.

421 回
KAIHUKU no ori
KAITOO o motomeru
KONKAI no SENKYO

SHUJUTSUGO no KAIHUKU o matte, SHACHOO ni hanasu tsumori desu.
KAISHA-gawa ni ikura motomete mo, KAITOO ga eraremasen deshita.
KONKAI no kyampu wa totemo tanoshikatta no de, mata RAINEN iku tsumori
Chiisai toki, yoku koma o mawashite asobimashita.   (desu.

422 及
KYUUDAITEN
HUKYUURITSU
oyobi mo tsukanai

Nan to ka KYUUDAITEN wa, toranakereba narimasen.
Nihon no terebi no HUKYUURITSU wa, TAIHEN takaku narimashita.
Oyobazu nagara, nan to ka yatte mimashoo.

KOOHUKU na KATEI 423
HUKOO na kodomo
KOOUN na hito
saiwai ni mo

幸

Sachiko-san ga KOOHUKU de atta to wa, ichigai ni wa iemasen.
Sono ko wa, JIKO de RYOOSHIN o nakushita HUKOO na kodomo
    nan desu.
KOOUN ni mo, KONDO Yooroppa e RYOKOO suru koto ni narimashita.
Rondon de, Ooyama-san ni aete saiwai deshita.

SHINKOKU na JITAI 424
IMI SHINCHOO
hukai umi

深

KOOGAI wa SHINKOKU na MONDAI ni natte imasu.
Ano kata no itta kotoba wa, nakanaka IMI SHINCHOO desu.
Tazawa-KO wa, Nihon de ICHIBAN hukai mizuumi desu.

SAIGO no SHUDAN 425
ima no DANKAI de wa
DANDAN-batake
KAIDAN o noboru

段

Doo SHIYOO mo nai no de, SAIGO no SHUDAN o toru koto ni shi-
Ima no DANKAI de wa, mada HAPPYOO dekimasen.   (mashita.
DoitsuGO ga DANDAN hanaseru yoo ni nari, totemo omoshiroi desu.
KAIDAN kara suberiochite, ooKEGA o shimashita.

HANDAN o ayamaru 426
DANTEI o kudasu
OODAN HODOO
kotowari naku

断

HANDAN o ayamatte, tonde mo nai SHIPPAI o shite shimaimashita.
Sugu ni DANTEI o kudasu wake ni wa ikimasen.
Michi o OODAN suru toki wa, ki o tsukenakereba narimasen.
Sonna koto wa, o-kotowari shimasu.

HAKAI-TEKI KOOI 427
INSHUU no DAHA
YAKUSOKU o yaburu

破

Kono machi wa, SENSOO de miru kage mo naku HAKAI saremashita.
Warui SHUUKAN wa, DAHA shite ikanakereba narimasen.
YAKUSOKU wa, itsumo yaburanai yoo ni shite imasu.

SAIGAI o husegu 428
SHINTAI SHOOGAISHA
SUIGAI TAISAKU
DAIHIGAI

害

con'd

428 JIZEN ni, SAIGAI o husegu yoo ni ki o tsukemashoo.
con'd Ano kata wa GENGO SHOOGAI no tame, chiisai toki kara, TAIHEN
害   KUROO sarete iru soo desu.
   Kono HEN wa, KYONEN no TAIHUU de SUIGAI o ukemashita.
   Kinoo no KASAI de, KAISHA wa ooki na HIGAI o koomurimashita.

---

429 KEMPOO KAISEI
憲
   GOGATSU mikka wa, KEMPOO KI'NEMBI de, SAIJITSU ni natte imasu.

---

430 yoi JOOTAI
     GENJOO IJI
状   JOOKYOO HANDAN

   Ima no JOOTAI de wa, RAINEN TOBEI dekiru ka doo ka wakarimasen.
   CHOOSADAN ga GENJOO o shirabe ni kimashita.
   GENZAI no JOOKYOO de wa MURI mo arimasen.

---

431 ooki na SONZAI
     IZONSEI ga tsuyoi
存   HOZONBUTSU

   Uchihara-san wa, EIGYOOBU de KICHOO na SONZAI desu.
   Moo ICHININmae na no de, oya ni IZON shinai SEIKATSU o shite imasu.
   Amari nagaku HOZON shinaide, meshiagatta HOO ga yoroshii desu.

---

432 hujiiro no YOOHUKU
     huji no hana
藤
   Katoo-san wa, YOOHUKUYA ni itte, hujiiro no wanpiisu o kaimashita.

---

433 TOCHI no BAIBAI
     KAOKU no BAISHUU
買   kaimono no memo
     HON o kau

   ICHIba de wa, asa hayaku kara, YASAI no BAIBAI ga okonawaremasu.
   Kono TOCHI wa BAISHUU sareru koto ni narimashita.
   Kaimono o suru toki, memo o motte iru to BENRI desu.
   O-miyage ni nani o kattara yoi ka, mada kimete imasen.

---

434 SENKYOKEN
     SAIKENKYO
挙   KYOSHIKI o ageru

   KONKAI no SENKYO wa, mare ni miru GEKISEN deshita.
   KENKYO sareta mono no naka ni wa, na no shirareta hito mo imashita.
   RAINEN no GOGATSU ni, Haruko-san-tachi wa, KYOSHIKI o ageru koto ni
         kimatta soo desu.

KETTEI-TEKI na DAGEKI 435
NAIKAKU no DATOO
DASAN-TEKI
打

Sutoraiki ga nagabikeba, KAISHA-gawa ni totte ooki na
    DAGEKI desu.
YATOO wa, NAIKAKU no DATOO o mezashite HISSHI desu.
Amari DASAN-TEKI na no de, kanoJO wa minna kara iyagararete
    imasu.

BUTAI SOOCHI 436
DAIdokoro no KAIZOO
DODAI no SHUURI
TAIHUU no me
台

HatsuBUTAI o itsu humimashita ka.
SAIKIN no ie wa, DAIdokoro ga modan ni narimashita.
Amari ie ga hurui no de, DODAI kara shikkari naosanakereba
    narimasen.
Natsu no owari ni wa, kanarazu to itte ii hodo, Nihon wa
    TAIHUU ni osowaremasu.

KONNAN na SAGYOO 437
HINKON TAISAKU
HENJI ni komaru
困

SHIgoto ni wa KONNAN ga tsukimono desu.
SEIHU wa HINKON TAISAKU ni noridashimashita.
O-kane ga nakute komarimashita.

KATEI KYOOSHI 438
ISHI no SHINDAN
Yamamoto-SHI
師

Ano kata wa, moo SANJUUNEN mo KYOOSHI o shite imasu.
NYUUSHA suru tame ni, ISHI no SHINDANSHO ga HITSUYOO desu.
KOOSHI ni Yoshida-SHI o maneite imasu.

SEISHIN HAKUJAKU 439
UNCHIN no SEISAN
精

Amari SHIgoto ga ooi no de, chichi wa SEISHIN-TEKI ni
    tsukarete imasu.
Norikoshi no UNCHIN o doko de SEISAN shitara yoroshii desu ka.

HOOSOOKYOKU 440
UNSOOTEN
SOOGEIKAI
purezento o okuru
送

Yuube no HOOSOO de, sono JIKEN o shirimashita.
Kuruma de UNSOO shita baai, nanNICHI gurai kakarimasu ka.
Kinoo, hurui SENSEI to atarashii SENSEI no SOOGEIKAI ga
    arimashita.
Tookyoo ni iru otooto ni, o-kane o okurimashita.

441　ZOOSEN-GAISHA
造　JINTAI no KOOZOO
　　SEIZOO moto
　　tatemono no KAIZOO
　　SOOZOORYOKU
　　ie o tsukuru

Nihon no ZOOSEN wa SEKAI-TEKI ni YUUMEI desu.
Kinoo katta HON wa, JIDOOSHA no KOOZOO ni tsuite no HON desu.
Watakushi no KAISHA de wa, o-mocha no SEIZOO o shite imasu.
HEYA o KAIZOO shimashita no de, itsuka mi ni kite kudasai.
SEISHO ni wa, TENCHI no SOOZOO ga shirusarete imasu.
Yamamoto-san no tsukutta ie wa, nakanaka modan desu.

442　mori-DAKUSAN
沢　KOOTAKU no aru ishi

SHOOTAI sareta tokoro, mori-DAKUSAN no go-CHISOO ga YOOI sarete
　　arimashita.
Kono shinamono wa, KIN-mekki shite KOOTAKU o dashita mono desu.

443　TOSHI no HATTEN
展　TENKAI suru KESHIKI
　　KOOSHOO ga SHINTEN suru

Kono machi wa, koko NI, SANNEN de ichijirushiku HATTEN shimashita.
GANKA ni TENKAI suru KESHIKI wa, JITSU ni subarashikatta desu.
KOOGAI wa, ooki na SHAKAI MONDAI ni SHINTEN shimashita.

444　YUSHUTSUHIN
輸　YU'NYUUZEI
　　TARYOO no YUKETSU

Kinu no YUSHUTSU wa, kono tokoro MAItoshi GENSHOO shitsutsu arimasu.
YU'NYUU CHOOKA o megutte, SEIHU wa RINJI KAIGI o hirakimashita.
SHUJUTSU ga ookikatta no de, ano kata wa TARYOO no YUKETSU o shita
　　soo desu.

445　RIKUGUN SHIREIKAN
陸　TAIRIKUSEI KIKOO
　　JOORIKU no JUMBI

Chichi wa moto RIKUGUN SHOOSA deshita ga, ima wa DAIGAKU KYOOJU desu.
Oosawa-san wa, nagai aida CHUUGOKU ni ita sei ka, TAIRIKUTEKI na
　　KANji no suru hito desu.
JOORIKU o MOKUZEN ni hikae, TAIHUU ni mimaware, hune wa ayauku
　　shizumi-soo ni narimashita.

446　HEN na KOOI
為　hito no tame o omotte

Anata no KOOI wa, yoi KEKKA o umimashita.
Minna no tame ni naru yoo na SHIgoto o shitai to omotte imasu.

SHOORAI YUUBOO 447
DAISHOOGUN
SHOOGI-daoshi   将
RIKUGUN TAISHOO

SHOORAISEI no aru SHIgoto o, korekara wa, mi ni tsuketa
         HOO ga ii desu.
Tokugawa Ieyasu wa, Sekigahara no tatakai no nochi,
         SEII TAISHOOGUN to natte SEIKEN o nigirimashita.
DENSHA ga KYUU ni tomatta no de, minna wa SHOOGI-daoshi
         ni narimashita.
Ano ko wa KINJO no gaki-DAISHOO desu.

SHOOKOHIN 448
HOSHOOtsuki
HIKOKU no SHOOGEN   証
SEISEKI SHOOMEISHO

SAIBAN no toki, KENSATSU-gawa wa HIKOKU no SHOOKOHIN o
         narabemashita.
Kono shinamono wa HOSHOO-zuki desu kara, ANSHIN shite
         tsukau koto ga dekimasu.
SAIBANCHOO ga HIKOKU no SHOOGEN o motomemashita.
DAIGAKU e SHINGAKU suru tame ni wa, KOOKOO no SEISEKI
         SHOOMEISHO ga HITSUYOO desu.

Nihon KOKUYUU TETSUDOO 449
TEKKOOGYOO   鉄

Nihon KOKUYUU TETSUDOO o RYAKU shite, KOKUTETSU to
         yonde imasu.
Chichi wa KAISHA no TEKKOO DAIIKKA de hataraite imasu.

HIKAKU ni naranu hodo 450
HAMPIREI   比

Amerika to HIKAKU shite, Nihon no JINKOO MITSUDO wa
         monosugoku takai desu.
Otooto wa, ima, GAKKOO de HIREI to HAMPIREI no HOOSHIKI o
         BENKYOO shite imasu.
KONDO dekita biru wa, ima made no ni kurabemono ni narimasen.

---

omoigakenai YUUJIN 451
GAKKOO no tomodachi
YUUKOO KANKEI   友
utsukushii YUUJOO
                                      (mashita.
SAKUJITSU DENSHA no naka de, omoigakenai YUUJIN ni deai-
YAKYUU no SHIai o, tomodachi to ISSHO ni mi ni ikimashita.
Nihon to Chuugoku no YUUKOO KANKEI ga, yoku natte kimashita.
Ano hutari wa, utsukushii YUUJOO de musubarete imasu.

452 領 SENRYOO shita TOCHI
DAITOORYOO SENKYO
TOO no KOORYOO

Nagai aida SENRYOO sarete ita TOCHI ga, HENKAN saremashita.
Amerika no DAITOORYOO SENKYO wa, yoNEN ni ICHIDO okonawaremasu.
TOO no KOORYOO o matomeageru no ni, ISSHUUKAN kakarimashita.

---

453 規 YUUBINBUTSU no KITEI
DAIKIBO na SOOSA
KISOKU tadashii

KYUURYOO wa KAISHA no KITEI ni shitagatte SHIharawaremasu.
Mada kono SHIgoto no KIBO wa chiisai desu ga, kore kara DANDAN
    ookiku naru deshoo.
KISOKU tadashii SEIKATSU o shite ireba, karada c kowasanakute
    sumu deshoo.

---

454 警 KEISATSU SHOCHOO
HUJIN KEIKAN
KEIKAI TAISEI

KONDO, KEISATSU no SHOCHOO ga kawarimashita.
Kono mae no demo de wa, KEIKANTAIgawa ni mo, kanari HUSHOOSHA
    ga deta soo desu.
GOKUAKU HANNIN no SOOSA ni wa, KEIKAI ga TOKU ni HITSUYOO desu.

---

455 個 KOJIN no IKEN

MINSHU-SHUGI no SHAKAI de wa, KOJIN no IKEN ga SONCHOO sarete
                                                        imasu.

---

456 紙 natsukashii tegami
SHIMBUN SHIJOO

Inaka no haha kara, natsukashii tegami o uketorimashita.
Sono MONDAI wa, SHIJOO de kanari hageshiku tatakarete imashita.
Kaimono ni itta tsuide ni, SHITSU no ii kami o GO, ROKUMAI
        katte kite kudasai.

---

457 授 DAIGAKU no KYOOJU
JUGYOO no NAIYOO
HAKUSHIGOO o sazukaru
SHUGEI o sazukeru

Hujimoto-san wa, dansu KYOOSHUUJO de, ima, tappu dansu no
    KYOOJU o ukete iru soo desu.
Hino SENSEI no JUGYOO no NAIYOO wa, totemo KOODO desu.
Ano utsukushii koe wa, TEN kara sazukatta mono deshoo.
Uchi no ko wa ashi ga HUJIYUU na no de, SHUGEI o sazukete
        moratte imasu.

SHOOHICHI SHOOKA huryoo hi ga kieru DENKI o kesu		458 消 (mashita.

SHOOHISHA no IKEN o SANKOO ni shita SHINSEIHIN ga, uridasare-
TOKAKU TAIRYOKU ga yowatte iru toki ni, SHOOKA HURYOO ga
        okoriyasui desu.
DENKI ga kietari, tsuitari shite imasu.
Yoku hi o keshite kara, yasunde kudasai.

SAIDAI no CHUUI   459
CHUUMOKU no mato
CHUUMON no shinamono   注
mizu o sosogu

Ame no hi no UNTEN ni wa, SAIDAI no CHUUI ga HITSUYOO desu.
Aporo JUUICHI-GOO wa, SEKAI no hitobito no CHUUMOKU no
        mato ni narimashita.
CHUUMON no shinamono o, o-todoke ni mairimashita.
MAIasa ROKUJI ni okite, hana ni mizu o sosoide imasu.

IPPAN no hitobito   460
ZEMPAN-TEKI ni   般

IPPAN no hitobito wa, JOONAI ni hairu koto ga dekimasen.
ZEMPAN-TEKI ni mite, madamada KAIZEN sarenakereba narimasen.

BUKI to suru   461
BUSOO KEIKAN
BUSHIDOO   武

Minna te ni te ni BUKI o motte tatakaimashita.
KEIKAN no BUSOO ga monomonoshii no de, nanigoto ga
        okotta no ka to omoimashita.
"BUSHI ni NIGON nashi" to iwarete imasu.

ICHIOKUNIN   462
                              億
Nihon no JINKOO wa ICHIOKUNIN o koemashita.

JITSUGEN no KANOOSEI   463
KYOKA no SHINSEI   可

Yoi AN desu ga, KANOOSEI ga usui desu.
SHINSEI shite KYOKA o morawanakereba, sono KAIKAN wa
        SHIYOO dekimasen.

---

ikuNIN ka no hitobito   464

IkuNIN ka no hitobito wa, SAICO made JIBUN no IKEN o   幾
        SHUCHOO shimashita.

465 HOOKOO SHIJIKI

示　　SENSEI no SHIJI o aoida ue de, KESSHIN suru tsumori desu.
　　　BUCHOO to yoku shimeshi awasete kara, SHOODAN ni OOzuru koto
　　　　　　　ni shimasu.

---

466 MANZOKUKAN
　　　MANSHUU TETSUDOO
満　　HUHEI HUMAN
　　　shio ga michiru

　　　MANZOKU ni SHIgoto mo dekinaide, doo suru no desu ka.
　　　Chichi wa, SENZEN, MANSHUU de JIGYOO o shite imashita.
　　　Ano ko wa itsumo HUHEI bakari itte imasu ga, nani ka HUMAN
　　　　　　　na no kashira.
　　　MAN'IN DENSHA o itsumo sakete, noru yoo ni shite imasu.
　　　Shio ga michiru no o mita koto ga arimasu ka.

---

467 mata to nai KIKAI

又　　Kono hanashi wa mata no KIKAI ni itashimashoo.

---

468 YOhodo no CHUUI
　　　YOYUU tappuri
余　　hanashiai no YOCHI
　　　YOKEI na o-SEWA

　　　Kono HEN wa abunai desu kara, YOhodo no CHUUI ga HITSUYOO desu.
　　　Moo sugu SHIai to iu no ni, YOYUU MANMAN desu.
　　　Madamada hanashiai no YOCHI ga aru to omoimasu.
　　　Machigatte, sukoshi YOKEI ni haratte shimaimashita.
　　　JIKAN ga sukoshi amatta no de, ashita no YOSHUU o shimashita.

---

469 KOOGI NAIYOO
　　　KOOENKAI
講　　KOOWA JOOYAKU

　　　KOOGI NAIYOO ga totemo muzukashii no de, yoku kikanakereba
　　　　　　　wakarimasen.
　　　SENSEI no KOOENKAI ga, ashita Kanda no KYOORITSU KOODOO de aru
　　　　　　　soo desu.
　　　Itsu KOOWA JOOYAKU ga musubareta ka, oboete imasu ka.

---

470 SATSUJINHAN
　　　JISATSU MISUI
殺　　iki o korosu

　　　　　　　　　　　　　　　　　　　　　　　　　　　　(imasu.
　　　KEISATSU de wa, SENGETSU okotta SATSUJIN JIKEN o CHOOSA shite
　　　Ano kata no GO-SHUJIN wa, BYOOKI ni nayande, TETSUDOO JISATSU
　　　　　　　o shita soo desu.
　　　Jitto iki o koroshite, sono ba o mimamorimashita.

KitaCHOOSEN no hitobito 471
SHINSEN na YASAI
(imasu. 鮮
NISSEKI o TSUUjite, KitaCHOOSEN e kaetta hito ga TAKUSAN
SHINSEN na YASAI o, dekiru dake ooku tabeta HOO ga
yoroshii desu.

TEIAN ga tooru 472
ROORYOKU o TEIKYOO suru
TEISHUTSU KIGEN 提
ZENTEI to suru

TEIAN ga tootte, iyoiyo JIKKOO sareru koto ni narimashita.
ROORYOKU o TEIKYOO shite moratta no de, kono SHIgoto wa
wariai hayaku owarimashita.
Repooto no TEISHUTSU KIGEN ga sematte imasu.
BEIKA SHINGIKAI wa, SEISANSHA to SHOOHISHA no IKEN o ZENTEI
to shite SHINGI shimashita.

GEN'AN no KENTOO 473
tadachi ni KENKYO suru
KENSATSUKAN 検
TANKENKA

Sono KEN ni tsuite wa, yoku KENTOO suru HITSUYOO ga arimasu.
Ano hito wa nusumi no GENKOOHAN de, tadachi ni KENKYO
saremashita.
KENSATSUgawa wa, SHOOKOBUKKEN ni tsuite surudoku TSUIKYUU
shimashita.
Roojaa-san wa, JUUNEN mae, Ahurika TANKENTAI ni kuwawatte
itta soo desu.

YOOGOSHA 474
HOGOSHA
BENGOSHI 護

YUUJIN no tachiBA o YOOGO shite agemashita.
Inaka kara dete kita JUUYONSAI no onna no ko wa, KEISATSU
ni HOGO saremashita.
Nan to ittara yoi ka, BENGO ni kurushimimashita.

SHIKYUU DEMPOO 475
ICHIMEI NAISHI NIMEI
KONNICHI ni itaru 至

Kinoo haha kara DEMPOO ga ari, SHIKYUU kaeranakereba narimasen.
ICHIMEI NAISHI NIMEI no KYUUJIN KOOKOKU ga arimashita.
Kinoo ni itatte, sono SHINSOO ga hakkiri shimashita.

---

atarashii YOOHUKU 476
GAKKOO no SEIHUKU
oya ni HUKUJUU suru 服
con'd

476 con'd 服
ISSAKUJITSU, depaato de atarashii YOOHUKU o kaimashita.
KOOKOO no NYUUGAKU SHIKEN ni ukattara, sugu SEIHUKU o kau tsumori desu.
Sono BAai, oya no IKEN ni HUKUJUU subeki da to omoimasu.

477 返
tegami no HENJI
SHAKKIN o kaesu
moto no SHOKUGYOO ni kaeru

Ashita made ni, hakkiri shita HENJI ga itadakitai n desu.
Ano hito kara, mada, o-kane o kaeshite moratte imasen.
Arai-san wa, mae no SHIgoto ni kaetta soo desu.

478 略
SHINRYAKU sareta RYOODO
Nihon no SENRYAKU
BUNSHOO no CHUURYAKU
RYAKUshite kaku

KYOOSANKOKU kara no SHINRYAKUSHA to YUUKAN ni tatakaimashita.
SENRYAKU wa SHOOHAI no ooki na pointo desu.
Kono BUN o CHUURYAKU shite kaite mo ii desu ka.
Ano hito no JI wa amari RYAKUshite iru no de, totemo yomi-nikui desu.

479 良
RYOOSHIN-TEKI
TOCHI no KAIRYOO
HURYOOHIN

Kono shinamono wa RYOOSHIN-TEKI ni dekite imasu.
Madamada KAIRYOO no YOCHI ga arimasen.
HURYOOHIN wa nozoite kudasai.

480 類
JINRUIGAKU
hana no SHURUI

GENSUIBAKU wa JINRUI o HAMETSU ni michibiku KIKEN ga arimasu.
Ano hito wa hana no SHURUI o TAKUSAN shitte imasu.

481 楽
SHUUKYOO ONGAKU
GAKKI o tsukau
tanoshii hitotoki
KYUUKA o tanoshimu

Ashita no ONGAKUKAI ni ISSHO ni tsurete itte itadakemasen ka.
GAKKIYA de, otooto wa gitaa o katte kimashita.
ICHINENJUU de natsu wa, watakushi ni totte ICHIBAN tanoshii KISETSU desu.
Dono yoo ni shitara, KYUUKA o tanoshimi nagara, YUUIGI ni sugoseru ka to kangaete imasu.

BISHOO o ukaberu   482
ookina waraigoe
hito ni warawareru   笑

YUUJIN no Matsuda-san wa, itsumo BISHOO o ukabete imasu.
Asoko de ooki na waraigoe de hanashite iru kata wa, donata
Sonna koto o suru to, hito ni warawaremasu.   (desu ka.

SHOOCHIKUBAI no MOYOO   483
umiBE no matsubayashi   松

o-SHOOGATSU ni SHOOCHIKUBAI no ikebana o kazarimasu.
Watakushi no ie no chikaku ni ooki na matsubayashi ga arimasu.

---

dare hitori to shite   484
dare ka   誰

Dare hitori to shite soko e ikitagarimasen.
Dare ka oide ni narimashita ka.

GEN'IN KEKKA   485
                                                          因
Nani ka GEN'IN ga nakereba, sonna koto wa okoru hazu ga ari
                                                  (masen.

YUUMEI na KAJIN   486
KABUKI o miru
suki na uta   歌
RYUUKOOKA o utau

Yosano Akiko wa watakushi no suki na KAJIN desu.
KABUKI wa huruku kara aru Nihon no GEIJUTSU desu.
Suki na uta kara nanKYOKU ka erande hiite kudasai.
Uta o utau no wa doomo nigate desu.

BOORYOKU ni yoru KAKUMEI   487
KYOOIKU no KAIKAKU
KAKUSHINHA no hitobito   革

BOORYOKU ni yoru KAKUMEI o kuudetaa to iimasu.
NIJUUISSEIKI ni okeru KYOOIKU no KAIKAKU ga sakebarete imasu.
KAKUSEI ni wa KAKUSHINHA ga ooi desu.

GIMOMBUN   488
GIGOKU JIKEN
utagau YOCHI ga nai   疑
utagawashii ashidori

GIMON na TEN ga arimashitara, dondon SHITSUMON shite kudasai.
ZOOSEN GIGOKU JIKEN wa SEKEN o odorokasemashita.
Moshi utagattara, kiri ga arimasen.
Sore wa utagawashii JIKEN to shite, mada o o hiite imasu.

489 血

KETSUEKI no KENSA
TARYOO no YUKETSU
chi no nijimu yoo na DORYOKU

KENKETSU no tame KETSUEKI no KENSA o ukemashita.
Oji wa SHUJUTSUGO, TARYOO no YUKETSU o shimashita.
Imooto wa chi o miruto, ki ga tooku narimasu.

490 興

SENGO no HUKKOO
KOOHUNZAI
KYOOMI o ushinau

Nihon no SANGYOO wa, SENGO, mezamashii HUKKOO buri o misemashita.
Koohii o nomisugi, KOOHUN shite nemurenakatta n desu.
Nihon no REKISHI no koto nara, KYOOMI ga arimasu.

491 財

ZAISAN no SOOZOKU
ZAIKAI no YUURYOKUSHA

Oji wa ISSHOO kakatte, are dake no ZAISAN o kizuki agemashita.
SEIJIKA ni wa ZAIKAI no YUURYOKUSHA ga ooi desu.

492 察

KEISATSUKAN
KENSATSUgawa no tachiBA
surudoi KANSATSURYOKU

KEISATSU no SHIgoto wa SEKININ ga omoi no de, TAIHEN desu.
KONDO no SAIBAN de, KENSATSUgawa no SHUCHOO ga toorimashita.
JIBUN de KANSATSU shita kotogara o, ari no mama ni shirushite
　　　　　　　go-rannasai.

493 或

aru hi
aruiwa

Aru hi, Ginza de Hujita-san ni atta koto ga arimasu.
Mada hakkiri shite imasen ga, aruiwa yama e iku ka mo shire-
　　　　　　　　　　　　　　　　　　　　　　　　(masen.

494 影

EIKYOO ga ookii
mabara na hitokage
kage mo katachi mo nai

Kodomo ni totte, terebi no EIKYOORYOKU wa totemo ookii desu.
YUUgata ni nattara, hitokage ga mabara ni narimashita.
Ano kata wa, nan to naku kage no usui kata desu.

495 危

KIKEN KUIKI
KIKI ga semaru
abunai tokoro

Kono HEN wa KIKEN KUIKI desu kara, oyogu koto ga dekimasen.
Moo sukoshi osokattara, KIKI o nogarerarenakatta deshoo.
Ayaui tokoro o tasukete itadaki, arigatoo gozaimashita.

KAKO no omoide 496
KYONEN no dekigoto
saru SANGATSU
去

Kako no koto ni kodawatte mo, shikata ga arimasen.
Imooto wa, KYONEN, baiorin o naraihajimeta bakari desu.
Atsui natsu ga sari, iyoiyo DOKUSHO no shiizun ni narimashita.

KYOOHUSHIN 497
osoraku
hito o osoreru
osoroshii yume
恐

Ano ko wa KYOOHUSHIN ga tsuyokute, itsumo nani ka ni obiete
Osoraku sore wa MONDAI ni naru deshoo.   (imasu.
Shinu wake de mo arumai shi, nani mo osoreru HITSUYOO wa
YUUBE osoroshii yume o mimashita.   (arimasen.

---

kumiai no KIKOO 498
BUNSHOO no KOOSEI
atama no KOOZOO
KEKKOO na hanashi
構

Kumiai no KIKOO ga kawari, KIYAKU no ICHIBU ga KAISEI
            saremashita.
Sawamura-san wa, terebi BANgumi no KIKOO o TANTOO shite imasu.
Enjin ga doo iu KOOZOO ni natte iru no ka, sappari wakarimasen.
Sore wa TAIHEN KEKKOO na hanashi da to omoimasu.

YOSANGAKU 499
DENSHI KEISANKI
算

KONDO no SOOKAI de HONNENDO no YOSAN ga KETTEI shimasu.
SOOGAKU ga ikura ni naru ka, KEISAN shite mite kudasai.

TAISETSU na YOOSO 500
CHOOKOKU no SOZAI
SOBOKU na JUUMIN
sunao na kodomo
zubu no shirooto
素

SEIKOO no TAISETSU na YOOSO wa DORYOKU suru koto desu.
Ano BANgumi wa, takumashii GYOMIN no SEIKATSU o SOZAI ni
    shita rupo desu.
Kono mura no hitobito wa minna SOBOKU na JUUMIN desu.
Kodomo o sunao ni sodatetai to negatte imasu.
Watakushi no machi de shirooto nodo JIMAN TAIKAI ga
            okonawaremashita.

Alphabetical Index of Characters

ON-yomi and KUN-yomi
↓
TOOYOO KANJI
↓
NLRI Frequency Rank Order, and Page Number for Characters 1-500
↓
Page Number in Nelson's Dictionary
↓

A	亜	---	49	akiraka	明	152	477
A	阿	1128	928	a(kiru)	飽	---	967
abi(ru)	浴	1351	550	AKU	悪	295	53
abura	油	879	542	AKU	握	814	447
a(geru)	上	29	223	ama	尼	---	341
a(geru)	揚	1042	447	ama(i)	甘	1101	615
AI	哀	---	116	ama(ru)	余	468	145
AI	愛	268	590	ame	雨	989	940
ai	相	111	498	ame	天	277	34
aida	間	31	920	ami	網	1091	708
aji	味	169	247	a(mu)	編	877	712
aka(i)	赤	406	853	AN	安	165	312
aka(rui)	明	152	477	AN	行	18	801
akatsuki	暁	---	483	AN	案	353	320
aki	秋	886	666	AN	暗	753	480
akina(u)	商	375	119	ana	穴	---	671

A -- ana

anado(ru)	悔	---	147	atama	頭	234	843
ane	姉	1217	303	atara(shii)	新	80	467
ani	兄	575	241	a(taru)	当	68	337
ao(i)	青	393	947	atata(kai)	暖	---	486
ao(gu)	仰	1363	134	a(teru)	充	807	112
ara(i)	荒	843	777	a(teru)	当	68	337
araso(u)	争	107	87	ato	跡	1145	858
arata	新	80	467	ATSU	圧	397	230
arata(meru)	改	289	355	atsuka(u)	扱	922	425
ara(u)	洗	1232	546	atsu(i)	厚	1025	231
ara(wasu)	表	178	71	atsu(i)	暑	---	483
ara(wasu)	著	651	781	atsu(i)	熱	636	586
ara(wasu)	現	67	610	atsuma(ru)	集	224	937
are(ru)	荒	843	777	a(u)	合	33	138
a(ru)	有	245	738	a(u)	会	16	136
aru(ku)	歩	267	519	awa(i)	淡	---	556
asa	麻	1297	990	aware(mu)	哀	---	116
asa	朝	217	749	ayama(ru)	誤	905	831
asa(i)	浅	765	545	ayashi(i)	怪	1256	398
ase	汗	---	536	ayau(i)	危	495	87
ashi	足	338	857	ayu(mu)	歩	267	519
aso(bu)	遊	585	889	aza	字	515	311
ata(eru)	与	334	26	azuka(ru)	預	1300	957
atai	価	342	148	azamu(ku)	欺	---	517
atai	値	828	156	BA	馬	890	970

BA	婆	---	305	BATSU	閥	1340	924
ba	場	49	275	BEI	米	155	690
BAI	売	313	270	BEN	弁	543	234
BAI	倍	602	155	BEN	便	769	152
BAI	梅	1403	501	BEN	勉	749	97
BAI	培	---	273	beni	紅	1137	696
BAI	陪	---	931	BETSU	別	227	198
BAI	媒	---	306	BI	尾	623	342
BAI	買	433	718	BI	美	339	721
BAI	賠	1404	851	BI	備	201	161
ba(keru)	化	104	162	BI	微	1190	390
BAKU	麦	1289	989	BI	鼻	1065	995
BAKU	幕	1036	786	BIN	便	769	152
BAKU	暴	556	487	BIN	敏	1341	457
BAKU	縛	---	713	BIN	貧	507	181
BAKU	爆	309	588	BO	母	317	525
BAN	伴	930	141	BO	募	---	782
BAN	板	876	495	BO	墓	1090	786
BAN	蛮	---	120	BO	慕	---	787
BAN	番	519	920	BO	暮	878	787
BAN	晩	668	484	BO	簿	---	689
BAN	盤	893	640	BO	模	797	510
BATSU	伐	---	133	BOO	亡	795	109
BATSU	抜	637	427	BOO	乏	669	80
BATSU	罰	1339	719	BOO	忙	1411	395

BOO	坊	1124	269	BU	分	28	171
BOO	妨	1410	302	BU	武	461	51
BOO	防	326	927	BU	侮	---	147
BOO	忘	726	114	BU	歩	267	519
BOO	房	1343	416	BU	部	52	897
BOO	肪	---	741	BU	無	179	597
BOO	昌	1344	479	BU	舞	638	762
BOO	某	---	616	BUN	文	89	462
BOO	剖	---	201	BUN	分	28	171
BOO	紡	---	696	BUN	聞	184	924
BOO	望	314	609	buta	豚	---	746
BOO	傍	1194	161	BUTSU	仏	700	127
BOO	帽	1295	359	BUTSU	物	95	597
BOO	棒	1067	504	BYOO	平	98	43
BOO	貿	550	848	BYOO	苗	---	772
BOO	暴	556	487	BYOO	秒	---	665
BOO	膨	---	753	BYOO	病	502	629
BOO	謀	915	838	BYOO	描	812	441
BOKU	木	225	490	CHA	茶	851	776
BOKU	牧	---	596	CHAKU	着	410	723
BOKU	墨	---	593	CHAKU	嫡	---	307
BOKU	撲	296	451	CHI	池	650	535
BON	凡	1156	193	CHI	地	45	267
BON	盆	---	178	CHI	知	73	646
BOTSU	没	1296	537	CHI	治	88	540

CHI	治	88	540	CHIN	沈	929	538
CHI	致	747	760	CHIN	珍	913	609
CHI	恥	1333	734	CHIN	朕	---	744
CHI	値	828	156	CHIN	陳	1398	931
CHI	遅	1147	886	CHIN	賃	684	850
CHI	痴	---	631	CHIN	鎮	1399	916
CHI	置	312	719	CHITSU	秩	1395	666
CHI	稚	---	668	CHITSU	窒	---	675
chi	千	335	81	chi(rasu)	散	969	459
chi	血	489	800	CHO	著	651	781
chi	乳	---	103	CHO	貯	1236	848
chichi	父	226	591	CHOO	丁	928	26
chichi	乳	---	103	CHOO	弔	---	55
chiga(u)	違	274	886	CHOO	庁	873	362
chigi(ru)	契	1209	298	CHOO	兆	---	190
chii(sai)	小	126	331	CHOO	町	570	621
chiji(mu)	縮	945	715	CHOO	長	90	918
chika(i)	近	149	873	CHOO	重	136	96
chikara	力	38	204	CHOO	頂	1062	956
chika(u)	誓	---	831	CHOO	鳥	852	985
CHIKU	竹	1009	681	CHOO	帳	---	358
CHIKU	逐	---	879	CHOO	張	553	375
CHIKU	畜	---	606	CHOO	彫	---	98
CHIKU	蓄	---	786	CHOO	朝	217	749
CHIKU	築	872	688	CHOO	跳	---	585

CHOO	超	1334	856	DA	堕	---	273
CHOO	脹	---	747	DA	惰	---	405
CHOO	腸	---	750	DAI	大	5	288
CHOO	徴	912	391	DAI	内	77	58
CHOO	調	219	835	DAI	代	87	132
CHOO	澄	---	569	DAI	台	436	235
CHOO	潮	1149	570	DAI	弟	548	176
CHOO	聴	767	735	DAI	第	83	683
CHOO	懲	---	410	DAI	題	51	488
CHOKU	直	214	217	DAKU	諾	---	834
CHOKU	勅	---	207	DAKU	濁	---	571
CHUU	中	12	56	da(ku)	抱	654	432
CHUU	虫	1183	794	dama(ru)	黙	1013	585
CHUU	仲	951	134	DAN	団	336	258
CHUU	忠	1184	396	DAN	男	203	621
CHUU	注	459	541	DAN	段	425	524
CHUU	宙	---	314	DAN	断	426	466
CHUU	抽	---	431	DAN	弾	705	377
CHUU	昼	1148	51	DAN	暖	---	486
CHUU	柱	1032	496	DAN	談	394	834
CHUU	衷	---	72	DAN	壇	---	279
CHUU	鋳	---	913	da(su)	出	8	66
CHUU	駐	888	973	DATSU	脱	826	746
DA	打	435	423	DATSU	奪	1182	298
DA	妥	979	599	DEN	田	61	620

DEN	伝	331	135		E	回	421	258
DEN	電	332	943		E	会	16	136
DEN	殿	1185	99		E	依	961	148
de(ru)	出	8	66		E	恵	1208	400
DO	土	360	264		E	絵	1100	704
DO	奴	981	300		e	江	761	536
DO	努	634	205		e	重	136	96
DO	度	72	364		e	柄	1122	496
DO	怒	1150	397		eda	枝	1050	494
DOO	同	54	184		ega(ku)	描	812	441
DOO	胴	---	745		EI	永	566	75
DOO	堂	789	340		EI	英	361	773
DOO	動	47	208		EI	泳	---	539
DOO	童	1186	680		EI	栄	990	497
DOO	道	123	887		EI	映	368	479
DOO	働	137	162		EI	営	388	252
DOO	銅	---	911		EI	詠	---	826
DOO	導	501	331		EI	鋭	1097	913
DOKU	毒	1035	526		EI	影	494	380
DOKU	独	205	602		EI	衛	287	392
DOKU	読	323	833		EKI	役	266	381
DON	鈍	---	908		EKI	易	383	477
DON	曇	---	487		EKI	疫	---	628
dono	殿	1185	99		EKI	益	605	180
					EKI	液	---	556

EKI -- GATSU

EKI	駅	1098	972	GA	画	176	50
EN	円	260	183	GA	雅	---	595
EN	延	1099	369	GA	賀	1310	848
EN	沿	---	540	GA	餓	---	967
EN	炎	---	576	GAI	外	69	283
EN	宴	---	320	GAI	劾	---	206
EN	援	354	446	GAI	害	428	320
EN	鉛	1307	909	GAI	街	837	387
EN	塩	1161	277	GAI	慨	---	407
EN	遠	675	891	GAI	概	1258	509
EN	園	686	264	GAI	該	---	827
EN	煙	1130	584	GAKU	岳	---	92
EN	演	413	569	GAKU	学	15	309
EN	縁	991	713	GAKU	楽	481	508
era(bu)	選	341	893	GAKU	額	659	958
era(i)	偉	987	159	GAN	丸	710	80
e(ru)	得	167	386	GAN	元	408	108
e(ru)	獲	1132	606	GAN	含	803	142
ETSU	悦	---	402	GAN	岸	815	348
ETSU	越	594	856	GAN	岩	1262	348
ETSU	謁	---	834	GAN	眼	505	643
ETSU	閲	---	926	GAN	顔	355	959
				GAN	願	711	101
GA	我	380	90	gara	柄	1122	496
GA	芽	---	772	GATSU	月	66	489

EKI -- GATSU

GE	下	75	30
GE	外	69	283
GE	解	142	820
GEI	迎	805	872
GEI	芸	551	770
GEI	鯨	---	984
GEKI	劇	760	100
GEKI	撃	407	450
GEKI	激	733	571
GEN	元	408	108
GEN	幻	1268	360
GEN	玄	1172	606
GEN	言	44	821
GEN	弦	---	375
GEN	限	370	929
GEN	原	113	231
GEN	現	67	610
GEN	減	679	563
GEN	源	626	564
GEN	厳	819	100
GETSU	月	66	489
GI	技	528	427
GI	宜	---	314
GI	偽	---	160
GI	義	62	724
GI	儀	966	164
GI	疑	488	212
GI	戯	---	100
GI	擬	---	453
GI	犠	---	599
GI	議	130	841
GI	欺	---	517
GIN	吟	---	245
GIN	銀	574	912
GO	五	40	33
GO	互	524	33
GO	午	1106	82
GO	呉	1371	176
GO	後	48	383
GO	悟	---	402
GO	娯	---	305
GO	御	371	388
GO	期	247	748
GO	碁	1370	653
GO	誤	905	831
GO	語	211	832
GO	護	474	841
GOO	号	691	243
GOO	合	33	138
GOO	拷	---	434

GOO	剛	---	73	GYOO	行	18	801
GOO	郷	731	896	GYOO	形	306	380
GOO	強	133	376	GYOO	暁	---	483
GOO	業	74	79	GYOO	業	74	79
GOO	豪	1000	121	GYOO	凝	---	192
GOKU	極	311	506	GYOKU	玉	942	607
GOKU	獄	1081	605	GYUU	牛	1102	596
GON	言	44	821				
GON	権	162	511	HA	波	790	540
GON	厳	819	100	HA	派	286	545
GU	具	534	642	HA	破	428	651
GU	愚	---	405	ha	刃	---	80
GUU	宮	643	321	ha	羽	1160	726
GUU	偶	1267	159	ha	葉	275	782
GUU	遇	1206	866	ha	歯	1083	997
GUN	軍	36	187	haba	幅	1291	359
GUN	郡	1365	896	habu(ku)	省	546	94
GUN	群	758	724	HACHI	八	116	171
gurai	位	319	142	hada	膚	---	794
GYAKU	逆	678	876	hadaka	裸	1353	808
GYAKU	虐	---	793	hage(masu)	励	1304	89
GYO	御	371	338	hage(shii)	激	733	571
GYO	魚	903	982	haha	母	317	525
GYO	漁	559	568	HAI	拝	982	432
GYOO	仰	1363	134	HAI	杯	1189	493

HAI	肺	---	743	HAKU	博	875	222
HAI	背	622	743	HAKU	薄	1153	790
HAI	俳	1188	156	ha(ku)	吐	---	243
HAI	配	308	899	ha(ku)	掃	1392	442
HAI	排	1288	443	hama	浜	1066	549
HAI	敗	420	847	HAN	凡	1156	193
HAI	廃	1120	366	HAN	反	146	229
HAI	輩	1338	951	HAN	半	324	75
hai	灰	1044	230	HAN	帆	---	357
haji	恥	1333	734	HAN	犯	791	600
haji(meru)	始	321	304	HAN	伴	930	75
hajime(te)	初	279	803	HAN	判	187	198
haka	墓	1090	786	HAN	坂	1037	269
haka(ru)	図	719	260	HAN	板	876	495
haka(ru)	計	210	823	HAN	版	892	594
haka(ru)	測	978	560	HAN	班	1290	609
haka(ru)	量	671	483	HAN	畔	---	624
hako	箱	1179	687	HAN	般	460	763
hako(bu)	運	157	888	HAN	販	1121	846
HAKU	白	252	46	HAN	飯	932	966
HAKU	伯	89	141	HAN	搬	---	448
HAKU	拍	---	430	HAN	煩	---	583
HAKU	泊	1405	540	HAN	頒		956
HAKU	迫	698	874	HAN	範	931	687
HAKU	舶	---	764	HAN	繁	---	714

HAN	藩	---	791	HATSU	髪	699	979
hana	花	642	771	hatsu	初	279	803
hana	鼻	1065	995	haya(i)	早	409	476
hanare(ru)	離	539	940	haya(i)	速	766	880
hana(su)	話	125	828	hayashi	林	655	494
hana(tsu)	放	325	470	ha(zukashii)	恥	1333	734
hane	羽	1160	726	heda(teru)	隔	---	934
hara	原	113	231	HEI	丙	---	42
hara	腹	896	751	HEI	平	98	43
hara(u)	払	725	422	HEI	兵	243	90
hare(ru)	晴	949	484	HEI	併	1292	148
hari	針	846	907	HEI	並	831	177
haru	春	609	480	HEI	柄	1122	496
ha(ru)	張	553	375	HEI	陛	---	929
hashi	端	887	680	HEI	閉	---	921
hashi	橋	713	513	HEI	弊	---	371
hashira	柱	1032	496	HEI	幣	1293	359
hashi(ru)	走	703	854	HEKI	壁	1155	280
hata	畑	918	576	HEKI	癖	---	632
hata	旗	1316	472	HEN	片	707	593
hata	機	158	513	HEN	辺	653	871
hatake	畑	918	576	HEN	返	477	872
hatara(ku)	働	137	162	HEN	変	254	117
hata(su)	果	250	71	HEN	偏	1294	160
HATSU	発	102	633	HEN	遍	---	886

HEN	編	877	713	hidari	左	374	353
he(rasu)	減	679	563	hi(eru)	冷	708	190
he(ru)	経	71	702	higashi	東	108	93
HI	比	450	527	hikae(ru)	控	---	441
HI	皮	1242	638	hika(ru)	光	345	336
HI	妃	---	300	HIKI	匹	---	212
HI	否	549	49	hi(ku)	引	263	372
HI	批	536	426	hiki(iru)	率	799	119
HI	肥	---	741	hiku(i)	低	652	143
HI	非	222	949	hima	暇	1356	486
HI	彼	56	382	hime	姫	1166	304
HI	卑	---	94	hi(meru)	秘	853	666
HI	飛	526	962	HIN	品	372	249
HI	疲	---	628	HIN	浜	1066	549
HI	被	555	805	HIN	貧	507	181
HI	秘	853	666	HIN	賓	---	328
HI	費	352	847	hira(ku)	開	290	922
HI	悲	748	950	hiratai	平	98	43
HI	碑	---	653	hirugae(ru)	翻	1244	727
HI	罷	---	720	hiro(i)	広	389	362
HI	避	854	895	hiro(u)	拾	1052	435
hi	日	3	473	hiru	午	939	359
hi	火	595	574	hiru	昼	1148	51
hi	灯	954	575	hisa(shii)	久	607	80
hibi(ku)	響	757	955	hiso(mu)	潜	---	570

hitai -- honoo

hitai	額	659	958	HOO	抱	654	432
hita(su)	浸	---	550	HOO	法	100	543
hito	一	1	19	HOO	奉	1193	92
hito	人	2	122	HOO	胞	---	742
hito(shii)	等	151	684	HOO	封	724	330
HITSU	匹	---	212	HOO	峰	794	349
HITSU	必	188	74	HOO	倣	---	155
HITSU	泌	---	539	HOO	砲	427	651
HITSU	筆	722	684	HOO	崩	1407	350
hitsuji	羊	---	720	HOO	訪	957	825
hiya(su)	冷	708	190	HOO	報	310	276
HO	歩	267	519	HOO	飽	---	967
HO	保	163	154	HOO	豊	750	843
HO	捕	584	439	HOO	縫	---	712
HO	浦	1192	550	hodoko(su)	施	783	471
HO	補	793	807	hogaraka	朗	---	744
HO	舗	---	164	hoka	外	69	283
ho	帆	---	357	hoko(ru)	誇	1105	828
ho	穂	---	669	HOKU	北	282	211
HOO	方	25	470	homare	誉	---	828
HOO	包	---	84	HON	本	6	64
HOO	芳	---	770	HON	奔	---	297
HOO	邦	1123	896	HON	翻	1244	727
HOO	宝	1408	314	hone	骨	1109	975
HOO	放	325	470	honoo	炎	---	576

hitai -- honoo

hoomuru -- hukumu

hoomu(ru)	葬	---	782	HU	普	894	181
horo(biru)	滅	796	565	HU	腐	1243	368
ho(ru)	彫	---	98	HU	敷	955	461
ho(ru)	掘	1207	442	HU	膚	---	794
hoshi	星	1230	480	HU	賦	---	851
ho(su)	干	939	359	HU	譜	---	840
hoso(i)	細	736	701	HUU	風	316	960
hos(suru)	欲	1043	842	HUU	封	724	330
hotoke	仏	700	127	HUU	夫		
HOTSU	発	102	633	huchi	縁	991	713
HU	不	103	37	huda	札	1215	491
HU	夫	220	82	hude	筆	722	684
HU	父	226	591	hue	笛	---	682
HU	付	792	130	huka(i)	深	424	558
HU	布	855	357	HUKU	伏	---	134
HU	扶	---	426	HUKU	腹	896	751
HU	府	168	363	HUKU	服	476	742
HU	怖	723	397	HUKU	副	956	202
HU	附	778	928	HUKU	幅	1291	359
HU	負	503	845	HUKU	復	536	387
HU	赴	---	855	HUKU	福	583	661
HU	浮	830	552	HUKU	複	1038	809
HU	婦	591	306	HUKU	覆	1154	812
HU	符		682	hu(ku)	吹	947	245
HU	富	895	325	huku(mu)	含	803	142

hoomuru -- hukumu

hukuro	袋	1180	805		huyu	冬	1326	281
humi	文	89	462		HYAKU	百	218	46
hu(mu)	踏	1033	859		HYOO	氷	---	75
HUN	分	28	171		HYOO	拍	---	430
HUN	粉	---	691		HYOO	表	178	71
HUN	紛	---	696		HYOO	俵	---	155
HUN	噴	---	255		HYOO	票	1191	812
HUN	墳	---	279		HYOO	評	358	826
HUN	憤	1046	409		HYOO	漂	---	567
HUN	奮	1342	299		HYOO	標	706	510
hune	舟	1327	763	I				
hune	船	518	764		I	以	118	126
hu(reru)	触	1114	819		I	衣	1129	803
hu(ru)	振	697	439		I	位	319	142
hu(ru)	降	862	930		I	医	772	213
huru(i)	古	320	215		I	囲	801	259
huru(u)	震	908	945		I	依	961	148
huru(u)	奮	1342	299		I	易	383	477
huse(gu)	防	326	927		I	委	540	664
hushi	節	745	685		I	為	446	77
huta	二	11	106		I	胃	---	622
hutatabi	再	252	47		I	威	728	413
huto(i)	太	257	296		I	尉	1306	98
HUTSU	払	725	422		I	異	593	625
HUTSU	沸	---	539		I	移	625	667

I	偉	987	159	imo	芋	---	769
I	違	274	886	imooto	妹	1412	303
I	意	86	955	i(mu)	忌	---	355
I	維	673	707	IN	引	263	372
I	遺	1096	894	IN	因	485	258
I	慰	---	408	IN	印	571	70
I	緯	---	711	IN	姻	---	304
i	井	517	83	IN	音	558	954
ICHI	一	1	19	IN	員	127	249
ICHI	壱	---	269	IN	院	412	929
ichi	市	305	110	IN	陰	988	932
ichijiru(shii)	著	651	781	IN	飲	900	966
ie	家	46	321	IN	隠	962	934
ika(ru)	怒	1150	397	IN	韻	---	956
ike	池	650	535	ina	否	549	49
IKI	域	674	273	ine	稲	1034	668
iki	息	786	759	inochi	命	249	149
ikidoo(ru)	憤	1406	409	ino(ru)	祈	1314	656
ikioi	勢	293	209	inu	犬	1210	600
iki(ru)	生	9	616	i(reru)	入	65	169
IKU	育	259	114	iro	色	405	768
i(ku)	行	18	801	i(ru)	居	281	343
iku	幾	464	361	i(ru)	射	823	863
ima	今	50	127	i(ru)	鋳	---	913
imashime(ru)	戒	1162	413	isagiyo(i)	潔	1366	569

isa(mu)	勇	983	207	JAKU	寂	---	323
isa(ru)	漁	859	568	JI	示	465	655
ishi	石	347	648	JI	次	150	190
ishizue	礎	927	654	JI	自	14	755
isoga(shii)	忙	1411	395	JI	耳	923	731
iso(gu)	急	533	399	JI	寺	763	266
ita	板	876	495	JI	地	45	267
itadaki	頂	1062	956	JI	字	515	311
ita(i)	痛	768	630	JI	児	597	168
ita(ru)	至	475	759	JI	似	695	134
ito	糸	---	695	JI	事	10	105
itona(mu)	営	388	252	JI	侍	---	148
ITSU	一	1	19	JI	治	88	540
ITSU	逸	1251	884	JI	持	94	435
itsu	五	40	33	JI	時	24	481
itsuwa(ru)	偽	---	160	JI	滋	1379	559
i(u)	言	44	821	JI	辞	784	762
iwa	岩	1262	348	JI	慈	---	182
iwa(u)	祝	1272	657	JI	磁	---	653
iya(shii)	卑	---	94	JI	璽	---	55
izumi	泉	1116	637	ji	路	835	858
J				JIKI	直	214	217
JA	邪	---	595	JIKI	食	207	964
JAKU	若	391	773	JIKU	軸	---	866
JAKU	弱	630	192	JIN	人	2	122

JIN	刃	---	80	JOO	城	907	272
JIN	仁	---	126	JOO	浄	1143	545
JIN	任	349	133	JOO	盛	808	639
JIN	尽	1227	342	JOO	常	190	339
JIN	迅	---	872	JOO	剰	1225	202
JIN	神	191	657	JOO	情	183	404
JIN	陣	619	929	JOO	畳	1388	626
JIN	尋	---	379	JOO	場	49	275
JITSU	日	3	473	JOO	蒸	---	783
JITSU	実	37	317	JOO	静	744	948
JO	女	60	299	JOO	錠	---	914
JO	如	337	301	JOO	嬢	---	307
JO	助	248	205	JOO	醸	---	901
JO	序	1029	362	JOO	譲	1224	841
JO	叙	---	238	JOO	壌	---	279
JO	徐	1328	385	JOKU	辱	1390	870
JO	除	646	929	JU	寿	906	89
JOO	丈	1387	80	JU	受	298	589
JOO	上	29	223	JU	授	457	443
JOO	冗	---	187	JU	就	---	120
JOO	成	160	412	JU	需	738	944
JOO	条	213	282	JU	儒	---	165
JOO	状	430	592	JU	樹	1218	513
JOO	定	95	516	JUU	十	22	214
JOO	乗	610	95	JUU	充	807	112

JUU	住	377	142	KA	化	104	126
JUU	重	136	96	KA	加	237	204
JUU	柔	---	645	KA	可	463	42
JUU	拾	1052	435	KA	仮	993	137
JUU	従	329	385	KA	何	43	146
JUU	渋	1382	556	KA	花	642	771
JUU	銃	1383	912	KA	果	250	71
JUU	縦	1273	714	KA	価	342	148
JUU	獣	---	605	KA	佳	---	149
JUKU	熟	1219	585	KA	河	614	541
JUN	旬	---	210	KA	架	---	496
JUN	巡	---	872	KA	科	369	665
JUN	盾	1220	94	KA	荷	1254	779
JUN	純	925	697	KA	華	901	779
JUN	准	---	191	KA	家	46	321
JUN	殉	---	522	KA	夏	936	52
JUN	循	---	387	KA	菓	---	781
JUN	順	1028	352	KA	貨	687	847
JUN	準	776	223	KA	過	230	887
JUN	遵	---	893	KA	禍	---	661
JUN	潤	1142	569	KA	嫁	1309	306
JUTSU	述	631	874	KA	暇	1356	486
JUTSU	術	322	386	KA	歌	486	517
KA	下	75	30	KA	寡	---	328
KA	火	595	574	KA	箇	---	686

KA	課	755	834		KAI	回	421	258
ka	日	3	473		KAI	快	994	396
ka	香	861	969		KAI	改	289	355
ka	蚊	---	795		KAI	戒	1162	413
kabe	壁	1155	280		KAI	怪	1256	398
kabu	株	1111	501		KAI	界	164	622
kachi	勝	419	748		KAI	皆	780	527
kado	門	376	920		KAI	悔	---	400
kae	替	1059	483		KAI	海	206	547
kaeri(miru)	省	546	94		KAI	械	937	503
kaeri(miru)	顧	1369	960		KAI	絵	1100	704
ka(eru)	代	87	132		KAI	階	328	933
ka(eru)	返	477	872		KAI	開	290	922
ka(eru)	変	254	117		KAI	塊	---	277
ka(eru)	帰	265	378		KAI	解	142	820
ka(eru)	換	660	447		KAI	壊	802	280
ka(eru)	替	1059	483		KAI	懐	1311	410
kagami	鏡	1205	917		kai	貝	---	845
kagaya(ku)	輝	1165	340		kaiko	蚕	---	52
kage	陰	988	932		kaka(geru)	掲	1103	441
kage	影	494	380		kaka(ru)	係	221	151
kagi(ru)	限	370	929		ka(karu)	掛	1135	445
KAI	介	658	126		ka(keru)	欠	774	516
KAI	灰	1044	230		ka(keru)	駆	---	972
KAI	会	16	136		kako(mu)	囲	801	259

KAKU -- KAN

KAKU	各	363	282	kami	髪	699	979
KAKU	角	881	819	kaminari	雷	---	943
KAKU	画	176	50	kammuri	冠	1312	187
KAKU	拡	729	421	KAN	干	939	359
KAKU	革	487	952	KAN	甘	1101	615
KAKU	客	606	319	KAN	刊	---	360
KAKU	核	---	500	KAN	汗	---	536
KAKU	格	403	501	KAN	完	559	313
KAKU	郭	---	896	KAN	肝	---	741
KAKU	覚	512	816	KAN	官	202	315
KAKU	隔	---	934	KAN	冠	1312	187
KAKU	較	858	867	KAN	看	1163	94
KAKU	閣	504	924	KAN	巻	938	356
KAKU	確	343	654	KAN	陥	1075	929
KAKU	獲	1132	606	KAN	勘	1260	207
KAKU	嚇	---	255	KAN	乾	---	221
KAKU	穫	---	671	KAN	貫	995	526
ka(ku)	欠	774	516	KAN	患	1016	402
ka(ku)	書	121	736	KAN	間	31	920
kaku(reru)	隠	962	934	KAN	閑	1201	921
kama(eru)	構	498	509	KAN	款	---	517
kamba(shii)	芳	---	770	KAN	喚	---	251
kami	上	29	223	KAN	堪	1359	275
kami	神	191	657	KAN	棺	---	504
kami	紙	456	698	KAN	敢	1017	459

KAKU -- KAN

KAN	換	660	447	ka(neru)	兼	1104	180
KAN	寒	1313	326	kangae(ru)	考	63	729
KAN	勧	1076	209	kao	顔	355	959
KAN	漢	1077	566	kara(i)	辛	973	869
KAN	寛	---	327	kare	彼	56	382
KAN	幹	838	222	ka(reru)	枯	---	497
KAN	感	105	406	kari	狩	---	602
KAN	管	996	686	kari(ni)	仮	993	137
KAN	関	84	924	ka(riru)	借	682	157
KAN	慣	1358	408	ka(ru)	刈	---	195
KAN	監	615	640	karu(i)	軽	841	866
KAN	緩	---	712	kasa(neru)	重	136	96
KAN	歓	1259	517	kashiko(i)	賢	---	851
KAN	還	1164	895	ka(su)	借	682	157
KAN	憾	---	410	ka(su)	貸	950	848
KAN	館	532	968	kata	方	25	470
KAN	環	965	614	kata	片	707	593
KAN	観	302	818	kata	形	306	380
KAN	簡	882	688	kata	肩	1171	416
KAN	艦	1261	765	kata	型	904	272
KAN	鑑	---	917	kata(i)	堅	1136	273
kanarazu	必	188	74	kata(i)	難	351	939
kanashi(mu)	悲	748	950	katamu(ku)	傾	759	162
kane	金	79	904	kata(meru)	固	820	260
kane	鐘	1053	917	katana	刀	1286	194

kataru -- KEI

kata(ru)	語	211	832		KE	家	46	321
KATSU	活	132	547		KE	懸	1317	411
KATSU	括	---	434		ke	毛	897	528
KATSU	渇	---	555		kega(reru)	汚	836	536
KATSU	割	414	202		KEI	兄	575	241
KATSU	滑	---	566		KEI	刑	817	197
KATSU	轄	---	869		KEI	系	884	89
katsu	且	1222	42		KEI	形	306	380
ka(tsu)	勝	419	748		KEI	径	---	381
ka(u)	買	433	718		KEI	茎	---	772
ka(u)	飼	---	967		KEI	京	303	114
kawa	皮	1242	638		KEI	係	221	151
kawa	川	196	351		KEI	契	1209	298
kawa	側	280	159		KEI	計	210	823
ka(waru)	代	87	132		KEI	型	904	272
ka(waru)	変	254	117		KEI	恵	1208	400
ka(waru)	換	660	447		KEI	啓	---	250
ka(waru)	替	1059	483		KEI	掲	1103	441
kayo(u)	通	97	882		KEI	経	71	702
kaza(ru)	飾	1054	966		KEI	景	617	483
kaze	風	316	960		KEI	敬	1079	459
kazo(eru)	数	159	460		KEI	軽	814	866
KE	化	104	126		KEI	傾	759	162
KE	気	55	529		KEI	携	---	448
KE	仮	993	137		KEI	継	1170	707

kataru -- KEI

KEI	警	454	840	KEN	遣	---	894
KEI	鶏	---	987	KEN	絹	---	706
KEI	競	1019	681	KEN	権	162	511
kemono	獣	---	605	KEN	憲	429	329
kemuri	煙	1130	584	KEN	賢	---	851
KEN	犬	1210		KEN	謙	---	838
KEN	件	171	133	KEN	繭	---	791
KEN	見	20	813	KEN	験	385	974
KEN	券	---	199	KEN	顕	1367	969
KEN	肩	1171	416	KEN	懸	1317	411
KEN	建	278	370	ke(su)	消	458	551
KEN	県	842	338	KETSU	欠	774	516
KEN	研	284	650	KETSU	穴	---	671
KEN	剣	818	201	KETSU	血	489	800
KEN	倹	---	155	KETSU	決	138	538
KEN	兼	1104	180	KETSU	結	109	705
KEN	軒	1080	864	KETSU	傑	---	161
KEN	健	734	160	KETSU	潔	1366	569
KEN	険	662	931	kewa(shii)	険	662	931
KEN	乾	---	221	kezu(ru)	削	1174	201
KEN	堅	1136	273	KI	己	618	355
KEN	検	473	505	KI	机	1263	491
KEN	圏	1318	264	KI	気	55	529
KEN	間	31	921	KI	危	495	87
KEN	献	1048	604	KI	企	513	133

KI -- KIN

KI	忌	---	355	KI	旗	1316	472
KI	岐	---	348	KI	器	520	254
KI	汽	---	538	KI	輝	1165	340
KI	希	816	357	KI	機	158	513
KI	奇	921	297	KI	騎	---	974
KI	祈	1314	656	ki	木	255	490
KI	季	---	664	ki	生	9	616
KI	紀	616	695	ki	黄	1199	991
KI	軌	1264	864	ki	着	410	723
KI	起	246	855	ki(bamu)	黄	1199	991
KI	帰	265	378	KICHI	吉	199	265
KI	鬼	1361	981	ki(eru)	消	458	551
KI	飢	---	966	KIKU	菊	---	781
KI	記	209	824	ki(ku)	聞	184	924
KI	既	902	769	ki(meru)	決	138	538
KI	寄	677	324	kimi	君	204	245
KI	基	251	274	kimo	肝	---	741
KI	規	453	816	KIN	今	50	127
KI	揮	---	446	KIN	斤	---	466
KI	喜	781	276	KIN	近	149	873
KI	幾	464	361	KIN	均	1021	270
KI	貴	676	849	KIN	金	79	904
KI	棋	1315	504	KIN	菌	---	780
KI	期	247	748	KIN	琴	---	612
KI	棄	1045	120	KIN	勤	690	208

KI -- KIN

KIN	筋	1022	684	KO	固	820	260
KIN	禁	732	660	KO	呼	541	247
KIN	緊	840	708	KO	拠	756	430
KIN	謹	---	839	KO	枯	---	375
kinu	衣	1129	803	KO	弧	---	497
kinu	絹	---	706	KO	故	523	455
kiri	霧	---	946	KO	孤	968	309
ki(ru)	切	208	195	KO	個	455	157
ki(ru)	着	410	723	KO	庫	1173	365
kishi	岸	815	348	KO	虚	1204	793
kiso(u)	競	1019	681	KO	雇	1368	417
kita	北	282	211	KO	湖	1320	560
kita(eru)	鍛	---	915	KO	鼓	---	994
KITSU	喫	---	252	KO	誇	1105	828
KITSU	詰	967	829	KO	顧	1369	960
kiwa(meru)	窮	1202	675	ko	小	126	331
kiyo(i)	清	469	557	ko	子	42	308
kiza(mu)	刻	884	199	ko	粉	---	691
kizu	傷	845	163	KOO	口	200	239
kizu(ku)	築	872	688	KOO	工	173	352
kizu(tsukeru)	傷	845	163	KOO	孔	---	308
KO	己	618	355	KOO	公	212	173
KO	戸	627	415	KOO	甲	1372	61
KO	去	496	265	KOO	巧	1373	353
KO	古	320	215	KOO	功	735	353

KOO	広	389	362		KOO	荒	843	777
KOO	交	269	113		KOO	後	48	383
KOO	考	63	729		KOO	恒	---	401
KOO	江	761	536		KOO	高	135	976
KOO	光	345	336		KOO	校	233	501
KOO	好	262	301		KOO	候	999	155
KOO	后	---	86		KOO	航	1139	763
KOO	向	192	69		KOO	耕	---	730
KOO	仰	1363	134		KOO	降	862	930
KOO	行	18	801		KOO	貢	1321	355
KOO	孝	---	217		KOO	康	821	366
KOO	抗	680	426		KOO	黄	1199	991
KOO	坑	---	269		KOO	控	---	441
KOO	更	608	49		KOO	硬	---	652
KOO	攻	588	354		KOO	絞	---	703
KOO	肯	---	519		KOO	港	1212	560
KOO	幸	423	272		KOO	項	1138	355
KOO	効	714	206		KOO	慌	---	405
KOO	拘	1024	431		KOO	鉱	---	909
KOO	侯	---	155		KOO	構	498	509
KOO	厚	1025	231		KOO	綱	1374	708
KOO	皇	535	637		KOO	酵	---	900
KOO	香	861	969		KOO	稿	---	669
KOO	紅	1137	696		KOO	衡	---	392
KOO	郊	---	896		KOO	興	490	183

KOO 鋼	1108	915	
KOO 衡	---	392	
KOO 購	1213	852	
KOO 講	469	839	
koba(mu) 拒	941	426	
koe 声	299	270	
ko(eru) 肥	---	741	
ko(eru) 越	594	856	
ko(geru) 焦	1276	936	
kogo(eru) 凍	---	191	
ko(i) 請	743	834	
ko(i) 濃	1152	571	
koi(shii) 恋	899	118	
kokono(tsu) 九	112	80	
kokoro 心	64	393	
kokoro(miru) 試	478	830	
kokoroyo(i) 快	994	396	
kokoro(zasu) 志	681	269	
KOKU 石	347	648	
KOKU 克	---	216	
KOKU 告	398	245	
KOKU 谷	692	842	
KOKU 国	4	261	
KOKU 刻	844	199	
KOKU 黒	552	992	

KOKU 酷	1376	900	
KOKU 穀	---	525	
koma(kai) 細	736	701	
koma(ru) 困	437	259	
kome 米	155	690	
ko(mu) 込	396	871	
KON 今	50	127	
KON 困	437	259	
KON 金	79	904	
KON 恨	---	400	
KON 根	390	502	
KON 混	596	557	
KON 婚	693	305	
KON 紺	---	699	
KON 献	1048	604	
KON 魂	---	982	
KON 墾	---	279	
kona 粉	---	691	
kono(mu) 好	262	301	
koomu(ru) 被	555	805	
koori 氷	---	75	
koo(ru) 凍	---	191	
ko(rasu) 懲	---	192	
ko(rasu) 凝	---	410	
koromo 衣	1129	803	

korosu -- kuraberu

koro(su)	殺	470	524		KU	宮	643	321
ko(ru)	凝	---	192		KU	駆	---	972
koshi	腰	1041	750		KUU	空	384	672
ko(su)	越	594	856		ku(u)	食	207	964
kota(eru)	答	565	684		kuba(ru)	配	308	899
koto	言	44	821		kubi	首	525	969
koto	事	10	105		kuchi	口	200	239
koto	琴	---	612		ku(chiru)	朽	---	491
kotobuki	寿	906	89		kuda	管	996	686
koto(naru)	異	593	625		kuda(keru)	砕	---	650
koto(waru)	断	426	466		kuda(ru)	下	75	30
KOTSU	骨	1109	975		ku(iru)	悔	---	400
ko(u)	請	743	834		kujira	鯨	---	984
koya(su)	肥	---	741		kuki	茎	---	772
koyomi	暦	---	233		ku(mu)	組	122	699
KU	九	112	80		kumo	雲	1252	942
KU	口	200	239		kumo(ru)	曇	---	487
KU	工	173	352		KUN	君	204	245
KU	久	607	80		KUN	訓	1023	824
KU	区	544	212		KUN	勲	---	585
KU	句	860	210		KUN	薫	---	789
KU	功	735	353		kuni	国	4	261
KU	供	340	149		kura	倉	1087	156
KU	苦	344	774		kura	蔵	977	787
KU	紅	1137	696		kura(beru)	比	527	450

korosu -- kuraberu

kurai	位	319	142	KYAKU	却	940	228
kura(i)	暗	753	486	KYAKU	客	606	319
kura(su)	暮	878	787	KYAKU	脚	1266	746
kurenai	紅	1137	696	KYO	巨	1203	212
ku(reru)	暮	878	787	KYO	去	496	265
kuro(i)	黒	552	992	KYO	拠	756	430
ku(ru)	来	27	91	KYO	居	281	343
ku(ru)	繰	1118	716	KYO	拒	941	426
kuru(u)	狂	1078	600	KYO	挙	431	135
kuruma	車	231	864	KYO	虚	1204	793
kurushi(mu)	苦	344	774	KYO	許	639	825
kuruwa	郭	---	896	KYO	距	---	858
kusa	草	649	775	KYOO	凶	---	194
kusa(i)	臭	1176	758	KYOO	兄	575	241
kusari	鎖	---	916	KYOO	叫	1046	243
kusa(ru)	腐	1243	368	KYOO	共	106	175
kuse	癖	---	632	KYOO	狂	1078	600
kusuri	薬	958	789	KYOO	供	340	149
KUTSU	屈	1134	343	KYOO	京	303	114
KUTSU	掘	1207	442	KYOO	享	---	114
kuwa	桑	---	238	KYOO	協	193	217
kuwada(teru)	企	513	133	KYOO	況	883	539
kuwa(eru)	加	237	204	KYOO	峡	---	349
kuwa(shii)	詳	1329	828	KYOO	狭	1018	601
ku(yamu)	悔	---	400	KYOO	胸	839	745

KYOO -- magaru

KYOO	恭	---	400	KYUU	求	297	77
KYOO	脅	1362	207	KYUU	吸	1168	244
KYOO	恐	497	401	KYUU	究	261	671
KYOO	郷	731	896	KYUU	泣	782	542
KYOO	教	58	457	KYUU	糾	---	695
KYOO	強	133	376	KYUU	急	533	399
KYOO	経	71	702	KYUU	級	373	695
KYOO	境	567	278	KYUU	宮	643	321
KYOO	橋	713	513	KYUU	球	688	609
KYOO	興	490	183	KYUU	救	804	457
KYOO	鏡	1205	917	KYUU	給	404	704
KYOO	響	757	955	KYUU	窮	1202	675
KYOO	競	1019	681	M			
KYOO	驚	997	975	MA	麻	1297	990
KYOKU	曲	1020	70	MA	摩	---	990
KYOKU	局	228	342	MA	魔	---	991
KYOKU	極	311	506	ma	真	195	220
KYUU	九	112	80	ma	間	31	920
KYUU	弓	---	372	maboroshi	幻	1268	360
KYUU	久	607	80	machi	町	570	621
KYUU	及	422	80	ma(chi)	待	366	383
KYUU	旧	661	61	mado	窓	1119	675
KYUU	丘	1167	84	mado(wasu)	惑	986	403
KYUU	休	573	136	mae	前	53	178
KYUU	朽	---	491	ma(garu)	曲	1020	70

KYOO -- magaru

magi(reru)	紛	---	696	manuka(reru)	免	1298	168
mago	孫	---	310	mane(ku)	招	972	432
MAI	毎	592	526	maru(i)	丸	710	80
MAI	米	155	690	ma(su)	増	365	279
MAI	妹	1412	303	mata	又	467	236
MAI	枚	1125	493	mato	的	7	637
MAI	埋	---	272	MATSU	末	531	84
mai	舞	638	762	matsu	松	483	494
mai(ru)	参	350	235	ma(tsu)	待	366	383
maji(ru)	交	269	113	matsu(ri)	祭	1214	659
maka(seru)	任	349	133	matsurigoto	政	23	456
ma(keru)	負	503	845	matta(ku)	全	70	139
maki	牧	---	596	ma(u)	舞	638	762
makoto	誠	848	828	mawa(ru)	回	421	258
MAKU	幕	1036	786	mayo(u)	迷	934	874
MAKU	膜	---	752	mayu	繭	---	791
ma(ku)	巻	938	356	ma(zeru)	混	596	557
mame	豆	---	843	mazu(shii)	貧	507	181
mamo(ru)	守	364	311	me	目	91	641
MAN	万	215	27	me	芽	---	772
MAN	満	466	562	me	雌	---	520
MAN	慢	1245	408	megu(mu)	恵	1208	400
MAN	漫	---	568	me(gumu)	芽	---	772
mana(bu)	学	15	309	megu(ru)	巡	---	072
manako	眼	505	643	MEI	名	140	286

MEI -- miya

MEI	命	249	149	mida(reru)	乱	557	761
MEI	明	152	477	midori	緑	1196	709
MEI	迷	934	874	migi	右	384	242
MEI	盟	603	640	mijika(i)	短	870	647
MEI	鳴	1068	254	miki	幹	838	222
MEI	銘	---	911	mikotonori	詔	---	826
mekura	盲	1347	114	mimi	耳	923	731
MEN	免	1298	168	MIN	民	30	42
MEN	面	117	951	MIN	眠	832	643
MEN	綿	1346	709	mina	皆	780	527
meshi	飯	932	966	minami	南	401	219
me(su)	召	---	197	minamoto	源	626	564
mesu	雌	---	520	minato	港	1212	560
METSU	滅	796	565	mine	峰	---	349
me(zasu)	芽	---	772	miniku(i)	醜	---	901
mezura(shii)	珍	913	609	mino(ru)	実	37	317
MI	未	624	85	mi(ru)	見	20	813
MI	味	169	247	misao	操	1235	452
MI	魅	---	982	misasagi	陵	---	930
mi	三	21	28	mise	店	622	364
mi	身	174	862	mi(tasu)	満	466	562
mi	実	37	317	mito(meru)	認	357	831
michi	道	123	887	MITSU	密	527	323
michibi(ku)	導	501	331	mi(tsu)	三	21	28
mi(chiru)	満	466	562	miya	宮	643	321

MEI -- miya

miyako	都	621	114	MON	問	41	920
mizu	水	166	532	mono	物	95	597
mizuka(ra)	自	14	755	mono	者	19	729
mizuumi	湖	1320	560	mo(ri)	盛	808	639
MO	茂	1195	772	mori	森	1115	504
MO	模	797	510	mo(ru)	漏	---	568
mo	喪	---	73	mo(ru)	盛	808	639
MOO	毛	897	528	moo(su)	申	509	61
MOO	盲	1347	114	moto	下	75	30
MOO	耗	---	730	moto	元	408	108
MOO	望	314	609	moto(zuku)	基	251	274
MOO	猛	1299	604	moto(meru)	求	297	77
MOO	網	1091	708	MOTSU	物	95	597
mo(chi)	持	94	435	mo(tsu)	持	94	435
mochi(iru)	用	177	619	motto(mo)	最	99	484
mo(eru)	燃	1401	587	mo(yasu)	燃	1401	587
moo(keru)	設	270	825	moyoo(su)	催	---	162
MOKU	木	255	490	MU	矛	1246	645
MOKU	目	91	641	MU	武	461	51
MOKU	黙	1013	585	MU	務	244	646
momme	匁	---	82	MU	無	179	579
momo	桃	---	500	MU	夢	771	786
MON	文	89	462	MU	霧	---	946
MON	門	376	920	mu	六	124	110
MON	紋	---	697	mugi	麦	1289	989

muka(eru)	迎	805	872	na	菜	---	781
muka(u)	向	192	69	nae	苗	---	772
mukashi	昔	612	477	naga(i)	長	90	918
muko	婿	---	306	naga(reru)	流	235	553
muku(iru)	報	310	276	nage(ku)	嘆	---	253
mune	旨	970	211	nage(ru)	投	510	428
mune	胸	839	745	nagusa(meru)	慰	---	408
mura	村	241	493				
mura(garu)	群	758	724	na(i)	無	179	579
murasaki	紫	---	703	naka	中	12	56
mure	群	758	724	naka	仲	951	134
mu(reru)	蒸	---	783	nakaba	半	324	75
muro	室	568	319	na(ku)	鳴	782	542
mushi	虫	1183	794	nama	生	9	616
musu(bu)	結	109	705	namari	鉛	1307	909
musume	娘	1085	305	nami	並	831	177
mu(tsu)	六	124	110	nami	波	790	540
MYAKU	脈	---	744	namida	涙	779	550
MYOO	名	140	286	NAN	男	203	621
MYOO	妙	770	303	NAN	南	401	219
MYOO	明	152	477	NAN	軟	---	865
MYOO	命	249	149	NAN	難	351	939
N				naname	斜	---	465
NA	納	1237	697	nana(tsu)	七	147	102
na	名	140	286	nani	何	43	146

nao(su)	直	214	217		NI	二	11	106
nara(beru)	並	831	177		NI	尼	---	341
nara(u)	習	764	727		NI	弐	---	46
na(reru)	慣	1358	408		NI	児	597	168
na(ru)	鳴	1068	254		ni	荷	1254	779
na(ru)	成	160	412		nibu(i)	鈍	---	908
nasake	情	180	404		NICHI	日	3	473
natsu	夏	936	52		ni(eru)	煮	---	577
naya(mu)	悩	914	402		niga(i)	苦	344	774
ne	音	558	954		ni(geru)	逃	721	875
ne	根	390	502		nigi(ru)	握	814	447
ne	値	828	156		nigo(ru)	濁	---	571
ne	寝	1226	327		NTKU	肉	811	738
neba(ru)	粘	---	691		niku(mu)	憎	---	408
nega(u)	願	711	101		NIN	人	2	122
NEI	寧	---	328		NIN	任	349	133
nemu(ru)	眠	832	643		NIN	妊	---	302
NEN	年	13	87		NIN	忍	---	395
NEN	念	333	148		NIN	認	357	831
NEN	粘	---	691		ni(ru)	似	695	134
NEN	然	144	577		ni(ru)	煮	---	577
NEN	燃	1401	587		nishi	西	198	811
ne(ru)	寝	1226	327		niwa	庭	600	365
ne(ru)	練	813	709		niwatori	鶏	---	987
NETSU	熱	636	586		no	野	170	903

NOO	納	1337	697	nu(ru)	塗	---	277
NOO	能	285	236	nushi	主	34	110
NOO	悩	914	402	nusu(mu)	盗	953	639
NOO	脳	829	746	NYO	女	60	299
NOO	農	229	870	NYO	如	337	301
NOO	濃	1152	571	NYOO	尿	---	342
no(biru)	延	1099	369	NYUU	入	65	169
no(biru)	伸	1330	142	NYUU	乳	---	103
no(beru)	述	631	874	NYUU	柔	---	645
nobo(ru)	上	29	223				
nobo(ru)	登	1151	634	O	汚	836	536
nochi	後	48	383	O	悪	295	53
noki	軒	1080	864	o	小	126	331
noko(ru)	残	382	522	o	尾	623	342
no(mu)	飲	900	966	o	雄	538	936
no(ru)	乗	610	95	o	緒	664	708
no(seru)	載	1002	222	OO	大	5	288
nozo(ku)	除	646	929	OO	王	754	607
nozo(mu)	望	314	609	OO	央	919	60
nozo(mu)	臨	1094	754	OO	応	362	363
nu(gu)	脱	826	746	OO	欧	641	516
nu(u)	縫	---	712	OO	段	---	524
nu(ku)	抜	637	427	OO	押	657	433
numa	沼	1386	539	OO	往	1308	382
nuno	布	855	357	OO	皇	535	637

OO	桜	---	500	oka(su)	冒	1344	479
OO	翁	---	180	oki	沖	1284	537
OO	黄	1199	991	oko(nau)	行	18	801
OO	奥	920	99	o(koru)	起	246	855
OO	横	511	511	oko(ru)	興	490	183
o(u)	負	503	845	okota(ru)	怠	---	236
o(u)	追	547	877	OKU	屋	236	344
o(biru)	帯	869	358	OKU	奥	920	99
obiya(kasu)	宵	1362	207	OKU	億	462	164
obo(eru)	覚	512	816	OKU	憶	992	410
ochii(ru)	陥	1075	929	o(ku)	置	312	719
o(chiru)	落	327	783	oku(reru)	遅	1147	886
odayaka	穏	---	670	oku(ru)	送	440	875
odoro(ku)	驚	997	975	oku(ru)	贈	---	852
odo(ru)	踊	---	859	omo	面	117	951
o(eru)	終	392	700	omo(i)	重	136	96
oga(mu)	拝	982	432	omo(u)	思	26	622
oogi	扇	---	417	omomuki	趣	971	856
ogina(u)	補	793	807	omote	面	117	951
oo(i)	多	128	285	omote	表	178	71
oo(kii)	大	5	288	ON	音	558	954
o(iru)	老	640	728	ON	恩	1131	401
oka	丘	1167	84	ON	温	964	561
oka(su)	犯	791	600	ON	遠	675	891
oka(su)	侵	741	152	ON	穏	---	670

on	御	371	388	oto	音	558	954
onaji	同	54	184	otoko	男	203	621
oni	鬼	1361	981	otooto	弟	548	176
onna	女	60	299	otoro(eru)	衰	---	118
onoono	各	363	282	oto(ru)	劣	1071	87
o(reru)	折	910	428	o(tosu)	落	327	783
o(riru)	降	862	930	otozu(reru)	訪	957	825
oroka	愚	---	405	OTSU	乙	---	102
oro(su)	卸	---	228	otto	夫	220	82
o(ru)	織	611	715	o(waru)	終	392	700
osa(eru)	押	657	433	o(wasu)	負	503	845
osa(meru)	収	516	237	oya	親	315	816
osa(meru)	治	88	540	ooyake	公	212	173
osa(meru)	修	529	157	oyo(bu)	及	422	80
osa(meru)	納	1237	697	oyo(gu)	泳	---	539
osa(nai)	幼	1248	360	R			
oo(se)	仰	1363	134	RA	裸	1053	808
oshi(eru)	教	58	457	RAI	来	27	91
o(shimu)	惜	---	403	RAI	雷	---	943
osore	虞	---	794	RAI	頼	604	958
oso(reru)	恐	497	401	RAKU	落	327	783
oso(u)	襲	1177	998	RAKU	絡	---	703
o(su)	押	657	433	RAKU	楽	481	508
o(su)	推	683	444	RAKU	酪	---	900
osu	雄	538	936	RAN	卵	---	90

RAN	乱	557	761	RETSU	烈	1198	576
RAN	覧	1414	816	RI	吏	---	86
RAN	濫	---	572	RI	利	180	662
RAN	欄	---	515	RI	里	857	902
REI	令	587	128	RI	理	59	610
REI	礼	959	655	RI	痢	---	630
REI	冷	708	190	RI	裏	727	121
REI	励	1304	89	RI	履	---	345
REI	例	294	149	RI	離	539	940
REI	鈴	1197	909	RIKI	力	38	204
REI	零	---	943	RIKU	陸	445	932
REI	霊	---	945	RIN	林	655	494
REI	隷	---	936	RIN	厘	---	231
REI	齢	1305	997	RIN	倫	---	155
REI	麗	---	989	RIN	鈴	1197	909
REKI	歴	389	233	RIN	輪	1070	868
REKI	暦	---	233	RIN	隣	1015	935
REN	恋	899	118	RIN	臨	1094	754
REN	連	101	881	RITSU	立	35	676
REN	廉	---	368	RITSU	律	898	382
REN	練	813	709	RITSU	率	799	119
REN	錬	---	914	RO	炉	---	576
RETSU	劣	1071	87	RO	路	835	858
RETSU	列	656	521	RO	露	880	946
RETSU	裂	834	806	ROO	老	640	728

ROO	労	145	206	RYOO	涼	---	556
ROO	郎	264	896	RYOO	猟	---	604
ROO	浪	---	550	RYOO	陵	---	930
ROO	朗	---	744	RYOO	量	671	483
ROO	廊	1249	366	RYOO	僚	917	164
ROO	楼	---	507	RYOO	領	452	957
ROO	漏	---	568	RYOO	漁	559	568
ROKU	六	124	110	RYOO	寮	---	328
ROKU	緑	1196	709	RYOO	療	1303	632
ROKU	録	960	914	RYOO	糧	935	694
RON	論	110	835	RYOKU	力	38	204
RU	留	670	624	RYOKU	緑	1196	709
RU	流	235	553	RYUU	柳	1069	496
RUI	涙	779	550	RYUU	留	670	624
RUI	累	---	624	RYUU	流	235	553
RUI	塁	---	626	RYUU	隆	---	931
RUI	類	480	959	RYUU	粒	---	691
RYAKU	略	478	625	RYUU	硫	---	652
RYO	旅	752	471				
RYO	虜	800	794	S			
RYO	慮	833	794	SA	左	374	353
RYOO	了	1014	103	SA	佐	381	141
RYOO	雨	288	47	SA	作	120	144
RYOO	良	479	766	SA	砂	1269	650
RYOO	料	395	690	SA	査	576	496
				SA	差	694	722

SA	唆	---	249	SAI	最	99	484
SA	詐	---	826	SAI	裁	577	222
SA	鎖	---	916	SAI	歳	715	
sabi(shii)	寂	---	323	SAI	載	1002	
sada(meru)	定	93	316	SAI	債	---	162
saga(su)	捜	1088	438	SAI	催	---	162
sa(geru)	下	75	30	SAI	際	189	934
sagu(ru)	探	871	443	saiwa(i)	幸	423	272
SAI	才	005	104	saka	坂	1037	269
SAI	切	208	195	saka(eru)	栄	990	497
SAI	西	198	811	sakai	境	567	278
SAI	再	252	47	sakana	魚	903	982
SAI	災	863	352	saka(rau)	逆	678	876
SAI	妻	629	303	saka(ru)	盛	808	639
SAI	砕	---	650	sakazuki	杯	1189	493
SAI	栽	---	219	sake	酒	1051	550
SAI	殺	470	524	sake(bu)	叫	1046	243
SAI	宰	---	320	sa(keru)	裂	834	806
SAI	彩	---	380	sa(keru)	避	854	895
SAI	斎	1323	996	saki	先	115	166
SAI	採	944	443	SAKU	作	120	144
SAI	細	736	701	SAKU	削	1174	201
SAI	済	131	555	SAKU	咋	663	479
SAI	菜	---	781	SAKU	索	---	220
SAI	祭	1214	659	SAKU	酢	---	900

SAKU	策	256	683		SATSU	札	1215	491
SAKU	搾	---	448		SATSU	刷	1377	92
SAKU	錯	---	914		SATSU	殺	470	524
sa(ku)	咲	---	249		SATSU	察	492	328
sa(ku)	裂	834	806		SATSU	撮	1082	452
sakura	桜	---	500		SATSU	擦	---	453
sama	様	216	509		sato(ru)	悟	---	402
samata(geru)	妨	1410	302		sawa	沢	442	537
samu(i)	寒	1313	326		sawa(gu)	騒	1393	974
samurai	侍	---	148		sazu(keru)	授	457	443
SAN	三	21	28		SE	世	81	63
SAN	山	148	346		SE	施	783	471
SAN	参	350	235		se	背	622	743
SAN	蚕	---	52		se	畝	---	118
SAN	惨	1175	403		se	瀬	---	573
SAN	産	92	679		SEI	井	517	83
SAN	散	969	459		SEI	生	9	616
SAN	酸	---	900		SEI	世	81	63
SAN	算	499	686		SEI	正	139	44
SAN	賛	1324	851		SEI	成	160	412
saso(u)	誘	1413	831		SEI	西	198	811
sa(su)	刺	1378	200		SEI	声	299	270
sa(su)	差	694	722		SEI	征	1231	381
sato	里	857	902		SEI	性	119	398
SATSU	冊	---	60		SEI	制	161	200

SEI	青	393	947	SEKI	昔	612	477
SEI	姓	1385	303	SEKI	隻	---	936
SEI	牲	---	598	SEKI	席	620	365
SEI	星	1230	480	SEKI	責	599	847
SEI	政	23	456	SEKI	惜	---	403
SEI	省	546	94	SEKI	跡	1145	858
SEI	盛	808	639	SEKI	積	647	670
SEI	清	569	557	SEKI	績	1056	714
SEI	晴	949	484	SEKI	籍	1332	689
SEI	婿	---	306	seki	関	84	924
SEI	聖	1030	612	sema(i)	狭	1019	601
SEI	誠	848	828	sema(ru)	迫	698	874
SEI	歳	715	519	se(meru)	攻	588	354
SEI	勢	293	209	se(meru)	責	599	847
SEI	精	439	692	SEN	千	335	81
SEI	静	744	948	SEN	川	196	351
SEI	製	521	808	SEN	占	378	226
SEI	誓	---	831	SEN	先	115	166
SEI	請	743	834	SEN	泉	1116	637
SEI	整	825	520	SEN	専	589	330
SEKI	夕	1055	283	SEN	染	---	497
SEKI	石	347	648	SEN	宣	849	319
SEKI	斤	---	84	SEN	洗	1232	546
SEKI	赤	406	853	SEN	浅	765	545
SEKI	析	---	493	SEN	扇	---	417

SEN -- SHI

SEN	船	518	764	SHA	社	82	655
SEN	施	783	471	SHA	舎	1110	148
SEN	践	---	858	SHA	者	19	729
SEN	戦	32	413	SHA	砂	1269	650
SEN	銑	---	911	SHA	射	823	863
SEN	銭	926	911	SHA	赦	---	854
SEN	線	506	711	SHA	斜	---	465
SEN	選	341	893	SHA	捨	1140	442
SEN	遷	---	893	SHA	煮	---	577
SEN	潜	---	570	SHA	謝	1026	839
SEN	薦	---	789	SHAKU	勺	---	210
SEN	繊	---	715	SHAKU	尺	---	341
SEN	鮮	471	983	SHAKU	石	347	648
SETSU	切	208	195	SHAKU	赤	406	853
SETSU	折	910	428	SHAKU	昔	612	477
SETSU	拙	---	431	SHAKU	借	682	157
SETSU	窃	---	674	SHAKU	釈	775	902
SETSU	雪	1005	941	SHAKU	爵	---	591
SETSU	設	270	825	SHI	子	42	308
SETSU	接	399	444	SHI	士	386	280
SETSU	節	745	685	SHI	氏	223	529
SETSU	摂	---	448	SHI	支	185	454
SETSU	説	240	832	SHI	止	415	518
SHA	写	696	187	SHI	示	465	655
SHA	車	231	864	SHI	仕	271	129
				SHI	市	305	110

SEN -- SHI

SHI	史	300	60	SHI	視	514	659
SHI	四	114	256	SHI	詞	---	826
SHI	司	864	242	SHI	紫	---	703
SHI	糸	---	695	SHI	歯	1083	997
SHI	旨	970	211	SHI	飼	---	967
SHI	次	150	190	SHI	資	141	850
SHI	自	14	755	SHI	試	578	830
SHI	死	238	521	SHI	詩	1049	829
SHI	至	475	759	SHI	嗣	---	253
SHI	私	17	663	SHI	誌	737	831
SHI	伺	---	141	SHI	雌	---	520
SHI	志	681	269	SHI	賜	---	851
SHI	刺	1378	200	SHI	諮	---	837
SHI	枝	1050	494	shiba	芝	1271	769
SHI	使	239	150	shiba(ru)	縛	---	713
SHI	始	321	304	shibo(ru)	絞	---	703
SHI	姉	1217	303	shibu(i)	渋	1382	556
SHI	祉	---	656	SHICHI	七	147	102
SHI	思	26	622	SHICHI	質	359	851
SHI	姿	560	304	shige(ru)	茂	1195	772
SHI	施	783	471	SHIKI	式	356	371
SHI	指	292	436	SHIKI	色	405	768
SHI	紙	456	698	SHIKI	織	611	715
SHI	師	430	73	SHIKI	識	416	840
SHI	脂	---	744	shi(ku)	敷	955	461

shima -- shitashii

shima	島	379	97		SHIN	森	1115	504
shi(meru)	占	398	226		SHIN	新	80	467
shime(ru)	湿	---	560		SHIN	寝	1226	327
shi(meru)	締	1089	712		SHIN	慎	---	407
shi(meru)	絞	---	703		SHIN	震	908	945
shime(su)	示	465	655		SHIN	請	743	834
shimo	下	75	30		SHIN	審	742	328
SHIN	心	64	393		SHIN	親	315	816
SHIN	申	509	61		SHIN	薪	---	789
SHIN	臣	580	754		shina	品	372	249
SHIN	辛	973	869		shino(bu)	忍	---	395
SHIN	身	174	862		shi(nu)	死	238	521
SHIN	伸	1330	142		shio	塩	1161	277
SHIN	侵	741	152		shio	潮	1149	570
SHIN	信	181	153		shira(beru)	調	219	835
SHIN	神	191	657		shira(seru)	知	73	646
SHIN	針	846	907		shirizo(keru)	退	666	876
SHIN	真	195	220		shiro	城	907	272
SHIN	振	697	439		shiro(i)	白	242	635
SHIN	娠	---	305		shi(ru)	知	73	646
SHIN	浸	---	550		shirushi	印	571	70
SHIN	紳	---	699		shita	下	75	30
SHIN	深	424	558		shita	舌	---	761
SHIN	進	156	885		shitaga(u)	従	329	385
SHIN	診	1178	826		shita(shii)	親	315	816

shima -- shitashii

shita(washii)	慕	---	787	SHOO	召	---	197
SHITSU	失	346	85	SHOO	匠	---	213
SHITSU	室	568	319	SHOO	肖	---	338
SHITSU	疾	---	628	SHOO	抄	---	426
SHITSU	執	924	274	SHOO	床	1223	363
SHITSU	湿	---	560	SHOO	青	393	947
SHITSU	漆	---	567	SHOO	松	483	494
SHITSU	質	359	851	SHOO	昇	1275	477
shizuka	静	744	948	SHOO	承	701	89
SHO	処	418	281	SHOO	沼	1386	539
SHO	初	279	803	SHOO	招	972	432
SHO	所	129	416	SHOO	姓	1385	303
SHO	書	121	736	SHOO	性	119	398
SHO	庶	1274	367	SHOO	相	111	498
SHO	暑	---	483	SHOO	昭	508	479
SHO	署	1221	719	SHOO	星	1230	480
SHO	緒	664	708	SHOO	政	23	456
SHO	諸	272	836	SHOO	省	546	94
SHOO	小	126	331	SHOO	荘	---	775
SHOO	少	153	83	SHOO	笑	482	682
SHOO	升	---	82	SHOO	症	---	628
SHOO	井	517	83	SHOO	称	946	666
SHOO	生	9	616	SHOO	消	458	551
SHOO	正	139	44	SHOO	将	477	592
				SHOO	紹	1277	699

SHOO	章	717	955	SHOO	礁	---	654
SHOO	訟	---	824	SHOO	償	1084	165
SHOO	商	375	119	SHOO	鐘	1053	917
SHOO	渉	740	555	SHOKU	色	405	768
SHOO	唱	---	250	SHOKU	食	207	964
SHOO	粧	---	692	SHOKU	植	598	505
SHOO	硝	---	652	SHOKU	殖	---	523
SHOO	掌	---	340	SHOKU	飾	1054	966
SHOO	焦	1276	936	SHOKU	触	1114	819
SHOO	詔	---	826	SHOKU	嘱	---	254
SHOO	証	448	827	SHOKU	織	611	715
SHOO	象	561	844	SHOKU	職	253	735
SHOO	勝	419	748	SHU	手	57	418
SHOO	焼	868	578	SHU	主	34	110
SHOO	晶	---	483	SHU	朱	---	86
SHOO	装	648	806	SHU	守	364	311
SHOO	詳	1329	828	SHU	取	194	731
SHOO	傷	849	163	SHU	首	525	969
SHOO	照	718	584	SHU	狩	---	602
SHOO	奨	---	298	SHU	修	529	157
SHOO	精	439	692	SHU	殊	1027	522
SHOO	彰	---	380	SHU	酒	1051	550
SHOO	障	530	934	SHU	珠	---	609
SHOO	賞	868	340	SHU	衆	232	801
SHOO	衝	1113	392	SHU	種	417	668

SHU	趣	971	856
SHUU	収	516	237
SHUU	囚	---	256
SHUU	舟	1327	763
SHUU	州	865	69
SHUU	秀	739	662
SHUU	周	824	186
SHUU	宗	579	314
SHUU	秋	886	666
SHUU	臭	1176	758
SHUU	拾	1052	435
SHUU	修	529	157
SHUU	終	592	700
SHUU	習	764	727
SHUU	執	924	274
SHUU	週	1141	884
SHUU	集	224	937
SHUU	衆	232	801
SHUU	就	906	120
SHUU	愁	---	405
SHUU	酬	---	900
SHUU	醜	---	901
SHUU	襲	1177	998
SHUKU	叔	---	238
SHUKU	祝	1272	657
SHUKU	宿	785	324
SHUKU	肅	---	73
SHUKU	淑	---	555
SHUKU	縮	945	715
SHUN	春	609	480
SHUN	俊	---	151
SHUN	瞬	1112	645
SHUTSU	出	8	66
SO	阻	1117	928
SO	祖	702	657
SO	租	---	666
SO	素	500	698
SO	粗	---	691
SO	組	122	699
SO	措	975	440
SO	疎	---	627
SO	訴	1006	827
SO	塑	---	277
SO	礎	927	654
SOO	双	1057	237
SOO	早	409	476
SOO	壮	---	592
SOO	争	107	87
SOO	走	703	854
SOO	宗	579	314

SOO	相	111	498	soo	添	---	556
SOO	送	440	875	soda(teru)	育	259	114
SOO	草	649	775	so(eru)	添	---	556
SOO	荘	---	775	soko	底	562	364
SOO	奏	---	298	SOKU	即	850	767
SOO	捜	1088	438	SOKU	束	911	89
SOO	倉	1087	156	SOKU	足	338	857
SOO	桑	---	238	SOKU	則	746	845
SOO	掃	1392	442	SOKU	促	1007	151
SOO	窓	1119	675	SOKU	息	786	759
SOO	巣	---	79	SOKU	速	766	880
SOO	喪	---	73	SOKU	側	280	159
SOO	創	976	202	SOKU	測	978	560
SOO	葬	---	782	so(meru)	染	---	497
SOO	装	648	806	SON	存	431	309
SOO	想	197	405	SON	村	241	493
SOO	僧	---	163	SON	孫	---	310
SOO	層	810	345	SON	尊	704	182
SOO	遭	---	892	SON	損	1058	449
SOO	総	307	710	sona(eru)	供	340	149
SOO	操	1235	452	sona(eru)	備	201	161
SOO	燥	---	587	sono	園	686	264
SOO	霜	---	946	sora	空	304	672
SOO	騒	1393	974	soso(gu)	注	459	541
soo	沿	---	540	soto	外	69	283

SOTSU -- suna

SOTSU	卒	787	114	SUI	衰	---	118
SOTSU	率	799	119	SUI	酔	1004	899
SU	子	42	308	SUI	推	683	444
SU	主	34	110	SUI	遂	974	886
SU	州	865	69	SUI	睡	---	644
SU	守	364	311	SUI	穂	---	669
SU	素	500	698	SUI	錘	---	914
su	巣	---	79	suji	筋	1022	684
su	酢	---	900	su(kasu)	透	---	880
SUU	枢	---	494	suke	助	248	205
SUU	崇	---	350	suki	好	262	301
SUU	数	159	460	suko(shi)	少	153	83
su(u)	吸	1168	244	suko(yaka)	健	743	160
su(beru)	統	273	703	su(ku)	好	262	301
sude(ni)	既	902	767	su(ku)	透	---	880
sue	末	531	84	suku(u)	救	804	457
sugata	姿	560	304	suku(nai)	少	153	83
su(giru)	過	230	887	suma(u)	住	377	142
SUI	水	166	532	sumi	炭	1061	349
SUI	出	8	66	sumi	墨	---	993
SUI	吹	947	245	su(mu)	住	377	142
SUI	垂	---	92	su(mu)	済	131	555
SUI	炊	---	576	su(mu)	澄	---	569
SUI	帥	---	72	SUN	寸	847	329
SUI	粋	1331	690	suna	砂	1269	650

SOTSU -- suna

suru -- TAKU

su(ru)	刷	1377	92
surudo(i)	鋭	1097	913
susu(meru)	勧	1076	209
susu(mu)	進	156	885
su(teru)	捨	1140	442
suzu	鈴	1197	909
suzu(shii)	涼	---	556

T

TA	太	257	296
TA	他	172	129
TA	多	128	285
ta	田	61	620
taba	束	911	89
tabe(ru)	食	207	964
tabi	旅	752	471
tada(chini)	直	214	217
tada(shi)	但	---	141
tada(shii)	正	139	44
tadayo(u)	漂	---	567
ta(eru)	耐	1281	730
ta(eru)	堪	1359	275
ta(eru)	絶	613	705
taga(i)	互	524	33
tagaya(su)	耕	---	730
TAI	大	5	288
TAI	太	257	296
TAI	台	436	235
TAI	対	39	464
TAI	体	96	143
TAI	耐	1281	730
TAI	退	666	876
TAI	待	366	383
TAI	怠	---	236
TAI	胎	1008	742
TAI	帯	869	358
TAI	泰	---	540
TAI	逮	---	884
TAI	袋	1180	805
TAI	隊	225	933
TAI	替	1059	483
TAI	貸	950	848
TAI	滞	---	565
TAI	態	330	407
tai(ra)	平	98	43
taka(i)	高	135	976
takara	宝	1408	314
take	竹	1009	681
take	岳	---	92
taki	滝	---	564
TAKU	宅	522	311

suru -- TAKU

TAKU	択	1283	425	tano(shimu)	楽	481	508
TAKU	沢	442	537	tano(mu)	頼	604	958
TAKU	卓	---	226	tao(reru)	倒	667	156
TAKU	拓	---	430	ta(riru)	足	338	857
TAKU	託	---	823	tashi(kameru)	確	343	654
takumi	巧	1373	353	ta(su)	足	338	857
tama	玉	942	607	tasu(keru)	助	248	205
tamago	卵	---	90	tataka(u)	戦	32	413
tamashii	魂	---	982	tatami	畳	1388	626
tami	民	30	42	tate	縦	1273	714
tamo(tsu)	保	163	154	tatematsu(ru)	奉	1193	92
TAN	反	146	229	ta(teru)	立	35	676
TAN	丹	---	82	ta(teru)	建	278	370
TAN	炭	1061	349	TATSU	達	154	886
TAN	胆	---	742	ta(tsu)	立	35	676
TAN	単	348	78	ta(tsu)	断	426	466
TAN	淡	---	556	ta(tsu)	裁	577	222
TAN	探	871	443	tatto(i)	尊	704	182
TAN	短	870	647	tawamu(reru)	戯	---	100
TAN	嘆	---	253	tawara	俵	---	155
TAN	端	887	680	ta(yasu)	絶	613	705
TAN	誕	---	834	tazu(neru)	尋	---	379
TAN	鍛	---	915	tazusa(eru)	携	---	448
tane	種	417	668	te	手	57	418
tani	谷	692	842	TEI	丁	928	26

TEI	体	96	143	TEKI	敵	553	461
TEI	低	652	143	TEN	天	277	34
TEI	呈	---	245	TEN	店	632	364
TEI	弟	548	176	TEN	典	1011	177
TEI	廷	1285	369	TEN	点	175	227
TEI	抵	889	431	TEN	展	443	344
TEI	定	93	316	TEN	添	---	556
TEI	邸	1240	896	TEN	転	554	865
TEI	底	562	364	TEN	殿	1185	99
TEI	訂	---	823	tera	寺	763	266
TEI	帝	788	116	te(rasu)	照	718	584
TEI	貞	---	227	TETSU	迭	---	874
TEI	逓	---	879	TETSU	哲	1064	250
TEI	庭	600	365	TETSU	鉄	449	910
TEI	停	952	159	TETSU	撤	---	451
TEI	程	276	667	TETSU	徹	980	392
TEI	提	472	447	TO	土	360	264
TEI	堤	1335	275	TO	斗	---	465
TEI	艇	---	765	TO	吐	---	243
TEI	締	1089	712	TO	図	719	260
TEKI	的	7	637	TO	途	590	879
TEKI	笛	---	682	TO	徒	633	385
TEKI	摘	874	450	TO	都	621	897
TEKI	適	1063	892	TO	登	1151	634
TEKI	滴	---	567	TO	渡	564	562

TO -- toko

TO	塗	---	277
to	戸	627	415
TOO	刀	1286	194
TOO	冬	1336	281
TOO	灯	954	575
TOO	当	68	337
TOO	豆	---	843
TOO	投	510	428
TOO	東	108	93
TOO	到	777	760
TOO	逃	721	875
TOO	凍	---	191
TOO	倒	667	156
TOO	桃	---	500
TOO	党	76	339
TOO	透	---	880
TOO	唐	---	366
TOO	島	379	97
TOO	討	582	823
TOO	盗	953	639
TOO	悼	---	403
TOO	陶	---	931
TOO	塔	---	275
TOO	筒	---	683
TOO	等	151	684

TOO	答	565	684
TOO	登	1151	634
TOO	痘	---	630
TOO	統	273	703
TOO	湯	1287	561
TOO	踏	1033	859
TOO	稲	1034	668
TOO	頭	234	843
TOO	糖	---	694
TOO	謄	---	753
TOO	闘	367	927
TOO	騰	---	754
too	十	22	214
tobo(shii)	乏	669	80
to(bu)	飛	526	962
todokoo(ru)	滞	---	565
todo(keru)	届	1357	343
to(geru)	遂	974	886
toi	問	41	920
tooge	峠	---	349
too(i)	遠	675	891
to(jiru)	閉	---	921
to(keru)	溶	---	565
to(keru)	解	142	020
toki	時	24	481
toko	床	1223	363

TO -- toko

tokoro -- tsuide

tokoro	所	129	416	to(ru)	取	194	731
TOKU	匿	---	213	to(ru)	採	944	443
TOKU	特	186	598	to(ru)	執	924	274
TOKU	得	167	386	too(ru)	通	97	882
TOKU	督	601	644	toshi	年	13	87
TOKU	読	323	833	totono(eru)	整	825	520
TOKU	徳	635	391	TOTSU	突	542	671
TOKU	篤	---	688	to(u)	問	41	920
to(ku)	解	142	820	to(zasu)	閉	---	921
to(ku)	説	240	832	TSU	都	621	897
to(maru)	止	415	518	tsu	津	1086	544
to(maru)	泊	1405	540	TSUU	通	97	882
to(meru)	留	670	624	TSUU	痛	768	630
tomo	友	451	237	tsubasa	翼	985	727
tomo	共	106	175	tsubo	坪	---	271
tomo	供	340	149	tsubu	粒	---	691
tomona(u)	伴	930	141	tsuchi	土	360	264
to(mu)	富	895	325	tsu(geru)	告	398	245
tomura(u)	弔	---	55	tsugi	次	150	190
TON	豚	---	746	tsu(gu)	継	1170	707
tona(eru)	唱	---	250	tsuguna(u)	償	1084	165
tonari	隣	1015	935	TSUI	対	39	464
tono	殿	1185	99	TSUI	追	547	877
tora(eru)	捕	584	439	TSUI	墜	---	278
tori	鳥	852	985	tsu(ide)	次	150	190

tokoro -- tsuide

tsui(yasu)	費	352	847	tsuno(ru)	募	---	782
tsuka(eru)	仕	271	129	tsuranu(ku)	貫	995	526
tsuka(reru)	疲	---	628	tsu(reru)	連	101	881
tsuka(u)	使	239	150	tsuru	弦	---	375
tsu(keru)	付	792	130	tsurugi	剣	818	201
tsuki	月	66	489	tsuta(eru)	伝	311	135
tsu(kiru)	尽	1227	342	tsutome	務	244	646
tsu(ku)	付	792	130	tsuto(meru)	勤	690	208
tsu(ku)	突	542	671	tsuto(meru)	努	634	205
tsu(ku)	着	410	723	tsutsu	筒	---	683
tsukue	机	1263	491	tsutsumi	堤	1335	275
tsukuro(u)	繕	---	715	tsutsu(mu)	包	---	84
tsu(kusu)	尽	1227	342	tsutsushi(mu)	慎	---	407
tsuma	妻	629	303	tsuyo(i)	強	133	376
tsu(meru)	詰	967	829	tsuyu	露	880	946
tsume(tai)	冷	708	190	tsuzu(ku)	続	400	707
tsumi	罪	645	719	tsuzumi	鼓	---	994
tsu(moru)	積	647	670				
tsu(mu)	摘	874	450	U			
tsu(mu)	積	647	670	U	右	384	242
tsumu	錘	---	914	U	有	245	738
tsumu(gu)	紡	---	696	U	宇	1073	311
tsuna	綱	1374	708	U	羽	1060	726
tsune	常	190	339	U	雨	989	940
tsuno	角	881	819	uba(u)	奪	1182	298
				uchi	内	77	58

ude -- WA

ude	腕	1415	748	urana(u)	占	378	226
ue	上	24	223	ure(eru)	憂	1349	54
u(eru)	飢	---	966	u(ru)	売	313	270
u(eru)	植	598	505	uruo(u)	潤	1142	569
ugo(ku)	動	47	208	urushi	漆	---	567
uji	氏	223	529	uruwa(shii)	麗	---	989
u(kabu)	浮	830	552	ushi	牛	1102	596
ukaga(u)	伺	---	141	ushina(u)	失	346	85
u(keru)	受	298	589	ushiro	後	48	383
u(keru)	請	743	834	usu(i)	薄	1153	790
uketamawa(ru)	承	701	89	utaga(u)	疑	488	212
uma	馬	890	970	utai	謡	1092	838
u(mareru)	生	9	616	uta(u)	歌	486	517
ume	梅	1403	501	u(tsu)	打	435	423
u(meru)	埋	---	272	u(tsu)	討	582	823
umi	海	206	547	u(tsu)	撃	407	450
u(mu)	生	9	616	utsu(ru)	映	368	479
u(mu)	産	92	679	utsu(ru)	移	625	667
UN	運	157	888	utsu(su)	写	696	187
UN	雲	1252	942	utsuwa	器	520	254
unaga(su)	促	1007	151	utta(eru)	訴	1006	827
uo	魚	903	982	uyama(u)	敬	1079	459
ura	浦	1192	550	uzu(meru)	埋	---	272
ura	裏	727	121	W			
ura(mu)	恨	---	400	WA	和	85	664

WA	話	125	828		ya	屋	236	344
wa	輪	1070	868		ya	家	46	321
wai	賄	---	850		yabu(reru)	敗	420	847
waka(i)	若	391	773		yabu(ru)	破	427	651
waka(reru)	別	227	198		yado(ru)	宿	785	324
wake	訳	685	825		yake(ru)	焼	868	578
wa(keru)	分	28	171		YAKU	役	266	381
WAKU	惑	986	403		YAKU	約	258	695
wa(ku)	沸	---	539		YAKU	訳	685	825
WAN	湾	1354	560		YAKU	薬	958	789
WAN	腕	1415	748		YAKU	躍	1039	861
wara(u)	笑	482	682		ya(ku)	焼	868	578
ware	我	380	90		yama	山	148	346
wa(ru)	割	414	202		yamai	病	502	629
waru(i)	悪	295	53		yanagi	柳	1069	496
wasu(reru)	忘	726	114		yasa(shii)	優	639	165
wata	綿	1346	709		yashina(u)	養	586	725
watakushi	私	17	663		yashiro	社	82	655
wata(ru)	渡	564	562		yasu(i)	安	165	312
wazawai	災	863	352		yasu(mu)	休	573	136
wazura(washii)	煩	---	583		yato(u)	雇	1369	417
Y					ya(ttsu)	八	116	171
	YA	夜	318	115	yawara(gu)	和	85	664
	YA	野	170	903	yawa(rakai)	柔	---	645
	ya	矢	1270	646	YO	与	334	26

YO	予	283	104	YOO	謡	1092	838
YO	余	468	145	YOO	曜	1350	488
YO	誉	---	828	yo(bu)	呼	541	247
YO	預	1300	957	yo(i)	良	479	766
yo	世	81	63	yoko	横	511	511
yo	代	87	132	YOKU	抑	798	426
yo	夜	318	115	YOKU	浴	1351	550
YOO	用	177	619	YOKU	翌	1093	727
YOO	幼	1248	360	YOKU	欲	1043	842
YOO	羊	---	720	YOKU	翼	985	727
YOO	洋	411	546	yome	嫁	1309	306
YOO	要	78	811	yo(mu)	読	323	833
YOO	容	402	320	yoro(kobu)	喜	781	276
YOO	庸	---	367	yoru	夜	318	115
YOO	葉	275	782	yo(ru)	因	485	258
YOO	揚	1042	447	yo(ru)	寄	677	324
YOO	摇	---	447	yoshi	由	134	60
YOO	陽	856	933	yosoo(u)	装	648	806
YOO	溶	---	565	yo(ttsu)	四	114	256
YOO	腰	1041	750	yo(u)	酔	1004	899
YOO	様	216	509	yowa(i)	弱	630	192
YOO	踊	---	859	YU	由	134	60
YOO	窯	---	675	YU	油	879	542
YOO	養	586	725	YU	愉	---	405
YOO	擁	984	452	YU	輸	444	868

yu	湯	1287	561	yumi	弓	---	372
YUU	友	451	237	yu(reru)	揺	---	447
YUU	右	384	242	yuru(su)	許	689	825
YUU	由	134	60	yutaka	豊	750	843
YUU	有	245	738	yuzu(ru)	譲	1224	841
YUU	勇	983	207				
YUU	幽	---	72	ZA	座	644	365
YUU	郵	1348	897	ZAI	在	182	266
YUU	雄	538	936	ZAI	材	806	493
YUU	猶	---	604	ZAI	剤	---	996
YUU	遊	585	889	ZAI	財	491	846
YUU	裕	---	807	ZAI	罪	645	719
YUU	誘	1413	831	ZAN	残	382	522
YUU	憂	1349	54	ZAN	暫	---	487
YUU	融	751	981	ZATSU	雑	545	938
YUU	優	639	165	ZE	是	1229	479
yuu	夕	1055	283	ZEI	税	909	668
yu(u)	結	109	705	ZEI	説	240	832
yubi	指	292	436	ZEN	全	70	139
YUI	唯	1040	250	ZEN	前	53	178
YUI	遺	1096	894	ZEN	善	665	181
yuka	床	1223	363	ZEN	然	144	577
yuki	雪	1005	941	ZEN	禅	1224	661
yu(ku)	行	18	801	ZEN	漸	1223	567
yume	夢	771	786	ZEN	繕	---	715

zeni -- ZUI

zeni	銭	926	911
ZETSU	舌	---	761
ZETSU	絶	613	705
ZOO	造	441	880
ZOO	象	561	844
ZOO	像	720	163
ZOO	増	365	279
ZOO	憎	---	408
ZOO	蔵	977	787
ZOO	贈	---	852
ZOO	臓	---	753
ZOKU	俗	1279	152
ZOKU	族	301	472
ZOKU	属	581	345
ZOKU	賊	---	850
ZOKU	続	400	707
ZON	存	431	309
ZU	豆	---	843
ZU	図	719	260
ZU	頭	234	843
ZUI	随	948	931
ZUI	髄	---	976

zeni -- ZUI

Officially Recommended Changes, 1971

In 1971, after many years of study, the Japanese Language Council of the Ministry of Education recommended to the Ministry the reinstatement of nearly 500 ON-yomi and KUN-yomi (Chinese and Japanese pronunciation) words and syllables for certain of the 1850 General Use Characters. At the time the following pages were in preparation it was not known if all, or only a portion of these items, which were not found in the approved list of 1946, would be approved for reinstatement.

Nevertheless, it is significant to note that continued widespread usage of certain General Use Characters to represent this list of words and syllables has resulted in official action. The student is advised to be informed of the changes which are finally approved, and modify this list accordingly.

Officially Recommended Changes, 1971

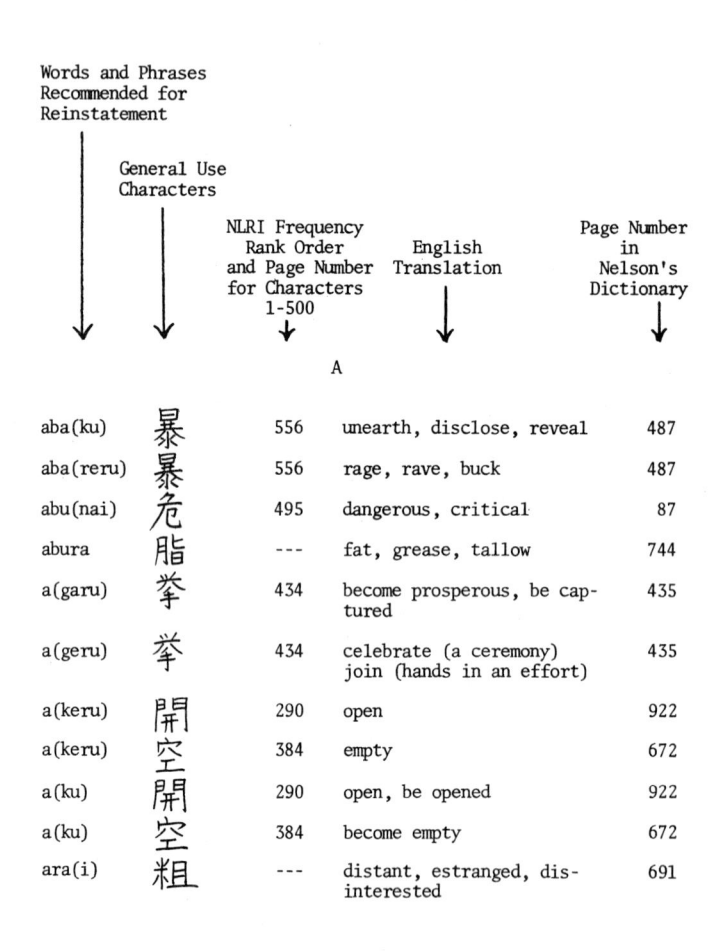

Words and Phrases Recommended for Reinstatement

General Use Characters

NLRI Frequency Rank Order and Page Number for Characters 1-500

English Translation

Page Number in Nelson's Dictionary

A

aba(ku)	暴	556	unearth, disclose, reveal	487
aba(reru)	暴	556	rage, rave, buck	487
abu(nai)	危	495	dangerous, critical	87
abura	脂	---	fat, grease, tallow	744
a(garu)	挙	434	become prosperous, be captured	435
a(geru)	挙	434	celebrate (a ceremony) join (hands in an effort)	435
a(keru)	開	290	open	922
a(keru)	空	384	empty	672
a(ku)	開	290	open, be opened	922
a(ku)	空	384	become empty	672
ara(i)	粗	---	distant, estranged, disinterested	691

a(ru)	在	182	there is, have, exist	266
ase(ru)	焦	1296	be in a hurry, be hasty	936
ashi	脚	1266	foot, leg, paw	746
atari	辺	653	vicinity	871
atata(ka)	温	964	warm, mild	561
atata(kai)	温	964	warm, mild, genial	561
atata(maru)	温	964	get warm, warm oneself, sun oneself	561
atata(meru)	温	964	to heat, to warm	561
ato	後	48	back, rear	383
a(u)	遭	---	encounter, meet	892
awa(remu)	哀	---	to pity, have mercy on	116
awa(seru)	併	1292	put together, unite	148
awa(teru)	慌	---	be confused, lose one's head	405
awatada(shii)	慌	---	busy, bustling, hurried	405
ayatsu(ru)	操	1235	manipulate, operate, steer	452
ayama(chi)	過	230	fault, error	887
ayama(ru)	謝	1026	apologize, be floored	839
ayama(tsu)	過	230	to mistake	887
azaya(ka)	鮮	471	vivid, clear, brilliant	983

B

BACHI	罰	1339	retribution, divine punishment	719
BAKU	博	875	gain, receive	222
BAN	判	187	size (of paper or books)	198

BATSU	末	531	end, powder	84
BE	辺	653	vicinity	871
BOKU	目	91	item, division, viewpoint	641
BON	煩	---	trouble, worry	583
BU	奉	1193	offer, do respectfully	92
BU	不	103	clumsy, ugly	37

C

CHI	質	359	nature (of a person)	851
CHO	緒	664	beginning, inception, end	708
CHUU	沖	1284	offing, open sea, rise high in the sky	537

D

DE	弟	548	faithful service to those older	176

E

e(mu)	笑	482	smile, bloom, split, open	682

G

GE	夏	936	summer	52
GEN	眼	505	eye	643
GEN	験	385	beneficial effect (of austerities)	974
GON	勤	690	service, duty, business	208

H

ha	端	887	end, tip, edge	680
haba(mu)	阻	1117	obstruct, prevent, impede	928
ha(e)	栄	990	shine, be brilliant	497
ha(eru)	映	368	shine, be brilliant	479
ha(eru)	生	9	grow, spring up, cut (teeth)	616
hagane	鋼	1108	steel	915
hai(ru)	入	65	enter, break into, join	169
haka(ru)	諮	---	consult with	837
haka(ru)	謀	915	plan, devise, deceive	838
ha(ku)	履	---	put on (the feet)	345
HAN	凡	1156	mediocrity	193
hana	華	901	flower	779
ha(neru)	跳	---	leap, spring up, hop	858
hata	端	887	side, edge	680
HATSU	法	100	law, ordinance, prohibition	543
ha(yasu)	生	9	grow, cultivate, wear (a beard)	616
hazuka(shimeru)	辱	1390	humiliate, put to shame	870
hazu(mu)	弾	705	spring, bound, rebound	377
hazu(reru)	外	69	be off, come off	283
hazu(su)	外	69	take off, remove	283
HEI	病	502	sickness, illness	629
hi	燈	---	lamp, light, counter for lights	575

hi	氷	---	ice, hail	75
HI	泌	---	flow, soak in, penetrate	539
hii(deru)	秀	739	surpass, excell	662
hi(ku)	弾	705	play on (an instrument)	377
hi(meru)	秘	853	conceal, keep a secret	666
hito(ri)	独	205	alone, on one's own	602
hodo	程	276	limits, extent, degree	667
hoko	矛	1246	halbert, arms	645
HON	反	146	opposite, antagonism	229
ho(shii)	欲	1043	desire, want	842
HOTSU	法	100	law, ordinance	543
HU	風	316	wind, air, appearance, custom	960
HU	歩	267	pawn (in chess)	519
hu(eru)	殖	---	increase, multiply, accrue	523
hu(eru)	増	365	increase	279
hu(kasu)	更	608	sit up late	49
hu(keru)	老	608	get late, grow old	49
hu(keru)	老	640	grow old	728
hu(ku)	噴	---	spout, emit, flush out	255
hukura(mu)	膨	---	swell	753
huku(reru)	膨	---	swell	753
humi	文	89	letter	462
husa	房	1343	tuft, fringe, lock (of hair)	416
huta	双	1057	a pair, a set, comparison	237
hutokoro	懐	1311	bosom, breast	410

hu(yasu)	増	365	increase	279
HYOO	兵	243	soldier, army	90

I

I	唯	1040	merely, willingly, meekly	250
ida(ku)	抱	654	hug, embrace, entertain (hope)	432
ikoi	憩	---	rest, relax, repose	409
ikusa	戦	32	war, fight, battle	413
irodo(ru)	彩	---	color, paint, make up	380
i(ru)	要	78	require, need, waylay	811
itada(ku)	頂	1062	be crowned with, wear, receive	956
ita(meru)	傷	849	hurt, injure, spoil	163
ita(mu)	傷	849	feel a pain, hurt, be hurt	163
ita(mu)	悼	---	grieve over	403
ita(su)	致	747	do, perform	760
itsuku(shimu)	慈	---	love, be affectionate to, pity	182

J

JAKU	着	410	putting on, arrival	723
JI	除	646	division (in math), excluding	929
JU	従	329	subordinate, follow	385

K

kado	角	881	corner, angle, edge	819

KAI	街	837	street, avenue, town	387
kaka(eru)	抱	654	hold or carry under or in the arms	432
ka(karu)	架	---	hang	496
ka(karu)	懸	1317	hang on, be suspended from	411
ka(keru)	架	---	hang	496
ka(keru)	懸	1317	hang, set up, put on	411
kama	窯	---	kiln, oven, furnace, stove	675
kamo(su)	醸	---	brew, cause, give rise to	901
kana(deru)	奏	---	play (an instrument)	298
kaori	香	861	fragrance, perfume, aroma	969
kao(ru)	薫	---	smell, be fragrant	789
kara	空	384	emptiness, vacancy	672
kara	唐	---	Chinese, Korean, foreign	366
karada	体	96	body, health	143
kara(maru)	絡	---	twist around, get caught in	703
kara(mu)	絡	---	coil around, get twisted	703
karo(yaka)	軽	814	light, easy	866
ka(ru)	狩	---	hunt	602
kashira	頭	234	head, hair, leader	843
kata(i)	硬	---	hard, solid, tough, rigid	652
kataki	敵	553	enemy, competitor, revenge	461
katamari	塊	---	lump, chunk, clod	277
katawara	傍	1194	nearby, beside	161
katayo(ru)	偏	1294	lean, incline, be biased	160

kate	糧	935	food, provisions, bread	694
KAtsu	合	33	fit, suit	138
katsu(gu)	担	---	shoulder (a load)	431
ka(u)	交	269	cross (a road)	113
kawa	革	487	leather, hide	952
kawa	河	614	river, stream	541
kawa(kasu)	乾	---	dry, desiccate	221
kawa(ku)	乾	---	dry, dry up	221
kawa(ku)	渇	---	be thirsty, dry up	555
kawa(su)	交	269	exchange (messages), dodge	113
KE	華	901	flower, petal, shining flower	779
kemu(i)	煙	1130	smoky	584
kemu(ru)	煙	1130	smoke, smolder	584
kibi(shii)	厳	819	severe, strict, stern	100
ki(ku)	利	180	take effect, do (a person) good	662
ki(ku)	効	714	be effective	206
ki(ku)	聴	767	hear, listen to, inquire	735
kita(nai)	汚	836	dirty, filthy, unclean	536
KITSU	吉	199	good luck, joy, congratulation	265
kiwa	際	189	side, edge, verge	934
kiwa(maru)	極	311	terminate, reach an extreme	506
kiwa(meru)	極	311	investigate thoroughly, master	506
kiwa(meru)	究	261	investigate thoroughly, master	671
kiwa(mi)	極	311	height, acme, extremity	506

kiza(shi)	兆	---	signs, omen, symptoms	190
kiza(su)	兆	---	show signs or symptoms of	190
ko(eru)	超	1334	cross, go beyond, exceed	856
KON	建	278	build, raise	370
KOO	神	191	divine, solemn, awe-inspiring	657
KOO	耗	---	decrease	730
koro(bu)	転	554	fall down, tumble	865
koro(garu)	転	554	roll over, tumble	865
koro(gasu)	転	554	knock down, roll over	865
koro(geru)	転	554	roll over, tumble over	865
ko(su)	超	1334	cross, pass, spend, tide over	856
koto	殊	1027	especially, exceptionally	522
kowa(i)	怖	723	fearful, frightful, terrible	397
kowa(reru)	壊	802	be broken, be demolished	280
kowa(su)	壊	802	break, destroy, tear up	280
KU	庫	1173	storehouse	365
KU	貢	1321	tribute	355
kura(u)	食	207	eat, drink, receive (a blow)	964
kutsugae(ru)	覆	1154	overturn, capsize, fall	812
kutsugae(su)	覆	1154	overturn, capsize, overthrow	812
kuzu(reru)	崩	1407	crumble, collapse	350
kuzu(su)	崩	1407	demolish, destroy, level	350
KYA	脚	1266	leg, skid, undercarriage	746
KYOO	香	861	incense, fragrance	969

M

ma	馬	890	horse	970
machi	街	837	town, quarters	387
makana(u)	賄	---	board, supply, finance	850
maru(i)	円	260	round, circular	183
masa	正	139	right, correct, sure	44
masa(ru)	勝	419	excel, surpass, outrival	748
masu	升	---	a measuring box	82
matata(ku)	瞬	1112	wink, blink	645
mawa(ri)	周	824	a round, a turn	186
ME	女	60	woman, girl, female	299
mijime	惨	1175	sad, pitiful, wretched	403
mi(ru)	診	1178	diagnose, examine	826
mitsu(gu)	貢	1321	support, finance	355
mogu(ru)	潜	---	dive, get into, crawl into	570
MON	聞	184	hearing	924
MOO	亡	795	the late, dying, being destroyed	109
moppa(ra)	専	589	mainly, solely	330
mori	守	364	nursemaid, baby sitter	311
moto	基	251	basis, foundation, origin	274
moto	本	6	beginning, foundation, root	64
MU	謀	915	plan, device, deceive	838
muzuka(shii)	難	351	hard, difficult, delicate	939

N

NA	南	401	hail	219
naga(i)	永	566	long, lengthly	75
nago(mu)	和	85	be softened, get quiet	664
nago(yaka)	和	85	mellow, matured, refined	664
nagu(ru)	殴	---	hit, beat, thrash	524
na(i)	亡	795	the late, the deceased	109
nama(keru)	怠	---	be lazy, be idle, neglect	236
name(raka)	滑	---	smooth	566
NAN	納	1337	supply, store	697
nao(ru)	治	88	be mended, get well	540
nao(su)	治	88	mend, heal, repair	540
nara(u)	倣	---	imitate, follow	155
natsu(kashii)	懐	1311	dear, longed for, yearning for	410
natsu(kashimu)	懐	1311	yearn for	410
natsu(keru)	懐	1311	win over, win another's heart	410
natsu(ku)	懐	1311	become attached to	410
nengoro	懇	---	kind, courteous, hospitable	410
NI	仁	---	kernel	126
nii	新	80	new	467
nina(u)	担	---	carry on the shoulder	431
nise	偽	---	sham, counterfeit, imitation	160
nobo(ru)	昇	1275	rise, ascend, go up	477
noga(reru)	逃	721	escape, avoid, evade, shirk	875

noga(su)	逃	721	let go, set free, let escape	875
NYAKU	若	391	young	773

O

O	悪	295	evil, wrong, vice	53
odo(kasu)	脅	1362	threaten, scare	207
odo(ru)	躍	1039	leap, skip, throb	861
odo(su)	脅	1362	threaten	207
ogoso(ka)	厳	819	austere, majestic, dignified	100
oku(reru)	後	48	be late, be delayed	383
oko(ru)	怒	1150	become angry, be offended	397
omo	主	34	main	110
omomu(ku)	赴	---	proceed to, get, become	855
onore	己	618	oneself, myself, yourself	355
oo(u)	覆	1154	cover, veil, hang over	812
o(riru)	下	75	come down, go down, step down	30
o(rosu)	下	75	take down, lower, pull down	30
osa(eru)	抑	798	stop, check, restrain, control	426
oso(i)	遅	1147	late, slow	886
o(u)	生	9	grow	616

R

RAI	礼	959	salutation, bow, courtesy	655
RICHI	律	898	law, regulation	382
ROO	糧	935	food, provisions, bread	694

RYOO	霊	---	spirits who possess men	945
RYUU	立	35	standing	676
		S		
sa	再	252	again, twice, re-	47
SA	茶	851	tea	776
saba(ku)	裁	577	judge	222
sachi	幸	423	happiness, blessing	272
saga(su)	探	871	search	443
sage(ru)	提	472	take along, carry in hand	447
SAI	財	491	money, wealth, assets	846
sakana	魚	903	fish	982
saka(ru)	盛	808	prosper, flourish, copulate (animals)	639
SAKU	冊	---	book counter, volume, book	60
sa(ku)	割	414	cut up, cleave	202
sa(masu)	覚	512	awake, wake up	816
sa(masu)	冷	708	cool, let cool, dampen	190
sa(meru)	覚	512	awake, be disillusioned	816
sa(meru)	冷	708	cool, get cold, abate	190
sasa(eru)	支	185	support, maintain, sustain	454
sa(su)	指	292	point to, indicate, name	436
sato(su)	諭	---	admonish, charge, remonstrate with	838
SATSU	早	409	quick, fast, speedy	476
sawa(ru)	障	530	hinder, interfere with, hurt	934

sawa(ru)	触	1114	touch, feel	819
seba(maru)	狭	1018	narrow, become narrow	601
seba(meru)	狭	1018	make narrow, contract, reduce	601
SECHI	節	745	season, occasion, honor	685
sei	背	622	stature, height	743
SEI	情	183	feeling, emotion, passion	404
SEKI	寂	---	lonely, lonesome	323
se(ru)	競	1019	compete, vice, bid	681
SETSU	殺	470	kill, murder, butcher	524
SHI	矢	1270	arrow	646
shiawa(se)	幸	423	good fortune, happiness	272
shibo(ru)	搾	---	wring, squeeze, press	448
shi(iru)	強	133	force, coerce, constrain	376
shiita(geru)	虐	---	oppress, tyrannize	793
shi(maru)	閉	---	be closed, be locked	921
shi(meru)	閉	---	shut, close	921
shi(miru)	染	---	soak in, permeate	497
shimi	染	---	stain, blot, spot	497
SHIN	津	1086	port, harbor, ferry	544
shiro	代	87	price, substitution, materials	132
shiru(su)	記	209	write down, inscribe, mention	824
shitata(ru)	滴	---	drip, drop	567
shizuku	滴	---	drop	567
shizu(maru)	鎮	1399	get quiet, calm down, grow still	916

shizu(meru)	鎮	1399	pacify, calm, soothe	916
SHOO	上	29	upper part, government	223
SHOO	声	299	voice, tone, alarm	270
SHOO	従	329	secondary, incidental	385
SHOO	清	569	purity	557
SHUU	祝	1272	celebration, congratulations	657
sokona(u)	損	1058	harm, hurt, injure, damage	449
soko(neru)	損	1058	harm, hurt, injure, damage	449
so(meru)	初	279	begin to	803
somu(keru)	背	622	look away from, avert	743
somu(ku)	背	622	act contrary to, go back on	743
SO	想	197	idea, conception, thought	405
SOO	贈	---	presenting	852
sooroo	候	999	classical verbal ending corresponding to colloquial -masu	155
sora(su)	反	146	bend, warp	229
so(ru)	反	146	warp, curve, lean backward	229
sosono(kasu)	唆	---	tempt, seduce, instigate	249
SU	数	159	strength, fate, law, numbers	460
sube(ru)	滑	---	slide, glide, skate	566
sugu(reru)	優	639	excel, surpass, have advantage over	165
sui	酸	---	sour, acid, tart	900
sumiya(ka)	速	766	speedy, prompt, swift	880
su(reru)	擦	---	rub, chafe, wear, become sophisticated	453

su(ru)	擦	---	rub, chafe, strike	453
susu(meru)	薦	---	recommend, advise	789
suta(reru)	廃	1120	become useless, get out of date	367
suta(ru)	廃	1120	become useless, decline	367
suwa(ru)	座	644	squat down, sit down	365

T

tabi	度	72	occasion, reception	364
TAI	代	87	period, age, generation	152
take	丈	1387	height, stature, length	80
takigi	薪	---	firewood, kindling, fuel	789
ta(ku)	炊	---	cook, boil	576
TAKU	度	72	save, redeem, reclaim	364
takuwa(eru)	蓄	---	store, lay in stock, save	786
tama	球	688	ball, bowl, sphere, blub	609
tama	弾	705	bullet, round	377
tama	霊	---	soul, spirit	945
tame(su)	試	578	attempt, try, experience	830
TAN	壇	---	stage, rostrum, dias	279
ta(rasu)	垂	---	suspend, hang down	92
ta(reru)	垂	---	hang, droop, drop	92
tataka(u)	闘	367	wage war, fight, struggle against	927
tata(mu)	畳	1388	fold, fold up, furl, shut up	626
tate	盾	1220	shield, buckler	94

tato(eru)	例	294	compare to, speak figuratively	149
tatto(i)	貴	676	valuable, precious, noble	849
tayori	便	769	news, tidings, connection	152
tayo(ru)	頼	604	rely on, have recourse to	958
tazu(neru)	訪	957	call on, visit, look up	825
TO	度	72	save, redeem, reclaim	364
TO	頭	234	head	843
to(bu)	跳	---	jump, leap, spring	858
to(gu)	研	284	sharpen, grind, scour	650
toko	常	190	ever, endless	339
TON	団	336	bedding, bedclothes	258
tona(ru)	隣	1015	adjoin	935
TOO	道	123	way, teachings	887
TOO	読	323	reading	833
tooto(bu)	尊	704	value, respect, honor	182
tooto(i)	尊	704	precious, valuable, noble	182
to(ru)	撮	1082	take (pictures)	452
to(ru)	捕	584	catch, arrest, capture	439
totono(eru)	調	219	prepare, arrange, fill orders	835
totono(u)	調	219	be prepared, be arranged	835
totsu(gu)	嫁	1309	marry off, get married	306
to(u)	問	41	question, inquiry	920
TSU	通	97	pass, run	882
tsuchika(u)	培	---	cultivate, foster	273
tsudo(u)	集	224	meet, assemble, congregate	937

tsu(gu)	接	399	join, piece together, splice	444
tsukama(eru)	捕	584	catch, arrest, capture	439
tsukama(ru)	捕	584	be caught, be captured	439
tsuka(u)	遣	---	use, handle, employ	890
tsuka(wasu)	遣	---	send, dispatch, give	890
tsu(keru)	就	906	place (something) in	120
tsu(ku)	就	906	settle in (place), take a seat	120
tsura	面	117	face, surface	951
tsuto(meru)	務	244	serve, fill a post, serve under	646
tsutsushi(mu)	謹	---	be discreet, be careful	839

U

ubu	産	92	childbirth	679
ui	初	279	first (time)	803
ui	憂	1349	sad, unhappy, gloomy	54
une	畝	---	ridge (in a field)	118
ure(i)	愁	---	sad, unhappy, gloomy	405
u(reru)	熟	1219	ripen	585
u(ru)	得	167	get, acquire, earn, find	386
uru(mu)	潤	1142	be dimmed, be clouded	569
uto(i)	疎	---	distant, estranged, disinterested	627
uto(mu)	疎	---	neglect, shun, alienate	627
uyauya(shii)	恭	---	respectful, reverent	400

W

wa	我	380	I, oneself, self	90
warabe	童	1186	child	680
waza	技	528	skill, work, performance	427
waza	業	74	deed, act, work, art	79
wazura(u)	患	1016	be ill, suffer from	402

Y

YAKU	疫	---	epidemic	628
YAKU	益	605	gain, benefit, profit	180
ya(meru)	辞	784	resign	762
yasa(shii)	易	383	easy, simple	477
yawa(raka)	軟	---	soft	865
yawa(rakai)	軟	---	soft	865
yo(i)	善	665	good, good-natured, pleasing	181
yogo(reru)	汚	836	get dirty, be stained	536
yogo(su)	汚	836	stain, soil, pollute	536
yo(mu)	詠	---	recite, chant	826
YU	遊	585	play, visit, taking a holiday	889
yue	故	523	reason, cause, circumstance	455
YUI	由	134	cause, significance	60
yuru(i)	緩	---	loose, slack	712
yuru(meru)	緩	---	loosen, unbend, unfasten	712
yuru(mu)	緩	---	loosen, lessen, relax	712
yuru(yaka)	緩	---	loose, easy, gentle	712
yu(saburu)	揺	---	swing, shake, rock	447
yu(suburu)	揺	---	swing, shake, rock	447
yu(suru)	揺	---	swing, shake, rock	447

Z

| ZAN | 惨 | 1175 | disaster, cruelty, wretchedness | 403 |